TO WALK
WITHOUT
NOV
FEAR

TO WALK WITHOUT FEAR

The Global Movement to Ban Landmines

Edited by
Maxwell A. Cameron,
Robert J. Lawson,
and Brian W. Tomlin

Toronto Oxford New York
Oxford University Press
1998

Oxford University Press
70 Wynford Drive, Don Mills, Ontario M3C 1J9
http://www.oupcan.com

Oxford New York Athens Auckland Bangkok Bogotá Buenos Aires
Calcutta Cape Town Chennai Dar es Salaam Delhi Florence
Hong Kong Istanbul Karachi Kuala Lumpur Madrid Melbourne
Mexico City Mumbai Nairobi Paris São Paulo Singapore Taipei
Tokyo Toronto Warsaw
and associated companies in Berlin Ibadan

Oxford is a trade mark of Oxford University Press

Canadian Cataloguing in Publication Data

Main entry under title:

To walk without fear : the global movement to ban landmines

Includes bibliographical references and index.
ISBN 0-19-541414-4

1. Land mines. 2. Land mines—Government policy. 3. Land mines
(International law). I. Cameron, Maxwell A. II. Lawson, Robert J.
III. Tomlin, Brian W., 1944-   .

UG490.T62 1998   327.1'743   C98-931857-5

Cover photographs: *Top*: © G. Varela/Explorer/Publiphoto.
Bottom: Kevin R. Morris/Tony Stone Images.
Cover and Text Design: Brett Miller

Courtesy of ICBL.

DEDICATION

For the thousands of people around the world who worked to ban land-mines so that future generations may walk without fear.

TABLE OF CONTENTS

PREFACE

This book is the product of an unusual, perhaps unique, collaboration among academics, government officials, and members of non-governmental organizations. It began with discussions between the editors even as the Ottawa Process was just beginning. As the momentum for a ban began to build throughout 1997, it seemed clear that the diplomatic process was in some ways unprecedented, and that the lessons learned from this could be of major significance. We decided to bring together diverse communities, in a way analogous to the Ottawa Process itself, to produce a book that would have a little of something for everyone. For the academics, it would contain solid, credible analyses of the process and the outcome. For government officials, it would provide a record of what had occurred, analysis of what could be learned, and evaluations of what might be replicated. For NGOs, it would contain their own descriptions of their campaigns and assessments of why and how they succeeded. Finally, we wanted to provide the general public with a book that was full of new facts and information, rich in narratives and images, and sufficiently inviting to encourage them to pursue the issues further.

The book pulls together an eclectic group of key government officials, leading members of the international and national ban campaigns, and knowledgeable academic observers to describe, explain, and assess various aspects of the Ottawa Process and its outcome. Chapters were developed through a series of policy workshops, seminars, intensive focus-group discussions with government officials and NGO members, and a 'lessons learned' exercise that brought together over 200 NGO and government participants immediately after the signing of the convention. The process has not been entirely smooth, which is not surprising for a book of such experimental character. Certain participants were forced, for reasons beyond their control, to drop out along the way, leaving gaps and omissions that we wish we could have filled but could not under the pressures of time. We would have liked to have had more analysis of the campaigns in developing nations. Analysis of the role of the media in the Ottawa Process remains to be done, and there are other gaps. But if the book stimulates others to take up these challenges and contributes to a lively debate on the origins and legacy of the movement to ban mines, it will have been successful. In particular, our goal has been to reach across the 'solitudes' that often define the worlds of policy, academic research, and public advocacy.

Readers should be aware that we have not attempted to write a purely academic account of the movement to ban anti-personnel mines. Many of the chapters in this book are written by the players themselves—key actors in the process, whether outside or inside government. While their views do not necessarily reflect the position of the organizations they work for, they were not expected to step outside their roles as officials or advocates in contributing to this book. We thought it more interesting to let the NGOs describe some of the various national and international campaigns that formed part of the movement to ban landmines. These chapters should be read as dispatches from the trenches rather than dispassionate academic treatises.

A book like this accumulates substantial debts. We are grateful to many colleagues, including Simon Dalby, John English, Beth Fischer, Debbie Grisdale, Fen Hampson, Allan Maslove, Maureen Appel Molot, Dean Oliver, and Harald von Riekhoff. A number of people in the Canadian Department of Foreign Affairs and International Trade helped with the research and logistics of the project, including Jeff Woods, Wendy Winch, Alex Lofthouse, Tommy Hall, Sarah Taylor, and Kerry Buck. Students who worked hard as research assistants included: Alexis Diamond, Faiza Warsame, Colleen Hoey, Suzannah Baum, Denis Orbay, Brian Finlay-Dick, Joaquin Zuckerberg, and Niall Cronin. Logistical and organizational support was professionally and cheerfully provided by Elizabeth James and Doris Whitteker. We also thank Richard Tallman for editing the manuscript to exacting standards, and Oxford University Press for its enthusiastic support for this project.

Max Cameron and Brian Tomlin are grateful to the supportive environment for policy research at Carleton University, and to the Non-proliferation, Arms Control and Disarmament Division in the Department of Foreign Affairs and International Trade for financial support for the research project. Oxford University Press generously allowed us to publish several of the chapters in the *Canadian Foreign Policy* journal.

Maxwell Cameron, Robert Lawson, Brian Tomlin
Ottawa
August 1998

CONTRIBUTORS

The Honourable Lloyd Axworthy is Canada's Minister of Foreign Affairs.

J. Marshall Beier is a doctoral candidate in Political Science at York University.

Maxwell A. Cameron is Associate Professor at the Norman Paterson School of International Affairs and Associate Director of the Centre for Negotiation and Dispute Resolution at Carleton University.

Philippe Chabasse is the Co-Director of Handicap International.

Deborah Chatsis is a lawyer in the United Nations, Human Rights, and Humanitarian Law Section of the Canadian Department of Foreign Affairs and International Trade.

Ann Denholm Crosby is Associate Professor of Political Science at York University.

Miguel de Larrinaga is a doctoral candidate in Political Science at the University of Ottawa.

Thomas Desch is the Senior Adviser in the Legal Division of the Austrian Ministry of Defence.

Michael Dolan is Professor of Political Science and former Director of the Institute of Political Economy at Carleton University.

Robert G. Gard, Jr, is Lieutenant General, USA (Ret.), President Emeritus, Monterey Institute of International Studies, and Military Adviser, Vietnam Veterans of America Foundation.

Stephen Goose is Program Director in the Arms Division of Human Rights Watch and a member of the Co-ordination Committee of the International Campaign to Ban Landmines.

Mark Gwozdecky is the Co-ordinator of the Mine Action Team in the Canadian Department of Foreign Affairs and International Trade.

Thomas Hajnoczi is the Head of the Department of Disarmament in the Austrian Ministry for Foreign Affairs.

Laird Hindle is an MA student in the Norman Paterson School of International Affairs, Carleton University.

Don Hubert is a Desk Officer in the Peace Building and Human Development Division of the Canadian Department of Foreign Affairs and International Trade.

Chris Hunt is a doctoral candidate in Political Science at Carleton University.

Robert Lawson is the Senior Policy Adviser in the Mine Action Team in the Canadian Department of Foreign Affairs and International Trade Canada.

David Long is Associate Professor at the Norman Paterson School of International Affairs at Carleton University.

Ralph Lysyshyn is the Director-General of the International Security Bureau in the Canadian Department of Foreign Affairs and International Trade.

Stuart Maslen is Adviser, Mines Unit, International Committee of the Red Cross.

Richard Price is Assistant Professor of Political Science at the University of Minnesota.

Ken Rutherford is co-founder of the Landmine Survivors Network.

Claire Turenne Sjolander is Associate Professor of Political Science at the University of Ottawa.

Jill Sinclair is the Ambassador for Mine Action in the Canadian Department of Foreign Affairs and International Trade.

Noel Stott is with the South African Campaign to Ban Landmines.

Brian W. Tomlin is Professor at the Norman Paterson School of International Affairs and Director of the Centre for Negotiation and Dispute Resolution at Carleton University.

Celina Tuttle is Co-ordinator of Mines Action Canada.

Alex Vines is a Research Associate with Human Rights Watch.

Mary Wareham is Senior Advocate, Human Rights Watch, and former Co-ordinator of the United States Campaign to Ban Landmines.

Valerie Warmington is the Co-Chair of Mines Action Canada.

Jerry White is co-founder of the Landmine Survivors Network.

Jody Williams is an International Ambassador for the International Campaign to Ban Landmines, formerly Co-ordinator of the ICBL, and co-recipient of the 1997 Nobel Peace Prize.

ABBREVIATIONS

ADEMO	Association for Disabled People of Mozambique
AHD	Anti-handling device
AMA	American Medical Association
AP mines	Anti-personnel mines
APL	Anti-personnel landmine
AT mines	Anti-tank mines
ATACMS	Army Tactical Missile System
AV mines	Anti-vehicle mines
BAT	Brilliant Anti-Armour Technology
BF	Belgian francs
CARICOM	Caribbean Community
CBO	Congressional Budget Office
CCIC	Canadian Council for International Co-operation
CCW	Convention on Certain Conventional Weapons
CD	Conference on Disarmament
CEM	Combined Effects Munition
CENTAM	Central American governments
CFE	Treaty on Conventional Forces in Europe
CIDA	Canadian International Development Agency
CMAC	Cambodia Mine Action Centre
COREMO	Revolutionary Committee (Mozambique)
CUSO	Canadian University Services Overseas
CWC	Chemical Weapons Convention
DFAIT	Department of Foreign Affairs and International Trade (Canada)
DHA	Department of Humanitarian Affairs (UN)
DIA	Defense Intelligence Agency (US)
DMZ	Demilitarized zone
DND	Department of National Defence (Canada)
DOD	Department of Defense (US)
DPKO	Department of Peacekeeping Operations (UN)
DSAA	Defense Security Assistance Administration (US)
ECU	European Currency Unit
EOD	Explosive ordnance disposal
EU	European Union
FLEC	Front for the Liberation of the Cabindan Enclave
FMS	Foreign military sales
FNLA	National Front for the Liberation of Angola
FRELIMO	Mozambique Liberation Front
FSTC	Foreign Science and Technology Center (US Army)
HALO	Hazardous Areas Life-Support Organisation
HI	Handicap International
ICBL	International Campaign to Ban Landmines

ICRC	International Committee of the Red Cross
IDA	Institute for Defence Analysis (Chapter 7)
	Non-Proliferation, Arms Control and Disarmament Division, DFAIT (Chapter 9)
IDC	Regional Security and Peacekeeping Division, DFAIT
IDD	International Security Bureau, DFAIT
IHL	International humanitarian law
IPU	Inter-Parliamentary Union
IR	International relations
JSOW	Joint Standoff Weapon
JSTARS	Joint Surveillance and Target Attack Radar System
LSN	Landmine Survivors Network
MAC	Mines Action Canada
	Mine Action Centre (Chapter 16)
MAG	Mines Advisory Group
MBFR	Mutual and Balanced Force Reduction Talks
MFDC	Movement of Democratic Forces of Casamance
MK	Umkhonto we Sizwe (South Africa)
MLRS	Multiple Launch Rocket System
MPLA	Popular Movement for the Liberation of Angola
NATO	North Atlantic Treaty Organization
NGOs	Non-governmental organizations
NPA	Norwegian People's Aid
NSC	National Security Council (US)
OAS	Organization of American States
OAU	Organization for African Unity
PCO	Privy Council Office
PHR	Physicians for Human Rights
PLAN	People's Liberation Army of Namibia
ROK	Republic of Korea
SADARM	Sense and Destroy Armor Munitions
SADC	Southern African Development Community
TNT	Trinitrotoluene
UN	United Nations
UNDP	United Nations Development Program
UNGA	United Nations General Assembly
UNICEF	United Nations Children's Fund
UNITA	National Union for Total Independence of Angola
USAID	United States Agency for International Development
USAMCCOM	US Army, Armament, Munitions and Chemical Command
UXO	Unexploded ordnance
VVAF	Vietnam Veterans of America Foundation
WAM	Wide Area Munition
ZANLA	Zimbabwe African National Liberation Army
ZIPRA	Zimbabwe People's Revolutionary Army

CHAPTER 1

TO WALK WITHOUT FEAR

Maxwell A. Cameron, Robert J. Lawson,
and Brian W. Tomlin

Courtesy of John Rodsted.

There is a path to the Kavungo River in eastern Angola, and the people of the village of Kavungo learned to walk along the path in fear.[1] For generations, the rich soil, abundant game, and fish from the river provided residents of surrounding villages with a secure livelihood. But in 1983 rebel forces attacked government troops and the path to the river became a raging battlefield. The battle was brief, but intense enough to cause the villagers to flee, and it left in its wake the usual detritus of war: spent cartridges, burnt hamlets, abandoned livestock, and a more enduring and dangerous legacy—innumerable anti-personnel (AP) mines, buried along the war-path, ever-alert and ready to strike.

AP mines provided no decisive advantage to either side in the battle along the Kavungo River, nor were they used in accordance with rules of war drafted by experts in Geneva. Strewn haphazardly to provide momentary perimeter security for units in a highly mobile and irregular conflict, live mines were simply left in the ground as the soldiers moved on—a modern version of salting the enemy's soil in order to poison the land.

Besides, it was simply more costly and dangerous to dig up the mines for reuse in other battles than to buy new ones. Mines were cheap, costing as little as $3–$5 each. In any case, the mines in this war were free, provided in batches of tens of thousands by superpowers and their allies waging what was supposed to be a 'Cold War'. When the fighting ended, the visible scars of war along the path to the river healed quickly, vegetation covering what rot and rust failed to consume. Beneath the path, however, the mines remained untouched by the passage of time, although some shifted from where they were originally placed under the pressure of rain and run-off. Government forces retook the area the next year, allowing the local population to begin to drift back to their land. After months of surviving in the bush, the dispersed villagers had little choice but to try to rebuild their lives in the midst of a precarious peace. The mines were waiting.

The villagers knew that the path to the river was mined, but remaining confined to their hamlets meant a slow death by starvation. Thousands of random footsteps, heavy with loads of water, firewood, and food, beat back nature's intrusions upon the path to the river. Miraculously, not a single foot fell on the detonator of a mine for many years. But on a cool summer morning in 1990, two village women were struck by a small blast mine. That the footstep detonating the mine was that of a civilian, not a soldier, was not a subtlety that the mine was designed to appreciate. In fact, the mine performed exactly as intended.

WHAT ARE ANTI-PERSONNEL MINES?

AP mines are at the root of a global humanitarian crisis. Every year they claim 26,000 casualties, many of whom are innocent civilians. An AP mine can take its deadly toll many decades after it was first laid; it is not a weapon that respects a cease-fire and it is indifferent to the distinction between civilians and soldiers. All casualties of war are lamentable, but AP mines are designed to inflict particularly horrific injuries on their victims. When a mine is stepped on, a chain reaction is set in motion. It begins with the mechanical pressure that triggers a detonator, igniting a booster charge of high-quality explosive material. The booster charge then sets off a more powerful explosion of trinitrotoluene, better known as TNT. Shock waves explode outward faster than high-velocity bullets, often at speeds of around 6,800 metres per second, driving metallic fragments, broken bones, bacteria, earth, and burning plastic into the victim's body.

Mines are activated in different ways. Small blast mines, often less than 10 centimetres in diameter, lie inconspicuously in hiding until activated by the weight of a foot. Others, like the American claymore, are activated by a trip-wire and project shards of metal in the direction of the victim. 'Bounding mines' are fragmentation mines that jump into the air before exploding, spraying fragments across a larger area. Perhaps the most insidious are the 'butterfly' mines, which look like toys and must be bent or twisted to explode.

Each type of mine causes a specific pattern of injury. Small blast mines traumatically amputate part of the foot or leg of the victim. The degree of injury depends on the size and placement of the mine. If the mine is small, upper body injury is unlikely; but larger blast mines will often blow off much of the leg, leaving the tibia (shin bone) exposed and the remaining muscles 'smashed and pushed upward, giving the injury a grotesque cauliflower-like appearance'.[2] Wounds from such blasts can affect the opposite leg, genitals, buttocks, thigh, abdomen, and chest areas. Fragmentation mines like the claymore are among the most lethal in the deadly arsenal of landmines. They have a 25-meter-radius 'kill zone' and are capable of causing injury in a radius of up to 200 meters. Traumatic amputation is less common because victims activating these mines are almost invariably killed. Those victims outside the kill zone frequently suffer injuries from penetration of the abdomen, chest, and brain. The butterfly mines traumatically amputate one or both hands at the wrist and cause damage to chest and face, including the eyes.

The physical harm caused by landmines varies widely according to the position of the mine, the type of footwear worn, the length of delay before treatment, the quality of medical attention received, and the age and health of the victim. Doctors working without advanced facilities must rapidly diagnose the condition of the wounded patient—observing such symptoms as 'pallor of extremities, cold pulseless limbs, pronounced haematoma, and cardiovascular instability'—before making such decisions as whether to amputate a limb.[3] Often, well-meaning efforts can make matters worse: a limb may be lost due to the poor application of a tourniquet or inadequate sterilization. Wound patterns vary greatly. The irregular fragments ejected from landmines, because they are not streamlined like bullets, become wobbly and shimmering in their trajectory, causing distinctive wounds. Low-velocity fragments 'core out holes and damage those tissue which they actually enter' whereas high-velocity fragments 'cause temporary cavitation with immense destructive effect'. Wounds caused by AP mines are more likely than gunshot wounds to produce 'soft tissue defects, bony injuries, wound contamination, and skin defects'.[4]

Cleaning the wounds is difficult but essential to avoid infection and the need for further surgery, even amputation. One of the mine victims from Kavungo who stepped on a small blast mine had her tibia amputated at mid-calf, but not all the necrotic tissue was removed; when the wound turned gangrenous she had to be amputated at mid-thigh.[5] Mine injuries are especially devastating for children whose growing limbs may require repeated surgery over the course of many years. Successful treatment and recovery depend heavily on getting the wounded to medical attention as soon as possible, yet the vast majority of victims, according to a study by the International Committee of the Red Cross (ICRC) based on the records of 757 cases, receive medical attention between six and 24 hours after they are wounded.[6]

The emotional harm caused by landmines is less tangible but no less real. A majority of amputees experience the sensation of having 'phantom pain'—a sensation that can be mildly discomforting or acutely painful. Amputees experience sensations ranging from a stabbing feeling, pins and needles, shooting (like electrical shocks), cramping, crushing, and burning.[7] For some victims, phantom pain becomes a debilitating post-traumatic stress disorder that leaves them unable to function normally for years, even decades.[8] Other sources of discomfort include 'anxiety, low self-esteem, body image concerns, loss of a sense of wholeness, social isolation, decreased sexual activity, and depression'.[9] The level of social discomfort depends on social cues conveying the stigmatization of amputees. In Buddhist cultures, the 'concept of karma may encourage some to believe they were "fated" or "destined" to be injured because of something they had done or failed to do in a previous incarnation'.[10] Depression may be caused by difficulties finding work, the experience of discrimination based on disability, or a sense of dependency.

Landmines harm even those who are not direct victims. They are laid with the intent of inflicting pain in order to produce a deterrent psychological effect on others. In principle, they shape the battlefield by channelling the enemy into disadvantageous positions, enhancing the effectiveness of other weapons by pinning enemy forces down and reducing their mobility; they also reputedly protect friendly forces and facilities against attack. In practice, however, they are used to demoralize the adversary, terrify and control civilian populations, and overburden the adversary's support systems and resources. The distinction is not semantic: landmines are used not just to take or protect things of value, they are also used to destroy value.[11] Not only do they weaken an enemy militarily, they hurt the enemy, cause suffering, and inflict pain. The military utility of mines must be measured not merely in terms of their effect on the balance of military strength, but also on their capacity to inflict grief and pain on soldiers and civilians alike. In this sense, they are weapons of terror.

Finally, AP mines have long-lasting social, economic, and environmental implications. They impoverish communities seeking peace and
reconstruction after a conflict is over by denying access to arable land or
pasture for grazing. If starvation results, the delivery of food aid and development assistance may be hindered. AP mines also impede the work of
humanitarian relief organizations and UN peacekeeping personnel. Most
mine-afflicted countries are poor, and many lack the resources to provide
wheelchairs, prosthetics, or even crutches for mine victims. Given the
gravity and scope of the humanitarian crisis, how did participants in the so-
called Ottawa Process respond?

WHAT WAS THE 'OTTAWA PROCESS'?

The Ottawa Process was a 'fast-track' diplomatic process. In only 14
months, from October 1996 to December 1997, these countries negotiated
a Convention banning the use, production, transfer, and stockpiling of AP
mines (see Appendix B). By the standards of international negotiations,
the Ottawa Process was extraordinarily fast and effective. Much of this success was due to the work of the International Committee of the Red Cross
(ICRC) and a broad range of non-governmental organizations (NGOs) led by
the International Campaign to Ban Landmines (ICBL).

The ICBL was composed of over 1,000 NGOs from over 60 countries. It
is a good example of what has been dubbed 'global civil society'—a network of social groups and organizations that transcends national boundaries.[12] It is a loosely organized and unstructured network—with only a
handful of key full-time and paid activists—that draws on the resources,
both financial and human, of a broad spectrum of member organizations
interconnected by fax machines, the Internet, periodic conferences, and a
common goal. By bringing the plight of the most vulnerable victims of war
to the attention of the media and public opinion around the world, the
ICBL set the agenda for the ban movement.

The ICRC and ICBL went beyond calling attention to the mines issue;
they participated actively in the negotiation of the Ottawa Convention. In
the Ottawa Process, three innovations came together: (1) a partnership
was built between states and NGOs, allowing 'two-track diplomacy' in
which both states and NGOs participated in the development of the
Convention; (2) small and medium-sized states worked together in a coalition of the like-minded; and (3) negotiations were held outside normal
channels and mechanisms in order to place AP mines on a diplomatic path
to extinction.

The Ottawa Process started in January 1996, when Canada began working with a global coalition of pro-ban countries, international organizations, UN agencies, and NGOs to accelerate progress towards a global ban on AP mines. The first major step was to hold a conference in Ottawa, called 'Towards a Global Ban on Anti-Personnel Mines', which brought representatives of over 50 countries and 24 observer states to discuss a strategy for achieving a ban. What was unusual about this conference was that it occurred outside the normal diplomatic forum for negotiating international humanitarian law—the UN Convention on Certain Conventional Weapons (CCW). Earlier in 1996, the CCW had concluded a review conference in which restrictions and prohibitions on AP mines were discussed. However, the talks ended with only modest improvements in the international restrictions on the use of AP mines, which under international law remained legal.

Thus, when Canada's Minister of Foreign Affairs, Lloyd Axworthy, invited all participants of the October 1996 Ottawa conference to work with Canada to negotiate a treaty banning AP mines by December 1997, he created a major diplomatic controversy. At first, it was unclear how many other countries would join the Canadian initiative. Some countries saw the Geneva Conference on Disarmament as an alternative, but only a limited number of countries participate in that process, and it is hampered by the same consensus-based procedures that made the CCW ineffective. Without a realistic alternative, the Ottawa Process became the only game in town.

During 1997, the momentum behind the Ottawa Process grew. Austrian officials prepared a draft treaty to serve as the basis for multilateral consultations in Vienna (February), Bonn (April), and Brussels (June). In Brussels, 97 countries signed a declaration calling for a comprehensive ban treaty and for convening a final conference in Oslo to complete a treaty based on the Austrian draft. The September conference in Oslo, called an 'International Total Ban on Anti-Personnel Land Mines', adopted the text that was formally signed in Ottawa in December.

In retrospect, the movement to ban landmines benefited from the nature of the issue, fortuitous circumstances, and risk-taking leadership. It was easy to present the issue to the public in terms of a simple moral and political choice: to keep a weapon based on limited military utility or ban it on the grounds of massive and indiscriminate humanitarian costs. Ban advocates were fortunate to have the support of prominent individuals like Diana, Princess of Wales, and Archbishop Desmond Tutu, and last-minute changes of government in France and the United Kingdom brought momentum to the movement. Moreover, courageous leadership was critical: the ban would not have been achieved—at least not with such spectacular speed—had Canadian Foreign Minister Lloyd Axworthy been unwilling to go out on a diplomatic limb. Although the Ottawa Process will never be replicated in exactly the same way, there are important lessons to be drawn from it that tell us much about the nature of the post-Cold War international order.

WHAT LESSONS HAVE WE LEARNED FROM THE BAN MOVEMENT?

Many of the chapters in this book were written by the key actors in the Ottawa Process—NGO leaders and government officials who played crucial roles in the drive to ban AP mines, and who here describe their firsthand experiences, and their feelings and assessments. Furthermore, academic contributors to the book, while they were not participant-observers in the Ottawa Process, did have access to the documentary record and to the recollections of participants as a source of information about the events that occurred. As a result, the book provides an accurate description of the reflections of many of the key players. Nevertheless, those writing and those interviewed represent only a small proportion of the hundreds of officials and NGO members who participated in the global movement to ban AP mines. This larger cast of participants came together in Ottawa on 2–4 December 1997 to attend the conference to sign the Convention to ban AP mines.

Representatives from 157 countries participated in three days of workshops and discussions, and 122 signed the convention in Ottawa. The conference was also attended by over 400 delegates from NGOs and international organizations. After the signing was complete, a forum was held with NGO members and officials from the core group of countries that led the ban movement to reflect on the Ottawa Process and draw lessons from it. The editors of this volume decided that the conference and the forum provided a unique opportunity to secure from a much wider cross-section of participants a description of their perceptions and evaluations of the Ottawa Process.

We approached Ekos Research Associates, Inc., a firm with a strong reputation for work on policy using deliberative polling techniques,[13] and asked them to design a survey and conduct focus group discussions with delegates at the Ottawa conference. A self-administered questionnaire was designed in conjunction with contributors to this volume. The questionnaire sought to elicit the views of a wider cross-section of participants on key aspects of the ban Convention—the decision to sign, its impact, compliance issues—as well as on the Ottawa Process itself. The purpose of the

Mines do not discriminate between civilians and soldiers. Courtesy of John Rodsted.

Tun Channareth, Cambodian Campaign to Ban Landmines. Courtesy of John Rodsted.

Prosthetic limbs in a field hospital. Courtesy of John Rodsted.

A hidden killer. Courtesy of John Rodsted.

questionnaire was not to estimate the views of the population of participants, since random selection methods were not feasible. Instead, we simply wanted to secure a basis for a wider examination of perceptions and
evaluations in order to draw some conclusions about the lessons that participants had drawn from their Ottawa Process experience. To probe more
deeply into the reasoning behind the perceptions and evaluations that
were offered by respondents to the questionnaire, we also held a series of
focus group discussions with conference participants.[14]

In describing the results of the survey, we prefer not to present a statistical summary, which would normally be used to extrapolate to the population from which a sample has been drawn. As noted above, we did not
sample delegate opinion, and we make no claim to represent the views of
all of those who attended the Ottawa conference. All we can do here is
present the principal tendencies in the aggregated views of a relatively
large number of participants in the Ottawa Process, and describe the reasoning behind these views that was offered in the focus group discussions.[15]
Most of the issues raised by the participants are analysed in greater detail
in subsequent chapters.

Asked to identify the factors that influenced their country's decision to
sign the Convention, delegates most frequently cited the pressure exercised
by NGOs, particularly as a presence at the table during the treaty negotiation process where they were able to influence policy decisions. In addition, a recurring theme throughout the focus group discussions was the
importance of the role played by regional blocs of states supporting a ban,
in effect shoring up national resolve to adhere to anti-AP mine positions as
part of a cohesive movement. Asked whether the failure of some countries
to sign the Convention would affect its implementation, only 16 per cent
expressed the view that this would have a large negative impact. In the
focus groups, there was a strong sense that these nations simply could not
isolate themselves from what was perceived to be a powerful world movement against AP mines, that in the end they would be forced to conform
and sign.

Delegates thought that the ban Convention would have its most dramatic effects in areas related most directly to AP mines issues. They were
virtually unanimous in their view that the Convention would result in the
provision of more resources for mine clearance, expanded assistance to
mine victims, and increased research and development in mine-clearance
technologies. Almost 80 per cent also expressed the view that the AP
mine ban would result in increased global security. Most focus group participants noted that the Convention would make it increasingly difficult to
deploy or traffic in AP mines, even for non-signatories, as public opinion

and international law begin to weigh heavily against their use. Furthermore, the Convention will now place real limits on AP mine production and distribution and, as a result, the available supply of mines will begin to dry up.

This whole discussion raised the issue of compliance, and respondents were asked how confident they were that countries would abide by the rules of the ban Convention. Only one-third expressed great confidence that other countries would comply with the rules, although two-thirds felt very confident that their own country would do so. However, an additional 60 per cent of respondents were moderately confident that other countries would abide by the rules. The focus groups were very clear as to the reasons why they felt compliance would be the norm. There was now a powerful world force working against those who would continue to use mines, whether non-signatory nations or irregular forces (rebels, guerrillas). More important than the formal compliance rules was the fact that a moral norm had been established, one that labelled AP mines as bad weapons that should not be used. Compliance was also enhanced, they believed, by the lack of wriggle room in the Convention: you either have mines or you do not, and this makes compliance much more straightforward than arms control agreements with more complicated rules for deploying certain types of weapons.

Finally, respondents were asked for their views on the Ottawa Process itself and its continuing effects. First, however, delegates offered a characterization of the Ottawa Process. It was seen as unorthodox diplomacy, distinguished by the following characteristics: small and medium powers had taken the lead on the issue; the process was conducted outside of regular diplomatic channels and negotiations were conducted on a fast-track schedule; the core group of pro-ban states was cross-regional and represented diverse interests and views; and NGOs were active participants throughout the negotiation process. If the Ottawa Process were to be repeated on other issues, these are the characteristics participants would look for.

To examine views about the potential longer-term effects of the Ottawa Process, respondents were asked to rate its impact, positive or negative, in a number of areas. A large majority felt that there would be a positive impact on government-civil society relations, multilateral diplomacy, international activism by small and medium powers, and North-South cooperation on disarmament issues. For many in the focus group discussions, the Ottawa Process was a sign of the changing times. For example, a coalition of NATO members and non-aligned states on a security issue would have been all but impossible during the Cold War. Similarly, the discovery that small and medium powers could not only lead but also redefine the rules of the game was a revelation for many, and they believed that it would be difficult for the major powers to get this particular genie back in the bottle.

Clearly, survey respondents and focus group participants see promise in the Ottawa Process, although only a bare majority believe that it has gone a long way towards establishing a new model for handling international disarmament issues. If the lesson learned by participants is truly that a coalition of small and medium powers in concert with NGOs can take issues outside of regular diplomatic channels and fast-track an outcome over the objections of major powers, then the major powers surely learned the same lesson and may be determined to see that it never happens again. As a result, the next time may be more difficult, requiring even greater determination and effort than the campaign to ban AP mines. The focus group discussions revealed that participants were acutely aware of the slender thread on which the Ottawa Process was hung: leadership was provided by a small group of core countries, and within each only a handful of individuals did the work and promoted the cause. The same was true for the NGOs: although there was a large coalition of organizations active on the issue, the process was driven by a very small group of people. In addition, the chapters in this book reveal just how serendipitous their achievement was, depending as much on good fortune as superior planning.

If the model provided by the Ottawa Process is to have application to other issues, then it will likely have to become more deliberate, with some formal institutionalization of roles. A small step in this direction may have occurred when Canada and Norway signed the Lycoen Declaration in May 1998, establishing a new partnership on human security. The two countries laid out an agenda for action that includes AP mines, human rights and international humanitarian law, women and children in armed conflict, small arms, child soldiers and child labour, and the establishment of an International Criminal Court. Declaring the partnership open to like-minded states, Canadian Foreign Affairs Minister Lloyd Axworthy stated:

> Instead of having an ad hoc coalition that reacts every time one of these issues emerges, we want to organize ourselves and other countries, as well as NGOs and organizations like Amnesty (International) and the Red Cross, around these principles and objectives. . . . we can actually choose what our priority is, how we can best use our resources and how we can undertake within the larger international system a very concerted, co-ordinated, collaborated drive toward these matters.[16]

Axworthy referred to the failure of Europe and the United States to agree at the G–7 summit in May 1998 on an appropriate response to Indian nuclear tests, and, in language reminiscent of the landmine experience, said that, in the absence of consensus within traditional institutions, it was necessary to develop a different track. Canada and Norway are taking their partnership 'one step at a time', but they are clearly aiming at the assembly of a group of like-minded nations that would act in concert on a range of human security issues. If successful, this could represent the institutional-ization of the model developed for the Ottawa Process and the emergence of a new force to challenge great power dominance on these critical inter-national issues.

Three basic lessons are to be learned from the Ottawa Process. First, partnership pays. Governments working together with global civil society can achieve diplomatic results far beyond what might have been possible in the Cold War era. But partnership requires that both governments and NGOs overcome their mutual ambivalence about working together. Second, small and medium-sized states can, in partnership with global civil society, overcome great power opposition; the US does not always have to lead in the new post-Cold War environment. Finally, traditional diplomatic fora and mechanisms can and should be subverted where they represent an obstacle to the achievement of policy goals that are widely demanded by world opinion. Multilateralism is fine as long as states are prepared to move as fast as the slowest in the pack, but coalitions of the like-minded are preferable when the public wants results.

The emergence of global civil society holds the promise of making existing international institutions more democratic, transforming them through innovation and experimentation, and anchoring them in world opinion. The era of nation-states is, of course, far from over, but the fact that an entire category of weaponry, widely used by armies around the world, has now been banned from the arsenals of over 120 states following negotiations of astounding rapidity suggests that world politics has been transformed since the Cold War in ways that we are only beginning to intimate. The Ottawa Process provides reason to believe that global civil society is a basic ingredient of this transformation.

TO WALK WITHOUT FEAR

Although we do not usually think of landmines as weapons of mass destruc-tion, more people have been killed by AP mines than by nuclear and chem-ical weapons combined. From this perspective, landmines truly are 'weapons of mass destruction in slow motion'.[17] Most victims of AP mines are silent, anonymous, nameless casualties. They tend to be among the world's most impoverished and marginalized peoples: front-line soldiers on the Thai-Cambodia border, displaced populations in Afghanistan, Kurdish rebels in Iraq, peasants along the border between Nicaragua and Honduras, or warring factions in the torn states of Bosnia-Herzegovina and Croatia. Tun Channareth, a young Cambodian soldier, was in some ways a typical victim and an exemplary survivor. He described, in broken but poignant English, how he wanted to die after stepping on a mine:

> I saw my legs, bone broken; saw everything lost. I take my own gun and try to kill myself. I cannot do so. After that, I chose the best way to kill myself. I try to find another AP mine but I cannot because both my legs are broken already. Then I saw my friend carry ax. . . . I beg him: 'It is the best for me, when I cut my leg already, then the blood will come out then I will die fast.' But I cannot beg him. He does not allow me and he answers to me: 'Wait a moment, I will bring you to hospital.'[18]

Tun Channareth recovered from his injury, in spite of the amputation of both his legs, and went on to organize a successful petition-drive and collected over a million signatures in support of a mine ban, which he presented to the Prime Minister of Cambodia. He became a founding member of the Cambodian Campaign to Ban Landmines and a familiar symbol of the international campaign, whose image was seen and felt in the capitals of the world as the ban movement gathered momentum. By overcoming his disability and leading the Cambodian campaign, Channareth became a symbol of a global movement; if he could transform his suffering and pain into a single-minded drive to ban mines, could not a world movement transform the private loss of all victims and survivors of AP mines into a public problem that demanded a solution?

Susan Walker of Handicap International used a phrase that captured the movement's humanitarian logic: 'Even soldiers, good soldiers, don't want to kill civilians. War is war, and innocent people have to die, but not 50 years after the war.' Once the issue was framed as a humanitarian problem, it became the common concern of publics around the world. But this did not happen spontaneously or miraculously. It occurred as the result of a co-ordinated grassroots strategy that mobilized a succession of powerful images and messages that were designed to stir and awaken, alarm and outrage, inspire and mobilize the public into action. Images and symbols played a powerful role in mobilizing public opposition to AP mines. Particularly stirring were images of dozens of prosthetic limbs lining field hospital walls, of mountains of shoes in Paris, of child amputees speaking with Diana, Princess of Wales, of children's art against mines, and media portrayals of the dangerous work of courageous deminers in Kuwait or Mozambique. Even Batman and Superman joined the campaign, with comic book stories that helped explain the AP mine issue to children.

This book tells the story of how it was possible to mobilize the world to ban an entire category of weapons in spite of the fact that AP mine survivors were often people like Tun Channareth, who were hurt in isolated, remote parts of the world, received only rudimentary medical attention, were stigmatized and misunderstood by their societies, and yet whose voices were ultimately heard and became part of a platform for international action. It is the story of an international movement that brought together a diverse collection of governments and non-governmental organizations, overcoming significant resistance from the countries that wield diplomatic might and military muscle—as well as manufacture AP mines— to negotiate and then sign and ratify an agreement to ban AP mines with 'no exceptions, no reservations, no loopholes'. It is a story of diplomatic triumph against all odds. And it is the history of an extraordinary alliance— derided by some as a 'coalition of angels'—of diplomats, generals, legislators, mine survivors, medical doctors, committed activists, and ordinary citizens who helped heal the physical, emotional, psychological, and social pain by creating a landmark in international humanitarian law: the ban on AP mines.

The chapters in this volume trace the problem of AP mines from the agony of victims in remote battlefields and villages, to a series of NGO conferences around the world, and culminating in a new diplomatic process that would lead to the signing of a ban treaty in Ottawa. We show how the issue of AP mines was transformed from the lowly file no diplomat wanted to touch to the high politics of public diplomacy and treaty-making. The book reflects a range of perspectives and interests. It contains the voices of those most directly involved in the campaign to ban AP mines, the NGOs— including mine survivors and leaders of national and international campaigns. Some contributors were champions of the Ottawa Process and major players in negotiating the treaty, while others were observers; some contributors celebrate the achievements and legacy of the process, while others are more sceptical. The presentation of a range of views should provide readers with interpretive tools to make their own assessments. Although we believe that banning AP mines was a major diplomatic triumph, it remains to be seen whether the signatories to the Ottawa Convention can maintain the political momentum and provide the resources necessary to ensure that the tasks of demining, assisting victims, and enforcing the Convention are carried out. The job will not be done until people in villages like Kavungo can, finally, walk without fear.

A path to the river. Courtesy of John Rodsted.

Notes

1. Imagery and story in this section is based on Philip C. Winslow, *Sowing the Dragon's Teeth: AP Mines and the Global Legacy of War* (Boston: Beacon Press, 1997), 21–9.
2. Gino Strada, 'The Horror of AP Mines', *Scientific American* 274 (May 1996): 42.
3. Ibid.
4. Roland Fasol et al., 'Vascular injuries caused by anti-personnel mines', *Journal of Cardiovascular Surgery* 30, 3 (1989): 472.
5. Winslow, *Sowing the Dragon's Teeth*, 27–8.
6. Robert M. Coupland and Adrian Korver, 'Injuries from anti-personnel mines: the experience of the International Committee of the Red Cross', *British Medical Journal* 303 (14 Dec. 1991): 1510.
7. Sonia W. Wartan et al., 'Phantom pain and sensation among British veteran amputees', *British Journal of Anaesthesia* 78, 6 (1997): 652.
8. Mamoru Murakota et al., 'Psychosomatic treatment of phantom limb pain with post-traumatic stress disorder: a case report', *Pain* 66, 2–3 (1996): 385–8.
9. Bruce Rybarczyk et al., 'Social Discomfort and Depression in a Sample of Adults with Leg Amputations', *Archives of Physical Medicine and Rehabilitation* 73, 12 (Dec. 1992): 1169.

10. Eric Stover et al., 'The Medical and Social Consequences of AP Mines in Cambodia', *Journal of the American Medical Association* 272, 5 (1994): 334.

11. Thomas Schelling, *Arms and Influence* (New Haven: Yale University Press, 1966), 1–34.

12. Martin Shaw, 'Civil Society and Global Politics: Beyond a Social Movements Approach', *Millennium: Journal of International Studies* 23, 3 (1994): 650.

13. The literature on deliberative polls includes Daniel Yankelovich, *Coming to Public Judgement* (Syracuse, NY: Syracuse University Press, 1991); James Fishkin, *Democracy and Deliberation* (New Haven: Yale University Press, 1991); James Fishkin, *The Voice of the People* (New Haven: Yale University Press, 1995).

14. Slightly more than 200 delegates responded to the self-administered questionnaire, consisting of approximately equal numbers of government officials and NGO members. The regional distribution of respondents was as follows: 32 per cent from North America, 21 per cent from Europe, 19 per cent from Africa, with the remaining 28 per cent from other regions. In addition, a total of 43 delegates participated in four focus groups, again with roughly equal numbers of governmental and non-governmental delegates.

15. A statistical summary of the survey results is available from the editors on request.

16. *Ottawa Citizen*, 28 May 1998, A18.

17. Kenneth Roth, 'Sidelined on Human Rights: America Bows Out', *Foreign Affairs* 77, 2 (1998): 2.

18. Quoted from 'One Step at a Time: The Campaign to Ban Land Mines', a videotape produced by Mines Action Canada and WETV with Corvideocom, Mar. 1998.

PART ONE

THE GLOBAL MOVEMENT FOR A BAN

CHAPTER 2

THE INTERNATIONAL CAMPAIGN TO BAN LANDMINES

Jody Williams and Stephen Goose

STOPPING THE 'COWARD'S WAR': THE ROOTS OF THE INTERNATIONAL CAMPAIGN TO BAN LANDMINES

Non-governmental organizations (NGOs) ultimately launched the campaign to eliminate AP mines. Numbed by the horrific impact of these weapons on civilian populations in almost every region of the world, by the late 1980s and early 1990s a growing number of diverse voices were raised calling for a ban on the weapon.

- A former British army sergeant went to Afghanistan in the late 1980s determined to begin agricultural development programs. Instead, what he found were so many of these 'seeds of death' that viable development was impossible until the mines were pulled from the ground. He helped launch one of the first NGO humanitarian mine clearance programs in the world—an organization that would later help to found the ICBL.
- In January 1991, after months in refugee camps on the Thai-Cambodia border caring for landmine victims, a member of the Women's Commission on Refugee Women and Children called for a ban on AP mines in testimony before the US Congress.
- In September of 1991, Human Rights Watch (Asia Division) and Physicians for Human Rights, after a field mission to Cambodia, issued their landmark work, *Landmines in Cambodia: The Coward's War*. They jointly called for a ban on AP mines.
- The Vietnam Veterans of America Foundation had opened its first prosthetics clinic in Cambodia in the summer of 1991. Quickly recognizing that providing prosthetic devices to mine victims without going to the root of the problem was no solution, they joined forces with Medico International of Germany to launch an advocacy campaign to ban AP mines.
- Fourteen hundred Australian citizens—educated by fieldworkers' stories of life in the Cambodian minefields—petitioned their government in February of 1992 to ban the use and production of AP mines.
- After years of providing prosthetic limbs to mine victims in dozens of countries, Handicap International decided to venture for the first time into political advocacy. Issuing *The Coward's War* in French

and working with the Mines Advisory Group and Physicians for Human Rights, Handicap International launched its campaign to 'Stop the Coward's War' with a petition calling for increased restrictions on mine use. Tens of thousands of French citizens would rally behind this call and press their government for action on AP mines.

Efforts to ban AP mines, or at least control their use, had begun in the 1970s. At that time, the International Committee of the Red Cross (ICRC), along with a handful of NGOs, had pressed governments to look at weapons that were indiscriminate or caused superfluous injury or unnecessary suffering. The impetus of this effort had been the impact on the world's psyche of the war in Vietnam—seeing civilians and soldiers alike mutilated for a lifetime by napalm and other weapons of war. One of the weapons of particular concern at that time was the landmine.

Many soldiers argue that they had never thought about the landmine as being much different from any of the other weapons at their disposal. But it does not take too long to educate soldier and civilian alike that AP mines are, in fact, quite different. They cannot discriminate between a combatant or a civilian. While the use of the weapon might be militarily justifiable during the days, weeks, or even months of the battle, once peace is declared the landmine does not stop killing—a unique feature that has earned the landmine the moniker the 'eternal sentry'. It is this long-term impact, coupled with its indiscriminate nature, that, in the view of the ICBL, makes the AP mine illegal.

A majority of the conflicts in the last half of this century have been internal conflicts, and in many of those wars AP mines have been used in great numbers. This proliferation of use has resulted in a global crisis—tens of millions of AP mines contaminate approximately 70 countries around the world. As is all too often the case, the majority of those countries are in the developing world where few have the resources to deal with the mess. Moreover, the problem extends beyond the mines already in the ground. Current estimates indicate that 100–200 million mines are stockpiled and ready for use in arsenals around the world.

Governments remained largely unaware of the degree of the landmine epidemic until the end of the Cold War. Yet the devastating, long-term consequences of AP mines were becoming all too apparent to those NGOs who were putting prosthetic limbs on victims, removing the detritus of war from the ground, providing aid and relief to war-torn societies, and documenting violations of human rights and the laws of war. It was the NGOs, as they tried to help war-torn societies like Cambodia, Afghanistan, and Somalia rebuild, who began to educate the public as to the degree and scope of the crisis. They showed that millions of AP mines were affecting every aspect of peacekeeping and every aspect of post-conflict reconstruction.

Ultimately, their all-too-real experience with the AP mine problem compelled these NGOs to join forces in an organized effort to achieve a global ban. Yet, even as the ICBL was launched, few would have ever predicted that within five years an international treaty banning the use, production, trade, and stockpiling of AP mines would be signed by over 120 countries in Ottawa, Canada. Fewer still would have imagined that this global citizens' coalition would be recognized as the driving force within the movement to ban AP mines, to the extent that it would be awarded the 1997 Nobel Peace Prize.

The Formation of the ICBL

The ICBL was formally launched after a meeting in the New York office of Human Rights Watch in October 1992. Six NGOs, which had taken a number of individual and joint steps in the direction of a ban campaign, agreed to initiate an international campaign by issuing a 'Joint Call to Ban Antipersonnel Landmines' and hosting the first NGO-sponsored international landmine conference in May of 1993. These organizations—Handicap International (France), Human Rights Watch (US), Medico International (Germany), Mines Advisory Group (UK), Physicians for Human Rights (US), and the Vietnam Veterans of America Foundation (US)—became the steering committee of the International Campaign to Ban Landmines, with Jody Williams of the VVAF appointed as its co-ordinator. These organizations, and the more than 1,200 other NGOs in some 60 countries around the world that have since joined the ICBL, were united behind the call for a total ban on AP mines. For the ICBL, the issue was simple and the call was clear. First, the world needed an international ban on the use, production, stockpiling, and transfer of AP mines. Second, resources for humanitarian mine clearance and for victim assistance had to be increased. To achieve these goals, the ICBL recognized that its member NGOs would have to work at the national, regional, and international levels to build public awareness and create the political will necessary to bring about a landmine ban.

A major strength of the ICBL was its ability to cut across disciplines to bring together a diverse array of NGOs to work towards a single goal. While united behind the call for a ban, this vast and diverse coalition has been tremendously flexible in its day-to-day work. Operating without a 'secretariat'—no central office or bureaucracy—member organizations were free to pursue the achievement of the campaign's goals as best fit their own mandate. Thus, for example, US-based NGOs would not try to dictate to

African NGOs how to operate, nor would African NGOs try to tell Asian or European colleagues how to move their governments and militaries towards a ban. It was clear that NGOs in the developed North, with their political culture of NGO/government dialogue, would not engage their governments precisely the same way that NGO partners in emerging democracies would. While the ICBL consistently called for increased and sustained resources for mine clearance and victim assistance, its primary focus was the achievement of an international ban treaty. Campaigners were clear that without a ban on the use, production, trade, and stockpiling of AP mines, it would be virtually impossible to stop mine proliferation, clean up the mess, and help mine victims reintegrate into society.

Beyond the call for the ban, much of the unity and success of the coalition can be traced to a commitment to a constant exchange of information—both internally among members of the ICBL as well as with governments, the media, and the general public. While the ICBL was quick to develop strong contacts in the international media, there was no overarching ICBL media strategy. The campaign certainly recognized the critical importance of favourable—and steady—coverage of the issue. But it was up to individual members to work with the media within their own contexts. Fortunately, many ICBL campaigners already had good contacts and significant experience with the media.

Most of the early news on AP mines was focused on the victim side of the equation and the tremendous difficulties faced by humanitarian de-miners. However, one by one, major media sources in almost all regions of the world began to endorse the concept of a global ban on AP mines. Prominent media outlets increasingly recognized the compelling story behind the global humanitarian crisis and the 'David vs Goliath' nature of NGOs taking on governments and militaries to ban a weapon used by armies for decades. In the face of media and public opinion increasingly united behind the view that AP mines were horrific and indiscriminate killers of women and children, militaries everywhere were very reluctant to try to justify publicly their 'need' for this weapon.

Within the ICBL itself, member organizations regularly communicated, through the ICBL co-ordinator, information on their political strategies and tactics, campaign activities, successes, and setbacks. This ability to provide its members with a sense of the overall activities of the campaign was key to the creation and maintenance of the momentum of the ICBL. One of the early communication tools used to maintain contact among ICBL members was the *Landmine Update*, a quarterly newsletter written and circulated by the ICBL's co-ordinator. Followed closely by NGOs and governments alike, the *Landmine Update* helped to chronicle the country-by-country activities of the ban movement—creating a sense of inexorable momentum towards the ban. Issues of the *Landmine Update* were supplemented by periodic mailings to ICBL members that provided information on UN resolutions, national legislation, organizational resolutions in support of the ban, and significant press clippings on various aspects of the AP mines problem.

While new communications technologies certainly helped facilitate communications within the ICBL, a bit of a mythology has developed surrounding the ICBL and its reliance on electronic mail. The ease and speed of communication within the ICBL provided by e-mail clearly had a great impact on the ability of civil society organizations from diverse cultures to exchange information and develop integrated global political strategies— for example, *Landmine Update* mailings were quickly replaced by e-mail circulation of the newsletter. However, e-mail alone did not 'move the movement'. When the ICBL was not much more than a handful of disparate NGOs, it was clear to the initiators of the campaign that in order to hold together NGOs of such diverse interests, these organizations would have to feel an immediate and important part of developments within the campaign. In the early years of the ICBL, this was achieved by extensive use of the fax machine. The fax was relatively new—it was 'exciting'. Information arriving almost instantaneously by fax was perceived to be more important—and thus more deserving of an immediate response— than regular mail. Therefore, the ICBL relied on fax and telephone communication in the early years for much of its almost daily communications. Even though this was somewhat expensive, the early work was undertaken largely in the North, where these costs were not as prohibitive as in the South. It was not until the ICBL was able to broaden its work from largely mine-producing countries to mine-affected countries that its members began to make the shift to electronic communication—a switch that was not fully achieved until late 1995 and early 1996. Once e-mail became established within the ICBL, its lower costs and increased reliability relative to telephone and fax made it particularly important in facilitating communication with campaigners in developing nations. Not only did it allow the campaign to share information and jointly develop strategies more effectively, but it was also crucial to joint planning of major activities and conferences, such as those held in Cambodia in 1995 and Mozambique in 1997.

Equally important as fax, phone, and e-mail in linking together the huge ICBL coalition has been networking through travel and the development of personal relationships—both within the campaign and between campaigners and various government and military representatives. Indeed, e-mail has been used relatively little for communications outside of the campaign. The much remarked upon close co-operation between governments and NGOs during the Ottawa Process was more the result of face-to-face meetings than anything else. From its very beginning, the ICBL has been built on networking, both individual and organizational. For example, upon agreeing to help launch a campaign, Williams's first meetings were with Human Rights Watch, Physicians for Human Rights, large religious organizations, UN agencies, and the office of Senator Patrick Leahy, who would prove so important to early momentum of the campaign and to movement within the US. The first travel abroad in the name of a landmine ban was to the offices of Medico International in Germany and then on to press the case of the campaign at a meeting of the European Network Against the Arms Trade, which brought together arms control groups from all over Europe and was a natural audience for 'converts' to the mine ban.

These types of meetings, coupled with the annual international meetings sponsored by the ICBL, helped spur the dramatic growth of the campaign's membership. Unlike in many coalition efforts, international meetings of the ICBL have never been devoted simply to sharing information. ICBL conferences have also included campaign capacity-building workshops and training sessions, along with the development of work plans at regional and international levels. NGOs have always left these important conferences with a clear sense of forward movement articulated through ICBL 'action plans'.

As noted above, the need for a ban on AP mines emerged from the fieldwork of NGOs who found themselves working in communities trying to survive, quite literally, in the middle of minefields—minefields supplied largely by the North. It was a sense of responsibility that motivated these groups to launch the ICBL. These NGOs also recognized that first steps by governments, if they were taken at all, would most likely be taken in those countries with a political culture in which NGOs could most effectively pressure governments to take action. Thus, for the first few years, much of the work was concentrated on expanding the campaign throughout North America, Europe, and Australia and New Zealand. Many of these countries had also been the most significant recent producers and exporters of anti-personnel mines. Large-scale expansion of the campaign throughout Asia and Africa did not occur until the ICBL network had been consolidated in the North and political momentum had begun to build.

Before the Ottawa Process: The Interplay of National and International Campaign Initiatives

The ICBL recognized that momentum behind the ban would be built through a combination of national and international initiatives. The objective of early political action was clear—education of the public and public officials about the landmine crisis would be essential to force changes in national and international policies and practices. The ICBL was painfully aware that only one treaty attempted to control the use of AP mines—the 1980 Convention on Certain Conventional Weapons (CCW). While the treaty was a dismal failure in reducing the impact of AP mines on civilian populations, it did provide a potential platform for further action on the issue. The CCW had entered into force in 1983. Since any signatory state could call for a review conference of the treaty 10 years after that date, the initial strategy of the campaign was to find a state willing to take on the issue.

The ICBL was not confident that a CCW Review Conference would result in a ban, but it did recognize that the review process would provide a platform from which to educate the public and governments alike on the nature and scope of the AP mine problem. There were other reasons for guarded optimism. Some states had begun to take unilateral action on the issue. The first unilateral initiative in the world was a one-year moratorium on the export of AP mines by the US in 1992. The moratorium was subsequently extended several times, and in 1997 the Clinton administration announced a permanent export ban. The moratorium was the result of an initiative undertaken by Senator Patrick Leahy and Congressman Lane Evans, who worked closely with US NGOs, most notably the Vietnam Veterans of America Foundation and a consortium of NGOs in Washington that work on arms control issues.

When speaking candidly about that first export moratorium, some members of the ICBL note that they wish they could claim 'strategic brilliance' in pressing for the moratorium and that they immediately recognized the global impact such legislation would have. But that was not exactly the case. NGOs did support the congressional initiative, but its success was much more the result of congressional strategy than NGO or grassroots pressure. While the ICBL immediately praised the initiative, it did not anticipate the tremendous political boost the export moratorium would provide to the ban movement. The simple fact that the US had just stopped the export of a legal weapon galvanized the imagination of the international community. Politicians, in particular, began to believe that if the US could take this step, perhaps significant movement against AP mines was possible.

The first country to respond to the US initiative was France. While in Cambodia in February 1993, French President François Mitterrand announced that his country was making official its 'voluntary abstention' from the export of AP mines, a policy that had been in place since the mid-1980s. Shortly after this announcement, under intense pressure from Handicap International and the French ban campaign, France called for a Review Conference of the CCW. Within a relatively short period of time more than a dozen countries announced comprehensive export moratoria. This led others to take even more 'radical' steps. In June of 1994, the Swedish parliament, under pressure from Sweden's national campaign headed by Radda Barnen (Swedish Save the Children), voted that the government 'should declare that an international total ban against anti-personnel mines is the only real solution to the humanitarian problem that the use of mines causes. Sweden should therefore propose solutions in order to achieve such a ban.' Sweden would later table an amendment to the AP mines protocol of the CCW. If there had been sufficient support, this would have effectively banned AP mines.

During this period the Italian senate, in a surprise move on 2 August 1994, ordered the Italian government to ratify immediately Protocol II of the 1980 Convention and to 'immediately activate the necessary legal instruments to launch a moratorium on the export of anti-personnel mines, to cease production of those mines by Italian companies or companies operating in Italy and support workers in that sector; and to promote de-mining in countries contaminated with anti-personnel mines.' This was a critical move on the part of a country that was considered to be one of the three most significant producers and exporters of AP mines in the world.

Shortly after the Italian initiative, in his address before the UN General Assembly on 26 September 1994, US President Bill Clinton called for the 'eventual elimination' of AP mines. His surprise statement set the stage for a US-sponsored resolution that not only urged states to enact export moratoriums, but in its final operative point encouraged 'further international efforts to seek solutions to the problems caused by anti-personnel land-mines, with a view towards the eventual elimination of anti-personnel land-mines.' The combination of Clinton's remarks and the resolution erroneously led many to believe that the US administration was finally following the lead on the issue shown in the US Congress and was signalling its willingness to move rapidly towards a ban.

The momentum on national fronts continued and in March 1995, Belgium became the first government in the world to ban the use, production, trade, and stockpiling of AP mines. Norway followed suit in June 1995. Senior representatives from both governments have on many occasions cited the pressures from NGOs as the key factor in bringing about their national bans. The tide was turning.

THE GROWTH OF THE ICBL AND ITS POLITICAL IMPACT

With the formal launch of the ICBL, its six founding NGOs had committed themselves to organizing the first international NGO conference on AP mines. Held in London in May 1993, the meeting was attended by some 70 representatives from approximately 40 NGOs. Just one year later, participation doubled for the campaign's second conference, held in Geneva. By this time, the ICBL's efforts were receiving important support from UN agencies. The Geneva conference, for example, was co-hosted by UNICEF, which provided all the logistical support, space, and support staff for the conference. This early and ongoing support from UNICEF was very important in increasing the institutional credibility of the campaign. In addition, by taking the political lead within the UN, UNICEF helped push the UN systems towards formal support for a ban.

By the time the campaign gathered for the Geneva conference it was clear that the ICBL had begun to generate significant momentum for action. Behind almost every domestic landmine initiative one could find evidence that national campaigns were making a difference. And yet the specific role played by member NGOs varied greatly from country to country—a reflection of the overall flexibility of the ICBL. In the US, for example, NGOs worked directly with Senator Leahy's staff to develop and move forward pro-ban legislation. Because of this immediate access and support 'at the top', the NGOs, while generating a great deal of media attention to the issue, did not work to build extensive grassroots support in the US at that time. In contrast, most European campaigns put a higher priority on directly engaging the public than on working with legislators or other government officials.

Movement by the French government was due primarily to the grassroots pressure developed by Handicap International, which led the NGO effort in France. In May 1992, HI had begun a country-wide petition campaign calling for a halt to the 'Coward's War', which gathered tens of thousands of signatures in support of the ban movement. Mitterrand is widely viewed to have initiated the CCW review process in response to the demands of the NGOs and the French public and to 'get them off his back'. The French campaign also held numerous meetings with French ministries and conducted a number of seminars at government offices on the issues related to a mine ban in an attempt to move forward French landmine policy.

In Italy, the dramatic shift in the Italian government's position in the summer of 1994 could be traced to the tremendously creative and hard work by the Italian national campaign—a group that did not seem to hold much promise of growth or impact less than a year before. Indeed, a meeting in Rome in December 1993 meant to build the Italian campaign had more participants from outside the country than from within. But from this inauspicious start, the Italian campaign blasted into the Italian public's consciousness in June 1994 by getting the most popular Italian national television talk show to begin to devote time every day to the issue of AP mines. The series culminated with members of the Italian campaign and the Italian Defence Minister appearing together on one of the shows, where the minister made the surprising declaration that Italy should ban the use of AP mines and end their production.

The Italian campaign was also able to convince the workers' representatives of Valsella Meccanotecnica—one of the world's biggest mine producers—and the trade unions of Brescia, the town where Valsella was located, to issue a press statement indicating that they 'agree with and support the campaign to ban landmines. It is mandatory to eliminate the production of every type of anti-personnel mine, including the so-called self-destructing and self-neutralizing mines.' Furthermore, the trade unionists asked the Italian government 'to take immediate initiatives to stop landmine production and trade, and . . . support all the humanitarian actions in favour of the victims.' Defence Minister Previti followed through with his public declaration, indicating in a letter to an Italian pro-ban senator that he had given the 'necessary instructions to start the procedure that will bring Italy to the unilateral commitment not to produce and export anti-personnel landmines.' And then, on 2 August 1994, the Italian senate passed legislation indicating that the government was formally undertaking 'to observe a unilateral moratorium on the sale of anti-personnel mines to other countries' and was readying 'the necessary instruments for stopping production of such devices by Italian companies or companies operating on Italian territory.'

Building on this success, the Italian campaign pressed its advantage and held three days of activities in Brescia on 23–5 September 1994. Events included a 'standing room only' concert to raise money for the campaign, a day-long seminar on AP mines, and a march to Castenedolo, the town where Valsella's production facility is located. From a couple of hundred people who began the 17-kilometre march, seemingly out of nowhere, thousands joined their ranks, including four women workers from Valsella, who also spoke at the rally culminating the march. The only women working at the plant, these four alone dared risk retribution from the factory owners. In a very moving display, they stood at the stage holding a banner declaring that in order to feed their own children, they should not have to produce AP mines that kill others' children. In a special session on 22 September, the town council of Castenedolo had voted unanimously to join the landmine campaign. The Italian campaign has been able to gain the support of municipal governments throughout the country, with more than 160 city councils passing resolutions in support of the ban movement.

As campaigns in the North continued to grow and generate success, ban campaigns began to emerge in the South, including in mine-affected countries such as Cambodia. In late July 1994, NGOs, the Cambodia Mine Action Centre (the national demining organization), and the UN Special Rapporteur on Human Rights had issued a statement to the press in Phnom Penh calling on the Cambodian government to 'declare a total and permanent ban on the import, stockpiling and use of AP mines; such a ban should include the destruction of all existing stockpiles of mines'. They also called on the UN Secretary-General to 'take a new and imaginative initiative' to 'completely redraft the 1980 Convention which has proved ineffective in preventing the global spread of landmines, with their devastating toll of death and suffering.' The next month, the NGO Forum on Cambodia together with local and international NGOs launched the Cambodia Campaign to Ban Landmines.

Early in 1995 the new Cambodia campaign decided to hold a major conference. After extensive consultations with other members of the ICBL, this grew into the third ICBL international conference, held in Phnom Penh in June 1995. It would be the first landmine conference held in a mine-infested country. It would also be the first major ICBL event organized primarily through e-mail. The Cambodian campaigners worked hard to build public awareness and support for the ban and the international conference. They launched a massive signature campaign, gathering names at temples, markets, and schools throughout the country: at every public event—any time or any place people would be gathered—the Cambodia campaign was there. Signatures were also gathered at the annual peace walk, held in late spring of every year, when thousands walk the length of the country to symbolize their cry for a peaceful, united Cambodia.

All of this creativity and excitement helped create a wildly successful international conference, with more than 450 participants from over 40 countries. Campaign networking grew dramatically as a result of the Cambodia conference, new information was exchanged, and plans of action developed. Importantly, six new national campaigns in the South were launched as a direct result of the conference. Finally, by the end of the conference, 340,000 Cambodian citizens, including King Sihanouk at the conference itself, had added their names to the Cambodian petition calling for an immediate ban on AP mines. This initiative helped spark other signature drives in national campaigns around the world, resulting in a million and a half signatures being gathered for presentation to the delegates of the CCW Review Conference, which opened only three months later in Vienna.

The ICBL and the CCW Review Process

Preparations for the review of the CCW landmines protocol began with a series of four governmental expert sessions held in Geneva in 1994 and early 1995. The formal negotiations began in Vienna in late September and were expected to take no longer than three weeks. During the CCW preparatory sessions, the ICBL urged delegates to take an aggressive approach to the landmine problem based on a serious assessment of the real impact of AP mines on the ground. However, from beginning to end, the preparatory sessions and the negotiations fell victim to an incremental approach that limited progress to adjustments within the existing framework of the treaty. It was abundantly clear that the international community simply was not ready to meet its then-stated goal of eliminating AP mines through the vehicle of an amended Protocol II of the CCW.

While not allowed inside the negotiations themselves, members of the ICBL still managed to have a significant impact on the process. The wealth of the ICBL's factual information on the landmine crisis, coupled with the skill and tenacity of its representatives at the meetings, strengthened relationships between the campaign and governments and firmly established the expertise of the NGO community on the landmine issue. These efforts would pay off later as the momentum for a ban continued to build. This period of NGO/government interaction helped pave the way for open cooperation between the ICBL and pro-ban governments during the Ottawa Process, and led to the ICBL's full participation in the meetings culminating in the ban treaty negotiations in Oslo in September 1997.

The ICBL sent a team of seasoned organizers to Vienna weeks in advance to work with Austrian NGOs preparing for the CCW conference. The campaign planned to hit delegates and the media of the world with a barrage of information about various aspects of the landmine crisis, as well as about the limited efforts to resolve the crisis at the Review Conference. Its media strategy included regular briefings on issues of concern to the campaign as well as the twice-weekly production of the CCW News, an ICBL newsletter on developments at the conference. While one of the newsletter's columns, 'The Good, The Bad and the Ugly', frequently roused the ire of governments, it also pressured them to bring their public statements in line with the realities of their negotiating positions—or vice versa. Not only did the ICBL give regular briefings to government delegates and the media, but delegates were also invited to explain their positions to campaigners.

The ICBL organized a range of advocacy activities at the conference site in Vienna and globally in support of its call for a ban. Activities included the delivery of six tons of shoes to the Austrian parliament by Pax Christi, UNICEF, and Save the Children Austria. The shoes symbolized unneeded shoes by countless present and future mine victims. A similar event was carried out the same weekend in Paris. During the conference, 1.7 million signatures of people from around the world calling for a ban were presented to the CCW Review Conference president, Ambassador Johan Molander of Sweden. The very moving ceremony featured mine victims from Afghanistan, Cambodia, Mozambique, and the US delivering signatures collected in 53 countries. Simulated minefields and photographic displays were presented in Vienna during the three weeks of the conference.

While the representatives of the International Campaign to Ban Landmines had not gone to Vienna with expectations of a ban, neither did they expect such limited changes in the treaty or the huge step backwards with the change in the AP mine definition. As it became increasingly clear that little of value to the ban movement would emerge from the review of the CCW, the campaign put tremendous pressure on governments extremely wary of 'bad press' on the issue. The ICBL worked to convince the media and friendly governments that not only were the negotiations *not* moving towards a ban, but they were, in fact, weakening the already horribly weak CCW landmine protocol. The certainty of bad press and a public backlash against the weak results of the negotiations produced a deadlock in Vienna, with governments deciding to meet again for two additional rounds of negotiation—one week in January of 1996 to deal with technical issues and two weeks in April and May to conclude the negotiations.

As the deadlock was developing during the Vienna session, members of the ICBL began discussing strategies to continue to build momentum beyond the Review Conference. A decision that turned out to be of pivotal importance in the next stage of the ban movement was made to put a priority on getting avowedly pro-ban governments to self-identify and work together as a bloc to move beyond the CCW impasse. While campaigners certainly did not believe there would be much enthusiasm for a new round of international meetings to deal with the landmine issue, it seemed clear that the only way to maintain movement would be to get a relatively small number of pro-ban states to work together on moving the issue forward. In addition, the ICBL began to talk much more seriously about regional work—trying to establish 'mine-free zones' as building blocks to a global ban.

When governments reconvened in Geneva in January, the ICBL invited pro-ban states to a meeting to discuss a co-operative way forward. To the surprise of many, eight states showed up for the first meeting. Fourteen came to a second meeting hosted by the Quakers at the beginning of the final negotiating session in April, and 11 to a third meeting at the end of the review conference in early May. Out of this series of meetings the Canadian government offered to host a conference that would bring together pro-ban governments, the NGO community, and international organizations to strategize on how to advance the cause of the ban.

More than 150 NGO representatives from 20 countries had participated in the final Geneva session. The campaign was as highly visible in Geneva as it was in Vienna. Advocacy activities included a simulated minefield that delegates encountered several times each day in the hall of the UN conference centre in Geneva, a 'Wall of Remembrance' with pictures of mine victims, and a clock registering another victim every 20 minutes. Photographic exhibitions, ban posters on buses, 'Ban Mines' stickers every-where, another mountain of shoes, and demining demonstrations all cul-minated in a campaign vigil at the gates of the UN building on the final day of the conference. The campaign held daily press briefings in the UN building and issued daily press communiqués. And at the ICBL's request, the closing plenary began with a minute of silence in remembrance of mine victims, past and future.

The movement to ban anti-personnel mines was quickly overtaking the CCW approach to controlling mines. The new landmines protocol was already largely irrelevant when it was finally agreed to on 3 May 1996. It was clear that many governments agreed to it, recognizing that it would make little difference in the short or long run, but resigned to the notion that it was the best that could be negotiated by consensus at the time. At the opening of the Review Conference, in Vienna in September 1995, only 14 nations had voiced support for an immediate ban. By the end of the conference, that number had grown to 41. On the final day of the confer-ence alone, five nations declared their support for a ban. But even more important than the numbers, many of these governments began to come together as an identifiable, cohesive bloc and to push for concrete steps to advance a ban domestically, regionally, and internationally.

As a clear symbol of the growing NGO/government partnership, on the last day of the CCW conference in May 1996 the ICBL held a joint press con-ference with the UN Department of Humanitarian Affairs, UNICEF, and the government of Canada. For each the message was the same—only a ban will do. And as awareness—and thus pressure on governments—grew, many governments began to approach the campaign about what it would take to be considered a 'pro-ban' nation. These states wanted to be invited to the Canadian conference and to be considered part of the ban movement.

THE ICBL AND THE OTTAWA PROCESS

When the Canadian government began floating the idea of hosting a meeting to strategize about a ban, some in the ICBL were sceptical, to say the least. One campaigner remembers wondering if the move was really designed to ensure that momentum for a ban would be sidetracked by more government discussions leading nowhere. But as the ICBL leadership began working closely with Canadian officials in the development of the meeting, it quickly became clear that Canada was genuinely interested in developing a concrete road-map leading to an international AP mine ban.

As planning for the Ottawa conference progressed, interest in the meeting continued to grow. Initially, planners had envisioned a relatively small meeting. Most believed it would be considered 'wildly' successful if even 20 states participated. But the 'Towards a Global Ban on Anti-Personnel Landmines' conference held on 3–5 October 1996 was more wildly successful than any had imagined. This historic meeting brought together 50 governments that had pledged support for a total ban on anti-personnel mines, as well as 24 observer states, dozens of NGOs from the International Campaign to Ban Landmines, various United Nations agencies, and the ICRC and other international organizations.

The Ottawa conference yielded three concrete results: a final declaration agreed to by the 50 participating governments recognizing the urgent need for a ban on anti-personnel mines; the conference Chairman's Agenda for Action, an outline of actions for reaching a ban rapidly; and, most importantly, the stunning announcement by Canada's Foreign Minister, Lloyd Axworthy, that Canada was prepared to hold a treaty-signing conference for a total ban in December 1997. As host of the meeting, the Foreign Minister gave opening and closing remarks to conference participants. Everyone anticipated the normal congratulatory statement thanking delegates for their hard work and support in developing the Ottawa Declaration and the Agenda for Action. Only a handful were aware of what would come next. As Mr Axworthy came to the end of his remarks, he rocked the diplomatic community by challenging governments to negotiate a simple and clear treaty banning AP mines and return to Ottawa—in the space of a little over one year—to sign the document! He further ruffled diplomatic feathers by clearly stating that Canada planned to work in open partnership with the ICBL to achieve this goal.

Amid the cheers of the ban campaigners, the silence of the diplomats was deafening. Even clearly pro-ban states were horrified. Canada had stepped outside of diplomatic processes and procedures and put them between a rock and a hard place. They had come to Ottawa to strategize on how best to achieve a ban treaty, and now they had a concrete, and extraordinarily ambitious, time frame in which to do it. The foot-soldiers of the campaign stood up and cheered while many diplomats literally hung their heads and wrung their hands.

The conference was also notable for the unprecedentedly high level of co-operation with and involvement by NGOs in both its planning and execution. Between May and October, members of the Canadian government and the ICBL had consulted frequently on nearly every aspect of the conference, including how best to ensure maximum attendance by governments. The ICBL was given a seat at the table as a full participant in the conference, while those governments unwilling to declare themselves pro-ban sat in the back as observers. Campaigners were actively involved in drafting the precise language of both the final declaration and the action plan. This extraordinary level of co-operation would become a defining feature of what would become known as the Ottawa Process. Between October 1996 and December 1997 the ICBL would work in close partnership with Canada and other pro-ban states of the Ottawa Process to help develop treaty language and build the political will necessary to ensure the success of the process.

Yet it was not clear in the first critical months after the Ottawa meeting that the Ottawa Process would survive. The Canadian government had to put a lot of diplomatic time, effort, and money into making the process work. Canadian diplomats shuttled the world over, soothing angry governments, reminding them of their own commitment to a ban 'as soon as possible', and working hard to form a core group that was regionally representative and that would 'deliver the goods'—an international treaty banning the use, production, trade, and stockpiling of AP mines in just over one year's time. During ICBL meetings in Ottawa in October and in Brussels in December, the ICBL declared the Ottawa Process to be its highest priority for the year and threw its full weight behind the effort. National campaigns pressed their governments to embrace the challenge and publicly support the Ottawa Process. Once shored up, the momentum appeared to build continuously. As the Process moved forward, the core group of pro-ban governments dedicated to the success of the treaty grew and worked closely with the ICBL.

Within the core group, Austria was given the task of developing a draft convention that ultimately became the basis for the Oslo negotiations. For its part, the ICBL developed its own treaty, which, in its view, established clear visions of what a total ban Convention would look like. Once this was drafted by the ICBL's treaty working group, members of the steering committee, beginning in January 1997 and several times thereafter, took the treaty to New York to meet with government officials at the United

Nations and educate them as to the ICBL's views on the essential aspects of a ban Convention. The ICBL's ad hoc treaty team pressed strongly throughout the Ottawa Process to ensure that the formal AP mine ban Convention would incorporate as much of the ICBL treaty as possible.

The details of the Ottawa Process are discussed in other chapters in this volume. The Ottawa Process was essentially a series of meetings designed to develop and negotiate the ban Convention as well as build the political will to sign it. Treaty language was developed at government-sponsored conferences in Vienna, Bonn, and Brussels, as well as in smaller meetings of the core group and through bilateral government consultations. The ICBL's views on treaty language were sought throughout the process, and the ICBL was an active participant in each of the government conferences. Moreover, pro-ban governments, the ICRC, and the ICBL hosted a number of conferences aimed at ensuring maximum support for the Ottawa Process and the December treaty-signing.

Over the course of the Vienna, Bonn, and Brussels meetings, the ICBL worked to expand its co-operative relationship with pro-ban governments. In a conscious move to emphasize the collaborative nature of the effort, the ICBL hosted a number of joint press conferences with its coalition partners. In Vienna this included the Austrian chairman of the conference, as well as representatives from the Canadian and Belgian governments and the ICRC. In Brussels, the day before the conference opened, the ICBL co-ordinator joined the Belgian Foreign Minister and Defence Minister as well as a representative from Canada at a high-profile press conference in the Brussels city hall. The ICBL co-ordinator was also asked to give one of three keynote speeches to open the conference, along with the Belgian Foreign Minister and the head of the Canadian delegation. During her speech, Jody Williams coined the refrain that the ICBL would adopt as its 'mantra' *en route* to the Oslo negotiations—the ICBL demanded nothing less than a comprehensive ban treaty with 'no exceptions, no reservations, no loopholes'. The conference ended with a joint press conference featuring the ICBL and the Belgian Foreign Minister.

Circling the Globe: Building Political Will on the Road to Ottawa
The ICBL threw its weight behind the Ottawa Process. In addition to participating in government-sponsored, treaty-oriented conferences, the campaign held its own series of meetings. The formats for some meetings already scheduled by the ICBL were modified to provide opportunities to build political will behind the Ottawa Process. Governments were invited to most if not all meetings in one form or another. Every meeting would

stress the development of co-operation between NGOs and governments on the road to the ban treaty.

NGO meetings were held in Ottawa and Brussels in 1996, and in Maputo, Tokyo, Stockholm, Sydney, New Delhi, Senegal, and Sanaa in 1997. Other conferences to help build political will were sponsored by the ICRC in Harare in April 1997 and Manila in July 1997, as well as by the Organization of African Unity (OAU) and South African government in Kempton Park in May and by the government of Turkmenistan in Ashgabat in June. Regardless of the sponsor, each of these conferences was characterized by a high degree of co-operation among the partners in the ban movement—the NGOs, ICRC, and pro-ban governments.

From Africa . . .

As noted above, as the CCW was winding to a disappointing close in May 1996, the ICBL decided to focus some of its political work on the creation of 'mine-free zones' as a way to build regional blocs in support of a ban. Central America declared itself the world's first mine-free zone in September 1996 as all six governments in the region committed themselves to no further use, production, trade, or stockpiling of the weapon by the year 2000. Caribbean nations forming the CARICOM followed suit in November.

The ICBL identified southern Africa as a next potential mine-free zone, largely because it constituted one of the most mined regions in the world. A 'mine-free zone' in Africa was seen as an important next step in building regional blocs, and Africa as a crucial region for the success of the Ottawa Treaty. A key failure for the CCW had been the lack of participation by mine-affected countries and the developing world in general. Thus, the ICBL decided to hold its 4th International NGO Conference on Landmines in southern Africa and sent Elizabeth Bernstein, its key conference organizer, to the region in August 1996. Although initial plans called for the conference to be held in Zimbabwe, it was decided after consultations with campaigners in the region to hold it instead in Mozambique. Organizers believed it to be extremely important that the conference be held in a seriously mine-contaminated country. Moreover, holding the conference in Mozambique would also help to strengthen the young campaign there—providing an opportunity for it to contribute to the organization of a major international conference.

The Mozambique campaign had been launched in November 1995 with a nationwide signature-gathering campaign in support of a ban. The campaign began modestly, as citizens both weary and wary after decades of

war were reluctant to promote a campaign not embraced by the government. But, in a prime example of how the landmine campaign helped to
empower civil society, the Mozambique campaign grew increasingly active
and influential, starting a newsletter, taking on a full-time co-ordinator,
lobbying parliamentary committees, and meeting with the Foreign
Minister and Speaker of the Assembly. The campaign grew to over 70 organizations and gathered over 100,000 signatures on the petition calling for
a total ban. Although the campaign repeatedly petitioned the Mozambican
President for a meeting to present the signatures, it was not until the week
before the conference itself that the audience was granted.

During the months of preparation leading up to the conference held on
25–8 February 1997 in Maputo, ICBL staff worked not only on conference
preparation itself but also on providing capacity-building and campaign
skills workshops throughout the region to help strengthen and build new
African ban campaigns. Indeed, four new campaigns were launched during
the course of the planning for the conference, in Zambia in September,
Zimbabwe in October, Angola in November, and Somalia in February
1997. In addition, because it was committed to building campaigns in and
networking throughout the South, the ICBL hosted a two-day South-South
meeting immediately prior to the Maputo conference. People from Africa,
Asia, and Latin America came together to share information, ideas, and
plans for the future. The co-ordinator of the ICBL participated in this
important South-South meeting to demonstrate the linkages between
these new campaigns and the ICBL overall.

The Maputo conference proved to be a crucial step in the Ottawa
Process—considered by the ICBL to be an unqualified success in expanding
the campaign throughout the continent, moving southern Africa towards
becoming a mine-free zone, and increasing support for the Ottawa treaty.
More than 450 participants from 60 countries listened as Mozambique's
President Joaquim Chissano opened the conference, titled 'Toward a Mine-
Free Southern Africa'. After four days of strategy sessions and informational
workshops, the conference ended with a final declaration endorsing the
Ottawa Process and calling on all governments to commit publicly to signing the ban treaty in December. South Africa announced a unilateral ban on
AP mines the week before the conference and Mozambique followed with its
own unilateral ban during the conference. In all, a total of 17 governments
addressed the meeting. Malawi and Swaziland used the occasion to announce
their support for the Ottawa Process and a December treaty-signing.

. . . to Asia . . .

A number of ICBL representatives travelled from Africa to Asia where on
6–7 March, the Japanese government hosted the 'Tokyo Conference on

Anti-Personnel Landmines'. Attended by 27 countries, the European Union, and 10 international organizations (NGOs were only allowed to attend the opening session), the primary aim of the conference was to discuss mine clearance and victim assistance. But taking advantage of the moment, immediately following the government meeting the Association to Aid Refugees/Japan and two other NGOs sponsored the 'NGO Tokyo Conference on Antipersonnel Landmines: Towards a Total Ban on Antipersonnel Landmines'. This first such NGO conference in Japan brought together over 200 participants to discuss landmine issues and to strategize on achieving a total ban. The joint appeal of the conference called on all governments to ban AP mines and to join the Ottawa Process.

While Japan clearly was not in the ban camp, this first NGO conference proved important to moving the Japanese government to sign the treaty. The conference helped to build NGO capacities in Japan, including the launch of the Japanese Campaign to Ban Landmines. The Association to Aid Refugees was able to build public awareness through a series of books on the issue, one featuring a young rabbit who wanted to see a world free of AP mines. The book and its hero 'Sunny the Rabbit' have raised significant funds for AP mine-related work and have become symbols of the ban movement in Japan. Exhibits of the original artwork of the book were shown throughout the country to raise awareness and funds, and were also featured in a landmine exhibit for the Nagano Olympics during its peace appeal, which focused on the ICBL.

. . . to Africa again . . .

Building on the results of the Maputo conference, the ICRC held a seminar in Harare, Zimbabwe, on 21–3 April 1997, during which military and foreign affairs officials from all 12 southern African states called on regional governments to establish a mine-free zone, immediately end all new deployments of AP mines, and commit to signing the ban treaty in December. The Maputo and Harare conferences helped lay the groundwork for the next meeting in Africa—the OAU and the government of South Africa's continent-wide conference on AP mines held in Kempton Park, South Africa, on 19–21 May.

There was significant ICBL involvement in the Kempton Park conference, particularly by the national ban campaigns in Africa. The ICBL was asked to deliver a keynote speech, along with South Africa's Vice-President and Archbishop Desmond Tutu. A surprising 41 OAU states were present, and Ambassador Jacob Selebi of South Africa served as the chair of the political working group. Zimbabwe became the third southern African state to ban AP mines unilaterally. Zimbabwe, Botswana, Lesotho, Mauritius, Sierra Leone, Cape Verde, Burundi, Uganda, Tanzania, and

Guinea-Bissau all issued statements for the first time pledging full support of the Ottawa Process. Egypt was the only country to state strongly its opposition to the Ottawa Process. However, it did make the declaration that it no longer produced or exported mines, and noted that it was in favour of the eventual elimination of AP mines.

On the final day of the Kempton Park meeting, South Africa destroyed 25 per cent of its AP mine stockpile. Six NGO representatives were invited to fly on the military plane to witness the destruction, which was set off by South Africa's Defence Minister, Joe Modise. Later in the day, at the close of the conference, Modise said, 'Like Archbishop Tutu and the others who have spoken at this conference, I appeal to representatives here today to strive to make our African continent and the whole world an anti-personnel landmine-free zone and a safer place for our children and for succeeding generations.' The very strong final declaration and action plan that emerged from the Kempton Park meeting was forwarded to the June OAU summit in Harare and helped forge the basis of African-wide strength in maintaining the integrity of the ban treaty during the Oslo negotiations later that year.

. . . to Europe . . .

Directly from Kempton Park, ICBL representatives travelled to Stockholm to take part, on 23–5 May, in a seminar on AP mines for NGOs and governments from Eastern and Central Europe and the Baltics. The aim of the meeting was to increase awareness of the mine issue and the Ottawa Process. Organized by the Swedish UN Association, Swedish Save the Children, and the Christian Council of Sweden, the seminar was divided in two parts—a day-long information exchange followed by a two-day capacity-building workshop for NGOs. Eight governments presented statements on their AP mine policies (Bulgaria, Croatia, Estonia, Latvia, Lithuania, Poland, Romania, Slovenia). Romania and Slovenia declared for the first time their intention to take part in the Ottawa Process and to sign the ban treaty in December 1997. Croatia repeated its commitment to the Ottawa Process, and Poland declared that it had prolonged indefinitely its moratorium on all AP mine exports. Some 20 NGOs from 14 Central/Eastern European and Baltic countries took part in the two-day workshop, including representatives from the ICBL and the ICRC. During two working group sessions, the NGOs explored a range of ways of raising the mine issue in their countries. Concrete goals and activities were established through the development of country 'action plans'. There was a strong feeling among the participants that the ban issue could move forward considerably in many countries with a minimum amount of public pressure. Immediately following the Stockholm meeting, an ICBL delegation spent one day in Norway (a staunchly pro-ban state) and one day in Finland (a strongly anti-ban state), meeting with campaigners, government officials, parliamentarians, and media.

The midway point between the Ottawa challenge and the treaty-signing in December was the June conference hosted by Belgium. The centrepiece of this 'make-or-break' conference was the Brussels Declaration that committed states to participate in the Oslo negotiations on the basis of the Austrian draft text, with a view to signing the convention in December 1997. Only weeks before the meeting, most observers were estimating that 60–75 governments would endorse the Brussels Declaration. By the end of the conference more than 90 had signed on, and that number subsequently grew to over 100. Among those announcing their support for the ban convention during or shortly after the conference were major producers, exporters, and users of mines such as France, the United Kingdom, Italy, Spain, the Czech Republic, Hungary, Bosnia, and Angola.

The Belgian Campaign to Ban Landmines hosted the ICBL's participation at the Brussels conference. More than 130 NGO representatives from 40 countries took part. Campaign activities included a cycle race from Paris to Brussels with the participation of landmine survivors, the display of a 'Giant Pair of Jeans' with one leg symbolically shredded, a Public Awareness Day with a demining demonstration, an official presentation of a 'landmine victim' outfit for the *Mannekin-Pis* (the famous symbol of Brussels), a simulated minefield government delegates had to cross each day entering the conference, and a variety of displays and exhibits. In addition, the week was observed by communities of faith around the world as International Days of Prayer for Victims of Landmines, with hundreds of individuals and groups in 39 countries sending messages to Brussels.

The success of the Belgian conference, which virtually guaranteed that an impressively large number of governments would come to Oslo to negotiate a true ban treaty, indicated that momentum was unstoppable at that point. On the negative side, the ICBL felt compelled to issue a press statement criticizing the United States delegation for 'testing the waters to see how many holes can be shot in the treaty in order to accommodate US policy'. During the Brussels meeting, a senior US official summoned numerous delegations to a hotel for bilateral meetings outside the conference to press them regarding their positions on the treaty, the Ottawa Process, and the preferred US option of negotiating any treaty in the Conference on Disarmament. The US—while signing the various pro-ban declarations and showing up at all the meetings—was clearly not of a 'like mind' with those governments honestly seeking a ban treaty with no exceptions, reservations, or loopholes. The US was pressing for a treaty with an explicit exception for Korea and for its own 'smart' mines—a stance it would take to an embarrassing conclusion at the Oslo negotiations.

. . . to Asia and the Middle East

In the wake of the Brussels conference additional meetings were held by NGOs in Australia, India, Senegal, Yemen, and elsewhere to continue building political will for the Ottawa Process. The ICRC held a seminar in the Philippines, in co-operation with the Philippine Campaign to Ban Landmines. The government of Turkmenistan hosted a ban meeting, with assistance from the Canadian government and with significant NGO participation. The ICBL attempted to put the ban issue on the agenda of every possible international meeting, including the G–8 meeting in Denver, the Commonwealth Heads of State meeting in Edinburgh in October, and the Francophonie meeting in Vietnam in November. At the latter two meetings, for example, ICBL members released detailed fact sheets on the landmine positions of each participating government and put out a press statement praising those that had joined the Ottawa Process and criticizing those that had not.

The Oslo Negotiations and the Return to Ottawa

When the historic ban convention negotiations opened in Oslo, the ICBL was ready, having put extensive time and resources into preparation for this critically important meeting. Hosted by its Norwegian counterpart, Norwegian People's Aid (NPA), the campaign began months before the negotiations opened preparing the groundwork for the arrival of campaigners both to take part in the negotiations themselves and for a four-day NGO forum to plan for ICBL action in the post convention-signing period. This strategic thinking has proved important to the campaign's ability to sustain and increase its momentum after the Convention was signed in Ottawa in December.

NPA was able to secure excellent facilities for the ICBL inside the negotiating site in Oslo. The campaign's office and meeting rooms were directly opposite the negotiation room itself, providing all campaigners—not just the official ICBL delegation to the negotiations—invaluable contact with government delegates throughout the three weeks of the conference. Landmine exhibits and banners were hung inside and outside the conference site. Regular briefings and press conferences laid out important developments in the negotiations and government delegations were invited to give their positions to the campaigners as well.

The opening of the treaty negotiations was marked by the tragic death of Diana, Princess of Wales. While this tragedy did not shift the negotiating process or government positions, it certainly greatly increased media attention to the process unfolding in Oslo. The number of accredited journalists covering the negotiations had already jumped measurably with the decision of the US to participate. This increased attention might have made it that much more difficult for governments to seriously consider any changes that would affect the integrity of the mine ban treaty.

Eighty-nine governments came to the Oslo negotiations as full participants. They were greeted with huge banners hung across the central square facing the conference centre, exhorting them to negotiate a treaty with 'no loopholes, no exceptions, and no reservations.' Based on their commitments made in the Brussels Declaration, nearly all of the 89 were, in fact, prepared to negotiate a comprehensive treaty, based on the Austrian draft. But a handful of nations, most notably the United States, were not of that mind. The US administration, worried about public opinion and the all-too-obvious contradiction of still claiming the leadership of the ban movement while not participating in ban treaty negotiations, decided at the last moment to go to Oslo. Perhaps to their surprise, this decision was not met with universal enthusiasm. For the ICBL—as well as many governments—it was clear that the US was not in Oslo as a 'like-minded' participant in the negotiations, but rather to put its full weight behind modifying the treaty to accommodate existing US policy.

Under the rules of procedure for the negotiations, which were agreed to on the first day, the ICBL was invited as an official observer with the same status as observer governments. This meant that ICBL representatives were permitted to be present at all sessions, including smaller working group sessions, and to make oral interventions at any point. The ICBL could not make formal proposals for treaty language, but did circulate informally suggested language. The ICBL did not have voting privileges, but, as it turned out, not a single vote was taken. It is believed that this is the first occasion on which NGOs were given official status in international negotiations of a disarmament/arms control or humanitarian law treaty.

The three-week negotiations were brilliantly presided over by South Africa's Ambassador to the UN in Geneva, Jacob Selebi. Rather than waste significant time with the usual government declarations pontificating great intentions, Selebi went immediately to the meat of the negotiations and opened discussion on core articles of the treaty, forcing sticking points into the open within the first two days of the conference. And every time a sticking point was on the table, the ICBL pressed its view, both inside the negotiations and to the general public through the media.

Creative campaigners proved tremendously skilful in distilling often seemingly complicated issues into simple slogans that allowed no doubt as to the position of the ICBL. Government delegates—to the dismay of some—were met daily as they entered the conference room with a new slogan. For example, when the US tried to redefine—more than once—its AP mines in order to avoid their inclusion in the treaty, the campaign asked the question: 'When is an AP mine not an AP mine?—When it's American.' When the US then tried to create a loophole in the definition, saying that an AP mine 'near' an anti-tank mine is actually an anti-handling device, the campaign came up with the slogan 'Near is Too Far'. The majority of these slogans featured US 'initiatives' to destroy the integrity of a true ban treaty.

The US from the very outset made a set of interlocking demands that the head of the US delegation told other diplomats were, in essence, non-negotiable. The demands included a geographic exception for Korea, a change in definition to exempt certain US 'smart' mines, and a nine-year delay in the effective date of the treaty. The ICBL denounced these demands as measures that would gut the treaty and render it largely meaningless. The campaign produced fact sheets and newsletters, held briefings, and lobbied delegates to reject all of the US demands. For its part, the US cajoled and arm-twisted with great vigour. Most dramatic was the US push for a 24-hour delay on the final day of the negotiations, when the conference was on the verge of completing a treaty strongly supported by the ICBL. The 24-hour delay, quite surprisingly supported by the Canadian government, was a period of tremendous tension. While President Clinton and other high officials of the US administration were calling counterparts around the world in their last-ditch effort to find support, the ICBL was holding press conferences to denounce the delay, pressing delegates to hold firm, and engaging in street theatre to dramatize the tense hours.

But amazingly, the world held firm. In the face of the tremendous pressure from the US, governments did not bend to the will of the 'world's sole remaining superpower'. In this instance, governments repeatedly said 'no' to US demands. And each 'no' empowered others to say 'no' and to hold firm in their intention to give the world a mine ban treaty with no exceptions, no reservations, and no loopholes. On 17 September the US finally withdrew its demands, leaving the treaty intact. As the negotiations were gavelled to a close the diplomats were cheered and thanked by the NGO community—perhaps for the first time in their diplomatic lives. Other campaigners were at the door as delegates filed out of the conference. The cheers, hugs, and chants did not end until the last delegate had left the site of the momentous Oslo negotiations.

The Oslo negotiations were historic for a number of reasons. For the first time, smaller and middle-sized powers had come together, to work in close co-operation with the NGOs of the International Campaign to Ban Landmines, to negotiate a treaty that would, for the first time, remove from the world's arsenals a weapon already in widespread use. Smaller and middle-sized powers had not yielded ground to intense pressure from a superpower to weaken the treaty to accommodate its own interests. Perhaps for the first time, negotiations ended with a treaty stronger than the draft on which the negotiations were based. The treaty had not been held hostage to rule by consensus, which would have inevitably resulted in a greatly weakened document.

The Oslo negotiations gave the world a treaty banning AP mines that is remarkably free of loopholes and exceptions. It not only establishes a new international norm, but also provides the framework for the total elim-ination of the weapon from the planet and for assistance to mine victims. It is not a perfect treaty—the ICBL has concerns about the provisions allow-ing anti-handling devices on anti-vehicle mines as well the retention of mines for training purposes. The campaign would like to see the treaty apply directly to non-state actors as well as stronger language regarding vic-tim assistance. But, given the close co-operation with governments that resulted in the treaty itself, the ICBL is confident that these issues can be addressed through the annual meetings and review conferences provided for in the treaty.

THE NOBEL PEACE PRIZE

The ICBL, its co-ordinator, Foreign Minister Axworthy, the ICRC, and oth-ers connected with the landmine movement had been nominated, some multiple times and in various combinations, for consideration for the 1997 Nobel Peace Prize. During the Oslo negotiations, the Norwegian media reported that the ICBL was a front runner for the prize. Despite great inter-est, particularly by Norwegian media, all requests for interviews on the topic were declined. The ICBL was clear that its focus was the treaty, and that the treaty was the 'prize' it sought.

At the same time, there was recognition that being awarded the Nobel Prize would add significant stature and weight to the ICBL and enhance its ability to continue to press for a maximum number of signatory states in Ottawa in December—and beyond, for quicker entry into force and universalization of the treaty—and ultimately for the total elimination of anti-personnel mines and sustained assistance for mine victims.

On 10 October, the Nobel Committee announced that it had awarded the 1997 Nobel Peace Prize jointly to the ICBL and its co-ordinator, Jody Williams. The immediate and sustained media attention to that announcement proved invaluable to maintaining the high visibility of the landmine issue. At the conclusion of the negotiations in Oslo, many had wondered how many countries would ultimately appear in Ottawa to sign the treaty—many felt that 'success' would best be measured by holding close to the number of states that had participated in the negotiations. Clearly, that measure of success was far surpassed—with 122 nations signing over the course of the two-day ceremony in Ottawa, and several more coming on board once the treaty opened for signature at the UN.

One significant example of the impact of the Peace Prize on the decision of some states is Japan. It was the view of most that Japan had participated in the Oslo negotiations primarily to support the demands of the US. On most points, the Japanese essentially mirrored the American positions, and when the US finally withdrew its proposals for the treaty Japan remained the lone voice still expressing reservations. It seemed at this point extremely unlikely that Japan would sign the ban treaty. But in a rather startling public statement, not long after the Peace Prize, Japan's newly appointed Foreign Minister, Keizo Obuchi, announced his intention to review Japanese policy with a mind to being able to sign the treaty. In his statement, he mentioned that the Peace Prize had given new and added weight to the issue. Japan not only signed, but the mine ban became the centrepiece of the Peace Appeal for the Nagano Winter Olympics, and the ICBL's Chris Moon, an ex-deminer and survivor of a landmine blast, carried the Olympic torch into the stadium during the opening ceremonies.

CONCLUSION: THE OTTAWA SIGNING OF THE MINE BAN CONVENTION

The Japanese Foreign Minister himself ultimately signed the ban Convention in Ottawa—along with 121 other countries. While not signing the Convention, even countries such as the US, Russia, and China—the latter participating for the first time in any session of the Ottawa Process—were in Ottawa as observers. Not only did significantly more countries sign the treaty than had participated in its negotiation, three ratified it simultaneously—signalling the political will of the international community to bring this treaty into force as soon as possible. Governments also made public commitments of approximately half a billion dollars for treaty implementation, mine clearance, and victim assistance.

This remarkable achievement is reflected in the words of the Nobel Committee in making its announcement of its 1997 Peace Prize recipients. The Nobel Committee noted that the ICBL had taken an idea viewed as Utopian and made it virtual reality, and that—just as significantly—it had helped form, with governments, a new model of diplomacy that could, hopefully, be applied to other issues of global humanitarian concern. AP mines have been used since the US Civil War and the Crimean War, yet the ICBL and small and mid-sized governments came together to take them out of the arsenals of the world. This model clearly demonstrates that in the post-Cold War world, civil society and governments do not have to see each other as adversaries, but can work together and address humanitarian concerns with breathtaking speed. It shows that such a partnership can form the basis of a new kind of 'superpower' in the post-Cold War world.

CHAPTER 3

THE CANADIAN CAMPAIGN

Valerie Warmington and Celina Tuttle

Mines Action Canada (MAC), a coalition of Canadian NGOs working to achieve a comprehensive international ban on anti-personnel (AP) mines, contributed to building a large and diverse international coalition against AP mines and to developing a broadly agreed upon framework for responding to the landmine crisis. This chapter offers a perspective on why Canada was able to move beyond the status quo to play the role it did in moving AP mines to the forefront of the diplomatic and public agendas. Importantly, it considers not only what has been achieved as a result of the Ottawa Process but also what remains to be achieved. In this light, the ban Convention is seen as a milestone on a longer and in many ways more challenging road ahead.

THE CANADIAN CAMPAIGN TO BAN LANDMINES

The landmines issue came to the fore in Canada during a period of great stress for the Canadian NGO community. NGOs had been experiencing a slow chipping away of their budgets for several years, including dramatic cutbacks in the few years prior to the formal emergence of Canada's campaign to ban landmines. Indeed, development education, one of the primary tools used during the campaign, had lost 100 per cent of the government funding it had previously enjoyed. Ongoing NGO programs were being threatened by a loss of funding and yet here was a serious emerging issue that demanded the attention of the NGO community and a portion of its dwindling resources.

The politically contentious nature of the AP mine issue was also of initial concern to some Canadian NGOs. It was recognized from the outset that effective action in response to the landmine crisis would require a significant amount of political advocacy on an issue that could be viewed as having more to do with disarmament than with development. However, Canadian NGOs were traditionally somewhat cautious with respect to undertakings that could lead them to exceed the proportion of funds legally allowed to be devoted to lobbying government—exceeding this proportion could jeopardize an organization's charitable status. In the past this constraint had steered some NGOs away from direct involvement in disarmament issues, despite the obvious links between disarmament and development and humanitarian issues.

In spite of these constraints, in early 1993 a handful of Canadian NGOs began circulating and responding to information produced by members of the International Campaign to Ban Landmines (ICBL), protesting Canada's lack of action in response to the humanitarian problem of landmines. Within a year the Canadian group had expanded to include development, social justice, faith, health, peace, disabled people's, and disarmament organizations. By the fall of 1994, this loose coalition had agreed to formal objectives and a mandate and had requested meetings with government. The Mines Action Canada (MAC) coalition was formally launched in March 1995 with the appointment of a co-ordinator, the selection of a steering committee, and registration of membership in the ICBL.

It is worth recalling that Canadian NGOs had already begun raising the landmines issue during the course of the foreign and defence policy reviews initiated by the newly elected Liberal government in 1993. During the election the Liberals had pledged to adopt a broader definition of security—one encompassing both sustainable development and 'capable' defence. Throughout both reviews, NGO representatives advocated reductions in defence budgets and argued that the primary goal of Canada's foreign policy should be global social justice and sustainable development. Throughout 1994 NGOs and individual Canadians pressed for the 'democratization' of the defence and foreign policy-making process. NGOs wanted a meaningful role in policy development and a sense that Canadian foreign policy reflected their values and experiences as organizations active in the fields of development assistance and peacebuilding.

Although the concrete outcomes of these review processes were considerably weaker than had been hoped for by the NGO community, the Foreign Policy Review did produce a degree of imperative for the government to consult with NGOs on issues of foreign policy concern. Perhaps more important was the development within government ranks of an awareness that consultation with NGOs was becoming an increasingly important and substantive element of the policy development process. On this basis, MAC insisted on and was granted regular meetings with officials during which NGOs were updated on the government's activities and policies with respect to landmines.

Initially, the polar opposite positions of the government and MAC on landmines produced little common ground from which discussions could progress. Government/NGO meetings were often mutually frustrating events, as entrenched positions were repeated to no discernible positive effect. However, these meetings, which began in early 1995, did provide MAC with an opportunity to provide the government with information on the humanitarian and socio-economic impact of landmines, and to discuss the relationship between these impacts and Canadian policy. However, while the government became increasingly aware of the grave socio-economic and humanitarian consequences of AP mines, it maintained that it was impossible to address these issues outside of the existing Canadian negotiating position within the Review Conference of the CCW.

Laying the Foundations

Ultimately, a strengthened relationship between the government, NGOs, and the public was critical to moving the landmine issue forward. This was particularly true in Canada, where NGOs played an important role in initiating and implementing the Ottawa Process and where ongoing public interest kept the political stakes high. However, the collaborative nature of the NGO-government relationship during the Ottawa Process itself contrasted sharply with early phases of this relationship. Prior to the Ottawa Process, the Canadian government was highly defensive in response to NGO calls for a total ban. Arguments against AP mines based on humanitarian impact were countered with arguments based on military utility. NGOs were advised not to confuse 'intent with effect' and were assured that the Canadian military used landmines responsibly and according to accepted doctrine. NGOs argued that by not opposing AP mines within the context of the CCW review, Canada was supporting an unacceptable status quo.

Although it had been formally reported that Canadian Forces had not used AP mines since Korea, officials argued the safety of Canadian soldiers would be jeopardized without them. They also argued that efforts to push CCW discussions further would be counter-productive to international efforts to resolve the problem. Canada would no longer be considered a serious player within the context of the negotiations. MAC pointed out that the entrenched positions of China, Russia, the US, and others, coupled with the CCW requirement for consensus decisions, would ensure that Canada would have limited impact on the outcome of discussions regardless of its position. MAC argued that Canada should adopt a morally strong stance in favour of a ban on AP mines. Such a stance would move Canada beyond the 'lowest-common-denominator' results of the CCW and accurately reflect growing public opposition to AP mines.

Of major concern to NGOs at the time was the bureaucratic separation of the humanitarian and military aspects of the landmines problem within the Department of Foreign Affairs and International Trade—the lead department in the CCW negotiations. While the Human Security Division of the department was mandated to consider the humanitarian implications of landmines, the Arms Control and Disarmament Division, supported by the Department of National Defence, dealt with technical and legal/treaty concerns. While Defence and the Arms Control Division were represented on Canada's delegation to the CCW negotiations, the Human Security Division was not. MAC argued that consideration of the humanitarian problems associated with landmines in isolation from issues related to the ongoing production, trade, stockpile, and use of AP mines was preventing the development of an effective Canadian response to the AP mine crisis.

MAC also began to argue that in failing to support a ban on AP mines, Canada should also be willing to accept responsibility for the associated humanitarian cost of their ongoing use. News that Canadian-made AP mines had been found in Iraqi arsenals, coupled with reports of Iraqi deployments of AP mines against its Kurdish population, underlined the validity of the NGO perspective. Overall, it was clear to MAC that humanitarian concerns had been poorly considered in the development of Canadian policy around AP mines and that such concerns were being ignored within the CCW negotiations. Indeed, throughout the CCW review process, Canada and other countries were openly accused of short-changing humanitarian need and neglecting development concerns in favour of military expedience. MAC began to insist that someone with humanitarian expertise be placed on the official Canadian delegation to the CCW Review Conference.

Mobilizing Public Opinion

Mines Action Canada understood that the campaign's ultimate success would depend on its ability to reach the public with information on existing government policy and motivate Canadians to press for change. One of the key challenges would be to bring the media on side. To this end, NGOs directed media attention to the links between AP mines and international humanitarian law (IHL). Following the lead of the International Committee of the Red Cross, over the summer of 1995 MAC began to argue publicly that AP mines were indiscriminate by nature and thus illegal under IHL regardless of how or in what circumstances they were used. In response to government arguments that AP mines posed little threat to civilians if used responsibly in accordance with proper military doctrine, MAC highlighted data from mine-affected areas that demonstrated that in the years since the original CCW was signed, responsible use and military doctrine had offered little assurance of safety to civilian populations. Moreover, MAC argued, the proposed amendments to the CCW offered little additional assurance of safety in the future. Images of seriously injured children, women, and men were used to underline the reality of the risk to civilians and the merits of NGO arguments for a ban. Stories accompanying these images described what the person was doing at the time of his or her accident. Innocent day-to-day activities like playing, planting food, collecting water, and walking to work or school became recognized as high-risk activities for those in mine-affected areas. Almost overnight, the media began referring to landmines as indiscriminate killers. The Canadian public began to empathize strongly with people forced to live with mines.

Again following the ICRC's lead, MAC introduced the idea of proportionality to the public—a tenet of IHL that demands that the weapons and means used to accomplish military objectives not be so out of proportion that they inflict massive destruction on civilians and societies at large. MAC also distributed data questioning the actual military utility of AP mines in relationship to their extensive socio-economic impacts. Information on the loss of agricultural land, the erosion of food security, the loss of access to markets and livelihoods, and the diversion of primary health-care funds to provide emergency treatment for landmine victims was circulated as it emerged.

By the September 1995 round of the CCW negotiations, MAC's efforts to disseminate information and inspire a public response to government policy began to pay off. In fact, the demand for information from media and the public began to overwhelm MAC's capacity to respond. To capitalize on this interest, a series of information packages were sent to the constituency offices of all Canadian members of Parliament (MPs) between June and August of 1995. Over the summer, Canadian musician Bruce Cockburn and Mozambican singer Chude Mondlane undertook a cross-Canada tour to raise awareness around the landmine situation in Mozambique. Upon arrival in Ottawa, Cockburn handed petitions demanding meaningful action on landmines, signed by thousands of Canadian citizens, to Liberal MP Jane Stewart, who was supportive of a ban. Stewart later visited Cambodia for a firsthand look at the impact of landmines through a program arranged by MAC member organizations. Keith Martin, Svend Robinson, Bill Blakey, and other opposition MPs repeatedly questioned Canada's position on landmines in the House of Commons.

Support for a ban from the Canadian public and the media continued to grow. Letters calling for stronger government action began to pour into the Departments of Foreign Affairs and National Defence and the Prime Minister's Office. Documentaries and public service announcements about landmines were aired on radio and television more frequently and media coverage in general increased. MAC members set up a 1–800 line staffed by volunteers to facilitate and respond to requests for information.

Mines Action Canada began to rely heavily on data generated in mine-affected communities to demonstrate the potential for ongoing casualties to landmines regardless of the restrictions and precautions proposed within the CCW. For example, the Department of National Defence stated that proposed changes regarding minefield mapping and marking would ensure the safety of civilians in mined areas. The coalition countered such arguments in the media by drawing on evidence provided by mine clearance agencies to demonstrate that mines are not static once in the ground but move in response to floods, landslides, and other natural phenomena. Moreover, efforts to mark minefields were not always effective since communities in dire need of resources often use minefield markers for other purposes. Thus, the proposed new standards offered little if any advantage over the very limited restrictions already contained in the CCW. Increasingly, the Canadian media and the public adopted positions in favour of an outright ban on production, export, stockpiling, and use of AP mines.

The First Cracks Appear
In September 1995, as delegates headed to Vienna for what was expected to be the final round of CCW negotiations, the Canadian government maintained that to seek stronger restrictions against AP mines than those already proposed would marginalize Canada as a contributor to the discussions. To propose a ban, even as a symbolic gesture, would significantly damage Canada's reputation within the international arms control community. Despite mounting public pressure for a ban and nearly two years of preliminary negotiations, states participating in the September 1995 session of the CCW review failed to agree on even modest new restrictions on AP mines. States could only agree to reconvene in Geneva in January 1996 to review the technical aspects of the Convention with a view to finalizing the negotiations in May.

The virtual collapse of the September 1995 CCW negotiations was used by MAC as an opportunity to step up pressure on the Canadian government for stronger action against AP mines. Meanwhile, MAC briefed members of the Canada delegation to the Inter-Parliamentary Union (IPU), who were prepared to raise the landmine issue at the next IPU meeting, in Istanbul. In November 1995, MAC hosted the launch of a National Film Board documentary on the day-to-day life of a Cambodian landmine survivor, *Than and the Invisible War*. Guest speakers from organizations working in mine-affected communities addressed an audience of several hundred people. MAC continued to circulate information through NGO, academic, and other networks.

By the late fall differences began to emerge between the positions of the Department of National Defence and the Department of Foreign Affairs. In November 1995, in response to a question put forward by a MAC member at a gathering of NGOs, Foreign Minister André Ouellet stated that Canada should take the lead in the ban campaign and declare a total ban on AP mines. However, in subsequent media scrums, Defence Minister David Collenette continued to defend the use of AP mines. Although the government tried to downplay the increasingly obvious divide in government policy, MAC worked to exploit this opening. Was it the Canadian military that dictated arms control policy in Canada, or was the military subject to civilian authority in such matters? Mines Action Canada continued its letter-writing campaigns urging Canadians to voice their opinion at this critical time. CBC television's *National Magazine* began researching Canadian policy on landmines. Pro-ban editorials appeared regularly in major Canadian newspapers. The government was unusually quiet.

Canada's Moratorium

MAC's efforts finally produced a measure of practical political progress. On 17 January 1996, during the resumed CCW negotiations, the Canadian government announced a moratorium on the production, transfer, and operational use of AP mines. Despite previous government concern, rather than undermining Canada's contribution to the negotiations, the move prompted indications of support from other governments, many under pressure from their own publics for action. NGOs welcomed the government's announcement as an improvement over previous Canadian passivity. However, Canadian NGOs remained sceptical because of the ambiguous nature of the moratorium, which essentially banned the use of landmines unless needed, and did not seek to reduce or eliminate stockpiled mines. Shortly after the announcement of the moratorium, André Ouellet resigned from politics and Lloyd Axworthy became Canada's new Minister of Foreign Affairs. Concerned that the change in leadership might jeopardize progress achieved thus far, MAC pushed for legislation to strengthen the moratorium and ensure its sustainability through future changes in ministers or governments.

In March 1996, the release of an ICRC study on the military utility of AP mines brought into serious question the arguments advanced by many states within the CCW negotiations. The report suggested that military arguments in support of AP mines were based on assumptions rather than sound analysis. In Canada, the report was launched with a press conference on Parliament Hill. MAC provided opposition party leaders and interested MPs with copies of the report and again questioned Canada's insistence on retaining stockpiles and the right to use landmines. Information on the devastating humanitarian impacts of landmines continued to be broadly circulated.

The shift in Canada's AP mine policy provided a new opening for the development of a humanitarian approach to the issue. Within weeks of the announced moratorium, MAC was invited to appoint a representative to the official Canadian delegation to the final CCW negotiating session. Although this opportunity was welcomed, the invitation created a dilemma for the coalition. MAC did not want to be perceived as endorsing the 'legitimate use' of landmines by becoming a full participant in the CCW negotiations, nor did members wish to forgo the opportunity to gain first-hand knowledge of and contribute directly to these otherwise closed-door discussions. In the end, it was decided the potential for MAC to bring a humanitarian perspective to the discussions outweighed other concerns and considerations. The CCW Review Conference reconvened in April 1996 with Mines Action Canada represented as a member of the Canadian delegation.

Throughout this final session, MAC's representative was integrally involved in discussions with the Department of Foreign Affairs and the Department of National Defence on the delegation's daily negotiating objectives and strategies. On several occasions the MAC representative was asked to take the chair and to speak on behalf of Canada, consequently engaging in difficult debates with both China and India. Although MAC and others argued strongly in favour of humanitarian progress whenever possible, the rituals and nuances of traditional international diplomacy proved to be only too effective in blocking substantive progress.

For those concerned with addressing the humanitarian impact of AP mines, participation in the CCW review was a painfully frustrating and dis-heartening experience. Virtually every effort to strengthen the Convention was met with consensus-blocking opposition from intransigent states. While ultimately some progress was made, NGOs saw the overall outcome of the CCW as an abysmal failure. The highlight of the final session was Canada's announcement on the last day that it would host a meeting for those interested in pursuing further discussions on AP mines, easing NGO fears that the issue would fall off the international agenda.

Building Expectations

In the wake of the CCW process, Canadian NGOs and the Canadian public continued to agitate for a legislated ban, stockpile destruction, and a for-mal announcement of the date of the promised Canadian meeting. By mid-summer 1996 MAC became integrally involved in the substantive planning for the October Ottawa meeting and related public activities. The MAC coalition had expanded to include more than 40 NGOs and an extensive network of interested Canadians, and had developed a solid reputation with the Canadian media. MAC put its entire capacity to work focusing attention on the upcoming Ottawa conference. A poster contest was sponsored; simulated minefields and demonstrations of mine clearance techniques were organized; exhibits were erected in a number of key locations; a film festival and a benefit concert featuring popular Canadian musicians were held. MAC distributed more information packages through its ever-expanding networks. Speaking tours of landmine survivors and others with experience in mine-affected communities were organized. Increasing numbers of media interviews were requested of Mines Action Canada and its member organizations, many of which were passed on to NGO resource people from around the world.

MAC's efforts effectively heightened the expectations of Canadians that further progress could be achieved on the AP mine issue. These expectations were rewarded by the announced destruction of two-thirds of Canada's stockpiles on 2 October and the unexpected launch of the Ottawa Process with Foreign Minister Axworthy's challenge to the world, issued on the last day of the conference, to negotiate a treaty banning anti-personnel landmines to be signed by December 1997. Ironically, the move by Canada to initiate the Ottawa Process was an example of unilateralism, a concept not often endorsed by NGOs sensitive to unilateral actions based on 'national security interests'. However, in this instance unilateralism was a welcomed response to a global humanitarian crisis that demanded decisive action. Nor was Axworthy's decision made in complete isolation from previous developments on this issue. One need only to recall the dismal outcome of the CCW review to understand the inspiration behind this diplomatic initiative and the rapidly mounting support for it throughout the 14 months prior to the ban Convention opening for signature.

Unexpectedly high attendance at the October meeting further confirmed indications of growing international political support for banning AP mines. Public support was even more apparent, particularly in Canada—landmines were front-page news. Belief that a ban was right and possible to achieve began overcoming scepticism within the Canadian public. It is believed these conditions prompted the Canadian government to offer an alternative to the slow proceedings of traditional negotiating fora such as the Conference on Disarmament (CD) and the five-year wait before the next review of the CCW. NGOs supported the newly initiated Ottawa Process because it afforded greater potential for progress. It kept AP mines on the immediate international agenda. It offered hope that efforts to deal with AP mines would not be relegated to the long and tortuous deliberations of the CD. Importantly, the Ottawa Process allowed for the participation of states and NGOs excluded from discussions in the CD.

CONCLUSION: THE PUBLIC VOICE

The relative openness of the Ottawa Process gave NGOs a stronger voice within the international policy development process on landmines. This was critical to keeping negotiations focused on the humanitarian intent of the treaty. Throughout the Ottawa Process, although the working relationships needed for continued progress became closer than many governments and NGOs were used to or comfortable with, the necessary exchange of information and open discussions ensured that the interests of mine-affected communities were better represented at the negotiating table. Consequently, the Convention responded to the urgent need to stop the spread of AP mines and to direct future international efforts towards the existing problem on the ground.

In support of this outcome, MAC contributed substantively throughout the Ottawa Process as a representative on official Canadian delegations. In addition, the coalition was also represented at official bilateral meetings with governments in the Asia-Pacific region aimed at informing them about the Ottawa Process. MAC provided significant and substantive assistance to the planning of the May 1997 OAU conference in South Africa— a conference critical to securing African support for the Ottawa Process and the ban on AP mines. MAC also worked closely with the Canadian government in planning and implementing both the October 1996 and December 1997 Ottawa conferences.

Although Mines Action Canada was represented on Canadian delegations throughout the Ottawa Process, this did not preclude substantive disagreement with the government on specific issues, the proposed US exception for the use of AP mines in Korea being a case in point. During negotiations of the final treaty text in Oslo this issue emerged under the guise of a 'transition period'—a point of concern compelling NGOs to protest in the streets. MAC members angrily delivered a press release directly to reporters at the Press Gallery in Ottawa. The release, entitled 'Canada Accused of "Selling Out" Humanitarian Treaty to US Policy', challenged the Prime Minister's statement that some exceptions on the use of AP mines were acceptable because of 'technical elements of a military nature'. It was during such times that the existence of an informed and concerned public was most vital.

A relatively sophisticated awareness by the general public was also crit-ical to initiating and sustaining actions undertaken within the Ottawa Process. Initially, the Canadian campaign faced great odds in mobilizing public opinion. NGOs were suffering from devastating cutbacks in govern-ment funding and had little remaining capacity for public education and outreach. Furthermore, a poor economy combined with both federal and provincial cutbacks to social programs had produced an angry and disillu-sioned public. Other issues, such as Canadian unity, the inquiry into the torture and murder of a Somali youth by members of the Canadian Airborne Regiment while on peacekeeping duty, followed by yet another inquiry into Canada's HIV-contaminated blood supply, determined that Canadian attention was focused domestically. It seemed unlikely that Canadians would take action on an issue far removed from their own immediate concerns.

It was also expected that constant exposure to media images of poverty, famine, war, and other human suffering would lead people to categorize landmines as yet another issue outside of their control. NGOs recognized that without providing avenues for public action and tangible evidence of progress, support for the campaign's work on landmines would be weak. Consequently, the coalition made every effort to provide simple avenues for public participation, to promote the positive results of public action, and to give Canadians a sense of ownership in the campaign to ban land-mines. Many people have conveyed to MAC a renewed motivation and optimism for their having been involved and actively continue to follow the issue.

MAC saw evidence of its success in the fact that the Ottawa Process was both supported and driven by public opinion. MAC members worked tire-lessly to generate public interest in the AP mines issue, which could then be used to guide political responses to the crisis. Thus, public concern for mine-affected people compelled the Canadian government and other gov-ernments to take action and provided the necessary strength to resist efforts to weaken the Convention during its negotiation. Of concern to MAC members now is their belief that the near-singular focus of interna-tional attention on the Convention has left many in mine-affected com-munities feeling their immediate problems have been overlooked. Future work undertaken within the context of the Convention must focus now on those living and working in mine-affected communities. The commitment and determination demonstrated by participants in the Ottawa Process must focus squarely on the tasks of removing landmines from the ground and helping individuals and communities cope with the aftermath. Every effort must be made to work with those in mine-affected communities so they benefit from the Convention and its attendant public interest. These communities must be centrally involved for effective implementation. Once again, media and public attention must be directed to the realities of landmines on the ground.

Will the Convention produce the anticipated reductions in human suffering? In part, the answer lies in how signatory governments interpret and fulfil their obligations. To this end, analysis and documentation of the Ottawa Process must extend beyond the negotiation and entry-into-force of the ban Convention. The co-operation and commitment of signatory states will be tested in days to come. Already discussions are being held and pressures felt in the context of NATO stockpiles and military transfers of mines. The outcome of these discussions will be a measure of the Convention and of the commitment and strength that it invokes.

This chapter does not fully describe the complex interplay of personalities, timings, coincidences, and other events that ultimately drove the Ottawa Process. Nor does it comprehensively describe the tremendous challenges that lie ahead. Those involved in the Ottawa Process are confident that success is possible and that this humanitarian crisis can be resolved. However, the true effectiveness of the Ottawa Process will only be measured over time. Landmines are still killing and maiming—laying waste to potential and dreams. Until people the world over can walk safely and without fear of landmines, we have not achieved our goal.

CHAPTER 4

THE FRENCH CAMPAIGN

Philippe Chabasse

France's position on anti-personnel (AP) mines evolved slowly compared to the rest of the international community, but by French standards the pace of change was quite radical. I hope to illustrate the principal stages of this evolution by examining relations between five key national actors engaged on the issue—political leaders and high-ranking officials on one side, the media, public opinion, and members of parliament on the other. Handicap International (HI) acted as a permanent link among these different groups, and this chapter will inevitably present a single-sided analysis, neglecting to take into account the particularly complex national administrative decision-making mechanisms of France.

THE REVOLT OF THOSE CLOSE TO LANDMINE VICTIMS: 1992

The first public information event on the impact of AP mines took the form of a conference organized by Handicap International, in May 1992, at the Senate Palace in Paris. This conference presented and analysed the French-language version of a report on landmines in Cambodia written in 1991 by Human Rights Asia Watch and Physicians for Human Rights (PHR) titled *Landmines in Cambodia: The Coward's War*. To be involved in *The Coward's War* event, Handicap International had to move well beyond its traditional mandate to help handicapped individuals who were victims of conflicts and/or in underdeveloped countries. HI began to publicly denounce the indiscriminate use of anti-personnel mines and the insufficient means available for controlling their intolerable consequences. At the same time, the association began direct involvement in training programs for mine clearance in Cambodia initiated by the United Nations.

The Coward's War report was a first step in what would become known as the International Campaign to Ban Landmines (ICBL). Working with the UK-based NGO Mines Advisory Group (MAG), Handicap International revised *The Coward's War* in 1992 after two field visits to Cambodia and then translated its revisions into French. The idea of an NGO network on the AP mine issue was suggested by Rae McGrath, director of MAG, and Eric Stover of PHR as they presented the report in Paris. Parallel contacts on the same theme were made between Medico International and the Vietnam Veterans of America Foundation.

The significance of the 1992 Paris conference was not the number of attendees (only a hundred or so NGO representatives, as well as students, journalists, and political personalities attended) but rather that it launched a call for signatures soliciting a ban on landmines. The first signatories included a diverse group—Elie Wiesel, Simone Weil, the president of the European Parliament, ex-ministers Jean-François Deniau and Bernard Kouchner, Javier Perez de Cuellar, and Barbara Hendriks. Handicap International maintained consistency and momentum on the issue in subsequent years by repeating this call for signatures in support of the ban.

Press reaction to the conference was modest, but the distribution of *The Coward's War* report to all French and Belgian legislators, as well as to all members of the European Parliament, had far-reaching consequences. The report motivated the President of the European Parliament and two Belgian senators to become involved in the issue. By the end of 1992 the first European parliamentary resolution calling for an immediate moratorium on the export of landmines was passed. Less than three years later, a Belgian law banning AP mines, prepared through a partnership between parliamentarians and NGOs, became the first model for unilateral and total bans.

Our will to be involved in the fight to ban landmines was reinforced in October 1992 in New York at a meeting of six NGOs—Handicap International, Vietnam Veterans of America Foundation, Human Rights Watch, Physicians for Human Rights, Mines Advisory Group, and Medico International—a group that would become the steering committee of the new ICBL. This meeting awakened us to the need to develop contacts with government authorities and to inform public opinion. Contacts were soon established with the French Foreign Affairs Ministry, while several articles on the injuries and severe distress caused by AP mines appeared in the media and began influencing French public opinion. Contacts were established with high-ranking officials and their international lawyers with remarkable ease. These men and women, responsible for negotiating and implementing international treaties, discovered for the first time the magnitude of the global landmine problem and pressed the NGO community for more evidence and documentation. Victims' testimonies were heard in the corridors of ministries and it soon became apparent that, contrary to our expectations, no doors were really closed—they just had not yet been pushed open.

The combination of journalistic and governmental interest prompted HI to organize a second landmines conference in February 1993, to which we invited representatives of the French government and the Mines Advisory Group, as well as US Senator Patrick Leahy, a leading advocate on the ban issue within the US. Two factors were responsible for the official French decision to go public on the landmines issue. Several days before the conference, Senator Leahy wrote to Handicap International encouraging the association to convince the French government to convene a meeting for the revision of the 1980 Convention on Certain Conventional Weapons (CCW). We forwarded this letter to the Foreign Affairs Ministry, which demonstrated a renewed interest in the issue. Fear of American leadership on the landmines issue had clearly motivated the French authorities to take action.

Handicap International sent another letter to François Mitterrand, President of the Republic, alerting him to the urgent need for action. This letter was given directly to the President by his wife, Danielle Mitterrand, president of the France Liberté Foundation, together with the first 15,000 signatures already received from the French population. In this manner the President's diplomatic and political advisers were bypassed. Landmines had suddenly become both an issue of personal importance to the President and an issue of international image for the Foreign Affairs Ministry. This laid the foundation for the events that followed. During an official visit to Cambodia on 11 February 1993, President Mitterrand called for a Review Conference of the CCW, proclaimed an indefinite French moratorium on the export of landmines, and called on other countries to join in this initiative.

Despite France's leadership in bringing landmines back onto the international agenda through the CCW review process, official support in Paris for a total ban remained elusive. However, it is clear in retrospect that the CCW review was a major event in the evolution of an AP mine ban. At the very least, it ensured that all future activities on the issue were organized and united in a progressive context.

GAINING MOMENTUM: 1993–1994

The CCW Review Conference process was transparent enough to allow Handicap International to document the positions taken by various countries during the proceedings. Conferences, television programs, and the distribution of field reports followed, and the number of signatures calling for the ban increased to 130,000 by June 1994. The growing interest in the ban allowed us to observe the impact of public pressure on the development of official policy. In November 1993, the spokesman for the French Ministry of Defence declared that 'there is a real and terrifying problem [with antipersonnel mines] for which we have some of the responsibility, [and] attitudes must change.' Jean-François Deniau, ex-Minister for Foreign Affairs, said, 'these anti-people mines must be prohibited, a ban must be imposed on this blind weapon which, once set, no longer obeys any human control. It no longer has a master.' Despite the growth in public interest, however, HI's efforts to activate members of parliament and senators with a new report about the consequences of the mines on civilian populations in Iraqi Kurdistan had no effect. At this stage our support base was obviously fragile.

In June 1994, during the International Arms Trade Show, Eurosatory, a press conference on landmines was organized by Handicap International, Médecins sans Frontières, UNICEF, and Greenpeace. Together with the Catholic Committee against Hunger and for Development, and Agir Ici, these groups would become the founding members of the French Campaign to Ban Landmines.

Handicap International's annual campaigns for action revolved around the theme 'NO to antipersonnel mines'. Thousands of posters and pamphlets were distributed, and TV and radio spots were produced. Greenpeace published a special newsletter dedicated to mines in September 1994, Médecins sans Frontières included a special chapter on the subject in its annual report, and Agir Ici launched a campaign denouncing the production of landmines by some firework manufacturers. Even the French Red Cross eventually agreed to make its international law expertise available to all other associations in the network.

The personal work of Madame Taubira-Delanon, a member of parliament for French Guiana, led to a gradual mobilization of activity of members of parliament, who presented a first draft of a law banning anti-personnel mines before the National Assembly in March 1995. The text was prepared in collaboration with NGOs and was co-signed by 110 members of parliament. In the same year, draft acts were prepared by both socialist and communist groups. These propositions had no direct influence on the position of the government, but they identified several members of parliament sympathetic to the campaign.

A BAN CHAMPION ENTERS THE GOVERNMENT: 1995

During the 1995 presidential electoral campaign Handicap International interviewed the candidates on the question of AP mines. Unfortunately, in stark contrast to Great Britain's 1997 experience, the government's position on landmines did not figure in the public debate around the election. However, through these interviews, good quotable statements were obtained. Jacques Chirac, the soon-to-be President of the Republic, assured us several days before the vote that he would give 'his full support to all the efforts which will be made internationally to ban the use of landmines as quickly as possible'. Lionel Jospin, who became Prime Minister two years later, wrote that he would defend 'without hesitation the total banning of mines and [fight] to stop France manufacturing such arms'.

Notwithstanding these positive developments, the most important event for the evolution of the French position was Xavier Emmanuelli's appointment as Secretary of State for Humanitarian Affairs. A well-known figure in non-governmental humanitarian action for more than 15 years, Dr Emmanuelli was a friend of several NGO leaders. Shortly after his nomination he declared that 'the fight against the proliferation of anti-personnel mines is one of my priorities.'

Through this very privileged contact inside the government, the mass of information collected via the international campaign network was transmitted to the highest officials. NGOs were often the first to be informed of the evolution of the position of certain countries and obtained detailed information on personalities, locations, and meetings important to the decision-making process. This privilege allowed us to send timely letters and organize public events for maximum effect.

Our 'shadow' work assumed a new dimension with the success of the first large-scale public demonstration, organized in four French cities on 23 September 1995. During the 'One Mine, One Victim, One Shoe To Say No' event, the public was invited to place a shoe on a pyramid of protest, symbolizing the injury sustained by a landmine victim. Several tens of thousands of persons participated in these events, which were covered by all the national media and by several international press agencies. The shoes were subsequently sent to Vienna to prolong the protest in the presence of delegations participating at the CCW Review Conference. The shoe pyramid idea was taken up for use over the following months in Switzerland, Italy, Germany, and Canada as well as other areas of the world. Three days after these successful demonstrations, during the opening session of the CCW review in Vienna, Dr Emmanuelli announced France's decision to stop the production of AP mines of all types and to progressively reduce stocks by destruction.

For the NGO community, this announcement had an emotional and psychological impact similar to the signature of the Ottawa Convention two years later. The decision was a positive step, despite the fact that it mentioned nothing about the continued use of mines and though it would not affect the daily situation of the victims. After three years of effort, we finally realized the capacity of NGOs to influence political decisions. Given the size of the French armaments industry and the network that governs it, we had covered a lot of ground in a short period of time.

French NGOs were then confronted with a difficult situation. On the one hand, we could lay claim to a solidly mobilized civil base of 180,000 signatories to the ban, a network of highly sensitive journalists, and NGOs recognized as credible representatives on the subject. Furthermore, the movement enjoyed the support of the President of the Republic and one of his ministers. On the other hand, we were faced with a military hierarchy that supported the CCW review process while firmly defending its prerogative to use mines. The mandate of diplomats remained limited to the revision of Protocol II, a commitment sufficient only to stem the passion of the NGOs and to be perceived as progress.

The French government had great trouble finding a single voice with which to speak on landmines, especially given the spectacular failure of the CCW conferences in Vienna and Geneva in 1995–6. Indeed, Handicap International representatives highlighted the contradictory positions of French government representatives at a news conference on 19 April 1996, several days before the end of the Geneva conference. The Ministry of Defence reiterated its belief in the utility of AP mines for protection of troops and installations. The Ministry of Foreign Affairs viewed a total ban as a significant long-term objective while considering the increasing number of unilateral bans being announced worldwide. The Secretary of State for Humanitarian Affairs pointed to the conclusions of the ICRC report, *Anti-Personnel Landmines: Friend or Foe?*, which doubted the military usefulness of mines, and declared that it 'will be difficult for France not to come to the same conclusion in the end'. The failure of the CCW process lent more weight to ban supporters, even inside the French government. Public opinion proved loyal when the second 'shoe pyramid' operation, on 28 September 1996, attracted even greater popular impact and media interest than the first.

A pooling of effort, inside and outside the government, developed before the first Ottawa conference on 2 October 1996. France took advantage of this new international platform to announce two major evolutionary elements in its position. First, officials had prepared a draft act confirming a ban on manufacture and sales to be put before the National Assembly that would oblige the Ministry of Defence to give an annual report on the destruction of stocks. Second, the government had given up the use of mines, except 'in the case of absolute necessity to protect its forces'. Though these steps were perceived as an appreciable new concession from the military, they had no international repercussions when contrasted with the dramatic launch of the Ottawa Process. They did, however, prove the value of maintaining public and political pressure on the heavy French interministerial machinery.

The 1996 Ottawa conference was also an occasion for a 'first' in the government/NGO relationship in France, with an NGO representative being invited to participate in the official government delegation. Recommended by the Secretary of State for Humanitarian Affairs and backed up by several highly placed officials, this integration needed final approval by the Prime Minister's cabinet. Such a level of transparency was new in French political culture, where formal collaboration with NGOs is seldom accepted, even on social or environmental issues. The decision was helped by Handicap International's unquestionable leadership role on the issue.

FRANCE, ONE OF THE GUARDIANS OF THE INTEGRITY OF THE TREATY: 1997

Worried, even shocked, by the Canadian challenge to have a ban treaty signed in 14 months, French diplomacy took several months to see more than a political scoop in the pronouncement made by Canadian Foreign Affairs Minister Lloyd Axworthy. Roughly three months into 1997, several high-ranking French officials and diplomats realized that the Ottawa Process could not be turned back. Great Britain's change of position in April 1997 accelerated this realization.

The official change in the French position took place under paradoxical conditions. The National Assembly was dissolved on 9 May and the draft act for the law banning manufacture and sales disappeared without having been presented to members of parliament. On 1 June 1997, the Socialist Party won the elections but the new government no longer included a Secretary of State for Humanitarian Affairs. All at once, we had lost the opportunity for parliamentary debate as well as the major support of someone inside the government, just at the moment the Brussels conference was announced.

We were fortunate that the scale of the movement and the strength of support, both inside and outside governmental structures, were such that the final steps in the evolution of French policy were completed rapidly. In fact, the new political environment turned out to be extremely supportive in several ways. The Socialist members of the previous legislature had submitted a draft act for a total ban in 1995. The new Prime Minister was clearly an advocate for a total ban. Several high-ranking officials, also long-time supporters of a total ban, were given key cabinet posts as Minister for Defence and Minister for Co-operation and for Development, and we also had supporters in positions close to the Prime Minister. Three weeks after the election, France announced in Brussels that it would sign the Ottawa Convention and that it would ban all uses of AP mines before the end of 1999, or earlier if the Convention entered into force early.

Armed with this apparently unambiguous national position, the French adopted an understandably tough negotiating position in Oslo. In fact, France became one of the key players to resist the American attempts to influence the negotiations. This strong position was made possible by the participation of NGOs on the delegation, the personality of the head of the French delegation, and the rigidity of the American delegation.

France had unwittingly initiated the political process leading to a ban on AP mines in 1993 when Mitterrand invited the world to revise the CCW. In Oslo in 1997, France reclaimed its place in the movement for a ban, a place that had been momentarily lost on account of slow policy evolution and diplomatic caution. Today there are questions as to whether French policy-makers will learn from the experience of the Ottawa Process. Can France accept a regulatory system where the five permanent members of the UN Security Council are not the only masters of the game? Can France recognize that a coalition of medium-influence countries can impose views on bigger powers? Can France accept that NGOs and the media will invite themselves to discussion tables and destabilize a traditional balance of power?

WHAT REMAINS AFTER OTTAWA?

French diplomacy can be seen as a reflection of our society: confident yet compartmentalized. French administrative 'machinery', which spurred the evolution of society 30 years ago, is now so rigid that it prohibits all possibilities of a new social dynamic. French diplomacy, which for a century allowed France to shine, is perhaps the victim of the same syndrome—it protects accepted views and fails to anticipate evolutionary trends.

The Ottawa Process has nevertheless been successful at breaking down some of the barriers between the state and the NGO community. The infusion of the stories of mine victims into the corridors of international power has created a different climate for policy-making. Spectacular public demonstrations by NGOs, their tenacity, and the seriousness of their analysis and arguments have progressively transformed the traditional diplomatic perception of NGOs as irresponsible sleepy dreamers. A few high-ranking officials were open to an alliance with the NGOs, and this cleared internal administrative impediments and allowed politicians to overcome the obstacles to a total ban.

We are still far from any idea of a mature partnership between NGOs and government, but in a country where every relationship between the state and its civil society is suspect or based on confrontation, this is perhaps a first victory.

CHAPTER 5

The South African Campaign
Noel Stott

Since the launch of the South African Campaign to Ban Landmines (SACBL) in 1995, South Africa's position progressed from that of being a major exporter and producer of mines in Africa to a point where it would spearhead African resistance to any delay or weakening of a total and immediate global landmine ban negotiated in Oslo in September 1997. Both government consciousness and public awareness of the scourge of landmines, especially in southern Africa, grew to such an extent that the 'new' South African government was able to participate fully in the process towards, and the signing of, the Convention on the Prohibition of the Use, Stockpiling, Production and Transfer of Anti-Personnel Mines and on their Destruction (the Ottawa Convention) in Ottawa, Canada, in December 1997. A number of factors contributed to this development, not least of which was the international post-Cold War context and the over-arching transformation process under way after the first democratic election in South Africa in April 1994. Beyond these important factors, there was also the SACBL, a network of NGOs affiliated to the International Campaign to Ban Landmines (ICBL), which directly contributed to the energy with which the South African government dramatically altered its position between 1993 and 1997 to become one of the leading nations of the Ottawa Process.

The objective of this chapter is to analyse the ways in which the SACBL was able to influence meaningfully the South African policy process with respect to anti-personnel mines. This chapter will also provide a brief overview of South Africa's contribution to the landmines situation in southern Africa, South Africa's changing position, and the role played by the SACBL in the development of the government's new AP mine policy. A brief discussion of the SACBL as a new social movement is provided at the conclusion of this chapter.

Landmines in Southern Africa

Southern Africa is probably the most heavily mined region in the world, with Mozambique and Angola listed by the United Nations as among the most mine-contaminated countries.[1] An estimated 20 million mines lie buried in the soils of southern Africa, many unmapped and unmarked. Only Lesotho and Mauritius are unaffected. According to Human Rights Watch researcher Alex Vines, mines have killed and injured over 250,000 people in the region since 1961, when the first known mine casualty was recorded in Angola.[2]

Although South Africa has stood out as a significant producer, exporter, and user of mines in the region, landmine use on South Africa's own soil was limited. The South African Defence Force and police occasionally mined African National Congress (ANC) infiltration routes in what are now the Northern and North-West provinces. ANC insurgents also placed AP mines on border tracks and farm roads. During the 1980s, a number of incidents in which military personnel and civilians were either killed or injured were reported along South Africa's borders with Zimbabwe, Botswana, and Mozambique, as well as between then South African-occupied Namibia and Angola. These events sparked off the apartheid government's 'strong objections to the violations of international law and the reluctance of neighbouring countries to ensure that their territories are not used for terrorist [sic] activities'.[3] More recently, the use of landmines has been the subject of Truth and Reconciliation Commission amnesty hearings.[4]

Locally produced mines have been found in many southern African countries. South Africa supplied mines (which were locally produced, bought from other countries, or captured from enemy supplies) to rebel forces in the region, such as UNITA and Renamo. The Human Rights Watch Arms Project has confirmed that South African-made mines have been reported in Angola, Mozambique, Namibia, Zambia, and Zimbabwe and have been used as far afield as Afghanistan, Eritrea, Rwanda, Somalia, Iraq, and Cambodia. However, because South Africa produced mines that were identical to the Chinese Type 72 and the Italian Valmara 69, which are among the most common in the world, these allegations are contentious.

It is believed that South Africa began producing mines in the 1970s or earlier, when the military and arms producers also began developing landmine-related products such as mine detectors and anti-mine armoured vehicles. However, it is difficult to establish the true dimensions of the commercial production of mines, as much of the country's arms trade was conducted in secret to circumvent the UN-imposed arms embargo between 1963 and 1994. Estimates of sales range from 3,900 mines to 17,000.[5] In more recent times South Africa has also been involved in extensive research and design of so-called 'smart' (or short-life) anti-personnel mines.

THE SOUTH AFRICAN STATE'S PROGRESSIVE POSITION

The first democratic general election and presidential inauguration of mid-1994 brought the new South Africa into being. Prior to this historic event,

President F.W. de Klerk, in compliance with UN General Assembly Resolution 48/75 (K) of 16 December 1993, had declared a moratorium on the export, marketing, and transit of all types of landmines. By September 1995, the new government of National Unity had acceded to the 1980 Convention on Certain Conventional Weapons (CCW). Notwithstanding South Africa becoming a state party to the CCW on 13 March 1996 and the announcement of a total ban on the marketing, export, and transit of all landmines, the government maintained its position that mines were still vital for defence purposes.

To the further dismay of the SACBL, the South African government announced at the CCW Review Conference in April-May 1996 that while the South African military would *suspend* its use of landmines, it would not support an outright ban, which ran contrary to the recommendations of its Parliamentary Standing Committee on Foreign Affairs.[6] Moreover, South Africa continued to argue that the way forward was to manufacture and use only 'smart mines'. One newspaper editorial later commented that 'South Africa has now halted the export of landmines, but to its enduring shame still continues to manufacture them.'[7]

However, on 19 February 1997, the South African government's position on AP mines would change radically. In an apparent about-turn, Defence Minister Joe Modise informed the press that 'Cabinet decided . . . to ban the use, development, production and stockpiling of anti-personnel landmines—with immediate effect.' He pledged that South Africa 'will do everything possible to help rid the world of the menace of the anti-personnel landmine.'[8]

Since then the South African government has been a vocal supporter of a total and immediate global ban on AP mines and has been at the forefront of diplomatic initiatives on this issue, both in Africa and internationally. Actions taken by the South African government included hosting the Organization of African Unity's landmines conference in May 1997, entering into bilateral agreements for the training of deminers from neighbouring countries, the signing of memoranda calling for the worldwide elimination of AP mines with countries such as New Zealand, co-sponsoring UN General Assembly resolutions, and, importantly, chairing the treaty negotiations in Oslo in September 1997 and the early destruction of all its AP mines stockpile as required by the Ottawa treaty.

THE ROLE OF THE SACBL

In June 1995, a number of South Africans representing various NGOs, concerned about South Africa's role in causing the devastating effects of landmines in southern Africa, attended the ICBL's Third International Conference to Ban Landmines. Organizations attending the conference, entitled The Human and Socio-Economic Impact of Landmines: Towards an International Ban and held in Phnom Penh, Cambodia, included the Ceasefire Campaign, the African Centre for the Constructive Resolution of Disputes, and the Centre for South-South Relations. During the meeting the South African delegation committed to establishing a national campaign, and in July the Ceasefire Campaign launched a co-ordinated campaign against AP mines as one of its demilitarization activities.

For strategic reasons and in keeping with the *modus operandi* of other national campaigns under the umbrella of the ICBL, the campaign was restructured in early 1996 as the South African Campaign to Ban Landmines. Permanent members of the co-ordinating committee of the SACBL included Oxfam–UK & Ireland, the Group for Environmental Monitoring, the Anglican Church, and the Catholic Justice and Peace Commission, as well as a small group of volunteers, many of whom were active in the anti-apartheid struggle. The SACBL, while being administratively and financially accountable to the Ceasefire Campaign, acted as a semi-autonomous structure with respect to policies and programs.

Both the SACBL and the global call to ban AP mines managed to receive wide support in South Africa. This was reflected in the fact that the activities of the SACBL were endorsed by more than 100 NGOs, community-based organizations, and religious groups (churches and church co-ordinating structures and interfaith bodies), as well as student movements from across the country. These institutions are active in sectors that range from land, environment, disability, and conflict resolution, to human rights. The SACBL thus mirrored the diverse, multisectoral approach and integrated strategy of the ICBL.

THE SACBL AS A NEW SOCIAL MOVEMENT

The SACBL was reflective of a new social movement primarily due to its international association, its decentralized nature, and its orientation as a network. Within the context of the new South African state, the role played by the SACBL has been consistent with that of an extra-governmental organization challenging government policy, but it has also been quite different in that it quickly learned how to adapt and seize the opportunities presented by the changing national political environment on the AP mine issue.

The SACBL rapidly learned to throw the advocacy net as wide as possible, what to focus on, who to target, and when to act. It was also quick to understand the differences and tensions between the different actors and levels of government that were the targets of its advocacy efforts—lawmakers in Parliament, drafters of policy in the ministries, and implementers in the various departments. Furthermore, the SACBL recognized the need to argue *for* something as opposed to *against* something. It was important to acknowledge and praise progress when appropriate. This paradoxical tactic of critiquing and encouraging played a fundamental role in the success of the SACBL. Unprecedented access to senior political and bureaucratic officials also greatly facilitated the eventual symbiosis of governmental and non-governmental activities and policy positions.

As noted above, the SACBL would ultimately have a somewhat fluid membership of 100 NGOs. The development of the movement was interesting in that it did not reflect the expected collective identity of demilitarists. Rather, it was a group of supporters reflecting a wide range of organizations working in such areas as the environment, religious communities, development, and disabled peoples. This diverse and broad participation supported the SACBL's success. Member organizations from a wide range of political tendencies and social affiliations were not necessarily against all weapons *per se*, but they were united against the effect of anti-personnel landmines on their particular constituencies. While the network was diverse, the organization of work was closely co-ordinated by a core group of committed individuals. Organizations that officially supported the SACBL were under no obligation to the SACBL. They were each involved in activities, but to varying degrees.

This same structure works successfully for the ICBL, which is also a decentralized organization with a relatively small steering committee of members from various countries. Activities are co-ordinated through the development of a broad program of action. The onus is then on each national campaign to implement the program using the means appropriate to its context. As such, the SACBL operates within its own political context, but its status and coherence are augmented through association with the ICBL. The affiliated members of the national and international campaign served to enhance the campaign as a representative movement of civil society acting on behalf of the 'victims' of landmines. Thus, the tightness of the AP mine issue, coupled with the ideological inclusiveness of the SACBL, helped to build a movement very much like a new social movement. The SACBL had a dual status. It was a local social movement with the capacity to share resources and affect changes nationally, but at the same time it was part of and had access to the resources of a global civil society movement, the ICBL.

This active involvement in a cause to ban a weapon responsible for a social, political, economic, and environmental crisis allowed national campaigns to impact substantially on individual nation-states. While new social movement theorists argue that the state is no longer the location around which social movements converge, the SACBL reflected a strong focus on the nation-state. Global solidarity, an effective tool in the national landmine campaigns, was exploited to achieve gains from governments. However, this did not axiomatically indicate a powerless state. The alliances forged by the landmines issue placed both national and international movements in a position to influence governments. The government of South Africa became accessible to extra-governmental organizations engaged in the landmines campaign. The SACBL was able to develop and put into practice the concept of 'critical solidarity'—supporting success, criticizing when necessary. But it was not only the SACBL that articulated itself in international terms. The discourse of the South African government on the AP mine issue was also grounded in internationalism. By taking the bold step of abandoning its program to develop smart mines, the government articulated its recognition of the global landmines crisis as a humanitarian issue and not a security issue. This propelled its concern about the crisis beyond the boundaries of South Africa.

The formation of the ICBL and the SACBL also coincided with the return of South Africa to the international community. For both the government and South African civil society the campaign to ban landmines represented a very concrete opportunity to give back what the people of South Africa had been receiving over the many years of the anti-apartheid struggle—solidarity. And what more fundamental issue could be taken up to express this solidarity than a campaign to ban landmines, especially given the previous South African government's history of destabilizing the region and the new government's indebtedness to the ordinary people of the region who bore the brunt of their countries' support of the liberation movements.

The SACBL believed firmly that, as South Africans, they had a moral obligation to propagate the ideals and philosophies formulated during the struggle against apartheid. They also believed that the South African government had a duty to place these ideals at the centre of the continuing global struggle for justice, peace, and human rights.

While the SACBL made effective use of mass media and information networks in lobbying the government on the AP mine issue, it also directly targeted the formal institutions of the state. The SACBL focused its efforts on a myriad of important state institutions, meeting with representatives of the relevant standing committees of Parliament as well as with officials from the Departments of Defence and Foreign Affairs. Lobbying was deliberately focused on Parliament—letters were sent directly to all parliamentarians, cabinet, and ANC working groups. Briefing papers were distributed and the campaign gave submissions to the parliamentary portfolio committees on Defence and Foreign Affairs. Ultimately, several individuals in Parliament became key supporters of the campaign.

It is important to note, as well, that members of the SACBL who were involved in the anti-apartheid struggle did not only seek alliances with their historical partners now in government. They worked to attract élite and influential sympathizers, including Archbishop Desmond Tutu, asking them to meet with all political parties to lobby on the issue and to use opposition parties by requesting them to ask questions in Parliament. In what may be considered an inspired move, the SACBL, rather than tackling the military utility of landmines by itself, arranged a press conference with top military veterans from both the previous apartheid forces and the liberation movements' armies—the South African Council of Military Veterans, Azanian People's Liberation Army, and Umkhonto we Sizwe. At this press conference a letter to President Mandela calling for the banning of anti-personnel landmines was presented to the public.

CONCLUSION

There is little doubt that the prevailing political context, both nationally and internationally, enhanced the ability of the SACBL to influence South Africa's policy process on the AP mines issue. The organizational structure, ideological inclusiveness, and strategies employed by the SACBL were particularly well suited to this task. To facilitate its interventions in state policy, the SACBL used an assortment of techniques, some indicative of its status as part of a new social movement and others more clearly related to traditional lobbying and advocacy methods.

The SACBL took advantage of its unprecedented access to senior state officials and the desire of the new South African government to re-enter international society as a recognized progressive force. In addition, the SACBL's association with the ICBL enabled it to engage with the state as part of a transnational social movement. As such, the SACBL, and the landmines campaign more generally, traversed two domains—local and global.

It is for these reasons that, in recognizing the SACBL's role in the campaign, both Defence Minister Modise and Deputy Foreign Minister Aziz Pahad could credit South African NGOs with taking the lead in uniting African nations throughout the treaty negotiations and could 'state unequivocally that government was ably informed in reaching this decision [to ban anti-personnel landmines with immediate effect] by the efforts of the South African Campaign to Ban Landmines.'[9]

NOTES

1. Kristian Harpviken, 'Landmines in Southern Africa: Regional Initiatives for Clearance and Control', *Contemporary Security Policy* 18, 1 (Apr. 1997).
2. Alex Vines, *Still Killing: Landmines in Southern Africa* (London: Human Rights Watch, 1997), 1.
3. *Citizen*, 6 May 1987.
4. South Africa, Truth and Reconciliation Commission—Armed Forces Hearings and Umkhonto we Sizwe (MK) appearance, 10 Oct. 1997.
5. Vines, *Still Killing*, 130.
6. *The Star*, 6 May 1996.
7. *Eastern Province Herald*, 15 Jan. 1997.
8. Catholic Justice and Peace, *Annual Report*, 1997.
9. *Business Day*, 16 March 1998.

Poster: Internation Committee to Ban Landmines. Courtesy of ICBL.

A 'shoe mountain' in Paris.
Courtesy of John Rodsted.

Canadian official Jill Sinclair navigates 'minefield' at Brussels conference. Courtesy of John Rodsted.

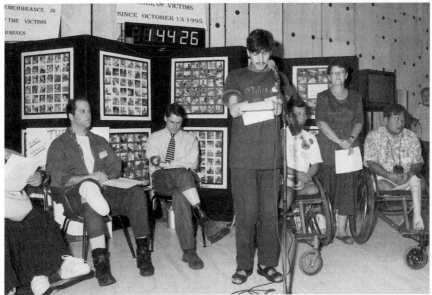

Landmine survivors at CCW conference in Geneva, 1996. (Note clock counting victims.) Courtesy of John Rodsted.

Susan Walker of Handicap International in Washington, DC. Courtesy of John Rodsted.

Jody Williams and Tun Channareth (on behalf of the ICBL) receive the 1997 Nobel Peace Prize. Courtesy of John Rodsted.

Members of the ICBL celebrate the signing of the ban Convention in Ottawa, December 1997.
Courtesy of John Rodsted.

Poster: International Committee of
the Red Cross. Courtesy of ICRC.

CHAPTER 6

THE ROLE OF THE INTERNATIONAL COMMITTEE OF THE RED CROSS

Stuart Maslen

This chapter traces the development of international humanitarian law governing weapons, particularly anti-personnel mines.[1] It outlines the role of the International Committee of the Red Cross (ICRC) and the broader Red Cross and Red Crescent Movement in the development of international humanitarian law, the efforts to translate medical field experience into international policy, and the successful adoption and signature, in 1997, of the Ottawa treaty. At the same time, it stresses the need to move towards a more preventive approach to control particularly abhorrent weapons so as to avoid needless repetition of the kind of enormous human and social suffering engendered by landmines.

INTERNATIONAL HUMANITARIAN LAW AND THE CONTROL OF WEAPONS: A HISTORICAL PERSPECTIVE

International humanitarian law (IHL), the branch of international law that regulates the conduct of warfare with a view to minimizing the suffering inflicted on civilians and combatants alike, has long been concerned with the dangers posed both by certain means (weaponry) and by methods of warfare (the way weapons are used). For instance, a prohibition on the use of poison in warfare had been widely recognized as a customary rule for many centuries. In 1862, at the end of his seminal work *A Memory of Solferino*, Henry Dunant—the father of the Red Cross Movement—drew attention to the dangers posed by the 'new and frightful weapons of destruction which are now at the disposal of the nations'.[2] Likewise, as customary rules of warfare began to be codified in international treaties in the late nineteenth century, governments became concerned by the ever-increasing proliferation of particularly destructive weapons.

In 1868, at an international conference convened by the tsar of Russia, assembled governments adopted the St Petersburg Declaration, which prohibited the use of exploding bullets, a new invention that in most cases caused the death of victims. This declaration was followed by an agreement reached at the 1899 Hague International Peace Conference to prohibit the recently developed dumdum bullets, which expanded on entering the body, causing appalling internal injuries. The Hague Declaration concerning expanding bullets was adopted only after a vote was taken and in spite of objections by two of the major military powers of the time, Great Britain and the United States. Yet, despite such initial opposition, the prohibition on dumdum bullets has since become part of customary international law, applicable to all states and to all armed conflicts.

In 1918, following the widespread use of chemical weapons in World War I, the ICRC protested 'with all the force at our command' against such means of warfare and called publicly for their prohibition.

> Far from attenuating the evils of war, progress in the science of aeronautics, ballistics and chemistry might well be said only to have aggravated suffering and especially to have extended it to all the population, so that war will soon be all-destroying and without mercy.
>
> We wish today to take a stand against a barbaric innovation which science is bringing to perfection, that is to say making it more lethal and more subtly cruel. This innovation is the use of asphyxiating and poisonous gas, which will it seems increase to an extent so far undreamed of.
>
> We now hear of new volatile poisons, large-scale production of which is all the easier as the raw material is ready to hand. We are shown missiles loaded with these poisonous gases spreading death—and a horrible death it is—not only among the fighting forces, but behind the lines among an inoffensive population over a wide area in which all living things will be destroyed. We protest with all the force at our command at such warfare, which can only be called criminal. And if, as seems likely, the enemy is forced to counter-attack or resort to reprisals to compel the perpetrator of this odious practice to give it up, we can only see ahead a struggle which will exceed in barbarity anything which history has known so far.[3]

In 1925, the Geneva Protocol on Poisonous and Asphyxiating Gases banned the use of chemical and bacteriological warfare. The norms created by this Protocol were subsequently strengthened by the negotiation of the 1972 Biological Weapons Convention, which became binding international law in 1975, and the 1993 Chemical Weapons Convention, which entered into force in April 1997. These two Conventions also banned the production, stockpiling, and transfer of chemical and biological weapons.

A fundamental and universally applicable rule of IHL holds that the right of the parties to a conflict to use weapons against an enemy is not unlimited. Two further customary principles, derived from this general rule, prohibit the use of weapons of a nature either to cause superfluous injury or unnecessary suffering, or to strike soldier and civilian without distinction. Both of these principles have obvious relevance to mines, which are difficult, if not impossible, to direct against military targets alone, and which, by design, inflict horrific injuries on the human body, usually resulting in permanent and severe disability. Customary law also provides that where existing IHL is inadequate or non-existent, soldiers and civilians alike are protected by the principles of humanity and the dictates of public conscience; this is the so-called 'Martens Clause', named after the nineteenth-century Russian diplomat who first proposed it.

As early as the 1950s, the ICRC had identified landmines as one of a number of conventional weapons of specific concern. Its 1955 Draft Rules for the Protection of the Civilian Population, as revised in 1958, addressed the issue of mines under a section on weapons 'with uncontrollable effects' and put forward requirements for the recording of minefields and post-conflict exchange of minefield information.[4] At that time, however, states were generally reluctant to envisage the adoption of new international instruments regulating means and methods of warfare.

Following the proliferation of new weapons in the 1960s, and in particular the use of new means and methods of warfare in Indochina, the ICRC again sought to promote the development of IHL in this field. In 1973, the ICRC published a report, based on discussions by governmental and non-governmental experts, entitled *Weapons That May Cause Unnecessary Suffering or Have Indiscriminate Effects*. Although the discussions focused primarily on incendiary weapons such as napalm, mines were clearly identified as weapons that 'may expose non-combatants to a grave and prolonged hazard'.[5]

At the request of the Twenty-second International Conference of the Red Cross,[6] in 1974 the ICRC convened a Conference of Governmental Experts on the Use of Certain Conventional Weapons (Governmental Experts Conference) in Lucerne, Switzerland. The need for specific legal control of both manually placed and remotely delivered landmines was again discussed. A number of experts believed that mines (and booby traps) were indiscriminate by their very nature, while others asserted that mines, as was the case with other weapons, could be used with or without discrimination. Thus, although some experts felt that at least certain types of anti-personnel mines ought to be banned, others were convinced 'that a complete ban on such weapons was both impracticable and unjustified'.[7]

A second session of this conference was held in Lugano, Switzerland, from 28 January to 26 February 1976. Early in the session, experts from France, the Netherlands, and the United Kingdom introduced a working paper entitled 'Land Mines and Booby-Traps and Proposals for the Regulation of Their Use'. The proposals included draft articles dealing with definitions, the recording of minefields, the use of remotely delivered mines, and the use of mines, booby traps, and other devices in populated areas. These proposals ultimately became the basis for the provisions of Protocol II to the 1980 Convention on Certain Conventional Weapons, adopted under the auspices of the United Nations.

Although the results of the two sessions of the Governmental Experts Conference were integrated in the work of the 1974–7 Diplomatic Conference convened by the Swiss government to codify and strengthen IHL in general, agreement on the regulation of specific conventional weapons proved impossible. Instead, the 1977 Protocol I additional to the Geneva Conventions of 1949 provides in general terms for the legal regulation of the use of all conventional weapons in accordance with customary principles of IHL. Article 35 states in part:

1. In any armed conflict, the right of the Parties to the conflict to choose methods or means of warfare is not unlimited.
2. It is prohibited to employ weapons, projectiles and material and methods of warfare of a nature to cause superfluous injury or unnecessary suffering.

Article 51, para. 4 provides as follows:

Indiscriminate attacks are prohibited. Indiscriminate attacks are:
(a) those which are not directed at a specific military objective;
(b) those which employ a method or means of combat which cannot be directed at a specific military objective; or
(c) those which employ a method or means of combat the effects of which cannot be limited as required by this Protocol; and consequently, in each such case, are of a nature to strike military objectives and civilians or civilian objects without distinction.

Following the adoption of the two 1977 Additional Protocols, the UN General Assembly decided that a conference should be held under UN auspices to conclude a Convention regulating the use of certain conventional weapons.[8] The result of this conference, the two sessions of which were held in 1979 and 1980, was the UN Convention on Certain Conventional Weapons (CCW) and its three annexed Protocols.[9] Landmines, including anti-personnel mines, were covered by the Protocol on Prohibitions or Restrictions on the Use of Mines, Booby-traps and Other Devices (Protocol II). Although Protocol II specified clearly that mines should not be directed against individual civilians or the civilian population as such, it applied only to international armed conflicts and provided no mechanism for ensuring compliance with its provisions. It therefore did little to add to existing customary law governing weaponry, and its provisions were all too often unknown or ignored by belligerents involved in later armed conflicts.

RESPONDING TO THE CRISIS

The 1980s saw a rapid expansion of the use of landmines, especially anti-personnel mines. In the conflicts waged in Afghanistan, Angola, Cambodia, and Mozambique, to name but a few, mines were used on a huge scale and with little thought for the requirements of international law. Children, women, the elderly—no one was spared the indiscriminate suffering sown by this weapon. At the beginning of the 1990s, the outbreak of conflicts in the former Yugoslavia, in the Russian Federation (Chechnya), and in other countries of the former Soviet Union (Armenia, Azerbaijan, Georgia, and Tadjikistan, in particular) brought the scourge of landmines to Europe and Central Asia, with a consequent large number of casualties among soldiers and civilians alike. Day after day, ICRC field staff were confronted with ever-increasing numbers of mine-injured persons requiring emergency first aid, complicated, time-consuming surgical operations, and prolonged rehabilitative assistance.

Landmines inflict horrendous wounds on the human body. Depending on the type and emplacement of the mine, a victim may be showered with metal or plastic fragments, or have one or more limbs torn off by the force of the blast. At the beginning of the 1990s, the ICRC began to collect data about the war-wounded treated in its surgical hospitals. Surgeons soon noticed that a substantial percentage of the wounded, and an overwhelming number of amputees, were mine victims. The information collected and its subsequent analysis clearly showed that mines were increasingly present in many conflict and post-conflict situations and that the number of mine victims was steadily rising. As a first step towards alerting the world to the epidemic of mine injuries, in 1992 the ICRC published *Mines, A Perverse Use of Technology*. The powerful and shocking photographs of mine victims featured in the publication were, sadly, no more than a simple reflection of the daily reality in the field.

Recognizing that the growing humanitarian catastrophe had to be tackled as a matter of urgency, in April 1993 the ICRC convened an international symposium in Montreux, Switzerland, bringing together humanitarian, legal, medical, and military experts to discuss the nature and extent of the landmine crisis and possible responses to it. Attention focused on the need to address the threat posed by anti-personnel mines. Many participants stated that prohibiting the use of all anti-personnel mines would be the best solution, not only from the humanitarian point of view but also because restrictions on the use of a weapon were more difficult to monitor than its complete prohibition. In particular, representatives of the International Campaign to Ban Landmines (ICBL) asserted their determination to seek a total prohibition of all anti-personnel mines. Other participants, however, felt that such a prohibition was unrealistic and declared that governments would agree to it only if their military establishments found it acceptable. All the participants agreed, however, on the need to strengthen the existing IHL rules applicable to all landmines, and especially anti-personnel mines.[10]

THE REVIEW CONFERENCE OF THE 1980 CCW AND PROTOCOL II AS AMENDED

In February 1993, at the urging of the French Handicap International and aware of the need to strengthen without delay IHL applicable to landmines, the French government called on the UN Secretary-General to convene a first Review Conference of the 1980 CCW. In accordance with UN General Assembly Resolution 48/79, meetings of governmental experts were convened in 1994 and early 1995 to prepare the Review Conference, the first session of which was held in Vienna from 25 September to 13 October 1995.

In the report it prepared for the Review Conference,[11] the ICRC reiterated its conviction, first expressed by the organization's president Cornelio Sommaruga, in February 1994, that a prohibition on the production, stockpiling, transfer, and use of all anti-personnel mines was the only practical solution to the crisis from a humanitarian standpoint. In the years prior to 1994, the ICRC studied a variety of possible measures to respond to the mines crisis. It finally came to the conclusion that the only effective solution would be the total prohibition of anti-personnel mines. It pointed out, however, that the prohibition could not be effective without a careful and precise definition of the weapon. Throughout the difficult negotiations in the CCW review process, the ICRC participated as an expert observer, maintaining its view that a total ban on anti-personnel mines was necessary and that anti-vehicle/anti-tank mines should be both detectable and self-neutralizing, while commenting constructively on the proposals by states to amend and strengthen CCW Protocol II. In May 1995, the ICRC provided all states parties to the CCW with detailed comments on the 'rolling text' of a revised Protocol II, which had been prepared for the Review Conference by a group of governmental experts during 1994 and 1995.

The final text of the Protocol adopted on 3 May 1996, after three sessions of a conference originally slated for only one three-week period, was extremely disappointing. Constrained by the practice of consensus used in disarmament negotiations, agreement was reduced to the lowest common denominator. Despite some progress—extension of the scope of the Protocol to include internal armed conflicts, clear responsibility for mine clearance attributed to the user, and new protection for humanitarian field personnel—the resulting provisions were widely considered to be overly complicated and difficult to put in practice. Convinced of the urgent need for strong action, the ICRC, in its statement to the closing session of the Review Conference, characterized the restrictions imposed on the use of anti-personnel mines as 'woefully inadequate'. It again called for a total prohibition of anti-personnel mines as the only effective response to the mines crisis.

Speaking at the same session, the head of the Canadian delegation, Ambassador Mark Moher, announced Canada's intention to convene a strategy conference of pro-ban states in Ottawa later in the year. This laid the foundations for what would become known as the Ottawa Process.

Towards the Prohibition of Anti-Personnel Mines: ICRC Campaign Strategy

As the first session of the Review Conference had closed in Vienna in October 1995 without any agreement on strengthening IHL control of land-mines, the prospect of an early international total ban on anti-personnel mines appeared remote. To persuade the international community of the need to move swiftly towards the elimination of anti-personnel mines, the ICRC had developed a three-pronged campaign strategy combining a detailed study of the military utility of anti-personnel mines, support for unilateral national and regional responses to the mines problem, and stigmatization of anti-personnel mines in the public conscience.

Support for the International Process

A central element of the ICRC mines campaign, conducted in co-operation with national Red Cross and Red Crescent societies and their international federation, was public advocacy on the effects of mines and the need for their total prohibition. This advocacy initiative comprised:

- a public advertising and information campaign;
- dissemination of campaign materials and specialist and general publications on the humanitarian costs of landmines;
- the provision of relevant legal and medical expertise.

Thus, in November 1995, for the first time in its history, the ICRC launched a major public advertising campaign designed to raise public awareness of the mines scourge and to highlight the need for the prohibition of anti-personnel mines. Using a combination of evocative TV spots and print announcements placed free of charge in the national and international media across Africa, Asia, Europe, and the Americas (to a commercial value of several million US dollars), together with hard-hitting videos on the mines problem and necessary responses to it, the campaign reached a worldwide audience of hundreds of millions of people with the unequivocal message: 'Landmines must be stopped.' In 1997 the movement's campaign communication strategy focused on support for the Ottawa Process, in particular the signature of the Ottawa treaty. New print announcements to be launched in 1998 are continuing this support, now targeting the importance of early ratification of the treaty and the need to ensure mine clearance and victim assistance programs over the long term.

Another important part of the campaign process has been the array of specialist and non-specialist literature on mines published and disseminated by the ICRC, covering the different aspects—humanitarian, legal, medical/rehabilitative, and military—of the mines problem. A guide to the Ottawa treaty has been printed in all UN languages and new and revised publications on the mines issue are put out regularly. The ICRC's Web page (http://www.icrc.org) has a special section devoted to landmines, which is regularly updated. Finally, presentations on the various issues involved have been made at hundreds of international, regional, and national seminars and other events to strengthen awareness of the problem and to further stigmatize anti-personnel mines.

Military Utility

It is generally understood that no rule of IHL can expect to be universal unless it enjoys widespread acceptance and respect within military circles. With a view to developing a better understanding of military doctrine regarding landmines, the ICRC had already held a symposium of military experts on anti-personnel mines in January 1994.[12] The majority of the participants were professional military officers, including combat engineers, familiar with current tactical doctrine and trends within their own armed forces. The symposium concluded that anti-personnel mines were the most cost-effective system available to the military and that no alternative fulfilled the military requirement in the way they did.[13]

It was clear from discussions in the CCW Review Conference the following year, however, that a further, more detailed study of the problems of actual use and effectiveness of anti-personnel mines in modern conflicts would be necessary. The sparse literature available on the utility of land-mines tended to concentrate only on doctrine, without a corresponding analysis of their effectiveness in actual combat. Moreover, a distinction was rarely made between the utility of anti-personnel mines *per se* and that of anti-vehicle mines or landmines in general. Accordingly, the ICRC com-missioned an analysis of the 'Military Use and Effectiveness of Anti-per-sonnel Mines' by a retired brigadier, Patrick Blagden, aided by a leading military historian. Blagden combined a background in combat engineering and weapons research with the British Army with recent experience with the landmines issue in more than a dozen countries as Senior Demining Adviser to the UN's Department of Peacekeeping Operations. The study looked at the actual use and effectiveness of anti-personnel mines in 26 conflicts since and including World War II.

In February 1996, the ICRC convened a meeting of senior military experts from eight countries to discuss Brigadier Blagden's report. As well as adding substantial material to his research, the experts drafted and unan-imously adopted a set of conclusions: these included assertions that the military value of anti-personnel mines was questionable and that their lim-ited utility was far outweighed by the appalling humanitarian consequences of their use in actual conflicts. These officers found that anti-personnel mines are by their nature very difficult to use in compliance with interna-tional law and military doctrine, and the experience of actual combat situ-ations has shown this to be true. On this basis, the meeting concluded that the prohibition and elimination of anti-personnel mines should be pursued as a matter of urgency by governments and the entire international com-munity.[14] These conclusions have since been endorsed by 55 senior mili-tary commanders from 19 countries, in their personal capacity.

A similar conclusion was put forward by 15 senior retired US Air Force, Army, and Navy commanders in an open letter to US President Bill Clinton, sponsored by the Vietnam Veterans of America Foundation. The 15 commanders, who included General H. Norman Schwarzkopf, the com-mander of Operation Desert Storm, declared that a permanent and total international ban on the production, stockpiling, sale, and use of anti-per-sonnel mines was not only humane, but also militarily responsible. They further asserted that given the wide range of weaponry available to military forces today, anti-personnel mines were not essential and that banning them would not undermine the military effectiveness or safety of US or other countries' armed forces.

The conclusions of the Blagden study—titled *Anti-Personnel Landmines: Friend or Foe?*—showed it was essential to broaden the dialogue on military utility with those concerned. In co-operation with the Organization of African Unity and the government of Zimbabwe, in April 1997 the ICRC sponsored a meeting in Harare of defence and foreign ministry officials from the 12 states of the Southern African Development Community (SADC). The participants agreed that the limited value of anti-personnel mines was outweighed by their cost in humanitarian terms, that the global scourge of landmines was unacceptable, and that it had to be stopped. They called on SADC states to end immediately all new deployments of anti-personnel mines and to launch an initiative for the establishment of a regional zone free of these weapons.[15]

In an attempt to remedy the relative lack of professional dialogue on anti-personnel mines in Asia, in July 1997 the ICRC convened, in co-operation with the Philippines government and the country's Red Cross Society, a regional seminar for experts in Asian military and strategic studies. Participants from 14 countries gathered in Manila to examine the experience of anti-personnel mine use in the region. The military value of anti-personnel mines was again considered in the context of the long-term human, social, and economic costs incurred in many of the conflicts in which these weapons have been used. Particular attention was paid to the difficulties and extremely high costs of post-conflict mine clearance. The final declaration of the seminar called on states from the region to participate in the Ottawa Process and appealed to the international community to pursue the prohibition and elimination of anti-personnel mines as a matter of urgency.[16]

Even with the signature of the Ottawa Convention by 124 states as of February 1998, the debate surrounding the military utility of anti-personnel mines will doubtless continue in the years to come. A number of important military powers remain to be convinced of the need to adhere to the treaty and to end the use of all anti-personnel mines. The ICRC is planning to convene regional seminars during 1998 to further discussion among governments on the military utility of anti-personnel mines and to encourage even greater support for the early elimination of this weapon.

Promoting a Regional Response to the Mines Crisis

As early as 1995, recognizing that Africa had become the continent worst affected by landmines, the ICRC embarked on a drive to alert African governments to the problem and to mobilize support for a regional response to it. In co-operation with the Organization for African Unity (OAU), the ICRC convened four regional seminars to discuss the mines issue— two in Addis Ababa, Ethiopia, one in Harare, Zimbabwe, and one in Yaounde, Cameroon. At the Harare seminar, held on 2–3 March 1995, the participants called on states to 'seriously consider working towards a total ban of anti-personnel landmines'. In their view, the serious problems created by landmines—in particular, that they inflicted immense suffering on their victims, rendered vast areas of land unusable, and had extremely negative effects on postwar reconstruction and development—outweighed any military benefit.

The importance of southern Africa, which includes some of the world's most heavily mine-infested countries, was reflected in the ICRC's decision to hold another regional seminar, described above, in Harare in April 1997, two months after the International Campaign to Ban Landmines (ICBL) had convened a major international conference in Maputo, Mozambique. These two initiatives were followed in May 1997 by the First Continental Conference of African Experts on Landmines, organized by the OAU and held in Kempton Park, South Africa. The conference adopted a Plan of Action calling for the elimination of anti-personnel landmines in Africa and the establishment of Africa as mine-free zone.

The idea of such a regional mine-free zone had first been raised in the context of Central America. In May 1996, following the conclusion of the First Review Conference of the 1980 CCW, the ICRC hosted a regional seminar in Managua, Nicaragua, in co-operation with the Nicaraguan Ministry of Foreign Affairs and the Nicaraguan Red Cross. During the two-day seminar, officials from Costa Rica, El Salvador, Guatemala, Honduras, Mexico, Nicaragua, and Panama and representatives of intergovernmental, regional, and non-governmental organizations discussed the regional mines problem and possible legal and diplomatic responses to it, as well as mine clearance and assistance to mine victims. At the end the participants issued a solemn, united message: 'Eliminate mines for good.' The conclusions of the seminar led to the idea of a regional initiative for a mine-free area in Central America. This proposal, which was endorsed by foreign ministers of Central American states, was adopted as the goal for the entire Western hemisphere by the Organization of American States barely a month later, in June 1996.

The positive impact of this regional approach[17] on the international process was clearly evidenced by the unity and sense of purpose shown at the Oslo Diplomatic Conference in September 1997 by Central American states and by African states, especially those from southern Africa. The significance of the South in the final treaty negotiations was further demonstrated by the appointment of Ambassador Jacob Selebi, South Africa's representative to the Geneva-based Conference on Disarmament, as chair of the Oslo conference. His adroit management of the negotiations, combined with the unshakeable determination of many states to come up with a strong and effective international legal instrument, helped to ensure that the Ottawa Convention spelled out a clear and unambiguous norm against anti-personnel mines.

THE OTTAWA PROCESS

From the outset, the ICRC has firmly supported the Ottawa Process. At the closing session of the October 1996 conference, Towards a Global Ban on Anti-Personnel Mines, ICRC President Cornelio Sommaruga was quick to congratulate the Canadian Foreign Minister, Lloyd Axworthy, for his courageous challenge to the world community of states to return to Ottawa before the end of 1997 to sign a treaty totally prohibiting anti-personnel mines.

In February 1997, at the Experts Meeting on the Text of a Convention to Ban Anti-Personnel Mines convened in Vienna by the Austrian government, the ICRC outlined what it considered the key issues to be addressed in such a convention. First, the ICRC reiterated the crucial importance of an unambiguous definition of an anti-personnel mine (in CCW Protocol II as amended, anti-personnel mines were defined as mines 'primarily' designed to be triggered by a person, thereby introducing a potentially harmful vagueness into the definition). Second, if a prohibition was to be effective, the new treaty should comprehensively ban the production, stockpiling, transfer, and use of anti-personnel mines and require their destruction. A phased approach should begin with an immediate prohibition on new deployments, production, and transfers. A second phase, which should be as short as practical constraints permit, could provide for the phased destruction of existing stockpiles and the clearance and destruction of mines already deployed.

Third, the ICRC noted that compliance monitoring would be an important element of a regime put in place to end the use of anti-personnel mines, and suggested that the best method would be for an independent mechanism to investigate credible reports of the use of the weapon following the entry into force of a new treaty. But while supporting the maximum possible verification of a ban treaty, the ICRC specifically encouraged states not to allow this question to stand in the way of the basic norm prohibiting anti-personnel mines. It reminded states that previous norms of humanitarian law prohibiting the use of specific weapons had been enacted without provisions on verification, but this did not prevent them from being very largely respected.

Finally, the ICRC addressed the issue of universality of the treaty. Universality is an important objective and the ICRC, in keeping with its mandate under IHL, has devoted a great deal of time and effort to promote existing agreements. It must be said that no major instrument of humanitarian law attracted universal adherence from the outset. Indeed, a number of states took decades to ratify the 1925 Geneva Protocol and, as already noted, in 1868 two of the major powers of the day voted against a prohibition of dumdum bullets. And yet the vast majority of states have observed the norms laid down by these agreements.

The ICRC's statement to the Vienna conference ended with the following words:

> The ICRC is convinced that the 'public conscience' of people throughout the world is revolted both by the indiscriminate nature of anti-personnel mines and by the horrific suffering they have caused. The question now before us is whether there is sufficient political will to establish an absolute prohibition on these weapons and to ensure respect for such a norm. . . . Sixteen months has been a long time for those living in mined areas. Ten more is long enough. But there is nothing inevitable about the loss of two thousand limbs and lives each and every month. Crucial decisions which your governments will make this year can stop this carnage.

Throughout the subsequent conferences and meetings of the Ottawa Process, the ICRC steadfastly maintained its position on these questions. In April 1997 in Bonn, where the issue of verification was specifically addressed, the ICRC made informal proposals for a legal obligation to bring to trial or to extradite for trial suspected treaty violators irrespective of their nationality or the alleged place of commission of the violation. Although the Ottawa Convention requires national implementation measures,[18] including, in most cases, national legislation, it does not provide for compulsory universal jurisdiction in case of serious violations of the core prohibitions.

At the Brussels International Conference for a Global Ban on Anti-Personnel Mines, hosted by the Belgian government in June 1997, states gathered to adopt the Brussels Declaration, adherence to which became the prerequisite for a place at the negotiating table at the subsequent Diplomatic Conference in Oslo. A total of 107 states signed the Brussels Declaration, which stated that a total anti-personnel mine ban treaty should provide for a comprehensive prohibition of anti-personnel mines, the destruction of existing stockpiles as well as of mines cleared, and international co-operation and assistance in the field of mine clearance. The Declaration welcomed the convening of the Oslo Diplomatic Conference, decided to forward to the conference the latest draft ban treaty as prepared by the Austrian government, and affirmed the objective of concluding and signing such a treaty in Ottawa before the end of 1997.

In addition to these measures, a number of states and the ICBL, as well as the ICRC, pointed out the crucial importance of international support for assistance to mine victims. In its formal comments on the third (and final) draft of the treaty,[19] the ICRC called for the inclusion of a provision requiring each state party in a position to do so to provide assistance for the care and rehabilitation of landmine victims and for mine awareness programs. The relevant provision incorporated in the final text of the treaty expressly mentioned the possibility of channelling assistance to mine victims through components of the International Red Cross and Red Crescent Movement,[20] and set out an obligation to promote the social and economic reintegration of survivors of mine explosions. As ICBL representatives rightly noted during the negotiations in Oslo, comprehensive assistance to mine victims demands more than surgical care and physical rehabilitation. Unfortunately, all too few receive even this minimum amount of care.[21]

When the Oslo Diplomatic Conference opened on 1 September 1997, a number of key issues still remained to be resolved. As a result of vigorous efforts by both the ICRC and the ICBL, the definition of an anti-personnel mine had been amended in the draft treaty under consideration. Although the text still contained an exception for anti-vehicle mines equipped with anti-handling devices (which, if remotely delivered, can have much the same effects as anti-personnel mines), the word 'primarily' had been removed, thus eliminating the source of considerable ambiguity.

Equally central to the credibility of the treaty were the general prohibitions relating to the development, production, stockpiling, transfer, and use. As the ICRC had noted in its formal report to the First Review Conference of the 1980 Convention on Certain Conventional Weapons, the core prohibition on use could be effectively implemented only if it was supported by corresponding duties not to manufacture, supply, or maintain stocks of the weapon.[22] It was essential that such a prohibition not be subject to 'exceptions, reservations, or loopholes'. Thus, the vast majority of states at the Diplomatic Conference declared their support for a clause expressly prohibiting reservations to any of the provisions of the treaty.[23] With respect to the possibility of withdrawal from the treaty, the ICRC supported the Austrian draft, which did not allow for effective withdrawals during armed conflict. Indeed, such a possibility would have run counter to the spirit of the treaty by allowing the waiver of its core obligations just when they are most needed—during armed conflict.

Both before and during the Oslo Diplomatic Conference, the nature and extent of the obligation to clear and destroy emplaced anti-personnel mines were discussed in some detail. The ICRC felt, as did a number of others, that an open-ended commitment to clear all anti-personnel mines 'as soon as possible' was inadequate, as it risked detracting from some of the undoubted urgency that would be contained in a specified time period. The shortest possible time frame was desirable from a humanitarian point of view; on the other hand, a number of countries are so severely contaminated by mines that too short a period would be unrealistic and might deter their adherence to the treaty. For this reason, the ICRC proposed that the obligation to clear anti-personnel mines laid in minefields within 10 years should be maintained, but that states needing more time could apply for an extension period.[24] In this way progress in mine clearance and the need for greater international assistance and support could be objectively assessed. Given the difficulty of distinguishing 'minefields' from 'mined areas', at the Diplomatic Conference the obligation of states to demine within 10 years of the treaty coming into force was expanded to include all emplaced anti-personnel mines, but with the possibility for severely mine-affected states to be granted extension periods of up to 10 years at a time.

Finally, as regards the facilitation of compliance, the ICRC reiterated its position that arrangements to clarify issues related to implementation of the Convention were desirable as they would build confidence in its effectiveness. It also reaffirmed, however, that disagreements over such measures should not be permitted to stand in the way of establishing the norms set out in Article 1, which were of fundamental importance. Articles 7 and 8 of the treaty (on transparency measures and facilitating and clarification of compliance, respectively) represent a workable compromise between those who saw the treaty essentially as an instrument of humanitarian law and those who favoured a more disarmament-oriented approach. It is to be hoped, of course, that states adhering to the treaty will put its provisions into effect expeditiously, including the duty to report annually on progress made towards implementing their treaty obligations.

THE IMPLICATIONS OF THE OTTAWA PROCESS FOR INTERNATIONAL HUMANITARIAN LAW

The analysis of the humanitarian costs of anti-personnel mines on the basis of existing humanitarian law principles led the ICRC to conclude that the only effective solution to the humanitarian emergency posed by these weapons was their total prohibition. The vast majority of the international community shared this view. International humanitarian law has been markedly strengthened by the adoption in 1997 of the Convention on the Prohibition of Anti-Personnel Mines and on their Destruction. But the credibility of IHL demands that the Convention be fully adhered to, both legally and in practice.

For the ICRC, and indeed the wider Red Cross and Red Crescent Movement, the experience of the mines campaign has been reinvigorating after the constraints of the Cold War. Dozens of national Red Cross and Red Crescent societies, including many new to campaigning, have felt empowered to advocate for the needs of mine victims present and future, for whom the Ottawa Process may bring hope of an end to the misery. Thus, the campaign has been in perfect accord with the fundamental Red Cross principle of neutrality, which prohibits the various components of the movement from taking sides in a conflict or favouring political parties or causes. The principle of neutrality is intended to ensure that all victims of war may receive protection and assistance—it is therefore a means to an end, not an end in itself.

Landmines are, however, only one weapon among many, and the legality of all of these means of warfare must be considered on the basis of IHL principles. Directed energy weapons, such as acoustic weapons or high-powered microwaves, are no longer confined to the realms of science fiction, and a new generation of 'non-lethal' weapons is now poised to appear. Article 36 of the 1977 Protocol I additional to the Geneva Conventions of 1949 provides that in the study, development, acquisition, or adoption of a new weapon, states party to the Conventions are under an obligation to determine whether the use of the weapon would be prohibited by international law, including IHL. Moreover, fuel-air explosives, small-calibre ammunition, naval mines, and cluster bombs represent 'unfinished business' as far as IHL is concerned.

The success of the Ottawa Process marks a welcome return to the traditional approach to the development of international humanitarian law whereby treaties are adopted without a consensus rule. Despite the successful adoption of Protocol IV to the 1980 CCW on blinding laser weapons, the consensus rule that has governed negotiations within the United Nations of the 1980 CCW and its formal review process has demonstrated its limitations with respect to the mines issue. With this in mind, for future CCW negotiations (a Second Review Conference is scheduled to take place in 2001), it may well be necessary to review the practice of adopting agreements by consensus.

The Ottawa Process has also shown that civil society has a crucial role to play in strengthening international law. The complementary role played by key governments, the ICBL (which presciently called for a total ban of anti-personnel mines in 1992), and the ICRC augurs well for the future development of IHL. The ICBL, for example, has been able to criticize specific governments directly, which is not possible for the ICRC. On the other hand, the ICRC, with its network of professional military officers working with armed forces on IHL issues, has access to military circles that non-governmental organizations do not.

In one other respect, the failure of the CCW review process to bring about a widely sought prohibition of anti-personnel mines has illustrated the importance of stigmatizing a weapon in the public mind. Just as law, even international law, is a social creation, so the mobilization of public consciousness worldwide was a key element in the success of the Ottawa Process. When confronted with powerful evidence of the limited military utility of anti-personnel mines, especially in comparison with their enormous humanitarian costs, the public was first appalled—and then persuaded that a total ban was necessary.

But the global mobilization necessary to achieve an international legal norm prohibiting anti-personnel mines has also clearly demonstrated that the international community must seek a more preventive approach to the control or prohibition of weapons at odds with IHL norms, and a more dynamic method of developing international humanitarian law. The Ottawa Process has raised public awareness of the limits that must be placed on the conduct of warfare. As a result, future expectations of state behaviour and vigilance may be higher and more demanding. The ICRC is discussing with medical experts possible objective medical criteria to determine whether the health effects of a given weapon are of a nature to cause superfluous injury or unnecessary suffering.[25] But, in the final analysis, the Ottawa Process has substantiated the need for an international social dynamic that permits legal intervention to prevent, rather than respond to, human carnage. Shutting the stable door after the horse has bolted is not an adequate long-term approach to the regulation of weapons. And, regrettably, mines are only one cruel weapon among others.

NOTES

1. A more detailed review of the ICRC's role in the development of international humanitarian law governing landmines will be published later this year. Many of the documents referred to in this article are available on the ICRC's Web site, which is to be found at [http://www.icrc.org].

   This article represents the views of the author alone and does not necessarily reflect the views of the ICRC.

2. H. Dunant, *A Memory of Solferino*, English version, American Red Cross, 1939, 1959 (Geneva: ICRC, 1986).

3. See *Bulletin international des Sociétés de la Croix-Rouge* (ICRC, Geneva), Apr. 1918.

4. *Draft Rules for the Limitation of the Dangers Incurred by the Civilian Population In Time of War*, 2nd edn (Geneva: ICRC, 1958), Article 15.

5. *Weapons That May Cause Unnecessary Suffering or Have Indiscriminate Effects: Report on the Work of Experts* (Geneva: ICRC, 1973), 25, para. 58.

6. Teheran, Nov. 1973, Resolution XIV.

7. Conference of Government Experts on the Use of Certain Conventional Weapons, *Report* (Geneva: ICRC, 1975), 69–71, paras 247–59.

8. UN General Assembly Resolution 32/152, 19 Dec. 1977.

9. The formal title of the Convention is the United Nations Convention on Prohibitions or Restrictions on the Use of Certain Conventional Weapons Which May Be Deemed to Be Excessively Injurious or to Have Indiscriminate Effects.

10. *Report of the Montreux Symposium on Anti-Personnel Mines* (Geneva: ICRC, 1993).

11. *Report of the International Committee of the Red Cross for the Review Conference of the 1980 United Nations Convention on Prohibitions or Restrictions on the Use of Certain Conventional Weapons Which May Be Deemed to Be Excessively Injurious or to Have Indiscriminate Effects* (Geneva: ICRC, Feb. 1994).

12. The results of the symposium can be found ibid., Annex II.

13. Ibid., 57.

14. *Anti-Personnel Landmines: Friend or Foe?* (Geneva: ICRC, 1996).

15. Final Declaration of Participants at the Regional Seminar for States of the Southern Africa Development Community, Anti-Personnel Mines: What Future for Southern Africa?, 20–3 July 1997.

16. Ibid.

17. The ICRC as well as the ICBL had also strongly encouraged unilateral prohibitions and restrictions on mines at the national level. In May 1996, by the end of the CCW Review Conference, more than 40 states supported a total international ban on anti-personnel mines and 25 states had unilaterally suspended or renounced the use of anti-personnel mines.

18. See Article 9.

19. Comments of the International Committee of the Red Cross on the Third Austrian Draft (13/5/97) of the Convention on the Prohibition of Anti-personnel Mines, Informal Working Paper for the Oslo Negotiations, Sept. 1997.

20. Article 6, para. 3.

21. At the request of a number of donor governments, the ICRC prepared proposals for the international community on how to improve the quality of and access to assistance for mine victims. These proposals are contained in Dr

Robin Coupland, ed., *Assistance for Victims of Anti-Personnel Mines: Needs, Constraints and Strategy* (Geneva: ICRC, Oct. 1997).

22. *Report of the International Committee of the Red Cross for the Review Conference of the 1980 United Nations Convention* (Geneva: ICRC, Feb. 1994), 11.

23. Article 19 of the Ottawa Convention represents the first time that a 'no-reservations' clause has been included in a humanitarian law treaty.

24. A similar extension period is contained in section C (paras 24–8) of the Verification Annex of the 1993 Chemical Weapons Convention.

25. See R.M. Coupland, ed., *The SIrUS Project: Towards a Determination of Which Weapons Cause 'Superfluous Injury or Unnecessary Suffering'* (Geneva: ICRC, 1997).

CHAPTER 7

THE ROLE OF THE LANDMINE SURVIVORS NETWORK

Jerry White and Ken Rutherford

When the Ottawa Convention was signed in December 1997, it included a clause to provide humanitarian relief for the hundreds of thousands of men, women, and children who have been maimed by landmines. It was an unprecedented achievement that came about through the efforts of many people. But, most importantly, landmine survivors themselves played a central role in ensuring that the people most wounded by these inhumane devices would not be forgotten in the first treaty to ban their use. Landmine victim statistics are well known to many people, but after a while the numbers become mind-numbing. It is easy to forget that there is a face and a name behind each landmine casualty. Also less well understood is the personal horror that each victim experiences in the moments after an explosion. Landmines tear off limbs and shoot shrapnel and dirt into the body. Even one's own bones become projectiles. If the eyes are not blinded during an explosion, a victim can see his own body torn, mangled, and bleeding. Without nearby help, the unfortunate victim usually dies alone.

The voices of landmine survivors were first heard at the international level at the Vienna CCW conference in September 1995. In an unusual development, representatives of NGOs working directly with landmines and landmine victims were invited to speak to the delegate assembly. It was not just another diplomatic discussion with government officials stating the same stale points of view. Instead, people who were experiencing the tragedy firsthand were helping to set the tone of the discussions. During their speeches, persons injured by landmines from Afghanistan, Cambodia, and the United States provided powerful evidence for urging the ban on these weapons.

THE VOICES

Ken Rutherford (United States): 'In December of 1993, I was working in Somalia with the International Rescue Committee. I was inspecting a program site near the border with Ethiopia when my car hit a landmine. After the explosion, I saw my foot lying on the floorboard of the car. I thought, "Is it mine?" I kept trying to put it back on. I dragged myself out of the car and called for help on my radio. I am here today because of the resources I had at my disposal. I had a radio, airplanes evacuated me to a hospital, and

I returned to the United States to receive, to date, over $300,000 in medical care. Needless to say, most mine victims are not so lucky.'

Jerry White (United States): 'I was only four years old when Syrian soldiers, retreating during the 1967 Arab-Israeli War, laid Soviet-supplied mines in the Golan Heights. My mine waited silently in the ground for 17 years before it exploded under my right foot while I was hiking in an unmarked minefield. I wasn't a soldier. I was a student taking a break from studies to explore the Middle East. There were no fences and no signs to keep me out. I was lucky I had friends with me and a farmer nearby who heard the blast. All the talk about fencing and marking minefields is a distraction from the real problem: how to stop the proliferation of landmines. Even in a small, security-conscious state like Israel, fences break down, signs fade, fall, or are stolen, and mines shift.'

Abdul Rahman Sahak (Afghanistan): 'Can you think for a moment what a human being would suffer in this situation? Imagine the extent of the injuries and pain while struggling between life and death with blood all around. I am proud to be a spokesman for my country. I would like to join the voices of my disabled brothers and sisters . . . to call for a total ban on production of all types of mines.'

As the UN landmine conference unfolded, however, the disabled participants felt they were being relegated to the conference sidelines. While most conference attendees were respectful, there was a sense that no one quite knew what to do about the needs of the survivors. As landmine survivors themselves, the authors saw a need to increase the volume and to become more a part of the process. The authors discussed the need for more representation for landmine survivors both within the ICBL and at conferences. If this debate was about landmines, then who was more suited than survivors to provide evidence of the indiscriminate nature of the weapon?

GENEVA: THE UN CCW CONFERENCE

In April 1996, at the follow-up conference in Geneva, the issue causing the most disappointment was that the needs of the victims, mostly civilians injured through no fault of their own, were not being discussed. Our landmine-disabled friends had travelled a great distance to Geneva, only to discover apathy concerning their needs. Did no one really care, or had the needs of survivors not been properly communicated? One of the slogans of the international campaign had been 'to speak for those who cannot speak for themselves'. Perhaps the time had come for landmine survivors to start speaking on their own behalf.

At that time, in Switzerland, the authors decided to create a new international organization, the Landmine Survivors Network (LSN), to become a powerful advocate for those disabled by mines and to offer practical assistance to one of the most vulnerable populations in the world. It was a radical concept in some ways: a new NGO staffed by landmine survivors to empower and offer peer support to other survivors. The authors recognized that in the fellowship of suffering that survivors share, there is also empowerment and strong motivation to do whatever it takes to end the suffering. A strong bond began to form among mine victims, along with a strong desire to work together towards a global ban and to find help for the wounded.

Together, the survivors decided to increase the pressure on governments and international organizations. First, Ken Rutherford and Tun Channareth, a Cambodian landmine survivor, introduced the 'Wall of Remembrance', a photographic collection of mine victims in Battambang Province, Cambodia. The victims were injured between the closing of the Vienna CCW conference in October 1995 and the opening of the Geneva CCW conference in April 1996. During this brief period there were more than 230 mine accidents in a province of fewer than 250,000 Cambodians. Behind the Wall of Remembrance display, the ICBL had set up an electronic counter that clicked every 22 minutes to signal another mine victim injured somewhere in the world. Like the Wall of Remembrance display, the scoreboard only counted victims since the end of the UN CCW landmine conference in Vienna. By the end of the Geneva conference the haunting clicker had registered nearly 15,000 new victims.

Tun Channareth, known as Reth by his friends worldwide, has been an inspiring leader in the global movement to rid the world of anti-personnel mines. Reth lost both his legs to a landmine in 1982 near the Thai-Cambodian border. His friend had to carry him nearly 30 kilometres to a medical post for emergency care. Reth has travelled the world and met with scores of world leaders and various groups to discuss the impact of mines on countries such as Cambodia and call for much-needed assistance for mine-contaminated communities. At the conference Reth told the delegates that 'if it were their children being blown up' they would have already banned landmines. He then asked, 'How can so many clever people sit together for two weeks and fail to do what ordinary people back home are asking them to do?'

The second way that landmine survivors amplified their voices at the Geneva CCW was at a press conference organized by Jerry White and a team of budding LSN 'associates' working under the umbrella of the ICBL. In the main lobby of the United Nations conference centre, survivors read a statement, 'We Are Outraged'. Survivors from Cambodia, Afghanistan, Mozambique, England, Bosnia, and the United States voiced their anger and frustration with the world's diplomats and politicians. One by one, the survivors removed their prosthetic limbs, describing their personal encounters with mines and calling on the world's diplomats to ban these weapons. In their statement, the mine-injured asked, 'Why do you covet weapons that primarily kill civilians and do not discriminate between soldiers, women, and children? Most of the delegates here have never seen a minefield or experienced firsthand the horror caused by landmines. One short visit to a mine-infected country would do wonders to cure the indifference of the world's politicians and diplomats.' The press conference included testimonies from the authors, Tun Channareth, and other persons with disabilities who had travelled on crutches and in wheelchairs to speak out.

MORE VOICES

A young Cambodian boy, Kherm Man So, recounted: 'I was blown up in Cambodia . . . in January. I was going to school with two friends when they picked up a landmine and were killed. We didn't know it was a mine. I am 14 years old and now have only one leg. Why did they just make it easier to make new mines?'

A brave Bosnian survivor, Pero Jakic, recalled: 'I was injured by a mine while visiting my burnt-out house in Sarajevo. Mines will prevent families from returning to their villages. My closest neighbour and her 17-year-old son were killed by a landmine when they went back to visit their former home. I came here to describe what people are suffering in Sarajevo and other parts of the world. I would like the whole world to know that producers of mines must stop now so that people don't die and so that there are no more handicapped.'

Mozambique's leading disability rights advocate, Farida Gulamo, said: 'For years, I have witnessed the human suffering and economic devastation caused by landmines in my country. Mozambique's richness is in its agriculture, but landmines have devastated the rural areas where farmers can no longer safely grow crops. It saddens me to watch these diplomats discuss ways to improve mines. Don't they see the humanitarian crisis?'

Usman Fitrat, 25 years old and from Afghanistan, shared his own poignant story: 'I was 11 years old when my mother and cousin were mercilessly killed by landmines on the way home from a local health clinic. Ten days later, I lost both my hands and my left eye in a mine explosion. My own grandmother saw it and thought I was dead. Let me ask one question: What was my fault and that of several hundred thousands of innocent

people who have been killed or maimed by mines in Afghanistan? I con-
demn the use of mines and can't believe that this conference has agreed to
their continued use.'

British mine-clearance expert Chris Moon also spoke forcefully: 'I
accept the loss of my right lower leg and hand with good grace because I
chose to run humanitarian mine-clearance teams. For this reason, I do not
consider myself a victim but want to point out that people in mined areas
have no choice. Blown up by a mine in Mozambique in March 1995, I have
sympathy for mine victims. In fact, I ran in the London Marathon a year
after my accident to assist those less fortunate because I believe actions
speak louder than words.' True to his word, Chris continues to raise money
for landmine survivors through actions. In 1997, he also ran marathons in
Cambodia, Mozambique, and Australia and ran 150 miles in the Sahara
Desert to raise over $150,000 to make artificial limbs for amputees in
Vietnam. Chris also raised awareness of the Landmine Survivors Network
when he carried the Olympic torch during the opening ceremony of the
1998 Winter Olympics at Nagano, Japan.

In Geneva, landmine survivors met in small groups and targeted their
messages one-by-one to intransigent government delegations. In sum, survivors said they came to Geneva 'to put a human face on the mass suffering caused by landmines. We have travelled a long distance with crutches,
artificial limbs, and wheelchairs to tell our personal stories in the hope that
the world's diplomats would listen to our plea to ban anti-personnel landmines from the earth. But this conference has turned a deaf ear to our cries.
We have no choice but to denounce the CCW's shameful agreement.' The
statement concluded: 'We were warned that this conference would not
address our desire for an immediate and total ban. But we had no idea that
the conference would settle for such a reprehensible agreement. Therefore,
we cannot support it and we must express our outrage.'

DEFINING VICTIM ASSISTANCE

What, exactly, is meant by victim assistance? What kind of structure is
needed to co-ordinate assistance? Which categories of humanitarian relief
should be included? The LSN began to define survivor assistance to include
the 'care and rehabilitation provided for the immediate and long-term
needs of mine victims, their family members and/or dependants, and mine-
affected communities. Victim assistance includes, but is not limited to,
emergency and medical care; access to prosthetics, wheelchairs and other
assistive devices; social and economical reintegration; psychological and
peer support; accident prevention programs; and legal and advisory

services.' The definition of 'victim assistance' was derived from discussions with other NGOs active in the ICBL as well as from informal discussions with government and UN representatives.

Looking into the needs of the victims, especially in developing countries, the LSN was nearly overwhelmed by the desperation of thousands of survivors with no access to affordable care. Aside from the emergency and acute medical care required immediately following a mine blast, the production and training for the use of assistive devices, including prosthetics, wheelchairs, crutches, and specially designed transportation, are of urgent necessity. There is also a need for psychosocial support programs, data collection of mine-affected populations, mine awareness programs, social reintegration, employment opportunities, and legal services. It was obvious that, to offer this range of services, landmine survivors would need to enlist the help of all governments and NGOs pushing for a ban treaty. Today, an enormous gap exists between rehabilitative care available in affluent countries and what most mine victims receive in developing countries recovering from years of war. For example, the American authors of this chapter have received care approaching a combined cost of $800,000.[1] This is in contrast to the United Nations estimate that the average lifetime care of a landmine victim is between $5,000 and $7,000.

Another question was how to define landmine victims. In consultation with other NGOs, the LSN proposed a broad definition: 'human beings impaired due to physical, psychological, social or economic harm or injury caused by the explosion of landmines; family members and/or dependants of the mine-disabled or mine fatalities; all human beings affected by the existence of mines who, due to the threat of mines, could not or cannot pursue their normal activities.'

In late 1995, very few people in the campaign were pushing for victim assistance. Several organizations such as Veterans International, Handicap International, and the International Committee of the Red Cross (ICRC) were, of course, providing prosthetics and other assistance in the field, but NGOs were not lobbying for such assistance to be part of the talking points for solving the landmine problem. The pursuit of a global ban was the central, unrelenting focus of the ICBL. On the surface, at least, it seemed logical that wealthier states would resist the inclusion of landmine victim assistance in the treaty, as many of them do not have landmine-disabled populations. Any mine victim assistance provided by these states would necessarily go to foreign populations. And poorer countries, those most affected by landmines, have limited means and infrastructure to support the growing number of survivors. Victim assistance seemed a no-win situation for garnering political support.

Meanwhile, the United Nations was still talking about legitimizing new types of landmines, and a global ban seemed years, if not decades, away. Some members of the campaign, though reluctant to say so publicly, believed that insisting on victim assistance measures would just muddy the waters and potentially give governments another excuse for not committing to a ban of any sort. Landmine survivors respectfully disagreed. As the debate continued over the next few months, much was made of 'the poor victims'. One of the biggest challenges was to convince other campaigns that survivors were more than just 'poster children' for the ban movement. Strangely, it was as if amputees had to demonstrate that though landmines had blown off limbs and left horrible scars, survivors' minds, dreams, and humanity were still intact.

The Landmine Survivors Network, now an official NGO, decided to take its concerns regarding the need for victim assistance directly to policy-makers. Not willing to wait until other campaigners understood the centrality of victim assistance to the larger issue of banning landmines, the LSN charged ahead by setting up independent meetings with the UN Department of Humanitarian Affairs, the American Red Cross, and the US National Security Council, Department of Defense, State Department, and Agency for International Development (USAID). We hammered away at the same message—of course, a global ban was imperative, but a 'paper' treaty that did not take into account the urgent need to help rehabilitate hundreds of thousands of survivors would be a tragically missed opportunity. To our thinking, victim assistance had to be a part of any meaningful discussion on how to stop the mass suffering caused by mines. Solving the landmine problem would require an integrated approach that took into account the need for accelerated mine clearance and survivor assistance.

In a May 1996 letter, Jerry White, Ken Rutherford, and Marianne Holtz, an American nurse who lost both legs to a landmine in Zaire in 1995, strongly urged US President Clinton to remember that 'most mine victims are civilians, including women and children. Many have trouble supporting their families and many are ostracized and denied proper medical attention or rehabilitation.' The President's response communicated his desire to secure a special exemption for mines in Korea and that he had instructed the Secretary of Defense to look into improving demining technology. No mention was made about victim assistance. In his defence of US policy, the President seemed blind to the humanitarian need for urgent action to protect civilian populations.

In October of 1996, the LSN demonstrated a prototype of the first database designed to track the needs of mine victims worldwide and the limited resources to help them. As word of the LSN's new information strategy started to reach mine victims in all regions, it began to serve as a small clearinghouse of information and resources. By 1998, the database contained profiles of scores of landmine survivors and their families in Mozambique, Angola, Bosnia, Cambodia, Jordan, Lebanon, and Afghanistan. It also contains detailed information on over 1,000 organizations and has been used by media and NGOs alike as a source of information about the world's mine-affected people and communities. But, while a database is useful to keep track of needs, it cannot meet those needs. Only by engaging the international community in a global effort would the LSN succeed in its efforts to respond to the pleas of landmine survivors.

OTTAWA CONFERENCE, 1996

At the October 1996 landmine conference in Ottawa, the LSN called for an integrated approach to mine action, including a ban, accelerated mine clearance, and increased assistance for survivors. At the time, the call for a global ban was receiving the greatest attention. The CCW was still calling for legalizing some mines and for increasing the metallic content of older mines so that they would be easier to detect. The ICBL and its members, including the LSN, were calling for nothing less than an immediate and comprehensive ban without loopholes. Victim assistance and demining were secondary goals of the ICBL, however. The LSN approached the ICBL co-ordinator to determine whether its leadership would object to the LSN's efforts to promote effective victim assistance in Ottawa. There was no response, so the LSN took matters into its own hands and prepared to fight for the rights of survivors. As the victims who had stared out from silent photographs for too long, the Landmine Survivors Network believed it was time to be heard.

The LSN found an ally in Jill Sinclair, an official in Canada's Department of Foreign Affairs and International Trade. Sinclair understood Canadian Foreign Affairs Minister Lloyd Axworthy's sympathy for mine victims, and her office helped arrange for the LSN to make a presentation to the plenary meeting of the Ottawa conference. Speaking on the final day of the conference, Jerry White made a statement that was intended as a wake-up call:

> Despite all the talk about the human suffering of mine victims, it seems that we still have trouble putting our money where our mouth is. What is really being done to help these victims? Very little, I'm afraid. I do not doubt that every person in this audience is horrified and personally moved by the stories of landmine victims—you'd need a heart of stone not to be.

I am also convinced that individuals, NGOs, and governments all want to help. But why is it that victim assistance has not moved beyond the rhetorical level? Survivors tend to be awfully strong and motivated people. They want a chance to be productive again, not to become dependent on charity.

White ended his statement by encouraging the Canadian government to honour its own survivors—the brave peacekeepers now threatened by landmines spread throughout the former Yugoslavia. He reminded the Canadians of Mark Isfeld, 'one of Canada's finest military sons, who was killed removing mines in Croatia in 1994 on his third peacekeeping duty'. Mark's father, Brian Isfeld, was sitting among the governmental and NGO delegates as White went on to describe how 'Mark cared deeply about stopping landmines from killing children. He would take candy and little dolls knit by his mother, Carol, to hand out to the children where he served.' Brian and Carol Isfeld are landmine survivors. They, like hundreds of thousands of families worldwide, know what it means to have your life suddenly and forever changed by losing a loved one to these cruel and unpredictable weapons.

By the end of the Ottawa conference, victim assistance had received rhetorical support as something that should be included in the treaty. The American and Irish delegations seemed keenly interested in pursuing the issue, and Canada appeared ready to take a leadership role. Without their early interest, victim assistance might very well have stayed on the shelf. But now, there was a glimmer of hope that mine victims would get the support they needed to help each other on the road to recovery.

The LSN privately urged the ICBL members to help landmine survivors get proper care instead of just flying them around the world to speak at international landmine conferences. Usman Fitrat, for example, was given a false eye during his trip to the Ottawa, thanks to the *pro bono* assistance provided by Canadian eye specialists, Thomas Dean and Dr A.G. Watson, who enthusiastically heeded the call by the LSN to help mine victims, and the Boston-based Physicians for Human Rights pitched in to make sure Usman made it to all his eye appointments between media interviews and panel discussions.

MOZAMBIQUE NGO LANDMINE CONFERENCE

In February of 1997, the Fourth International NGO Landmine Conference was held in Maputo, Mozambique—an appropriate venue as Africa is the most mined-contaminated continent in the world, with Angola alone having tens of thousands of amputees from landmine explosions. Once again, the LSN was asked to identify and invite survivors to participate in the conference. We came with high hopes, even arranging for Bosnian landmine survivors to join us in Maputo. While eager to embrace the survivors, conference participants appeared unsure of how best to include their disabled guests in the dialogue on the treaty and the role of victim assistance. This was something that required focus through the eyes of survivors themselves. The challenge was to communicate effectively survivors' needs without offending the incredibly committed and hardworking conference planners.

LSN organized a dinner for the disabled gathered in Maputo. It was a wonderful opportunity for survivors from across the world to relax and talk openly. How should survivors play an active role? What were our own goals? It came out during the dinner that there was a frustration with the portrayals of victims in the international campaign. Survivors were shown almost exclusively as 'victims', many photographed only in their worst moments of pain and anguish. By showing the horrible effects, the media had assigned to mine victims an aura of tragedy and helplessness. Yet most of the survivors didn't see their own lives as over after a landmine explosion. Most felt lucky to have survived. It was clear at that special dinner in Maputo that the survivors who gathered to eat and talk were some of the strongest and most motivated people we had ever met. It was in Maputo that survivors started to address more pointedly the campaign language that often depicted the disabled as helpless victims. LSN was determined to add images of strength, empowerment, and survival. Extraordinary strength is required to overcome disfiguring injury and sometimes ostracism. Somehow, that message needed to come out, as well as a realistic portrayal of the human suffering. We would now work toward empowerment.

RAISING THE PROFILE OF SURVIVOR ASSISTANCE IN THE ICBL

Throughout 1996–7, the ICBL issued periodic statements on the status of the campaign, dealing primarily with the platforms it currently supported. Survivors began to push for stronger language on the need for effective victim assistance. At the very least, we argued, the issue deserved its own bullet, instead of being lumped in as an inconspicuous clause together with the issue of demining efforts. During strategy sessions the response was usually supportive, but there still was no initiative by the ICBL as a whole to advocate for the rights of the victims. Instead, most members were overwhelmingly concerned with the ban and with building support for that. Some in the campaign leadership felt that the LSN was being counter-productive to the overriding goal of the campaign, which was, of course, a total ban on landmines.

OAU Conference in Johannesburg

In May of 1997, the Organization of African Unity (OAU) hosted a conference on landmines. As with previous conferences, not enough survivors were invited, and again, we had a small voice. The LSN had pushed consultants and conference organizers to include victims and disability support issues in panel discussions, and urged that disabled persons and rehabilitation specialists be invited to speak, including Farida Gulamo from Mozambique and Abraham Gebreyesus from Eritrea. During the conference, Ken Rutherford arranged a small press conference with Gebreyesus and Mozambican survivor Luis Wamuce, who posed the question to the government participants: 'What are you doing to help the victims?'

African delegates quoted statistics on landmines and the casualties, but there was little indication that they understood or had much contact with the real people behind the numbers. To put a face on the issue, Rutherford, Wamuce, and Gebreyesus told their stories and pushed for social and economic support of mine victims and their families. Wamuce, a secretary for the Association for Disabled People of Mozambique (ADEMO), urged the OAU 'to adopt and implement victim assistance policies so that landmine survivors can be more easily reintegrated back into society.' The LSN succeeded in having mine victim assistance included in the OAU final declaration and action agenda. In addition, the LSN called for co-ordination of data collection and development of a comprehensive database on assistance for survivors. These recommendations were incorporated in the final OAU conference proceedings. One of the wonderful benefits of arranging for Abraham Gebreyesus to attend the OAU conference was that he was introduced to Lieutenant General D.P. Knobel, who assured him that South Africa could arrange a corneal transplant operation that Abraham had been waiting for since he was 11 years old when a landmine accident caused blindness and the loss of his right hand.[2]

Diana, Princess of Wales

Perhaps the greatest contribution to the issue of victim assistance came from Diana, Princess of Wales. In January 1997, Diana had visited Angola as a guest of the British Red Cross and HALO Trust, a British NGO working to clear landmines. Photographic images of her walking through minefields and meeting with landmine-disabled persons were beamed around the world. During her visit, she called on her own country to ban landmines.

At the time, the British position was similar to that of the United States—unwilling to give up these weapons and wishing to develop new types of mines. Diana's remarks in the minefields of Angola put her at odds with Britain's Tory government. Many back home criticized her 'political' statements, while most of the world applauded her courage and honesty. Without a doubt, the Princess of Wales, more than any other individual, caused global awareness of the devastation caused by landmines to skyrocket. Her willingness to use her celebrity as a lightning rod for the issue was an invaluable service to the International Campaign to Ban Landmines. Wherever she went, cameras followed, sending pictures of the Princess in minefields to living rooms throughout the world.

In an effort to encourage the Princess's work on landmines, the LSN and the Mines Advisory Group (MAG), a demining organization, co-hosted a seminar at the Royal Geographical Society in London, entitled 'Responding to Landmines'. Rae McGrath, MAG's founder, had invited the Princess to deliver the keynote address. Kensington Palace agreed, with the understanding that the seminar was geared to address the practical needs of those working or living in minefields, including demining and victim assistance. It was at the Royal Geographical Society on 12 June that the Princess delivered her first major speech on landmines, describing with emotion her reaction to what she saw firsthand in Angola: 'I am not a political figure. I'd like to reiterate now, my intentions are humanitarian. That is why I felt drawn to this human tragedy.'

With the Princess's involvement, the media was hooked. Landmines and the human suffering they caused were now in the headlines. Diana understood her contribution to the cause. She realized better than anyone that the media would closely follow any move she made. Why not take them to mine-infested countries! Thus, by the summer of 1997, it seemed that landmine survivors had found a compassionate spokesperson for their cause and an ally to help alleviate their suffering.

Bad Honnef Conference
Also in June 1997, members of the German Campaign to Ban Landmines arranged a workshop in Bad Honnef, Germany, to develop guidelines for integrated mine action programs from a development point of view. Again, the focus of Medico International, Jesuit Refugee Service, Miseoror, the LSN, and other international organizations was to draft a set of guidelines for people seeking to help mine-affected communities and the growing number of victims. The Bad Honnef guidelines emphasized community and development. Among them were:

- The needs and aspirations of people affected by mines are the starting point for mine action programs.

- Mine action programs support the reconstruction and development of the community and aim at rebuilding the socio-economic and cultural infrastructure.
- Empowerment and training of the community to carry out all aspects of mine action programs are the ultimate goal.
- Mine-affected people have a right to participate in political and economic decision-making, to shape their own lives, and to have their dignity restored.

Brussels Conference

Later that same month, a conference in Brussels, Belgium, reviewed the draft treaty and lined up those countries willing to be counted as ban supporters. Just before the opening of the conference, the LSN and other sympathetic NGOs, such as Medico International, Jesuit Refugee Service, and Handicap International, discovered that there was not one word on victim assistance in the first draft of the treaty. It was a devastating discovery. Time was getting short, and a serious push was needed to lobby the government delegates. There were only a dozen survivors present in Brussels, and all 12 prepared a joint statement emphasizing the need to include language on victim assistance: 'We ask you to re-read the current draft of the treaty and consider how it appears to us landmine survivors. There is virtually nothing in it to urge governments to take responsibility for the victims. Yet people are bleeding and dying even as we speak. To this day, the real needs of mine-affected communities are not being addressed. Survivors remain an afterthought. Their numbers grow each day, but without your help they have little hope of ever receiving proper medical attention or rehabilitation.' The reaction from delegates and the International Committee of the Red Cross was positive. Several governments, particularly South Africa, responded by indicating they would not support a treaty without provisions for the survivors.

Although most campaigners were enthusiastic, one of the ICBL steering committee members expressed dismay that the LSN had 'surprised' him with its statement and suggested that, in the future, the LSN would be better advised to consult first with the treaty committee, which had been working for months on the draft. Others in the campaign were also not supportive of adding victim assistance to the mix. The LSN had to identify its allies in the campaign and determine what chance victim assistance had to be included in the treaty. It did not look promising, since the priority for most organizations was simply to achieve a global ban as soon as possible. At the eleventh hour, victim assistance would complicate the negotiations. Furthermore, wealthier 'donor' countries would be wary of any language that would oblige them to put their money in the 'tin cup' of poorer mine-affected countries.

The LSN decided to turn international law to its advantage by enlisting the services of the Washington-based law firm of Arnold & Porter, who agreed to work *pro bono* to research legal precedents and draw up a memo regarding mine victim assistance proposals that could be included in the treaty. The LSN discussed its initiative with the Canadians, and Axworthy's office offered support by faxing a list of core group contact information so the LSN could approach other countries directly. Again, this independent initiative was not well received by some in the campaign leadership. The LSN was accused of pursuing its own agenda rather than that of the campaign. Nevertheless, we persisted, and throughout the summer, Arnold & Porter's attorneys, led by Anthony O'Donnell, searched for precedents and ways to legitimize the inclusion of victim assistance language in the treaty.

A VISIT TO BOSNIA

Meanwhile, the LSN was busy planning a secret trip to Bosnia with Diana, Princess of Wales. In late July 1997, the LSN's co-founders visited Kensington Palace to brief the Princess on its mission to survey the rehabilitative needs of Bosnia's landmine victims. Diana had repeatedly offered her help to the LSN and immediately picked up on the idea of survivors helping survivors. She wanted to join us in Bosnia. That summer afternoon, drinking tea in Diana's plush living-room, we started to brainstorm her three-day visit to Bosnia. The Princess's overriding interest was to meet privately with the survivors and their families. She did not want to discuss policy, meet government officials, or detonate another mine, as she had done in Angola. She insisted on direct contact with those who had suffered.

In Bosnia, her impact on the survivors was spectacular. She listened attentively to their gut-wrenching stories, holding their hands and stroking their scarred limbs. She resolved to do more for them in the future. It was to be her last public act of charity. When Diana lost her life in a car accident in Paris on 31 August landmine survivors lost a true and irreplaceable friend and ally.

OSLO CONFERENCE

Only days after Princess Diana's death, the Oslo conference commenced to negotiate the final treaty draft to be signed in Ottawa in December. The conference chair, Ambassador Jacob Selebi, from South Africa, was seen as a potential ally. He had, however, set a disciplined agenda within the first three days of the conference. With each passing day, it would be increasingly difficult to add new items or proposed language to the table. In Oslo,

Susan Walker of Handicap International was working to build pressure on governments to get victim assistance into the treaty. She took the lead to ensure that the ICBL platform included some of our proposed draft language on victim assistance. The ICRC was also very supportive. Language worked its way into the draft and was ready for debate, though the LSN was not allowed to sit in on any negotiating sessions. Instead, survivors had to lobby the delegates individually between sessions and after hours. We met with the Germans, the Norwegians, the Americans, the Austrians, the ICRC, the ICBL—in fact, with anyone who had time and was willing to speak with us about victim assistance.

Thankfully, Ambassador Selebi was sympathetic to the inclusion of victim assistance on the agenda. With the encouragement of Canadian Foreign Affairs officials Jill Sinclair and Bob Lawson, the LSN had circulated its memo by Arnold & Porter to the core group of countries working on treaty proposals. Even though the draft treaty did not impose on states direct obligations to assist civilian victims, it did require states to ban and destroy landmines because they were recognized as endangering civilian populations. The LSN hoped the inclusion of mine victim assistance language 'would require states to accept certain affirmative duties toward individuals.'

The LSN argued there were substantial reasons to include humanitarian relief in the ban treaty. First, the primary purpose of the treaty is to protect individuals from the type of excessive and unnecessary injury landmines inflict. The inclusion of language relating to victim assistance furthers the purpose of the treaty by protecting individuals from the long-term injuries that landmines cause. In other words, landmine victim assistance programs were necessary to prevent mine victims' permanent inability to function, work, or otherwise participate as productive members of society. Thus, the inclusion of mine victim assistance was necessary for the Convention to provide a complete response by the international community to the dangers posed by landmines.

Second, the inclusion of victim assistance provisions within the Convention is consistent with international humanitarian law. The Geneva Conventions of 12 August 1949 and the 1977 Protocols Additional to the Geneva Conventions constitute the framework within which humanitarian law pertaining to the protection of civilians, combatants, and prisoners of war has developed. Although these provisions primarily restrict what states can do within the context of war, they also require states to accept certain affirmative obligations towards individuals.

Finally, many international instruments refer to assistance or compensation to victims as a humanitarian duty of states. More significantly, a strong argument can be made that states are legally obligated to assist or compensate mine victims. The use of mines violates two basic principles of international humanitarian law. Landmines scattered over large areas likely to be used by civilians during or after a conflict do not distinguish between military and civilian targets. This violates the principle of discrimination, which holds that weapons must be able to discriminate between civilian and military targets. Landmine injuries also inflict much more severe injuries than other conventional weapons and often result in excessive injury or suffering to civilians. This violates the principle that prohibits attacks that produce 'unnecessary suffering or superfluous injury'. Violations of humanitarian law trigger a duty to compensate or assist victims of those violations. Therefore, the unlawful use of landmines generates a legal obligation to assist mine victims.

In the end, victim assistance made it into the landmine treaty due to the efforts of many people, but full credit must be given to the landmine survivors around the world. In the keynote address at the opening plenary for the Mine Action Forum at the Ottawa conference, the Canadian Minister of Foreign Affairs, Lloyd Axworthy, stated that one of the lessons to be learned from the Ottawa Process was that international public opinion will not tolerate 'weapons that cause massive civilian casualties'. In other words, the large and growing number of landmine victims caused the ban dream to become reality.

The Ottawa Convention is the first international arms control agreement that addresses the humanitarian needs of the victims of a particular weapon system. On victim assistance, it states in the Preamble that signatory states wish 'to do their utmost in providing assistance for the care and rehabilitation, including the social and economic reintegration of mine victims'. Article 6 of the treaty elaborates on this issue:

3: Each State Party in a position to do so shall provide assistance for the care and rehabilitation, and social and economic reintegration, of mine victims and for mine awareness programs. Such assistance may be provided, inter alia, through the United Nations system, international, regional or national organizations or institutions, non-governmental organizations or institutions, the ICRC, national Red Cross and Red Crescent societies and their International Federation, non-governmental organization, or on a bilateral basis.

7: States Parties may request the United Nations, regional organizations, other States Parties or other competent intergovernmental or non-governmental fora to assist its authorities in the elaboration of a national demining program to determine, *inter alia:* . . . assistance to mine victims . . . .

By the time of the signing ceremony in Ottawa, there had been a significant change in the role victim assistance played in the campaign. The catch-phrase 'victim assistance' had become one of the three main pillars of the campaign. In Ottawa, there were several panels on the issue, including 'Addressing Psycho-Social Reintegration for Mine Victims'. Mine-disabled persons were now an official and welcome part of the discussion.

Landmine survivors believe they have won a battle, but the war is not over. It's time to give the treaty legs, so to speak. Though the treaty only 'urges' victim assistance, we believe justice demands that more be done for the survivors and their families. New battles on the horizon include how to raise significant funding to support rehabilitation programs and how best to spend money on community-based programs to help survivors heal and recover from trauma.

There are still mixed signals coming from various signatory governments. For example, more than 100 foreign ministries failed to respond to a letter the LSN distributed asking governments to describe their intentions to promote victim assistance. The letter, signed by more than 20 organizations, urged governments 'to commit significant resources to help rehabilitate the growing numbers of mine victims worldwide'. To this end, the LSN issued a challenge to governments: 'For every three dollars pledged for demining, at least one additional dollar should be directed toward rehabilitation and assistance for landmine victims.'

As of mid-1998, fewer than 10 governments had responded to the LSN query on victim assistance programs. Though Canada immediately pledged $100 million to support mine action, including support for mine victims, there are questions about how the money will be spent and how much will end up helping mine victims. Norway pledged $100 million over five years to support mine clearance and victim assistance, but some fear that victim assistance could be reduced to a simple donation to the Red Cross and will not address the range of survivors' needs for rehabilitation and social and economic integration. The British government also pledged to give money towards victim assistance and mine clearance. When asked, government officials could not say when or where the support would be given. Though the treaty calls for reporting and tracking progress on mine clearance, there was no mention of creating a similar mechanism for tracking rehabilitation services. The LSN will continue to monitor governments and ask for concrete victim assistance. We plan on developing a report card to evaluate each signatory's true commitment to comprehensive survivor assistance.

ICBL GENERAL ASSEMBLY MEETING

The ICBL held a meeting in Frankfurt, Germany, in February 1998 to restructure the Nobel Prize-winning coalition and chart out future strategy and actions. The Landmine Survivors Network and other organizations were added to the steering committee. At the meeting, the LSN pushed for the creation of the first global task force on survivor assistance. Survivors are now heading up this new effort on behalf of the ICBL.

In preparation for the Frankfurt meeting, the LSN drafted a short list of 'victim assistance goals' and solicited feedback from a selection of NGOs interested in working on victim assistance. The key organizations to offer input included Handicap International, Jesuit Refugee Service-Cambodia, Physicians for Human Rights, and the Kenyan Campaign to Ban Landmines. The LSN redrafted its goals and proposed them to the conference. The following goals were adopted by the ICBL:

1. The ICBL will press governments to commit $3 billion over the next 10 years to support victim assistance, including social and economic reintegration.
2. The ICBL will press governments to support a whole range of landmine victim assistance activities: acute care, supply of prosthetics and wheelchairs, physical therapy, psychosocial support, data-gathering, landmine awareness, social reintegration, land tenure, and legal and employment services.
3. The ICBL and national campaigns will promote sharing of landmine victim information and assistance strategies among members and other groups to effect the best possible rehabilitation outcomes for mine victims.
4. The ICBL will promote and involve landmine victims and landmine-infested communities in the planning and implementation of mine assistance programs.

Victim assistance is now an established pillar of the ICBL. The treaty language, coupled with the goals established by the ICBL in Frankfurt, mean we have much work to do to ensure that survivors and their families receive the attention, care, and compassion they deserve.

CONCLUSION

Landmine survivors worldwide commend Canada for its leadership to make our dream for a treaty become reality. We also commend our allies in the ICBL and Red Cross who have helped to move this issue so far and fast. Unlike most organizations, the LSN does not want its constituency to grow in size. To the contrary, we long for the day when there are no more land-mine casualties and no man, woman, or child will experience that terrible pain of losing a limb, eyesight, or life to this inhumane weapon. For the present, we want to see increased resources dedicated to rehabilitate the thousands of innocent and often impoverished mine victims around the world. It won't be easy, as the world's attention focuses elsewhere and the media spotlight turns to new issues.

The challenges for effective victim assistance include: lack of reliable data, and information-gathering exercises that leave most survivors empty-handed; limited information-sharing and collaboration among service providers and local disability groups; and too much attention focused on 'limbs only' (prosthetics) relative to the attention paid to the psychosocial impact of landmine injury and the survivors' needs for social and economic integration.

For the hundreds of thousands of landmine disabled, healing will begin when the weapon that disfigured our bodies and took away the innocence of daily life is banned and proper rehabilitation services become available worldwide. Our scars bear witness to the cruelty and inhumanity of anti-personnel mines. But survivors worldwide believe this weapon can be stopped and that it is within the international community's grasp to help turn victims into survivors who rightfully take their place as valued mem-bers of their communities. No one can make the journey alone. We are joining together to demand action and drawing strength from each other, and from humanitarian organizations, and from the states committed to implementing *all* aspects of the Ottawa Convention. Survivors worldwide will monitor the progress closely.

NOTES

1. Ken Rutherford's rehabilitation has cost nearly $400,000 in less than four years; Jerry White's rehabilitation costs come to roughly $400,000 in the 14 years since his accident.

2. Abraham was examined by a specialist and in August 1997 returned to Johannesburg to undergo surgery. He has regained sight in his right eye and was fitted with a prosthesis on his right arm. The LSN wants to recognize the com-bined efforts that accomplished this act of healing: the South African Surgeon General, Christian Outreach (a British organization), and the fund-raising efforts (swim- and bike-a-thons) of Rae McGrath (founder of the UK-based Mines Advisory Group) to raise money for the operation. When Abraham arrived in Oslo, Norway, for the September 1997 ban treaty negotiations, the LSN nominated him to receive the 1997 Reebok Human Rights Prize, which he was awarded at a ceremony in New York City in March 1998.

CHAPTER 8

THE CRISIS OF ANTI-PERSONNEL MINES
Alex Vines

INTRODUCTION

Anti-personnel landmines have become a widely used tool of war since 1940. According to the United Nations these weapons claim some 2,000 victims a month,[1] and the International Committee of the Red Cross (ICRC) estimates that over the last 50 years these weapons have probably inflicted more death and injury than nuclear and chemical weapons.[2] Although mines were originally designed to counter the use of tanks and other armoured vehicles, in the second half of the twentieth century they have been increasingly used to target humans. Changing patterns of war resulted in an increasing use of anti-personnel landmines, which were easy to use and spread terror where they were used. According to the UN, each year 2–5 million new mines are put in the ground, adding to 'one of the most widespread, lethal and long-lasting forms of pollution' the world has ever known.[3]

This chapter examines the proliferation of anti-personnel (AP) mines since 1940. It describes the boom in manufacture and the way these mines were transferred. It also looks at southern Africa, the most mine-contaminated region in the world, to assess the humanitarian, economic, and environmental impact of this proliferation. Finally, the upsurge of use of landmines in Senegal in 1998 is described to demonstrate that although the Ottawa Convention was signed in December 1997, proliferation will continue in conflict hot spots unless the treaty enters in force, landmine eradication quickens, and stockpiles are destroyed.

THE FIRST ANTI-PERSONNEL MINES

Early precursors to the modern landmine were developed during World War I, when German soldiers used buried artillery shells with exposed fuses to block the advance of French and British tanks. The invention in the 1920s of easy-to-handle, powerful, and lightweight explosive trinitrotoluene (TNT) led to the development of the first reliable anti-tank pressure mines. During World War II, these flat steel cylinders, measuring about 30 centimetres in diameter and containing about 10 kilograms of TNT, were used extensively by all parties. According to the US Defense Intelligence Agency (DIA), more than 300 million anti-tank landmines were used during World War II, including 220 million deployed by the

Soviet Union, 80 million by Germany, and 17 million by the United States.[4]

However, these anti-tank mines had one major weakness: they could easily be removed by enemy troops, who would replant them in their own minefields. To keep mine-clearing soldiers at bay, both German and Allied troops began seeding their anti-tank minefields with small metallic or glass containers holding a pound or less of explosive. These early anti-personnel mines were activated by the direct pressure of 15 to 40 pounds, or by a few pounds of pull on a tripwire. Soldiers also booby-trapped anti-tank mines to prevent removal. In the early stages of the war, most of these devices were improvised with hand grenades or simple electric fuses. Later, more complex machine-made fuses were rigged to explosive charges that would easily detonate when pressure was applied or when an electrical circuit was closed.

It was not long before improvised explosive devices and anti-personnel mines were being used as weapons in their own right, rather than merely to protect anti-tank mines. Both weapons were used to demoralize troops or terrorize civilians. Japanese soldiers, for instance, often booby-trapped harmless, everyday objects such as pipes, flashlights, radios, and fruit cans. The practice of booby-trapping the bodies of dead or wounded soldiers, although officially denied, was also common.

North Africa was one of the main laboratories of landmine warfare and design in World War II. The roots of present-day landmine use doctrine and counter-mine warfare were developed in North Africa. Mines initially were used in North Africa to protect strong points in fighting between British and Italian forces on the Egyptian-Libyan border. The British broke an Italian thrust into Egypt in 1940 by using mines extensively, causing the Italians significant numbers of casualties and making them mine-shy and overcautious.

The Italians used air-delivered scatterable mines dropped over British positions. During the four-week Battle of Gazala in early 1942 the British laid over 500,000 mines to defend the Libyan fortress of Tobruk and the nearby Gazala line. The German offensive across the Sahara came to a halt at El Alamein in June 1942, a battle in which both sides again used mines in massive quantities.[5] Field Marshal Erwin Rommel, commander of German forces in Africa, relied heavily on mines to compensate for shortages of weapons and men. He used lifted British, French, German, and Italian mines by tens of thousands to create a 'minegarden' to defend against the British. At El Alamein, each side incorporated the other's minefields in its own defences, making it the largest minefield the world has ever seen. Millions of these mines still need clearing in Egypt.[6]

Advances in mine technology, as in all areas of weaponry, accelerated in the decades following World War II, particularly in response to changing battlefield requirements and the development of new military technologies. In the early 1960s, the United States first introduced the use of a new and sophisticated class of contact anti-personnel mines, known as 'scatterables', to stop the flow of men and material from North to South Vietnam through Laos and Cambodia. American pilots dropped so many of these mines they referred to them as 'garbage'. They were scattered from the air and landed on the ground without detonating. When stepped on, the device, which weighed only 20 grams, could tear off a foot.[7]

For all these tactical advantages, scatterable mines had drawbacks. Because of the hit-and-run nature of the Vietnam War, American ground forces often found themselves retreating through areas that their own pilots had previously saturated with mines—sometimes only a few days or hours before. These areas were not 'minefields' in any traditional military sense; they were simply zones randomly scattered with surface mines. The boundaries of these areas were therefore not precisely knowable. Vietnamese forces, which used several dozen types of improvised or simply manufactured mines, proved that advanced technology was not needed to deploy landmines with deadly effectiveness. In 1965, one year for which detailed statistics are available, 65–70 per cent of US Marine Corps casualties were caused by mines and booby traps.[8]

With the proliferation of low-intensity conflicts since the 1970s the landmine, like the automatic rifle, became a weapon of choice for many government and guerrilla armies around the world. They are not only durable and effective, but also readily available from governments as well as from the vast global network of private arms suppliers. Mines are also easy and relatively cheap to manufacture locally. As scientists invent new high-technology devices, older but equally lethal models have been unloaded on the surplus arms market or supplied directly to armies or guerrilla groups, usually in developing countries.

PROLIFERATION OF ANTI-PERSONNEL MINES

Over 100 companies and government agencies in 52 countries have manufactured more than 344 types of anti-personnel landmines. Human Rights Watch estimated in 1993 that manufacturers had probably produced an average of 5–10 million AP mines per year over the past 25 years, about 10 times the volume identified in past published reports.[9]

The number of mines planted around the world is difficult to estimate, but the US State Department estimates that between 85 million and 90 million landmines are currently implanted in the soil of at least 62 nations. The senior mine warfare analyst at the US Defense Intelligence Agency's Foreign Science and Technology Center estimates that some 400 million mines had been emplaced since World War II.[10] This would imply the existence of well over 100 million deployed and stockpiled anti-personnel landmines over the last 25 years, meaning that for several decades annual global production could have been as high as 10 million units.[11] The main anti-personnel landmine producers over the last 25 years were:

- United States (37 models)
- Italy (36)
- the former Soviet Union (31)
- Sweden (21)
- Vietnam (18)
- Germany [former East and West combined] (18)
- Austria (16)
- former Yugoslavia (15)
- France (14)
- China (12)
- United Kingdom (9)

The largest producers were China, Italy, and the former Soviet Union, measured by the numbers of their mines found around the world. The US has also been a major producer. Beyond these top producers, opinion is divided on who were major players. Important exporters were:

- in Western Europe: Belgium, and possibly also Austria, France, Greece, and Sweden;
- in Eastern Europe: former Czechoslovakia, former East Germany, and former Yugoslavia;
- in the developing world: Egypt, India, Israel, Pakistan, Singapore, South Africa, and possibly also Chile, Iran, Iraq, South Korea, and North Korea.[12]

Who Bought These Mines?
Only a very small number of states around the world, such as San Marino, Andorra, and Saint Lucia, appear never to have maintained AP stockpiles. All others have at some point purchased landmines. Reconstructing the export of AP mines is difficult, but it is possible in some cases. Data obtained under the US Freedom of Information Act reveal that the US has exported more than 4.3 million conventional AP mines since 1969.[13] US exports of conventional AP mines peaked in 1975, at more than 1.4 million. That year's shipments of mines to Cambodia, Chile, and Iran

represent one-third of all reported 'foreign military sales' (FMS) exports of conventional landmines in the 24-year period from 1969 to 1993. Other sales over the period were to Iran under the Shah (2.5 million); Cambodia (622,000); Thailand (437,000); Chile (300,000); El Salvador (102,000); Malaysia (88,000); and Saudi Arabia (88,000). Other confirmed purchasers of US AP mines were Australia, Belize, Brunei, Canada, Denmark, Ecuador, El Salvador, Ethiopia, Greece, Indonesia, Jordan, Lebanon, Morocco, the Netherlands, New Zealand, Oman, Peru, the Philippines, Singapore, Somalia, South Korea, Switzerland, Taiwan, Turkey, and the United Kingdom.[14] In the 1980s the US only exported under FMS 70,000 conventional AP mines. El Salvador was the largest recipient, accounting for about half the mines, followed by Lebanon and Thailand.[15]

The US figures do not include licensed production of US-designed mines in other nations; illegal or unauthorized copies of US mines produced in other nations; and covert shipments during the Cold War of US landmines to rebel clients in Afghanistan, Cambodia, Nicaragua, or elsewhere. Mines deployed by US troops in conflict (as in Vietnam or the Persian Gulf) are not included either.

Italy has also played an important role in exporting landmines. Italy's three landmine producing companies—Valsella, BPD, and Technovar—were probably the world's most aggressive exporters in the 1980s and early 1990s. Two of them, BPD and Valsella, are 50 per cent owned by Italy's largest private manufacturing firm, Fiat.[16] Unlike other producers, these three Italian firms specialized in landmine-related products. All three have been involved in both direct exports and licensed overseas production. According to the US Defense Intelligence Agency their licensing and co-production agreements involved partners in at least five countries—Egypt, Greece, Portugal, Singapore, and Spain—making it difficult to determine where particular Italian-designed mines actually originated. There also exist reports of past sales through 'front companies' in Nigeria and Spain, production of Italian-designed landmines in Iraq, Cyprus, and South Africa, and smuggling via Jordan and Paraguay.[17]

Italian government documents on Valsella exports in the period 1980–6, provided to Human Rights Watch by the Geneva-based P. Network press agency, disclosed shipments of 100,000 AP mines to Indonesia, 90,000 to Paraguay (for covert shipment to South Africa), and smaller or unspecified quantities to Dubai, Finland, Gabon, Greece, Jordan, Kuwait, Morocco, Nigeria, Pakistan, Singapore, and Thailand. These customers paid between $6.15 and $17.17 per unit for scatterable AP mines. Chartered Industries of Singapore purchased parts and components for local assembly of 7 million mines, including the Valmara 69 and scatterable VS–50 AP mines for prices as low as $3 to $4.50 per mine. Fiat's other mine-making subsidiary, BPD Difesa e Spazio, has been especially active in foreign licensing and co-production. Its most successful product, the plastic-cased, helicopter-scatterable SB–33, has been sold directly to the Netherlands and Spain as well as to Argentina and Iraq. BPD products also reached the global market via factories in Greece, Spain, and Portugal.[18]

It has been less easy to reconstruct the shipments made by the two other main global producers of anti-personnel landmines, the former Soviet Union and China. Prior to the breakup of the Soviet Union, Soviet landmines were sold and shipped as military aid around the globe. Products ranged from wooden box mines to mine-scattering systems. Russian AP mines have been identified as having been used in most conflicts, such as Afghanistan, Angola, Cambodia, Iran, Iraq, Mozambique, North Korea, Syria, Vietnam, Zimbabwe, throughout the Warsaw Pact countries, and in many other places around the world. Soviet-origin mines were also locally manufactured in many Eastern European nations, as well as in Vietnam and China.[19]

China has also maintained a strong production capacity. Most of its conventional anti-personnel mines have been based on Soviet designs and have been among the cheapest on the market. Chinese AP mines have been found in a range of countries, including Angola, Cambodia, Iraq, Laos, Mozambique, Nicaragua, and Somalia. Chinese exports have been difficult to track, although a landmine clearance expert identified a shipment of Chinese landmines and cluster weapons in the East African port of Djibouti destined for Sudan.[20] Other developing countries have also contributed to the proliferation of AP mines. In addition to China, at least seven developing nations in Asia, eight in Latin America, four in the Middle East, and four in sub-Saharan Africa produced AP mines in recent years. This count excludes the many nations where there is evidence of locally improvised landmine-type devices. Some of these countries in the South became notable exporters of conventional landmines. Notable exporters would include Egypt and Israel in the Middle East, Pakistan and Singapore in Asia, Brazil and Chile in Latin America, and South Africa.

The overall result of this proliferation has been a world where few countries have not been touched by the impact of landmines, from being directly affected to having aid workers or peacekeepers killed or maimed. Every significant armed conflict since 1945 saw an increasing use of AP mines. During the UN operation in Korea in 1951–3, the US, Canadian, British, Australian, New Zealand, Turkish, Chinese, and North and South Korean forces all used AP mines. In Indochina and Vietnam between 1958 and 1968, initially French forces but later the Americans and North and

Table 1: Countries That Have Produced Anti-Personnel Landmines

Country	No. of Models	Country	No. of Models
Argentina	3	Korea, North	4
Austria	16	Korea, South	3
Belgium	8	Mexico	1
Brazil	2	Netherlands	3
Bulgaria	3	Nicaragua	1
Canada	1	Pakistan	4
Chile	5	Peru	1
China	12	Poland	1
Cuba	1	Portugal	8
Cyprus	1	Romania	3
Czechoslovakia (former)	6	Singapore	3
Denmark	4	South Africa	5
Egypt	5	Spain	8
El Salvador	1	Sweden	21
France	14	Switzerland	5
Germany (combined)	18	Taiwan	4
Greece	2	Uganda	3
Guinea-Bissau	1	United Kingdom	9
Hungary	7	United States	37
India	2	USSR (former, including	31
Iran	1	Russia, Belarus, Ukraine)	
Iraq	2	Venezuela	1
Israel	3	Vietnam	18
Italy	36	Yugoslavia (former)	15
Japan	2	Zimbabwe	3
Total			350

Source: Human Rights Watch database, compiled from press reports, industry directories, manufacturers' literature, declassified military documents, and Human Rights Watch field research.

South Vietnamese used AP mines in an indiscriminate manner. India-Pakistan, 1947–8, 1965, 1971; India-China, 1962; Arab-Israeli wars, 1967, 1973; the internal conflicts in the Philippines, 1945–present; Cambodia, 1978–present; Croatia, 1991–5; Ecuador-Peru, 1995—these and many other areas of conflict have seen AP mines used indiscriminately with little or no concern for international law.[21] On the historical evidence, the ICRC in its 1996 study of 26 conflicts since 1940, concluded:

> It would therefore be unwise to base the continued use of landmines on the premise that mines can be used in a lawful and responsible fashion. The historical evidence would indicate that they rarely are, whether by 'developed' armies, 'third-world' armies or insurgents, and that their effects cannot be limited as doctrine presumes. . . . the real effects of AP mine use [are] a horrific world-wide legacy of mine infestation.[22]

The list of countries that have had AP mine incidents on their soil is even longer, too long to list. In cases such as Africa, a continent of more than 50 countries, it is easier to list those that have not—Cape Verde, Gambia, Cote D'Ivoire, Burkina Faso, Ghana, Togo, Benin, Cameroon, Equatorial Guinea, Gabon, Sao Tome, Lesotho, Seychelles, Madagascar, Mauritius, and the Comoros.

SOUTHERN AFRICA: THE WORLD'S MOST CONTAMINATED REGION

The humanitarian and socio-economic impact of landmines is best illustrated in southern Africa. Southern Africa is the most mine-affected region in the world. For over 30 years landmines have been killing and maiming civilians throughout the region. The first known mine casualty occurred in Angola in 1961. By 1998, 11 of the 14 countries in the Southern Africa Development Community (SADC) had recorded landmine incidents.[23]

A conservative estimate is that southern Africa today has some 20 million mines in its soil. Mines have claimed over 250,000 victims since 1961. The use of anti-personnel landmines has been widespread in the colonial and post-colonial wars that have plagued much of southern Africa for the last three decades. During this period many millions of landmines were imported into southern Africa, while a smaller number were manufactured there. Sixty-eight types of AP mines from 22 countries have been found in southern Africa. These countries are: Austria, Belgium, China, Cuba, former Czechoslovakia, Egypt, France, former East Germany, former West Germany, Hungry, Israel, Italy, Portugal, Romania, former Soviet Union, South Africa, Spain, Sweden, United Kingdom, United States, former Yugoslavia, and Zimbabwe.[24]

In southern Africa, in every war since 1961, every group has used landmines in contravention of international humanitarian law. The Portuguese colonial forces, minority-rule South African units, Rhodesian forces, the Popular Movement for the Liberation of Angola (MPLA), the National Front for the Liberation of Angola (FNLA), and the National Union for Total Independence of Angola (UNITA) in Angola, the People's Liberation Army of Namibia (PLAN), Umkhonto we Sizwe (MK) in South Africa, the Revolutionary Committee (Coremo) and the Mozambique Liberation Front (Frelimo) in Mozambique, and the Zimbabwe African National Liberation Army (ZANLA) and Zimbabwe People's Revolutionary Army (ZIPRA) in the Rhodesian war have all been guilty of contravening inter-national law. The same is true in the post-colonial wars in Angola and Mozambique, where the two governments, supporting forces (such as Cubans, Tanzanians, and Zimbabweans), and rebel groups (such as UNITA, Renamo, and Angola's Front for the Liberation of the Cabindan Enclave (FLEC) have used landmines in a manner in which civilians were the great-est victims. In Zaire, now the Democratic Republic of Congo, landmines were laid in 1997 by forces loyal to then President Mobutu and by those supporting current President Laurent Kabila.[25]

Only some 500,000 mines have been removed since serious clearance operations began in 1991. Despite international clearance efforts in Angola, landmines continue to be planted by UNITA forces. In recent years landmines have also been used in criminal acts in Angola, Mozambique, and Namibia. Criminal groups linked to drugs and gun-running have also laid mines in central Mozambique to stop the restoration of state control in remote areas. Some of these mines were found on access roads to the Cahora Bassa hydroelectric power line rehabilitation project, thereby threatening the viability of this multinational, multimillion-dollar com-mercial project. In addition, landmines have been available in Angola, Mozambique, Namibia, and Zambia in exchange for food or second-hand clothing. Mines were offered in the South African press for as little as US $25 for home protection.[26]

Not all landmines have reached southern Africa through open, legal channels. In former Rhodesia and apartheid South Africa, landmines were purchased in contravention of UN sanctions. For example, parliamentary investigations in Paraguay into arms transactions during the reign of former dictator Alfredo Stroessner uncovered information about Italian and Greek landmine sales to South Africa. In one previously unreported 1980s transaction, 90,000 mines, loaded onto a Danish ship in the Italian port of Ortobello ostensibly for delivery to the Paraguayan defence ministry, were actually diverted to South Africa. In another transaction, a Paraguayan general allegedly provided a false end-use certificate for a secret sale of 45,000 'Booster M 125 C1' mines sold to South Africa by the Greek

Powder and Cartridge Company. It is not known if these were anti-personnel or anti-tank mines since neither the Greek company's name nor the designation of the mines appears in any publicly available guides to landmines and their producers.[27]

South Africa also used stocks of landmines captured in its invasions of Angola in the 1980s to supply insurgent forces in Angola, Mozambique, and Zimbabwe, as well as the illegal Rhodesian regime. The US government supplied landmines to UNITA rebels in Angola until 1991. More recently, from 1993 to 1997, UNITA rebels in Angola purchased weapons, including landmines, in contravention of UN sanctions.[28]

The provenance of landmines transferred to southern Africa can be complex. For example, in the 1970s French landmines removed from the ground in Algeria were later sold to Mozambique. Today, mines removed from the ground in Angola by both the government and UNITA are sometimes preserved for reuse or sale.[29] As well at least two countries in southern Africa, South Africa and Zimbabwe, have produced and exported anti-personnel landmines. In 1997, both nations pledged no further production or export.[30]

Limited Military Utility

A close look at southern Africa's landmine legacy over the last 30 years reveals few, if any, examples where anti-personnel mines have provided significant or lasting military advantages. Government minefields in Mozambique were quickly breached by Renamo rebels during the 1977–92 war. In Angola, government mine belts around the main towns did not stop UNITA from capturing several of them. In the 1960s and 1970s, saboteurs simply shovelled their way across the minefield protecting the Kariba power station in Rhodesia, did their damage, and left.[31] In 1988, South Africa scrapped plans to build a 30-kilometre-long minefield along Namibia's northern border in part because it determined that such a barrier would only delay any potential invasion by some 30 minutes.[32]

The use of anti-personnel mines has provided short-term military advantages in some cases, but often at tremendous cost to civilians and often in contravention of humanitarian law. This was the case in Mozambique in 1972–3 for the Mozambique Liberation Front (Frelimo) in its Tete offensive against the *aldeamentos* (protected villages) during its nationalist struggle against Portuguese colonialism.[33] UNITA, in both the 1977–92 and 1992–4 wars, used landmines to deny food production and access to water sources in certain areas of Angola, resulting in horrendous civilian suffering.[34]

Soldiers and guerrillas alike fear and dislike landmines. In Mozambique, Renamo had to offer special privileges to its forces to clear and use them. An Angolan sapper (mine specialist) from the Angolan Armed Forces (FAA) admitted in October 1996 that 'I hate mines. They destroy the lives of Angolans on a daily basis and make our country poorer. They are the worst sort of environmental pollution you can find.'[35]

Human, Social, and Environmental Costs

Landmines are blind weapons that cannot distinguish between the footfall of a soldier and that of an old woman gathering firewood. They are inherently indiscriminate weapons. Landmines recognize no cease-fire and, long after the fighting has stopped, they can maim or kill the children and grandchildren of the soldiers who laid them. An old man who planted a landmine in northern Angola in 1965 recently returned to help find it. The mine was still operational, still waiting after 30 years to claim a victim.[36]

The ongoing threat created by live landmines can prevent civilians from living in their homes and using their fields, and can seriously threaten the ability of an entire country to rebuild long after the war has ended. Simple fear of landmines, whether they are present or not, denies land and homes to people.

With independence in 1980, Zimbabwe inherited the lengthy border minefields from the Rhodesian government, which the Rhodesians boasted constituted the second largest man-made barrier in the world, after the Great Wall of China. Initially the minefields were demarcated on both sides by security fencing with prominent signs. By 1977 the Rhodesians stopped demarcating the minefields on the hostile side and stopped maintaining them. As a result, minelaying became uncontrolled and unrecorded and booby-trapping flourished. The minefields remain lethal today, claiming new victims.[37]

These minefields also pose an environmental threat to wildlife and livestock. Although many of the minefields had been demarcated by fences, concrete beacons, and warning signs, 90 per cent of the fencing is now gone, removed by local people and converted for their own use, leaving only concrete posts in place. Although these posts act as a warning to humans, they do not stop livestock and game from entering the minefields, and thousands of animals have been killed or injured. Since 1980, 9,084 cattle have been reported killed in minefields, representing a loss of income. Many people have been injured trying to save or retrieve livestock that has strayed into minefields. Cattle are not just food for these people— they play a critical social and economic function. A cow represents family wealth, insurance against periods of hardship, and a form of payment for rituals, such as marriages. The loss of cattle is therefore very significant.[38]

In Mozambique's Maputo province, the village of Mapulenge, which had been the centre of a community of 10,000 people, was deserted for four years because local people had been told it was badly mined. A three-month mine clearance operation in the village in 1994 uncovered only four mines. These, and the spreading of rumours, had been sufficient to depopulate the area for four years. Four anti-personnel mines costing US $40 resulted in years of fear and tens of thousands of dollars spent before the community felt safe to return. Also in Mozambique, the UN concluded a contract for the clearance of 2,010 kilometres of roads in 1994. Many of these roads had been closed for years.[39] Yet clearance produced only 28 mines, although other pieces of unexploded ordnance were also uncovered. Rumours spread by soldiers and guerrilla fighters that they have laid land-mines, when they have not, have played an equally devastating role in southern Africa's conflicts over the last 30 years. A simple rumour that an area has been mined can deny land for agricultural production for years or, in some cases, can deny people access to a cemetery to honour their ances-tors. Although no mines had in fact been planted, these areas will still need to be cleared professionally before a community is confident to use that land again.

In Namibia, on 22 December 1995, a 12-year-old boy named Absalom Luuwa lost his left leg when he stepped on a South African R2m2 anti-per-sonnel mine in a minefield the South Africans laid around Ruacana before Namibian independence in 1990. Absolom's family was devastated. He could no longer walk to school and was sent 80 miles away to a hostel. His family cannot afford to pay for his medical treatment. The whole commu-nity is frightened by the threat of landmines and has moved the local school several miles away, making children lose more study time. The councillor of Ruacana, Absalom's uncle, explained in April 1996:

> This minefield has been cleared twice, by the South Africans and now by the Namibian Defense Force with U.S. military help. But these mines still kill and maim. We don't trust anybody now about these mines— Americans, South Africans and our government. The solution is to ban these mines, and those who make these killers should pay for their legacy. Ruacana cries because of mines. Our families want them eradicated. If you can do it for small-pox, you can do it for landmines.[40]

Anti-personnel mines are also notable for the particularly egregious nature of the injuries they cause. The majority of landmine explosions that do not cause death result in traumatic or surgical amputation. In Angola there are some 70,000 victims seriously maimed by landmine injuries. As reported in the *British Medical Journal* in 1991:

> Landmines . . . have ruinous effects on the human body: they drive dirt, bacteria, clothing and metal and plastic fragments into the tissue causing secondary infections. The shock wave from an exploding mine can destroy blood vessels well up the leg, causing surgeons to amputate much higher than the site of the primary wound.[41]

The result for the individual is not one but, typically, a series of painful operations, often followed by a life at the margins of a society heavily dependent on manual labour. Sylvie Maphosa, a pregnant Lusaka housewife, stepped on a landmine in 1991 laid over 15 years before, while collecting firewood outside Lusaka. She cannot walk and speaks with difficulty. She sustained severe head wounds and had her right limbs shattered in the explosion.[42]

The landmine legacy in southern Africa has serious environmental consequences. In Zimbabwe, the border minefields have become a haven for tsetse flies. Wildlife also suffer. The Hwange and Gonarezhou national game parks have reported many mine incidents involving wildlife and there have been several cases of buffalo wounded by landmines attacking people living near the game parks. Without fencing, there has been considerable triggering of mines in remote areas by game animals. Many hundreds of elephants were killed towards the end of the Rhodesian war by mines. An elephant would wander into the minefield and initiate an explosion, and once wounded it would stagger into other mines, setting off further explosions. A dead animal in the minefield would result in additional mine incidents from scavenging animals attempting to feed on its body.[43]

Landmines have also threatened the development of Zimbabwe's premier tourist attraction, Victoria Falls. Minefields that start in Kazungula encircle the resort town and continue due east for some six kilometres to the western shore of Lake Kariba. These minefields have some 66,000 anti-personnel mines placed in them. Tourists who are hiking, kayaking, or bungee jumping pass through cleared paths in these minefields. But the fields are poorly fenced and there is a danger of tourists straying into the minefields or that mines could be washed into the cleared areas. Further expansion of Victoria Falls is also hampered by the minefields because the town's sewage system cannot be expanded to cope with increased tourist demand, resulting in frequent spillages and raw effluent flowing into the Zambezi River.[44] As well, mines used by poachers in Angola's Mupa National Park have decimated elephant stocks.[45]

THE USE OF LANDMINES IN 1998 AND BEYOND

Despite the impressive moves to achieve a worldwide ban in the use, transfer, and stockpiling of anti-personnel landmines in 1997, in a number of ongoing conflicts around the world these mines are freshly laid or minefields are consciously maintained. The range is great, and includes the US-maintained minefield along the North-South Korea border, along the Greek-Turkish division of Cyprus, and on some of Israel's borders. Other examples reported in 1998 are fresh mines laid by rebels in Angola, Cambodia, Russia, Rwanda, and Uganda, by warring groups in Afghanistan, by rebels and the government in Sudan, and by highwaymen in Albania.

One region that has seen a serious upswing of landmine use in 1998 is the Casamance province in Senegal. The separatist Movement of Democratic Forces of Casamance (MFDC) has fought for independence from Senegal since 1982, although landmines only started to be used in 1993. By 1997 travellers in the province were increasingly at risk from anti-tank and anti-personnel landmines laid on roads and in farmland. Between June 1997 and January 1998, 32 people were killed by mines and 109 suffered amputations. Women and children are conspicuous among the mine-victim patients at Ziguinchor's regional hospital.[46] By December 1997, the Senegalese armed forces claimed to have disarmed over 1,600 mines manufactured in Belgium, Portugal, Spain, and Russia, although mine-clearing can be a risky business. The Senegalese authorities report that several of their deminers have been shot at by the MFDC while trying to clear landmines. Most of the mines appear to be second-hand, from porous arsenals and old minefields in neighbouring states. An anti-personnel landmine is reportedly available in Guinea-Bissau markets for under $30 (home-made mines cost much less). A proportion of the landmines in Casamance are Guinea-Bissau leftovers from the PAIGC liberation struggle against Portuguese colonialism.[47]

On 7 February 1998, the Guinea-Bissau army launched a campaign to destroy its landmines by blowing up some 2,300 anti-personnel and anti-tank mines near Bissau. Foreign diplomats and Senegalese army officials were there to monitor the destruction. The destruction followed a scandal in Guinea-Bissau, where MFDC separatists had been buying up old stocks of weapons from Guinea-Bissau. The chief of staff of the Guinea-Bissau national armed forces, Ousmane Mane, was suspended in late February by Minister of Defense Samba Lamine for dereliction of duty because a number of weapons captured in Casamance were taken from the military depot of the Bissau army. An investigation into the affair has been set up. The

Senegalese authorities also claim that mines come from Gambian military arsenals.[48]

The Senegalese army denies using landmines in Casamance. The Minister of the Interior, Abdouramme Sow, stated at the opening of a workshop on landmines that 'it is not the vocation of the Senegalese army to use anti-personnel landmines' and promised to work for wide adherence to the Ottawa treaty and to ensure the protection of people 'within the framework of territorial integrity'.[49] Privately, the Senegalese military admits it has a stockpile of anti-personnel landmines, including claymores, that have been used in regional peacekeeping operations such as ECOMOG in Liberia. One official said that the claymores had been supplied by the US.[50]

The MFDC separatists are split on their use of landmines. Hardliners want to step up the fight at any cost, while its political leader, Father Augustine Diamacoune Senghor, currently under house arrest in Zinguinchor, is said to be shocked by the rebels' use of anti-personnel mines. The MFDC admitted using landmines in November 1997 but promised not to do so again, although its international representatives deny they use them. However, in 1998 the laying of landmines continued and in February 1998 the MFDC military wing in Casamance, following NGO pressure, pledged not to use anti-personnel landmines in their fight against the government. The MFDC also e-mailed Human Rights Watch in December and claimed that the Senegalese military was using landmines in Casamance:

> 1. We are informed that landmines are buried by Senegalese forces in the ricefields of Kandialang, Bouraf and Boutoute suburbs of Zinguinchor, the Capital of Casamance area to discourage the progression of Independentist forces. 2. Our Movement denies the use of vehicle mines in the road of Zinguinchor-Cap Skirring. The explosion of two of them in December killed 7 persons, all civilians.[51]

Not all the landmines used in Casamance are laid for political or military reasons. The Senegalese authorities believe that an increasing number are laid where looting has taken place, resulting in an increase in crime over the last six months. They claim bandits and highwaymen have been using the devices to cover their tracks and frighten the locals.

The upsurge of mine warfare in Casamance is a reminder that non-states parties also need to be locked into the Ottawa Process. It also illustrates how yesterday's landmines can be used in tomorrow's next-door conflicts. Guinea-Bissau has been at peace since 1975, but it is only now, in the late 1990s, clearing the minefields and destroying redundant military stockpiles left from the liberation struggle.

A lesson from Casamance is that mine clearance and destruction of anti-personnel landmine stockpiles are an urgent priority everywhere. Otherwise, other countries may find themselves in a few years time like Senegal, with rebel forces engaging in a war fuelled by a trade in second-hand landmines. But there is also some hope in the Casamance example. Rebel forces and governments now know that using landmines is publicly abhorred. Five years ago, few governments and most rebel groups would never have been divided about using anti-personnel landmines. The MFDC rebels' contacts with NGOs to discuss the use of landmines demonstrates that they are aware of the negative publicity attached to using AP mines.

CONCLUSION

Since 1940 an extraordinary proliferation of anti-personnel landmines has taken place around the world. By the 1990s almost every conflict had seen the use of AP mines, with serious longer-term humanitarian, economic, and environmental consequences. A study by the Centre for Defence Studies at the University of London on the military utility of landmines concluded that 'the only way to use an anti-personnel mine well, is to use it badly.'[52] One cannot deny that anti-personnel landmines have at times brought short-term military advantage to those who use them. But whereas these mines may have had a short-term military utility, the post-conflict impact is utterly disproportionate to their limited benefits. That is the lesson drawn from conventional and unconventional warfare over the last 60 years. It is also why the momentum for a global ban is growing. Already, over 120 countries have supported a ban by signing the Ottawa Convention, including many past producers such as Argentina, Austria, Brazil, Britain, France, South Africa, and Italy. Others, such as Russia, India, and Pakistan, are being encouraged to join in an effort to ensure that AP mines are eradicated in the next century.

NOTES

1. 'Assistance in Mine Clearance', Report of the UN Secretary-General, document A/49/357, 6 Sept. 1994.
2. ICRC, *Anti-Personnel Landmines: Friend or Foe? A Study of the Military Use and Effectiveness of Anti-Personnel Mines* (Geneva: ICRC, 1996), 9.
3. 'Assistance in Mine Clearance', Report of the UN Secretary-General.

4. US Defense Intelligence Agency and US Army Foreign Science and Technology Center (DIA/FSTC), 'Landmines Warfare—Trends & Projections', Dec. 1992, DST–1160S–019, p. 2–1. This document was obtained by Human Rights Watch through the Freedom of Information Act. Lieutenant Colonel Sloan (p. 4) states that in the past 55 years over 650 million mines have been emplaced.

5. Ahmad Lutfi, 'Egypt: Unearthing the Lethal Menace', *African Topics* (London) no. 22 (Jan.-Mar. 1998).

6. Alex Vines, 'The Killing Fields: Landmines in North and West and Central Africa', *African Topics* (London) no. 18 (June-July 1997).

7. Human Rights Watch and Physicians for Human Rights (HRW and PHR), *Landmines: A Deadly Legacy* (New York: Human Rights Watch/PHR, 1993), 17.

8. DIA/FTSC, 'Landmines Warfare', 2–1.

9. HRW and PHR, *Landmines: A Deadly Legacy*, 36.

10. Thomas Reeder at ADPA Symposium, 7–9 Sept. 1993.

11. HRW and PHR, *Landmines: A Deadly Legacy*, 50.

12. Ibid., 55.

13. US Army, Armament, Munitions and Chemical (USAMCCOM), letter to Human Rights Watch, 25 Aug. 1993, and attached statistical tables; US Department of Defense, Defense Security Assistance Administration (US-DSAA), Foreign Military Sales of Anti-Personnel Mines for the period FY 1983–1993 to date JF171 as of 8/11/93. This document was obtained by Human Rights Watch through the Freedom of Information Act.

14. Ibid.

15. Ibid.

16. *Wall Street Journal*, 27 Feb. 1991; Valsella Meccanotecnia, 'Company Profile' (undated), 1; Fiat Group, *1991 Annual Report*, 98.

17. HRW and PHR, *Landmines: A Deadly Legacy*, 77–8.

18. Ibid., 80.

19. Ibid., 88–90.

20. Ibid., 90–1.

21. Shawn Roberts and Jody Williams, *After the Guns Fall Silent: The Enduring Legacy of Landmines* (Washington: Vietnam Veterans of America Foundation, 1995).

22. ICRC, *Anti-Personnel Landmines: Friend or Foe?*, 39.

23. The three countries that have not had landmine incidents on their soil are Lesotho, Mauritius, and the Seychelles.

24. Human Rights Watch, *Still Killing: Landmines in Southern Africa* (New York: HRW, 1997), 1. Since publication, Human Rights Watch has established that Egyptian AP mines have been used in Angola.

25. Ibid. Landmines continue to be laid in areas of eastern Congo and were laid by mercenary forces in support of President Mobutu around Kisangani airport in 1997.

26. Sue Wixley, 'Backyard Land-Mine Sales', in Jacklyn Cock and Penny Mckenzie, eds, *From Defence to Development: Redirecting Military Resources in South Africa* (Cape Town and Ottawa: David Phillip and International Development Research Centre, 1998), 149.

27. HRW and PHR, *Landmines: A Deadly Legacy*, 60.

28. Africa Watch, *Landmines in Angola* (New York: HRW, 1993).

29. HRW, *Still Killing: Landmines in Southern Africa*, 2, and ongoing research by Human Rights Watch.

30. Alex Vines, 'Still Killing: Landmines in Southern Africa', in Cock and Mckenzie, eds, *From Defence to Development: Redirecting Military Resources in South Africa*, 148-62.

31. ICRC, *Anti-Personnel Landmines: Friend or Foe?*, 30.

32. HRW, *Still Killing: Landmines in Southern Africa*, 110.

33. Portuguese Military Intelligence, 4 Seccao/CMD/ZOT, situation report from May 1972 to July 1974.

34. Human Rights Watch, *Angola: Arms Trade and Violations of the Laws of War Since the 1992 Elections* (New York: HRW, 1994), 118.

35. HRW, *Still Killing: Landmines in Southern Africa*, 2–3.

36. Ibid., 3.

37. Peter Swift, *Taming the Landmine* (Alberton: Galago Books, 1986), 84.

38. Martin Rupiah, *Deadly Legacy: Landmines in Zimbabwe* (Harare: Southern Africa Political and Economic Series, 1998).

39. HRW, *Still Killing: Landmines in Southern Africa*, 3.

40. Ibid., 120.

41. Rae McGrath and Eric Stover, 'Injuries from Landmines', *British Medical Journal* 303 (14 Dec. 1991).

42. *The Weekly Post* (Lusaka), 29 Nov., 5 Dec. 1991.

43. HRW, *Still Killing: Landmines in Southern Africa*, 159.

44. Rupiah, *Deadly Legacy: Landmines in Zimbabwe*.

45. 'Hunted Elephants', Dumbo Internet page of MGM Stiftung Menschen gegen Minen Web site (includes photograph): http://www.dsk.de/mgm.

46. Barbarcar Diagne and Alex Vines, 'Senegal: Old Mines, New Wars', *African Topics* (London) no. 22 (Jan.-Mar. 1998).

47. Ibid.

48. Ibid.

49. Statement by Minister of Interior Abdouramme Sow, Dakar, 2 Nov. 1997.

50. A Senegalese military official communicated this to Human Rights Watch, Dakar, 3 Nov. 1997.

51. MFDC e-mail to Human Rights Watch, 15 Dec. 1997.

52. Chris Smith, ed., *The Military Utility of Landmines . . . ?* (London: Centre for Defence Studies, King's College, University of London, 1996), 2.

CHAPTER 9

THE MILITARY UTILITY
OF ANTI-PERSONNEL MINES

Robert G. Gard, Jr

BACKGROUND

All may be fair in love, but not in war. The modern system of the international law of war is rooted in customary humanitarian practices of the medieval period. The widely accepted principle of the need to conciliate military requirements with humanitarian considerations was formalized in 1868 by the Declaration of St Petersburg: 'There are limits at which the necessities of war ought to yield to the requirements of humanity.' This was reinforced in 1907 by Article 22 of Hague Convention IV, Respecting the Laws and Customs of War on Land: 'The right of belligerents to adopt a means of injuring the enemy is not unlimited.'[1]

On 8 August 1945, France, the United Kingdom, the USSR, and the US entered into an agreement on the 'Prosecution and Punishment of the Major War Criminals of the European Axis'.[2] Subsequent rulings by the International Military Tribunal at Nürnberg delineated in detail the recognized concepts of 'proportionality' and 'military necessity', which require nations to take into account the effects of military operations and the use of weapons on non-combatants. These concepts are now well established in international treaty law and are incorporated in military regulations. For example, according to the United States Army field manual on *The Law of Land Warfare*, 'proportionality' means that the 'loss of life and damage to property must not be out of proportion to the military advantage to be gained' by the conduct of a military operation.[3] The manual states as basic principles that noncombatants must be protected from 'unnecessary suffering' and that the law of war 'requires that belligerents refrain from employing any kind or degree of violence that is not actually necessary for military purposes and that they conduct hostilities with regard for the principles of humanity'.[4]

International humanitarian law is concerned with weapons themselves, as well as how they are used. It prohibits the use of weapons that cause unnecessary suffering or civilian casualties disproportionate to the concrete and direct military advantages anticipated by their use. These criteria were applied in agreements to ban the use of exploding bullets at St Petersburg in 1868 and expanding dumdum bullets at the 1899 Hague International Peace Conference; in the Geneva Protocol of 1925, prohibiting the use of poisonous and asphyxiating gases; in the Biological

Weapons Convention of 1972; and in Protocol IV of the 1996 revisions of the Convention on Certain Conventional Weapons, which bans the use of blinding lasers.

One of the four landmark conventions signed in Geneva in 1949 dealt with the Protection of Civilian Persons in Time of War. Because of advances in the lethality of weapons, an international conference was held in the mid-1970s to update the provisions of the Geneva Conventions. Protocol I Additional to the Geneva Conventions of 1949, Relating to the Protection of Victims of International Armed Conflicts, was signed in December 1977. It amplified the principle of 'proportionality' in international humanitarian law by prohibiting both the employment of weapons 'of a nature to cause superfluous injury or unnecessary suffering' (Article 35), and 'a method or means of combat' that is 'of a nature to strike military objectives and civilians . . . without distinction' (Article 51). These provisions iterated UN General Assembly Resolution 2444, passed unanimously in 1968, advocating the prohibition of the use of weapons that cause unnecessary suffering or have indiscriminate effects.

The companion principle to 'proportionality' is 'military necessity', which permits reasonably necessary violence, other than measures specifically prohibited by international law, that is indispensable to the accomplishment of the military mission of securing the submission of the enemy armed force. However, consistent with the principle of 'proportionality', the military utility of a weapon should be considered in relation to the humanitarian costs of its employment. In deciding whether or not to subscribe to a treaty banning the use of anti-personnel mines, for example, nations are obligated to assess not only the effectiveness of these weapons, to determine if they are indispensable to legitimate military operations, but also whether they are proportional in their effects. The issue, therefore, is not whether AP mines might under some circumstances have marginal military utility, but rather whether their use is not only essential but also proportional in relation to the military utility they may provide.

The use of mines is addressed in Protocol II of the 1980 Convention on Prohibitions or Restrictions on the Use of Certain Conventional Weapons which may be Deemed to be Excessively Injurious and to have Indiscriminate Effects. It was revised in May 1996 to prohibit the employment of mines in a way that 'may be expected to cause incidental loss of civilian life, injury to civilians . . . which would be excessive in relation to the concrete and direct military advantage anticipated'. This international treaty banned the placing of non-self-destruct, or 'dumb', mines in unmarked or uncontrolled locations because there was general agreement that the resultant humanitarian costs exceed their military utility to a degree sufficient to warrant a prohibition on such uses of the weapon. However, there are continuing claims of 'military necessity' for appropriately marked and controlled 'dumb' minefields, as well as for the use of self-destruct, or so-called 'smart', AP mines.

DETERMINING MILITARY UTILITY

There is no formula or specific set of criteria on which to base a determination of the point at which the putative military utility of AP mines is exceeded by the humanitarian costs of their employment. This is a complex problem involving subjective judgement; and for a nation to deny its military the use of a weapon that could assist in prevailing against opposing forces while reducing friendly casualties, there must be a compelling case that the weapon is not indispensable to legitimate military operations and that its utility is clearly outweighed by the resultant killing and wounding of innocent civilians. Since Alex Vines has addressed in Chapter 8 the humanitarian crisis caused by AP mines, this chapter focuses on the military utility of the weapon.

What evidence exists for the military utility of AP mines? One obvious source is the professional judgement of active-duty military officers responsible for the conduct of combat operations. It is understandable, however, that military professionals are reluctant to forfeit any weapon that might have even marginal utility. This is especially true in the case of the United States, whose professional military doctrine evolved from a traditionally restricted role for its military forces as a result of the nation's isolation for most of its history from foreign power centres. Until recently, the mission of the US military has been regarded by civilian officials, the body politic, and military professionals themselves as limited to destroying the enemy armed force as soon as feasible with the fewest possible friendly casualties.

This tradition persists in the US Department of Defense. General John M. Shalikashvili, then Chairman of the Joint Chiefs of Staff, stated in 1995 that 'Congress and the American people expect us to fight and win conflicts with minimum casualties.'[5] The Under-Secretary of Defense for Policy stated in 1997 that AP mines are necessary 'to safeguard American lives and hasten an end to fighting'.[6] At a press briefing in 1996 addressing US policy on AP mines, Secretary of Defense William Perry maintained that the US military establishment is 'responsible for preparing and executing our nation's war plans with maximum effectiveness and minimum casualties to US forces'.[7]

Protecting one's soldiers from harm is a laudable and appropriate objective; but it must be balanced against other priorities, including consideration of non-combatant casualties. In fact, restrictive 'rules of engagement' that increase the risks to US military forces are now routinely imposed in combat theatres or in operations that may lead to employing military force. However, in opposing a ban on AP mines, US military leaders invoke the primacy of protecting American soldiers. In a letter to the chairman of the Senate Armed Services Committee, the Joint Chiefs of Staff and the commanders of the US major combatant forces stated: 'The lives of our sons and daughters should be given the highest priority when deciding whether or not to ban . . . the use of self-destructing anti-personnel land mines.'[8]

Regardless of their personal views, it would be extremely difficult for responsible active-duty military professionals, especially the US Joint Chiefs of Staff, to advocate the prohibition of any weapon that might under some circumstances save the lives of their nation's soldiers. Moreover, military professionals, particularly in the United States, are not expected to determine the point at which military needs should yield to humanitarian considerations. In democratic societies, that judgement is an appropriate responsibility of elected civilian leadership.

It is instructive to recall the debate in the United States over the Geneva Protocol of 1925, which banned the use of poison gas. Although now there is nearly universal agreement, even among US military professionals, that the use of chemical weapons should be prohibited, representatives of the US War Department, the Pentagon of its day, argued that chemicals were one of the most effective weapons ever known, decisive in offensive operations; that it would not be possible to prevent the use in war of a weapon that is militarily effective; and that the treaty was impractical, unenforceable, and ineffective.[9]

The parallels with the position of the US military regarding the treaty to ban AP mines are striking. In the case of the Geneva Protocol, however, the US signed the treaty over the objections of the War Department; and although military professionals were able to persuade the US Senate to deny its consent to ratification of the Protocol for 50 years, every US President, from Warren Harding forward, in his role as commander-in-chief of the armed forces, ordered compliance with the prohibition against the use of chemical weapons, even when the chief of staff of the Army recommended their use against entrenched Japanese positions on outlying islands towards the end of World War II in order to save the lives of American soldiers.[10]

In justifying his decision to decline to sign the Ottawa Convention to ban AP mines, US President Bill Clinton echoed the position of the US Joint Chiefs of Staff: 'there is a line that I simply cannot cross . . . the safety of our men and women in uniform. We will always, always do everything we can to protect our own.'[11] None the less, a year earlier, in May 1996, the President had deplored the civilian casualties caused by AP mines and had recognized the need for a universal ban on the use of the weapon to deal with the humanitarian problems: 'To end the carnage, the United States will seek a worldwide agreement as soon as possible to end the use of all anti-personnel land mines.' At the same time, however, in announcing his decision on the US position regarding the Convention to ban AP mines, the President stated that the US 'will reserve the right to use . . . "smart mines" . . . because there may be battlefield situations in which these [mines] will save the lives of our soldiers.' There is no evidence that the President weighed the military utility of AP mines to US forces against the impact of retaining them on international efforts to ameliorate and eventually solve the humanitarian problems caused by their continued use. In his words, 'as Commander-in-Chief, my responsibility is . . . to safeguard the safety, the lives of our men and women in uniform.'[12] Although the President suggested that AP mines have only marginal military utility by stating that there 'may be' operations justifying their use, it is evident that he has acceded to the position of the Joint Chiefs of Staff. In fact, probably due to political vulnerability regarding his actions during the Vietnam War, the President stated in a brief discussion with the author on the AP mine issue that he could not 'risk a breach with the Joint Chiefs'.[13]

Research Studies of Utility

More objective analyses of the military utility of AP mines can be expected from independent research organizations. In 1994, the Office of the US Secretary of Defense commissioned the Institute for Defense Analyses (IDA) to conduct a study of the military utility of AP mines in high-intensity mechanized land warfare, the situation considered by the US military as the most compelling for retaining use of the weapon. The IDA, a highly respected independent research organization, was established to conduct objective studies for the Department of Defense; it certainly cannot be considered unsympathetic to the genuine needs of the US military. Recently retired military officers with combat experience participated in the study.[14]

While one can support different positions by citing various sections of the IDA study, its principal conclusion is that AP mines have only a 'quite modest' military utility, and that 'the set of attack types that cannot be affected directly by AT [anti-tank] mines alone is relatively small (and thus, a mine inventory consisting solely of AT mines would still provide a substantially robust mine warfare capability).'[15] While AP mines are judged to be useful in static defensive situations, the study concludes that they are of marginal utility in a defence that also employs tactical offensive operations; the doctrine of modern armed forces in mechanized warfare is to conduct a defence with aggressive counterattacks. The study determined that the use of AP mines by both sides during US offensive operations would probably yield a 'negative net military utility' for US forces.[16]

At the request of the Chairman of the Joint Chiefs of Staff, General Shalikashvili, the Dupuy Institute conducted a study in April 1996 entitled 'Military Consequences of Landmine Restrictions'.[17] An independent non-profit organization, the Dupuy Institute specializes in research and analysis of issues related to armed conflict by merging operations research techniques with historical trends and combat data. Following additional analysis, the president of the Dupuy Institute, a recently retired US Army major-general, wrote a memorandum to General Shalikashvili on 2 January 1997, concluding that 'our historical research, when coupled with probable future engagements, indicates that a total ban on this [AP] type of mine, if eventually adhered to by most nations, will only benefit US ground forces in the long run.' On the basis of the study, he recommended 'that the United States support a total ban on anti-personnel mines'.[18]

The principal arguments for the utility of anti-personnel mines include: (1) to shape the battlefield by denying the enemy access to mined areas, and to channel enemy forces into positions vulnerable to friendly attack; (2) to defend borders against infiltration and positions or facilities against hostile action; (3) to enhance the effectiveness of other weapons by halting the movement of enemy forces, thereby increasing their vulnerability; and (4) to protect friendly forces by deploying mines to deter or delay an enemy attack.

The effectiveness of mine barriers in channelling the enemy is highly suspect. Techniques to breach passage through minefields are well developed; these include the use of flails, rollers, ploughs, explosive-filled hoses, and fuel-air explosives. The vulnerability of minefields was clearly demonstrated in the Gulf War; in about two hours, coalition forces breached Iraqi defences that employed some 9 million protective mines.[19] During the Korean War, the Chinese cleared corridors through minefields by simply moving troops through them, as did the Iranians during the Iraq-Iran War.[20] General Alfred Gray, retired commandant of the US Marine Corps, stated in a speech to the American Defense Preparedness Association in September 1993: 'I know of no situation in the Korean War, nor in the five years I served in Southeast Asia, nor in Panama, nor in Desert Storm-Desert Shield where our use of mine warfare truly channelized the enemy and brought them into a destructive pattern.'[21]

A significant problem is created by attempting to deny an enemy access to areas by deploying mines: it also limits the rapid manoeuvrability of friendly forces, requiring them to breach or bypass their own minefields. Worse yet, employing AP mines inflicts friendly casualties; in rapidly moving combat operations, or in the general chaos of battle, friendly forces inadvertently manoeuvre into areas mined by their own or other friendly units. A publication of the US Army Training and Doctrine Command states that 'the most important lesson from recent operations is that close combat operations remain violent, fast-paced and hard to predict' and that battle space will be 'fluid', requiring 'agility' and 'flexibility' of 'non-contiguous' units in conducting 'active defense' operations.[22] Mined areas obviously present a threat to forces operating in this manner.

Proponents who support the need for AP mines claim that their military utility was demonstrated during the Gulf War. While the mining of beaches by the Iraqis did prevent an amphibious assault by US Marines, it appears unlikely that the deployment of 'smart' mines on the flank of the US VII Corps was necessary to deter a counterattack by outgunned Iraqi troops who had been bombarded for some 38 days prior to the coalition ground attack. There is stronger evidence that the employment of mixed mine systems by coalition forces in fact impeded the manoeuvrability of their own troops and slowed their operational tempo. A follow-up report of the 1st Infantry Division expressed 'grave concern about minefields created by US weapons'. The report noted that 'casualties would have been even higher' had there been a requirement for dismounted assaults, operations often necessary in mechanized warfare when foot troops are vulnerable to AP mines.[23]

During the ground offensive phase of the Gulf War, XVIII Corps sent a message to its units on 28 February 1991, cautioning all soldiers 'to leave unexploded mines alone'. It noted that 'several severe injuries' had resulted from soldiers disturbing unexploded munitions, and warned that the 'rapid Allied advance' could encounter 'activated Gator minefields, consisting of anti-personnel and anti-armor mines' that had been dispersed on 'airfields, MSRs [main supply routes], approaches and bridges, and assembly areas'. The message directed that 'extreme caution must be exercised in moving/maneuvering through areas where air strikes have been conducted.'[24]

The name 'scatterables' has been applied appropriately to US self-destruct mines. The Gator system delivered by the Air Force is made up of canisters, each containing 72 anti-tank and 22 anti-personnel mines; some 600 mines can be spread over a wide area in a single sortie. Even though coalition forces in the Gulf War had six months to prepare for the ground attack against static Iraqi positions, it is evident from the XVIII Corps message that precision in delivery and the recording of the location of the mines, required by the Convention on Conventional Weapons signed by the US, could not be accomplished; the advancing units were directed to move with caution through all areas that had been attacked by friendly air forces. Although he later endorsed US retention of 'smart' mines, General Gray asked: 'What the hell is the use of sowing all this if you're going to move through it. . . . We have many examples of our own young warriors trapped by their own minefields. . . . We had examples even in Desert Storm.' He noted that 'We kill more Americans with our own mines than we do anyone else.'[25]

Given the negative consequences to coalition forces of the employ- ment of AP mines in the Gulf War, it is not surprising that the commander- in-chief of that operation, General Norman Schwartzkopf, joined 14 other retired senior US military officers in signing the open letter to the President, which was published as a full-page advertisement in the *New York Times* by the Vietnam Veterans of America Foundation. The letter states that AP mines are not essential and urges the President to fulfil the commitment he had made to ban all AP mines as soon as possible as an action 'not only humane but militarily responsible'.[26] The proclivity of Western democratic societies, especially the US, to accord high priority to preventing friendly casualties reinforces the conclusion in the IDA study that the two-sided use of AP mines in offensive operations is probably a net disadvantage to the US.

The International Committee of the Red Cross (ICRC) analysed the military use and effectiveness of AP mines in 26 conflicts between 1940 and 1995. The general conclusions, endorsed as of 12 May 1997 by 55 active and retired military officers from 19 countries, are consistent with the IDA study: 'No case was found in which the use of anti-personnel mines played a major role in determining the outcome of a conflict'; they had 'little or no effect on the outcome of hostilities'; they had only 'limited effect on unprotected infantry'; and while 'these weapons had a marginal tactical value under certain specific . . . conditions . . . the effects are very limited and may even be counterproductive.'[27]

The ICRC study also addressed the utility of AP mines in protecting extensive national borders from infiltration or attack. This type of defence has been employed along the India/Pakistan and China/Russia borders and between countries in Africa. Experience has shown that such defences are not only dangerous to the country that employs them in inflicting casual- ties on its own civilians and soldiers, but also expensive in terms of the resources required to maintain them. To be effective, such minefields must be covered by observation and aimed fire; and they require frequent maintenance and repair when mines are triggered or neutralized by animals, innocent civilians, or enemy infiltrators. The study concluded that border minefields have not been effective in preventing infiltration, but that they have resulted in numerous non-combatant casualties and the killing of livestock.[28]

Both the IDA and ICRC studies acknowledge that AP mines can be useful in static defensive situations and for close-in protection of facilities against dismounted personnel. However, employment of these indiscriminate weapons for such purposes often causes civilian casualties and alienates the local population. There are discriminating weapons available that are as effective as AP mines. Most simply, protective barriers of various kinds can be installed, and non-lethal sensors, including trip flares, can be placed around a position or facility to detect infiltrators; aimed fire and weapons such as claymore mines, which are not victim-activated, can be employed to stop incursion. More sophisticated detection equipment is available: radars that can identify people at considerable distance, even through heavy rain; infrared and night vision devices that can see people several hundred metres away; and a variety of mechanical, electronic, and electro-optical sensors.[29] Also, 'a wide range of [additional] non-landmine responses to counter infiltration and night/bad weather surveillance are becoming available.'[30]

Moreover, even minefields under close control of defending forces can cause unintended and counter-productive casualties. The US base at Guantanamo Bay, Cuba, has been protected by a minefield, now in the process of being cleared. Of the 23 people killed by these mines, five were Cubans; the others were US personnel, including five sailors who accidentally walked into the minefield. According to the South Korean Ministry of Defence, between 1992 and 1997 there were 78 casualties, 35 killed and 43 injured, one-third civilian, caused by the minefields emplaced in the closely guarded military control area just south of the demilitarized zone that separates South from North Korea.[31]

Recent Conflicts and Peacekeeping
As described by Vines in Chapter 8, AP mines have proved highly effective when used to terrorize or control civilians, purposes contrary to international law. The placement of even a limited number of mines on trails, and in or near villages, wells, and fields used for agriculture or grazing, prevents their use by the civilian population. Also, civilians can be confined to village areas around which AP mines are emplaced. Precisely because AP mines are indiscriminate and can be concealed easily, they inherently are weapons of terror. Since civilians lack the equipment and training for

demining, a single casualty, or very few casualties, can serve to inhibit the movement of the local populace, as has been demonstrated in Cambodia, Bosnia, and several countries in Africa.[32] The commander of the American sector in Bosnia stated on 5 October 1997 that the situation there cannot be returned to normal and the refugees cannot be resettled until the serious mine problem is brought under control. At the current rate of removal, he said, it would require 50–100 years to solve that problem.[33]

Peacekeeping forces attempting to operate in areas where mines have been sown have suffered casualties and have been restricted in their operations. Despite strenuous efforts to train UN and NATO peacekeeping troops to avoid mines in Bosnia, they have suffered more than 300 casualties from mine accidents. In their paper on 'The APL [AP mine] Threat to the US', Department of Defense officials noted that 'mines are a major threat in all types of combat operations and will be the major threat in most Operations Other than War.'[34] A principal incentive in convening the Review Conference to revise Protocol II of the Convention on Conventional Weapons was to minimize the kinds of problems encountered in Bosnia by regulating the use of AP mines in internal conflicts.

The principal uses of AP mines up to the time of the Gulf War were in defensive operations to channel and delay the enemy and to protect borders and installations. Before remotely delivered scatterable mines were developed, it usually was not feasible to employ mines in offensive operations to protect exposed flanks against counterattack and to impede enemy movement in their own rear areas.

While some military professionals continue to claim that AP mines are necessary for close-in defence against dismounted troops or infiltrators, the principal arguments advanced by the US military for continuing the use of AP mines are based on the need to protect remotely delivered anti-tank (AT) mines from rapid neutralization. The contention is that without AP mines mixed in, enemy forces would be able to breach AT minefields in about 10 minutes, which would allow for only one attack by air or other weapons while the halted enemy forces are most vulnerable. With AP mines deployed with the AT mines, it is claimed, the enemy would need to spend some 20 to 30 additional minutes breaching the minefield, thereby permitting three, instead of one, attacks while their units present stationary targets.

Proponents for the continuing use of 'smart' AP mines also claim that they do not contribute to the humanitarian problem caused by 'dumb' mines. US smart mines are programmed to self-destruct in up to 15 days, with an estimated 90–95 per cent reliability. The remaining 5–10 per cent deactivate by exhaustion of their batteries within 90 days, with a claimed reliability of 99.9 per cent. However, 'smart' AP mines are no more able than the 'dumb' variety to discriminate among an enemy, an innocent civilian, or a member of a friendly armed force before, or at the time, they self-destruct. Also, AP mines are considered by many physicians to cause excessive suffering in their victims. ICRC surgeons state that mine injuries are 'horrific', requiring long-term medical care if the patient survives. Fragmentation mines shower victims with metal or plastic fragments. Blast mines, which tear off limbs, drive ground debris, plastic fragments, and shattered bones deep into the wounds they create, requiring a series of complex surgeries.[35]

Moreover, the capability of remote delivery of 'smart' mines encourages far more extensive use of mixed scatterable systems than was the case with 'dumb' mines. In addition to the objective of halting second- and third-echelon advancing enemy formations to make them vulnerable to attack by other weapons, there is the same justification for employing scatterables against myriad other rear-area targets such as artillery and rocket units, supply points, and command and control headquarters. This could result in the saturation with indiscriminate weapons of areas behind enemy front lines.

In the Gulf War, remotely delivered mines were used by coalition forces to try to close gaps in Iraqi protective minefields to slow the withdrawal of their troops; while this contributed to delaying the advance of coalition forces, it did not prevent the rapid breaching of mined areas and the escape of the majority of the Iraqi Republican Guard. Employing mixed 'smart' mine systems in enemy rear areas and to protect the flanks of troops in offensive operations inevitably will scatter them into locations occupied by civilians, who lack the capability to protect themselves from the mines. The ICRC study concludes that the use of 'smart' AP mines will increase, not reduce, the likelihood of civilian casualties.[36] While this is impossible to verify, the extensive deployment of scatterable mines almost certainly would cause large numbers of civilian casualties.

There is an additional problem regarding the arming of 'smart' mines. Mistakes in air speed, dropping height, and fuse settings add to the failure rate of the activating mechanisms of these weapons. Combined with those that do not self-destruct, this results in residual unexploded mines 'in an unknown condition'[37] that renders mined areas unusable pending meticulous hand-demining clearance. Some 1,700 such devices were found by CMS Environmental, Inc., the US contractor employed to clear mines from a sector of Kuwait following the Gulf War.[38]

Although at this writing over 120 states have signed the international treaty to ban AP mines, the US and other major powers, including China,

India, and Russia, have declined to do so; however, President Boris Yeltsin has declared that Russia would sign the accord,[39] and China and India have pledged not to deploy AP mines outside their own borders.[40] Even though President Clinton has stated the goal of achieving a ban on all AP mines as soon as possible, and although in 1996 the UN adopted a US-sponsored resolution advocating this objective, with 156 affirmative votes, none against, and only 10 abstentions, the current US position is that it cannot sign the Ottawa Convention because of its special responsibilities as the only world superpower and the need to protect its own military personnel. Yet the US Joint Chiefs of Staff and the major field commanders declared in their 1997 letter that 'we are ready to ban all APL [AP mines] when the major producers and suppliers ban theirs.'[41] Since anti-personnel mines are not employed to counter their use by enemy forces, this statement strongly suggests that senior US military leaders actually regard the military utility of AP mines as marginal rather than indispensable.

In 1996, then US Secretary of State Warren Christopher noted that AP mines 'probably kill more children than soldiers'; he expressed American 'determination to eliminate these deadly instruments of terror', noting that 'an international ban on landmines cannot happen without American leadership.'[42] During the debates on US adherence to the Chemical Weapons Convention (CWC), Senator Joseph Biden argued strenuously against withholding US ratification until all other states with a chemical weapons capability had acceded to the treaty.[43] On 8 April 1997, Secretary of State Madeleine K. Albright stressed

> the imperative of American leadership. The United States is the only nation with the power, influence and respect to forge a strong global consensus against . . . weapons of mass destruction. . . . I believe that—if the United States joins the CWC—most other nations will too. . . . But the problem states will never accept a prohibition of chemical weapons if America stays out, keeps them company and gives them cover.[44]

In urging congressional support of the CWC, Secretary of Defense William S. Cohen pointed out that the treaty 'will reduce the chemical weapons problem to a few notorious rogues', and Senator Biden noted that the rogue states would be 'isolated and targeted'.[45]

The US is advocating adherence by others to the international treaty to ban AP mines, while noting the lack of universal agreement and reserving exceptions for itself. If the US persists in this position, it seems evident that other nations will be encouraged to claim that they, too, have special circumstances that warrant exceptions. During 1994–5, the US and the

United Kingdom engaged in a campaign, the US-UK Landmine Control Regime, to try to persuade other countries that there should be a ban on 'dumb' mines but that self-destructing mines should be exempted. This was rejected as an attempt by advanced industrialized nations to deny AP mines to less developed countries or to require them to purchase 'smart' mines from technically advanced nations. The points made by Senator Biden and Secretaries Albright and Cohen supporting ratification of the CWC are equally valid for the international treaty to ban AP mines.

US spokepersons, including the President, have acknowledged the necessity of a total ban on all AP mines to deal effectively with the humanitarian problem caused by their use. In a background press briefing on 3 July 1997, a senior Department of Defense official, who identified himself as the director of AP mine policy, referred to the 'horrendous problem' of 26,000 casualties per year caused by mines and stated that 'a ban is a critical part' of solving the problem. He continued: 'we think the ban's essential', and 'we are willing, unilaterally, to ban the high-tech, self-destructing type landmine . . . because it is a landmine and we understand the problem.' He noted that 'The new international norm has been established. The world is going to do without landmines.'[46]

Nevertheless, the United States has declined to sign the international treaty to ban AP mines unless and until it can develop 'alternatives' to replace what it regards as the critical military functions of these weapons, including the defence of South Korea and the role of AP mines in protecting anti-tank mines. In an interview published on 23 November 1997, President Clinton stated that he would sign the treaty 'in a heartbeat' if the problems of Korea and the protection of anti-tank mines could be solved.[47] Therefore, the question of 'alternatives' to AP mines is important to the analysis of their military utility and critical to the willingness of the US to sign the Ottawa Convention. It is evident, however, that the US Department of Defense is not motivated to make a serious effort to find alternatives to AP mines.

Although President Clinton affirmed his commitment to a ban on AP mines in May 1996, and in late 1994 had indicated he had asked military officials to find a feasible alternative,[48] the American position remained ambivalent, at best. In May 1997 the Under-Secretary of Defense for Policy reported that 'Preliminary research indicates that effective alternatives should be feasible by integrating various elements of existing and near-future technologies, combat forces, and military doctrine.'[49] In October 1997, however, the Deputy Secretary of Defense issued a memorandum stating that the President had determined that 'the use of mixed systems containing both self-destructing anti-personnel submunitions [previously called anti-personnel mines] and anti-vehicle submunitions [previously called anti-tank mines] is necessary to meet security requirements', thereby in effect exempting AP mines in mixed systems from the search for alternatives. In fact, the memo directed the repackaging of the remote anti-armour mine artillery shell into a mixed system with AP mines.[50] In a letter responding to Senator Patrick Leahy's inquiry on the issue of alternatives to mixed systems, the Secretary of Defense repeated the claim that US mixed systems do not contribute to the humanitarian problem and stated that if the exploration by the Defense Advanced Research Projects Agency for 'new barrier system concepts' is successful, 'the results might also eventually be adopted to replace our current method of protecting mixed systems.'[51]

Although he has set 2003 as the year that the US will cease using AP mines, other than in those mixed systems, and an objective of ceasing their use in Korea by 2006, the President obviously has retreated a significant distance from his earlier position of seeking a ban on all AP mines as soon as possible. In an interview published on 23 November 1997, the retreat turned into surrender: when asked if he believed that the Defense Department had worked 'earnestly' to find alternatives, the President responded: 'It's not so easy to find alternatives', and 'I think that they are committed to the timetable that they're committed to.'[52]

In response to pressure from Senator Patrick Leahy, the Clinton administration modified its earlier position on mixed systems, which would have prevented the US from signing the Ottawa Convention. In a letter of 15 May 1998, the Assistant to the President for National Security pledged that the US will 'search aggressively for alternatives to our mixed anti-tank systems'. However, the lack of a genuine sense of urgency is obvious in the accompanying qualification that the 'the United States will sign the Ottawa Convention by 2006 *if* we succeed in identifying and fielding suitable alternatives.'[53] Without a deadline, the Department of Defense has no incentive to expedite the process or to conclude that alternatives are 'suitable'.

The President evidently is allowing the Department of Defense to take too narrow an interpretation of 'alternatives' or substitutes for AP mines. The IDA study noted that consideration of such options usually is restricted to 'symmetrical' substitutes, and it challenged the 'implicit premise that substitution is best pursued by duplicating the effects of landmine use'.[54] Several non-lethal alternatives, such as incapacitating darts, sticky foam, and string nets, have been suggested.[55] It is obvious, however, that the relevant question should be how to achieve an equivalent or better combat outcome in the absence of AP mines, not how to create some kind of weapon or weapons that replicate the current effects of AP mines.

In the Korean situation, AP mines are redundant for effective close-in defence south of the demilitarized zone (DMZ). Other means of detection of enemy movement are available—mountainous terrain channels invaders into narrow north-south invasion routes, which are under direct observation; hundreds of tank traps, trenches, and barricades are in place between the DMZ and Seoul; and weapons have been focused on routes of attack for years.[56] Retired Lieutenant-General James Hollingsworth, who designed the plan to defend the sector north of Seoul, observed: 'we have developed numerous methods other than APLs [AP mines] to halt the North Korean advance', and he characterized the military utility of AP mines in Korea as 'minimal, and . . . even offset by the difficulty our own APLs pose to our brand of mobile warfare.'[57] In refuting the need to employ AP mines in the defence of South Korea, retired General Jack Galvin, former US Supreme Allied Commander, Europe, stated that 'In offense, but also in defense, American forces rely on mobility', and that AP mines 'stifle and frustrate mobility'.[58]

However, for whatever military utility they may provide, about 1 million 'dumb' AP mines already are emplaced in the six mile-deep military control zone immediately south of the two-and-a-half-mile band of the DMZ, augmented by some 2 million more mines within the DMZ;[59] all of these minefields have been turned over to the South Koreans, so they are no longer a US responsibility.[60] Another million 'dumb' AP mines held in reserve could be emplaced in the military control zone prior to an American signing of the Ottawa Convention. There would be no obligation to remove these mines for 10 years after the treaty comes into effect, which will occur when 40 nations have ratified it; thus these mines could be left in place several years beyond the US target date of 2006 to replace them. Surely, by then, action could be taken to compensate for the loss of whatever contribution AP mines might make to the strength of the defence south of the border between the two Koreas.

The more complex problem is the mixed mine systems in the US inventory for use in more remote locations not directly under observation of US ground forces in Korea and elsewhere. It is argued that the AP mines offer important protection against the capability of enemy forces to neutralize the anti-tank mines more quickly than if AP mines were absent. However, other means are available to detect enemy personnel attempting to clear or detonate the AT mines, and there are effective anti-personnel weapons to interdict their capability to do so. The May 1997 report of the Under-Secretary of Defense for Policy concluded that 'much of what is already being developed can be leveraged into area denial operations' and that lethal alternatives can be achieved by 'precise real time surveillance systems to automatically detect, classify and track vehicles and/or people; precise firepower to immediately suppress movement of enemy forces; and command and control systems (a "man-in-the-loop") to cue the precise firepower.'[61]

Enemy movement can be ascertained by scattering non-lethal sensor devices with the anti-tank mines, and/or by making use of real-time overhead imagery with satellites, drones, and JSTARS, an aircraft that can circle at high altitudes and detect moving columns 100 miles away to identify, transmit, and display target information to fire support controllers. As demonstrated in the Gulf War, US forces possessed in 1991 the capability to detect and monitor enemy movements; and in 1995, looking to the near-term future, the Army's Training and Doctrine Command study described the emerging capability of 'a full suite of strategic, operational and tactical sensors [to locate and track enemy vehicles and personnel] linked to analytical teams that will fuse combat information into situational awareness across the battle space with greater clarity that ever before.'[62]

Weapons that can be brought to bear effectively on soldiers attempting to neutralize anti-tank mines include area denial bomblets, sometimes called 'cluster' submunitions. A tracked vehicle, the Multiple Launch Rocket System (MLRS), can fire a 'ripple' of 12 M26 rockets, each containing 644 submunitions that are dispensed in mid-air over the target and detonate on impact; they cover an area of up to 200,000 square metres to a range of 32 kilometres. The Extended Range MLRS can deliver rockets containing 518 of these submunitions to a range of 45 kilometres, and the Army Tactical Missile System (ATACMS) can deliver 950 bomblets to a range of 165 kilometres. Fighter aircraft can dispense up to 12 canisters of cluster munitions, each containing 650 bomblets designed to explode on impact or at random within a half-hour.[63]

Scheduled to be fielded in the spring of 1998 is an Improved Position Determining Launcher, a follow-on to the MLRS, that can fire inertially guided ATACMS, with a reduced payload but with greater accuracy and effectiveness, to a range of 300 kilometres; $142 million is included in the fiscal 1999 US Defense budget for procurement of this system.[64] A Navy version (NTACMS) of the inertially guided missile can attack personnel or materiel targets to ranges in excess of 150 nautical miles.[65] Consistent with the need to protect civilians from AP mines, all bomblets should contain backup self-destruct mechanisms that will activate promptly if the bomblets do not explode on impact, or very shortly thereafter if so programmed.

Weapons already in the inventory provided the basis for the conclusion of the letter to the President signed in 1996 by 15 senior retired US military officers: 'Given the wide range of weapons available . . . banning [AP mines] would not undermine the effectiveness or safety of our forces.'[66] Even more promising as substitutes for AP mines in their function of protecting anti-tank mines are weapons that do not require anti-tank mines to halt armoured vehicles. Anti-tank submunitions have been under development for more than 20 years, and various weapons entering the US arsenal can destroy armoured vehicles on the move.[67]

A companion approach to substituting other weapons to perform the functions of AP mines is to modify military doctrine and tactical concepts to compensate for the absence of these mines. A Defense Department news release noted that the President's policy on AP mines 'directs fundamental changes in war plans, doctrine and tactics of the US military with the goal of eliminating reliance on anti-personnel land mines.'[68] William Perry, then Secretary of Defense, stated that the principal purpose of AP mines is 'to delay and disrupt, slow down . . . infantry. . . . There are other ways of doing that, too, that have to do with tactics, techniques and other weapons. That broad approach involves changes across the board in the way we fight . . . in tactics and doctrine as well as in systems.'[69] The report of the Office of the Under-secretary of Defense for Policy noted that the Secretary of Defense, in June 1996, directed the Chairman of the Joint Chiefs of Staff to change 'war plans, joint doctrine, and training to reduce and eliminate the reliance' on AP mines, and directed the services (Army and Marine Corps) to 'begin development of tactics and Service doctrine eliminating the need to rely on self-destructing APL [AP landmines] in anticipation of prompt international agreement to ban all APL.'[70]

In January 1997, a senior US military official observed that 'the Joint Staff and services have initiated the necessary doctrinal and tactical changes . . . such that there will not be a requirement for APLs . . . and doctrinal manuals are already under revision.'[71] The director of AP mine policy in the Office of the Secretary of Defense stated on 3 July 1997: 'the President's policy put us on a very clear course . . . of modifying the way we fight wars . . . and the way we train our people.' He went on to say that 'the quote [from the President] was to end the reliance on anti-personnel land mines', and he stated that 'most of the items that are at issue, we've done already . . . and we are unilaterally taking those steps right now to do without landmines.'[72] On 19 September 1997, Secretary of Defense Cohen affirmed that 'we have . . . changed military doctrine, planning and tactics to enable us to move away from reliance on those weapons.'[73] The stated willingness of the US Joint Chiefs of Staff and the major field commanders to ban all AP mines if the major producers and suppliers follow the ban is strong evidence that the US military has identified other means to substitute for the use of AP mines.

CONCLUSION

Typically, arms control treaties fail to receive universal endorsement at the time they initially are negotiated. However, when treaties are accepted by a significant number of countries, they establish an increasingly accepted international norm that stigmatizes actions contrary to its provisions, and previously reluctant nations tend to comply. This was the pattern in the case of the Geneva Protocol; in 1943, although the US had not ratified the treaty, President Roosevelt stated that the use of poison gas had been 'outlawed by the general opinion of mankind'.[74] Even the professional military come to accept such prohibitions, despite previous resistance; in 1994, the Chairman of the US Joint Chiefs of Staff expressed support for the Chemical Weapons Convention.[75]

With clear evidence that alternative means are available to substitute for the marginal military utility of AP mines, there is hope that the United States will join other nations in signing the treaty, thereby encouraging other holdouts to join. As noted by US officials, a total ban on anti-personnel mines is essential to solving the humanitarian disaster caused by their use. If the US, as the only remaining superpower, insists on continuing to use AP mines despite its superiority in advanced technology, other nations will be unlikely to comply with the provisions of the treaty. Should the President notify the Secretary of Defense of his intent to sign the Ottawa Convention as soon as it becomes effective, the US military would have more than ample time to complete plans to conduct operations effectively without them, provided funds are made available to remove AP mines from the mixed systems.

To return to the principal issue raised at the outset, is there ample justification of 'military necessity' for the use of AP mines to achieve legitimate military objectives, and, if so, can their employment be considered 'proportional' in view of the resultant humanitarian costs? From the evidence presented here, it is easy to concur with the 1995 testimony before the UK Parliamentary Foreign Affairs Committee by retired General Sir Hugh Beach, Royal Engineer and former Master-General of Ordnance, regarding the military utility of AP mines:

> there is no case known where AP mines as such have influenced a campaign, a battle or even a skirmish in any decisive way. They marginally

increase the usefulness of anti-tank minefields as instruments of delay and marginally raise the human cost of breaching them. . . . these effects (marginal not multiplicatory) while not negligible are nevertheless simply not worth the candle when measured against the scale of human suffering they cause.[76]

AP mines are indiscriminate weapons that cause disproportionate civilian casualties and unnecessary suffering. It is evident that their military utility is convincingly outweighed by the humanitarian costs of their use. There are situations in which AP mines can contribute marginally to the effectiveness of military operations; however, as explained in detail elsewhere in this volume, their use results in civilian casualties and suffering on a massive scale. Stigmatization of the weapon by means of an international prohibition against its use is essential to reduce and eventually stop the carnage. AP mines should be banned, and their use classified as a war crime.

NOTES

1. W. Michael Reisman and Chris T. Antoniu, *The Laws of War: A Comprehensive Collection of Primary Documents on International Laws Governing Armed Conflict* (New York: Vintage, 1994), 36.
2. Ibid., 318.
3. US Army, *The Law of Land Warfare*, Field Manual 27–10 (1956), 19.
4. Ibid., 3.
5. John M. Shalikashvili, letter to Congressman Ronald Dellums, 12 Sept. 1995.
6. Under-Secretary of Defense for Policy, 'Report to the Secretary of Defense of the Status of DoD's Implementation of the U.S. Policy on Anti-Personnel Landmines', May 1997.
7. White House, Office of the Press Secretary, 'Press Briefing by Secretary of State Warren Christopher, Secretary of Defense William Perry, and UN Ambassador Madeleine Albright', 16 May 1996.
8. Joint Chiefs of Staff, letter to Chairman, Senate Armed Services Committee, 10 July 1997.
9. John Ellis van Courtland Moon, 'Chemical Weapons and Deterrence: The World War II Experience', *International Security* (Spring 1984): 7–8, 17; Richard D. Burns, ed., *Encyclopedia of Arms Control and Disarmament*, vol. 2 (New York: Scribner, 1993), 662.
10. Moon, 'Chemical Weapons and Deterrence', 22.
11. White House, Office of the Press Secretary, announcement by President Clinton, 'Land Mine Ban Treaty', 17 Sept. 1997.

12. White House, Office of the Press Secretary, 'Statement by the President', 16 May 1996, 3.
13. Discussion with President Clinton, 30 Apr. 1996.
14. Institute for Defense Analyses (IDA), 'The Military Utility of Landmines: Implications for Arms Control', Document D–1559, June 1994, iv.
15. Ibid., 61, 60.
16. Ibid., 69.
17. Dupuy Institute, 'Military Consequences of Landmine Restrictions', Apr. 1996.
18. Nick Krawciv, 'Banning of Antipersonnel Mines', memo, 2 Jan. 1997.
19. International Committee of the Red Cross (ICRC), *Anti-Personnel Landmines: Friend or Foe? A Study of the Military Use and Effectiveness of Anti-Personnel Mines* (Geneva: ICRC, Mar. 1996; update, 12 May 1997), 37–8.
20. Ibid., 43.
21. Human Rights Watch (HRW), 'In Its Own Words: The US Army and Antipersonnel Mines in the Korean and Vietnam Wars', July 1997, 13.
22. US Army Training and Doctrine Command, 'Force XXI, Land Combat in the 21st Century', 1995, 4, 17–19. See also a paper presented by two Defense Department officials: Harry N. Hambric and William C. Schmidt, 'The Antipersonnel Mine Threat', manuscript, 1996, 1, 13, who argue persuasively that the 'widespread employment of landmines threatens to neutralize US advantages in fire power and mobility' and that these mines 'directly attack the basis of our current doctrine by limiting our tactical maneuverability and slowing our operational tempo.'
23. William M. Arkin, 'Treaty Barriers are within US, not in Korean fields', *San Jose Mercury News*, 20 Sept. 1997, 7P.
24. HRW, 'In Its Own Words', 12.
25. Ibid., 11.
26. 'Letter to President Clinton', *New York Times*, 3 Apr. 1996, A9.
27. ICRC, *Anti-Personnel Landmines*, 7, 8, 72.
28. Ibid., 21, 71.
29. Susan Feeney, 'Deadly Zone', *Dallas Morning News*, 24 Nov. 1997, 1.
30. IDA, 'The Military Utility of Landmines', 6.
31. Patrick L. Hatcher, 'US Position on Land Mines is a Dud', *Los Angeles Times*, 3 Dec. 1997, B7; 'Cohen defends landmines on Korean borders', Reuters news service, 21 Jan. 1998.
32. ICRC, *Anti-Personnel Landmines*, 22–3, 48–51.
33. 'Landmines Block Recovery', Associated Press, Tuzla, Bosnia, Oct. 1997; Steven Komarow, 'Proposal: Pay Bosnians to help clean land mines', *USA Today*, 6 Oct. 1997, 10A.
34. Hambric and Schmidt, 'The Antipersonnel Mine Threat', 1, 10–12.

35. ICRC, *Anti-Personnel Landmines*, 67.
36. Ibid., 55–6, 73.
37. *Jane's Intelligence Review*, 'Legislation and the Landmine', Special Report No. 16, Nov. 1997, 15.
38. ICRC, *Anti-Personnel Landmines*, 57.
39. Carey Goldberg, 'Peace Prize Goes to Landmine Opponents', *New York Times*, 11 Oct. 1997, 1.
40. Dele Oiojede, 'The Danger Zone', *Long Island Newsday*, 12 Dec. 1997, 7.
41. Joint Chiefs of Staff, letter to Chairman, 10 July 1997.
42. White House, Office of the Press Secretary, 'Press Briefing', 16 May 1996.
43. Joe Biden, 'Proposed CWC Killer Condition on Rogue States', memo, 21 Apr. 1997.
44. Madeleine K. Albright, 'Prepared Statement before the Senate Foreign Relations Committee', 8 Apr. 1997.
45. William S. Cohen, 'Ratify the Chemical Weapons Treaty', *Washington Post*, 6 Apr. 1997, 7; Biden, 'Proposed CWC Killer Condition on Rogue States'.
46. Senior Defense Department official, background briefing, 'Landmine Policy', 17 Jan. 1997, 1–4.
47. Susan Feeney, 'Bill Clinton on land mines', *Dallas Morning News*, 23 Nov. 1997, J1.
48. White House, Office of the Press Secretary, 'Statement by the President', 16 May 1996, 2–4; William Clinton, letter to Senator Patrick Leahy, 30 Nov. 1994.
49. Under-Secretary of Defense for Policy, 'Report to the Secretary of Defense', 1, 4.
50. Deputy Secretary of Defense, 'Anti-Personnel Landmine Alternatives', memo, 21 Oct. 1997.
51. Secretary of Defense, letter to Senator Patrick Leahy, 12 Jan. 1998.
52. Feeney, 'Bill Clinton on land mines'.
53. Samuel R. Berger, letter to Senator Patrick Leahy, 15 May 1998; emphasis added.
54. IDA, 'The Military Utility of Landmines', 18–19, 70.
55. Mark Hewish and Rupert Pengelley, 'In search of a successor to the anti-personnel landmine', *Jane's International Defense Review* (Mar. 1998): 36.
56. Hatcher, 'US Position on Land Mines is a Dud'; Michael O'Hanlon, 'Stopping a North Korean Invasion: Why Defending South Korea is Easier than the Pentagon Thinks', unpublished monograph, Brookings Institution, 17 Oct. 1997, 6, 31; Oiojede, 'The Danger Zone'.
57. Demilitarization for Democracy, 'The Landmine Myth in Korea', Aug. 1997, i, ii.
58. Jack Galvin, 'US land mines are not necessary for the defense of South Korea', *Boston Globe*, 15 Sept. 1997, 17.

59. Bill Gertz, 'In Korea's misnamed DMZ', *Washington Times*, 23 Jan. 1998, 5.
60. Oiojede, 'The Danger Zone'.
61. Under-Secretary of Defense for Policy, 'Report to the Secretary of Defense', 4.
62. US Army Training and Doctrine Command, 'Force XXI, Land Combat in the 21st Century', 16–17.
63. Lockheed Martin Vought Systems, 'MLRS Family of Munitions', n.d.; Lockheed Martin Vought Systems, 'Army Tactical Missile System', 1 Apr. 1997; Demilitarization for Democracy, 'Possible Solutions to Remaining US Problems with the Ottawa Treaty', 17 Oct. 1997, 3.
64. Lockheed Martin Vought Systems, 'Army Tactical Missile System'; G.E. Willis, 'Advances Will Expand Role, Power of Field Artillery', *Defense News*, 16–22 Feb. 1998, 12.
65. Lockheed Martin Vought Systems, 'NTACMS', Feb. 1998.
66. 'Letter to President Clinton', *New York Times*, 3 Apr. 1996, A9.
67. For these weapons, see Alliant Techsystems, 'TERM-KE 120mm Tank Munition (AM1007)', 1997; Alliant Techsystems, 'CBU–87B/B, Combined Effects Munition (CEM)', n.d.; Textron Defense Systems, 'Wide Area Munition (WAM)', n.d.; Hewish and Pengelley, 'In search of a successor', 37; Aerojet, 'Sense and Destroy Armor (SADARM)', n.d.; Alliant Techsystems, 'Sense and Destroy Armor (SADARM)', 1997; Willis, 'Advances Will Expand Role, Power of Field Artillery'; 'All Things Considered', National Public Radio, 13 Feb. 1998; Northrup Grumman Corporation, 'BAT Brilliant Antiarmor Submunition', 1997; Robert J. Bunker and T. Lindsay Moore, 'Nonlethal Technology and Fourth Epoch War', Association of the US Army, Feb. 1996, 5; Feeney, 'Deadly Zone'.
68. Assistant Secretary of Defense, Public Affairs, News Release 245–97, May 1997.
69. White House, Office of the Press Secretary, 'Press Briefing', 16 May 1996, 5.
70. Under-Secretary of Defense for Policy, 'Report to the Secretary of Defense', 3, 45.
71. Senior military official, background briefing, 'Landmine Policy', 17 Jan. 1997.
72. Senior Defense Department official, background briefing, 'Landmines', 3 July 1997, 3–4.
73. William S. Cohen, 'Necessary and Right', *Washington Post*, 19 Sept. 1997, A23.
74. Moon, 'Chemical Weapons and Deterrence', 14.
75. John F. Harris, 'Gas Weapons Ban Backed by Pentagon', *Washington Post*, 12 Aug. 1994, A34.
76. ICRC, *Anti-Personnel Landmines*, 44.

PART TWO

THE INTERNATIONAL RESPONSE

CHAPTER 10

THE OTTAWA PROCESS AND THE INTERNATIONAL MOVEMENT TO BAN ANTI-PERSONNEL MINES

Robert J. Lawson, Mark Gwozdecky, Jill Sinclair, and Ralph Lysyshyn

The signature of the Convention to ban anti-personnel mines by 122 countries in Ottawa, 2–4 December 1997, was an extraordinary accomplishment by almost any measure of what is considered to be success within international diplomacy. This was the Ottawa Process, a fast-track diplomatic initiative with the ambitious mandate to deliver what the vast majority of informed observers thought would be impossible—the negotiation and signature of a Convention banning anti-personnel mines in less than 14 months.

There were good reasons to be sceptical about this bold venture, despite the fact that the Ottawa Process was building on years of skilful advocacy work by organizations such as the International Campaign to Ban Landmines and the International Committee of the Red Cross. The idea of a treaty banning AP mines had only begun to enjoy the support of a small number of states when, in his concluding speech to the first Ottawa landmines conference of 3–5 October 1996, Canada's Minister of Foreign Affairs, Lloyd Axworthy, invited the entire international community to join Canada in negotiating a Convention to ban AP mines by the end of 1997. Only 14 months later Axworthy would welcome 2,400 representatives from 122 signatory and 35 observer governments and dozens of international and non-governmental organizations back to Ottawa to sign the ban Convention and to develop a global 'Agenda for Mine Action' to ensure that the Convention would be fully implemented, mines cleared, and mine victims cared for.

Axworthy's bold gamble and the successful global diplomatic campaign it launched were an indication that the end of the Cold War has opened up new opportunities for middle powers to influence the course of international affairs. While the Ottawa Process deployed many of the traditional skills and practices of Canadian multilateralism, it also brought to bear a unique combination of diplomatic strategies and tactics that was well suited to the opportunities offered by the new geopolitical landscape of the post-Cold War era. The following chapter explores the 'nuts and bolts' of the Ottawa Process from the perspective of the Canadian Foreign Affairs officials who were directly involved in the development and implementation of this ground-breaking initiative. Specifically, it examines the strategies, the tactics, the coalition-building, and the information-based diplomatic tools of the Ottawa Process from the first Ottawa landmines conference in October 1996 through to the early developments within what has become known as the Ottawa Process II—the implementation of the AP Mine Ban Convention in all of its aspects.

THE CHALLENGE

While early developments within the Ottawa Process are discussed in some detail in other chapters in this volume, it is worth recalling that its origins can be traced to a profound sense of frustration with the failure of traditional multilateral diplomacy to find a durable solution to the global AP mine crisis. Governments and international and non-governmental organizations supportive of an AP mine ban had emerged from the CCW negotiations determined to find a way to get around the diplomatic obstacles that those opposed to the ban had so easily erected under the cover of the CCW's consensus decision-making mechanisms.[1] Thus, a persistent theme of consultations undertaken by Canadian officials with pro-ban forces on the form and content of the first Ottawa landmines conference was how best to launch pro-ban states towards a ban while preventing more sceptical members of the international community from blocking progress. The challenge would be to find out which states were really supportive of the ban. Of the 41 states identified on the ICBL's May 1996 'Good List' as being supportive of the ban, what was rhetoric and what was reality?

Part of the solution would be to invite states to participate in the Ottawa conference on the basis of 'self-selection'. A draft Final Declaration of the Ottawa conference was widely circulated prior to the conference and states willing publicly to associate themselves with its content were invited to attend as participants. Those who could not support the Declaration would be welcomed as observers.

Additional pressure to maintain the integrity of the pro-ban forces would be provided by the complete integration of the ICBL, the ICRC, and other prominent supporters of the ban such as UNICEF into the Ottawa conference program. Through these organizations and their systematic campaign to educate diplomats previously unaware of the humanitarian crisis caused by these weapons, the moral scrutiny of those most affected by AP mines would be brought to bear on the diplomats charged with shaping and explaining their government's position on the ban issue.

The Ottawa conference of 3–5 October 1996, 'Towards a Global Ban on Anti-Personnel Mines', attracted 74 states, as well as a wide range of international and non-governmental organizations. Described as an 'exercise in unconventional diplomacy', the conference featured ministers and officials sharing plenary and workshop platforms with mine victims, parliamentarians, and representatives from international and non-governmental organizations active in advocacy for the ban, mine clearance, and victim assistance. During the conference itself, infused with the passion and clarity of vision of the ICBL, speaker after speaker, officials and advocates alike, called for action, not just rhetoric. In what was to be prophetic, ICBL co-ordinator Jody Williams repeatedly spoke of the need for governments to step forward and offer 'leadership'. Ultimately, 50 states, including the United States, France, and the United Kingdom, publicly supported the Ottawa Declaration, which included 'a commitment to work together to ensure the earliest possible conclusion of a legally binding international agreement to ban anti-personnel mines'.[2] Participants in the conference were invited to contribute to an 'Agenda for Action on AP Mines', which listed a number of activities to be undertaken by conference participants to build political will for an AP mine ban.

However, the real news of the conference was made during Foreign Minister Axworthy's dramatic final speech to the conference when he established a deadline for action on the ban—inviting states to work with Canada in negotiating a treaty banning AP mines to be signed in Canada by December 1997. Setting a deadline for action was one thing. Getting the job done was quite another. Thus, in the wake of the Ottawa conference the first task for Canadian officials was to complete a detailed assessment of the new political terrain surrounding the AP mine issue—terrain that had been radically altered by the Ottawa conference.

A COMPREHENSIVE BAN OR A STEP-BY-STEP APPROACH?

Axworthy's challenge had received the immediate endorsement of the UN Secretary-General, the ICRC, and the ICBL in the form of a standing ovation—an honour not often bestowed on foreign ministers by members of the NGO community. However, there was no shortage of critics within the diplomatic corps who questioned both the wisdom of rapid movement towards a ban and the unilateralist nature of Canada's gambit. Even many of those who supported an AP mine ban were sceptical, arguing that it would be simply impossible to negotiate a Convention banning a weapon in widespread use by dozens of states in less than 14 months.

While Canadian officials fully expected criticism from several quarters, they were, in some respects, more concerned about the practical concerns raised by sceptical potential allies. The Declaration and Agenda for Action on AP Mines that emerged from the Ottawa conference indicated a relatively high degree of political support for the concept of the ban in almost every region of the world. Canada's growing partnership with the ICBL and the ICRC held out the possibility of an even broader mobilization of public will for a ban Convention. Support for the ban had even begun to penetrate popular culture. The ban issue was becoming a hot issue for popular singers and media pundits. DC comics had enlisted Superman as well as Batman in the fight against AP mines.[3] However, what was missing was a vision of how all of this political will could best be focused on the complex task of preparing for and bringing to conclusion a multilateral negotiation within what was obviously a very tight time frame.

The development of such a vision would require ban supporters to consider a number of difficult and interrelated substantive and tactical questions. What kind of treaty instrument would be the best fit for the technical and political dimensions of the AP mine ban issue? A fully integrated and comprehensive ban convention would respond to the demands of the NGO/IO community and might make more sense from a technical perspective. However, it would also force states to make a single difficult choice— either you supported a total ban on the production, stockpiling, transfer, and use of AP mines or you did not. How many states would be willing to make such a choice, and would this group include those states that would be essential to the operational success of the ban? Of course, this question prompted what would become a central feature of the early debate over the Ottawa Process. How would one define success for the ban movement? Did it really need to be fully global in the first instance? Should the process address both sides of the supply and demand equation? Or would it be sufficient to capture a critical mass of user states in an effort to 'dry up' the demand for AP mines?

For those most concerned about the depth and breadth of participation in the Ottawa Process, there was also the option of developing a ban convention with four separate protocols for bans on the production, stockpiling, use, and transfer of AP mines, each of which, in theory, could be signed and implemented independently of the others. Recognizing that some states would only be willing to move towards a total ban over a longer time frame, the four-protocol model would provide a more inclusive framework for diplomatic action within the Ottawa Process. In particular, this approach had the potential to engage large states such as the US and Russia in the Ottawa Process—possibly bringing along a large number of smaller states on their diplomatic coat-tails. However, opinion within the US remained split on how to react to the Ottawa Process. The four-protocol model failed to attract the support of the US, which would turn to the Conference on Disarmament as the alternative to the Ottawa Process.

There were also important tactical considerations surrounding the four-protocol model. Providing states with the flexibility to pick and choose which of the ban elements they would adopt and when they would adopt them would effectively remove most of the political pressure for states to move quickly towards a total ban. States could potentially argue that they supported the idea of a total ban while delaying concrete action on its core elements (a halt to new use and destruction of stockpiles) for years if not decades. In short, the four-protocol model was a poor match for what had become the political mainspring of the Ottawa Process—the mobilization of public opinion and moral authority behind the very clear and easily communicated message—ban AP mines now.

Beyond the question of how the structure of the ban Convention might affect participation, there was the more fundamental question of what the nature of the AP mine issue itself suggested about the range of state participation that would be required to achieve success within the Ottawa Process. How one initially defined the AP mine problem was obviously closely linked to the search for corresponding solutions. In the wake of the CCW process and the Ottawa conference it was clear that the debate about the nature of the AP mine crisis had crystallized around one central question—how did states assess the humanitarian costs associated with AP mines relative to their actual military utility? How states answered this question was usually an accurate reflection of where they stood with respect to the Ottawa Process.

Initially at least, prominent critics of the Ottawa Process included all five of the permanent members of the United Nations Security Council. With relatively minor variations, each of these states argued that any response to the AP mine crisis would be largely ineffective if it did not address the security implications of a global ban. This approach would effectively place a completely different set of concerns and actors at the centre of the ban process. Traditional producers of AP mines and those states with significant security interests would need to be engaged as a matter of priority. Of course, genuine engagement with this particular set of states also presented a new range of quite daunting diplomatic challenges. What pressure could the Ottawa Process coalition bring to bear on states, such as the United States, Russia, and China, that for decades had collectively enjoyed a virtual veto capability over substantive progress within the Cold War multilateral arms control and disarmament agenda? Russia and China rejected the very notion of an AP mine ban. While the United States, whose President Clinton had called for an AP mine ban in 1996, the

United Kingdom, and France were, in principle, supportive of a ban, they were all openly critical of the Canadian initiative, arguing that this 'coalition of the angels' would have little practical effect on the global AP mine crisis. Informed observers noted that these states shared more than a distaste for the Ottawa Process and its strategic alliance with the NGO community. Each of these states continued to reserve the right to use AP mines. Each also favoured the negotiation of an AP mine ban treaty within the Conference on Disarmament in Geneva—a consensus-based forum that effectively gives each of them a veto over the pace of progress and the eventual content of a treaty.

Within this debate supporters of the AP mine ban had clearly arrived at the conclusion that the global AP mine crisis was fundamentally a humanitarian issue with somewhat limited implications for national security. By late 1996 a growing number of expert studies and individual interventions into this debate suggested that expert opinion was, at a minimum, quite divided on the question of the military utility of AP mines. An ICRC study undertaken by retired military officers concluded that there was little evidence to suggest that AP mines were as effective as military commanders often assumed. For states such as Canada, which were both active participants in international peacekeeping operations as well as significant contributors to humanitarian mine action, the costs associated with AP mine use could be clearly understood in both humanitarian and security terms. The global social and economic costs associated with mine use and subsequent mine clearance and victim assistance were estimated to be in the tens of billions of dollars. Peacekeeping and peace-building were clearly more difficult, costly, and dangerous within mine-affected countries.

Defined as primarily a humanitarian problem, it was decided that the central focus of the Ottawa Process would be the construction of a global coalition with the capacity to engage mine-affected states in the march towards a ban. The most direct and effective way to address the humanitarian crisis caused by the widespread use of AP mines would be to get those states that had used mines against civilian populations to halt any further use, thereby significantly enhancing the relative effectiveness of mine clearance and victim assistance efforts. States such as Cambodia, Angola, Mozambique, and Afghanistan, which were producing the majority of the world mine victims, should be among the first to sign the Convention. Defining the AP mine problem in primarily humanitarian terms also suggested that, as the Axworthy challenge implied, a profound sense of urgency needed to be injected into efforts to mobilize the international community in the fight against AP mines. The history of disarmament negotiations since World War II suggested that placing an excessive emphasis on engaging large mine-producing states such as Russia, China, and the United States would most certainly add years to the process. Moreover, considerable evidence suggested that efforts to establish a new international norm against the trade in landmines had, at least temporarily, yielded a radical reduction if not a total halt in the international flows of AP mines.

Thus, in the wake of a fairly extensive review of the options for action before them, Canadian officials concluded that the strategic thrust of the Ottawa Process would be directed towards the development of a comprehensive ban convention that, initially at least, would be targeted to engage directly the 'demand side' of the AP mine equation—mine-affected states and regions.

THE OTTAWA PROCESS CORE GROUP

Having worked through some of the theoretical questions associated with the drive towards a ban, by late fall of 1996 Canadian officials began to focus on a range of more practical concerns. First and foremost was the question of process management. Getting dozens of countries from all regions of the world to a single negotiating table to develop a ban convention in less than a year would require an almost unprecedented degree of diplomatic choreography. Canada clearly needed help, and looked for assistance through what would become known as the Ottawa Process core group.

The origins of the core group could be traced to the small group of countries that agreed to meet with the ICBL and ICRC to muse about a ban on the margins of the CCW process in early 1996—Austria, Belgium, Canada, Denmark, Ireland, Mexico, Norway, and Switzerland. Canada's traditional multilateral reflexes and experience had begun to kick in shortly after it decided to host the first Ottawa meeting. If the conference and the effort to secure a global ban were to have a chance of succeeding, Canada would need to work with a broad coalition of countries representative of the various international, regional, and political groupings. It was not, of course, until Foreign Minister Axworthy's dramatic announcement at the end of the October meeting that the goal became clearer, the need for a common front more urgent, and the potential membership of such a group more obvious.

A group of countries, including several of those that would later become members of the Ottawa Process, had been consulted in the period leading up to the first Ottawa conference. It was hoped that traditional arms control and disarmament supporters such as Australia might be part of the inner circle of countries supporting the ban. But the process of drafting the October 1996 Ottawa Declaration, as well as the Ottawa conference itself soon revealed a divergence in views between those ready to move quickly and decisively to a ban and those whose political statements were still somewhat ahead of their actual policy positions.

The first formal meeting of the Ottawa Process core group took place in February 1997, bringing together Canada, Norway, Belgium, Austria, Switzerland, Ireland, Mexico, South Africa, the Philippines, Germany, and the Netherlands. The group recognized that global reach would be key to the achievement of a ban, and thus the core group members would have a role to play in bringing along their own subregional and regional communities, from the OAS and OAU to the EU, the ARF, and the G–8. South Africa, with its regional leadership role and firsthand knowledge of the most intensely mine-affected region of the world, was a key member of the core group. Mexico, with its long-standing diplomatic traditions and early advocacy of a total ban, provided a key partner with whom Canada would work, through the OAS and bilaterally, to lobby in the Americas. The Philippines would become the core group's eyes and ears in Asia. Austria, Belgium, the Netherlands, and Ireland played a key role within the European Union, where France and the UK, until changes in government, were half-hearted supporters of the ban and firm advocates of the CD. Both Ireland and the Netherlands would assume the presidency of the European Union over the course of the Ottawa Process.

Austria, one of the earliest supports of the ban, had actually arrived at the Ottawa conference with a rough draft of an AP mine ban convention and would, before the end of the meeting, agree to be the 'pen' for a potential ban convention. Austria would also host an international experts meeting in early February to begin broad consultations on the draft convention. Belgium, the first state officially to ban AP mines, was named in the Ottawa Declaration as the host of the next global-level meeting on AP mines, to be held in June 1997. Switzerland would host several meetings of the core group in Geneva. Norway would provide a great deal of leadership within the core group and would ultimately host the formal negotiation of the ban Convention in the fall of 1997. For its part, Canada would work to provide strategic guidance for the core group—not as a taskmaster, but more as member of a well-integrated multinational team.

The core group worked with an extraordinary sense of common purpose, which reflected more than broadly synchronized national foreign policy objectives. It was a group of countries who drew strength from and were empowered by the feeling that they could—even as small and middle powers—effect change and make a difference. Over the course of about a dozen formal meetings, numerous informal discussions, and hundreds of hours of telephone consultations, a framework for action was developed and rapidly implemented. This intensive sharing of information, concerns, wild ideas, and careful co-ordination enabled the Ottawa Process to move forward decisively. The personal rapport and sense of common purpose that developed between the individuals who represented their countries in the core group were clearly key to its success. Over time the core group did broaden to include new members, particularly prior to the Brussels meeting when a number of new countries were invited: Brazil, Slovenia, France, the UK, Zimbabwe, Malaysia.

While the existence of a cohesive core group of middle and small powers would ultimately become one of the defining features of the Ottawa Process, it is worth recalling that the cohesion of the group developed over time—forged through the efforts to prepare for significant events or overcome specific diplomatic obstacles. Each of the key diplomatic meetings within the Ottawa Process was preceded by intensive telephone and fax diplomacy through which common policy objectives were established and tactical approaches developed. Proposals developed in Ottawa, Vienna, Oslo, Brussels, and Pretoria were quickly shared with capitals throughout the world through joint or reinforcing diplomatic *démarches* using common speaking notes. Embassies were also instructed to co-ordinate their actions with local NGOs and delegates of the ICRC. Diplomatic correspondence, usually reserved exclusively for national use, was often shared to provide insights into the challenges facing core partners within regional contexts. Bilateral ministerial meetings consolidated, at the highest political level, the intense working relationship at the bureaucratic level.

In Ottawa, Canada maintained close relations with core group embassies, providing regular briefings to ensure that information flowed quickly and openly among all partners so that all members of the group were working on the basis of common and complete information. The core group also worked co-operatively in a range of multilateral settings, in particular, in Geneva at the Conference on Disarmament and in New York at the United Nations. There, representatives of the core group states drafted joint resolutions, shared intervention notes, and worked together on the tactical management of resolutions and initiatives.

WORKING THE PROCESS

By February of 1997 the transition from 'ad-hocery' to a coherent and widely understood process had begun to transform Foreign Minister Axworthy's political challenge into a diplomatic 'fast track' leading to a legally binding international Convention. The diplomatic challenges of what had become known as the Ottawa Process were at least as enormous as the political risks. Little more than a dozen truly committed states would need to bring dozens of others into a process while avoiding the diplomatic traps that had stalled progress on a range of disarmament and humanitarian issues over the years, for example, the emergence of political cleavages along North-South and/or East-West lines. All regions of the world would need to feel they were helping to shape the destiny of the Ottawa Process rather than simply doing the bidding of others. The process and the resulting negotiations would need technical credibility through the early development of a clear understanding of the parameters of the ban Convention. The draft convention itself would also need to have political integrity— faithfully reflecting the core values of the coalition charged with promoting it.

There was also the critical question of political will and momentum. With little time to waste, the Ottawa Process would need to communicate to states that the ban was inevitable. The international community was moving decisively towards the ban and states could not afford to wait before taking action. The most frequently used metaphor was that of a train leaving the station. Those who were first on board would be welcome to help steer the train. Those who hesitated for too long may be forced to take the train to a destination chosen by others.

The track ahead was carefully laid—strategic political opportunities were chosen where countries could be challenged to demonstrate their commitment to the ban. For example, the fall General Assembly of the United Nations provided a perfectly timed opportunity to build on the political/diplomatic momentum for the ban developed through the substance of the Ottawa Declaration. A total of 50 states had supported the Ottawa Declaration and its call for the 'earliest possible conclusion of a legally binding international agreement to ban anti-personnel mines'. Canada worked closely with a number of states, including a very effective United States team led by Ambassador Karl F. Inderfurth, to seek the best possible language in the 1996 UN landmines resolution. A total of 156 states would vote on 10 December 1996 to support (none would oppose and 10 abstained) UN General Assembly Resolution 51/45S, which called on states 'to pursue vigorously an effective, legally binding international agreement to ban the use, stockpiling, production, and transfers of anti-personnel landmines with a view to completing the negotiation as soon as possible.'[4] The UN landmine resolution did not explicitly mention the Ottawa Process as the means through which to achieve the 'soon as possible' objective of this call for action, nor was the rival forum (the

Conference on Disarmament) mentioned. Moreover, the UN resolution represented an entirely new quality of multilateral legitimacy and profile for the ban and also provide a relatively clear mandate to move 'vigorously' on the diplomatic front. Supporters of the Ottawa Process could point to the UN resolution and note that December 1997 was a 'vigorous' deadline.

Ultimately, the Ottawa Process was really two processes proceeding on parallel tracks—each of which would provide unique contributions to the success of the overall process. Track one would include the concrete steps leading towards a formal diplomatic conference to negotiate the ban Convention. Track two would be charged with the development of political will and momentum through a series of multilateral initiatives and an extensive series of regional conferences.

The first stop on track one would be in Vienna in mid-February. Extensive discussions between Austria and Canada in early 1997 had yielded a draft plan for kick-starting the diplomatic process. Austria would host an experts meeting in Vienna on 12–14 February to review a draft Austrian ban convention text and discuss the elements of a possible AP mine ban convention. It would be the first test case, post-October 1996, to see just how many countries were truly committed to the ban concept. Research conducted by DFAIT officials on the AP mine policies of the world's governments indicated that, given the right conditions, potential support for the AP mine ban treaty could peak at somewhere over 100 states. In theory, with at least 156 supporters of the UN landmines resolution, this level of support was possible. In practice, however, few were willing to commit to a deadline and a ban convention that was not even on the table.

Canada worked closely with the Austrians to plan the formal invitations and prepare a concept paper to help launch the discussions. Talking points were developed for joint Austrian/Canadian *démarches* throughout the world to maximize participation in the meeting. To ensure participation from all regions, Canada, with generous financial support from other core group members, co-ordinated the provision of travel support for delegations from the developing world, particularly those states severely affected by mines. To the surprise and delight of Ottawa Process supporters, a total of 111 states attended the meeting to 'start the speedy elaboration of a draft text that can serve as a basis for negotiations'.[5] While core group members worked to focus the meeting on the draft Austrian text, delegation after delegation provided their views on the Ottawa Process and its rival forum, the CD, revealing a greater level of support for the Ottawa Process than expected.

In the wake of the Vienna meeting Canada developed a formal paper to map out the steps towards formal negotiations, which it circulated at a core group meeting in Vienna in early March. Of course, the first question was where and when would the negotiations take place? Canada used the Vienna meeting to informally approach Norway, which during the October conference had indicated an interest in hosting a meeting on AP mines. Canada took the Norwegians up on this offer, proposing that Norway consider acting as the venue for the diplomatic negotiations. Norway, with its firm commitment to the ban and, of course, all the positive connotations of the Oslo Middle East Accord, seemed an ideal place. Norway agreed. The remaining questions would be when and for how long. The generosity and rapidity with which Norway responded to the enormous diplomatic and organizational challenge of hosting an international negotiation were key to the ultimate success of the Ottawa Process.

Once the venue for the negotiations had been determined through consultations with Norway and then through approval of the core group, there remained a number of difficult and important questions related to diplomatic procedures. Would the negotiations work by consensus, potentially replicating the negative dynamics of the CCW process? Or would voting procedures be developed? How long would it take to produce a text? Could it be done in a single or multiple sessions? Some believed it could, and should, be done in days—basically adopting the existing Austrian text. Others, including Canada, believed that for the credibility of the process and technical integrity of the resulting Convention, several weeks would be needed. Would the conference work in all of the UN languages? Who would chair the conference and how would he or she be selected? Each of these issues had to be thought through and a course of action carefully choreographed.

As a stand-alone forum, there would be tremendous scope for flexibility in Oslo. But as a process accused by critics of illegitimacy because of its birth outside normal diplomatic channels, the establishment of a recognizable diplomatic conference, grounded in precedence and traditional diplomatic practice, would be crucial to building the confidence of certain key countries who were supportive, but still sceptical and suspicious. The decision to approach the skilled and internationally respected South African diplomat and senior ANC official, Ambassador Jacob Selebi, to chair the negotiations was first broached through the core group. Once Ambassador Selebi had agreed to chair, much of the preparation was done with core group partners, particularly Ambassador Selebi's own team, to ensure that he was given a working, functioning negotiation to drive forward. The development and circulation of draft rules of procedure for the Oslo negotiations were undertaken by Norway in co-operation with the core group.

GLOBAL OBJECTIVES, REGIONAL STRATEGIES

In parallel with efforts to solidify the diplomatic negotiation track of the Ottawa Process, Canadian officials were also engaged in a series of consultations with coalition partners on how best to convert a general level of political will for a ban into concrete support for the Ottawa Process from key governments and regions. What was clearly needed and was soon developed by Canada was a comprehensive 'critical path' that would break down the blizzard of ICBL, ICRC, and government-sponsored events into a coherent 'track two' for the Ottawa Process—bilateral and multilateral opportunities for Canada and its coalition partners to highlight the AP mine problem and emphasize the Ottawa Process solution. While the Ottawa Process would remain global in its scope and objectives, it was clear that support for the process could most easily be generated through an integrated series of regional strategies. This approach would also facilitate the engagement of mine-affected regions in the march towards the ban. In addition to getting states that had already deployed mines to halt any further deployments, the active participation of southern mine-affected states would also be critical to the coalition's efforts to prevent the emergence of a North-South split on key issues related to the AP mine ban.

The ICBL and the ICRC had already planned major conferences in Africa for February and April. Canadian consultations with the Organization for African Unity (OAU) in November yielded an agreement that it should work with Canada, South Africa, and the ICBL and the ICRC to host an Africa-wide landmines conference in Kempton Park, South Africa, in late May 1997—just a few weeks before the OAU summit scheduled for Harare in early June. As with other regions, Canadian officials worked to take advantage of the sequence of government/NGO-sponsored African meetings to increase progressively the familiarity with and support for the Ottawa Process. The draft Austrian ban convention was circulated at each of the three meetings prior to Harare. The final declarations of the Maputo and Kempton Park conferences would express support for the Ottawa Process and urge participants to become active in the other multilateral meetings leading to the negotiations in Oslo and the signature of the ban treaty in Ottawa.

An early and critical victory for the African strategy was South Africa's move to a unilateral ban on AP mines, announced on the eve of the ICBL's '4th International NGO Conference on Landmines', held in Maputo,

Mozambique, 25–8 February 1997. Mozambique announced its support for the ban during the conference itself. Attended by 450 NGO representatives from 60 countries, the Maputo conference was a critical juncture in the rapidly evolving partnership between Canada and the NGO community. The final declaration of the Maputo conference would commit the full support of the ICBL and its over 800 member organizations to the Ottawa Process. It would also reinforce the campaign's African strategy, calling on the South African Development Community (SADC) to 'take all measures to make the region a mine free zone' and urged the member states of the OAU to use the upcoming 'OAU Landmine Conference in South Africa in May and the OAU Summit in Zimbabwe in June to implement the OAU resolutions urging a continent-wide ban on anti-personnel landmines.'[6] With the active support and engagement of South Africa and the OAU, the Africa strategy was clearly on track. By the end of the Kempton Park conference on 19–22 May 1997, a total of 43 of the 53 members of the OAU would pledge their active support for the Ottawa Process. Regional strategies for the Americas, Europe, and Asia had also begun to yield results. Building on previous resolutions by the Organization of American States, the foreign ministers of Central America and the Caribbean Community and Common Market (including several mine-affected states) declared their full support for the Ottawa Process, the first regional grouping to do so. Regional and subregional government/NGO conferences to build political will for the Ottawa Process were organized for Stockholm, Sydney, Manila, Ashgabat, and New Delhi.

In total, some 10 global, regional, and subregional multilateral meetings would be held in the 11 months prior to the Oslo negotiations—each designed to 'pressure' national decision-making on the AP mine ban issue.[7] These meetings would also attempt to combine state-led diplomatic activism with NGO-led advocacy through the media and a growing number of prominent supporters of the ban movement, including Princess Diana, Archbishop Desmond Tutu, Gracia Machel, Jimmy Carter, and the new Secretary-General of the UN, Kofi Annan. Canadian diplomats, who normally take pride in their skills at 'quiet' diplomacy, provided dozens of backgrounder and on-record briefings to key journalists in the United States, the United Kingdom, France, Australia, Malaysia, the Philippines, and Japan. An AP mine ban newsletter was developed and widely circulated to all Canadian diplomatic missions and multilateral meetings. Editions of the newsletter were loaded onto a Web site linked to dozens of pro-ban sites maintained by NGOs. An Ottawa Process advocacy video was produced and hundreds of copies circulated in multiple-language formats.

Traditional diplomatic practice—private, regular, and repeated *démarches* on political leaders and officials around the world—would play an equally important role, particularly in regions such as Asia and Latin America where NGOs were either non-existent or carried little sway with governments. Canadian diplomats and political leaders, including Prime Minister Chrétien, travelled the globe conducting a 'full-court press'— sometimes working jointly with their equivalents from the core group—in pressing countries to alter their AP mine policies and to join the Ottawa Process. Similar pitches were made to delegations visiting Canada, as well as in a series of letters and carefully timed phone calls from the Prime Minister and Foreign Minister to their counterparts around the world. Countries, engaged by the attention accorded to them in letters and visiting delegations, were persuaded to take a first—and then a second and third—look at the issue, and to challenge the opposition to the mine ban offered by military establishments. This unique synergy that developed among the political, bureaucratic, and civil society supporters of the ban helped to develop the all-important momentum behind the Ottawa Process.

MOMENTUM, MOMENTUM, MOMENTUM

By the end of May, the Ottawa Process had reached a turning point. The second meeting on the draft text hosted by Germany in Bonn on 24–5 April 1997 was focused on its compliance provisions and had attracted a remarkable 120 states. Between early 1997 and late May, explicit support for the process had grown from approximately 30 countries to more than 70. A majority of African states were largely on board, thanks to the mobilization efforts flowing from the conferences in Maputo and Harare and culminating in the Africa-wide gathering in Kempton Park. In quick succession, new Labour governments in the UK and France, responding to NGO communities that had made landmines an election issue, reversed the policies of their predecessors and pledged support for the Ottawa Process. While these decisions suggested that the vast majority of European countries would eventually lend support to the movement, they also had wide-ranging influence worldwide. They also effectively undercut efforts, under way since January, to convince countries that what was needed was to translate the energy of the Ottawa Process into a negotiation in the Conference on Disarmament. The risk of two negotiating tracks (the Ottawa track and the CD), each competing with and draining the political will from the other, and generally confusing the issue, had been averted.

Suddenly, the Ottawa Process was more than a highly risky venture by a rump of small and middle-sized states. The all-important political momentum that coalition partners had hoped for was clearly developing. The train was leaving the station and countries were now forced to take the process seriously and to gauge carefully their participation in the next major milestone in the process—the Brussels conference scheduled for 24–7 June.

In the meantime, many countries awaited the US, which had promised to review its AP mine policies beginning in July. Foreign Minister Axworthy had sought and obtained an agreement from US Secretary of State Madeleine Albright that Canadian and US officials begin a substantive dialogue on the landmines issue, and the first of these discussions took place in Ottawa in mid-June. Canadian officials hoped that this dialogue could facilitate the required US inter-agency agreement that would allow for US participation in the Oslo negotiations. If the US could not be convinced to go to Oslo and participate in the shaping of the Convention, there was little hope of convincing the US to sign the treaty afterwards. Canadian officials would repeatedly offer to consult, discuss, and respond to any queries out of Washington in the hope of bolstering those within the Clinton administration sympathetic to the process.

The diplomatic centrepiece of the Brussels conference would be a political declaration that 'locked in' the commitment of states to the final stages of the Ottawa Process—the Oslo negotiations and the signature of the ban treaty in Ottawa in December. Featuring extensive exchanges of views on the draft Austrian text, which would now be forwarded to the Oslo as the basis for negotiations, the Brussels conference attracted a total of 155 states, 97 of which would sign the Brussels Declaration. Still, many doubted how many of these states would be prepared to sign a legally binding international convention as opposed to a political declaration. However, Brussels was clearly a watershed moment in the Ottawa Process. A commitment, even a political one, by the 97 countries that signed the Brussels Declaration was impossible to ignore. For the many countries inclined to follow an American lead on the issue, it was no longer possible to wait for a decision out of Washington. The deadline of a negotiation in Oslo was now too close and many more countries would soon decide that they had to be in Oslo, regardless of whether the US would be there.

THE OSLO NEGOTIATIONS

The Brussels Declaration would also become the price of admission for the Oslo negotiations. Once again, states would be invited to 'self-select' their participation in the next stage of the Ottawa Process, in this case on the basis of a Declaration that made it quite clear that the objective of the Oslo negotiations was to negotiate a 'comprehensive ban on the use, stockpiling, production and transfer of anti-personnel mines'.[8] The Brussels conference also provided an opportunity for Canada, Norway, and their core group allies to begin the delicate process of putting in place the diplomatic framework for the actual negotiations due to take place the first three weeks of September. Ambassador Jacob Selebi's name was circulated as the candidate of choice for the presidency of the Oslo conference. Draft rules of procedure for the conference were circulated, based on standard UN General Assembly rules of procedures, which would enable decisions to be taken by two-thirds vote if consensus could not be achieved. It had become difficult for sceptics to challenge the Ottawa Process. Explicit opposition to rapid action on the ban issue had almost become 'politically incorrect' at a time when there was no credible alternative to the formal diplomatic process that would shortly begin in Oslo.

The ICBL and the ICRC used the Brussels conference to launch an aggressive communications campaign focused on the media and state representatives preparing for the Oslo negotiations. Fearing that the rapid growth in the number of Ottawa Process participants would erode the core consensus on the need for a clear and unambiguous ban treaty, the core message of the ban campaign in the final months before Oslo would emphasize the need for a treaty with 'no exceptions, no reservations, and no loopholes'.

There was much to be done between Brussels and Oslo. Core group members remained in constant contact throughout the summer as the final preparations for Oslo proceeded. Taking advantage of the seasonal differences between the North and South, a final push was launched in Asia to engage regional leaders such as Japan, Malaysia (which had joined the core group in Brussels), Australia, and Indonesia. In August, when Europe is usually closed for business, core group partners met in Vienna, along with their legal experts, to begin to fine-tune the draft Austrian text that would be presented in Oslo as the basis for negotiations. While the Brussels Declaration clearly highlighted the Austrian text as the most legitimate basis for negotiations, it was also recognized that the entire text would, in theory, be open for negotiation. Thus, it would be important to take the ground, firmly and early, with the Austrian text to discourage others from presenting competing texts—a tactic with the potential to undermine the core group's Oslo game plan. A great deal of time in Vienna was devoted to thinking through such scenarios. A general negotiating strategy was developed, with bottom lines and alternative language on issues from definitions to entry-into-force provisions to compliance mechanisms. The positions of other players were also discussed and fall-back positions planned. Following the Vienna discussions, the core group was scheduled to meet in Geneva to have a final policy discussion of approach and tactics for the negotiations.

It was during the Geneva meeting that the United States asked to meet with the core group to explain its concerns and bottom lines for the negotiations. By then the United States had announced its intention to attend the Oslo negotiations as a full participant. In a widely circulated letter to other governments, US Secretary of State Albright made it clear that the United States would be seeking at least five substantive changes to the draft Austrian text. Specifically, US negotiators would be instructed to seek an exception for potential US AP mine use in Korea, a fundamental change in the definition of an AP mine, a delay in the entry-into-force (EIF) of the Convention, a strengthened verification regime, and a 'supreme national interest clause' that would enable parties to the Convention to withdraw rapidly from their obligations when their 'national interests' were threatened.[9] Media reaction to the US announcement that it would join the Ottawa Process was generally characterized by cautious optimism, with *The Economist* noting that the 'new convert' should be welcomed as long as 'its real intent is not to sabotage'.[10]

On 1 September, less than a year after Foreign Minister Axworthy's challenge, 87 full participants and 33 observer states gathered in Oslo to begin the negotiation of an AP mine ban convention. The drama surrounding the beginning of the Oslo negotiations was heightened by the tragic death of one of the ban campaign's most prominent supporters, Princess Diana, two days before the opening ceremony of the conference.

Members of the core group were relieved as the conference formally elected Ambassador Selebi to the conference presidency and adopted the agenda and rules of procedure without difficulty. With the formal diplomatic framework for the negotiations finally in place, including, if necessary, the option of voting to break deadlocks, Ambassador Selebi moved quickly to establish what would prove to become a diplomatically bold and administratively efficient work-plan for the conference. Areas of difficulty would be clearly identified within the first 24–48 hours of the conference and divided for further consultation and problem-solving drafting between the South African team and five 'Friends of the Chair'—Austria, Brazil, Canada, Ireland, and Mexico.[11]

The central fault-line of the Oslo conference quickly formed along the three most problematic US proposals—the Korean exception, the deferral of EIF, and changes in the AP mine definition—the core of what US negotiators repeatedly stated was an 'all-or-nothing package'. The potential for a compromise with the US appeared to be greatest on the issue of a deferral period, which could, in theory, provide time for US forces in Korea and elsewhere to make the transition to an AP mine-free doctrine and force structure. Here the United States enjoyed the public support of Australia, Japan, Poland, and Ecuador, as well as the private sympathy of an unknown but probably quite large number of states that saw the political and military-security value of having the last superpower sign the Convention. Precedent had been established by the 1997 CCW Landmines Protocol, which provided signatories with the option to defer compliance with key provisions for up to nine years. However, the deferral compromise had at least two important strikes against it. First, politically speaking, a Korea-specific deferral period that would provide the United States with special treatment was a non-starter. Yet, a more broadly defined deferral article could potentially undermine the practical effect and political credibility of the entire ban. Second, but perhaps more importantly, the exploration of potential compromises remained virtually impossible as long as US negotiators were unable to 'break their package'—allowing the deferral issue to be discussed in isolation from the vastly more problematic issue of the definition of an AP mine.[12]

The US delegation was quite transparent about its desire for a fundamental change in the definition of an AP mine, noting that the current definition would prevent the future use of US 'mixed-mine' systems such as 'Gator' and 'Volcano', which were pre-packaged and designed to deploy a mix of 'short-lived' AP mines and anti-tank mines.[13] US negotiators argued that AP mines within these mixed systems should be defined as 'anti-handling devices' since they performed essentially the same function as the anti-handling devices that other states attached to their anti-tank mines to protect them against enemy mine-clearance personnel. However, the US systems were not actually attached to the anti-tank mines they were designed to protect and thus would function exactly like AP mines, irrespective of their proximity to the anti-tank mines. Moreover, a ban treaty that legalized the use of AP mines to protect anti-tank mines would be legalizing a practice widely cited by military authorities around the world as the real reason for deploying AP mines in the first place. The short-lived, high-tech nature of the US mines did not alter the fact that they could not discriminate between civilian or soldier in the first place. Moreover, one prominent US ban supporter, Senator Patrick Leahy, noted, 'an effective international agreement that is based on stigmatizing a weapon cannot have different standards for different nations.'[14] A number of scheduled and 'special' consultations called at the request of the US and devoted to the definition problem failed to reveal any real support for the US position.

By the second week in Oslo it appeared that the inability of the US team to break open their package reflected a policy stalemate in Washington. Significant proportions of the American media and public, along with a bipartisan Senate and House of Representatives group led by Senator Leahy, were calling on President Clinton to 'seize the moment' to provide 'moral leadership' in the drive for the AP mine ban.[15] At the same time, Clinton received an unprecedented 'open letter' from 10 retired four-star American generals urging Clinton to reject the emerging ban treaty. Senator Jesse Helms (R-NC) also weighed in with a letter, calling on Clinton to recall the US delegation if the other delegations failed to 'recognize that the US negotiation position in Oslo is our *bottom line . . . not a starting point* for debate.' Helms would also argue that the negotiations had become a 'soap box forum for anti-American rhetoric', while the press release attached to the 'open letter' letter to Clinton complained about the 'contempt being expressed by those running the Oslo negotiations for the United States'.[16] In the absence of any significant movement by the US during the second week, negotiators moved on to resolve a number of other outstanding issues. After a three-day weekend the US package remained intact. Finally, despite a 24-hour delay in movement towards closure of the conference to provide Washington time to reconsider its bottom line, the package remained unbroken and the US end-game was never reached.

Notwithstanding the views of Jesse Helms and a limited number of retired generals, there was little that was anti-American or contemptuous about the diplomatic or NGO activities within and surrounding the Oslo negotiations. On the diplomatic side the US was late to take the Ottawa Process seriously and was simply unable to divert or reverse the political momentum of a multilateral 'ban-wagon' effect that had been gaining strength for several months. Further, the US inability to break its 'package' ensured that no accommodation could be found for its position, notwithstanding the determined efforts of many US friends, allies, and the chair of the negotiations. Highly mobilized mine-affected regions such as Africa and Central America had, given their relative numbers, become powerful advocates for a clear and unambiguous ban convention. For their part, the ICBL and the ICRC had waged a sophisticated communications campaign that delivered a blizzard of pro-ban newsletters, leaflets, posters, fact sheets, press releases, and press conferences, as well phone, radio, and television interviews to a highly attentive and well-informed international media. Foreign Minister Axworthy had argued in his address to the Oslo NGO forum that the government-civil society coalition behind the Ottawa

Process had indeed developed the 'power to change the dynamics and direction of the international agenda' on the AP mine issue.[17] On 17 September, the US team announced that it had no further proposals to make to the Oslo conference. The following day Ambassador Selebi brought formal closure to the Oslo conference against the backdrop of a prolonged standing ovation. A long and difficult journey begun by a few visionary NGOs in the early 1990s had produced what no one had expected—a clear and unambiguous Convention totally banning AP mines—the first treaty in history to ban a weapon that has been in widespread use by military forces throughout the world for decades.

THE JOURNEY BACK TO OTTAWA

While there was much to celebrate in the wake of the Oslo conference, there was little time for rest as the Ottawa Process coalition geared up for the final stretch back to Ottawa. Joint *démarches* with regional core partners were launched to sell the Olso text to the reluctant and previously indifferent. A Canadian resolution calling on states to sign the Convention would form the centrepiece of an intensive lobbying effort within the United Nations General Assembly in the fall of 1997. The final stage of the Ottawa Process 'public diplomacy' campaign was launched through a range of government- and NGO-sponsored media activities and letter, fax, and poster campaigns. A highly effective series of ICRC black-and-white public service announcements that tracked the journey of a young female mine victim from her hut in Cambodia to the site of the Convention signing conference in Ottawa declared that 'the people of the world want a ban on AP mines—now it's the governments' turn.' The public diplomacy campaign provided a dramatic boost on 10 October 1997 when the Nobel Committee announced that Jody Williams and the ICBL were the winners of the 1997 Nobel Peace Prize. A few weeks later, on 3 November, Williams and Valerie Warmington and Celina Tuttle of Mines Action Canada joined Prime Minister Chrétien, Foreign Minister Axworthy, and Defence Minister Art Eggleton outside of Ottawa to participate in the destruction of the last of Canada's stockpiles of AP mines. Finally, there was the task of preparing for the largest multilateral ministerial conference ever held in Canada.

While the primary objective of the second Ottawa landmines conference was to open the new AP Mine Ban Convention for signature, Canadian officials also planned to use the meeting to launch what would soon become known as Ottawa Process II. Thus, 'A Global Ban on Landmines: Treaty Signing Conference and Mine Action Forum' would feature 20 'Mine Action Roundtables' that would attract one of the best-ever collections of the world's AP mine experts for consultations on the future of global mine action efforts. Expert representatives from governments, the United Nations system, and NGOs would examine almost every aspect of the international response to the AP mine crisis, including the mobilization and co-ordination of resources for mine action as well as the ratification, universalization, and implementation of the Convention in all of its aspects, including mine clearance and mine victim assistance. The results of these consultations, as well as a listing of initiatives that states and international and non-governmental organizations would be undertaking to ensure progress on the AP mine issue, were included in a 114-page final report of the conference—An Agenda for Mine Action—which was provided to participants immediately following the close of the conference.[18]

The Ottawa conference would attract a total of 2,400 participants, including more than 500 members of the international media. Over a half-billion dollars would be pledged for mine action during the conference. Canada, South Africa, and Norway would sign the treaty almost simultaneously. Canada would also announce its immediate ratification of the new ban Convention as well as its intention to devote $100 million to mine action over the next five years. Officials also used the Ottawa conference to launch a 'lessons learned' exercise that collected the views of key players within the Ottawa Process as well as from the members of the broader AP mine action community using a range of survey and focus group-based instruments. Key members of the Ottawa Process coalition were also asked to attend a one-day 'Ottawa Process Forum' immediately following the formal Ottawa conference, which would examine the lessons learned from the process in more detail. An additional two-day seminar of consultations and planning for Ottawa Process II was hosted by Mines Action Canada for members of the NGO community on 6–7 December.

Taken together, the activities within and surrounding the second Ottawa landmines conference had succeeded in producing a comprehensive and widely consulted new 'road-map' for the second phase of the Ottawa Process. The success of the first Ottawa Process was underscored by the presentation of the Nobel Peace Prize to Jody Williams and the ICBL in Oslo on 10 December 1997. In the 424 days between the two Ottawa conferences, the Ottawa Process coalition had navigated a complex and very public diplomatic initiative to a successful conclusion that now enjoyed the support of 122 governments—an achievement described by Prime Minister Chrétien as 'without precedent or parallel in either international disarmament or international humanitarian law'.[19]

By the summer of 1998 Ottawa Process II was already breaking new diplomatic track records. With 126 signatories and 30 of the 40 state ratifications required for the Convention to enter into force deposited with the UN in less than eight months, it is clear that the new AP Mine Ban Convention will be the most rapidly implemented treaty of its kind in modern history. Moreover, as its supporters had hoped, the Convention's unique blend of disarmament law and deadlines for practical humanitarian action was already providing a widely supported framework for the co-ordination of the international community's response to the AP mine crisis. International meetings and activities forecast in *An Agenda for Mine Action*, including a Mine Action Workshop hosted by Canada in late March 1998, have succeeded in maintaining the momentum for action on AP mines.[20] The Ottawa Process coalition is continuing, through a range of global and regional initiatives, to press for the timely ratification, universalization, and full implementation of the Convention. In the first half of 1998 alone mine action was the central theme of multilateral action-oriented meetings in Ottawa, New York, Budapest, Geneva, Washington, Brussels, Moscow, Pretoria, Oslo, Karlsruhe, Ougadugo, and Bangkok. The mobilization of resources for mine action in the field continues to gain momentum. The pace of mine clearance, mine awareness, and victim assistance activities has significantly increased. Strategies to engage the hold-out states are being developed and implemented with concrete results. In late May the United States announced that it will work to sign the Ottawa Convention by 2006. Russia has halted the production of 90 per cent of various models of AP mines and will destroy 500,000 AP mines by the end of 1998.

FAST-TRACK DIPLOMACY

There is little doubt that much of the success of the Ottawa Process can be traced to the uniqueness of the AP mine issue itself. Once the true destructiveness of AP mines was made clear to publics, politicians, and policy-makers, the drive towards a ban was almost inevitable. However, there was nothing that was inevitable about the speed or concrete results of the Ottawa Process itself. There is no shortage of worthwhile issues that have rocketed to the top of the international agenda only to have their momentum blunted and potential solutions buried under the dysfunctions of multilateral 'business as usual'. The Ottawa Process clearly pushed the boundaries of multilateralism—building on Axworthy's bold gamble and drawing its strength from new sources of diplomatic influence in the post-Cold War era. International public opinion, transnational NGOs, and revolutions in telecommunications and the mass media have all begun to erode the traditional boundaries and prerogatives of diplomatic praxis.

The middle-power/civil society coalition forged by Canada around the AP mine issue was successful in harnessing a number of these new sources of influence—providing a dramatically expanded 'diplomatic tool-kit' for officials developing strategies to influence key decision-makers at state, regional, and global levels. 'Public diplomacy' efforts by key foreign ministers and senior officials were effectively combined with NGO-led civil society advocacy campaigns. Videos, posters, fax campaigns, e-mail, conference calls, and the Internet all facilitated the rapid co-ordination and transmission of the key messages of the constantly evolving Ottawa Process.

Multilateral diplomacy remains a contested terrain where middle powers such as Canada often have a home-field advantage. Canada's extensive experience with multilateralism provided a solid foundation upon which the framework of an issue-specific diplomatic initiative could quickly be constructed. But while the Ottawa Process may have emerged as an ad hoc response to the need for immediate multilateral action, it will produce more than a much needed international Convention banning AP mines. In a world in desperate need of rapidly organized multilateral responses to complex and large-scale threats to human health, security, and development, the Ottawa Process holds open the hope that multilateral diplomacy will continue to evolve as a flexible and effective instrument of global governance. With its clear objectives, deadlines for collective action, coalition-building across traditional political boundaries, and full use of the new tools of the Information Age, fast-track diplomacy in the style of the Ottawa Process is a welcome addition to Canada's multilateral tool-kit.

NOTES

1. The full title is the 'Convention on Prohibitions or Restrictions on the Use of Certain Conventional Weapons Which May Be Deemed To Be Excessively Injurious or To Have Indiscriminate Effects'.
2. Canada, *Towards A Global Ban on Anti-Personnel Mines: Declaration of the Ottawa Conference* (Ottawa, 1996).
3. Batman's *Death of Innocents: The Horror of Landmines*, 1996, was more advocacy-oriented, while Superman's *Deadly Legacy*, 1996, was produced in co-operation with DC Comics and UNICEF as a mine awareness project and was translated for use in mine-affected countries such as Bosnia.
4. United Nations General Assembly Resolution 51/45S, 'An International Agreement to Ban Anti-Personnel Landmines', adopted 10 Dec. 1996.

5. Ministry of Foreign Affairs, Austria, 'Austria to Host Next Meeting on Anti-Personnel Mines', in DFAIT, *AP Mine Ban: Progress Report* 1 (1997): 2.
6. Final Declaration of the 4th International NGO Conference on Landmines: Toward a Mine Free Southern Africa; Maputo, Mozambique, 25–8 Feb. 1997, 3.
7. Details on these conferences can be found in issues 1–5 of DFAIT's landmine newsletter, *AP Mine Ban: Progress Report*.
8. Brussels, Declaration of the Brussels Conference on Anti-Personnel Landmines, 1997.
9. Madeleine Albright, letter to Foreign Ministers, 20 Aug. 1997, in ICBL, *Report on Activities: Diplomatic Conference on an International Total Ban on Anti-Personnel Landmines, Oslo, Norway, September 1–18, 1997*, 18–20.
10. 'The New Convert', *The Economist*, 23–9 Aug. 1997, 14.
11. Report of the Diplomatic Conference on an International Total Ban on Anti-Personnel Land Mines, Oslo, 1–18 Sept. 1997, APL/CRP.5, 18 Sept. 1997.
12. The best 'open' source of information on the details of the Oslo negotiations is the newsletters and the releases of the ICBL, representatives of which were present in all formal and informal sessions of the Oslo negotiations.
13. Delegation of the United States, 4 Sept. 1997, 'Summary of U.S. Anti-Armour Landmine Systems', in ICBL, *Report on Activities*, 1997, 31.
14. Senator Patrick Leahy, 'Seize the Moment', *ICBL Ban Treaty News*, 9 Sept. 1997, 1.
15. Ibid.
16. Helms's letter was dated 8 Sept. 1997 and was 'leaked' to the media the following day. The 'open letter' to Clinton signed by the 10 retired generals was released on 11 Sept. 1997 by the Centre for Security Policy, an organization reported to be fully funded by defence industry contributions.
17. The Honourable Lloyd Axworthy, 'Notes for an Address by the Honourable Lloyd Axworthy, Minister of Foreign Affairs, to the Oslo NGO Forum on Banning Anti-Personnel Landmines—September 10, 1997', 1.
18. Those wishing to keep track of developments related to the Ottawa conference could also plug in to a 'real-time' audio feed of the various speeches and conference events via DFAIT's landmines Web site.
19. 'Message from the Right Honourable Jean Chrétien, Prime Minister—Canada', in United Nations, *Landmines: Demining News From the United Nations* (New York: UN, Dec. 1997), 2.
20. Canada, 'Years Not Decades: Agenda for Mine Action II', Chair's Summary, Mine Action Co-ordination Workshop, Ottawa, 23–4 Mar. 1998.

CHAPTER 11

ON A FAST TRACK TO A BAN:
THE CANADIAN POLICY PROCESS

Brian W. Tomlin

'[Landmines] should be banned not only in Canada but everywhere in the world.'

Canadian Foreign Affairs Minister André Ouellet,
9 November 1995

When André Ouellet made this statement during a consultation on Canadian foreign aid with non-governmental organizations, he knew that he was at odds with official Canadian policy on anti-personnel (AP) mines. And although he may have hoped for change, he could not have known that his words would serve as a catalyst in the process that dramatically transformed an element of Canadian foreign policy and, more significantly, culminated in an international prohibition on the production and use of a weapon of war, providing Jean Chrétien's Liberal government with a diplomatic triumph. If book were being made in Ottawa, these events would have been given virtually no chance of occurring, since the AP mines issue was not on the decision agenda of anyone who counted in the Ottawa policy arena. In fact, senior policy officials, from the Prime Minister's Office down to senior levels in Foreign Affairs, missed the issue almost completely, and in the end they had to board a train that was leaving without them.

Responsibility for the mines issue within Canada's national federal government was divided, as might be expected, between the Department of National Defence (DND) and the Department of Foreign Affairs and International Trade (DFAIT). Within DFAIT, the issue was buried in the Non-proliferation, Arms Control, and Disarmament Division (IDA) within the department's International Security Bureau (IDD). This welter of acronyms, alone, is enough to convey the easily recognized image of bureaucratic layers, where issues move at a snail's pace under the direction of careful civil servants. In a world where caution is the watchword, even high-priority issues have difficulty overcoming organizational inertia. And anti-personnel mines were not a priority in DFAIT.

At the time of Ouellet's statement, Canadian arms control priorities centred not on mines but on nuclear issues, especially non-proliferation. When Mark Gwozdecky returned from a diplomatic posting in Syria to take up his position as deputy director in IDA in August 1995, he assumed responsibility for the file on anti-personnel mines. His departing predecessor on the file advised him not to waste his time on mines, describing the file as a loser, both domestically and internationally. Gwozdecky was told, 'Nobody here is interested in this file, and nobody else in the world will let it go anywhere.' Gwozdecky initially was content to mouth government nostrums in his dialogue with earnest proponents of a ban from Mines Action Canada, the principal Canadian non-governmental organization active on this issue. Internationally, the mines issue was a morass, hopelessly tied up in the UN's consensus-based process, just where the major powers wanted it. In any case, the idea of an outright ban on the production and use of mines was not deemed to be a credible policy alternative for any government. These antecedent facts define the goals of this chapter. First, we want to explain how the issue of anti-personnel mines went from being that most wretched of policy dogs for bureaucrats—a loser—to the top of the Canadian government's decision agenda. Second, after the issue was identified as a top priority, we need to understand the policy process that led Canada to propose to the world that it follow the path that is now known universally as the Ottawa Process.

To accomplish this, the chapter will employ a policy model directed particularly at the explanation of both agenda-setting and the development of policy alternatives, the two key elements that require explanation here. John Kingdon has developed a revised version of the garbage-can model of policy choice, advanced originally by Cohen, March, and Olsen, to explain, first, why some issues become prominent on governmental policy agendas and, second, how alternative policy approaches to issues are identified and chosen.[1] Kingdon conceives the policy process as consisting of three separate streams—problem identification or recognition, policy alternatives generation, and politics—that flow through and around government, largely independent of one another. Conventionally, agendas are set by problems or politics, and alternatives are generated in the policy stream. At certain critical times, the three streams come together, and at that juncture major policy change can occur.

On the issue of anti-personnel mines, we want to understand how the mines issue rose to the top of the decision agenda, and why a Canadian-led initiative for a global ban on mines became the preferred policy alternative for the government of Canada. To accomplish this, we will examine the process by which particular solutions became joined to problems and the two were joined to favourable political forces. Kingdon argues that this coupling is most likely to occur when policy windows—defined as opportunities to advocate particular proposals or conceptions of problems—are opened, either by the appearance of compelling problems or by happenings in the political stream. Our analysis of the policy process surrounding the mines issue will include a search for the policy windows that opened and resulted in the Ottawa Process. In addition, we will examine the role played by policy entrepreneurs who, according to Kingdon, invest resources in pushing particular proposals or problems, prompt important people to pay attention, and couple solutions to problems and both to politics. We begin this analysis in the following section with a more complete specification of the model and its constituent elements.

STREAMS IN THE POLICY PROCESS: HOW AN IDEA'S TIME CAN COME

How do certain problems surface on the government's foreign policy agenda, and why is a particular policy alternative selected to address the problem? Thomas Risse-Kappen suggests that the answer lies in an understanding of how certain ideas intervene between international power-related factors and state interests and preferences, and that this, in turn, is dependent on the domestic structures of the state.[2] Risse-Kappen's emphasis on the role of ideas is well placed.[3] However, a reading of the public, as opposed to foreign, policy literature suggests that we have to move beyond domestic structures and probe into policy processes for an adequate understanding of agenda change and policy choice. As described above, Kingdon conceives of three process streams flowing through the public policy system: streams of problems, policies, and politics.[4] Each will be described in turn.

Problems

It is a fact that governments pay attention to some problems while ignoring others, obliging us to ask how it is that some problems capture the attention of important people in and around government and thereby obtain a place on the governmental agenda.[5] Kingdon argues that objective indicators of the presence of a problem are important, especially quantitative ones.[6] Problems are not self-evident from their indicators, however, but require a push from a focusing event to carry them on to a governmental agenda. Such an event may arise from a crisis or the creation of a compelling symbol, or out of the personal experience of a policy-maker. Even a focusing event is rarely sufficient to carry an issue to a prominent place on the policy agenda, however; instead, it typically serves only as a catalyst by reinforcing some pre-existing perception of a problem. Finally, problem identification is more likely when government officials receive feedback about the inadequacy of existing policies and programs.

In summary, the chances that a government will pay attention to one problem out of the multitude that circulate in the problem stream are enhanced by the presence of objective indicators, a focusing event, perceptions that a problem already may exist, and feedback about existing policies. All of these characteristics may be present, however, and a problem may still not make it onto the government's policy agenda. This is because the policy process consists of more than a stream of problems waiting to be identified; it also includes a stream of policy alternatives that must ultimately be linked to problems.

Policy Proposals

Kingdon argues that ideas about policy alternatives circulate in communities of specialists scattered within and outside government.[7] Individual ideas in this stream of policy proposals mutate and recombine in a process of continual refinement until some are ready to enter a serious decision stage as alternative choices.[8] Advocates for particular proposals or ideas are policy entrepreneurs, inside or outside of government, who are defined by their willingness to invest resources (time and energy, and occasionally money) in order to secure a future return (desired policies, satisfaction from participation, or career rewards). These entrepreneurs try to build acceptance for their pet proposals, softening up both the policy community and the larger public by pushing their ideas repeatedly and in many different forums.

If entrepreneurs are successful in communicating their idea in a policy community, then a take-off point may be reached where diffusion occurs rapidly and the idea becomes generally accepted.[9] This process of creating alternatives for policy-makers to consider proceeds independently of the process of problem identification. However, viable alternatives must exist before a problem can secure a solid position on the decision agenda. Even in this circumstance, problems and their alternative solutions exist alongside the political stream, which also exerts influence on the policy process.

Politics

In Kingdon's model, developments in the political stream have their most powerful effects on agendas. The stream is composed of elements related to electoral, partisan, and pressure group considerations of politicians and those who serve them. An important component of the political stream is what Kingdon refers to as the national mood.[10] He maintains that governmental participants' sense of the climate of opinion on an issue—gleaned from mail, media, and lobbyists, among other sources—can provide a fertile ground for certain ideas. Similarly, the component of organized political interests is important to those in government in so far as the interests all point in the same direction, thus providing a powerful impetus to move on that course.

The third major element in the political stream is composed of events within the government itself. Governmental actors affect policy agendas through two major processes: turnover and jurisdiction. According to Kingdon, agendas may change because some of the major participants change.[11] Furthermore, agendas are significantly affected by jurisdictional boundaries and by turf battles. The final component in the political stream is consensus-building. Unlike the policy stream, where consensus is built through persuasion and diffusion, consensus in the political stream is achieved through bargaining and coalition-building among participants in the selection of a course of action. As in the policy stream, however, once adherents of a particular alternative have grown sufficiently in number, then the balance of support will tip overwhelmingly in the direction of that option. The distinction between agendas and alternatives is useful analytically in distinguishing the effects of the various components of the political stream. Kingdon maintains that the mix of the national mood and elections has a strong impact on policy agendas, capable of overwhelming the balance of organized forces.[12] But once a problem is on the decision agenda, then organized forces can be expected to step back in to shape alternatives and outcomes.

Policy Windows

Much of the time, these three streams—problems, policies, and politics—flow through the policy system on largely independent courses. However, the streams come together at critical times, so that a problem is recognized, a solution is developed and available in the policy community, a political change makes the time right for policy change, and potential constraints are not severe.[13] This joining of the streams is most likely to occur when a policy window opens, and policy entrepreneurs play a critical role in this process.

Typically, a policy window opens because the policy agenda is affected by a change or event in the political stream, or by the emergence of a pressing problem that captures the attention of government officials. Kingdon distinguishes between the governmental agenda, which is the set of subjects to which people in and around government are paying serious attention, and the decision agenda, which consists of a smaller set of items from the governmental agenda being actively decided upon.[14] Events in the problem or political streams can, by themselves, structure the governmental agenda, but the probability that an issue will rise on the decision agenda is increased if a policy window opens and all three streams are joined.

Whether a window has, in fact, opened is a matter of perception, and may be a matter of debate, because only a test (successful advocacy) will determine its presence. The test must be done quickly, however, because policy windows may not remain open for long. It only takes the loss of one of the three elements to miss the moment of opportunity: if a problem does not remain sufficiently compelling, a solution is not available, or support is not forthcoming from the political stream, then the issue's place on the decision agenda may be lost and the window will close without action. It follows, then, that when a window opens, policy entrepreneurs have to be ready to take advantage of the opportunity to engineer, in Kingdon's terminology, the coupling of the streams that must occur at the open window. To be effective in doing so, entrepreneurs must have one or more of the following characteristics: a claim to a hearing, because of either their expertise on an issue or their leadership of organized groups; political connections or negotiating skills and the savvy to use them effectively; and persistence and tenacity.

This model of agenda-setting and policy alternative specification is designed to help us 'find pattern and structure in very complicated, fluid, and seemingly unpredictable phenomena'.[15] However, it is very much a probabilistic model, one that explicitly leaves room for a residual randomness in the way events will unfold in any particular policy episode. In addition, it is historically contingent: the direction of change depends heavily on initial conditions, and events may develop in different ways depending on which way they happen to start. In other words, the model can point to the kinds of structural change and forms of individual action likely to affect agendas and policy choice, but it cannot tell us precisely when those factors will operate to produce particular effects. Nevertheless, it provides a more comprehensive and integrated representation of the policy process than the major alternatives.[16] Models that focus on competing pressures in the generation and selection of policy alternatives capture important aspects of the political stream, but ignore the important role played by ideas in other parts of the process. Comprehensive-rational models focus on the orderly elements of choice, but overlook the larger policy process that is much less tidy, while incrementalist models that accurately capture the evolution of alternatives fail to describe the discontinuous process of agenda change. Kingdon's model, on the other hand, provides us with a comprehensive representation of the enduring streams in the policy process—problems, alternatives, and politics—and alerts us to the critical ingredients—windows of opportunity and the entrepreneurial initiatives that must couple the streams at the openings—that increase the likelihood of policy change. We now turn to apply the model in an analysis of how the mines issue rose to the top of the decision agenda, and why a Canadian-led initiative for a global ban on mines became the preferred policy alternative.

OF WINDOWS OF OPPORTUNITY AND POLICY ENTREPRENEURS[17]

First Window: Changing the Agenda

Throughout the summer and autumn of 1995, André Ouellet had been pressing Canadian Defence Minister David Collenette for a change in Canada's policy on AP mines.[18] Ouellet's awareness of the mines issue came largely from his ministerial responsibility for Canadian development assistance, some of which was allocated for demining operations in mine-affected regions of the world. Ouellet was struck by the futility of spending money for demining at the same time that new mines were being deployed around the world. His interest in doing something on the AP mines issue was encouraged by Michael Pearson, Ouellet's senior policy adviser. In an exchange of letters in the late summer, Ouellet proposed to Collenette that Canada destroy its stocks of mines as a way of taking the lead on the issue. In reply, Collenette presented the standard DND argument that landmines could not be eliminated until 'effective and humane alternatives' were found.

Ouellet tried a different tack. The United States was planning to introduce a resolution in the UN First Committee calling for a moratorium on the export of mines, and asked Canada to become a co-sponsor. Earlier, Canada's name had been included, mistakenly, on a list compiled by the UN Secretary-General of countries that had in place a moratorium on exports. Ouellet urged Collenette to bring Canada's policy into line with the position portrayed in the Secretary-General's report. Again, Collenette's officials advised him to reject Ouellet's request, arguing that the export moratorium was only the thin edge of the wedge in DFAIT's efforts to control DND weapons policy.[19] Collenette did not have a reputation as a minister who was willing to challenge the views put forward by his officials.[20] The bureaucrats' arguments did not satisfy Ouellet, however, and he was running out of patience with the Defence Minister. A conference to review the 1980 Convention on Certain Conventional Weapons (CCW) was held from 25 September to 23 October in Vienna, ostensibly to strengthen the existing regime governing the use of anti-personnel mines. Bells tolled throughout Vienna for landmine victims, and anti-mines groups pressed their case while national campaigns held days of action—and participating nations failed to reach consensus on the mines issue. On 11 October 1995, Ouellet again wrote to Collenette, stating that it was time for a change in

Canadian policy: he wanted to announce a Canadian moratorium on exports and to co-sponsor the US resolution in the UN, and he wanted to declare Canada's commitment to the eventual elimination of landmines. Reluctantly, DND agreed to the export moratorium, but insisted that this was as far as policy change could go. DFAIT officials agreed that no further changes in Canadian policy, beyond the export moratorium, would be pursued.

While the export moratorium may have satisfied DFAIT bureaucrats, it did not go far enough for their minister. If Collenette was inclined to follow the policy advice offered by his bureaucrats, Ouellet was much more of a free spirit. He was not afraid to set the cat among the pigeons in pursuit of his goals, and this he did on 9 November when he opined to a CBC (Canadian Broadcasting Corporation) reporter that Canada should destroy its stockpile of landmines and declare a total ban on the production, export, and use of the weapons.[21] The statement took officials in DFAIT's Non-proliferation, Arms Control, and Disarmament Division by complete surprise. By November 1995, Mark Gwozdecky had handed the AP mines file off to a new officer in the division, Bob Lawson.[22] Upon his arrival in IDA in October 1995, Lawson was told by Gwozdecky that an outright ban on landmines, however desirable, was not in the cards because DND would not countenance further changes in policy. On 9 November Lawson was engaged in preparations for the upcoming January CCW session in Geneva[23] when he received a telephone call from the CBC asking for a comment on Ouellet's statement. Begging off, Lawson secured a transcript of the minister's remarks and took it to Gwozdecky and Jill Sinclair, the director of IDA,[24] saying, 'You won't believe what just happened.' Lawson immediately faxed the transcript to Mines Action Canada (MAC) and followed up with a phone call. MAC took the statement and ran with it, flooding the minister's office with congratulatory messages on Canada's new policy.

Summary
Ouellet's statement offered a window of opportunity for policy entrepreneurs inside and outside of government to move the mines issue onto the governmental agenda. In Kingdon's model, policy windows open when the problem, policy, and political streams join, offering policy entrepreneurs an opportunity to advocate particular alternatives. In the problem stream, the chances of a problem securing attention are enhanced by the presence of objective indicators, a focusing event, perceptions that a problem already may exist, and feedback about existing policies. There were indicators aplenty on this issue, and statistics on the human costs of AP mines were used liberally by international and non-governmental organizations

(NGOs), which also provided extensive feedback to Ouellet about the inadequacy of Canada's current mines policy. The focusing event in the problem stream for Ouellet was the dissonance between Canadian demining activities and Canada's status quo position on the use of mines, a contradiction that dovetailed with the critique of Canadian policy that NGOs were presenting to the minister.

These developments in the problem stream were joined with conditions in the political stream to generate pressure in the direction of a change in the policy agenda. By Ouellet's reading, the national mood, reflected in public opinion polls[25] and the heavy flow of mail to the minister's office, was clearly supportive of a ban on landmines, and pressure from organized political interests, led by MAC, was overwhelmingly in this direction. Finally, Ouellet and his advisers had engaged DND in a skirmish over turf on landmines, and while they did not directly challenge the jurisdiction of DND on the issue, Ouellet was determined to keep up the pressure for a change in Canadian policy.

Change in the policy stream conspired with events in the other two streams to make change more likely. The UN mistake in placing Canada on a published list of countries with export moratoria in place provided a powerful argument for a change in Canadian policy, and the US request that Canada co-sponsor a UN resolution calling for an export moratorium provided the impetus for change. The alternative, to announce to the world that there had been an error, that Canada did not have such a moratorium in place, was unthinkable, and Defence Minister Collenette and his officials could not maintain their resistance to the export moratorium alternative. Their intransigence provoked Ouellet to act unilaterally, however, so that by the time DND finally gave in and agreed to an export moratorium, the policy window had opened and the mines issue was firmly entrenched on the governmental agenda. Policy entrepreneurs, inside and outside government, would seize the opportunity to begin moving Canada, and the world, in the direction of a complete ban. In the words of one official, 'Ouellet's statement broke the logjam and gave DFAIT the opening it needed.'

Second Window: Changing Policy

Collenette's formal agreement to a Canadian export ban, in a letter to Ouellet on 12 November 1995, was almost immediately overtaken by events in the policy stream. Emboldened by Ouellet's declaration in favour of a ban, mines action groups were pushing for further steps, and IDA officials now knew they had a minister who would take on DND and fight for policy change. And so, despite their earlier commitment to DND that the export moratorium would be the last step, in that same month of November IDA advised Ouellet to pursue with DND the possibility of declaring a comprehensive Canadian moratorium, not only on exports, but also on the production and use of anti-personnel mines. The DND response to this initiative was, by the normal standards of ministerial correspondence, unusually direct in its acerbity, stating that DND would agree, in principle, to 'acquiesce', but that they did so reluctantly, complaining that this latest policy shift represented 'movement of the goalposts' by DFAIT. In acquiescing, DND lost control of its policy turf on the issue—and soon discovered the extent to which the goalposts had moved. On 17 January 1996, DFAIT announced not only the comprehensive moratorium, but also Canadian support for a complete ban on production, transfer, and use. In the words of one DFAIT official, DND had bought into a ban, and this gave DFAIT the running room it needed on the issue.

January brought change in the political stream as well, when André Ouellet retired and was replaced by Lloyd Axworthy as Foreign Affairs Minister. Whereas Ouellet was a consummate politician whose policy streak did not run deep, Axworthy, a former professor of political science, was a minister genuinely interested in policy innovation, who saw politics as a way to advance policy goals. In the transition, Ouellet's senior policy adviser, Michael Pearson, stayed on in the same role for Axworthy and provided important continuity on landmines. Upon his arrival in Foreign Affairs, Axworthy requested the department to provide recommendations on what Canadian foreign policy priorities ought to be. In response, IDA sent two notes up to the minister, one identifying small arms and the other anti-personnel mines. Axworthy, guided by Pearson and seeing an opportunity to run with an issue, picked landmines as an immediate priority. He noted the prominent role played by NGOs on the issue and, anticipating the process that would unfold subsequently, indicated his interest in a partnership that would link NGO efforts with Canada's ability to champion the issue internationally. Axworthy signalled IDA to move forward on the policy front, extending the moratorium and pressing DND to agree to destroy Canadian stockpiles of mines. Congruent with Kingdon's model, turnover in the political stream elevated the mines issue to the decision agenda, where policy choices would be made. Although we have no way of knowing how the issue would have fared had Ouellet remained in office, officials and advisers agree that Axworthy gave the issue new urgency.

In the policy stream, the US export moratorium resolution in the UN also expanded Canadian policy options, because many of the large number of countries that supported the export moratorium were now prepared to go further. By March 1996, IDA had drafted a *Canadian Action Plan to*

Reduce the Global Use of Landmines. The plan proposed movement on two tracks. The first was continued Canadian participation in the CCW Review Conference, scheduled to meet in Geneva in April, which the Canadians were convinced would remain deadlocked. The second track consisted of an unremarkable proposal that contained the seeds of the Ottawa Process: IDA proposed that Canada host a small international meeting of officials and NGOs to develop an action plan on landmines.[26] By April, track two had grown to include a Canadian-sponsored UN resolution on landmines, and the small meeting was now called an 'International Landmine Strategy Session', to be held in September in Ottawa.[27] It also included a proposal to convert the January moratorium into a permanent ban on production, transfer, and use. Although DND refused the DFAIT request for a ban, Defence was now, effectively, sidelined on the landmines issue; DFAIT would pursue a ban on the international front while continuing to pressure DND to agree to destroy its stockpiles of landmines.[28]

Change was under way in the problem stream, as well. The CCW Review Conference was winding down in Geneva, and it was clear that no consensus would be achieved. If a ban was Canada's goal, then officials had to deal with the problem of international stalemate. Three of Canada's G-7 partners—France, the UK, and the US—wanted to refer the issue to the Conference on Disarmament (CD), but IDA was convinced that the CD, operating by consensus, would only replicate the deadlocked CCW.[29] Policy alternatives would have to take this problem into account. The UN resolution being prepared by IDA for introduction by Canada in the General Assembly originally contained a proposal to negotiate in the CD, but that was removed, and officials began to focus their energies on the session planned for 3–5 October in Ottawa. As conceived by IDA in May 1996, the session would include pro-ban states and NGOs from around the world, and its purpose would be to develop a strategic action plan detailing concrete global and regional initiatives for the elimination of anti-personnel mines. In addition, the session would issue a political declaration committing participating states to concrete actions to achieve the elimination of mines.

It is important to emphasize that IDA was on a very long policy leash on this issue, with decisions taken largely by Jill Sinclair and her staff. Following his attendance at the meeting of pro-ban states and NGOs in Geneva, Lawson was on the phone to Sinclair to report the results. They agreed that this was a leadership opportunity for Canada they could not afford to pass up, and so Sinclair authorized Lawson to announce Canada's intention to host the autumn meeting in Ottawa. Sinclair kept Michael Pearson generally informed about what IDA was doing, but otherwise there was not a lot of communication with the minister specifically on the issue.

Similarly, Sinclair's boss, Ralph Lysyshyn, director-general of the International Security Bureau, was preoccupied with issues related to Yugoslavia and NATO enlargement, and was content to let Sinclair handle the AP mines issue. It was not until later, when the Ottawa meeting was gathering momentum, that senior policy levels would become engaged.

Lawson's announcement, at the conclusion of the CCW conference in May, of Canada's intention to host the October meeting in Ottawa did bring some early ministerial attention to the issue, although it was not in a form that anyone welcomed. The announcement was picked up by the media and received some play in the Canadian press, much to the displeasure of the minister's office. The objection was not to the substance of the announcement (a small meeting, which in itself was a minor thing) but to the fact that an official, rather than the minister, was front and centre in the press coverage.[30] Officials know that this kind of ministerial displeasure is harmful to the maintenance of issues on decision agendas, but the gods smiled on Sinclair and her group in IDA by providing them with an opportunity to make things up to the minister. When German Foreign Affairs Minister Klaus Kinkel visited Ottawa shortly after the end of the CCW, an anti-mines event was staged on Parliament Hill, with Axworthy and Kinkel appearing before a 'shoe mountain' intended to depict graphically the limbs lost by AP mine victims. The event was a huge success, with lots of favourable press coverage, and Axworthy was re-engaged on the issue.

Although the number of countries wanting to attend the Ottawa meeting was growing, there was still substantial opposition to the movement to ban mines, and officials in IDA were concerned that opponents might attend the session simply to sabotage it. The problem centred on the invitation list. Clearly, they did not want firm opponents in attendance, because, as one official put it in a mixed metaphor, 'once you let the rats in, they could scuttle the boat.' On the other hand, they reasoned, how could you not invite countries like France, the UK, and the US? A solution to this dilemma was proposed by Mark Gwozdecky to the IDA group in June 1996, and it was deceptive in its simplicity. The meeting would, in principle, be open to all states, but each would determine for itself whether it should attend. The criterion for such a determination would be the draft political declaration that Canada was preparing for endorsement by the session, which included a reference to countries taking unilateral steps towards a ban. Governments would be given the declaration in advance, and they would decide whether it was something they could endorse and, therefore, whether they should attend the meeting. In fact, a desire for eligibility might also lead some to change their AP mines policy unilaterally in advance of the meeting. This self-selection principle worked like 'magic' (as one official described it): any rats who attended would have to be prepared to face intense scrutiny in the presence of a core group of pro-ban states and NGOs; and any who signed the declaration would be held to it by the international coalition of NGOs, determined to make certain that countries would live up to their commitments.

The Canadians were especially keen to bring the US on side, for obvious reasons. In May 1996, US President Bill Clinton announced American support for efforts to conclude an international agreement to ban mines. Coming two weeks after the unsuccessful conclusion of the CCW, Clinton's announcement was very positively received by Canadian officials, especially, as one said, since the meeting planned for Ottawa was now the only show in town. Axworthy responded to Clinton's announcement in a letter to US Secretary of State Warren Christopher in which he invited the US to work with Canada to ensure that the planned Ottawa meeting would facilitate progress towards an international agreement. Christopher agreed, and during the spring and summer, Canadian officials travelled to Washington several times to work with their American counterparts in an effort to bring the US into the tent.

When, at the conclusion of the CCW, Canada circulated the resolution it was preparing for the UN General Assembly, the Americans objected that, since they had introduced the export moratorium resolution in the General Assembly the previous autumn, they saw the UN as their show. Canada agreed to withdraw its UN resolution in favour of one sponsored by the US, but only if the Americans would agree not to refer to the CD in their resolution. This the Americans agreed to, even though they eventually decided that the CD was their preferred forum for negotiations.[31] When IDA circulated the political declaration it was drafting for the Ottawa session to the US, the Americans expressed real concerns, objecting that the Canadians were moving too far, too fast. As a result, Canada agreed to remove language referring to 'zero by 2000' (no new mine deployments by the year 2000) from the declaration, and in return the US agreed to consider coming to Ottawa.

The United States was also concerned about Canadian plans for extensive participation by NGOs at the Ottawa session. The issue of who should be invited to the Ottawa meeting engaged IDA in extensive consultations with the International Campaign to Ban Landmines (ICBL), particularly with ICBL leaders Steve Goose and Jody Williams. The ICBL wanted the hurdle for participation to be set very high, in order to keep the rats out, while IDA wanted to engage those states that were wavering on the borderline. IDA officials and ICBL representatives co-operated closely on the resolution of the invitees issue, and in the process forged an alliance that would last throughout the Ottawa Process. Over the course of the summer of 1996, IDA's Lawson conducted weekly conference calls with ICBL members (principally Goose and Williams), and they worked out joint plans for the upcoming meeting. Jill Sinclair, knowing that Axworthy had a history of working with NGOs, reinforced the importance of offering the ICBL and other NGOs a central role in the plans DFAIT was formulating. The Canadians went further, deciding that the ICBL should have a seat at the table for the October meeting, a first for the ICBL. Any reservations that DFAIT officials had about how extensive the role of NGOs should be were largely overcome by the trust that had developed between them and the ICBL's Goose and Williams. In addition, a representative from Mines Action Canada would be a member of Canada's delegation at the session.[32] To encourage other governments to do likewise, Canada agreed to increase the number of delegates that could be accredited to the Ottawa session by one if the national delegation included an NGO. Despite this strong commitment to NGO participation, Canada, nevertheless, felt compelled to assuage the concerns of the US, and other countries, over the unwanted scrutiny that would result from NGO participation. As a result, IDA appealed to the NGOs to agree to a formula whereby the session would have open and closed meetings, the former including NGOs and the latter for governments only.

It is clear from the written record, and is confirmed through interviews, that Canadian officials were not proceeding according to some grand plan but were feeling their way as policy alternatives were developed over the summer of 1996. The issue was still being managed by IDA, with minimal oversight by senior management, who saw nothing more than a small planning session being organized for the autumn. As one senior manager said, 'We had no idea where the thing was headed.' As plans for the Ottawa strategy session were firmed up, and as more and more countries indicated their desire to participate, however, thoughts in IDA turned to what should be done in the period following the Ottawa session. Two options were put on the table for presentation to Axworthy, the first a UN resolution, the second a forum for negotiations. Regarding the latter, Jill Sinclair argued that the CD was unacceptable because of its consensus format, and instead she promoted the idea of a 'stand-alone forum' for 'like-minded' states who would bring pressure to bear on those opposed to a ban; in other words, another version of the Ottawa strategy session, this time constituted as a negotiating forum. At a meeting to discuss options, Mark Gwozdecky raised the prospect of Ottawa hosting such an ad hoc forum. Ralph Lysyshyn was also in attendance and, drawing on his experience with the 'Open Skies' conference that was held in Ottawa in 1990, when he was

serving as IDA director, he said that such an initiative would be very expensive, probably somewhere in the range of $2 million. In the current fiscal
climate, said Lysyshyn, this was simply not possible. The idea was
dropped.[33]

As the summer progressed, DFAIT energies were increasingly directed to
the organization of the Ottawa session, but there was still time available to
continue to chip away at DND's turf on the policy front. Although DFAIT
had given up its efforts to convince DND to agree to convert the Canadian
moratorium into a permanent ban, officials continued to pressure DND to
agree to destroy its stockpiles of landmines. Throughout the summer, DND
resisted DFAIT pressures on stockpile destruction. DND officials felt they
were still being 'nickelled and dimed', as Foreign Affairs continued to move
the goalposts after each DND policy concession.[34] Finally, in September
1996, Sinclair and Lysyshyn became concerned that the interdepartmental
turf war was diverting too much energy and generating anxiety among
senior people in DFAIT. They asked the Privy Council Office (PCO) to get
involved and broker a deal between the two departments so that Canada
could announce plans to destroy its stockpiles on the eve of the Ottawa
strategy meeting.[35] Jim Bartleman, the PCO foreign policy adviser, presented various options to the Prime Minister, and he opted for compromise
language whereby one-third of stocks would be destroyed immediately,
with the remainder to be destroyed 'in the context of successful negotiations'. That neither party was happy with the trade-off may be a reflection
of its Solomon-like wisdom.[36]

Summary
The export moratorium created the opening DFAIT officials needed to move
alternatives forward in the policy stream, to a comprehensive moratorium
with the prospect of a complete ban in sight. NGO policy entrepreneurs had
softened up the security policy community, as well as the larger public, with
continual messages about the need to ban mines, and officials had found an
alternative in the policy stream that might address the problem. The problem stream shifted, as well, and the focus became how to engineer agreement on an international ban convention. The requirement for consensus
in the CD ruled it out as a forum, and the time was ripe for an alternative
forum in which a preponderance of pro-ban states could carry the day. The
political transition from Ouellet to Axworthy had moved the landmines
issue onto the decision agenda where choices among alternatives would be
made. The streams of problem definition, policy alternatives, and political
forces had joined again, and policy entrepreneurs had seized the opportunity to organize the October 1996 meeting of like-minded states in Ottawa.

The session would provide a test of the effectiveness of an alternative forum as a policy vehicle on the landmines issue.

Third Window: The Ottawa Process

Near the end of September the upcoming meeting finally caught the attention of the minister's office, which meant that senior officials in the Foreign Affairs bureaucracy also became interested. And when they saw what was about to happen, they were suddenly very nervous. This was partly because the minister's attention was drawn by the international flak he was starting to get over the structure of the meeting. The Russians, for example, were complaining about the self-selection principle, accusing Canada of behaving outrageously. In addition, the small planning session that had been conceived in the late spring had grown into a major event, and senior managers were concerned that proper arrangements had not been made. These anxieties were transmitted down to Ralph Lysyshyn, who began making adjustments to relieve the heat. In essence, Lysyshyn offered assurances that this was not really a big deal, that there was no need to be concerned. His ministrations ranged from major to minor: the original plan to have the meeting adopt an action plan was dropped in favour of a 'Chairman's Agenda for Action', to which not everyone would have to agree; and plans to have a special logo for the conference were dropped as well, in the interest of keeping the profile low.

Jill Sinclair was also becoming concerned as the conference approached, but for different reasons. The Canadian initiative had attracted a large number of countries, and a very large NGO contingent, and she was convinced that the session had to produce some concrete, and dramatic, result in order to sustain the momentum that had built up in the past month. About a week before the scheduled start date, Sinclair met with Ralph Lysyshyn in his office to explain her concern and propose that the meeting issue a call for countries to begin negotiations within a specified period of time, say two years. Lysyshyn rejected the proposal. In the first place, he said, a significant number of countries attending the meeting would be antagonized by even this modest proposal. Nevertheless, an initiative that would capture public attention would be worth their antagonism. However, only bureaucrats, said Lysyshyn, could get excited about a commitment to begin to talk in two years; the significance would be lost on the broader public, and Canada would garner no credit. Sinclair left, her problem unresolved, and was swept up in last-minute preparations for what had originally been billed as 'a small international meeting of officials and NGOs to develop an action work plan on land mines'.[37]

The Ottawa strategy session that opened at the federal government's Conference Centre in the old Ottawa train station on Wellington Street on 3 October 1996 was attended by 50 governments pledged to support a ban on landmines, as well as 24 observer states. In addition, the ICBL, the International Committee of the Red Cross (ICRC), various UN agencies, and a host of other NGOs were in attendance. IDA's self-selection process worked as hoped. The assembly was dominated by the core group of states committed to a ban, supported and guided by the participating NGOs. Any rats in attendance were sure to be subject to intense, and sometimes critical, scrutiny. A defining moment in this regard occurred during a 'Prestige Panel' chaired by Christine Stewart, Canada's Secretary of State for Latin America and Africa.[38] The head of the French delegation, Michel Duclos, chose to make a statement during the panel, and he misjudged the moment badly. Duclos's statement of the French position, while it may have been perfectly suited to a forum like the CD, was most certainly not suitable for the Ottawa conference, dominated as it was by pro-ban countries and NGOs. Distilled to its essence, the French position boiled down to this: France was prepared to ban landmines, until it needed them. This position was typical of countries that did not want to be seen by their publics to be opposing a ban, but that also did not want an international agreement in the short (or even medium) term. The French position was fully anticipated by the Canadians and their NGO allies. When Duclos finished speaking, Jody Williams took the floor to respond to the French statement. A self-described practitioner of what she herself calls 'in-your-face diplomacy', Williams slammed the French representative in front of the entire assembly. 'Your policy is contradictory', she told him. 'You are saying that you want to ban landmines, except when you want to use them. I suppose this is better than a stick in the eye, but it is not what we are looking for here.' While some delegates, from both governments and NGOs, were aghast at Williams's public scolding of France, US Senator Patrick Leahy, a leading American proponent of a ban, and others jumped in to echo Williams's condemnation of prevarication on the issue.[39] While this episode confirmed IDA hopes that any rats who decided to attend would face intense scrutiny in a forum intolerant of equivocation, it also confirmed the worst fears of the US, and other doubters, that the session would create a bandwagon effect and inexorable pressure to support a ban. It was what Foreign Minister Axworthy called the mobilization of shame, and it was deliberately intended to move countries in the direction of a ban.

As the meeting got under way, primary emphasis was placed on negotiating the terms of what was now called the Ottawa Declaration. Since it was clear that the Declaration would affirm the commitment of signatories to seek an early conclusion of a ban agreement, the attention of the delegates shifted to the exact means of achieving this end, reflecting their determination to do more than declare a commitment and instead to produce some concrete results. As noted previously, the Canadians had already decided that, instead of attempting to have the conference adopt a common action plan, they would produce a 'Chairman's Agenda for Action', describing the concrete activities that would, or in some cases should, be taken by governments and NGOs to activate a global ban effort. The Agenda was constructed by asking delegates to propose follow-up activities to be undertaken, and then Jill Sinclair and Bob Lawson sat at a computer with the ICBL's Jody Williams and Steve Goose late into the night on Friday, 4 October, and wrote the text of the Agenda. The fact that the Chairman's Agenda did not have to be negotiated meant that its drafters did not have to restrict their text to the lowest common denominator agreement among the delegates, thus sustaining the momentum generated by the session.

Earlier on Friday morning, Ralph Lysyshyn, from his position as Chair of the meeting,[40] could see a problem emerging, and it related back to the proposal that Jill Sinclair had made to him a week earlier, which he had rejected. During bilateral discussions prior to the conference, the French had insisted that any statement about further negotiations that might emerge from the Ottawa meeting had to include a reference to the CD. As noted earlier, because its consensus format was likely to produce deadlock, the CD was not an acceptable negotiating forum for Canada, and so the Canadians equivocated, replying to the French that negotiations did not necessarily have to occur in the CD, but without having an alternative firmly in mind. Now, as the conference proceeded, first France and then Italy and the United States made their statements to the meeting, and each argued, in turn, that any follow-up negotiations should be undertaken in the CD. Listening to these statements, Lysyshyn surveyed his counterparts around the table, international security bureaucrats like himself from the 50 countries formally attending the meeting. He realized that, of the 50, probably 25 or 30 were simply there to ensure that their governments were represented in the meeting; they neither knew nor cared a great deal about the AP mines issue, nor did they believe particularly in the need for a ban. As a result, they could be expected to follow the lead of the major powers and direct the issue to the CD, where it would be buried.

If this was the problem, then Lysyshyn could also see an opportunity unfolding. As noted previously, Lysyshyn had been preoccupied with other international security issues and had left the anti-personnel mines issue largely to Sinclair. Now, at the conference, he could see for the first time how broad the international coalition was on this issue, and he was impressed by the presence of very senior UN officials, there to lend their support to the initiative. He was also aware of the enormous coverage being given to the event, and to Canada's leadership role, in the Canadian press. This thing was, Lysyshyn realized, a hell of a lot bigger than he had thought originally, and there was an opportunity here for Canada to secure its leadership role on the issue. And if it did not do so, chances were that somebody else would. The most likely candidate to usurp Canadian leadership was Belgium. A founding member of the core group of pro-ban states, Belgium had previously taken a leading role on the AP mines issue, and before the Ottawa meeting convened the Belgians had declared their intention to host a follow-up meeting. The Belgian Foreign Affairs Minister had a background in international development and a particular interest in the humanitarian dimension of the AP mines issue. Just as Lysyshyn could see momentum building in the conference for action following the Ottawa meeting, he could also see the Belgians positioning themselves to take over the lead on the issue.[41]

Between problem and opportunity, Lysyshyn thought he saw an opening. Recall Kingdon's description of the joining of the policy streams where, occasionally, a viable policy alternative is linked to a pressing problem under favourable political conditions and, as a result, a policy window opens. In this circumstance, a policy entrepreneur has to be ready with the alternative and savvy enough to take advantage of the opening. While sitting in the chair that Friday morning, Lysyshyn came up with an idea, and he decided to move. The idea was drawn from his previous experience as IDA director, the position now occupied by Jill Sinclair, and it concerned a previous negotiation initiated by Canada. Earlier in the summer, as mentioned previously, Mark Gwozdecky had raised the prospect of Ottawa hosting a stand-alone forum to negotiate a ban on landmines, and Lysyshyn had estimated the cost at $2 million, based on his experience with the Open Skies conference held in Ottawa in 1990. Open Skies held other lessons for Lysyshyn as well.

Early in 1989, the US National Security Council (NSC) staff was conducting a wide-ranging review of American strategic relations with the Soviet Union. While in Washington in April 1989, Lysyshyn met with an NSC staffer who said they were considering all options as part of the review, even a resurrection of the Open Skies concept, a regime proposed originally by the Eisenhower administration in 1955 to permit the US and the Soviet Union to monitor each other's strategic arsenals.[42] Back in Ottawa, Lysyshyn suggested to his boss, John Noble, director-general of the

International Security Bureau, that they should push the US to move forward on the Open Skies idea.[43] Noble secured agreement, and Lysyshyn returned to Washington to meet with NSC officials. Prime Minister Brian Mulroney was scheduled to meet with US President George Bush in early May, and Lysyshyn informed the Americans that Mulroney was going to raise the Open Skies idea for discussion with Bush. On 4 May 1989, Mulroney did so in a meeting with Bush at the White House. Urging Bush to move forward with Open Skies, Mulroney also argued that the negotiations should include not just the two superpowers, but the entire membership of NATO and the Warsaw Pact. The negotiations would not take place in Vienna, traditional site of arms control negotiations between the superpowers, but instead would open in Ottawa in February 1990, with plans to reconvene in Budapest, Hungary, only three months later to conclude the final text of a treaty.[44]

Open Skies provided Lysyshyn with the idea for a viable policy alternative that would keep the AP mines issue from being buried in the CD and would secure a leadership role for Canada. Open Skies had drawn together an ad hoc collection of negotiating parties who deliberated outside of the traditional forum for negotiation, according to an unusually short timetable. The same could be done here, thought Lysyshyn. He also saw a parallel between the political state of play on the AP mines issue and that which had prevailed on Open Skies: in each, public opinion was strongly supportive of action, and political leaders were looking for something that they could say yes to. At noon on Friday, Lysyshyn phoned his boss, Assistant Deputy Minister Paul Heinbecker. He said that he thought the issue was ripe, but that a lot of people were out to kill it. Either way, things could move quickly, and if Canada did not do something dramatic, the issue would either be derailed into the CD or it would move forward with somebody else in the lead. It was obviously an issue that Axworthy liked, and Lysyshyn thought there was an opportunity here for Canada to do something. Heinbecker asked what he had in mind, and Lysyshyn laid out his idea that Canada should offer to host a follow-on negotiation to conclude an international ban treaty before the end of 1997. He told Heinbecker that he had not discussed the idea with anyone in the Canadian group, and that he would not put the idea to the minister unless he was promised the resources to host the negotiating session. When Heinbecker asked for an amount, Lysyshyn repeated his earlier estimate of $2 million, figuring he could do just about anything with that amount of money.[45] Three hours later, Heinbecker phoned back to tell Lysyshyn that he had his $2 million and should proceed, and that in the meantime he and

Gordon Smith, the Foreign Affairs deputy minister, would give Axworthy a preliminary briefing.[46]

With his marching orders in hand, Lysyshyn met with Sinclair and Gwozdecky to describe his proposal and instruct them as to the content of the speech they would have to prepare for Axworthy. The speech was ready Saturday morning. Now, a critical decision for Lysyshyn was whether any other state delegations should be told about the Canadian plans. Since, by this time, government offices would be closed in Europe and Asia, delegations could do little but say they disagreed or that they would consult their governments. Lysyshyn did not want to register either response, and opted instead to let them be surprised. This required a little dissembling on his part. While he was reading a draft of Axworthy's speech at the Conference Centre on Saturday morning, Lysyshyn was joined by the head of another national delegation. When the latter inquired, innocently, whether anything was up, Lysyshyn replied in the negative. Similarly, when another head of delegation asked whether there was any reason why he should not plan to leave the conference a bit early, Lysyshyn reassured him that there was not.

The draft of Axworthy's speech was faxed to Michael Pearson for review on Saturday morning.[47] Pearson joined the Canadian group, telling them that Axworthy had some idea of what was being proposed and had agreed to go along. At that point, Peter Herby of the ICRC was briefed on the Canadian plan and was asked to arrange a statement of support from ICRC President Cornelio Sommaruga. In addition, Bob Lawson briefed Jody Williams and arranged a statement of support from her. When Axworthy arrived, Lysyshyn described to him the enthusiasm and momentum that was building in the conference and outlined the closing statement that had been prepared, in which Axworthy would offer to host a meeting to sign an international convention before the end of 1997. The action was risky, said Lysyshyn, particularly the stipulation of an imminent deadline: it would anger a large number of countries, including the US, the UK, France, Russia, and China;[48] Canada would be accused of grandstanding, failing to consult, and playing outside the rules; and there was a danger that the initiative would fail. Nevertheless, Lysyshyn told Axworthy that the issue was ripe for bold action, and that the bandwagon emerging in the conference would be led by somebody else if Canada did not seize the initiative. Finally, he said that, in his judgement, the challenge would work, that an international treaty would be achieved. After Lysyshyn had finished his presentation, Axworthy said simply, 'It's the right thing. Let's do it.'

That afternoon, Axworthy invited delegates to gather again in Ottawa no later than December 1997 to sign a ban treaty, and his announcement touched off a minor uproar, composed in equal parts of jubilation and consternation. Along with the core group of states and many NGOs that were overjoyed with Axworthy's bold initiative, there were a number of allies that thought it foolhardy. To offset the latter view, Sommaruga and Williams made their prearranged statements in support of Axworthy's position, after which Lysyshyn adjourned the meeting. The Ottawa Process was launched.

Summary

In this final stage of a policy process that began with André Ouellet's declaration of support for a ban almost a year earlier, the three policy streams converged once again, this time to launch a quest for an international ban treaty. And once again, the streams were joined by resourceful policy entrepreneurs who recognized a window of opportunity and seized the chance to advance an evolving policy alternative. In the problem stream, the NGO policy community stepped up its pressure for a ban, and Jill Sinclair identified the need to sustain the momentum that had been generated in the lead-up to the Ottawa strategy session. Waiting to be joined with this problem was the alternative that was formulated by Ralph Lysyshyn in the policy stream, namely, extending the idea of an ad hoc forum of self-selected states to apply to an international negotiation, with a deadline for completion attached.

Congruent with Kingdon's model, the consensus around the idea of an alternative forum of like-minded states grew until, in Ottawa, a tipping point was reached when the number of adherents had grown sufficiently that the success of the idea seemed assured. Even with that, it is not difficult to imagine the impediments to such an idea that might arise in the political stream. However, in this case DFAIT had the field to itself, with DND sidelined since the summer, and within DFAIT there was no effective opposition to Lysyshyn and Sinclair on the issue. Most importantly, when problem, policy, and politics were aligned in Ottawa on 4 October 1996, Lysyshyn played a critically important entrepreneurial role and was savvy enough to present a *beau risque* to a minister not afraid to take one.

CONCLUSION

The Ottawa Process originated in a series of conjunctions of events in three streams of the policy process. First, the landmines problem was elevated to the governmental agenda when a pressing problem combined with pressure for an export moratorium from a minister who was willing to challenge DND's jurisdiction and was dissatisfied with the dissonance between

Canada's demining activities and Canadian landmines policy. The issue moved from the governmental to the decision agenda with the transition to a new minister, anxious to find an issue to run with. When this occurred, the problem was redefined to focus on the need to avoid the Conference on Disarmament process, and the preferred policy alternative shifted to a comprehensive unilateral moratorium and an international ban. The decision to organize the October 1996 strategy session did not solve the problem, of course, but created a new imperative to sustain the momentum building in support of an international ban, while still avoiding the CD. An inchoate idea of organizing a group of like-minded states for the negotiation of an international ban circulated through the policy stream, along with other alternatives, as DFAIT officials searched for ways to address the landmines problem. When an extraordinary negotiating forum with a deadline for concluding a convention was finally identified as the preferred alternative, the idea was delivered on fertile political ground: DFAIT was firmly in control of the anti-personnel mines file, there was substantial public and pressure group support for action, and the minister was eager to do something.

As Kingdon's model alerts us, however, while the conjunctions can open windows of opportunity, they do not guarantee that change will occur. Without policy entrepreneurs, the streams are not joined, no conjunctions occur, and the windows close. It may be tempting to conclude, in hindsight, that there was an inevitability to the launch of the Ottawa Process, that it was driven by inexorable forces behind an idea whose time had come. A careful analysis reveals that this simply was not the case. The policy process streams were joined by fortuitous events at a number of critical junctures, and policy entrepreneurs needed as much dumb luck as they did skill in their efforts to take advantage of the windows of opportunity that opened at those moments. If there is a lesson from this Canadian policy process, it is this: substantial changes in agendas and policies occur neither comprehensively nor incrementally; instead, they result from the alignment of a complex array of conditions associated with problems, policies, and politics and the associated actions of knowledgeable players who are lucky and skilful enough to be able to exploit these opportunities to bring about change.

NOTES

An earlier version of this chapter appeared in *Canadian Foreign Policy* 5, 3 (Spring 1998). Financial support for the research undertaken for this article was provided by the Non-proliferation, Arms Control, and Disarmament Division in the

Canadian Department of Foreign Affairs and International Trade. Able research assistance in the preparation of the article was provided by Colleen Hoey of the Norman Paterson School of International Affairs.

1. John W. Kingdon, *Agendas, Alternatives, and Public Policies*, 2nd edn (New York: HarperCollins, 1995); Michael Cohen, James March, and Johan Olsen, 'A Garbage Can Model of Organizational Choice', *Administrative Science Quarterly* 17 (Mar. 1972): 1–25.
2. Thomas Risse-Kappen, 'Ideas Do Not Float Freely: Transnational Coalitions, Domestic Structures, and the End of the Cold War', *International Organization* 48 (Spring 1994): 185–214.
3. For discussions of the role of ideas in policy formulation, see Giandomenico Majone, *Evidence, Argument, and Persuasion in the Policy Process* (New Haven: Yale University Press, 1989); and, on international policy, Judith Goldstein, 'The Impact of Ideas on Trade Policy', *International Organization* 43 (Winter 1989): 31–71; Judith Goldstein and Robert Keohane, eds, *Ideas and Foreign Policy* (Ithaca, NY: Cornell University Press, 1993).
4. Kingdon, *Agendas*, 19.
5. On problem definition and agenda setting, see David Rochefort and Roger Cobb, eds, *The Politics of Problem Definition* (Lawrence: University of Kansas Press, 1994); Deborah Stone, 'Causal Stories and the Formation of Policy Agendas', *Political Science Quarterly* 104, 2 (1989): 281–300.
6. Kingdon, *Agendas*, 90.
7. Ibid., 117. For discussions of the role of policy communities, see Paul Sabatier and Hank Jenkins-Smith, eds, *Policy Change and Learning* (Boulder, Colo.: Westview Press, 1993); Michael Atkinson and William Coleman, 'Policy Networks, Policy Communities and the Problems of Governance', *Governance* 5, 2 (1992): 154–80; Peter Haas, 'Introduction: Epistemic Communities and International Policy Coordination', *International Organization* 46, 1 (1992): 1–35.
8. See Colin Bennett and Michael Howlett, 'The Lessons of Learning: Reconciling Theories of Policy Learning and Policy Change', *Policy Sciences* 25 (1992): 275–94.
9. Kingdon, *Agendas*, 140.
10. Ibid., 145, 146.
11. Ibid., 153.
12. Ibid., 164.
13. Ibid., 165.
14. Ibid., 166. This is a variation on the distinction between systemic and institutional agendas originally proposed in Roger Cobb and Charles Elder, *Participation in American Politics: The Dynamics of Agenda-Building* (Boston: Allyn and Bacon, 1972).

15. Kingdon, *Agendas*, 224.
16. Ibid., 206.
17. Information for the following analysis was drawn from confidential government documents and interviews. The interviews involved discussions with those government officials who were centrally involved in the anti-personnel mines issue during the period under study. They were conducted on the understanding that there would be no direct attribution or quotation without permission.
18. Ouellet's interest in the issue was manifest even earlier. In 1994, Cornelio Sommaruga, president of the ICRC, had urged Jean Chrétien to support a ban on anti-personnel mines, believing that Canada's status as a G–7 member would lend credence to the movement to ban mines. Ouellet encouraged the Prime Minister to support a ban, and Chrétien raised the issue at the G–7 summit in Naples in the summer of 1994. However, the issue did not remain a priority, and it was left to Ouellet to secure a place for it on the governmental agenda.
19. He did so in a letter to Ouellet dated 22 August 1995. The official reason for DND opposition to the export moratorium was that, because Canada had not produced mines since 1992, they had to retain their ability to import components for mines held by Canada. In addition, Canadian supplies of claymore mines were running low, and replacements would have to be imported.
20. In fairness, Collenette had to deal with his officials on issues that were more difficult and carried a higher priority for him, including deep cuts in defence spending and fallout from the inquiry into the actions of Canadian peacekeeping troops in Somalia. In this context, he may have preferred not to take them on over mines as well.
21. As reported in the *Toronto Star*, 10 Nov. 1995, A12.
22. Lawson was new to the division, but not to the issue. A former member of the Canadian Forces, he had served as technical adviser on arms control and verification at DND.
23. The CCW Review Conference in Vienna had ended in stalemate, as previously noted. Canadian Ambassador Mark Moher played an instrumental role in securing an extension of the talks, to January, for technical issues, and to April 1996 when two final sessions were scheduled to take place in Geneva. Clearly, Canada was still, at this point, officially committed to the CCW.
24. Sinclair had become director of IDA in August 1994, moving over from her position as deputy director in the Regional Security and Peacekeeping Division (IDC).
25. A Gallup International review of national public opinion in the spring of 1996 showed 73 per cent of Canadians in favour of an international agreement to ban the use of mines (with only 8 per cent opposed). In comparison,

22 per cent of Americans opposed a ban (with 60 per cent in favour). Poll results provided by the Canadian Red Cross Society.

26. This memorandum was intended to provide authorization for Bob Lawson to issue an invitation to selected (pro-ban) countries while attending the CCW in April in Geneva. For a description of the meeting between Lawson and other government officials and NGOs in Geneva, see the *Ottawa Citizen*, 29 Nov. 1997, B1.

27. September would become October, of course. Originally, IDA planned to have this meeting in June 1996, expecting it to be very small and informal. However, initial soundings with other countries revealed substantial interest, indicating that it would be a bigger meeting than expected and requiring more time for planning.

28. While DND was sidelined on the matter of policy choice, Defence officials did continue to participate in the policy process and were actively involved in planning the Ottawa strategy session.

29. Several developing countries, Mexico and Indonesia prominent among them, maintained that the first priority of the CD should be nuclear weapons, not landmines. Nor could Canada count on support from the major powers. The UK, for example, bitterly opposed Canada on the landmines issue prior to the change to a Labour government in Britain in the spring of 1997.

30. Of course, the fault was not Lawson's, who had been authorized to make the announcement to the press. Undoubtedly, had the media interest been anticipated, other arrangements would have been made.

31. Even after they had opted for the CD, the Americans stuck to their agreement with Canada, resisting French efforts to add a CD reference to the UN resolution.

32. MAC was also part of the Canadian delegation at the final session of the CCW in May 1996.

33. The idea was not dropped permanently, however. In October, Lysyshyn would draw again on his experience with Open Skies to considerable effect, as described below.

34. In the face of DND's resistance to stockpile destruction, the DND military adviser assigned to DFAIT suggested to Lysyshyn that he ask Defence officials when they had last actually used anti-personnel mines. The answer, as it turned out, was during the Korean War, a fact that did little to buttress DND arguments about necessity.

35. To strengthen the DFAIT case, Lysyshyn reminded the PCO about the Prime Minister's statement in support of a ban at the G–7 meeting in Naples in 1994. The reminder was necessary because the PCO did not recall the statement.

36. IDA was concerned that DND officials, if asked why a portion of the stockpiles were being retained, might refer to needing them in the event of hostilities,

undermining Canada's declared support for an unconditional ban. In fact, Collenette did make such a reference, but the press missed it. The next day, Collenette resigned as Defence Minister, and DFAIT simply let the point go.

37. *Canadian Action Plan* prepared in March 1996 (see note 26).

38. The panel included prominent ban proponents such as US Senator Patrick Leahy, UNICEF Deputy Executive Director Stephen Lewis, and ICRC President Cornelio Sommaruga.

39. Ironically, Duclos subsequently became a firm supporter of the Ottawa Process.

40. Lysyshyn was in the chair because Canada was hosting the meeting.

41. Belgian leadership would also make the CD track more likely, especially since the head of the Belgian delegation in Ottawa was scheduled to take up a position as Belgium's ambassador to the CD, where he might be tempted to take the issue.

42. The Soviets rejected the proposal.

43. For a discussion of the reasons behind Canada's interest in Open Skies, see the Foreword by former Secretary of State for External Affairs Joe Clark in Michael Slack and Heather Chestnutt, eds, *Open Skies: Technical, Organizational, Operational, Legal, and Political Aspects* (Toronto: Centre for International Strategic Studies, York University, 1990).

44. For discussions of the Open Skies negotiations, see Peter Jones, 'Open Skies: A New Era of Transparency', *Arms Control Today* 22, 4 (1992): 10–15; Slack and Chestnutt, eds, *Open Skies*; Jonathan Tucker, 'Back to the Future: The Open Skies Talks', *Arms Control Today* 20, 8 (1990): 20–4.

45. The figure was truly invented, since Lysyshyn had no idea what the Open Skies conference in 1990 had actually cost.

46. During their meeting with Axworthy on Friday evening, Smith called Robert Fowler, Canada's Ambassador to the United Nations, to ask if he thought Lysyshyn's idea was crazy. Fowler assured them it was not. Mary Fowler, the Ambassador's wife, worked in the UN's Department of Humanitarian Affairs and was attending the Ottawa meeting. By early Saturday morning, the UN people were aware of Canadian plans, and Mary Fowler approached Lysyshyn to tell him she knew what he was up to and to offer a written statement of support from the UN Secretary-General.

47. In a reversal of usual roles, Pearson thought the bureaucrats had gone over the top with some of their language, and he toned it down for the minister.

48. Rarely in the past had Axworthy been persuaded not to rock the policy boat because it would upset allies, so this was not a particular concern for him now. Nor did he believe that Canada's quarrel was with the US government; rather, it was with the Pentagon.

CHAPTER 12

RHETORIC AND POLICY REALITIES IN THE UNITED STATES

Mary Wareham

President Bill Clinton defended his administration's decision not to sign the Ottawa Convention by saying that 'our refusal to sign does not indicate a lack of dedication to our common goal of eliminating antipersonnel landmines from the face of the earth.'[1] He repeated his mantra of leadership on this issue of global concern, went on to cite his place in history as the 'first world leader to call for the elimination of antipersonnel landmines', and claimed his policies were consistent with that commitment.

This chapter will outline the significant gap between rhetorical leadership and policy realities resulting in the President's refusal to relinquish anti-personnel (AP) mines. It analyses the US Campaign to Ban Landmines (USCBL), leadership on the ban issue in the Congress, specifically legislative initiatives of Vermont Democratic Senator Patrick Leahy, and shows how Congress, rather than the administration, was the key influence in any movement in American landmine policy. It will also examine how the USCBL repeatedly attempted to pressure the administration to formulate a coherent policy to match its rhetoric. Finally, the international context will be analysed to show how early US leadership towards a ban on AP mines was ultimately overtaken by an actual global commitment to do away with these insidious devices. It will offer reasons for the US refusal to sign the Ottawa Convention and will look to policy options for the future.

USCBL AND CONGRESS: EARLY LEADERSHIP IN THE BAN MOVEMENT

The United States was an early leader on a landmines ban, but then, as now, real leadership has been the result of the interplay between the USCBL and Congress and has not emanated from the White House. The USCBL, like most national ban campaigns, was created by an NGO whose field-based experience with mine victims resulted in its concluding that the only way to deal effectively with the global landmine crisis was to seek a ban on AP mines. In 1991, Human Rights Watch (HRW) and Physicians for Human Rights (PHR) had issued their joint report, *Landmines in Cambodia: The Coward's War*, in which they were among the first to call publicly for a ban on landmines. But it was the Vietnam Veterans of America Foundation (VVAF) that took the next step.

In mid-1991, the VVAF had opened a prosthetics clinic in Cambodia. Only a few months later, at the end of November, its president, Robert O. (Bobby) Muller, and Thomas Gebauer, head of the German NGO Medico International, partners in several field-based projects, met in Washington to discuss the possibility of initiating a coalition effort to ban anti-personnel mines. At Gebauer's suggestion, Muller hired Jody Williams, a long-time activist on Central American policy, to take on the building of a campaign.

With the VVAF's decision to campaign against AP mines, it was obviously wise to seek congressional partners in what would likely be a long process. The most important leadership from Capitol Hill originated from the office of Senator Leahy. One of the very first meetings on the Hill was between Williams and Leahy staffer Tim Rieser. Leahy's support was likely, given his involvement in the landmine issue dating to the late 1980s when he visited a field hospital on the Honduran border during the armed conflict in Nicaragua.[2] There he met an adolescent boy who had lost a leg to a landmine and was living at the hospital—he was moving around on a homemade crutch. In response to Leahy's questions, the boy said he didn't know where the mine had come from or who had laid it—all he knew was that the landmine had changed his life forever. Unable to shake the image of the boy, Leahy returned to Washington and established the War Victims Fund, a $5 million annual congressional appropriation to provide assistance to victims of landmines.

When Rieser met with Williams on 4 December 1991, he was supportive of the idea of a ban campaign. Although conceding it would be a tough battle to win, Rieser thought such an initiative could highlight the as yet little-known problem of landmine contamination and perhaps lead to more stringent conditions governing their use or even measures to outlaw their sale. Rieser told Williams that Leahy would be willing to enter information about such a campaign into the Congressional Record.[3] Thus began what would become the core of a USCBL/congressional partnership in the movement to ban AP mines.

The World's First Landmine Export Moratorium
Tim Rieser's words in that first meeting on the Hill the previous December proved prescient. In 1992, Patrick Leahy's first legislative step would be a one-year moratorium on exports and transfers of AP mines from the United States. Throughout the early months of 1992, the work between Leahy's office and the VVAF developed on the landmine issue. In June, Muller met with Leahy to thank him for his leadership and to offer support to Leahy's contemplated legislative initiative. By this time Muller had also enlisted

the involvement of Congressman Lane Evans, a Vietnam-era veteran from Illinois who would take up landmine legislation on the House side of Congress.

Early grassroots support for the Leahy legislation was rooted primarily in arms control groups working in Washington. Tom Cardamone, a VVAF employee working with Williams, had met with various groups to learn how they had worked to get the Chemical Weapons Convention enacted into law. As one arms control activist said, 'I was impressed with the way he was looking for a comparable model, and chemical weapons were not comparable—it was a nightmarish model negotiated through the CD—but he wanted to find out how groups working for many years against an indiscriminate and inhumane weapons system had achieved what they did.'[4]

Later that spring, Williams and Cardamone attended a bimonthly meeting of the Washington coalition, the Arms Transfer Working Group (ATWG), and briefed its members on the campaign. Not everyone there understood the relevance of the issue immediately, but shortly thereafter Williams circulated a letter asking ATWG member groups to endorse the ICBL. As another member of ATWG notes, 'I remember during these ATWG meetings the question keep coming up of "why are we singling this issue out?" At that point I had been convinced by Jody [Williams] on the inhumane nature of the weapon and its impact and I helped to convince people not only to work for the export ban but a worldwide ban.'[5] Landmines became a core agenda item for the ATWG, which formed the core of lobby efforts for the export moratorium.

Skilfully shepherded through Congress, the Leahy-Evans export moratorium was signed into law on 23 October 1992 by President George Bush. The amendment also called on the US to 'seek verifiable international agreements prohibiting the sale, transfer, or export, and further limiting the use, production, possession, and deployment of antipersonnel landmines.' Separate language in the Defense bill also called on the President to submit, within 180 days, a report on demining activities in certain nations. Senator Leahy also called on the US government to ratify the 1980 Convention on Conventional Weapons (CCW), a task that was finally completed in early 1996. Leahy's initiative placed the United States in the lead as the first country to enact domestic legislation on landmines and gave tremendous impetus to the ban movement internationally.

Growth of the USCBL and Congressional Leadership

Early and relatively easy legislative victories helped build momentum in the young coalition effort that would become the USCBL. The US movement was also greatly strengthened by the fact that the NGOs had a powerful and influential champion in Senator Leahy. That the issue was an 'easy sell' to the media also helped build public awareness in support of the ban cause. NGOs were also encouraged that the defence industry had not mounted an aggressive campaign in support of AP mines, something they encountered frequently on other defence-related issues. With the ban movement having seized the moral high ground through the media, in these early days the Pentagon's presence on the Hill was minimal. Few uniformed military officials wanted to defend a weapon already seen as an indiscriminate killer of innocent civilians.

Groups outside of the ATWG began signing up to the cause, and in June 1993 NGOs met in Boston to develop a broader-based US-coalition to eliminate landmines. NGOs were increasingly able to broaden the coalition to include not only peace and disarmament and religious groups but new constituencies—humanitarian groups such as Save the Children USA and World Vision, which were concerned by the impact of mines on their programs. By late 1995, US organizations had agreed that closer co-ordination, based in Washington, would greatly benefit campaign efforts. This agreement led to a meeting in March of 1996 in Washington where the USCBL adopted a more formal structure as a co-ordinated country campaign. Nine NGOs volunteered to serve as a USCBL steering committee, the core group responsible for overall strategic planning. Three founders of the ICBL— HRW, PHR, and the VVAF—were among the nine volunteers for the USCBL steering committee. Since February 1996, the VVAF has employed the co-ordinator of the USCBL. In addition, at the March meeting, member organizations were invited to participate in task forces on media, grassroots, and legislative affairs. By March 1996, some 70 US-based NGOs had endorsed the USCBL's goals and thus became members of the USCBL.

When in May of that year President Clinton pledged to 'seek a worldwide agreement as soon as possible to end the use of all anti-personnel land mines', the campaign called for the US to set a time frame for its policy— and demanded that it ban landmines *now*! By early 1998 over 300 NGOs had endorsed this call, including over a dozen city and county councils and state legislatures. Like the ICBL, a key strength to the USCBL was its broad-based membership involving groups from a wide range of fields: human rights, children's, women's, humanitarian, veterans', peace, arms control, and major religious constituencies. While the USCBL initially concentrated its work on providing constituent support for legislative action on landmines, as the network grew its work diversified and the campaign and individual NGOs carried out a range of actions to build public awareness of the global landmine crisis, to continue to support US legislative initiatives, and to press the Clinton administration to turn its leadership rhetoric into reality.

Stigmatizing Producers and Building Grassroots Support

In the early morning of 7 May 1996 the first US demonstration against a local landmine manufacturer was held by over 250 people outside the headquarters of Alliant Techsystems in Hopkins, Minnesota. The demonstration was followed by meetings between the Minnesota Campaign to Ban Landmines and public relations officers of Alliant Tech, whose arguments were predictable: 'it's not our [self-destruct] mines that cause the problem' and 'we will stop producing mines when the Department of Defense stops ordering them.'[6] A religious order, the School Sisters of Notre Dame, purchased shares in Alliant Tech in order to be able to provoke discussion about AP mines at the company's annual general meetings of shareholders.

At the conclusion of that demonstration at Alliant Tech, a 27-year-old woman from New Hampshire, Ariel Brugger, left on an interfaith pilgrimage that would take her 1,600 miles by foot through America's heartland calling for a ban on landmines. Only 18 months later, the Ban Bus to Ottawa would retrace parts of her route. Brugger's walk concluded in Lafayette Park, opposite the White House, on 29 July 1996 with speeches from Senator Leahy and the supreme patriarch of Cambodian Buddhism and leader of Cambodia's Peace Walks, Samdech Preah Maha Ghosananda. At the same time as the walk, the Women's Commission for Refugee Women and Children organized a speakers' tour of three American cities featuring Cambodian, American, and Rwandan landmine survivors.

During this period, Human Rights Watch had begun following up on sections of its *Deadly Legacy* report by preparing research into US-based manufacturers of AP mines and their components. *Exposing the Source*, the results of the year-long investigation, documented 47 US companies in 23 states that have been involved in producing and supplying AP mine components. Made public in April 1997, the report's release had been purposefully delayed by months. Before launching its 'Stigmatization Campaign', HRW began dialogue with the producer companies to give them the opportunity to 'voluntarily renounce' any future production of mines or their components and thus be praised, rather than stigmatized. These negotiations resulted in 19 companies, including Motorola and Hughes Aircraft, renouncing future mine production activities. The USCBL distributed the report to campaigners across the country and urged them to help stigmatize the producers, which included General Electric ('the company that brings good things to life') and major defence contractors Lockheed Martin and Alliant Techsystems, the biggest US landmine producer. Outside Alliant

Tech's headquarters in Minnesota, demonstrations continued and protestors were arrested *en masse* and prosecuted for trespassing.

Building public awareness in the US was given a significant boost when, in late 1996, Warner Brothers DC Comics published *Batman: Death of Innocents*, a comic book about AP mines featuring an introduction by Senator Leahy and articles by Jody Williams, Colonel David Hackworth, and landmine survivor Jerry White. The comic, which was published in conjunction with a Superman comic on mine awareness for Bosnian children, reached thousands of American children and adults, resulting in numerous requests for more information on how to participate in the call for a ban. Actions against producers continued while campaigners also sought to build a public understanding of US landmine policy. Part of the problem for the USCBL throughout was the lack of a clear administration policy on anti-personnel mines other than the rhetorical call for their eventual elimination. This changed on 16 May 1996 when President Clinton announced his new landmine policy. Now the challenge for the USCBL was in explaining a complicated policy to the public and media. In truth, the campaigners claimed, the President's announcement meant 'no real change', and privately more than a few administration officials concurred.

When the United States reluctantly agreed to participate in the October 1996 strategy conference in Ottawa and Foreign Minister Lloyd Axworthy called on nations to come back in December 1997 to sign an agreement banning AP mines, the USCBL joined the ICBL in welcoming Axworthy's bold challenge to the world. But this decision, like others taken by the US administration—such as its January 1997 decision to take negotiations to the CD instead of participating in the Ottawa Process—received little media attention in the US, making the work of campaigners that much harder. As one noted, 'The action message to grassroots at this time asking them to call the White House hotline and urge that US-led negotiations not go [to] this dead forum called the Conference on Disarmament was such an obscure sell for the grassroots.'[7] While the USCBL co-ordinator kept the campaign up-to-date with the Ottawa Process and CD efforts, the primary focus was kept on the need for a domestic ban on the weapon.

The USCBL continued its varied actions to press Clinton to 'do the right thing'. Timed to coincide with a much-publicized summit meeting between the President and Canada's Prime Minister Chrétien, the VVAF announced with an advertisement in the *Washington Post* on 7 April its intention to intensify domestic lobbying on the ban to make the December treaty-signing deadline a real objective for the administration. Brian Isfeld, father of the first Canadian peacekeeper killed in Bosnia (because of a mine), came to Washington to talk to media and campaigners about why the US should sign the treaty in Ottawa. At this time the USCBL began its efforts to obtain the support of 164 members of the House of Representatives who wrote to President Clinton to urge him to participate fully in the Ottawa Process. In July 1997, the letter was unveiled at the same time as the introduction of Senate and House landmine elimination legislation.

The USCBL planned a series of events to mark the one-year anniversary of the President's promise to ban AP mines: 26,000 mine victims later, 'where's the ban?' the campaigners asked. On 15 May, at a film première in the US Capitol, Senator Patrick Leahy accepted signatures from 110,680 Americans calling for a ban on landmines. US campaigners also sent thousands of postcards addressed to the President at the White House urging him to ban AP mines and sign the treaty in December. The events concluded with a 16 May 1997 rally outside the White House featuring Cambodian landmine survivor and activist Tun Channareth. The Web site of the USCBL featured a clock that started ticking on 16 May and rose by one every 22 minutes, indicating another landmine victim somewhere in the world, to symbolize the humanitarian nature of the USCBL call for the President to keep his promise.

Back on the Hill

As the USCBL continued to grow, Leahy and Evans sought repeatedly to bring the landmine issue back to Congress. In September of 1993, they sought a three-year extension of their 1992 export moratorium. To the surprise of many, the bill won the rare unanimous support of the Senate in a clear vote of 100 to 0. With the moratorium extension in place, Leahy's next step was to garner political, public, and media support for the ban by holding Senate hearings on the global landmine crisis. The 13 May 1994 hearings featured emotional testimony by recently wounded landmine survivor Ken Rutherford and statements from the VVAF and HRW. The hearing received prepared statements in support of a ban from notable figures— UNICEF executive director James P. Grant, UN Secretary-General Boutros Boutros-Ghali, the president of the American Red Cross, Elizabeth Dole, former US President Jimmy Carter, former Secretary of State Cyrus Vance, and former US Ambassador to the United Nations Herbert S. Okun.

These hearings set the stage for new legislation introduced on 21 June 1994. The Senator, along with over 50 Senate co-sponsors, entered a bill that would require a one-year moratorium on the production and procurement of AP mines by the US government. Evans introduced a parallel bill in the House of Representatives. For the first time, legislative initiatives met significant resistance on the part of the Secretaries of State and Defense. In a letter to Leahy, they said they were 'committed to working toward an effective international AP landmine control regime' and that a 'broad spectrum of options is under discussion, ranging from a total ban on APL to export controls on all types of APL, production and/or stockpiling restrictions, and transparency measures', but they felt that the current legislation would be 'counter-productive to the goal we all share of developing as quickly as possible an effective AP landmine control regime.' The Secretaries added that such legislation would 'prejudge the US negotiating position, restricting our ability to conduct effective consultations with countries critical to a control regime'.[8]

NGOs stepped up their lobbying efforts to build support in Congress for this and other legislation. The World Federalists, 20/20 Vision, and other grassroots NGOs, including those representing major US religious denominations such as the US Catholic Conference, began including landmines in their legislative action alerts to members. Peace Action Education Fund made up 10,000 'Landmines Lotto' scratch-and-win cards explaining US policy to send to activists across the country in their monthly grassroots mailings. Ultimately, the production moratorium was never voted on. Leahy agreed to forgo a vote in order to 'give the Administration time to develop its own landmine policy'.[9] This scenario was repeated again with the 1997 ban legislation that was never voted on. The strategy was indicative of Leahy's repeated attempts to prod the administration into developing a true ban policy.

While a possible moratorium on production had gone nowhere in 1994, with the new congressional year, additional steps were being contemplated. On 15 June 1995, Senator Leahy and Congressman Evans held a press conference to mark the introduction in the Senate, with 49 co-sponsors, of new legislation. Seeking to 'support proposals to implement the United States goal of the eventual elimination of antipersonnel landmines', starting in 1999, the bill would place a one-year moratorium on the use of AP mines, 'except along internationally recognized borders or in demilitarized zones' in marked and guarded minefields.[10] In August, the bill passed the Senate by a vote of 67–27. As a provision in the annual foreign aid spending bill, it was signed into law by President Clinton on 12 February 1996.

To date, the 1999 use moratorium remains unchanged despite attempts to water it down. Given the movement of the US administration away from a ban, it is now clear that the 1998 legislative year will prove the final test for the moratorium. In fact, while the President is extremely sensitive to how the landmine issue has turned out, he may turn a blind eye to Pentagon lobbying against the moratorium. In February 1998, the commander of US forces in Korea testified against the moratorium in Senate Armed Services Committee hearings—which may be a portent of things to come.[11]

THE GAP BETWEEN RHETORIC AND POLICY REALITIES

Even though the international ban movement was still quite young, not too long after the first US export moratorium France announced its own moratorium to enshrine its 'voluntary abstention' from exports of AP mines during the past several years. In addition, responding to pressure from the French campaign, led by Handicap International, the French government had set in motion the process to review the CCW. Clearly, 'competition' among governments for leadership on the issue had already begun.

At the United Nations

Not to be left behind, the US took the issue to the United Nations. The ban movement actually had strong advocates in US representatives at the UN in both Ambassador Madeleine Albright and her chief arms control deputy, Karl ('Rick') Inderfurth. Exchanges between their offices and that of Senator Leahy led to his speaking for the US delegation to introduce, on 11 November 1993, a resolution calling for a moratorium on the export of AP mines. While the US domestic moratorium covered all AP mines, both 'smart' (or self-destructing) and 'dumb' (or non-self-destructing) AP mines, the wording of the UN resolution was more ambiguous and a signal of battles yet to come. The resolution called on states to agree to a moratorium on the export of 'antipersonnel landmines that pose *grave dangers* to civilian populations' (emphasis added). The resolution, with more than 70 co-sponsors, passed by consensus on 17 November. On 7 December 1993— in one of the first landmine policy initiatives by the Clinton administration—letters were sent to 44 mine-producing countries asking them to ban exports of AP landmines for three to five years and requesting them to join US efforts to stop the spread of mines.

By the next session of the General Assembly, many states had enacted some form of export moratorium. The US had already begun work on another resolution to strengthen the export moratorium 'movement'. After being lobbied behind-the-scenes by Senator Leahy and his staff, President Clinton included a quite unexpected phrase in his address before the UN General Assembly in September 1994. While his words calling for the 'eventual elimination' of AP mines placed him squarely in the rhetorical lead, briefing papers released after the speech delineated the qualifiers. While Clinton had said that the world should work for the 'ultimate goal of the eventual elimination of APLs', he added that this elimination would occur *as viable and humane alternatives are developed*.[12]

Campaigners have continued to use the President's words to try to hold him to his promise, but the initial excitement generated by his call was quickly tempered. On 7 October 1994, the US State Department held a briefing for the USCBL to outline policy initiatives signalled by the President's UN speech a week earlier. This included a proposed 'Landmine Control Regime' calling for reduced reliance on those types of AP mines that cause the greatest danger to civilians (i.e., 'dumb' AP mines), restricted availability of AP mines, and reinforcement of landmine use restrictions contained in the 1980 CCW. The NGO community told the administration—both at the briefing and in a letter to President Clinton signed by the heads of 28 US-based NGOs—that it viewed the proposed control regime as 'a giant step backwards in what has until now been a promising US leadership initiative'. While supporting the goal of the eventual elimination of landmines and steps that would move in that direction, the USCBL could not support the control regime itself. After the briefing, one campaigner described the State Department and Arms Control and Disarmament Agency (ACDA) officials as being 'very keen on trying to see if they could convince [campaigners] that we had a joint humanitarian concern and that our [the NGOs'] calculations on how to deal with it were naïve and their landmine control regime was the real humanitarian initiative.'[13]

Despite the fact that the USCBL did not buy the argument, US diplomats pushed ahead with the control regime proposal, convening a closed-door meeting of 31 countries in Budapest on 29–30 June 1995. The US and Britain presented a 12-point program—now called the 'US/UK landmines control regime', that would bind signatories to cut stocks and stop exports of conventional AP mines; however, stocks would be replaced with so-called self-destruct mines.[14] This control regime was formulated to try to seize the initiative before the soon-to-open CCW Review Conference and to ensure that little meaningful change would occur. While the control regime ultimately went nowhere in the CCW, the US still is trying to incorporate elements of it in its continued attempts to move the issue in the CD.

During the CCW Review

After four governmental preparatory meetings, the CCW Review Conference opened for three weeks in Vienna in September and October 1995. Pressure from the ICBL resulted in governments being unable to agree on revisions to its Landmines Protocol and forced delegates to reconvene in January 1996 and from 22 April to 3 May 1996 in a final Geneva meeting.[15] The American negotiating team throughout the two-and-a-half-year CCW review was led by Michael Matheson, principal deputy legal adviser at the Department of State, and included State Department lawyers and representatives from the ACDA and the Pentagon. Officials with experience dating back to the original negotiations of the 1980 CCW were also involved.

US NGOs prepared for the conference by attending meetings held at HRW, where tasks involving grassroots, media, and lobbying work were assigned in order to 'hit the ground running' in Vienna. Letters were collected from a wide range of US NGOs and distributed to lobby the US delegates to the meeting. The NGOs viewed the American position as obstructionist during the CCW because of its attempts to exempt US self-destructing and self-deactivating AP mines. The NGOs viewed this as an open door for other nations to put forward their exemptions for the Protocol.

In Vienna, USCBL participants were struck by the international campaign's lobbying during the proceedings. 'The way that the campaign operated there was unlike anything I had encountered before in any arms control or disarmament initiative', Lora Lumpe remembered. 'They [the NGOs] had a newsletter, mines laid out on the floor, videos showing between delegates' meetings and very aggressive lobbying, pigeonholing, and brow beating of the delegates, who were clearly there to do as little as possible in terms of reforming this Protocol. It was power like I had never seen.'[16]

By the Geneva sessions, while continuing to focus on the handful of countries blocking consensus on a number of issues, the ICBL began criticizing nations, particularly the US, the UK, Australia, Germany, and South Africa, for insisting that they were progressive on the elimination of AP mines while they claimed they could only pursue 'realistic' solutions. When the conference finally ended on 3 May, the ICBL concluded that 'the revised Landmines Protocol is woefully inadequate and is unlikely to make a significant difference in stemming the global landmines crisis.'[17] The head of the US delegation, Matheson, on the other hand, listed what he called 'ground-breaking achievements' to hail the revised Landmine Protocol as 'a vital step toward a ban'.[18]

From the inception of the CCW review, the ICBL had very low expectations for meaningful results from the negotiations, but it recognized the process as a significant platform from which to develop the growing ban movement. By the opening of the Vienna session, only 14 nations had pledged support for an immediate ban. By the end of the review in May, that number had grown to 41, with five nations declaring support for a ban on the last day of the CCW conference alone. The ICBL put pressure on those nations professing to support an immediate total ban to take domestic and international actions consistent with that position. One result of this pressure was the meetings of 'pro-ban' governments with the ICBL during the Geneva review sessions, which ultimately led to the beginning of the Ottawa Process and the December 1997 mine ban treaty. The US, never seen as truly pro-ban, was never invited to take part in these informal pro-ban government meetings in Geneva.[19]

Who's Driving This Policy?

'Who's driving this policy?' has been a favourite question of the VVAF's Bobby Muller. The question underscores the confused and inconsistent decision-making process within the Clinton administration, which led to its inability to sign the Ottawa Convention. While an 'Interagency Working Group' (IWG) made up of representatives of agencies in the government dealing with various aspects of the landmine issue[20] technically has been charged with the development of landmine policy, its real formulation has been much more complicated. Ultimately dominated by the Pentagon, other competing interests have had a hand in the dips and swings of US policy on AP mines.

Among the most important policy-makers was then US Ambassador to the United Nations, Madeleine Albright.[21] Her involvement has gone far beyond the two US resolutions in the UN. In March 1996, after a trip to severely mine-contaminated Angola, Albright wrote a confidential letter to the President, the Chairman of the Joint Chiefs of Staff (JCS), General John Shalikashvili, Defense Secretary William J. Perry, Secretary of State Warren Christopher, and other high-ranking US officials. She bluntly stated that US policies on the issue would not see the elimination of landmines 'within our lifetimes' and concluded that a new policy was 'urgently needed'.

Elements of the letter were leaked to the *New York Times*.[22] That, along with a Mary McGrorey article in the *Washington Post* describing sensitive points discussed in a meeting with Bobby Muller that Albright insisted had been off the record, resulted in Muller being angrily denied access to her office. But at least one official claimed that the letter 'appeared written to be leaked'.[23] Albright's letter and the pending conclusion of the CCW review were among several catalysts for General Shalikashvili to order a full-scale military review of the weapon, which came to public attention in March 1996 with a front-page article in the *New York Times* claiming that

General Shalikashvili was reportedly inclined 'to eliminate all anti-personnel landmines'.[24]

During this same period, the VVAF had begun soliciting support for a ban from senior retired military figures. The goal was to provide President Clinton with the military and political cover necessary should he decide to support a total ban. The VVAF's discussions with retired three- and four-star generals sent ripples through the Pentagon and hastened internal discussions for the AP mine review. On 3 April 1996, 'An Open Letter to President Clinton' appeared in the *New York Times*. The full-page letter, the result of the VVAF's work, contained signatures from 15 retired military leaders in support of a ban. Important former military leaders such as General Norman Schwarzkopf, Commander of Operation Desert Storm; General David Jones, former Chairman, Joint Chiefs of Staff; General John Galvin, former Supreme Allied Commander, Europe; and Lieutenant General James Hollingsworth, former I Corps (ROK/US Group) signed the letter, which stated that an AP mine ban was not only 'humane' but also 'militarily responsible'. (Colin Powell declined to sign, but only because he said he wanted to give Shalikashvili time to complete his internal review.) The letter itself became an international news story.

As the military review reached its conclusion and a policy announcement became imminent, hopes for a total and immediate ban were high. Campaigners knew that discussions even included time frames for a US ban on all AP mines, ranging from as early as 1999 to 2014. There was hope, too, that Korea would be a 'muddy' statement involving a finite exception mandated by the President. One congressional staffer described the intense negotiations as 'a state of war'. But the outcome proved to be a worst-case scenario.

The military review involved getting reports from all seven of the US regional Commanders-in-Chief (CINCs) around the world on their perceived utility of AP mines. CINC staff prepared position papers drawn largely from existing military doctrine and training manuals claiming mines were needed for existing war plans. Yet only the CINC responsible for Korea argued forcefully for the retention of AP mines. In subsequent JCS meetings the findings of the various reports were examined and toughened up. Then, on 10 May General Shalikashvili took the conclusions of the JCS to the White House.

Within an hour, campaigners learned details of the findings and reacted in anger. The USCBL urged the President to reject the advice of the JCS. In addition, because of their fundamental involvement in the ban issue, NGOs decried the lack of consultation with them during the review process. Trying to deflect criticism, the National Security Council (NSC) hastily convened a late-night meeting with VVAF representatives. There they were told that there was still time for them to have a say in the final policy decision. Just at that moment, an official unwittingly stuck his head in the door to inform that the President had just signed off on the Joint Chiefs' policy.

Muller was outraged: '[L]ast week the President stressed his personal concern over landmines by describing the hours he has committed to addressing this problem, and by noting that he keeps an AP landmine on his desk in the Oval Office. This proposal would make a mockery of the President's concern, and would run a dagger through the heart of our international campaign to ban this weapon.'[25] Still trying to influence the President, Muller invited two of the 'Open Letter' generals to attend a White House fund-raising dinner prior to the announcement and argue the case for a total ban with the President. There they were told by the President that 'he couldn't afford a rupture with the Joint Chiefs of Staff' and were asked for help to 'get them off my back'. An exasperated Muller pointed out to the President that this was exactly what he was trying to do.

Six days after the JSC presented its military review to the White House, President Clinton announced a policy reflecting word-for-word the JCS proposal. The policy contained four main elements. First, the US pledged to lead negotiations towards an international agreement to ban AP mines. Second, an immediate ban was placed on the use of 'dumb' or non-self-destruct AP mines, except on the Korean peninsula or for training purposes, and plans were to destroy stocks by the end of 1999. Third, the US reserved the right to use so-called 'smart' or self-destruct and/or self-deactivating AP mines in any conflict situations until an international ban takes effect, and finally, an exception was made for the use of AP mines in Korea in any negotiation on a ban 'until alternatives become available or the risk of aggression has been removed'. The President ordered the Pentagon to search for alternatives to AP landmines.

In a briefing after the announcement, Secretary of State Warren Christopher listed the Conference on Disarmament as a possible negotiating venue, saying '[w]e will begin to consult immediately with our allies on the best way to achieve this.'[26] The next day, campaigners were called into the White House to be briefed on the policy by Nancy Soderberg, the NSC officer in charge of the issue. She defended the policy announcement as a 'new concrete road map toward a total ban', stressing that 'this time we mean it' and calling for regular consultations with NGOs 'to keep us honest'.[27] She offered no specific policy prescription for the avenue leading to an international ban but noted that the Conference on Disarmament could offer some success.

Senator Leahy described the 16 May policy announcement as a lost opportunity and 'old mines in new bottles'. HRW's Stephen Goose, chair of the USCBL steering committee, described the President as being 'completely out of touch with the rapidly growing momentum of the international movement to ban mines'.[28] Campaigners denounced the policy as 'smoke and mirrors' offering no concrete road-map to achieve a ban. Some administration officials confided that the policy announcement was handled badly, noting 'there were too many zigs and zags on the way to the policy announcement'.[29] Hopes and expectations leading up to the announcement had been high—perhaps too high, given the years of leadership rhetoric and the clumsily handled process itself. But with hopes dashed, the gloves were now off and the stage was set for the events over the 20 months leading to the signing of the Ottawa Convention.

A Two-Track Approach: The CD and the Ottawa Process

From the aftermath of its May policy announcement until the October 1996 strategy meeting in Ottawa, there was little movement by the Clinton administration on its landmine policy. In a series of meetings prior to the Ottawa meeting, the administration kept promising an 'immediate' decision on the path they would take towards a ban, but no decision ever materialized. At the same time, officials claimed to have no idea or information on what Canada was hoping to achieve from the Ottawa meeting and continually dismissed it as a 'pep rally', 'an exercise in symbolism', and a 'coalition of the willing' that would beat up on the United States.

During 1996, while repeatedly asking the administration to take the upcoming Ottawa meeting seriously, the USCBL pointed to three domestic policy steps the administration could take to demonstrate a serious commitment to an ultimate ban: (1) turn its export moratorium into a permanent export ban; (2) at a minimum, adopt a moratorium on AP mine production; and (3) encourage greater transparency by taking the lead and establishing a global registry for AP mines.

Prior to the opening of the international strategy meeting in Ottawa in October 1996, the government of Canada decided to divide government participation at the meeting into full participants and observers by asking nations interested in attending to sign a declaration stating their intention to ban the use, production, stockpiling, and transfer of AP mines. In the US, within the IWG there was disagreement over whether to endorse the declaration that in draft form asked nations to support the banning of AP mines by the year 2000. Once Canada dropped these words and stressed that the declaration was a political statement, the US decided to attend as a full participant. Thomas McNamara headed the US delegation to

Ottawa, taking with him officials from the Pentagon, the NSC, the State Department, and Inderfurth, a US representative at the UN. Ultimately, 50 governments joined the meeting as full participants, with another 24 nations attending as observers.

After three days of meetings, the Ottawa conference closed with the final declaration recognizing the urgent need for a ban on AP mines. To reach that goal, the participants had helped elaborate a Chairman's Agenda for Action, outlining actions for reaching a ban rapidly. But few were prepared for the meeting's dramatic ending with the announcement by Canada's Foreign Minister Lloyd Axworthy that not only was Canada prepared to hold a treaty-signing conference for a total ban in December 1997, but it would sign such a treaty no matter how many other states joined it. Campaigners cheered with the realization that their call for a ban would have a government partner to drive the process forward to a concrete deadline. Most diplomats left Ottawa, however, shocked and amazed at the statement. Many of the US delegation had left Ottawa that morning, but in the aftermath of the Ottawa meeting the United States sent a sharply worded *démarche* to Canada and called in Canadian officials to express US anger at Axworthy's shock announcement. Every indication was that the US would not join Canada in support of an immediate ban, but would likely pursue its own course in the Conference on Disarmament.

From that time until its last-minute January 1997 CD announcement, there was even less movement within the administration on the path to negotiate an international ban. One notable exception was a UN General Assembly resolution originally drafted by Canada but introduced, with 84 co-sponsors, by Ambassador Albright on 4 November 1996. The resolution passed the General Assembly on 10 December by a vote of 156 to 0, with 10 abstentions. Its key elements, along with an acknowledgement of the Ottawa conference and its follow-up meeting to be held in Brussels in June, included operative paragraphs urging states to 'pursue vigorously' an international agreement to ban use, stockpiling, production, and transfer of AP mines 'with a view to completing the negotiation as soon as possible'. In his statement to the UN General Assembly that fall, President Clinton had again tried to demonstrate leadership by appealing to all nations 'for the swift negotiation of a worldwide ban on anti-personnel landmines'. He said, 'The United States will lead a global effort to eliminate these terrible weapons and to stop the enormous loss of human life.'

Despite these fine words, which gave the appearance of US commitment to a speedy ban, 1997 began with Clinton's announcement that the US would not join the Ottawa Process but instead seek to negotiate a ban through the UN's CD. Two policy changes were announced at the same time to attempt to placate the USCBL. The administration would support turning Senator Leahy's export moratorium into a permanent ban and also would cap its inventory of stocks at current levels. At first, administration and Pentagon officials did not know what the current stockpiles totalled—research later revealed the US had 14 million AP mines.

In a conference call to the USCBL, the NSC's Robert Bell defended the CD decision by promising that 'if we're wrong about the CD and experience shows that it's going nowhere, we will reassess and are prepared to switch to a more promising venue.'[30] Bell repeatedly cited his own experience in negotiating the Comprehensive Test Ban Treaty by claiming that if the political will were there, the seemingly unachievable could be achieved. Describing 70 per cent of CD members as 'pro-ban' and 18 per cent 'in opposition', Bell claimed that the political will was there. Unconvinced, the USCBL called the decision a 'go slow approach in order to satisfy US military leaders who are still reluctant to abandon the weapon'.[31] Only a week after the announcement, the US Ambassador to the CD, Stephen Ledogar, was already making statements fearing a stalemate at the CD, thus using the forum as a way to deflect criticism of American policy and blame inaction on other participating nations.[32]

Throughout 1997, nations including the US attempted unsuccessfully to place landmines on the CD agenda. By June, one senior administration official said '[p]rogress has been glacial, it's been very disappointing.'[33] Later that month, a special co-ordinator was appointed to try to push the issue forward among CD members; but by 15 August, that co-ordinator—Australian Ambassador Campbell—stated that there was little point in the CD taking any decisions on a possible mandate on landmines until the outcome of the Ottawa Process was known in December. Clearly, the political will was not to be found in the CD—and even if it had been, pro-Ottawa nations were determined to block any attempt to undercut the true ban movement by allowing a 'mandate' to form in the CD.

Throughout 1997, US diplomats were sent to Ottawa Process meetings, where they continued to defend the CD negotiation policy while making somewhat unconvincing attempts to influence the shaping of the Austrian draft of the ban treaty. In the June Brussels meeting, US delegates alienated NGOs and government allies alike with their unseemly conduct that saw the delegation to the conference headed up by a mid-level official while Ambassador McNamara conducted aggressive bilateral discussions with country delegations in isolation from the conference at a downtown hotel. In their bilaterals, US diplomats pressed for consideration of an explicit exception in the treaty for new use of all mines in Korea and the continued use of so-called smart mines indefinitely anywhere in the world.

In short, they attempted to influence the treaty text while still refusing to fully join the Ottawa Process and endorse its December 1997 deadline. US delegates bristled, however, at a news story that they were trying to persuade other nations not to support the mine ban treaty. In the corridors of the Brussels meeting and beyond, much talk was made of US arrogance.

Ban Legislation in 1997

While the administration continued its losing battle to control the international ban process, Leahy took the issue again to Congress—again to put additional pressure on the government to make its joining the ban process inevitable. In July 1997, after months of discussions and behind-the-scenes lobbying by the NGOs and Capitol Hill allies, bipartisan legislation in the 'Landmine Elimination Act' was introduced in both Houses of Congress. The bill sought to ban new deployments of AP mines by the US after 1 January 2000. By the time of its introduction, the legislation had 59 senators and 190 representatives as co-sponsors. Although the legislation never came to a vote, Leahy argued that he and Senator Charles Hagel (R-Nebraska) withheld action on the legislation to give the administration time to participate in the Ottawa Process. A House letter signed by 164 representatives also signalled congressional support for US participation in the Ottawa Process. Senator Leahy had hoped that the President would respond to the pressure—and the bipartisan support—to 'seize this moment' and join with other nations in negotiating the mine ban treaty.

In the Landmine Elimination legislation, language on Korea highlighted differing points of view between the Congress and US NGOs calling for a ban. The relevant clause was not an explicit Korea exception (contrary to claims of American diplomats at the Brussels meeting) but rather a provision that would give the President the option to delay application of the bill for Korea, if he had issued a report and certified that landmine deployment was essential for South Korea's defence. It was a decision the NGOs and the bill's sponsors did not expect the President to exercise: the 'Korea clause' was included because the bill's sponsors wanted to show that they recognized Korea is a problem for the US military that required special attention. The more important aspect of the bill for US NGOs was the time frame of January 2000, which it set for an end to US use of mines. This time frame would put the US in a position to participate in the treaty negotiations.

Despite these attempts to address military concerns, the backlash against the legislation began in early 1997. The Pentagon began deploying staff to the Hill to lobby against the bill. Senator Jesse Helms, Chairman of the Senate Armed Services Committee, wrote a letter to Senate colleagues on 27 June 1997, arguing against the legislation—and attached similar letters from the Chairman of the Joint Chiefs of Staff, the Chief of Staff of the Army, and the General Counsel of the Department of Defense. Secretary of Defense William Cohen—a former Republican Senator and Armed Services Committee member—concurred with Helms, writing that his '[d]epartment strongly objects to elements of the proposal [to bar new deployments of anti-personnel landmines] and urges that it be modified in several important areas'.[34] This was disappointing to the bill's co-sponsors and to the NGO community, for while Cohen was in the Senate he had supported previous legislative initiatives by Leahy.

Subsequently, a letter signed by every member of the Joint Chiefs of Staff and all of the regional CINCs, dubbed the '64 Star' letter (16 four-star generals and admirals), was released opposing the ban legislation. These military officials stated that the legislation would 'unnecessarily endanger US military forces and significantly restrict the ability to conduct combat operations successfully'.[35] Several editorials against the legislation were published in the *Washington Post* and rebutted by ban advocates.[36]

The US in Oslo

In order to participate as a full member in the ban treaty negotiations in Oslo in September 1997, nations had to sign the Brussels Declaration endorsing the Austrian text as the basis for treaty negotiations and committing them to work toward the December 1997 treaty-signing deadline. By the end of the Brussels meeting, 89 governments had signed the Declaration, but not the US. After Brussels, members of the USCBL wrote to the President to urge him to 'abandon the caveats which constrain your current policy in order to fully participate in ban treaty negotiations this September in Oslo and sign the ban treaty in Ottawa this December'.[37] The USCBL asked the President 'how many more mine victims will it take before you stand up to the Pentagon and ban this weapon? The door is open for you to join over 100 nations in negotiating a comprehensive ban treaty with no reservations, no exceptions and no loopholes.'[38]

On 15 August, the President met with the Secretary of Defense, Secretary of State, and National Security Adviser Sandy Berger to discuss whether to participate in the Oslo negotiations after the IWG was unable to reach a decision. The State Department argued that the US should participate but the Defense Department was adamant that certain issues should be non-negotiable. Hillary Rodham Clinton, lobbied variously by UNICEF, Princess Diana, and others concerned with US policy, was rumoured to have encouraged her husband to let the US participate in the negotiations. Finally, the President agreed with Secretary Albright that for political and diplomatic reasons the US should join the negotiations, but to placate the JCS he agreed that the majority of proposals to change the treaty sought by the US were non-negotiable. On 18 August 1997 the administration announced its intention to participate in the three-week treaty negotiations in Oslo, Norway. Immediately, media applications for accreditation at the treaty negotiations shot up. With the 31 August death of Princess Diana, the conference was suddenly propelled into the world's spotlight. The US claimed that by attending it would bring on board other reluctant nations. Only two significant nations—Japan and Poland—joined the negotiations on the heels of the US announcement.

The US delegation came to Oslo proposing significant changes to the treaty that, according to the ICBL, if accepted, would have weakened it seriously. The non-negotiable changes were labelled variously as 'red lines' that could not be crossed and an integral 'package' that could not be broken up into separate pieces. They included a geographic exception for continued use of AP mines in Korea; a redefinition of AP mine so the US would be able to keep its AP mines mixed in canisters with anti-tank mines; and a transition period including two elements, first, a requirement that the treaty enter into force only when at least 60 countries have ratified it, including all five permanent members of the Security Council and at least 75 per cent of historic producers and users of AP landmines, and second, an optional nine-year deferral period for compliance with certain provisions. The US also called for verification provisions to be strengthened and for a 'supreme national interest clause' permitting a party to withdraw from the treaty when its 'supreme national interests are threatened'.[39] Prior to the opening of negotiations, the US demands had been sent around the world to heads of state and foreign ministers in a letter by Secretary of State Albright.

The tale of how the US failed to get any of its proposed changes to the treaty text inserted, except for strengthened verification and compliance, is a story retold by others in this book and one that will be retold and analysed for years to come. It was not only the failure of US diplomats in Oslo to influence the negotiations that ended in the US refusal to sign the mine ban treaty, but ultimately the original policy that was flawed since its first announcement in May 1996. Without effective changes to this policy, and with the US redefinition of AP mines, the US will never be able to sign the Ottawa Convention or any other agreement that bans AP mines.

The United States delegation to the Oslo negotiations was headed up by Eric Newsom, principal deputy assistant secretary in the Bureau of Political-Military Affairs at the Department of State and Senator Leahy's former chief of staff. In addition to four generals, the delegation also included officials from the days of the CCW review negotiations and even two staffers from the office of Senator Jesse Helms, sent to 'counsel' the delegation.

NGOs and certain government delegates alike held their breath in the opening session of the treaty negotiations as conference president Jacob Selebi was elected and the rules of procedure of the conference were adopted without debate. Nations agreed that the rules would allow for decisions to be made by a two-thirds majority vote, as opposed to consensus in which any one country could block progress. This represented a turn-around from the CCW review. A further significant step was the unchallenged and unprecedented granting of observer status to the ICBL. These measures set the framework for the next three weeks of negotiations and ultimately made it impossible for the United States to block progress or force its proposals into the treaty text. The conference chair asked nations with proposals to the treaty text to put them forward within the first three days.

When Newsom took the floor for the US, he clearly stated that the proposed changes being sought by the US were non-negotiable. He made it very clear that the US was not in Oslo to negotiate a ban treaty but to bend the treaty to accommodate existing US policy. He stated that the demands were interlocking and it was, therefore, an all-or-nothing package. This opening salvo displaying complete inflexibility set the stage for US isolation and embarrassment in Oslo.

By the end of the second week, the US had failed to get any of its proposals, except for strengthened verification and compliance measures, inserted in the text, and expectations ran high that the treaty would be concluded when the conference on Tuesday 16 September resumed after a long weekend. But the US asked for, and was granted, a 24-hour delay to allow for 'consultations' with other nations on its proposals, which had been modified slightly but at their heart remained the same interlocking package. Prior to this, the US had repackaged their proposals into five 'fundamental' but essentially unchanged concerns of which three (Korea, definitions, and deferral period) were labelled 'killer amendments' by the ICBL.[40] The ICBL claimed that the US was 'delaying the inevitable rejection of its demands for the treaty'.[41]

During that weekend and into the 24-hour delay period, tensions were mounting within the White House. The State Department and President were worried about the diplomatic and political ramifications of holding out, while the Joint Chiefs were threatening to go public with their opposition to any weakening in the US negotiating position. The Joint Chiefs were under pressure from, or perhaps were encouraging, retired military leaders who publicly demanded that the US not give in to the negotiators in Oslo. The President himself, along with Secretary Albright and National Security Adviser Berger, lobbied foreign capitols and ambassadors in a series of late-night, last-minute phone calls and faxes. But it was too little, too late.

When the conference reconvened on 17 September the US made a short statement that because it had been unable to gain any significant support it was regretfully withdrawing its proposals, and shortly thereafter the mine ban treaty was adopted. Later that day, a clearly upset President Clinton spoke to the press from the White House lawn, contending that the US could not 'in good conscience' sign the mine ban treaty because it failed to provide an adequate transition period to develop alternatives to AP mines used as a key part of its defence in Korea—and because it prohibited US anti-tank mines! He went on to note that as 'Commander in Chief, I will not send our soldiers to defend the freedom of our people and the freedom of others without doing everything we can to make them as secure as possible.'

Government delegates and ban advocates were shocked that the presidential statement obfuscated the terms of the treaty. Many speculated that he had, perhaps, been 'misinformed' in stating that the US could not give up anti-tank mines. As everyone involved in the ban movement clearly knows, the mine ban treaty allows use of anti-tank mines. But apparently the 'confusion' continues, as campaigners to this day are asked about the treaty's impact on anti-tank mines. Still struggling to demonstrate his leadership, the President also announced that the US would ban all AP landmines by 2003, except in Korea, where use would continue until 2006. Not surprisingly, this leadership proved hollow when administration officials later said the unilateral ban would not apply to US Gator, Volcano, and MOPMS AP mines, which they again called 'explosive devices'.

Senator Leahy described his deep disappointment that the US would not be among the signers of the treaty in Ottawa, claiming that the administration seriously underestimated the worldwide commitment for a ban. *USA Today* described the US refusal to sign: 'having blown the best chance ever to negotiate an acceptable international ban on landmines, the Clinton administration now finds itself churning in the wake of world affairs. The United States has joined a few nations, including rogue states like Iran and Iraq, on the outside of a remarkable process.'[42] Editorials in the *New York Times* and *Los Angeles Times* voiced similar sentiments. While most major US papers had urged the US to participate in the Oslo negotiations, in their aftermath some, such as the *Washington Post*, the *Washington Times*, and the *San Diego Tribune*, supported the President's decision not to sign.

As the treaty negotiations had wound down, ICBL members gathered informally in Oslo to discuss strategies to bring attention to the US position against signing the mine ban treaty later in the year. They decided to initiate a 'Ban Bus to Ottawa' and mapped out a route from California to Ottawa, taking into account key congressional districts, locations of land-mine producers, and sources of grassroots support. Just four weeks later, on 23 October 1997, the Ban Bus departed from Berkeley, California, and arrived—7,500 miles later—in Ottawa on 1 December 1997, having given over 100 presentations to audiences in over 75 cities. Public interest in the Ban Bus was heightened by media attracted to the issue by the 31 August death of Diana, Princess of Wales. In addition, the Afghan Campaign to Ban Landmines and Save the Children USA collected and delivered in December 1997 over 25,000 postcards to President Clinton, featuring art-work by Afghan children depicting their desires for a mine-free world. The Ban Bus and public awareness of the mine ban treaty in general were fur-ther boosted by the 10 October announcement to award the 1997 Nobel Peace Prize to the International Campaign to Ban Landmines and its co-ordinator, Jody Williams.

How and Why the US Miscalculated the Ottawa Process
Several questions can be posed from this outline of US policy regarding not only why the US refused to sign the mine ban treaty, but also when, if ever, it will relinquish the weapon. First, why did the US so badly underestimate the potential for success of the Ottawa Process? Was it because the US could not comprehend the potential for a new way of diplomacy—and a way outside its control—to succeed? For example, in May 1996 Secretary of State Warren Christopher, in describing how he envisaged the US lead-ing the world to an international ban, referred to a world of Western and Eastern and non-aligned group meetings: 'I think if we can move first, per-haps, to get the industrialized countries in support of this ban and then broaden out to the nonaligned countries, it's a long, difficult negotiation in most cases. But we've been through that before. We have procedures for moving on it. We have a forum in Geneva [the CD].'[43]

One observer of the Ottawa Process commented that, 'though the United States still can impose its will on the rest, the new power of NGOs and other nonstate actors gives a much larger role to small and medium-sized governments that decide to seize the baton.'[44] At the time of the Brussels meeting, the fact that the Ottawa Process might succeed dawned on the US delegation, who were surprised at the number of countries pre-sent even though 'most of them were not very important countries.'[45] US critics of the Ottawa Process and official US participants in the Oslo negotiations lamented the way that 'the United States is being relegated to the role of just another nation . . . with no more say or influence on decisions . . . than Mauritania, Malta and Malaysia.'[46]

One government official, noting his 'surprise' that the Ottawa Process 'got as far as it did', viewed the process as benefiting from a number of 'lucky' circumstances. For example, 'the way the US government took a low-profile attitude or approach toward presenting its views on the process. Very few articles defending the US were published and those that were published generally had run through the bureaucratic process to the extent that they were not very persuasive. They were few, far between, too little, and too late when compared to the series of Leahy initiatives that gathered public attention, the publicity surrounding the ban movement, and especially the Open Letter to the President in the *New York Times*.' These factors 'helped to create an impression overseas that the United States was going to ban mines very soon' when, in fact, the reality was quite the opposite.[47]

Second, did the US seriously believe that its policy proposals could be inserted in the treaty text at the last minute? One official noted that the US delegation was unable to reply to the questions posed by the negotiating nations in Oslo, such as: 'How long will it take you to find a solution to Korea and how long will it take you to find a replacement for mixed munitions?' The reply, after all, was 'we don't know that either one of those can be and there was no way we could answer. To find a replacement for mixed munitions is more a matter of decades than it is years. Is that what they wanted to hear?'[48] The lack of any idea of how long it would take to get rid of the weapon ran against a statement back in May 1996, by the Secretary of Defense, that 'we are prepared to give up the smart mines as part of an international agreement. And we believe that may be necessary to get the international agreement.'[49]

Leahy described the last 48 hours of the treaty negotiations as 'a genuine attempt to break the impasse' but one which 'proved to be an issue that could not be solved by the kind of frenzied all-night, 11th-hour scramble that sometimes has been raised to an art form in this administration. There simply are too many countries involved, and the issues are too serious for that.'[50] Campaigners, on the other hand, would argue that the US never had any intention of breaking the 'impasse' in any way other than one that would preserve US interests. In particular, the ICBL held that the US only went to Oslo as a public relations gesture and not because it sought 'meaningful' participation in a process that would end in a true ban treaty. Given the polar opposites of the goals of the US versus the majority of nations in Oslo, what genuine attempt was possible?

Was it acceptable for one of the world's most powerful nations to tell nations to give up their mines when it refused to lead by example and give up its own as well? One can speculate that the above factors, especially the muddled approach the US took towards the Ottawa Process, played into the hands of the core group of pro-ban governments driving the Ottawa Process by helping to bring on board nations attracted by the humanitarian nature of the issue and the diplomatic fact that the US was at odds with the process. But its muddled approach brings us back to the question, posed earlier, of who is driving the policy. After years of promises to lead the world to a ban 'as soon as possible', it became all too clear that the administration was not willing to match its rhetoric with real ban policies.

For months the administration delayed the decision on where to negotiate an international ban agreement. This delay can be explained, as one US official put it to an NGO representative during the final Geneva session of the CCW, as meaning that 'a stated goal without a stated deadline is no goal at all.'[51] Or perhaps the delay was an indication of the continuous internal 'turf battle' between agencies, not only over which forum the US should choose to negotiate a ban but more significantly over which agency would have the most 'control' of the landmine policy once that decision was made.

Senator Leahy claimed he was convinced that while the President wants to see these weapons banned, he could not risk becoming 'unpopular' with the Pentagon. Leahy viewed the Pentagon as being 'deeply reluctant to give up a weapon that has some utility, even if doing so would help pressure others to end the suffering of innocent people', but described the President's role as civilian leader to act when there are overriding humanitarian concerns. Why were the President and his advisers unwilling to aggressively challenge and prod the Pentagon into finding a workable solution? Why did the President accept at face value the recommendations of the Joint Chiefs of Staff in May 1996 and announce them as his own policy prescription? Why did the President and his advisers not recognize the weaknesses in the Pentagon's doomsday predictions about the consequences of removing AP mines from Korea, or why had they not been aware of the fact that the Pentagon was, at least internally, divided over some of the same arguments they had made at the White House?[52]

By Oslo, NGOs familiar with the issue from its inception had seen arguments ranging from 'safe' mines to 'smart' mines, and then to Korea and now to 'pure' AP mines and 'mixed-munition systems', indicating that the crux of the problem was that the Pentagon did not want to give up any weapon to a movement looking for a ban—because if they do, then what is next? Fearing this 'slippery slope' towards the elimination of future weapons and seeing the speed at which the issue was gaining support among governments, the Pentagon found it had an immediate threat on its hands and did anything it could to halt that movement in the US.

Finally, one must ask if there is the necessary political resolve to solve the current policy problems and put the US into a position to sign the treaty. The President seems to have taken the landmine issue personally. He reacted viscerally to a newspaper article in early 1996 claiming he 'waffled' on landmine policy. One can only imagine the feelings on landmine policy within the White House now that dozens of editorial boards and cartoonists have had a field day with his refusal to sign the mine ban treaty. In a November 1997 press conference with Canadian Prime Minister Jean Chrétien, reporters were surprised at the President's heated defence of his decision. Clinton repeated his claim to the leadership mantle by being 'the first world leader at the United Nations to call for a total ban', then went on to blame the way the 'treaty was worded and the unwillingness of some people to entertain any change to the wording of it'.[53]

Clinton then praised Chrétien for his nation's efforts, calling the mine ban treaty a 'magnificent thing', but he added that '[i]t is a great mistake to make this whole story about whether we will sign on to this.' If signing the treaty was not an objective of the US, then what exactly is its objective regarding the elimination of landmines? For the first time since his 1994 call, Clinton neglected to mention mines in his 1997 speech to the United Nations General Assembly, instead choosing to focus on speedy ratification through the Senate of the Comprehensive Test Ban Treaty, a measure intended to placate disappointed peace and disarmament NGOs whose agendas often include both nuclear disarmament and other issues such as landmines. One has to ask if the landmine issue is one that can be managed by the sort of clever public relations for which this administration has been famous.

One commentator viewed the refusal to sign as being indicative of a moral and ethical lapse in leadership on disarmament matters in general—a lapse resulting in deferral to the Pentagon in all military policy. The lapse can be traced back to Vietnam, as Joe Volk of the Friends Committee explains:

> President Clinton and his advisers, including his civilian officials in the Pentagon, did not have a Vietnam War experience. They sat out the biggest moral issue of their generation with a view to their future careers. A lot of other people either went into the military and took the risks in Vietnam or they went into the anti-war movement and took the risks to their future careers because the ethics of the situation made a difference

to them. The ethics of the landmine situation made no difference to the President or to many of his closest advisers, such as the vice-president, except where they could get cheap credit for it. So shaming Clinton doesn't do a damn thing. Other presidents could have been shamed into it. On other issues, for example, civil rights issues or race relations, Clinton can take moral decisions.[54]

Perhaps the President needs to continue to hear the drumbeat of 'ban landmines, sign the treaty', but he also needs a face-saving way to enable him to do the right thing. Just as Bobby Muller tried to do with the backing of the generals, and just as Senator Leahy attempted to do by holding back on his legislation and prodding the administration to act, the President needs to recognize these doors are open so he can walk through them.

The main issue needing to be solved is the one regarding the definition of AP landmines and the current push to define the problem away. After the Oslo negotiations and the President's announcement, few people in the media took an interest in the unilateral reclassification of AP mines into 'pure anti-personnel mines' and those AP mines contained in 'mixed-munition systems'.[55] One reporter called the move 'a classic bait-and-switch', while the VVAF ran advertisements in Washington newspapers calling the redefinition 'Bill Clinton's landmine dodge'.[56] A long-awaited Presidential Directive on the Search for Alternatives was still not complete at the time of writing. It likely will not, however, cover mixed-mine systems and can be reversed by the stroke of a pen.

According to one official, certain mine ban treaty signatory nations seem to believe that the US is going to sign the mine ban treaty in 2006 and that the mixed-munition systems are just transitional weapons. Inderfurth's statement to this effect during the treaty-signing conference in Ottawa was tempered by two qualifiers: 'if we are able to develop alternatives to mixed-munition systems and there is nothing promising available right now.' Leahy asked:

> if the use of antipersonnel mines near antitank mines is what prevents the United States from signing the treaty, then solve it. We run a little Rover around on Mars. If we can do that, we can solve this problem. If the Pentagon had spent the past three years since the President first called for a worldwide ban really trying to solve that problem rather than to keep from having to solve it, the United States might have been able to show the leadership on this issue that the world needs and, frankly, the world wants.[57]

In the future, the US may continue to move away from rather than towards the mine ban treaty. The President has asked his diplomats to redouble their efforts to negotiate an export ban through the CD, but 1998 did not look any more promising than 1997. Besides, to support restrictions on landmines, nations can choose to sign up to the amended Protocol of the CCW. To support the total ban they can sign the mine ban treaty. There is the possibility of having three international agreements on landmines from different fora setting different standards for different nations. On landmines, the CD is seen as important by the US because it includes certain nations with large stockpiles of AP mines and because it includes certain nations, especially from the Middle East, such as Iraq and Syria, that are party to neither the CCW nor the Ottawa Convention.

US officials have not sought advice regarding how to live without AP mines from other allies who have given up the weapon and signed the Convention. Rather, the US seems more concerned with NATO 'interoperability' and how the US will participate in joint exercises given that all NATO member states have signed the Ottawa Convention except for the US and Turkey. In February 1998, members of the ICBL held a demonstration outside the US Rhein-Main airbase in Frankfurt to protest US diplomatic efforts to encourage its NATO allies to allow the US to continue to hold stockpiles in Germany, Italy, Norway, Spain, and the UK, as well as in Japan and perhaps other nations, in direct violation of Article 1 of the Ottawa Convention.[58]

CONCLUSION: DEMINING THE PATH TOWARDS AN EVENTUAL BAN

After Oslo, some administration officials believed that the US had to be seen to be 'doing something' on the landmine issue, especially in the lead-up to the treaty-signing ceremonies. On 31 October 1997, Secretary of State Albright announced 'Demining 2010', aimed at harnessing financial and material support internationally from both private and public sectors to increase by five-fold—to $1 billion per year—resources necessary for humanitarian demining. The US pledged to expand its own demining program by increasing funding from $68 million to $77 million in 1998 and Inderfurth was appointed US Special Representative for Global Humanitarian Demining. Albright was quoted as saying that 'the best way to protect civilians from landmines is to pull mines from the soil like the noxious weeds that they are.'[59]

It was a difficult announcement for the ban supporters to swallow. No one can be against demining or victim assistance—both are central planks of the ICBL—but now the US would become the world's leader in clearing mines from the ground while continuing the right to use, produce, and stockpile them? NGOs were for the most part silent on the announcement, but some asked why the Clinton administration was only seeking funding, instead of providing it. They pointed to the provisions of the Ottawa Convention banning new deployments of AP mines and giving signatory nations a 10-year frame by which they must clear the mines in their territories.

Demining has always been central to the administration's landmine policy, but perhaps for reasons of deflecting attention from the ban policy. Since 1993, when the US Government Humanitarian Demining Program was launched, the United States has spent $153 million on demining, much of it on training and equipment for 15 countries. The US claims to have trained up to one-quarter of the world's deminers.[60] At a meeting with Ambassador Inderfurth prior to the treaty-signing, NGOs asked the administration to focus not only on where the money comes from but how it is spent, especially by the Pentagon. By February 1998, three top people in the Pentagon's demining program had resigned or been pushed out in a reorganization just three months before the major international conference on demining, and responsibility for the demining program was shifted over from the office of the Assistant Secretary of Defense for Special Operations/Low Intensity Conflict to the Defense Security Assistance Agency, which administers the Pentagon's arms export program.[61]

The demining policy is therefore in danger of becoming a mirror image of the US policy towards banning AP mines—a willingness to look like a leader while not providing the financial and political resources necessary to validate the leadership stance. While the groundwork has been laid by the USCBL for widespread public and media support for a ban, and while congressional initiatives have pushed the administration to take the issue seriously, one must conclude the US policy towards banning AP mines has been driven primarily by political rather than humanitarian considerations. These political considerations have not been persuasive enough for the administration to back up its rhetoric with a concerted effort to create a policy that requires the President, as Commander in Chief of the Armed Forces, to stand up and say AP mines have to go now.

NOTES

1. William Clinton, 'Letter to Members of the United States Campaign to Ban Landmines', c/o Ms Mary Wareham, 4 Feb. 1998.
2. Senate Subcommittee of the Committee on Appropriations, 'The Global Landmine Crisis' Hearing, 13 May 1994.

3. Jody Williams, 'Notes on meeting with Tim Rieser, Leahy's aid', memorandum to Bobby Muller, John Terzano, Tom Cardamone, and VVAF staff, 5 Dec. 1991.

4. Interview with Lora Lumpe, Director, Arms Sales Monitoring Project, Federation of American Scientists, 7 Apr. 1998.

5. Interview with Scott Nathanson, Senior Researcher, Demilitarization for Democracy, 9 Apr. 1998.

6. Rod Bitz, Alliant Techsystems, meeting with the author, 7 May 1996.

7. Interview with Lumpe.

8. Jody Williams, *Landmine Update* 8 (1994): 9.

9. Senator Patrick Leahy, 'Landmine Chronology', Feb. 1996.

10. Jody Williams, *Landmine Update* 11 (1995): 7.

11. 'U.S. Military Implications of the Ottawa Treaty', Senate Armed Services Committee hearings, 3 Feb. 1998.

12. White House, Office of the Press Secretary, 'U.S. Policy on Landmine Control Regime', 26 Sept. 1994, 2.

13. Interview with Joe Volk, Executive Secretary, Friends Committee on National Legislation, 9 Apr. 1998.

14. Williams, *Landmine Update* 11 (1995): 7.

15. Williams, *Landmine Update* 12 (1995): 12.

16. Interview with Lumpe.

17. Williams, *Landmine Update* 11 (1995): 7.

18. Michael J. Matheson, 'New Landmine Protocol is Vital Step Toward Ban', *Arms Control Today* 26, 5 (July 1996): 9.

19. The ICBL's definition of 'pro-ban' states did not include those nations that had called for 'eventual elimination' but only those that had voiced their support for an immediate total ban. States encouraged by the ICBL to meet as a pro-ban bloc in the last days of the CCW included Austria, Belgium, Denmark, Ireland, Mexico, New Zealand, Norway, Slovenia, Sweden, Cambodia, Colombia, Mozambique, Nicaragua, Peru. See Williams, *Landmine Update* 12 (1995): 12.

20. Most significant players in the IWG included representatives of the Joint Chiefs of Staff, the Office of the Secretary of Defense (OSD), the Arms Control and Disarmament Agency, and the National Security Council (NSC). The group was chaired by the State Department's Office of Political and Military Affairs (PM) principal assistant deputy secretary, Ted McNamara. Currently, the IWG on policy is chaired by the NSC's Robert Bell and the demining group is co-chaired by PM and OSD.

21. Since being appointed Secretary of State, Albright has been publicly silent on the landmine debate. Yet, many speculate that she is very active inside the administration. It is likely that the appointment of her UN deputy, Rick Inderfurth, as 'Demining Czar' for Clinton's October 1997 policy of demining

the world by 2010 originated with her and will allow her considerable influence on policy.

22. Raymond Bonner, 'Pentagon Weighs Ending Opposition to a Ban on Mines', *New York Times*, 17 Mar. 1996.

23. Confidential interview with a senior government official.

24. Bonner, 'Pentagon Weighs Ending Opposition'.

25. Robert O. Muller, 'Pentagon Proposal to Continue Landmine Use Denounced', statement of president, Vietnam Veterans of America Foundation, 10 May 1996.

26. White House, Office of the Press Secretary, 'Press Briefing by Secretary of State Warren Christopher, Secretary of Defense William Perry, and UN Ambassador Madeleine Albright', 16 May 1996.

27. Notes taken by author, 17 May 1996.

28. USCBL, '"New" Clinton landmines policy rejected by Campaign', press statement, 15 May 1996.

29. Confidential interview with a senior administration official.

30. Notes taken by author, 17 Jan. 1997.

31. USCBL, 'Clinton Announcement Sends "Mistaken" Signal on Landmines', press statement, 17 Jan. 1997.

32. Stephanie Nebehay, 'U.S. fears stalemate at Geneva arms talks', Reuters news service, 23 Jan. 1997.

33. Dana Priest, '56 in Senate to Press for Law Banning Use of Land Mines by U.S.', *Washington Post*, 12 June 1997.

34. Letter cited in Frank Gaffney, Decision Brief, No. 97–D 94, Center for Security Policy, 9 July 1997.

35. Frank Gaffney, Decision Brief, No. 97–D 97, Center for Security Policy, 14 July 1997.

36. See Patrick M. Cronin and Ted Sahlin, 'Hard Questions About Land Mines', *Washington Post*, 9 July 1997, A23; Chuck Hagel, 'Weapons We Do Not Need', *Washington Post*, 18 June 1997, A17; Robert Gard, 'Flawed Arguments For Land Mines', *Washington Post*, 16 July 1997, A19; David Isenberg, 'We Need a Land-Mine Ban', *Washington Post*, 17 July 1997, A18.

37. USCBL, 'Letter to President Clinton', 16 July 1997.

38. USCBL, 'Princess Diana Visits Bosnia's Landmine Survivors While President Clinton Sits on the Fence', press statement, 8 Aug. 1997.

39. See letter by Albright, reprinted in ICBL, *Report on Activities: Diplomatic Conference on an International Total Ban on Anti-Personnel Landmines* (Oslo, 1997).

40. ICBL, 'U.S. To Make Final Attempt to Maim Landmine Ban Treaty', press statement, 15 Sept. 1997.

41. ICBL, 'U.S. Delays the Inevitable', press statement, 16 Sept. 1997.

42. Cited by Senator Patrick Leahy, *Congressional Record*, 23 Sept. 1997.
43. White House, 'Press Briefing by Christopher, Perry, and Albright'.
44. Jessica Mathews, 'The New, Private Order', *Washington Post*, 21 Jan. 1997, A11.
45. Interview with Robert Sherman, director, Advanced Projects, US Arms Control and Disarmament Agency, Washington, 6 Apr. 1998.
46. Frank Gaffney, 'Welcome to the New World Order: U.S. "Red Lines" on the Landmine Issue Are Being Crossed with Impunity, Contempt', Decision Brief, No. 97–D 125, 4 Sept. 1997.
47. Confidential interview with a senior government official.
48. Ibid.
49. White House, 'Press Briefing by Christopher, Perry, and Albright'.
50. Leahy, *Congressional Record*, 23 Sept. 1997.
51. Interview with Volk.
52. Leahy, *Congressional Record*, 23 Sept. 1997.
53. Peter Baker, 'A Dispute Between Neighbors', *Washington Post*, 24 Nov. 1997.
54. Interview with Volk.
55. One exception was Dana Priest, 'Clinton Directive on Mines: New Form, Old Function', *Washington Post*, 24 Sept. 1997.
56. George Seffers, 'Pentagon Plan for Mixed System Mines Draws Criticism', *Defense News*, 3–9 Nov. 1997.
57. Leahy, *Congressional Record*, 23 Sept. 1997.
58. 'Anti-Landmine Protest outside U.S. Base in Germany', Reuters news service, 20 Feb. 1998; ICBL, 'ICBL Demands US Mines Out of Europe and Japan', press statement, 20 Feb. 1998.
59. State Department, 'Albright, Cohen Announce U.S. Demining Initiative', transcript, 31 Oct. 1997.
60. William S. Cohen, 'Statement on Landmine Policy and Demining', 18 Sept. 1997; William S. Cohen, 'Necessary and Right', *Washington Post*, 19 Sept. 1997.
61. Colin Clark, 'Departure of Demining Officials Called "Discouraging"', *White House Weekly*, 2 Feb. 1998.

Poster from the 4th International NGO Conference on Landmines. Courtesy of ICBL.

US Senator Patrick Leahy addresses NGO forum in Oslo. Courtesy of John Rodsted.

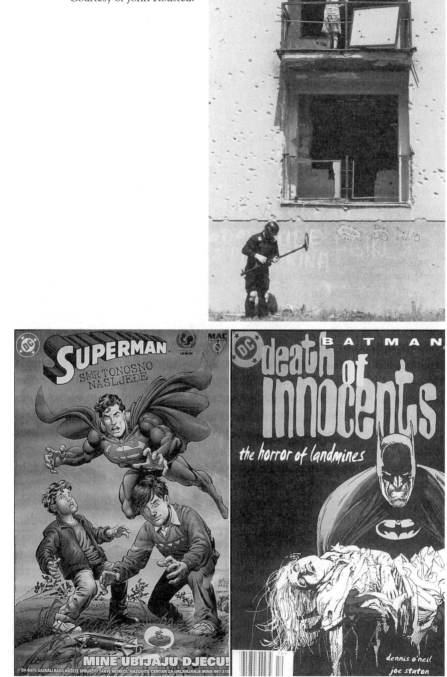

Norwegian deminer in Bosnia.
Courtesy of John Rodsted.

Batman and Superman join the campaign. Courtesy of DC Comics.

ICBL nerve centre in Oslo.
Standing: Mary Wareham,
Stephen Goose; seated: Jody
Williams, Norwegian diplomat
Steffen Kongstad. Courtesy of
John Rodsted.

Tun Channareth meets
UN Secretary-General Kofi
Annan in Oslo, 1997.
Courtesy of John Rodsted.

Jody Williams, ICBL Co-ordinator, Cornelio Sommaruga, President of the ICRC, UN Secretary-General Kofi Annan, and Canadian Prime Minister Jean Chrétien watch Canada's Foreign Minister Lloyd Axworthy sign the ban Convention. Courtesy of ICBL.

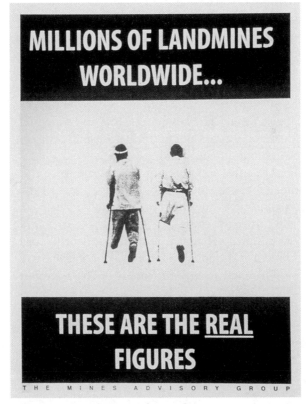

Poster: Courtesy of Mines Advisory Group.

CHAPTER 13

EUROPE AND THE OTTAWA PROCESS: AN OVERVIEW

David Long and Laird Hindle

Leadership of the Ottawa Process is usually attributed to the International Campaign to Ban Landmines and the Canadian government. Yet, at the beginning, the campaign to ban anti-personnel mines can with some justification be described as a European-led initiative. A number of European countries advocated a ban long before the Ottawa Process began and many became members of the core group proposing a comprehensive ban on the weapons, including EU member states Austria, Belgium, Germany, Ireland, and the Netherlands, as well as Norway and Switzerland. Half of the steering committee of the International Campaign to Ban Landmines were European NGOs (Medico from Germany, Handicap International from France, and the Mines Advisory Group from the UK). The European Parliament adopted a resolution in 1992 decrying the use of AP mines and called for a ban in 1996.

Ultimately, all but a few European states signed the Ottawa Convention in December 1997. However, at the beginning of the Ottawa Process, support among European governments for a comprehensive ban on anti-personnel mines was far from unanimous. Furthermore, with the notable exception of Germany, until the spring of 1997 the international campaign faced the opposition or, at best, lukewarm support of the European Great Powers. The key proponents and supporters of the ban on landmines in Europe were, by contrast, predominantly the smaller, more 'progressive', and often neutral states.

The mix of security and humanitarian elements to the landmine issue and the campaign to ban the weapon created a mix of reactions from the various European states, ranging from the highly active and influential in support of the Ottawa Process (for instance, Austria, Belgium, Ireland), through the initially reluctant, but subsequently converted (United Kingdom, France, Italy, much of Central and Eastern Europe), to the unconvinced and recalcitrant (for much of the time, Greece and, ultimately, Finland and Turkey). This contrast in positions was arguably exacerbated by Lloyd Axworthy's surprise call at the October 1996 Ottawa conference for a ban treaty by the end of 1997. The idea of signing a treaty briefly polarized European governmental positions and also momentarily congealed opposition to the move towards a comprehensive ban in the form of a call for the issue to be dealt with in the Conference on Disarmament (CD).

Thus, the story of the Ottawa Process in Europe is one of a few leading states, a number of followers, and a handful of holdouts. This chapter describes the range of behaviour and positions of European states regarding the ban on AP landmines and, in particular, within the Ottawa Process. While certain European states led the international campaign, and the majority followed, the tendency to follow was also evident in the policy of the European Union, despite the progressively solid support for the Ottawa Process among its member states during 1997.[1]

The explanation for this variation of behaviour lies in a number of factors at a number of levels. First of all, the domestic context of states was critical to early and/or enthusiastic adherence to the principles of a comprehensive ban called for in the Ottawa Process. Second, the international context was influential for a number of governments' decision to sign the Ottawa treaty, especially the active campaigning of the ICBL as well as the core group of states (led by the Canadian government), and the ultimate sense of a bandwagon that states could not afford to miss. Third, in Europe, there were regional influences associated in particular with the European Union as a forum for negotiation between EU member states and also as a means of harmonizing security policy in its Common Foreign and Security Policy. Finally, a number of contingent factors impacted on European states: notably, the changes of government in the UK and France in the middle of 1997; the failure of the traditional route for dealing with the landmine issue, initially the CCW and later the CD; and finally, the support and then the death of Diana, Princess of Wales.

In the confines of this chapter, it is difficult to do justice to the NGOs and their national campaigns to ban landmines conducted in the various European countries. Their role is considered to some extent in earlier chapters of this book, and while it is certainly true that NGO campaigns and the orchestration of the ICBL made up a good deal of the substance of the movement to ban anti-personnel mines, many other factors contributed to make for a state's signature to the Ottawa Convention. Therefore, this chapter's primary focus is on the policies of European states and the various influences on them and their decisions to sign or not sign.

ENTHUSIASTIC SUPPORTERS

As a group, the core group countries were the leaders of the state-level campaign to ban landmines. They are an integral part of what Jody Williams described as the new 'superpower'.[2] The core group was populated by a large number of European states, including the EU members, Austria, Belgium, Germany, Ireland, the Netherlands, Switzerland, and Norway. As well as being in the core group, many of these states had led the push for a comprehensive ban in the period prior to the Ottawa Process. During the Ottawa Process, each of these states played important roles in leading the landmine campaign in Europe and more broadly. Austria proposed a total ban on AP mines at the CCW Review Conference in 1995 and participated enthusiastically in the coalition of like-minded states and NGOs once that conference collapsed. It hosted the Experts Meeting on the Text of a Total Ban Convention in February 1997 and undertook to draft and amend the treaty text during 1997 (see Chapter 15). Belgium hosted the Brussels conference in June 1997 that locked states' commitments to sign a treaty banning landmines in Ottawa in December 1997. Switzerland, along with Austria, the Netherlands, and Germany, had supported the initial French proposal to draft a resolution for the UN General Assembly for a review conference of the 1980 Convention.[3] Germany lent credence to the campaign by virtue of its size and stature and hosted the Bonn conference on compliance verification in April 1997. Ireland and the Netherlands held the EU Council presidency through the difficult months after Canadian Foreign Affairs Minister Axworthy's surprise announcement at the October 1996 Ottawa conference. Norway, of course, hosted the critical Oslo Diplomatic Conference in the fall of 1997, where the treaty text was negotiated and finalized.

A predominant characteristic of the majority of the core group is that they are small to medium-sized states. In the case of AP mines, many of the smaller European states, such as Norway, Belgium, and Austria, were generally enthusiastic supporters of the Ottawa Process and the landmine campaign from the beginning. These states were among the first to adopt comprehensive ban legislation domestically that accorded with the goals of the Ottawa Process and the principles enunciated by the ICBL. In general, assessments of the foreign policy behaviour of European states tend to lump the smaller states together into a single category. They share a number of common characteristics shaping their foreign policies, such as their limited though not insignificant international influence, their progressive stance on international aid and assistance, and their relative security in the absence of germane and immediate threats to their borders.

While the specific developments differed in each case, these states were influenced by a number of similar factors. For instance, in each case the influence of the national NGO campaigns (under the umbrella of the ICBL) on government policy was clear and strong. National NGO campaigns were part of a network of European NGOs that formed the European Network Against the Arms Trade.[4] A manifestation of the influence of NGOs was the frequently close relationship between NGOs and government officials in these states, mirroring the experience in Canada. While NGOs were critical, then, the importance of governments and government officials should not be underplayed, since it was the officials who participated in the core group of states supporting the comprehensive ban. Without this initial catalyst, the ICBL campaign might have remained marginalized at the edges of the international conferences from which they were initially routinely excluded.

A cursory overview of the enthusiastic supporters highlights some further elements in common. First, the fact that these states are relatively progressive and active humanitarian members of the international community conditioned their reaction to the landmine issue—emphasizing the humanitarian impulse that drove the campaign forward. Regarding international security policy, Austria, Ireland, and Switzerland are neutral, while Belgium, Norway, and the Netherlands are members of NATO. At one level, neutrality would appear to limit those states' credibility on landmines as a security and disarmament issue, although the tradition of self-defence in Switzerland, for instance, has hardly made for the archetypal pacific society. The Benelux countries are not located in the heartland of NATO Europe. While Norway is not either, it does share a border with Russia and has commensurate security concerns associated with this. However, this has created more problems within NATO than it has for the Norwegians themselves. Norway has stated that its forces will not take part in exercises involving landmines and insists that the US remove any landmines it may possess on Norwegian territory.[5] This issue is one that will have to be addressed by other NATO members.

Second, in some cases, the relatively advanced policy regarding landmines was a result of the agreement of the relevant departments of government, especially Foreign Affairs and Defence, regarding the need for a ban, whether this was a result of genuine consensus or because in some cases the military and civilian analysts and policy-makers in defence departments were outmanoeuvred. However, even in pro-ban states, the military and civilian defence officials protested the prospect of a ban on use and transfer.

Third, because they are among the smaller and medium powers, their international influence is generally small. This is true not only in terms of the sheer political weight they carry but also because of the relatively small amount of resources these states have in the form of diplomatic missions abroad. Canada, by contrast, has much greater international reach, especially through its membership and active participation in a wide range of international organizations.

However, the relatively low level of international influence is mitigated in the case of Ireland and the Netherlands, which consecutively held the EU Council presidency (and were both in the EU Troika)[6] during the early months of the Ottawa Process, which amplified their influence within the EU and possibly internationally, albeit in the limited ways in which the president of the EU Council of Ministers has influence.[7] Within the EU, the international campaign was fortunate that these two pro-ban states were in the presidency during late 1996 and early 1997. A presidency less amenable to the Ottawa Process might have sought an EU consensus, which would inevitably have been a lowest common denominator and at the time among EU member states might well have meant taking the issue of AP mines to the Conference on Disarmament.

In general, early passage of ban legislation is a further characteristic of many of these enthusiastic supporters. Belgium prides itself as the first to legislate a ban, but it was quickly followed by Austria, Denmark, Germany, Ireland, the Netherlands, Norway, and Switzerland, all of which passed similar legislation banning the use, production, export, import, and stockpiling of AP mines in 1996. By the time of the second Ottawa conference many of these states had destroyed their stockpiles (with exceptions for training in demining as permitted in the treaty, Article 3.1) or were in the midst of completing their destruction.

This is an elementary analysis, however, and it is unable to provide an adequate understanding of the different experiences of each state. Furthermore, the description of a small, progressive European state active in international humanitarian affairs would have to include Finland, a state that notably did not sign the Ottawa Convention. In addition, a number of these states, for instance, Belgium, had been significant producers of AP mines in the not-so-distant past. Thus, the adoption of a pro-landmine ban stance is a recent development even for these states and it flew in the face of a potentially vocal domestic constituency, the arms industry.

Belgium is often held up as a campaign exemplary, and yet it went through a difficult process in legislating a ban. The process began relatively early. The Belgian campaign, headed by Handicap International, approached Senators Lalleand and Dardenne with a proposal to place legislation before the Senate. The legislation, passed on 2 March 1995, expanded existing legislation concerning the prohibition of certain weapons to include AP mines and extended it to include jurisdiction over the armed forces; modified laws governing trade to ban the production, export, and import of AP mines; and introduced a new piece of legislation calling for the destruction of existing Belgian stockpiles.[8] Final destruction of the Belgian stockpiles, save those for demining training, occurred in August 1997.

But this process was not without its opponents. The opposition of military officials to the mine ban in larger and more powerful states has garnered a good deal of attention. Smaller European states also faced this fierce opposition from their military officials. The Belgian military did not want to see the elimination of a valued military tool. Ministry of Defence officials were vocal in their opposition to the legislation and attempted to erect impediments to its implementation. They suggested many amendments and various exemptions to be included in the legislation. An exemption for Belgian forces serving under NATO was put forward. Three amendments were proposed and three amendments were voted down in both parliamentary committee and in plenary in the Belgian parliament.[9]

In some instances military and civilian defence officials did support a pro-ban stance, but this was not the norm. For example, Sweden's military command was divided over the issue of landmines. The Minister of Defence, Thage Peterson, along with some members of the Swedish military were supportive of the ban. They felt that AP mines were not necessary for the protection of Swedish territory. Yet, this sentiment was not reciprocated by the rest of the command staff, especially the Supreme Commander for Sweden's Defence Forces. The majority felt that there remained a military utility for mines.[10]

The Role of Germany

While the role of smaller European states was predominant in advancing the campaign, the larger states were also critical. Germany, in many respects, is in a special category of its own. As an early member of the core group, what it symbolized in the Ottawa Process was different from the smaller states. Because of Germany's geopolitical, diplomatic, and economic clout, its support for the AP mines ban was a great boost to the international campaign and, in particular, legitimized the campaign within the EU (and to some extent within NATO). While not a permanent member of the UN Security Council, Germany has considerable international influence, especially within the European Union. Along with the UK and France, Germany is one of the Big Three of EU politics. Critically, the European Big Three were never united against the Ottawa Process, a scenario some campaigners had feared. Analysis of a number of policy areas in the EU suggests that ban supporters were correct to be concerned at the prospect of Germany siding with the UK and France against the Ottawa Process. Generally, Big Three concurrence is a prerequisite for EU policy; their support is vital, their opposition deadly.[11]

A source of concern among supporters of the Ottawa Process was that Germany's membership in the core group was not without its ambiguities. German foreign and security policy tends to walk a fine line between European and transatlantic orientations as Germany maintains its most important relationships with France and with the US. Indeed, it has been suggested that the German position on landmines might have been influenced by a mistaken impression of the US position following President Clinton's statement in support of the eventual elimination of landmines in May 1996. The following July Germany announced a seven-point action plan calling for an international ban in a letter to the UN Secretary-General. Most likely, however, the German government position was a result of the influence of the domestic constituency, especially the strength of the German NGO campaign led by Medico and its bold position in favour of banning anti-tank as well as anti-personnel mines. However, in Europe, while the Dutch and Italian campaigns had similar goals, the position taken by the German campaign was seen as too radical. It was felt, by more pragmatic campaigns in the UK, France, and Belgium, that insistence on a ban on anti-tank mines would jeopardize the entire exercise.[12] German government support for the Ottawa Process was also founded on the relatively early concurrence on the issue of the foreign and defence ministers regarding the need for action. Furthermore, the rapport between German Foreign Minister Klaus Kinkel and Canadian Foreign Minister Axworthy cemented a relationship that was deeper than a misjudged piece of opportunism. Kinkel was personally strongly in favour of the ban, as was his party, the Free Democrats.

As a result, Germany not only adopted a pro-ban stance but made the legislative commitments relatively early. On 22 April 1996 the German government had renounced the use and production of AP mines and announced a plan to destroy German stockpiles. This was followed by the seven-point initiative for dealing with AP mines globally. The German position, nevertheless, was to complement the fast-track approach of the Ottawa Process with the use of other traditional arms control fora favoured by the United States, in particular, the CD. Such complementarity is not in principle a bad thing—it appears in the Preamble to the Ottawa Convention, after all.

Shortly after the first Ottawa conference in October 1996, with the shock of Foreign Minister Axworthy's statement still stinging the hesitant states, German support for dual tracking of the landmines issue in the Ottawa Process and the Conference on Disarmament signified something else entirely. In early 1997, the CD was the preferred route of the British, French, and American governments. German support for this route threatened to derail the fast-track option for a comprehensive ban by moving the discussion into a forum where the Great Powers would have considerable leverage, where the consensus (or more properly, the veto) rule would apply, and where a range of other arms control issues could easily get entangled with the landmines ban. The CD option was dismissed by other members of the core group and the ICBL as a distraction from the Ottawa Process. Even with the failure of the CD option, Germany (along with other European states) continued its call for dual tracking and its support for the Ottawa Process. Ironically, this led to doubts in the ICBL and the core group about the German commitment at the Oslo conference, where previously recalcitrant European states, notably the UK and France, were clearly unaffected by the blunt American overtures to move them away from the Ottawa Process.

INITIALLY RELUCTANT, SUBSEQUENTLY CONVINCED

For much of the international campaign to ban landmines, the majority of European states rhetorically supported some sort of action but hedged their commitments with caveats and reservations. When the Ottawa Process began, those states that were ready for the commitment were clearly distinguishable from those that were not. Outside the core group countries mentioned above, there was little appetite for a comprehensive ban. Yet, almost all European states in the end signed the Ottawa Convention. Why? Broadly there are three groups of reasons, varying according to the states' international stature and membership in European organizations: respectively, the UK and France as Great Powers and permanent members of the Security Council; other member states of the European Union; and the 10 states that were prospective members of the European Union.

The United Kingdom and France

The exemplars of the initially reluctant but subsequently convinced states are the UK and France. In each case, national campaigns to ban landmines, led by Handicap International in France and the Mines Advisory Group in the UK, had pressed for commitments in favour of the Ottawa Process. The international campaign was favoured by two fortuitous events: the extent of Labour's victory in the UK in May 1997 and the somewhat surprising victory of Jospin and the Socialists in France in June 1997. The new governments' positions were more amenable to a comprehensive ban, although it would be wrong to suggest that government policy in the UK and France was transformed overnight by the changes of government. The Conservatives and Gaullists had been shifting their positions on the landmine issue closer in line with the common EU position of the time in favour of an export moratorium, although it is true to say that neither had moved to a genuine acceptance of a total ban. It is worth remembering, furthermore, that a change in ministers does not mean a change in the bureaucracy. In the British Ministry of Defence, for instance, officials continued, even at the time of the December 1997 Ottawa conference, to advocate the military utility of landmines and to portray the humanitarian nature of the Ottawa Convention as meaning that it was not relevant to arms control nor did it supersede national security considerations in British defence policy.

On closer reading, the British and French declarations in favour of a comprehensive ban are noticeably non-comprehensive. France's initial declaration on 2 October 1996 renounced the use of landmines except 'en cas de nécessité absolue imposée par la protection de nos forces'.[13] This provoked the now celebrated riposte from Jody Williams, the co-ordinator of the ICBL, that the French position amounted to France not using mines unless they needed them! Even so, France was on the ICBL good list during the Ottawa Process, even with its caveat. The French government was very open about the escape clause in its declaration. It was reiterated when France officially adopted a pro-comprehensive ban stance at the Brussels conference and agreed to sign the treaty in December. The French continue to support not only the Ottawa Process but the CD. In this attitude France did not diverge greatly from the policies of other Security Council permanent members in its support for both processes, with a distinct preference for the latter. French policy barely wavered throughout the entire process and the election of Jospin's Socialists did not change this. The only recognizable change from the Gaullist position was an endorsement of the Ottawa Process as a means to a comprehensive ban.

By comparison, the United Kingdom's endorsement of a comprehensive ban seems to be more of a reversal of policy. Tony Blair's Labour government was much more willing to endorse the ban than John Major's Conservatives. Labour's overwhelming victory in May 1997 at first glance seemed to herald a tremendous change in British policy. This was partly that the adoption of a pro-ban stance fitted perfectly with Foreign Minister Robin Cook's vision of a more moral foreign policy. It was also a reflection of the fact that a number of Labour MPs, including International Development Minister Claire Short, had been active in the UK campaign. Labour had also made the manifesto commitment to 'ban the import, export, transfer and manufacture of all forms of anti-personnel mines [and] introduce an immediate moratorium on their use'.[14]

A further important influence, of course, was Diana, Princess of Wales, who single-handedly raised the profile of the international campaign, especially in the UK and particularly through her well-publicized visits to Angola and Bosnia with the International Committee of the Red Cross. It is easy, perhaps, to belittle the 'publicity stunt' aspect to the Princess's role. The significance of her role in terms of the profile of the campaign and to some extent the content and direction of the public debate on landmines in the UK is attested to, however, by the ire that she raised in Conservative government circles as a result of her remarks, not long before the UK general election, that Labour's policy on landmines was more sensible than that of the Tories. This intervention even provoked questions about the political role of the royal family.

In its last year in office the Conservative government had shifted from a minimum moratorium to a comprehensive moratorium on all AP mine exports to all states. Even use by British forces was to be curtailed. 'Dumb' mines were to be destroyed and a portion of them were to be replaced with so-called 'smart' mines. Of course, this change needs to be understood in the context of the Ministry of Defence's modernization plans. 'Dumb' mines were to be eliminated but were to be replaced with 'smart' mines.[15] Change, although not as drastic as some would believe, only occurred with Labour's victory. The new policy unveiled on 21 May 1997 appears to mirror the commitments of other pro-ban states. It included a timetable for destruction, a moratorium on operational use, a moratorium on the transfer and production of AP mines, and full support for the Ottawa Process.[16] However, the final section of the policy is of special interest, for it is more similar to France's position than it is to, say, Belgium's. Britain reserved the right to use AP mines for operations where the security of British forces would otherwise be jeopardized without them.

Other EU States

If the actual change in British and French policy was not quite as dramatic as it is sometimes presented, the impact of the changes of governments and policy in the UK and France was certainly dramatic. While the Ottawa Process had been gathering steam during the first months of 1997, especially after the failure of the CD to grasp the issue, the number of states signed on suddenly jumped after May-June when the UK and France clearly came on board. This contributed to the sense of growing, probably unstoppable, momentum at the Brussels conference.[17] In addition, the loss of support of the two European permanent members of the Security Council dealt a severe blow to the US in its opposition to the Ottawa

Process. It was subsequently left to ally itself with the Russians and the Chinese, among others.

Within Europe, a number of states that had been holdouts, including Italy and Spain, subsequently joined the Ottawa Process, leaving only a couple of smaller states not in favour. As some of Europe's primary exporters of landmines and with a business interest in the continuation of the legality of the transfer of these weapons, the Italian and Spanish governments' initial reservations were to be expected. Italy's decision to support the comprehensive ban followed the French decision, thus making it the thirteenth member of the EU to support the treaty.[18] Spain had previously endorsed a comprehensive ban, just prior to France and Italy, after the governing party came under pressure from the Spanish parliament to do so. The Italian decision did not come without some controversy.[19] It was only after a full-scale NGO assault on the government and after major Italian businesses had divested themselves of subsidiaries that produced AP mines that the decision was taken. That Italy joined the Ottawa Process demonstrates that, within Europe and more widely, what kept states from seeking a comprehensive ban was not, in the final analysis, the dubious profits to be made from selling AP mines.

EU Applicants

EU applicants constitute another category among the more recently converted states.[20] Here, the international campaign had an influence, in particular its snowballing impact. However, the EU and especially the prospect of EU membership had a major impact on states' decisions to sign the Ottawa Convention. Applicants for membership in the EU were faced with dilemmas similar to though arguably starker than those of the present member states regarding production and transfer of AP mines. During their years under Communist rule, large defence industries had been built in some countries, such as Czechoslovakia. Employing thousands of people, they have been hit hard by the transition to a democratic and capitalist system. Because of this defence industrial base, several applicant states, such as the Czech Republic and Poland, were producing large amounts of mines. Given the constraints of economic transition, the economic imperative is what underlies the motives for many of these states, and here there was a potential problem—whether to choose the immediate gains from selling AP mines or fall into line with the European consensus against exporting these weapons.

The foreign policies of Poland, the Czech Republic, Hungary, Slovenia, and Estonia (those that were ultimately selected as the first round of candidates for the next EU enlargement) are clearly oriented towards getting into the EU, as this represents not only a major step to international legitimacy and acceptance but, more importantly, a hoped-for route to prosperity. Many of these states were apparently unwilling to jeopardize their potential membership in the EU by not endorsing the treaty. This became evident as the EU progressed towards a more comprehensive position, and so did various other applicants. After the first EU Joint Action was taken (see Appendix in this chapter), all applicant states put in place, at a minimum, a limited export moratorium. Of the Eastern European states, Poland was the last to adopt a moratorium. This Polish reluctance continued throughout the entire process.

At the end of 1997, the EU announced which states would be given the first chance at membership among the applicant states. The decision reverberated through the positions subsequently taken on the AP mine ban by the EU applicant states. For example, Romania had hesitations about the Ottawa Convention despite being a signatory. Its reasons relate to the lack of international support and in particular that it is not in the first round of Central and East European countries to be admitted to NATO and the EU. The Romanian government indicated that, since it is not a member of any collective security organization and because of its geostrategic position, it would require AP mines for self-defence. A secondary reason was a lack of financial resources necessary to complete the destruction of stockpiles. Romania felt that due to the austerity measures imposed on it, in order to become a member of the EU, it would not have the discretionary funds available to destroy its AP mines.[21] Nevertheless, the Romanian government assured the international community that it would maintain an export moratorium. Romania was not the sole applicant whose position on AP mines was unclear, however. Poland, for instance, did not agree to sign the treaty until very shortly before the second Ottawa conference.

The overall pattern of eventual adherence is enlightening. The European states that have not signed the Convention are at the 'edges' of Europe and/or with clear security considerations for not signing. Even among those that finally signed the treaty, such as Poland and Romania, there was considerable reluctance due to concerns with the security implications of removing AP mines from their arsenal, even in the context of the pressure to be in line with the EU in anticipation of future membership.

However, possible EU membership likely affected the policies of Central, East, and Southeast European states. As well as their being heavily mine-affected countries, the general interest in international recognition surely motivated Croatia and Bosnia's decisions to sign. EU membership, however, did not overcome all broader concerns with international security, as is evident in the fact that the Baltic states did not sign the

Ottawa Convention, even though all are likely future EU members and Estonia in particular is in the first round of future admissions.

In summary, the subsequently converted seem to fall into two camps, the big players (France and the UK), which were clearly more influenced by domestic NGO activities and campaigns, and the rest of the initially unconvinced, which were more influenced by international factors, ranging from the influence of the ICBL (for instance, in its support of the Italian and other national ban campaigns), to negotiations and discussions within the EU and the change in stance of the UK and France.

THE EXCEPTIONS

Those European states that chose not to sign the Ottawa Convention are clearly marked by their location at the 'edges' of the European space and/or their recent involvement in a war, including Finland, Turkey, and Yugoslavia. The most interesting case in many respects is Finland. The fact that Finland did not sign the Convention is at once surprising and not surprising. It is not surprising since Finland has a 1,000+ kilometre border with Russia and has a history of being invaded and forcibly made part of the Russian Empire, as well as more recently being invaded by the Soviet Union during World War II. As a result, Finns are acutely aware of security considerations generally, and particularly in relations with their southern neighbour. Finnish neutrality is a function of the country's geopolitical location: as one Finnish official was said to have observed to one of his Scandinavian colleagues, 'we are your buffer zone'. The fact that Russia failed to sign the Ottawa Convention only compounded Finnish reasons for not signing.

On the other hand, the Finnish exception is surprising because Finns are generally well-regarded international citizens, especially with respect to humanitarian and development assistance. The landmine issue has prevented them from continuing an apparently time-honoured principle of Finnish foreign policy of being on the side of the angels. The Ottawa Process is an exception in Finnish foreign policy because the Finns are on the sharp end of the opposition of security and humanitarian concerns in the landmines issue. The Finnish response to calls for them to sign the Convention has been to plead their inability, given their geopolitical circumstances, and to look into alternative instruments and defence strategies to achieve their national security interests—in short, providing an alternative to the use of AP mines along the Finnish-Russian border. Meanwhile, Finnish stockpiles are currently in storage and are not deployed. The Finns reserve the right to use their stockpiles in case of future aggression but have promised not to acquire more landmines. At the same time, Finland has remained supportive of the long-term goals of the Ottawa Process.[22] Thus, in addition to their active support for demining and victim assistance, the Finns are saying 'not now' rather than 'no' to the Ottawa Process. Indeed, in an odd twist, it is *because* the Finns are good international citizens with a reputation and self-image for keeping international commitments that Finland has yet to sign the Ottawa treaty. Unlike some other states that have signed, Finland has qualms about signing a treaty it is likely to find difficult to ratify or to comply with once it is in force. Ironically, as the Ottawa Process unfolded in a hunt for signatures, less than complete commitment to ratification was better for the campaign than governmental forthrightness regarding possible difficulties with ratification of and compliance with the treaty. In this context, the Finns were painted as villains while states with less commitment to the ultimate goals of the comprehensive ban on landmines were applauded.

Of the states that have recently applied for EU membership, Turkey and the Baltic states are the only non-signatories of the treaty. Citing security reasons for the requirement to use AP mines in its defence, Turkey has continued to employ them. As with other states that remained outside of the Ottawa Process, Turkey has stated that it prefers the CD as the forum for negotiating a ban. The Baltic states are clearly concerned about their security in relation to Russia for reasons that parallel the concerns expressed in Finland, though even more immediately and dramatically given recent history in the Baltics.

Until shortly before the Ottawa conference in December 1997, the holdouts in Europe were much more numerous than these. The Greeks, for example, decided to join the Ottawa Process quite late in the day, in October 1997. Their statement at the Ottawa conference might best be described as terse: 'Greece fully subscribes to the principles enshrined within the Convention on the Prohibition of the Use, Stockpiling, Production and Transfer of Anti-Personnel Mines and on their Destruction and declares that ratification will take place as soon as conditions relating to the implementation of its relevant provisions are fulfilled.'[23] What the precise nature of these conditions are is not clear, but it is evident that Greece intends to determine when they are fulfilled.

The Greek decision can probably be best understood as, in part, currying favour with their EU colleagues, and, in part, embarrassing the Turkish government. Furthermore, while the Finns received some sympathy from their EU partners regarding their stance on AP mines, Greece did not receive such support. While Greece and Turkey have a tense relationship and both countries have borders touching on volatile situations, Greece was able to sign while Turkey was not, primarily because of the Kurdish insurgency in southeast Turkey and the currently unstable nature of the Turkish border with Iraq.

CONCLUSION

What does the pattern of behaviour of European states tell us? Generally, the decisions to sign the Ottawa Convention were influenced by considerations of humanitarianism, security, and profit. The profit motive fell by the wayside. Those states in Western and Central Europe that were producers, such as Belgium and Italy, decided that the humanitarian issue massively outweighed the dubious levels of profit to be made from the production of anti-personnel mines; or, like the Czech Republic, recognized that continued production and export of AP mines was inconsistent with the superordinate policy goal of joining the European Union and becoming an established member of the Western club; or, like Romania, judged that economic support would be forthcoming that would in various ways cover the costs of destruction of AP mines and perhaps assist in the broader transition of defence industries and economic transition away from military to civilian production.

The interpretation of the humanitarian and security elements of the treaty filter into European state policies in different ways. First, security considerations outweighed any commercial interest in determining continued opposition to the Ottawa Process. Opposition was stronger and lasted longer where perceived security interests were involved, for instance, in Finland compared to Italy. In so far as the commercial aspect applied at all with regard to state policy, for example with Italy, it was ultimately overcome. Second, states with less to fear on either security or economic grounds were most likely to be enthusiastic supporters of the Ottawa Process, for example, Ireland and the Benelux countries. (However, the historical experience of Belgians dating back to the two world wars certainly contributed to the depth of feelings engendered by the ban campaign.)

The core group countries tended to highlight the humanitarian aspect of the Ottawa Convention but linked it to arms control and security matters. However, this is perhaps easy for, say, the Netherlands to do, as it is not facing any direct or immediate threats to its national security. By contrast, among the initially reluctant states, the UK and France in particular initially opposed the Ottawa Process because of its security implications and eventually signed on the basis of its humanitarian aspects. Such a change was reconciled by officials by the policy of double-tracking (pushing for AP mines to be dealt with in the CD as well as through the Ottawa Process) and, conceptually, by denying the link of security and humanitarianism in the Ottawa Convention. The Ottawa Convention was interpreted, in this view, as humanitarian law only and not as an arms control treaty. Such attitudes demonstrate that the collapse of this opposition of humanitarianism and security—the conceptual heart of the Ottawa Process—continues to be contested terrain among states that have signed but have yet to ratify.

Those states in Europe that did not sign—Turkey, Finland, and Yugoslavia, for instance—did so because of the stark nature of the opposition of security and humanitarianism in their national context. It deserves to be restated that this is not an issue of whether AP mines have military utility so much as it is a question of whether they *might* be useful in the context of a perceived pressing threat to national security. Given the adherence of a number of states on the basis of their confidence in international security mechanisms, in particular the NATO alliance, Turkey's non-signature is notable. It speaks, however, to the radically different context with which Turkish officials are forced to cope. Furthermore, few Middle Eastern countries signed the Ottawa Convention, and Turkey in this respect is behaving normally. However, the fact that in this case Turkey behaves like its neighbours in the Middle East rather than in Europe should give European policy-makers pause for thought.

What is less obvious is what influence, if any, the European Union had on the policies of the member states. The decision to sign the Convention or not ultimately rested with the member states of the EU and not with the EU itself or its institutions.[24] From the perspective of those in favour of a ban, at the beginning of the Ottawa Process the priority of national over European decision-making was just as well, given the distinct possibility that the Great Powers would take landmines to the CD. As the Ottawa Process unfolded, EU policy increasingly lagged behind the large majority of the member states' policies because of the strictures of the consensus rule regarding foreign policy issues. This meant the concerns of Finland and of other hesitant states had to be taken into account alongside the vocal advocates of a ban. The EU was in microcosm an example of the sort of consensus diplomacy derided by the ICBL.

Arguably, the influence of the EU in terms of the prospect of future membership was stronger on applicant countries such as the Czech Republic and Hungary than it was on present members of the EU such as Greece. However, in each case (of members and possible future members), national security considerations weighed heavily, resulting in holdouts (Finland, the Baltic states) and hesitation (e.g., Greece, Poland). But while the EU did not take the lead on the AP mines ban, neither did it prevent or hinder the Ottawa Process. Indeed, while developments in the EU were relatively unimportant for those states that supported the ban, the peer pressure to take a common position upgraded the commitments of those states that were outside the Ottawa Process. For applicant states, this was a policy they needed to shadow, and for member states such as Greece and Finland, EU policy, though short of the comprehensive commitments in the Ottawa Convention, created legal commitments on transfer and production in advance of the treaty's ratification.

Finally, of course, the International Campaign to Ban Landmines had important impacts in all the democratic countries of Western Europe, though in different ways. Certainly the level of trust between certain government officials and certain NGOs that was so much a part of the Ottawa Process in Canada, Austria, and Norway was far from being the case in many of the countries in Europe, for instance, France, the UK (where, arguably, there is more trust between government ministers and some NGO representatives on this issue than of either with ministry officials), Spain, and Greece, to name just a few. The German case is an interesting one, furthermore, as here the government was in the vanguard of the international campaign and yet was heavily criticized by its national campaign to ban landmines.

In conclusion, a few European states made up the backbone of the international campaign to ban landmines. Yet, beyond these few, European states were divided over the prospect of a comprehensive ban. The proponents of the Ottawa Process benefited from the failure of the traditional avenues of arms control, specifically the Conference on Disarmament, as well as from the support of the UK and France after the spring 1997 elections. More generally, European states' policies varied according to a mix of national security concerns, EU membership or potential membership, and the status and influence of national NGO campaigns. The bandwagon effect of the campaign during 1997 also had an impact on the policies of some states.

APPENDIX: EU JOINT ACTIONS ON ANTI-PERSONNEL MINES

Because the use, stockpiling, production, and transfer of landmines are issues of national security, the mechanism for EU decision-making was the Common Foreign and Security Policy, and in particular, the Joint Action provision that enables the EU to take action in concert in areas of common concern. Given the differing positions of the member states and the supporting role played by the community institutions, the EU position is not immediately obvious. However, an educated observer might justifiably expect that EU policy would be as significantly affected by the snowball effect of the Ottawa Process as state policies were and that EU policy would move in line with member state policies. In fact, this is not the case. Prior to the Ottawa Process, the EU position was relatively advanced compared to general international community opinion and the national policies of member states. By comparison, while the EU position (exemplified by the 1997 Joint Action) advances on previous decisions of the Council, it exudes a hesitancy towards the Ottawa Process that appears unreflective of the current majority opinion of the member states that signed the treaty.

In all, the EU adopted three Joint Actions regarding landmines along with a number of enabling and complementary Council Resolutions. The Joint Action 95/170/CFSP (May 1995, complemented by Council Decision 96/251/CFSP in March 1996, two months prior to the CCW Review Conference) imposed a moratorium on the export of so-called 'dumb' mines to all states and all AP mines to certain states.

The next two Joint Actions were each finalized after long and arduous negotiations just a few days before the two Ottawa conferences. The timing of these Joint Actions indicates that the EU states endeavoured to caucus before these important discussions in order to generate a consensus. The Joint Action 96/588/CFSP (1 October 1996) was taken directly before the first Ottawa conference and committed the European Union to working actively towards the earliest possible achievement of an international agreement to ban AP landmines and to pushing for universal adherence to the 1980 Convention on Certain Conventional Weapons. It reiterated and extended the moratorium on exports of all AP landmines. While this was progress on previous EU policy, considerable ambiguity permitted the variations in member-state approaches to the AP mines question. Furthermore, as an agreement on exports, this Joint Action did not address stockpiling, production, or use—all considered too controversial for an EU decision.

Any semblance of the common position formulated in the Joint Action signed just before the conference disappeared immediately afterwards, however, in the wake of Lloyd Axworthy's surprise call for a ban treaty to be signed in a year. Though the member states had different positions beforehand, the impact of Axworthy's announcement was to bring further controversy into the EU's decision-making, and the EU predictably split along the lines we have set out above, between those states that supported the Ottawa Process, those that were more hesitant and argued for dual tracking with the Conference on Disarmament, and those that were totally opposed to the Ottawa Process. EU support for the Ottawa Process in early 1997 was not secure, as the lowest common denominator, especially among the Big Three (the UK, France, and Germany), was to take the landmines issue to the CD.

Shortly before the second Ottawa conference and the signing of the Ottawa Convention, and in the more general context of the decisions of all but one member state to sign, the EU Council made three decisions: two elaborating on and making provision for the implementation of the previous Council decision (97/818/CFSP and 97/819/CFSP) and a Joint Action that extended the moratorium to transfer and to production of anti-personnel mines (97/817/CFSP). The EU also committed to further support for demining and humanitarian assistance for mine victims. Though this last Joint Action is the most ambitious of the Joint Actions decided on, it lagged behind almost all member states' policies on AP mines at the time, in contrast to the earlier Joint Actions. The idea of member states committing to control production of landmines is in some respects a moot point in so far as many states had already committed unilaterally to such a position.

Actually, such a provision remained highly controversial since it suggests that the EU has a role in dealing with an issue that has strictly been viewed as a domestic prerogative of its members. Furthermore, the inclusion of a reference to the defence organization Western European Union in this Joint Action resulted in Denmark adding a statement for the Council minutes to the effect that 'Denmark will not participate in future Council decisions following up the joint actions on anti-personnel landmines' because 'Denmark does not take part in the elaboration or implementation of decisions and actions of the Union which have defence implications.' This was despite the fact that the Danes supported the Ottawa Process.

Over time, then, EU member states had moved quickly towards joining the Ottawa Process, particularly in the second half of 1997, but the EU made no such dramatic progress. The November 1997 Joint Action falls far short of adherence to the Ottawa Process, as there is no prohibition of use or stockpiling. Thus, far from upgrading or enhancing co-operation of EU states on the landmines issue, the EU reflected little more than the lowest common denominator among them. Indeed, this conclusion persisted and was made more stark as 'initially reluctant, subsequently convinced' states joined the Ottawa Process and the holdouts became marginalized. However, this gives only part of the story since the Joint Actions are legally binding on EU states now, whereas the Ottawa Convention only comes into force on ratification. As such, the force of the Joint Action is significant among those signatories of the Ottawa Convention, especially the less enthusiastic signatories such as Greece, and even more so for the non-signatory, Finland.

There are two reasons why the EU was hesitant. First, Finland, as we have seen, refused to sign the Ottawa Convention and the intergovernmental structure of the Common Foreign and Security Policy meant that Finnish opposition could effectively bring down any attempt at cooperation beyond what the Finns could accept. Second, while a number of states indeed signed the Ottawa Convention, it does not follow that they would support the involvement of the European Union in the wider aspects of the Convention and the ban on landmines. In the words of a European official, 'every word [in the Joint Action of November 1997] means something', that is, there was a delicate balance between differing national positions. The hesitancy reflected in the text conceals not only a gulf between states on the landmines issue, but between states and EU institutions on the right balance of European and national competencies.

NOTES

An earlier version of this chapter appeared in *Canadian Foreign Policy* 5, 3 (Spring 1998).

1. See *European Union Newsletter*, Delegation of the European Commission in Canada, 3 Oct. 1997.
2. See Chapter 2.
3. The drafting meeting hosted by the Netherlands included Austria, France, Germany, Sweden, and Switzerland.
4. The members of the European Network Against the Arms Trade were drawn from Belgium, Denmark, France, Germany, the Netherlands, Slovakia, Spain, Sweden, Switzerland, the UK, and international organizations based in Belgium and Geneva.
5. 'USA is storing mines in Norway', *Dagbladet*, 12 Sept. 1997.
6. The Troika consists of the immediate past, current, and next presidents of the Council and represents the EU internationally.
7. David Long, 'The EU and the Ottawa Process', paper presented at the European Community Studies Association of Canada annual meeting, Ottawa, 1998.
8. Martine Dardenne, 'Parliamentarians and the Agenda for Mine Action: Belgium', *A Global Ban on Landmines: Treaty Signing and Mine Action Forum*, 3 Dec. 1997, Ottawa.
9. Ibid.
10. International Campaign to Ban Landmines, 'Campaign Updates: Landmine Update #13', 1996. [http//:www.vvaf.org/landmine/international/updates/events/28.html]

11. Andrew Moravcsik, 'Negotiating the Single European Act: National Interests and Conventional Statecraft in the European Community', in Brent F. Nelson and Alexander C.G. Stubb, eds, *The European Union: Readings on the Theory and Practice of European Integration* (Boulder, Colo.: Lynne Rienner, 1994), 226.

12. Angelika Beer, 'The German Campaign to Ban Landmines', in ICBL, *Second NGO Conference on Landmines: Report on Proceedings*, 1994, 46.

13. Ministère des Affaires Étrangères, 'Interdiction des mines antipersonnel—Communiqué du ministère des affaires étrangères', *La politique étrangère de la France: texte et documents* (Jan.-Feb. 1997): 51.

14. Labour Party, *New Labour: Because Britain Deserves Better*, 1997, 38.

15. Chris Smith, ed., *The Military Utility of Landmines . . . ?* (London: Centre for Defence Studies, University of London, 1996), 94.

16. Foreign and Commonwealth Office, 'New UK Policy on Landmines', 1997.

17. Bob Lawson, 'Towards a New Multilateralism: Canada and the Landmine Ban', *Behind the Headlines* 54, 4 (1997): 22.

18. 'Des alliés de poids contre les mines antipersonnel', *Le Soir*, 25 June 1997.

19. Nicoletta Dentico, 'Country Report: Italy', in ICBL, *Second NGO Conference on Landmines: Report on Proceedings*, 1994, 50.

20. Ten states have applied to join the European Union: Bulgaria, the Czech Republic, Estonia, Hungary, Latvia, Lithuania, Poland, Romania, Slovakia, and Slovenia. Prior to these, Turkey had also applied to join the EU.

21. Valeriu Talabara, 'Parliamentarians and the Agenda for Mine Action: Romania', A Global Ban on Landmines: Treaty Signing and Mine Action Forum, 3 Dec. 1997, Ottawa.

22. Tarja Halonen, 'What Alternative to Anti-Personnel Mines?', 1997. [http:/www.vn.fi/vn/um/nr/english/topical/ default.html]

23. Statement issued in Ottawa by the Embassy of the Hellenic Republic, Dec. 1997.

24. For a fuller discussion of the influence of the European Union on its member states' decisions to join the Ottawa Process, see Long, 'The EU and the Ottawa Process'. For a discussion of the role of the EU in the landmines ban, see Geoffrey van Orden and Robert Cox, 'The European Union's Role in Overcoming the Tragedy of Anti-Personnel Landmines', *UNIDIR Newsletter*, special issue on The Elimination of Landmines (1997): 3.

CHAPTER 14

HARNESSING CHANGE FOR CONTINUITY: THE PLAY OF POLITICAL AND ECONOMIC FORCES BEHIND THE OTTAWA PROCESS

J.Marshall Beier and Ann Denholm Crosby

INTRODUCTION

The Convention on the Prohibition of the Use, Stockpiling, Production and Transfer of Anti-Personnel Mines and on Their Destruction, signed by representatives of 122 countries in Ottawa on 2–4 December 1997, has been widely hailed as a triumph of an emerging global civil society, transcendent of the particularistic interests of states in the international system.[1] Long a *cause célèbre* of a range of non-governmental organizations (NGOs), the scourge of anti-personnel (AP) landmines was successfully propelled onto the foreign policy agendas of states, including several that did not, in the end, become signatories to the Convention. To be sure, the outcome of the Ottawa Process, even if somewhat incomplete, is an auspicious one that promises to address the unambiguously deleterious effects of these weapons.

Rather less certain, however, is the soundness of prevailing accounts of the meaning of the Convention and its determinants. There is no questioning the fact that NGOs and other elements of what might be regarded as an emergent global civil society actively and persistently engaged in the motivation, framing, and unfolding of the Ottawa Process. Questions remain, however, as to whether the Convention is representative of the human security claims made on its behalf by a variety of involved NGOs, media commentators, signatory states,[2] and perhaps most notably by the man at the helm of the Ottawa Process, Canada's Minister of Foreign Affairs, Lloyd Axworthy,[3] and by US Congressman James McGovern in nominating the International Campaign to Ban Landmines for a Nobel Peace Prize.[4] Portraying the Convention as a practical application of the emerging discourse on 'human security' raises questions as to whether the Convention represents significant changes in state understandings about what constitutes security and for whom, and whether elements of an emergent global civil society acted as agents of that change or served as a conduit through which broader military, political, and economic forces could find new ways to realize old interests.

From a practical standpoint, the importance of coming to terms with these questions cannot be overstated in so far as they concern the potential of state/civil society partnerships as vehicles for substantive change in the ideas and practices that define global security relationships. With this in mind, this chapter turns to a consideration of the conceptual context ascribed to the Convention and its fit with the more tangible military, political, and economic realities of the landmines issue at the end of the millennium.

THE CONCEPTUAL CONTEXT OF THE CONVENTION

Plying the discourse of human security, Canada's Minister of Foreign Affairs suggested to the United Nations General Assembly in September 1996 that international security 'cannot be achieved until human security is guaranteed'. Human security, he continued, 'includes security against economic privation, an acceptable quality of life, and a guarantee of fundamental human rights' and encompasses 'the rule of law, good governance, sustainable development and social equity'.[5] In another venue, Axworthy placed this definition of human security within the context of peacebuilding and argued that peacebuilding 'aims to put in place the minimal conditions under which a country can take charge of its destiny, and social, political and economic development become possible'.[6]

The concept of human security, as described by Axworthy, sits well with the work of critical security theorists who, in exploring the meanings and practices of security in the post-Cold War world, focus on the individual, alone or in collectives, as the object of security—the entity to be secured, as opposed to the state.[7] According to these analyses, an examination of the history of international security relations, particularly during the Cold War, suggests that sovereign state security practices, rooted in the zero-sum games of arms races and strategies of nuclear deterrence, have done much to produce insecurities for the world's peoples. Quite apart from the abiding threat of nuclear war, the reality of regional wars and intra-state conflicts fuelled by the East/West relations of nuclear deterrence, the related global trade in arms, and the economic costs of traditional state-centric security practices have all served to compromise the ability of both states and peoples to provide secure environments for the quotidian business of living. On the basis of the experience of the Cold War, then, the ideas that support traditional state security practices have been seriously challenged.

With the end of the Cold War, these challenges have intensified for two reasons. First, as the relatively autonomous non-state forces of the global economy increasingly shape the political, economic, cultural, and ecological neighbourhoods of the world, the state's ability to address issues of environmental degradation, resource depletion, population movements, and distributive injustices involving gender, race, class, and ethnic dynamics is being increasingly eroded, as, therefore, is the state's ability to provide secure and just environments for its citizens. Second, and in relation to traditional state-centric security practices, using military force to address the conflicts that arise neither resolves the conditions that produce the conflicts nor addresses the kinds of insecurities produced by military means as experienced during the Cold War. Indeed, a resort to military means reinforces the hierarchical structures of power and privilege that sustain relations of inegalitarian exchange among the world's peoples.

Hence, from a critical security perspective, not only are traditional top-down ideas and practices inadequate for addressing contemporary problems, but the use of military force is seen as counter-productive for addressing the range of issues and relationships within a human security perspective and that require empathetic dialogue, co-operation, and compromise at all levels for their resolution. The pursuit of human security, then, is a demilitarized pursuit.

In this vein, critical security theorists argue that if state-centric security ideas and practices, and the structures supporting them, are to be transformed into global security initiatives with some meaningful semblance of egalitarian justice for the world's peoples, those transformative initiatives will emerge from within civil society. From an environmental security perspective, for example, Ronnie Lipschutz suggests that despite global macromanagement designs, local communities must work with local resources and live with the results.[8] Innovation, he argues, is most likely to come from those whose everyday dealings with the exigencies of specific resource and environmental conditions as they relate either to local production for local consumption, or to global market forces, require them first to imagine, and then construct, indigenously friendly forms of local management. These alternatives, rooted in historical experience but shaped by existing material, political, social, and cultural relations, emerge as working alternatives to management processes devised by macro-managers with macro perspectives. Writing from a more general critical perspective, Robert Cox also concludes that 'The struggle for change will take place primarily in civil society',[9] through the formation of counter-hegemonic authority systems capable of challenging the status quo.

In short, these authors, and others,[10] argue that with the erosion of the dominant Cold War structures of co-operation and conflict, ad hoc bargaining between, among, and within states, subnational groups, and transnational interests and communities will result in a remapping of international politics reflective of a global community with a global consciousness. In this endeavour, civil society is regarded as the agent of transition from traditional state-centric security formulations and practices to initiatives rooted in understandings of human security.

A combination of factors, specific to the contemporary era, is thought to facilitate this transition. A primary factor is the technological revolution in communication systems. Real-time television coverage of world events and the access provided by personal computers to e-mail and the Internet have created a more informed population worldwide, as well as the means to shape and rally world opinion. More to the point, the new communication technologies facilitate the identification of civil society expertise in specific issue areas and the organization of that expertise into networks of knowledge-based relations among the world's peoples. These relations are counter-hegemonic to the extent that they are informed by disillusionment with current political leadership and a recognition of the erosion of the state's ability to address human security issues, either alone or in existing fora of global governance. The existence of multiple global authority structures and the incoherence they bring to the management of global processes create the space for these counter-hegemonic, knowledge-based relations to develop, organize, and influence world processes. Hence, civil society, working co-operatively in specific but interacting issue-areas, is creating the basis for the emergence of new forms of political and social identity and action at all levels of governance.

The Ottawa Convention is portrayed as evidence of this new kind of security thinking in practice, primarily for three reasons. First, in terms of 'human security', the Convention goes beyond the traditional arms control prohibitions against development, use, stockpiling, production, and transfer. Signatory states are also obliged to destroy the crop of AP mines sown in upwards of 65 countries throughout the world and, when 'in a position to do so', to participate in the 'care and rehabilitation, and social and economic reintegration, of mine victims and for mine awareness programs'.[11] For these reasons, the Convention is more often described as a humanitarian initiative than as an arms control agreement and, indeed, one of its key undertakings is usually referred to as 'humanitarian demining'.

The Convention is therefore transformative in concept. Apart from recognizing the indiscriminate nature of a staple in the world's military stockpiles through an agreement to ban the weapon and by accepting a responsibility for both mine removal and the rehabilitation of mine victims and their communities, signatory states also implicitly recognize their own culpability in producing what is often described by those same states as a humanitarian crisis.

Second, in terms of the role of global civil society in pursuing transformative security practices, the Convention is a direct result of concerted co-operative efforts of non-governmental organizations worldwide. These NGOs were responsible for putting the issue on public and state agendas and for confronting and interfacing with government officials to bring 122 countries to the signing of the Convention in Ottawa. Moreover, the Convention relies heavily on the NGO community for verifying and implementing its conditions in concert with local, regional, and international fora of governance.[12]

Finally, the ability to identify and organize civil society expertise on the landmine issue, to co-ordinate NGO activity at all levels of involvement and across the range of activities covered by the Convention, to rally public opinion, and to interact with governments was facilitated by global communication technologies. Jody Williams, for instance, when not travelling for the cause, co-ordinated much of the work of the International Campaign to Ban Landmines (ICBL) from her home in Vermont through e-mail communication with more than 700 involved contacts and NGOs working in 40 countries.[13]

Taking these three points together, the NGO community has reflected many of the characteristics of civil society acting as an agent of transformative change. Yet, critical security theorists also remind us that in periods of change the past continues to shape the present.[14] The forces of the status quo overlap with the forces of transition, and within the interplay of overlapping forces change takes place, including the determination as to whether it will be of a reformative or transformative nature. If the forces of the status quo emerge with their interests essentially uncompromised, or indeed reinforced, then change is of a reformative kind. Hierarchical authority structures may become populated with new configurations of power interests and relationships reflecting current political, economic, and social exigencies, but the ideas supporting privilege within those structures and their practices remain intact.[15] As described by Antonio Gramsci in his discussions of passive revolutions, through processes of co-optation, assimilation, and/or evasion, the status quo may simply mould the transitionary agenda to its own purposes and subsume agents of change within its ranks.[16] If, however, the forces of transition succeed in altering the ideas, practices, and agents of governance fora so that the interests of the status quo are compromised, then transformative change may be under way.

With regard to the status quo in the context of potentially transformative human security initiatives, the Cold War created the conditions within major industrialized states for the development of a matrix of government, military, and economic relationships, each with its own particular interests in sustaining the ideas and practices that rooted security in military means. In his 1961 'Farewell Address to the Nation', US President

Dwight D. Eisenhower referred to this matrix of relationships as a 'military-industrial complex' and warned of its ability to shape foreign policy.[17] In the ensuing Cold War years, studies of the dynamics of the military-industrial complex demonstrated how the separate interests of the outwardly discrete realms of the military, the defence production industry, and the government coalesced to contribute to the production and reproduction of the East/West tensions of the Cold War.[18] In the post-Cold War world, the confluence of these status-quo interests made fighting the Gulf War ideologically and technologically possible and, as will be discussed later, continues to develop plans, programs, and technologies designed to define and/or sustain regional and global security environments through military means.[19]

The Cold War years were also witness to the increasing globalization of market forces, born in Western industrialized states and carriers of Western capitalist values and relations. Dominated by the interests of large transnational corporations, these market forces increasingly determined who would produce and consume what amounts of the world's commodities and where. In the post-Cold War era, this distribution of the world's natural, manufactured, and social resources, facilitated by state-driven neoliberal economic policies, has continued to favour industrialized states, often at the expense of so-called developing nations. The resultant growing gap between have and have-not populations is but one measure of the injustices in the distributive system, just as it is one criterion of what constitutes insecurity for vast numbers of the world's peoples and security for a privileged few.[20]

The point to be made in the context of the Ottawa Convention is that significant military, political, and economic interests, residing in industrialized states and born of the Cold War, have survived to sustain a militarized approach to securing state interests and addressing conflicts in the post-Cold War era. In their non-military hats, these political and economic interests also produce and/or exacerbate insecurities and conflicts for many of the world's peoples. Implementing the conditions of the Convention directly engages many of these interests wearing both their hats, and if the Convention is to be representative of humanitarian initiatives rooted in human security dimensions, its implementation cannot also reinforce the military, political, and economic forces that render people's lives insecure.

In its conception, agents, and methods, the Ottawa Convention appears to represent transitional forces in action in the area of global security initiatives. The central question is whether the Convention—and the articulation of state/NGO interests that brought it to fruition—compromises or reinforces status-quo economic, political, and military efforts to sustain traditional state-centric security ideas and practices. In other words, is it transformative or reformative? This question is explored in the context of the four pillars of the Convention—the ban on the use of AP landmines, the ban on their production, the obligation to demine the world's minefields, and the concomitant obligation to aid in the rehabilitation of mine victims and the reconstruction of their social and economic environments.

THE BAN ON THE USE OF ANTI-PERSONNEL LANDMINES

Anti-personnel landmines, when originally implanted by hand, were designed as defensive weapons to protect military installations, essential resources, and infrastructures, and/or to impede enemy advancement.[21] With the advent in the 1960s of the capability to deliver mines by rocket, artillery, and aircraft, they became an offensive weapon used for such additional purposes as saturating target areas and preventing the retreat of an enemy. In both their offensive and defensive roles, landmines were a staple in military equipment stores and their use was integral to military doctrine. During the Cold War, these features of the weapon, together with its being inexpensive to produce as well as easily manufactured, stored, and transported, established a place for landmines in the global arms trade and in arms transfers between states. By the mid-1990s, the proliferation of the weapon and its use by state militaries and guerrilla movements resulted in estimates of between 60 million and 110 million landmines sown in upwards of 65 countries, with another 100 million in the world's stockpiles.[22]

Some military experts remain convinced that mines are an essential weapon of modern warfare, but as Gard notes in Chapter 9, studies of their military effectiveness have suggested otherwise. With emphasis on the havoc wreaked upon civilian populations, these kinds of conclusions, together with the proliferation of the weapon, were cited by states as reasons for signing the Convention. However, major producers and users of AP landmines did not sign the Convention, including China, Iran, Israel, Russia, and the United States. Each of these states declared that the absence of functional alternatives to landmines was a factor preventing it from signing.[23]

Focusing narrowly on the ban against the use of landmines, then, the Convention does not represent a change in traditional state ideas about what constitutes security, for whom it is provided, or by what means. To be sure, the Convention recognizes the inappropriateness of subjecting civilian populations to the scourge of AP landmines and, not insignificantly, has been successful in removing one weapon from the arsenals of signatory states. Nevertheless, states signing the Convention did so in recognition of the dubious value of that particular weapon in military tactical manoeuvres, while those not signing cited the need to find an alternative method of fulfilling the landmine role in military endeavours. Neither of these reasons compromises the ideas and practices that legitimate the use of military force in securing state positions within hierarchical structures of power and privilege and the perpetuation of injustices endemic to those structures.

Drawing back from a narrow focus on the prohibition against the use of landmines, however, larger questions can be explored concerning the articulation of interests within the state/civil society co-operative effort to bring the Convention to fruition. What comes into view from this perspective is the extent to which the focus on the immediate goal of achieving the ban produced strategies that reinforced both state-centric security ideas in general and some post-Cold War security practices of Western industrialized states in particular. Instructive here for attempting to conceptualize the process of change is the interplay of the forces of the status quo and the perceived forces of transition in relation to their relative interests.

As was mentioned earlier, the Convention to ban landmines is often represented by involved politicians, government bureaucrats, NGOs, and media representatives as an example of human security rhetoric in practice. According to Jody Williams, however, the ICBL's agenda was singular: to eliminate the use by states of AP landmines because of their indiscriminate and inhumane nature. There was no intent on the part of the ICBL to situate the movement to ban landmines within the larger context of state-centric security practices.[24] By not doing so, the ICBL left largely unexamined the issue of states' responsibility for creating the humanitarian problem through their support for the production, stockpiling, use, transfer, and global trade in landmines.

Moreover, having been granted impunity by signing the Convention, states were able to take advantage of its portrayal as a humanitarian initiative by representing themselves as supporters of progressive human security programs. This is a legitimate representation in terms of the demining, rehabilitation, and reconstruction programs embodied in the Convention, but only if those programs are conducted in ways that do allow mined communities to, in Lloyd Axworthy's words, take charge of their own destinies so that 'social, political and economic development become possible'. As will be argued in the next section, however, the human security aspects of the Convention are tied in significant ways to Western concepts of what constitutes 'development'. Under these conditions, the destinies of land-mined peoples stand to be shaped from outside.

Segments of the NGO community also reinforced traditional state security practices by engaging states in the debate about landmines on their own terms. Especially noteworthy in this context is the degree to which the ICRC in particular took seriously the claims of non-signatory states that their signing of the Convention depended on their finding an alternative to landmines. A chapter in the ICRC study mentioned above is devoted to a discussion of possible alternatives to landmines and cites a range of possibilities, from 'slippery surfaces and foam' to other forms of 'munitions' and extending even to space-based 'remote surveillance methods'.[25] In reference to the latter alternative, the ICRC suggests that space-based surveillance and warning systems 'could, for countries with access to such technology, substitute for mine use. The early-warning capabilities of such devices could offer military advantages similar to the delaying effect of minefields. Upon detection, advancing forces could be targeted with ordnance other than mines, delivered by artillery, aircraft or direct fire.'[26]

By engaging these arguments, the ICRC explicitly indicates its support for the ideas and practices that allowed state militaries to use landmines in the first place. Using landmines to achieve military ends is challenged, but neither the broader practice of means nor the ends are questioned in themselves. Indeed, military casualties suffered by means other than landmines appear unproblematic. Nor does the study argue against initiatives that might allow advanced industrial states, those with access to space-based surveillance and warning technologies, to secure their positions of dominance through military means. In this, the ICRC implicitly lends its support to efforts by the industrialized states to militarize outer space. As General Joseph W. Ashy, Commander-in-Chief of the US Space Command, noted in a brief to the US Senate in March 1996:

> Traditionally, land, sea and air comprised the operating media of the military. The latter decades of the 20th Century have witnessed the emergence of a fourth operational medium for the military—space. The use of space and control of this space medium are essential to today's military operations . . . [where] joint operations, precision weapons, and information dominance are the hallmarks of a 21st Century fighting force.[27]

US defence programs supported by this perspective were budgeted $17 billion over the five-year period from 1995 to 1999, with a forecast core program budget of $50 billion through to the year 2010, exclusive of operational costs.[28] Hence, while millions of dollars are being sought and spent to take AP landmines out of the earth, billions are also being spent and budgeted to put weapons in space.

As the ICRC suggests, the surveillance, warning, and communication systems that constitute a major thrust to the militarization of space may be able to perform a significant role in landmine detection on earth. The systems, however, are designed first and foremost 'to protect U.S. forces, U.S. allies, and other important countries, including areas of vital interest to the U.S.'[29] With the exception of South Korea, only the major industrialized states, including Canada, have routinized institutional links with these US programs and all participation is on US terms.[30] In human security terms, the programs supported by these space-based defence technologies facilitate only those countries with access to them through US military command and control systems to 'take charge of their own destinies'. Under these conditions, the 'destinies' of most mined countries, as they pertain to the militarization of space, are in the hands of industrialized states.

Moreover, during the 45 years of constant war preparation that constituted the Cold War relations of nuclear deterrence, the design, production, and sale of the weapons of war were a lucrative business for the defence production industry, and especially so for those firms that could meet the increasing demand for high-tech weapons and delivery systems to be used in military initiatives on land, at sea, and in the air and space. The space-based programs described by General Ashy and funded by the US defence budget sustain the nexus of Cold War military, political, and economic interests in traditional state-centric security practices in the post-Cold War era, and the ICRC's implicit support for these programs leaves them unchallenged.

Hence, although the ICBL and the ICRC accomplished their immediate goal of achieving a Convention to ban landmines by being less than critical of the broader ethos of the military practices of industrialized states, they ultimately participated in legitimating both the ethos and the practices. The corollary, of course, is that if the NGO community had engaged states in fundamentally critical ways the Ottawa Convention likely would not have come to pass and this is informative for the prospects for success of future 'humanitarian' arms control initiatives now in the offing.

During the NGO Mine Action Forum held at the same site and at the same time as the state signing ceremonies in Ottawa, representatives of concerned NGOs, including the ICRC, called for the community to build on its success with the landmine issue by turning its attention next to the subject of small arms and light weapons. These include assault rifles, machine guns, light mortars, and hand- and rocket-propelled grenades, as well as landmines.[31] Addressing the uses of these weapons would involve states in a fundamental rethinking of conflict, what causes it, how to address it, and the relevancy of traditional military initiatives in these contexts. The coincidence of state/NGO interests as constructed to achieve the ban on landmines will not serve these purposes.

Still, change is incremental and state/NGO interests are not necessarily frozen in place by the coincidence of interests that produced the Convention, nor is the signing of it the end of the story. Implementing the Convention involves states and NGOs in co-operative endeavours to de-mine the world's minefields, to rehabilitate mine victims, and to recon-struct their social and economic environments. A persistent theme of pre-sentations during the NGO Mine Action Forum was that these programs were essentially about development and humanitarian issues.

In this regard, in the weeks prior to the signing of the Convention, the UN transferred responsibility for the implementation of the Convention from the Office of the Secretary-General to its military organization, the Department of Peacekeeping Operations (DPKO). Although the transfer serves to reinforce both the image and the role of the military in shaping global and regional security environments, the DPKO is mandated to work closely with the United Nations Development Program, UNICEF, and the World Bank in implementing the conditions of the Convention.[32] The mandated articulation of military, humanitarian, and development issues and interests in the implementation of the Convention creates spaces for the emergence of new roles for traditional militaries and for NGOs with egalitarian ideas about what constitutes security and for whom to exercise their influence. At the same time, traditional political-economic forces are poised to fill these same spaces with the pursuit of their own interests. It is to these elements of the Convention that this chapter now turns.

THE BAN ON LANDMINE PRODUCTION

Both private defence production firms and state production units originally produced AP mines under government contract for use by their national militaries in field operations and by their governments in arms transfers to 'client' states. The increase in demand for an inexpensive, easily trans-ported and deployed weapon, however, together with the cost-effectiveness of mass production, led mine-producing industries to extend production runs to supply foreign markets, including black markets, independently. Over time, and as part of the global trade in arms, an intricate web of credit, shipping, and financial structures developed to support the world-wide production of and trade in landmines.[33] By the mid-1990s, the world's production of landmines was estimated at about 5 million mines per year with approximately 100 firms in more than 55 countries engaged in legitimate production.[34]

Prior to the signing of the Ottawa Convention, then, the production and trade of AP mines were shaped by the same global market forces that determine the production and distribution of civilian consumer products. For this reason, country-specific bans on landmine production have not always been effective because producing firms have been able to react to a ban by moving production offshore to subsidiaries or affiliates in other parts of the world. When their governments banned indigenous production, for example, French and Italian manufacturers shipped explosives to Singapore for the production and assembly of mines there.[35] Such intrafirm trade, representative of 25 per cent of all contemporary global trade, is not amenable to government control.[36] In short, landmines are but one example of the globalization of commodity production and trade, fuelled and protected by a relatively autonomous market system.

However, it is most likely that the Convention banning AP mines will substantially curb the production and trade in the weapon. As the legitimate markets for the weapons wane due to the ban, so, too, will production for those markets. In addition, there will be less demand for illegitimate production; legitimate firms engaged in the secret production of the weapon will have less incentive to do so, while firms of non-signatory states will be increasingly limited to producing on contract to their own governments. Only the illegitimate production of the weapon for illegitimate use will remain unaffected, but this sector has generally produced for its own use and has not contributed greatly to the global trade in landmines.

Yet, in spite of private industry's involvement in the production of landmines and the real possibility of declining markets for the weapon due to the ban, there has not been a significant defence production industry lobby against the Ottawa Convention. This cannot be attributed to moral trepidation on the part of producer firms alone, for when targeted in a stigmatization campaign by Human Rights Watch, some of the larger US producer firms, including Alliant Techsystems, General Electric, Lockheed Martin, Raytheon, and Thiokol, publicly refused to renounce their future involvement in landmine production.[37] Rather, the lack of publicly expressed industry concern most likely indicates that the ban does not seriously compromise their economic interests.

Indeed, being generally priced in the $3 to $30 range per mine,[38] AP mines are not a high-profit commodity for defence production firms and are often used as the loss-leaders in the arms markets. In total, it is estimated that the trade in AP mines accounts for less than $100 million of the total $20 billion per year global arms trade.[39] Moreover, with approximately 100 million such mines in the world's stockpiles,[40] it is quite possible that the landmine market is saturated. Given these conditions, together with the proliferation in the use of landmines during the Cold War, the Convention's obligation to demine the world's minefields is arguably more profitable to the defence production industry than is the production of mines themselves.

DEMINING THE WORLD'S MINEFIELDS

Speaking at the opening plenary session of the Mine Action Forum in Ottawa in December 1997, Rafeeuddin Ahmed, associate administrator of the UN's Development Program, echoed the position of many demining and development NGOs by saying that the UN 'sees demining as a key component to sustainable development' and that, among other components of a successful program, demining initiatives must include a commitment to 'local expertise and resources'.[41] In this context, Lieutenant Colonel Chip Bowness, chief UN adviser to the Cambodian Mine Action Centre, later warned 'of a potential gap between support for local manufacturing and the interests of foreign industry that hopes to make money on the manufacture of humanitarian demining equipment'. What is really needed in impoverished countries, he suggested, 'is simple, easy to use and maintain, low-tech equipment'.[42] Despite the opinions voiced by these and other participants at the Mine Action Forum—some from indigenous demining NGOs—that demining must essentially be about locally controlled and directed humanitarian and development concerns, temptations to pursue high-tech demining initiatives that directly benefit firms in industrialized states are proving too hard for those same states to resist.

Although an AP mine can cost as little as $3 to buy, the cost of removing it from the ground can range from $300 to $1,000.[43] Depending on which estimate one uses of the number of mines presently in the ground, this means that the cost of demining the world's minefields ranges from $18 billion to $110 billion, with $33 billion being a commonly used figure. Since the Convention commits signatory states to undertake demining on a global basis and since some non-signatory states such as the US have also committed themselves to this endeavour, a plethora of demining contracts is potentially available and much of this work stands to be highly profitable for Western military experts and Western defence production industries.

A glossy catalogue published by the US Department of Defense (DOD) indicates the range of demining technologies presently available and/or in their research and development phases from US firms.[44] Available mine detection equipment ranges from pocket-size devices at a cost of $6,000 per unit to vehicle-mounted detectors at $500,000 a system. Mine-clearance equipment, which includes a 'supersonic air spade', ranges in cost from $20 for neutralizing foams, to $480 for a chemical neutralizer, to $350,000 for a 'tele-operated' remote-control backhoe.

In support of the US commitment to establish mine awareness programs in select countries,[45] the catalogue offers a range of US-produced materials, including multimedia awareness and demining training programs at a cost of $60,000 a system, educational comic books, a Mine Facts CD-ROM, and simulated mines for training indigenous populations and deminers in mine recognition. These simulated mines, which are 'accurate full scale inert replicas' of 'real' mines, cost $126 per unit, about 42 times the cost of the least expensive active mine they replicate. Many of these systems are examples of the output of US government research and development contracts, and they preview a new generation of more esoteric demining technologies currently in development. In 1996, for example, Westinghouse and Raytheon, the latter being a major producer of AP mines, competed for US DOD contracts worth between $40 million and $50 million for research and development in the area of airborne detection systems.[46]

Quite apart from its research and development funding of demining technologies, since 1993 the US has invested over $153 million in global demining initiatives and has budgeted another $80 million for demining operations in 1998.[47] US policy, however, determines that these funds, along with research and development investments, will reap their immediate dollar benefits at home. In support of its current mine-clearance operations in 18 countries, US policy is to provide 'training, expertise, and equipment support through programs administered by the Department of Defense'. This means that the US will provide demining technologies to those mine-affected countries that cannot afford them by way of purchasing them from US firms, which have developed them under US government funding. The administration of the mine-clearing operations and the training of indigenous deminers are then undertaken by US personnel. In addition, once an indigenous demining program is established, the ongoing maintenance of the equipment is also supplied by the US.[48] Not all funding for demining will be spent in this fashion, and demining will take place, but this is the phenomenon of tied-aid *par excellence*, and does not fulfil the criterion of commitment to 'local expertise and resources' as described by many of the demining NGOs speaking at the NGO Mine Action Forum.

Other industrialized countries have similar benefits built into their demining programs. Australia has earmarked $4 million over the next five years for research into demining technologies. Belgium will spend a proportion of its BF 63 million demining funds on 'high technology demining solutions'. The European Union (EU) has pledged ECU 15 million for 'development of appropriate technologies for humanitarian demining'. Sweden will spend Cdn $3 million on producing a 'multi-sensor mines detector', and the UK has pledged £30 million for a three-year demining technology program. These countries, and others, have also pledged the services of their military and technological experts in demining programs around the world.[49]

The UN is also supporting demining initiatives that reap substantial benefits for industrialized countries, their defence production industries, and their military and technology experts. In 1994, it awarded a $5 million contract to a consortium of British and South African firms for mine removal in Mozambique. The contract was controversial inasmuch as these firms had produced mines that had been used in that country.[50] In addition, the World Bank has also agreed to fund mine-clearing initiatives, but only if such initiatives can be 'justified on economic grounds' and shown to be 'an integral part of a development project or a prelude to a future development project or program to be adopted by the borrower'. To these ends, the World Bank 'requires that the borrower obtain competent independent technical, financial and legal advice on all aspects of project design and implementation', including possibly establishing 'a panel of internationally recognized experts to advise on the project'.[51]

Since the expertise required to support funding for demining/development projects resides primarily within industrialized states, these states and their resident experts ultimately benefit from the relevant conditions applied by the Bank. More to the point, since the World Bank defines 'development' largely within the context of neo-liberal market forces, which are themselves rooted in the economic interests of industrialized states and transnational corporations, its choices for funding particular demining programs are both economically determined and designed to reflect the interests of Western market forces.

Hence, although there are indigenously sensitive demining programs in existence, and although the continued articulation of NGO and state interests during the implementation of the Convention may succeed in prioritizing indigenous development and humanitarian interests at the expense of larger economic interests, at the time of the signing of the Convention its mandate to demine the world's minefields created markets for new and expensive demining technologies along with state programs to support the production, transfer, use, and maintenance of those technologies. In the process, defence production industries, largely Western in residence, have acquired research and development funds for new product lines and markets for their wares while Western military and technology experts have secured employment in demining and related development projects. To this extent, the interests of the status quo appear reinforced rather than compromised by the Convention.

REHABILITATION AND RECONSTRUCTION

As noted, the Ottawa Convention obligates signatory states 'in a position to do so' to participate in the 'care and rehabilitation, and social and economic reintegration' of mine victims. This is arguably the most expensive condition of the Convention. With regard to the 'care and rehabilitation' of landmine victims, to date there are some 250,000 landmine amputees worldwide, while the 60 to 110 million AP mines scattered throughout the world can remain active for up to 100 years and are currently producing an estimated additional 2,000 landmine victims a month.[52] Approximately one-third of these monthly victims require prostheses. In general, health-care costs per mine victim are estimated to average between $3,000 and $5,000[53] and include costs related to blood transfusions, malnutrition, disease related to poor and/or contaminated water supply, physical and psychological rehabilitation programs, and hospitalization and treatment for blindness, burns, infection, and blast-related injuries. Carolyn Taylor of the US Mine Victims Fund estimates that $3 billion will be needed for mine victim assistance in the next five to 10 years.[54]

In terms of the 'social and economic reintegration of mine victims', the funds required are equally substantial. Here, funding is needed primarily for the rebuilding of infrastructures, including roads, bridges, airports, power systems, water supplies, homes, businesses, hospitals, schools, and livestock replacement. Examples of the projected costs for some of these undertakings include $125 million to reconstruct 550 miles of the Cahors Bassa power lines in Mozambique[55] and $6.5 million to replace livestock lost to landmines in Afghanistan, Bosnia, Cambodia, and Mozambique.[56]

As with demining programs, large-scale state and private contributions are being made to mine victim assistance funds. For example, for assistance to mine victims the ICRC has been pledged ECU 8 million by the EU, US $100,000 by the Vatican, and US $20 million by Norway.[57] Also, and as with demining programs, although the assistance programs supported by these funds will benefit landmine victims directly, the funds will be spent on services largely supplied by industrialized states and/or transnational corporations. Two-thirds of world trade is now in services and this sector is dominated by transnational corporations engaged in the provision of many of those services most relevant to the rehabilitation of landmine victims and the reconstruction of their societies, including the areas of transportation, communications, finance, management, health, and education.[58]

Moreover, as the World Bank conditions for supporting demining programs indicate, its reconstruction funds will be tied to development programs that require vetting by technical, financial, and legal experts. The Bank's model of neo-liberal capitalist development more or less assures that that expertise will be of a similar persuasion and found to reside within industrialized states. In this self-perpetuating system, the dispersal of multilateral reconstruction funds is designed to bring potentially productive but presently mined areas and populations into the embrace of the Western-dominated global market system under its terms.

Joshua Malinga of the executive council of Zimbabwe's Disabled People's International argued at the Mine Action Forum that 'Victim assistance must concentrate on empowerment.'[59] If the implementation of the Convention's obligations to rehabilitate mine victims and reconstruct their social and economic environments is to reflect human security characteristics, co-operative state/NGO assistance in these areas would be directed towards 'empowering' mined communities to define, control, and manage their own social and economic rehabilitation. The political-economic interests facilitated by the Convention's mandate, however, have the propensity to define the context within which 'empowerment' takes place in terms consistent with the play of capitalist market forces and according to neo-liberal conceptions of what constitutes development. In this way, solutions to local problems are effectively globalized and, as Vandana Shiva has argued in a similar context, 'the North gains a new political space in which to control the South.'[60] The exercise of such control runs counter to the basic precepts of what constitutes human security.

CONCLUSION

Although it bears witness to several criteria cited by critical security theorists as representative of a human security initiative, the outcome of the Ottawa Process is not indicative of transformative change in either the international system or the established and enduring conceptions of security that help to sustain it. Rather, with respect to the traditional arms control elements of the Convention, such change is wholly reformative, conforming to the terms and bounds of pre-existing institutional and ideational structures. Significantly, these selfsame structures just as readily facilitated the global production, trade, and use of AP mines, and although signatory states may be circumscribed in the resort to a particular weapon that, at any rate, was of questionable utility, the means and ends it was intended to serve remain uncontested.

If the Ottawa Convention is ultimately to reflect the image of human security with which it has been painted, the mirror will have to be provided during its implementation when demining, rehabilitation, and reconstruction programs are undertaken. Here, however, in the paraphrased words of one voice from the NGO forum, 'There is a danger that the increased flow of international resources for mines action may be channelled in such a way that it supplants local community-based peacebuilding and development efforts amid a proliferation of NGOs and the imposition of external agendas.'[61] Indeed, at the time of the signing of the Convention, neo-liberal market forces of the industrialized world, both public and private, were poised to reap parochial advantages from the more pro-active obligations placed on signatory states by the Convention.

Hence, while states have accepted certain obligations in the realm of demining, rehabilitation, and reconstruction, these stand to be offset by the political and economic benefits likely to accrue to the industrialized states in the course of fulfilling them. In any event, should this turn out not to be the case in the realm of direct care and support for mine victims, states are left with what amounts to a loophole inasmuch as they are mandated to undertake such endeavours only when 'in a position to do so'. The ambiguity of this provision and the lack of a mechanism by which to make the determination mean that signatory states themselves will rule on their own fitness to address the needs of mine victims and, whatever their decision on the matter, their participation in lucrative demining activities will not be imperilled. Even the more proactive obligations of signatories to the Convention, therefore, are framed in ways that are likely to be beneficial to the interests of the most powerful and privileged actors in the global political economy or that at least do not jeopardize them in any meaningful way.

In terms of the Ottawa Process, what is clear is that the immediate practical agenda and, to some extent, the discourse of the anti-mine lobby have been adopted and merged with those of the forces of the status quo. Although civil society has gained a legitimate seat at the table, the extant system of power relations remains fundamentally unaltered, while innovations such as the notion of 'human security', in this instance, are effectively drained of their substantive content. And, far from carrying forward a sustained challenge to the status-quo interests implicated in the planting of the world's minefields, these integrated forces and movements serve to underwrite them. Ultimately, status-quo interests are sustained with the paradoxically solicitous support of the erstwhile forces of transition.

In the realm of determinants, then, all of this is consequential to the extent that it renders rather problematic the notion of global civil society as a significant source of transformative change in this instance. As well as being a determinant of the Ottawa Process, it would seem that in the end the NGO community was, at least in some measure, determined by it. The distinction is not merely an academic one: it has important implications in the realm of praxis as well. Being less than critical of the broader practices of privilege, the confluence of lead-NGO and state interests responsible for bringing the Convention to fruition reinforces the constraints put on those humanitarian and development NGOs working on demining, rehabilitation, and reconstruction programs from within a human security perspective.

This is instructive, too, for hopes expressed at the NGO Mine Action Forum to the effect that the successes of the Ottawa Process could be parlayed into similar efforts to address the use of small arms and light weapons. If status-quo interests are not served by such efforts, then rooting such hopes in similar processes are likely misguided and could produce unfruitful strategies for action. Perhaps the most instructive aspect of the Convention in this regard is that it was born more of general consensus than of fundamental contention.

NOTES

An earlier version of this chapter appeared in *Canadian Foreign Policy* 5, 3 (Spring 1998).

1. Canada's Minister of Foreign Affairs, Lloyd Axworthy, among others, credited 'the tremendous efforts made by NGOs' in contributing to 'the emergence of a truly global partnership' of peoples from 'Africa and Asia, from Europe to the Americas' dedicated to advancing the cause to ban landmines. Department of Foreign Affairs and International Trade (DFAIT), *AP Mine Ban: Progress Report No. 1* (Ottawa, Feb. 1997), 1.

2. For examples of these representations, see Canada, *An Agenda for Mine Action: A Global Ban on Landmines* (Ottawa, 2–4 Dec. 1997).

3. Lloyd Axworthy situated the ban on landmines within a human security context in 'Canada and Human Security: The Need for Leadership', *International Journal* 53, 2 (Spring 1997): 187–8.

4. As reported in *AP Mine Ban: Progress Report* (Feb. 1997), 6.

5. Axworthy, 'Canada and Human Security', 185.

6. Lloyd Axworthy, 'Building Peace To Last: Establishing a Canadian Peacebuilding Initiative', speech delivered at York University, 30 Oct. 1996.

7. For analyses of this type, see R.B.J. Walker, 'Security, Sovereignty and the Challenge of World Politics', *Alternatives* 15, 1 (1990): 3–27; Ken Booth,

'Security and Emancipation', *Review of International Studies* 17, 4 (1991): 313–26; Simon Dalby, 'Security, Modernity, Ecology: The Dilemmas of Post-Cold War Security Discourse', *Alternatives* 17, 1 (Winter 1992): 95–134. For the political economy elements of the argument, see Susan Strange, *The Retreat of the State: The Diffusion of Power in the World Economy* (Cambridge: Cambridge University Press, 1996).

8. Ronnie D. Lipschutz, 'From Place to Planet: Local Knowledge and Global Environmental Governance', *Global Governance* 3, 1 (1997): 83–102.

9. Robert W. Cox, 'An Alternative Approach to Multilateralism for the Twenty-first Century', *Global Governance* 3, 1 (1997): 103–16.

10. See, for example, James N. Rosenau, 'Citizenship in a Changing Global Order', in Rosenau and Ernst-Otto Czempiel, eds, *Governance Without Government* (Cambridge: Cambridge University Press, 1992), 272–94; Daniele Archibugi, 'The Reform of the UN and Cosmopolitan Democracy', *Journal of Peace Research* 30, 3 (Aug. 1993): 301–15; W. Kreml and C. Kegley, 'A Global Political Party: The Next Step', *Alternatives* 21 (1996): 123–34.

11. Article 6, para. 3 of the Convention on the Prohibition of the Use, Stockpiling, Production and Transfer of Anti-Personnel Mines and On Their Destruction.

12. See Ottawa Convention, Article 6, paras 3–5, Article 11, para. 4, and Article 12, para. 3.

13. Scott Baldauf, 'Nobel Laureate's Long Trip from Vermont Farm to Fame', *Christian Science Monitor*, 14 Oct. 1997.

14. See, for example, Justin Rosenberg, *The Empire of Civil Society* (London: Verso, 1994); Alexander Wendt, 'Anarchy Is What States Make of It', *International Organization* 46, 2 (1992): 391–425; John G. Ruggie, 'Territoriality and Beyond: Problematizing Modernity in International Relations', *International Organization* 47, 1 (1993): 139–74.

15. The Multilateral Agreement on Investment is an example of this kind of reformative activity.

16. Antonio Gramsci, *Selections from the Prison Notebooks*, Quinton Hoare and Geoffrey Nowell Smith, eds (New York: International Publishers, 1971), 106–14.

17. Dwight D. Eisenhower, 'Farewell Address to the Nation', 17 Jan. 1961, in William M. Evan and Steven Hilgarnter, eds, *The Arms Race and Nuclear War* (Englewood Cliffs, NJ: Prentice-Hall, 1987), 210–12.

18. In particular, see Seymour Melman, *Permanent War Economy* (New York: McGraw-Hill, 1974); John Kenneth Galbraith, *The Culture of Contentment* (Boston: Houghton Mifflin, 1992); Ann Markusen, 'The Militarized Economy', *World Policy Journal* 3 (Summer 1986): 495–516. A primary text on

the conjuncture of military, industry, and government interests is C. Wright Mills, *The Power Elite* (New York: Oxford University Press, 1956).

19. For an outline of these programs, see Ballistic Missile Defense Organization, *1995 Report to the Congress on Ballistic Missile Defense* (Washington, Sept. 1995). See also Kevin O'Brien, 'Canada and Aerospace Defence: NORAD, Global Warning and Theatre Missile Defence in the Evolving International Security Environment', Toronto, Canadian Institute of Strategic Studies, July 1995. For an analysis of Canada's involvement in the programs, see Ann Denholm Crosby, *Dilemmas in Defence Decision-Making: Constructing Canada's Role in NORAD* (Hampshire: Macmillan Press, 1998).

20. See Strange, *Retreat of the State*.

21. For a brief history of AP mines, see International Committee of the Red Cross, *Anti-Personnel Landmines: Friend or Foe?* (Geneva: ICRC, 1996), 9–39.

22. The lower estimate of the number of landmines presently in the ground is from the Canadian International Development Agency (CIDA). Both CIDA and the UN support the larger estimate of 110 million. Unless otherwise stated, the landmine-relevant figures used in the balance of the chapter are those most often cited by the UN and involved NGOs such as the ICBL, the ICRC, and Human Rights Watch. Although the accuracy of the data is contested by NGOs and governments alike, the use of the figures to rally support for the ban on landmines has meant that they have entered the public and private consciousness as fact and have that effect on the organization of ban-related activity.

23. From author's notes taken during the speeches made by signatory and non-signatory state representatives at the Convention signing ceremonies in Ottawa, 2–4 Dec. 1997.

24. This point was stressed by Jody Williams of the ICBL, and supported by Stephen Goose of Human Rights Watch, at the Ottawa Process Writers' Workshop held at Carleton University, Ottawa, 6–7, Mar. 1998.

25. ICRC, *Anti-Personnel Landmines*, 65–8.

26. Ibid., 67.

27. Testimony of General Joseph W. Ashy to the Senate Armed Services Committee, 21 Mar. 1996. Washington, Federal Document Clearing House, retrieved through Lexus Nexus News Service on the Internet.

28. Congressional Budget Office, 'The Future of Theatre Missile Defense', Washington, June 1994, 40–6.

29. *1995 Report to the Congress on Ballistic Missile Defense*, 2–1.

30. Ibid., 7–1–9.

31. Jeffrey Boutwell, Michael T. Klare, and Laura W. Reed, 'Introduction', in Boutwell, Klare, and Reed, eds, *Lethal Commerce: The Global Trade in Small*

Arms and Light Weapons (Cambridge, Mass: Committee on International Security Studies, American Academy of Arts and Sciences, 1995), 9.

32. From a speech delivered by Leon Terblanche, Mine Action Specialist with the Emergency Response Division of the United Nations Development Program, at the NGO Mine Action Forum. The talk is summarized in Canada, *An Agenda for Mine Action*, 62.

33. See ICRC, *Anti-Personnel Landmines*, 62–4; Michael T. Klare, 'The Global Trade in Light Weapons and the International System in the Post-Cold War Era', R.T. Naylor, 'The Structure and Operation of the Modern Arms Black Market', both in Boutwell, Klare, and Reed, eds, *Lethal Commerce*, 31–43, 44–57.

34. Shawn Roberts and Jody Williams, *After the Guns Fall Silent: The Enduring Legacy of Landmines* (Washington: Vietnam Veterans of America Foundation, 1995), 34.

35. United Nations Demining Database, 'Fact Sheet: Manufacturing and Trade' (New York: United Nations, 1997). [http://www.un.org/depts/dha/mct/trade.htm]

36. Strange, *Retreat of the State*, 48.

37. Human Rights Watch Arms Project, *Exposing the Source: U.S. Companies and the Production of Antipersonnel Mines* (New York: Human Rights Watch, Apr. 1997), 2.

38. The generally cited cost, here taken from Canadian International Development Agency (CIDA), *Anti-Personnel Mines and Development: CIDA's Approach* (Ottawa, Dec. 1997), 1.

39. Roberts and Williams, *After the Guns Fall Silent*, 34.

40. CIDA, *Anti-Personnel Mines and Development*, 1.

41. Canada, *An Agenda for Mine Action*, 2.

42. Ibid., 25.

43. CIDA, *Anti-Personnel Mines and Development*, 1. These are the figures used by the UN and major NGOs involved in the movement to ban landmines. (For a discussion, see Chapter 16.)

44. US Department of Defense, *Humanitarian Demining Equipment Catalogue: Taming the Demon* . . . (Washington: Office of the Assistant Secretary of Defense, Special Operations and Low Intensity Conflict, 1997).

45. US Government, 'Fiscal Year 1998 Humanitarian Demining Program: Fact Sheet', Washington, 1997, 1.

46. Steven Ashley, 'Searching for Landmines', *Mechanical Engineering—CIME* 118, 4 (Apr. 1996): 66.

47. See US Government, 'Fact Sheet', 1; Canada, *An Agenda for Mine Action*, 21.

48. US Government, 'Fact Sheet', 1.

49. Canada, *An Agenda for Mine Action*, 3–8.
50. Andrew Meldrum, 'On Deadly Ground', *Africa Report* 39, 4 (July-Aug. 1994): 57.
51. World Bank, 'Operational Memorandum: Demining—Operational Guidelines for Financing Land Mine Clearance', from Robert E. Hindle, Acting Director, OPR, 7 Feb. 1997.
52. CIDA, *Anti-Personnel Mines and Development*, 1.
53. 'Landmine-Related Injuries, 1993–1996', *Journal of the American Medical Association* 27, 8 (27 Aug. 1997): 621. But see Chapter 7, which calls into question these low figures.
54. Canada, *An Agenda for Mine Action*, 45.
55. Meldrum, 'On Deadly Ground', 58.
56. Neil Andersson, Cesar Palha da Sousa, and Sergio Paredes, 'Social Cost of Land Mines in Four Countries: Afghanistan, Bosnia, Cambodia, and Mozambique', *British Medical Journal* 311 (16 Sept. 1995): 719.
57. Canada, *An Agenda for Mine Action*, 8–9.
58. Strange, *Retreat of the State*, 51.
59. Canada, *An Agenda for Mine Action*, 34.
60. Vandana Shiva, 'Conflicts of Global Ecology: Environmental Activism in a Period of Global Reach', *Alternatives* 19, 2 (Spring 1994): 198.
61. Canada, *An Agenda for Mine Action*, 64.

CHAPTER 15

THE BAN TREATY

Thomas Hajnoczi, Thomas Desch, and Deborah Chatsis

THE IMPETUS FOR ACTION

Frustration can be a powerful and creative force. In April 1996, as the CCW Review Conference[1] reeled in the doldrums of finalizing amendments to Protocol II, which would bring limited and slow humanitarian progress to the issue of anti-personnel (AP) mines, the Austrian delegation to the conference gave up on it as the means towards a total ban. Among other pro-ban delegations, the Austrians floated the idea of a convention for a total ban of AP mines that, in their view, could be short, clear, and simple. The head of the Austrian delegation quickly drafted an outline of a convention and showed it to like-minded colleagues and non-governmental organizations (NGOs) attending the CCW Review Conference. The Austrian work on developing a text for the convention had begun.

In the following weeks it became clear that Canada would lay the foundations of the necessary political process at the Ottawa international strategy meeting in October 1996. Austria's intention of developing a first draft of a convention was warmly welcomed by Canada and the earlier outline, which had been further developed in Vienna, was circulated at the Ottawa conference. The chair of the Ottawa conference, Foreign Minister Lloyd Axworthy, gave Austria the task of elaborating a first draft of a ban convention and included this project in the plan of action prepared during the meeting.

THE DEVELOPMENT OF THE AUSTRIAN TEXT

States and NGOs drew several lessons from the CCW Review Conference process. The first was the importance of maintaining a clear message—based on principles of international humanitarian law (IHL), AP mines should be banned. Second, the focus would be on norm-building by a co-ordinated group of like-minded states rather than on an attempt to reconcile humanitarian and military considerations in a forum that included major mine-users or mine-producers, such as the CCW Review Conference or the Conference on Disarmament (CD).

Following the Ottawa strategy session in October 1996, a group of like-minded states met in Geneva in late 1996 to develop what would become known as the Ottawa Process. Freed from the constraints of UN multilateral negotiations and the need for consensus agreement, these states (the core group[2]) were able to set up a series of meetings and a work schedule leading to a diplomatic conference at which the formal negotiations would take place.

The normal procedure for negotiating a treaty is long and complicated. It often involves the establishment of preparatory committee meetings, lengthy negotiation over the rules of procedure, the identification of issues and proposals, the bracketing of differing versions, and, in a long, protracted process, the elimination of the brackets. This would have been tantamount to losing years—and tens of thousands of legs, hands, eyes, and lives. A fast track for developing a negotiating text was required. The question was how to develop a text based on the basic principles of IHL that banned AP mines without any loopholes, yet was widely acceptable.

A principle that guided the Austrians in elaborating the first version of the text was to keep it as short and clear as possible. To facilitate the acceptance of the text and minimize the duration of future negotiations, language from other treaties was taken over wherever possible. This would demonstrate that a convention could be negotiated quickly and that it was the lack of goodwill by states that kept the international community from achieving a total ban rather than the supposedly complicated nature of the issue. A simple text was less likely to open a Pandora's box of questions regarding the intricacies of verification mechanisms or trigger a North-South conflict on the questions of assistance and responsibility for mine clearance. As a result, the first version of the Austrian draft had only 13 articles, which set out a total ban in a very concise manner.

But this was only a beginning. Initially, the Austrian draft did not have any real political or legal status. It is not enough for a paper to be distributed by a state for it to become the main proposal in a treaty negotiation. It is only when states participate in a drafting exercise and are able to identify themselves with the text that it makes sense to convene formal negotiations. Thus, the Austrians were faced with two challenges: how to get states to comment on the text and incorporate their suggestions without putting the integrity of the draft treaty text at risk.

The Austrians and the core group embarked on a journey to move from a purely 'Austrian' paper to an internationally established draft that would become, with slight changes, the AP Mine Ban Convention. Soon after the October 1996 Ottawa meeting, all Austrian embassies were instructed to forward the first version of the draft text to their host states and to request comments and proposals for improvements from them. Indeed, in response to this request, the Austrian government received about two dozen substantial replies from all regions within a few weeks, including a number of responses from states that hitherto had been silent on the issue. Some states indicated that they were ready to sign the text as it then stood, others proposed amendments that were taken into account in redrafting the text. However, pursuing a bilateral track had its limits and would not build legitimacy beyond those states that responded to the request for comments and proposals. A multilateral process was needed to elicit comments from other states and intensify efforts towards a total ban.

To build legitimacy, Austria invited all states, the United Nations (UN), the International Committee of the Red Cross (ICRC) and the International Campaign to Ban Landmines (ICBL) to attend an 'Experts Meeting on the Text of a Total Ban Convention', held from 12 to 14 February 1997 in Vienna. This rather awkward title was chosen to make participation possible for all states, including those hostile to the Ottawa Process. It was unclear at that time what level of support for the Ottawa Process and the ban campaign there was among states, and it was with great surprise and relief that the Austrian chair announced that 111 delegations were present at the meeting. The unexpectedly high number illustrated that the process was gaining political momentum. It became increasingly politically desirable to be seen as part of the Ottawa Process.

The next step was to obtain a broad level of participation in the discussions on the draft text. A group of states (including the US, the UK, and France) that favoured the CD as the sole forum to negotiate a total ban treaty had clearly developed a strategy to undermine the meeting. They intended to make general statements to the effect that the CD was their preferred forum and remain silent on the substance of the text. Gradually, however, most of them became engaged in the discussion. To a certain extent, the statement of the Austrian chair that the text was provided only for the purpose of discussion (and would not bind any delegation) helped to build confidence. Even more effective were the many interventions by the members of the core group. The dissenters had to participate in the discussions as they did not want to leave the impression that the positions of the core group commanded the general support of the meeting. During those three days a common basis for approaching the problem developed. Apart from a few critical areas, the views expressed by various delegations attested to the acceptability of the structure and, to a considerable extent, the content of the Austrian draft.[3]

The many comments and suggestions obtained during the Vienna Experts Meeting, as well as in the written replies from states and the ICBL, necessitated a revised version of the text. While the first version had to be submitted to start the drafting process, the second had to be visibly improved and closer to the final product. The draft could only benefit from the collective wisdom of and discussions within the core group. Thus, a core group meeting was held in Vienna in March 1997 to revise the text. The second version of the Austrian text was circulated to states for comments and the final version of the Austrian draft was agreed upon at a core group meeting held in April 1997.[4]

When the new Austrian draft was circulated worldwide on 13 May 1997, it represented a collective effort not only of Austria and the core group but also, to a certain extent, of the approximately 70 states that had submitted comments, as well as the UN, ICRC, and ICBL. Nevertheless, the paper was attributable solely to Austria. This approach made it possible to view this paper as the result of extensive bilateral and multilateral negotiations while leaving Austria and the core group the discretion to take up only those proposals that were consistent with the objective—a total ban of AP mines.

By the late spring of 1997, the Austrian draft had won general support from a number of additional states, including France and the United Kingdom, which had changed their positions on the Ottawa Process in response to national policy reviews. It appeared as though the chances for another draft being put forward to compete with the Austrian draft were slim. Now, the transformation of a political process into a formal conference of states convened to negotiate a treaty on the basis of the Austrian draft was necessary.

THE POLITICAL FRAMEWORK AND NEGOTIATING FORUM

A significant broadening of political support for the Austrian text was achieved at the Brussels Conference on Anti-Personnel Landmines held on 24–7 June 1997. The first two days of the Brussels conference featured a 'critical lecture and substantive discussion of the main elements of a draft for the convention'. While support for the text was broadened, the level of discussion was kept general to ensure that the negotiations began only in Oslo. The Declaration of the Brussels conference 'welcomed the convening of a Diplomatic Conference by the Government of Norway in Oslo on 1 September 1997 to negotiate such an agreement and also welcomed the important work done by the Government of Austria on the text of a draft agreement which . . . [would be forwarded] to the Oslo Diplomatic Conference in order to be considered together with other relevant proposals which may be put forward there.' This served the purpose of further fuelling the political momentum behind the Ottawa Process.

At the beginning of the Oslo Diplomatic Conference the Austrian draft was adopted as the basic proposal for negotiation.[5] Amendments were tabled by a number of delegations, including even the Austrian delegation and other members of the core group. Improvements on a number of points were well warranted and had been prepared beforehand by the core group at a meeting in Vienna in August 1997. Hostile amendments were either not tabled or failed to attract enough support in the negotiations.[6] The conference adopted more detailed and concise language on several important articles, including the provisions related to the destruction of emplaced AP mines, international co-operation and assistance, and compliance. On the whole, the treaty resembles closely the final Austrian draft. The final product fulfilled the hopes of Austria and the core group. The integrity of the Convention—a total ban without any loopholes—had been successfully defended.

THE AP MINE CONVENTION

The Object and Purpose of the Convention

The 'Convention on the Prohibition of the Use, Stockpiling, Production and Transfer of Anti-Personnel Mines and on their Destruction' (the Convention) was adopted by 91 states on 18 September 1997 in Oslo without a vote and signed by 122 states in Ottawa on 2–4 December 1997.[7] It is the first international, legally binding agreement completely banning AP mines. The object and purpose of the Convention is to put an end to the suffering and casualties as well as to other severe consequences caused by AP mine use. Within the legal framework created by this Convention, states intend to contribute in an efficient and co-ordinated manner to the removal and destruction of AP mines placed throughout the world and to provide assistance for the care and rehabilitation of mine victims.[8]

The Convention is firmly rooted in international humanitarian law (IHL), and at the same time also contains important elements of disarmament law. As the Preamble indicates,[9] the Convention is based on the principle that the right of the parties to an armed conflict to choose methods or means of warfare is not unlimited, the principle that the employment in armed conflicts of weapons, projectiles, materials, and methods of warfare of a nature to cause superfluous injury or unnecessary suffering is prohibited, and the principle that a distinction must be made between civilian and military objects.[10] The Convention totally bans a specific type of weapon and provides for a compliance mechanism, in keeping with the disarmament tradition.[11]

Scope of Application

The earliest version of the Austrian draft contained a scope-of-application article stating that the Convention was to apply to AP mines, as defined in the Convention, and was also to apply in all circumstances, including armed conflict and times of peace. In the end, the negotiating states chose not to include a separate provision on the scope of application, because this was deemed unnecessary. Article 1 already makes it clear that the general obligations apply 'under any circumstances'. Furthermore, it was felt that an explicit provision on a comprehensive scope of application might either be regarded as stating the obvious and therefore redundant, or bear the risk of unintentionally creating a loophole.

Thus, the Convention's scope of application is comprehensive. Once it has entered into force,[12] it applies at all times.[13] The Convention, however, provides that even before its entry into force states may declare, at the time of the deposit of their instrument of ratification, acceptance, approval, or accession, that they will provisionally apply the general obligations under Article 1(1).[14] The personal (and thereby also the territorial) scope of application is—like that of other treaties—restricted to those states that have become parties to it.[15] It is therefore of vital importance for the ban of AP mines to become universal.[16]

The central subject of the Convention is the AP mine. The first draft of the Austrian text defined an AP mine as 'a mine[17] primarily designed to be exploded by the presence, proximity or contact of a person and that will incapacitate, injure or kill one or more persons.'[18] This definition was the same used in Amended Protocol II. While several states were dissatisfied with the definition, given its acceptance by the CCW Review Conference only months earlier, the Austrians decided to use it.

The chief criticism regarding this definition was with respect to the inclusion of the word 'primarily', which had been included in the definition by the technical subcommittee of the CCW Review Conference to prevent anti-vehicle (AV) mines, including those equipped with anti-handling devices (AHDs),[19] from falling within the definition.[20] Nevertheless, some states and NGOs objected to the CCW definition as the effect was to exclude weapons with more than one use ('hybrid mines'). It was argued that the development of this definition had prompted some manufacturers to rename their mines to avoid the application of Amended Protocol II.[21]

There was general agreement not to include AV mines within the Convention, as these weapons were considered to serve decisive military purposes and do not cause the same humanitarian problems as AP mines. Expanding the scope of the Convention to include AV mines might have prevented the majority of states from accepting it. Thus, the intention to exclude AV mines with AHDs from the definition had to be made explicit. Following the Vienna meeting in February 1997, the core group developed a definition that did not use the word 'primarily' but explicitly excluded AV mines.[22]

Several delegations expressed concern that the definition was too broad and would include munitions systems or weapons, such as unexploded ordnance, which, in their view, do not cause humanitarian problems, while others wanted the scope to be broader.[23] The risk in significantly expanding the scope to include all systems was that the support and momentum, so clearly focused on AP mines, might be lost and the negotiations in Oslo derailed. However, munitions adapted to work as AP mines would be covered by the Convention, as would 'booby traps',[24] as long as they otherwise fall within the definition of AP mine.

One delegation made several proposals to amend the definitions of both AP mine and of AHD[25] to exempt from the application of the Convention 'mixed munitions systems' of AV and AP mines deployed together. In such systems, the AP mines, equipped with self-destruction and self-deactivation features, serve the purpose of 'protecting' the AV mines from being removed or destroyed easily. The delegation argued that submunitions could be considered to function like AHDs. This was refuted by other delegations. The expression 'tamper with' was considered to cover only cases of intentional behaviour aiming at removing or destroying the AV mine in question.[26]

Another delegation proposed amending the definition of AHD to include the phrase 'or otherwise disturb'.[27] The effect of this amendment would have been the same as if the first proposal had succeeded, that is, it would have excluded from the definition of AP mine those munitions that detonate when unintentionally 'disturbed' by an otherwise innocent act, for example, a person stumbling over an AP mine deployed in a mixed munitions minefield. To limit the potential damage this amendment might cause, 'intentionally' was added to the text.[28]

The Core Obligations

Apart from what may be called mere 'technical' obligations, such as the obligation to settle disputes that may arise with regard to the application or the interpretation of the Convention'[29] the obligation of the states parties to meet regularly to consider any matter with regard to the application or implementation of the Convention,[30] and the obligation to bear the costs involved in the execution of the Convention,[31] the treaty obligations fall under either of two categories: (1) core obligations and (2) supplementary obligations to facilitate and support compliance with the core obligations.

Prohibition of the Use, Stockpiling, Production, and Transfer of AP Mines
As the title of the Convention indicates, the core obligations are the prohibition of the use, stockpiling, production, and transfer of AP mines, on

the one hand, and the obligation to destroy or ensure the destruction of all AP mines, on the other.

Article 1(1) prohibits the development, production, or acquisition as well as the stockpiling of AP mines by a state party to the Convention. Furthermore, the retention or the transfer of AP mines by a state party to anyone, be it another state party, a state not party to the Convention, or a private person, is prohibited, with the exception of a minimum amount of AP mines absolutely necessary for the development of and training in mine detection, mine clearance, or mine destruction techniques.[32] Also permitted by way of exception is the transfer of AP mines for the purpose of destruction.[33] Both the prohibitions and exceptions contained in these articles did not change significantly during the development of the text. The term 'transfer' is defined as involving, in addition to the physical movement of anti-personnel mines into or from national territory, the transfer of title to and control over the mines, but it does not involve the transfer of territory containing emplaced AP mines.[34]

A state party cannot evade its obligation under Article 1(2) to destroy its AP mines by simply shifting them across the border to another state's territory while keeping the title to and the control over the mines. Neither can it shift the ownership or possession of the mines to another person, for example, a private company, while still keeping the mines on its territory, and thus under its jurisdiction or control.[35]

Finally, Article 1(1) prohibits a state party to assist, encourage, or induce, in any way, anyone to engage in any activity prohibited to a state party under this Convention. This provision obliges a state party to omit any active support[36] of third parties, whether other states or private persons, while those third parties are engaging in prohibited activities. Further, Article 9 obliges states parties to pursue actively all appropriate ways and means to prevent and suppress any prohibited activity undertaken by persons or on territory under its jurisdiction or control.[37]

Mine Destruction

With regard to the obligation to destroy all AP mines, the Convention makes a distinction between AP mines kept in stockpiles and those lying in the ground, Article 4 covering the former and Article 5 the latter. Article 4 provides that each state party is obliged to destroy or ensure the destruction of all stockpiled AP mines it owns or possesses, or that are under its jurisdiction or control, within four years after the entry into force of the Convention for that state party.[38]

Although the terms 'jurisdiction' and 'control' have been used in other treaties, the terms have never been defined. There appears, however, to be an accepted understanding of them.[39] These terms would include a situation in which a state has sovereignty over an area with responsibility under international law for the persons or objects contained therein, or administrative or long-term control over an area, including when it is the occupying force in an area, but would appear to preclude short-term military control over an area by military or peacekeeping forces.[40]

Addressing the obligation of states with respect to emplaced mines proved to be more difficult. How could the Convention prescribe a certain period for mine-clearing in heavily mine-infested states, while knowing that in all likelihood this objective could not be achieved? Without any time-limit, however, pressure on states to clear the mines, a crucial function of the treaty, would be missing. An additional difficulty was coming up with definitions to distinguish clearly between those areas that could be cleared relatively quickly and those mine-infested areas that would take considerably longer. The solution taken in Oslo was to eliminate the distinction between the two types of mined areas and, knowing that most mine-affected states would not be able to clear all the AP mines within 10 years, to develop a mechanism that would give them more time to destroy the AP mines and avoid being in non-compliance with the Convention.[41] Thus, Article 5 provides that states parties that have in their territories areas that are considered dangerous due to the presence, or suspected presence, of AP mines have up to 10 years to destroy those mines.[42] If for some reason a state party is not able to meet this obligation, it may apply to a meeting of the states parties or a review conference[43] for an extension period of up to 10 years.

There are several advantages in taking such an approach. It avoids creating an arbitrary distinction between different areas containing minefields and will allow mine-affected states to deal with the burden of mine-clearance in a transparent fashion. It will give other states parties with AP mines in their territories the opportunity to seek renewal of the time period for those cases in which the AP mines do not pose a humanitarian danger to civilians and the benefits in clearing the area would be outweighed by the cost and the risks of clearing it. The application for extension will also provide mine-affected states with a forum (and an opportunity) to seek assistance from other states parties for the purposes of mine clearance.

Recognizing that all mine-affected states will not face the same challenges, the criteria for information to be included with the request is fairly general. The state party is to provide information on the progress achieved under national demining programs, the financial and technical means available to it, and circumstances that impede its ability to destroy the AP mines. The submission is also to include information on the humanitarian, social, economic, and environmental implications of the extension.[44] The request must be approved by a majority of votes of states parties attending the meeting. There is provision for a further renewal of the extension period, at which time the state party will have to submit further information on efforts undertaken to meet the obligation to destroy the AP mines.

Until all AP mines in mined areas are cleared and/or destroyed, states parties must identify areas under their jurisdiction or control in which AP mines are known or suspected to be emplaced, and ensure that such areas are perimeter-marked, monitored, and protected by fencing or other means to the standards set out in Amended Protocol II to the CCW.[45]

Compliance Mechanism

As a mix of IHL and disarmament, the Austrian text proved to be a fertile ground for discussions regarding various merits of IHL and disarmament law, particularly with respect to the issue of compliance. At the Vienna Experts Meeting it became clear that this issue was potentially the most difficult one and would need further and deeper consideration. Germany offered during the Vienna meeting to hold an experts meeting on verification and, at that time, joined the core group.

On 24-5 April 1997, 120 states as well as the UN, ICRC, and ICBL attended the Experts Meeting on Possible Verification Measures in Königswinter. That meeting served an important purpose—to consider in concrete terms the applicability of traditional verification measures for the various obligations. While some progress was achieved, no convergence of minds was in sight. Having dodged this controversial issue in the second version, the final Austrian draft had to find a viable middle ground. After numerous consultations, Austria presented a compromise solution that did not satisfy any side fully, but was conceptually acceptable for everyone.

In Oslo, the conference president selected a 'Friend of the Chair', Canada, to resolve the outstanding issue of a compliance mechanism. Thus, the Canadian delegation held a series of consultations in Oslo aimed at finding common ground between the two approaches. The compliance mechanism is a mix of the disarmament model of an intrusive verification regime and the IHL model of a fact-finding mechanism. The negotiations focused on questions relating to the scope of the fact-finding, i.e., whether the mission had to take place with the consent of the state against which an allegation of non-compliance had been made or whether this could be done through a decision of a meeting of the states parties.[46] After considerable discussion and negotiation, agreement was reached on the provisions of Article 8, which draws on important elements of a verification system while maintaining focus on a co-operative approach to clarifying compliance.[47] It allows for a formal exchange of information between states parties, allowing them to clarify situations in which they have reason to believe another state party may not be complying with its Convention obligations. In the event that this exchange of information does not sufficiently clarify the situation, the Convention allows for the possibility of a fact-finding mission of experts to the territory of the state in question to gather more information.

The clarification mechanism has five distinct phases. The *first stage* is the request for information regarding allegations of non-compliance.[48] A state or group of states ('requesting State Party') may submit a request for clarification, accompanied by all appropriate information, through the UN Secretary-General. The state party from which the clarification is sought ('requested State Party') must respond within 28 days.

The *second stage* concerns the response by the requested state. If the information is not provided to the requesting state party or is deemed to be unsatisfactory, the requesting state party may refer the matter to the next meeting of the states parties.[49] It may also request, through the UN Secretary-General, a special meeting of the states parties. Information on the allegation of non-compliance is to be provided to the states parties with the requested state party having the opportunity to respond to the information. The special meeting would be approved if one-third of the states parties agree, within 14 days, to its convocation.[50] Pending the convening of such a meeting, regular or special, states parties are urged to request the UN Secretary-General to exercise his or her good offices to facilitate the request for clarification.[51]

The *third stage* is the meeting itself, at which the request for further clarification is considered.[52] The states parties first have to determine whether to consider the matter further, taking into account all information submitted. The meeting must make every effort to reach a decision by consensus, but failing this, decisions will be taken by a majority of those present and voting. If further clarification is required, the meeting can authorize a fact-finding mission and decide on its mandate by a majority vote.[53] At any time, the requested state party may invite a fact-finding mission to its territory without the need for a specific decision to be taken.

The *fourth stage* in the clarification process is the fact-finding mission.[54] This mission is to consist of up to nine experts drawn from a list of names submitted by states parties held by the UN Secretary-General.[55] The experts are entitled to enjoy certain privileges and immunities during the course of the mission.[56] It must give 72 hours' notice before arriving in the territory of the requested state party, which must take the necessary administrative measures to receive, transport, and accommodate the mission and is responsible for ensuring the mission's security. The mission is entitled to bring along necessary equipment for the fact-finding, of which the requested state party is to be advised. The requested state party is to make all efforts to ensure that the fact-finding mission is given the opportunity to speak with all relevant persons and must grant access to all areas and installations under its control where relevant facts could be expected to be collected. This access is subject to security arrangements made by the requested state.[57] If the requested state party limits access for any of the given reasons, it must make every reasonable effort to demonstrate through alternative means its compliance with the Convention. Information provided in confidence and not related to the subject matter of the fact-finding mission is to be treated on a confidential basis. The mission may remain in the territory of the state party concerned for no more than 14 days, and at any particular site for no more than 7 days, unless otherwise agreed.

The *fifth stage* is the review of the information collected by the fact-finding mission.[58] The mission is to report its findings to the meeting through the UN Secretary-General. If the mission finds that the requested state party has not complied with the Convention, the meeting of the states parties can decide on appropriate action to be taken. Decisions are to be made by consensus but, failing that, the meeting can make decisions by a two-thirds majority of those present and voting.

The meeting may ask the requested state party to take measures to address the compliance issue within a specified period of time. It may also suggest to the states parties concerned ways and means to further clarify or resolve the matter under consideration, including the initiation of appropriate procedures in conformity with international law. These are not spelled out but could include, for example, suspension of the benefits arising out of the Convention, such as the provision of international co-operation and assistance, or referral of the matter to the United Nations.

The article specifically addresses the situation in which the non-compliance is found to be beyond the control of the requested state party. In such a case, it may make recommendations regarding the provision of international co-operation for the purpose of assisting the requested state party to achieve compliance.[59]

As a compromise between the IHL and disarmament models, the Convention clarification mechanism clearly is not as time-sensitive or intrusive as other inspection regimes,[60] nor is it bulky compared to IHL regimes.[61] There is a significant threshold for decisions to be taken by the meeting of the states parties (majority required to authorize a fact-finding mission, two-thirds to take action with respect to a finding of non-compliance). The sanctions for non-compliance are not spelled out clearly and, as with other treaties, the requested state party retains the ability to place limits on the fact-finding mission for security reasons.

Yet, this clarification mechanism is a remarkable achievement since it goes well beyond what has been accepted in other IHL treaties, such as the 1949 Geneva Conventions or Additional Protocol I. As it does not call for the creation of a new international organization but operates in an ad hoc manner, the costs to states parties will be relatively small. It may be that the clarification mechanism will rarely, if ever, be used, but, as with other fact-finding mechanisms, it will serve to encourage compliance.

The Supplemental Obligations

International Co-operation and Assistance

In developing the Convention, the core group was always aware of the need to take an integrated approach to the AP mine crisis: the prohibition and stigmatization of the use of AP mines, mine destruction, and victim assistance. Knowing that most of the mine-affected states were also developing states, a key part of the Convention would have to be that of international co-operation and assistance.

The first Austrian draft did not contain an article on international assistance.[62] In view of the comments made on this issue at the Vienna meeting, the Austrians included an article based on an article on technological co-operation and assistance contained in Amended Protocol II.[63] A further provision on victim assistance was included at the Oslo conference.[64]

Article 6 sets out the provisions regarding international co-operation and assistance. Paragraph 1 sets out the general obligation in this regard, that each state party 'has the right to seek and receive assistance, where feasible, from other States Parties to the extent possible.' While this obligation is qualified twice and does not impose a clear legal obligation on states parties to take specific action in this area, it does provide a clear political message on the importance of doing so.

States parties undertake to facilitate and shall have the right to participate in the 'fullest possible exchange of equipment and material, and scientific and technological information'. States both providing and receiving assistance have an obligation not to impose undue restrictions on the provision of mine-clearance equipment and related technological information for humanitarian purposes, for example, through import or export controls.[65] Other provisions in the article underline the political obligation on states parties to provide assistance for victims, as well as for mine clearance and destruction. States parties undertake to provide information to the United Nations for the purposes of mine clearance.[66]

States parties are entitled to request the UN, regional organizations, other states parties, or other competent intergovernmental or non-governmental fora to assist them with the elaboration of their national demining programs.[67] This can include information on: the scope of the AP mines problem, including the number of years required for mine clearance; the financial, technological, and human resources required for the program; possible mine awareness activities that could be undertaken; required assistance for mine victims; and the specifics on how the program is to operate.

Transparency Measures
Each state party must report annually on the measures it has taken towards meeting its obligations under the Convention.[68] The purposes of these transparency measures are to: assess implementation of the provisions of the Convention by states parties; provide baseline data for use in assessing compliance; provide confidence-building measures to alleviate security concerns of other states parties; and assist in demining efforts. In addition, they are to report on national implementation measures, including legislation and administrative and regulatory measures to implement the provisions of the Convention.[69] This could include changes to national military doctrine and military manuals. As well, they are to report on all types and quantities of AP mines stockpiled and, to the extent possible, on the location of all mined areas and any information on the AP mines contained in those mined areas.[70] The phrase 'to the extent possible' was included to alleviate the burden on severely mine-affected states that may not have information on the location of all mined areas.

States parties must provide information on all AP mines destroyed after the entry into force of the Convention, whether in stocks or in mined areas.[71] This will be useful in assessing requests for technical and financial assistance, as well as the request for an extension of the deferral period for the destruction of AP mines in mined areas. For those mined areas in which AP mines have not yet been destroyed, states parties are to provide information on the measures taken to provide an immediate and effective warning to the population.[72] Information on safety and environmental standards to be observed is also to be included.

Further, signatory states are to provide detailed information on each type of mine produced, to the extent known, and those currently owned or possessed by it, to facilitate identification and mine-clearance efforts of all states.[73] They must submit information regarding the types and quantities of AP mines they retain or transfer in accordance with the exception contained in Article 3 and must also provide information on the institutions authorized to retain or transfer such mines[74] and on the status of programs for the conversion or decommissioning of AP mine production facilities.[75] While there is no obligation in the Convention to convert or decommission the facilities, such action would be consistent with the prohibition on AP mines production contained in the Convention.

National Implementation Measures

The article on national implementation measures proved to be another area that combined IHL and disarmament law. The first draft of the Austrian text contained a provision on national implementation measures, similar to the final version, though it also included a provision making breaches of the Convention during armed conflict 'grave breaches', in accordance with the 1949 Geneva Conventions. There was some resistance to this at the Vienna Experts Meeting and within the core group, and the article included in the Austrian text was modelled very closely on Article 14 of Amended Protocol II,[76] itself a hybrid between IHL and disarmament law.

In accordance with Article 9, states parties agree to establish national implementation measures, including legislation or regulation, to prevent any person under their jurisdiction or control, on any territory under their jurisdiction or control, from using, stockpiling, producing, or transferring AP mines. This obligation can be fulfilled through legislative, administrative, or regulatory measures that prevent and suppress breaches of the Convention. Unlike similar provisions in the Chemical Weapons Convention or the Comprehensive Nuclear Test Ban Treaty, the Convention does not explicitly assume extraterritorial jurisdiction. The question of extraterritorial jurisdiction is left open for the states parties to decide.[77]

The question of application to non-state entities remains an important one in view of the number of internal armed conflicts and guerrilla movements. The clarification mechanism takes into account the fact that the state party may not have control over areas or installations, which would be considered in addressing the issue of compliance.[78] In addition, the Preamble was formulated to reiterate the basic principles that all parties to the conflict are bound by the principles of IHL underlying the ban.[79]

CONCLUSION

The Convention does not pretend to resolve the mines crisis. It does, however, establish a clear and unambiguous legal norm. This norm will have to be implemented by all states that ratify the Convention. The Convention sets up a comprehensive framework for action in addressing the anti-personnel mines crisis, including deadlines for action by states parties and provision for co-operation and opportunities for dialogue between states parties through the meetings (annually for the first five years) and review conferences.

The mechanisms contained in the Convention will ensure that states parties consider at least yearly the implementation of the Convention. A state cannot simply forget about the issue once it deposits its instrument of ratification, for it will be involved in a continuous political review process. In this context NGOs will play an important role, along with states parties, as watchdogs over the effective implementation of the Convention.

But implementation means much more than simply seeing to it that contraventions of the Convention do not occur. Provisions relating to the destruction of AP mines in mined areas, international co-operation and assistance, as well as transparency measures, will also provide opportunities for states to consider the progress of mine action, including victim assistance. The meetings and review conferences will be occasions to garner additional support for ongoing mine action, and will also serve as incentives for mine-affected states to give priority to mine action in their territories as they present their cases to the international community.

And what about those states that choose to stay outside the Convention? Obviously, they are not legally bound by the obligations. But, politically, the price for using AP mines has been raised considerably. There will be a certain stigma attached to their use if the political momentum behind the Convention is maintained. No treaty has begun with universality. However, few other treaties have been signed by 122 states within two days. This is only the beginning of the process, not the end. Continued domestic public and international pressure will ensure that additional states will become party to the Convention.

The Convention can serve as an invaluable tool towards resolving the AP mines crisis. It is up to all of us to maximize its impact.

NOTES

This article represents the views of the authors alone and does not necessarily reflect the views of their respective governments and departments.

1. Convention on Prohibitions or Restrictions on the Use of Certain Conventional Weapons Which May Be Deemed to Be Excessively Injurious or to Have Indiscriminate Effects (CCW).

2. The early core group included: Austria, Belgium, Canada, Ireland, Philippines, Mexico, Netherlands, Norway, South Africa, Switzerland, and, later, Colombia and Germany.

3. At the Vienna meeting, two other unofficial drafts of a proposed treaty were circulated by the Belgian delegation and the ICBL. Both of these drafts contained many of the same elements as the Austrian draft.

4. The final version of the Austrian text contained an article on compliance, revised by the Austrian delegation following an experts' meeting on the topic held in Königswinter, Germany, on 24–5 April 1997. This is discussed in more detail later in this chapter.

5. APL/CRP.3

6. The rules of procedure adopted by the conference (APL/CRP.2) provided that, for matters of substance, when consensus was not possible decisions would be taken by a two-thirds majority. These rules were based on the standard rules of procedure used at various UN conferences.

7. On signature, see Article 15.

8. See paras 1–3 of the Preamble.

9. See para. 11 of the Preamble.

10. These customary law principles have already been codified in Articles 22 and 23 of the Hague Regulations Respecting the Laws and Customs of War on Land 1907 and have been confirmed by Articles 35 and 48 of Protocol I 1977 Additional to the Geneva Conventions of 1949.

11. See Articles 1 and 8.

12. According to Article 17 the Convention shall enter into force six months after the deposit of the 40th instrument of ratification, acceptance, approval, or accession with the Depositary, i.e., the Secretary-General of the United Nations (see Article 21). For any state that deposits its instrument after that date, the Convention shall enter into force six months after that date.

13. See Article 20(1), which stipulates that the Convention shall be of unlimited duration. It was felt necessary during the preparatory phase, as well as during the negotiations, to include a possibility of withdrawal from the Convention (see Article 20, paras 2–4) in order to attract as many states as possible. This was restricted in two ways. First, a state wishing to withdraw must notify the other states parties, the Depositary, and the UN Security Council of its intent, explaining the reasons motivating its withdrawal. Second, if that state is engaged in an armed conflict at that time, the withdrawal shall not take effect before the end of the armed conflict.

14. See Article 18, which was included in the Convention during the negotiations upon a proposal made by the Belgian delegation.

15. Article 16 provides a variety of ways to express the will to become bound by the Convention. It also allows for accession, even before its entry into force.

The intention was to facilitate the adhesion to the Convention by as many states as early as possible. Note that in accordance with Article 19, reservations to the Convention are not permitted.

16. To that end, the states parties commit themselves in para. 10 of the Preamble 'to work strenuously towards the promotion of its universalization in all relevant fora including, *inter alia*, the United Nations, the Conference on Disarmament, regional organizations, and groupings, and review conferences of the Convention on Prohibitions or Restrictions on the Use of Certain Conventional Weapons Which May Be Deemed to Be Excessively Injurious or to Have Indiscriminate Effects'.

17. The Convention defines an AP mine as follows: 'Mine' means a munition *designed to be* placed under, on, or near the ground or other surface area and to be exploded by the presence, proximity, or contact of a person or vehicle.

    The rationale for making the changes was that if 'designed' was not removed, 'mine' would only cover those munitions which were *actually* placed under or near the ground, and would not include those in stockpiles. It was thought that this might cause problems with respect to the obligation to destroy stocks, thus the definition was amended.

18. Article 2(3).

19. 'Anti-handling device' was defined as a device intended to protect a mine and that is part of, linked to, attached to, or placed under the mine and that activates when an attempt is made to tamper with or otherwise intentionally disturb the mine.

20. This was confirmed by the interpretive statements made by a number of delegations at the conclusion of the CCW Review Conference, as well as by various statements of understanding made at the time of ratification of Amended Protocol II.

    See conference document CCW/CONF.I/SR.14, 6 June 1996 at 3, as well as the Statements of Understanding of States Parties to Amended Protocol II included in the UN Treaty Database [http:\\www.un.org\Depts\Treaty].

21. The ICRC made a statement to this effect at the February 1997 Vienna meeting.

22. Initially, the core group was not in favour of moving from the CCW definition, to avoid confusion of differing definitions. The change was made in response to the concerns expressed by some states and NGOs, but was also seen as a means of ensuring that AV mines would not be covered by the Convention. It became a starting negotiating position, being easier to retreat in negotiations than advance. Interestingly, the definition was not changed back to the CCW definition.

23. Not covered by the Convention are weapons used against persons but not designed to function as an AP mine, i.e., they are not designed to be triggered

by the victim. Thus, for example, directional fragmentation charges triggered by remote control are by definition not AP mines and do not fall under the Convention.

24. See Article 2(4) of Amended Protocol II for the definition of 'booby-trap'.

25. The Austrian draft contained a definition of AHD taken from Article 2(14) of Amended Protocol II, which provides: 'Anti-handling device' means a device intended to protect a mine and which is part of, linked to, attached to, or placed under the mine and which activates when an attempt is made to tamper with the mine. See Conference documents APL/CW.9 and APL/CW.9/Rev.1 for the amendments proposed by the US delegation.

26. APL/CW.9/Rev.1. After that proposal failed to gain acceptance, the US delegation proposed to change the definition of AHD to include those munitions 'near' to (though not connected to) AV mines. The result would have been to classify their submunitions (AO mines), which were 'near' AV mines, as AHD, not AP mines. This, too, was not successful.

27. See Conference document APL/CW.32 proposed by the UK delegation.

28. The UK delegation proposal to include the term 'or otherwise disturb' was orally amended by the Norwegian delegation, supported by a number of other delegations, to include 'intentionally'.

29. See Article 10.

30. See Article 11.

31. See Article 14.

32. See Article 3(1). The general understanding at the conference, supported by the statements of several delegations in the plenary sessions, was that the number would be relatively low, e.g., 1,000–2,000 mines.

33. See Article 3(2).

34. See Article 2(4). This provision was taken from Article 2(15) of Amended Protocol II. This was derived from the work done for the UN Conventional Arms Register: see A/RES/47/52 and A/47/342.

35. See Articles 4 and 5.

36. See, for example, the interpretive statement made by Canada at the time of ratification of the Convention:

It is the understanding of the Government of Canada that, in the context of operations, exercises or other military activity sanctioned by the United Nations or otherwise conducted in accordance with international law, the mere participation by the Canadian Forces, or individual Canadians, in operations, exercises or other military activity conducted in combination with the armed forces of States not party to the Convention which engage in activity prohibited under the Convention would not, by itself, be considered to be assistance, encouragement or inducement in accordance with the meaning of those terms in article 1, paragraph 1 (c).

37. See Article 9.

38. The first Austrian draft provided that the stocks were to be destroyed within one year of entry into force of the Convention, while later versions set the time limit at three years. It was only at the closing days of the Oslo Diplomatic Conference that the time limit was set at four years because some, particularly developing states, considered three years to be too short a time.

39. For example, the Biological and Toxin Weapons Convention, Chemical Weapons Convention, Amended Protocol II to the CCW, and the Comprehensive Nuclear Test Ban Treaty all use these terms without defining them.

40. This was the view of delegations at both the CCW Review Conference and the Oslo conference. Nevertheless, the proposal of the US delegation to qualify it as 'long-term' control (APL/CW.11) was not successful.

41. This solution was based on a proposal made by the ICRC at the Brussels conference to include a provision that would allow a state party to apply for an extension of the time period (for clearing minefields) if certain conditions were met. This proposal was based on a similar provision included in the Verification Annex of the Chemical Weapons Convention: Part IV(A), section C, paras 24–8.

42. See Article 5(1).

43. See Articles 5(3)–(6), 11(1)(f), and 12(2)(c).

44. Article 5(4).

45. These requirements are set out in Article 5 and the Technical Annex of Amended Protocol II.

46. The former proposal was put forward by the Mexican delegation (APL/CW.6) and the latter proposal by the German delegation (APL/CW.24 & 25).

47. Article 8(1) sets out the obligation of states parties to consult and co-operate with each other regarding the implementation of the provisions of the Convention, and to work together in a spirit of co-operation to facilitate compliance by states parties with their obligations under this Convention. The obligation to co-operate with respect to questions of compliance is drawn from Article IX of the Chemical Weapons Convention.

48. Article 8(2).

49. Article 8(3).

50. Para. 5 provides that the quorum for the meeting is a majority of states parties.

51. Article 8(4).

52. Article 8, paras 6 and 7.

53. Article 8(8).

54. Article 8, paras 9–14.
55. When the list is compiled, a state party has an opportunity to object to particular individuals on the list, but only with respect to fact-finding missions on territory or area under its jurisdiction or control. Nationals of the states parties involved (requested and requesting states) are not to be nominated to the mission. See para. 9.
56. The privileges and immunities are those set out in Article VI of the Convention on the Privileges and Immunities of the United Nations, adopted 13 Feb. 1946.
57. Para. 14 provides that the requested state may make arrangements for the protection of sensitive equipment, information, and areas, the protection of constitutional obligations, and the physical protection and safety of the members of the fact-finding mission.
58. Article 8, paras 17–20.
59. Para. 19 specifically mentions the co-operative measures referred to in Article 6.
60. See, for example, the verification systems set up by the Chemical Weapons Convention (Article IX and the Annex on Compliance) and the Comprehensive Test Ban Treaty (Article IV and the Protocol on Compliance).
61. Article 149 of the Fourth Geneva Convention allows for the possibility of holding an inquiry into alleged violations of the Convention, as does Article 90 of Additional Protocol I to the Geneva Conventions. Both of these mechanisms require the consent of all parties involved, which has proven to limit their potential.
62. Only the ICBL draft treaty contained a provision obliging states parties to co-operate with each other and to provide technical assistance in order to fulfil their obligations under the treaty.
63. Article 11 of Amended Protocol II concerns the provision of technical, material, and financial assistance to 'High Contracting Parties' to facilitate its implementation, with a focus on the technical specifications for AP mines set by the Protocol.
64. The Norwegian delegation proposed a paragraph on victim assistance (APL/CW.5).
65. Article 6(2).
66. Article 6, paras 3–6.
67. Article 6(7).
68. The information is to be provided to the UN Secretary-General within 180 days of the entry into force of the Convention for the state party and is to be updated annually, covering the last calendar year, and reported to the UN Secretary-General no later than 30 April of each year (Article 7, paras 1–2).

69. Article 7(1)(a) refers to the national implementation measures contained in Article 9.
70. Article 7, paras 1(b) and (c).
71. Article 7, paras 1(f) and (g).
72. Article 7(1)(i) refers to the obligation to provide warning to the population in accordance with Article 5(2).
73. Article 7(1)(h).
74. Article 7(1)(d).
75. Article 7(1)(e).
76. Article 14(1) of Amended Protocol II provides that: 'Each High Contracting Party shall take all appropriate steps, including legislative and other measures, to prevent and suppress violations of this Protocol by persons or on territory under its jurisdiction or control.'
77. The phrase included in the article, 'by persons or on territory under its jurisdiction or control', leaves open the possibility that a state asserting jurisdiction over its nationals outside of its territory could do so in this case.
78. Article 8(14) provides that the requested state party is to provide access to all areas and installations 'under its control' without mention of whether the state party has 'jurisdiction' over those areas or installations.
79. The preamble, para. 11, reinforces that 'all parties to an armed conflict' must respect the basic principles underlying this Convention.

CHAPTER 16

THE CHALLENGE OF
HUMANITARIAN MINE CLEARANCE

Don Hubert

The seeds of the campaign to ban landmines are to be found in the mine-fields of Cambodia. After years of responding to the human suffering caused by mines, a few individuals and organizations concluded that assist-ing victims was not enough. Irrespective of their efforts, the problem con-tinued to worsen. Two conclusions were drawn: that the further laying of mines must be prohibited; and that those already buried must be cleared. This volume explores in considerable detail efforts to prohibit the further use of mines. The purpose of this chapter is to describe and assess the efforts to remove those mines that have already been laid.

WHAT IS HUMANITARIAN DEMINING?

Humanitarian demining is most easily understood by contrasting it with the most well-developed approach to removing landmines—military breaching. According to traditional military doctrine, minefields are employed to channel enemy forces or at least to slow their advance. Not surprisingly, countermeasures were developed to reduce their effectiveness. The requirements were simple: clear a lane several metres wide as quickly as possible in the midst of combat. Breaching is normally achieved by det-onating the mines with either steel rollers or chain flails mounted on armoured vehicles, or with fuel-air explosives ignited at ground level. Alternatively, mines are simply pushed to the side with armoured ploughs. Regardless of the particular technique, all breaching methods share two characteristics that limit their broader utility. First, thoroughness is sacri-ficed in favour of speed. None of these techniques will consistently destroy more than eight out of every 10 mines encountered. Second, breaching techniques are designed to be effective in small, clearly defined areas, and usually on flat, open terrain.

Traditional military techniques for dealing with mines, however, are not limited simply to minefield breaching. Military personnel are also trained in 'lifting' mines where maps or records are available. The indis-criminate use of mines and the corresponding lack of maps and markings have been highlighted in recent years. Still, many minefields are clearly identified. Where the precise number and location of mines is known, as along parts of the former Iron Curtain in Germany, mine clearance is a rel-atively straightforward undertaking.

Military forces operating in so-called 'low-intensity conflicts' or peace-keeping operations have also developed techniques to deal with the threat posed by the indiscriminate use of landmines. In some respects the challenges they face are similar to those of the humanitarian deminer. In the absence of reliable markings, large areas are assumed to be mined until proven otherwise, and as clearance operations are not conducted under fire, thoroughness is more important than speed. Yet at the same time, clearance is undertaken only where mines directly affect ongoing operations and compromise the safety of personnel. For the most part, areas believed to be mined are simply avoided.

Humanitarian demining is set apart by its principal objective: to expedite the safe return of land and other productive resources to civilian use. Given the emphasis on safety, thoroughness is obviously of utmost importance. Current UN standards require a clearance rate of at least 99.6 per cent, but even this figure is arbitrary. It was established to facilitate commercial contracting and does not represent a consensus definition. For most humanitarian deminers, leaving even four mines in the ground for every one thousand cleared would be considered unacceptable. In addition to both anti-personnel and anti-tank mines, all other unexploded ordnance (UXOs) are also removed. Since humanitarian efforts are focused on land and other productive resources broadly conceived, the areas to be cleared are neither small nor well defined. Vast tracts of agricultural land must be certified mine-free, land that after years of disuse is commonly overgrown with thick vegetation. The task is further complicated by the need to clear difficult areas such as rice paddies, mountain passes, urban areas, and collapsed buildings.

Three Basic Tasks

The basic tasks of the thousands of humanitarian deminers working in countries around the world can be divided into three discrete categories: locating and marking the boundaries of mined areas; finding the precise location of individual mines and other explosives; and destroying or disabling the devices. The surveying of mined areas is the first stage of demining operations and begins with a review of the types of mines deployed, the tactics used by the warring factions, existing maps and records, available data on mine-related injuries, and interviews with former combatants and local inhabitants. This background information provides the basis for preliminary field inspections by small teams searching for signs of mining activity such as wooden posts or fence wire, battlefield relics, and human or animal skeletons. Preliminary inspections are followed by more detailed surveys. Using metal detectors, steel prods, and explosive-sniffing dogs, the boundaries of mined areas are identified and clearly marked.

Following detailed surveying, mine-clearance teams are brought to the area to locate and neutralize the devices. Mined areas are divided into a series of lanes, to ensure that an accidental detonation will not injure other workers, and areas cleared are distinguished from uncleared by plastic tape mounted on stakes. Demining teams are normally divided into pairs, one using a hand-held detector to identify metal buried beneath the ground, the other using a metal prod to locate the source. Any object encountered must be unearthed and identified. If the object is not a mine the clearance process continues. If a mine is uncovered, it is carefully marked and the pair of deminers move to a new different section of the minefield, perhaps a few feet away, to continue working.

The third task is the destruction of the device to ensure that it cannot be reused. Mines are either destroyed by high explosives where they are found or are disarmed and detonated in a centralized location. Both approaches have advantages and disadvantages.[1] Destruction *in situ* is the technique adopted by most organizations because it requires only minimal contact with the mine and is less prone to errors of judgement. However, this approach may scatter additional metal fragments through the minefield and is not well suited to mines positioned above the ground. It is also time-consuming and expensive. Where centralized detonation is adopted, it may still be necessary to destroy particularly unstable or damaged mines *in situ*, but the majority are rendered inoperable, placed in a trench, and destroyed with a single blast.

Finally, when the area has been completely cleared it can be returned to civilian use. Often, deminers will walk across the field in the presence of local inhabitants to prove that the land is now safe.

Humanitarian mine clearance is made more complicated by variations in terrain and landmine design. As noted above, years of disuse mean that mined areas are normally covered by dense vegetation that must be removed before metal detectors can be employed. However, as many commonly encountered mines are detonated by a tripwire, vegetation must be cleared with extreme caution. Tripwires entwined in dense undergrowth are detected using a long metal wand inserted at ground level and cautiously raised. When a tripwire is located it must be traced to its origins and the device neutralized before work can continue. Vegetation is not the only barrier restricting access to mines. More difficult still is the clearance of mines from collapsed buildings and walls where the devices may be buried deep beneath the rubble.

Metal detectors also have their limitations. Not surprisingly, mines are often placed in former battlefields strewn with metal fragments such as shell casings, each of which must be individually uncovered and inspected. It is not uncommon for deminers to uncover hundreds of harmless metal fragments for each mine destroyed. The reliability of metal detectors is also affected by the amount of natural iron in the soil. Where the iron content is high, the margin of error for metal detectors increases significantly. This problem is further exacerbated by plastic mines specifically designed to contain a minimum of metal in order to defy detection.

Unfortunately, the maliciousness of weapon designers has not been limited simply to low-metal mines. More sophisticated versions have also been fitted with 'anti-handling devices' that initiate detonation when an attempt is made to tamper with the mine. The objective of this design feature is simple—to maim or kill those who attempt to demine. Although these 'high-tech' mines are found in only a few mine-affected countries, in particular the former Yugoslavia, primitive technology can be rigged to the same effect.

This description, although brief, should be sufficient to establish that humanitarian demining is extremely labour-intensive. It is also expensive and dangerous. Given the variations in terrain and methods of mine deployment, statistics on the costs of clearing mines are not very meaningful. While the UN has estimated that clearance costs between $300 and $1,000 per mine, these figures mean little. It may take one team months to clear 10 mines from a large area while another team clears dozens from a dense minefield in a matter of hours. The statistics on the risks faced by deminers are more reliable, although again subject to wide variation. It is estimated that a deminer is killed or maimed for every 1,000–2,000 mines cleared.[2] Surprisingly, the danger appears to be greatest where mines are encountered only infrequently, increasing the probability of lapses in concentration. In countries where the amount of land to be cleared is numbered in the hundreds of square kilometres, manual mine clearance seems an impossible task; yet it remains the only method sufficiently reliable to render formerly mined areas safe.

A GEOGRAPHICAL HISTORY OF HUMANITARIAN DEMINING

Mines have been used in conflicts for more than a century, but clearance has never kept pace with deployment. Landmines were first used on a massive scale during World War II, and the legacy of those weapons is useful in placing the current crisis in context. Although most of the mines in

Western Europe have been cleared, millions of mines remain buried across huge tracts in North Africa and in parts of the former Soviet Union. These mines account for a significant proportion of those currently in the ground, yet for the most part they do not constitute part of the humanitarian crisis.

The devices that now threaten the lives and livelihoods of millions of people in dozens of countries were laid within the past three decades, and result largely from the use of mines as 'area denial' weapons. Whether distributed by remote delivery systems capable of scattering thousands of mines per minute or hand emplaced by military and irregular forces, these devices were commonly used to deny the use of land and infrastructure or simply to terrorize the population. In spite of the widespread use of mines in the 1970s and 1980s, significant mine-clearance operations were not undertaken, due largely to the protracted nature of many Cold War conflicts. During the late 1980s, with improving prospects for the resolution of these ongoing conflicts, the international community began to address the problem of uncleared mines. It was in this context that several dozen army engineers on the Afghan-Pakistan border made the first tentative steps in developing what is now known as humanitarian demining.

Afghanistan

Although estimates vary, there is no doubt that Afghanistan is among the most heavily mined countries. Government and Soviet forces were responsible for a majority of those deployed, but mines were widely used by opposition forces as well. Mined areas include military and strategic locations such as airports, power stations, military posts, and government buildings. Scatterable 'butterfly' mines were also dispersed widely through mountain passes, villages, and enemy bases.[3] With the decision of the Soviet Union to withdraw its forces from Afghanistan in 1989, it was widely believed that the pro-Soviet Najibullah regime would be defeated quickly and that a massive repatriation of the more than 5 million refugees displaced by the conflict would follow. Uncleared mines were identified as a significant barrier to such a return.

Mine-clearance activities were first undertaken as part of a short-term national reconstruction plan known as 'Operation Salam' developed by the UN co-ordination mission for Afghanistan in 1988. Small teams of military specialists from Australia, Canada, France, Italy, New Zealand, Norway, Turkey, the US, and the UK were sent to train and equip thousands of refugees in the hope that they could clear the communities to which they returned. For the specialists it was a new experience: this was the first systematic attempt to adapt military techniques for indigenous demining programs. Although 13,000 refugees eventually participated in the training, the sparse evidence available suggests that only a small percentage of those trained ever engaged in demining activities, that the quality of the demining undertaken was poor, and that the rate of accidents was very high.[4]

Contrary to expectations, the government did not fall, the war continued, and the massive repatriation failed to materialize. Yet the need for a systematic response to the landmine problem remained. The UN mission abandoned the 'spontaneous' mine-clearance approach and created four Afghan NGOs to respond to the landmine problem systematically. By the middle of 1990 these organizations employed 900 deminers supervised by a small number of foreign experts. Two other demining organizations were also active in the country. The British NGO HALO Trust was also training and supervising indigenous deminers, while RONCO, a commercial firm from the United States, established a centre for training explosive-sniffing dogs. Although fighting continued, with the capital falling to the advancing Taliban forces in 1995, mine-clearance operations still operated effectively. By that time the Afghan demining NGOs employed more than 3,500 people supervised by five foreign advisers at an annual cost of roughly $25 million.[5] The mine-clearance program in Afghanistan is not without its problems. The continuing conflict has resulted in further mines being deployed and has prevented the handover of the UN-led operation to a functioning central government, and the rate of accidents remains very high. But by focusing on detailed surveys, careful prioritization of land to be cleared, and a shift in emphasis to protecting lives and livelihoods, the program in Afghanistan has become among the most effective and efficient anywhere in the world.

Cambodia

A major humanitarian demining operation was also undertaken in Cambodia following the peace agreement signed in 1991. Early estimates suggested that there were between 4 million and 6 million mines, some laid in border areas and around military and strategic sites, but many deployed indiscriminately to terrorize the population.[6] Current estimates suggest that 3,600 square kilometres, or roughly 2 per cent of the total land area, may be mined.[7]

The United Nations mission to Cambodia, launched in late 1991, was given responsibility for 'assisting with clearing mines and undertaking training programmes in mine clearance and mine awareness'. A training unit was created to provide instruction to indigenous deminers, and a group was assigned to do surveying and mapping. However, the UN was preoccupied with the successful completion of other parts of its mission, most notably refugee repatriation and democratic elections, and did not develop a long-term country-wide demining strategy. As a result, though foreign technical advisers trained qualified indigenous deminers, the organizational capacity to deploy them was not developed. Much of the mine clearance undertaken during this early period was supervised not by the UN but by demining NGOs, including Norwegian People's Aid, Mines Advisory Group, and HALO Trust.

With no provision made for continued UN assistance, the departure of the UN mission in late 1993 nearly resulted in the collapse of the national demining program. The government had established the Cambodia Mine Action Centre (CMAC) in June 1992, but it remained undeveloped during the UN mandate. For a number of months the continued existence of humanitarian demining in Cambodia depended on the extraordinary efforts of a few non-governmental organizations and key individuals, including CMAC's chief technical adviser. Ultimately, the creation of a UN trust fund in 1994 offered a degree of financial security, and the declaration of CMAC as an autonomous institution independent from the military provided further stability. During this period CMAC began to pursue a broad action plan, including the prioritization of land for clearance, an expanded training program for indigenous deminers, an emphasis on minefield surveys and a national database, and mine awareness training. The results have been impressive. By late 1997, CMAC had cleared over 75,000 AP mines, 750 anti-tank mines, and 411,000 UXOs from 950 square kilometres.[8] The organization now is composed of more than 2,500 staff, has an annual budget of roughly $20 million, and works in close co-operation with the demining NGOs also operating in Cambodia.

In Cambodia, as in Afghanistan, the development of a sustainable mine-clearance program faced enormous challenges. In both cases conflicts were ongoing, central governments were weak or non-existent, and new strategies were being devised through trial and error. Guided by national realities, they have adopted radically different organizational structures. Yet these two programs are widely regarded as the most successful anywhere in the world. In other countries, where the challenges have been somewhat less daunting, similar accomplishments have been elusive.

Kuwait

Following the Gulf War, it was estimated that between 5 and 7 million mines had been deployed in Kuwait. Iraqi soldiers had laid millions of mines, while the US-led coalition had deployed several hundred thousand by remote delivery systems. The demining operation began in 1991 and lasted four years. Countries such as Egypt, Pakistan, and Bangladesh provided military specialists, but most of the demining was conducted by

American, British, and French companies. More than 4,000 expatriate deminers cleared 728 square kilometres using a combination of manual and mechanized techniques at a cost of $700 million,[9] the most expensive mine-clearance operation ever undertaken. The costs were also high in human terms. Eighty-four deminers were killed, more than the total American fatalities during the war itself, including all five mine experts in the Kuwaiti military.[10] Furthermore, as uncleared mines were found during quality assurance inspections, large areas are being resurveyed and may need to be recleared.

The operation in Kuwait offers compelling evidence of the immense challenge posed by uncleared mines. In comparison to other affected countries, conditions for mine clearance in Kuwait were reasonably favourable. The mines had been deployed recently, many minefields were clearly marked, and the terrain was relatively flat and free from vegetation. Yet clearance was extremely costly in terms of both money and lives. The ability of Kuwait to pay whatever was required also illustrates that a lack of funds is only one of many problems facing humanitarian deminers.

While operations in Kuwait may seem to have little in common with those in Afghanistan or Cambodia, they are also important for understanding the commercialization of humanitarian landmine clearance. Kuwait marked the beginning of demining as a lucrative corporate enterprise. If 5–7 million mines in Kuwait were worth $700 million, how much more could be made from the reported 80–110 million mines in 64 other countries? In addition to corporations, operations in the Gulf also resulted in a large number of expatriates looking for highly paid employment in other mine-affected countries. Some of these individuals were explosive ordnance disposal (EOD) specialists, but others had little specialized training. And if their approach to demining was of questionable effectiveness in Kuwait, there was no doubt that it was even less well suited to the circumstances faced by a majority of mine-affected countries.

Mozambique

As was the case in Cambodia, humanitarian demining in Mozambique was initiated under the auspices of a UN peacekeeping mission. The landmine problem facing Mozambique is the result of nearly three decades of war beginning in the mid-1960s. Most of the mines were laid during the 1980s by both government (Frelimo) and insurgent (Renamo) forces. Renamo used mines to isolate government forces, undermine the economy, restrict access to productive resources, terrorize the civilian population, and discourage the return of displaced persons. Many of the mines laid by Frelimo were intended to defend economic and strategic locations: mines were laid close to infrastructure, such as power lines, dams, and bridges, along border areas, and in rings around towns and villages. While tactics differed, evidence suggests that both parties used mines against the civilian population.[11]

The General Peace Agreement signed by the warring parties in October 1992 brought an end to the formal conflict and provided the basis for a UN peacekeeping mission. Early in the UN mission, a mine specialist was sent to prepare a plan of action. Completed in January 1993, the plan to deal with the estimated 2 million uncleared mines in the country focused on clearing routes to facilitate the return of refugees and the provision of humanitarian aid, and on training indigenous deminers.

Implementation of the plan, however, was little short of disastrous. Over the next 18 months the UN did not engage in any serious mine-clearance activity. By the fall of 1994 the Security Council had expressed concern at the lack of progress and donors were threatening to withdraw money.[12] Almost a year had lapsed before the former warring factions agreed to the plan of action. Further delays were then encountered in contracting commercial firms to undertake the priority road clearance. At fault were donor demands that the short list of companies be expanded, extreme inefficiencies within the UN bureaucracy, and concerns about the commercial biases of senior UN officials.[13] A contract for $4.8 million to clear 2,000 km of priority roads was ultimately awarded to a consortium of British, Mozambican, and South African firms, and the work was completed by the end of 1994. The lack of UN activity did not mean that no demining operations were under way, only that no co-ordinated country-wide strategy was being implemented. Commercial firms, including Gurka Security Guards, RONCO, Mechem, and Mine-Tech, were contracted by bilateral donors and companies, and HALO Trust and Norwegian People's Aid (NPA) began to work in the northern and central provinces of the country.

Responding to the criticism, the UN launched an Accelerated Demining Program in the autumn of 1994 to train and deploy 450 indigenous deminers in the south of the country. Attempts were also made to ensure the sustainability of the program following the departure of the UN mission. A national demining institution modelled on CMAC in Cambodia was proposed, but this met with opposition from the donor community, which believed that it would be expensive, unwieldy, and a duplication of existing capacity.

In spite of the abysmal start, recent mine-clearance operations supervised by the UN have been reasonably effective, clearing more than 9,000 mines and 1.5 million square metres by early 1997.[14] Still, no coherent national demining strategy exists. Although NPA and HALO operate effec-tive demining programs, they maintain a rigid geographic division of labour. The National Demining Commission is ineffective, the only coun-try-wide survey lacks sufficient detail to set priorities, and objectives are often established by donors on the basis of their own priorities. That the difficulties in establishing effective operations in Mozambique did not lead to disastrous consequences can be credited in part to good fortune: as de-mining continues it becomes increasingly clear that the scale of the land-mine problem is much more modest than originally believed.

Bosnia-Herzegovina

The former Yugoslavia is the site of a more recent major demining initia-tive. Since Yugoslavia was a leading producer with large stockpiles, mines were used widely by all parties to the conflict. In addition to military and strategic sites, mines have also been laid along roads and mountain trails, and in forests and urban areas. Clearance is particularly difficult due to the prevalence of low-metal mines and booby-trapping.[15] The Dayton Peace Agreement signed in December 1995 allocated responsibility for clearing mines to the former warring parties and called for those operations to be completed within 30 days of the start of the NATO mission.[16] While this deadline was completely unrealistic, soldiers under NATO supervision have undertaken mine-lifting in areas where records exist. These efforts, how-ever, are of limited use in addressing the humanitarian aspects of the mine problem. To date, these forces have not cleared high-priority land required for refugee returns or reconstruction activities, or areas retaining significant strategic importance. In addition, the technique adopted does not meet humanitarian standards.[17]

As part of the larger UN mission, a Mine Action Centre (MAC) was established in Sarajevo in early 1996. Yet by the end of that year only a few hundred mines had actually been cleared. In the absence of an integrated national demining strategy, a series of ad hoc initiatives were undertaken. The World Bank has provided more than $12 million in soft loans to develop private-sector capacity, but concerns have been raised about the reliability of the work and biases in the tendering process. American efforts have included $15 million, mostly to RONCO, for training commercial and army deminers, in addition to infrastructure and staff supplied to the MAC. The European Commission has focused its support on the development of a commercial demining sector and on strengthening the UN operation. Norway has been among the largest bilateral donors, providing $5.6 million mostly to NPA operations on refugee housing projects.[18] Due to ongoing disputes between former warring factions, inefficiencies within the

UN system, shoddy private-sector companies, and a lack of co-ordination among donors and mine-clearing organizations, however, only five of the 100 square kilometres of high-priority land had been cleared to humanitarian standards by late 1997.[19] There is currently some optimism surrounding mine clearance in Bosnia, but given the lack of co-ordination combined with ongoing political tensions and 'post-war profiteering', it may be unwarranted.[20]

Other Mine-Clearance Initiatives

The discussion above has focused on the major humanitarian mine-clearance operations undertaken to date. But there are other less well-developed programs. Since 1994 the United Nations has managed a Mine Action Centre in Angola, another seriously mine-affected country. From the start, however, these operations have been plagued with difficulties. In addition to the ongoing conflict and the lack of co-operation from the opposing factions, bureaucratic infighting, disputes over the division of labour between UN agencies, and a lack of consistent donor support all contributed to a very ineffective program.[21]

Demining in Somalia has also faced serious difficulties. In 1991 the European Commission supported a British company to conduct a basic survey and train 450 deminers. Although some mines were cleared, the accident rate was very high and deteriorating security conditions resulted in the collapse of the operations. Demining efforts were revived with the arrival of the main UN peacekeeping mission in 1993, and included contracts to several Somali firms and the establishment of a training school, but operations were again discontinued due to security concerns.[22]

Greater success has been encountered in Central America, though the scale of the mine problem there was much less severe. The Salvadoran government, with support from multilateral agencies, initiated a mine-clearance operation in 1993. The project was undertaken jointly by a Belgian firm and the national armed forces, and in 1994 it was reported that all mines had been cleared.[23] Nicaragua faces a more serious problem, estimated at more than 100,000 mines. Early work by the armed forces was complemented by an Organization of American States (OAS) initiative beginning in 1993. Despite inconsistent funding, mine clearance continues and current estimates suggest that the country may be declared mine-free by the year 2000.

Humanitarian demining is also being undertaken independently by NGOs in a number of countries, some of which are politically sensitive. For example, the Mines Advisory Group from Britain has been working in northern Iraq since 1992. With support from a number of bilateral donors and the European Community, they have undertaken surveys and mine awareness programs, as well as the training and supervision of hundreds of indigenous deminers. Surveys, training, and mine awareness programs have also been pursued by HALO Trust in Nagorno Karabakh and Chechnya.

AN INTEGRATED APPROACH TO HUMANITARIAN DEMINING

This brief review of humanitarian demining operations illustrates the diverse range of agencies and organizations involved. A list of only the most prominent organizations would include militaries, commercial firms, UN agencies, and NGOs. A wide range of technologies has also been used. Debates have raged about which approaches are most effective. It is widely accepted that the nature of the mine problem, and therefore the appropriate response, will differ depending on the country. Since 1995 there has been broad acceptance that an integrated approach is necessary to ensure that responses are tailored to specific needs. The relative merits of the main approaches can be assessed by reviewing the major debates relating to the actors (military versus civilian, expatriate versus indigenous, and commercial versus non-profit) and the technologies (mechanical versus manual and high-tech versus incremental).

Actors

Armed forces have traditionally been responsible for dealing with weaponry and explosives. Yet it is important to recognize that the ability to lay mines has little to do with the ability to clear them. There may be a certain justice in demanding, as in the former Yugoslavia, that the soldiers who laid the mines be responsible for their removal, but specialized training is required to meet humanitarian demining standards. Furthermore, following civil conflicts, the armed forces may be reluctant to clear mines that they believe may offer some strategic advantage.

An approach, widely employed by the United States, is to offer military-to-military training. While statistics on the number of deminers trained can be impressive, sustainability is questionable because of the high turnover in conscript armies and the lack of long-term funding and commitment. The technical skills of army engineers and specialists in explosive ordnance disposal are essential for mine-clearance training programs. Yet, evidence from over a decade of humanitarian demining indicates that these skills are only one part of a complex task, and seconded or retired personnel can be easily incorporated into civilian projects. Organizations with experience in humanitarian and development work may also have a comparative advantage in establishing sustainable programs in mine-affected countries.

The balance between military and civilian responses is particularly important during peacekeeping operations. In most cases, peacekeepers have been assigned initial responsibility for landmines. Troublesome transitions to humanitarian or developmental responsibility have invariably followed. A recent UN study distinguishes between operational demining required for the successful completion of the peacekeeping mission and broader humanitarian mine clearance.[24] Rather than simply giving operational demining priority in the early stages of an operation, the report suggests that the two be developed in parallel. Peacekeepers would retain control over operational demining while civilian agencies would be responsible for humanitarian programs.

The debate over whether humanitarian demining should be conducted by foreign specialists or indigenous personnel can be reduced largely to issues of cost and available expertise. It is generally accepted that between 20 and 25 indigenous deminers can be hired for the $150,000 per year it costs to employ a single foreign specialist. Unlike Kuwait, the vast majority of affected countries simply do not have the resources to hire thousands of outsiders. In emergency situations, where the existing capacity of the affected state is insufficient, expatriates may be required whatever the cost. But long-term sustainable mine clearance depends on the development of an indigenous cadre of demining specialists, often taken from the ranks of demobilized soldiers. The use of foreign technical advisers in initial training and supervision will still be necessary, but the objective of these advisers must be to work themselves out of a job. Where training, supervision, and management skills have been transferred, large demining programs currently operate with very few foreign experts.

In addition to Kuwait, commercial mine clearance has been widely undertaken in southern Africa and the former Yugoslavia. Although results are inconsistent, it does appear that commercial demining has a comparative advantage in large infrastructure projects such as roads, railways, and power lines. It has been argued, however, that there is a certain tension in commercial demining between speed and thoroughness. Contracts may encourage efficient working practice, but if the job turns out to be more difficult than expected, the contractor may be forced to choose between a financial loss or compromising standards. In the long run, shoddy work will affect the firm's reputation. But demining remains a relatively immature industry and there is no doubt that some active commercial firms have cut corners to ensure profit. Furthermore, even the assumption that commercial contracting, while perhaps more expensive, will get the job done more quickly may be unwarranted. The experiences in Mozambique and Bosnia indicate that due to contract delays, the mismanagement of tendering, and donor politics, the private sector is not necessarily faster. Ethical concerns have also been raised where mine producers themselves have been awarded demining contracts. This so-called 'double-dipping' has been strongly condemned in the humanitarian community, and UN agencies have implemented policies to avoid such firms. Production bans in many countries have rendered this issue less pressing, since few mine-clearance firms continue to produce, but some segments of the humanitarian community are ethically opposed to contracting former producers as well.

In contrast to commercial firms, NGOs are normally supported by project funding based on the length of time the work will be undertaken rather than a contract based on an amount of space cleared. Some have argued that this approach can potentially lead to inefficient practices. Still, each of the three main demining NGOs is well respected for the quality of its work and its cost-effectiveness. The HALO Trust, a British organization, is the oldest and perhaps most unusual of the three main demining NGOs. Founded in the late 1980s by a former British member of Parliament, the Hazardous Areas Life-Support Organisation (HALO) Trust employs ex-military personnel, shuns attention, and openly refused to support the campaign to ban mines. Focusing its demining efforts in countries such as Cambodia, Afghanistan, Angola, and Mozambique, the organization is noted for its willingness to work in particularly dangerous areas and for numerous innovations in humanitarian demining techniques. The Mines Advisory Group (MAG), another British NGO, was established in 1991 following several years of work in Afghanistan by its founder. MAG is one of the founding members of the ICBL and sits on the international steering committee. The organization currently manages operations in northern Iraq, Cambodia, Angola, and Laos. The third major demining NGO is Norwegian People's Aid. Founded in 1939 by the Norwegian labour movement, NPA is now one of Norway's largest non-governmental organizations and operates a wide variety of development projects. NPA began mine clearance in 1992 in Cambodia and now runs programs in Bosnia, Mozambique, Angola, and Iraq as well. It is particularly well known for its integration of demining within a developmentalist perspective and for its work with explosive-sniffing dogs.

The non-profit demining sector also includes government ministries. Broad agreement exists that each country should establish a national entity, normally a Mine Action Centre (MAC), to ensure the effectiveness and coherence of country-wide demining operations. While MACs are often set up by the United Nations, responsibility for overall co-ordination is transferred to the national government as their programs mature. An important question, however, is whether the MAC should limit its activities to co-ordination and regulation, as in Afghanistan, or whether it should also employ large numbers of deminers, as in Cambodia. The UN study on indigenous mine action strongly advocates separating the principal functions, with the MAC contracting out the implementation.[25] Others accept that contracting can be effective, but argue that the MAC should not be entirely dependent on other actors for field operations.

A final set of important actors are the multilateral and bilateral donors. United Nations contributions to mine clearance come from three principal sources. The UN Voluntary Trust Fund for Assistance in Mine Clearance was established in the fall of 1994 to provide funding for UN demining activities. More than $20 million was pledged at a major UN conference on mine clearance in Geneva in July 1995, but by November 1997 total commitments had only increased to $42 million. The EU, Japan, and Denmark have been major contributors, but donors in general have preferred to target their money more directly and avoid high UN overhead costs. Resources are also channelled through country-specific trust funds administered by UNDP and from contributions assessed to members of the UN as part of peacekeeping operations. Other major multilateral donors include the European Commission, the single largest funder of humanitarian demining, and the World Bank, which has loaned money to both Bosnia and Croatia. Major bilateral donors include the United States, though primarily through military-to-military assistance, Denmark, Germany, Japan, the Netherlands, Norway, Sweden, and the UK. The balance between these different sources of funding varies from country to country. In Cambodia, 90 per cent of the funding has been channelled through the UNDP trust fund, with the remainder coming from direct contributions, while in Mozambique bilateral funding accounts for three-quarters of total funds, with one-quarter coming from assessed contributions and the UN Voluntary Trust Fund.[26]

Technology

Technology for clearing mines has obviously not kept pace with the technology for deployment. The main tools used by humanitarian deminers around the world today, a metal detector and a prod, are remarkably similar to those used by sappers after World War II. Technological advancements are sought not only to increase productivity but to reduce the risk of accidents. Efforts initially focused on converting military breaching equipment to humanitarian use. By using mechanized equipment, it was hoped that large areas could be cleared without the need to locate each individual mine, and productivity would increase accordingly. This approach has been pursued by a number of companies, particularly from Germany,

Sweden, and South Africa, but with only modest success. Mechanical systems function well only on relatively flat, open terrain and are insufficiently thorough, missing some mines and leaving others in a partially destroyed state. Even under optimal conditions, subsequent manual clearance is required to achieve humanitarian standards. While insufficient on its own, mechanical clearance can be an important complement to manual approaches. By clearing away brush and tripwires and loosening the soil, mechanical clearance can significantly increase the productivity of manual deminers.

A range of innovative technologies for mine detection, such as detection infrared sensors, ground-penetrating radar, microwaves, and visible spectrum photography, have been proposed by commercial firms, defence research institutions, and universities. But devising systems that can accommodate the wide variation in mine technology and terrain with sufficient reliability is extremely difficult. Given the years already invested in unsuccessful military research, it would appear that advancements in this area are a long-term prospect. For the moment, the most efficient and reliable approach for distinguishing mined from unmined areas is explosive-sniffing dogs. A dog's sense of smell is far superior to even the best mechanical devices. Unfortunately, dogs can be temperamental, and they tire quickly in hot weather.

The utility of most research and development on demining technologies has also been limited due to minimal interaction between the research community and deminers in the field. What seems to make sense in a laboratory or a test site may be completely inappropriate when applied to real minefields. The most effective vehicle for mine clearance, for example, is not very useful if its weight cannot be supported by bridges in mine-affected countries. Field testing is important, but a more thorough initial assessment by researchers of the needs of humanitarian deminers would be much better.

An alternative approach to research and development, focusing on 'appropriate technology', has been largely neglected. As humanitarian mine clearance is conducted primarily by indigenous demining personnel, appropriate technologies must be transferable to severely mine-affected countries with extremely limited resources and minimal infrastructure. Advances are needed particularly in the areas of protective equipment for demining personnel and basic demining tools. Modified farm or excavation machinery has been used effectively for removing brush and clearing collapsed buildings. Through incremental improvements in existing technology, equipment can be developed that is easy to maintain with available resources and expertise. Although such an approach will not revolutionize landmine clearance, it can produce significant improvements in a timely fashion.

FROM MINE CLEARANCE TO MINE ACTION

The detection and removal of mines is commonly viewed as the principal solution to the landmines crisis. Yet according to the UN, the objective should not be mine clearance, but rather 'mine action':

> Humanitarian Mine Action is not about mines. Rather it is about people and their interactions with a mine-contaminated environment. The aim of a mine action programme is not therefore a technical engineering objective—to survey, mark and eradicate landmines—but a humanitarian and developmental aim which seeks to create an environment in which people can live more safely and in which economic and social development can occur free from the constraints imposed by landmine contamination.[27]

When mitigation of the effects of landmines is viewed as the overriding concern, demining may not be at the top of the agenda. As we have seen, mine clearance is an expensive, labour-intensive task, and evidence suggests that it takes years before effective mine-clearance operations, either commercial or non-profit, can be widely deployed. Alternatives still make available productive resources, reduce the number of casualties, and can be a more effective use of scarce funds.

Comprehensive minefield surveys are an essential component of any coherent response to the mines problem, yet in most severely mined countries they remain incomplete. Surveys obviously provide the basis for a rational allocation of resources, but their importance extends much further. Where thorough surveys have been conducted, initial estimates of the scale of the mines problem have been reduced by two or three times, land previously believed to be unusable has been returned to productive use, and resources are not wasted clearing land where no mines exist. The marking of mined areas is also part of the surveying process and helps to reduce casualties.

Mine awareness training is another crucial component of mine action. Programs aimed at teaching people how to live in a mined environment are particularly targeted at those unfamiliar with the local conditions, including returning refugees and internally displaced persons. Living safely in mined areas requires much more than simply knowing which areas are suspected to be dangerous. Wherever mines exist, local inhabitants must receive information on how to avoid encounters with mines and what the appropriate responses are in the event of an accident. It is also important to recognize that victims are frequently aware of the presence of mines, but choose to ignore the risks in order to cultivate crops or collect water and fuel. Securing alternative sources of basic necessities, therefore, can also significantly reduce the number of casualties.

Demining operations clearly remain a major component of mine action, but even here decisions about which land to demine first, and who benefits from the cleared land, become just as important as the technical operations. All mines are not equal in terms of their immediate threat or the degree to which they disrupt efforts towards post-conflict reconstruction and sustainable development. Systematic prioritization can transform a seemingly unmanageable crisis into a resolvable challenge. In Afghanistan, for example, all mined areas are assigned to one of five priority levels. The top priority is granted to those areas where mine incidents are frequent, where refugees will be immediately resettled, or where funds are immediately available for reconstruction activities. Lowest priority is assigned to areas where the existence of mines does not affect normal life. Current estimates suggest that all category-one land in Afghanistan will be cleared within three years.[28]

Once cleared, land in severely mined areas is highly valued. Past experience indicates that great care must be taken to ensure that demined areas serve the interests of those in greatest need. Taking the mine action perspective seriously also requires a new approach to assessing the effectiveness of clearance programs. The issue is not simply how many mines were removed or even how much land was cleared, two commonly cited output indicators. Rather, focus shifts to the human impact of operations: the number of displaced persons resettled, the resulting increase in agricultural production, and the reduction in casualties. Thousands of mines removed from a remote border minefield are likely to be of far less benefit than a single mine cleared from a footpath leading to a well.[29]

Mitigating the effects of landmines cannot be conceived simply as a technical problem. To be effective, interventions must always be linked to the broader objective of avoiding casualties and making productive resources available, and must be situated within the broad social and economic context. Daunting estimates notwithstanding, evidence now suggests that the most severe effects of the mines crisis can be dealt with in years, not decades.[30]

CONCLUSION

In assessing the challenge of humanitarian demining, it is worthwhile to reflect on the pressing questions as the enterprise begins its second decade. The most prominent issues centre on the availability and sustainability of funding. With the successful adoption of the Ottawa Convention, new resources have been pledged for humanitarian demining. But how will this money be spent? If taken seriously, the conclusion that the humanitarian tragedy can be resolved in a matter of years has important implications. Research and development strategies, whether they succeed or fail, will have limited impact if they do not produce technologies that can be widely deployed in the field within the next three to five years. There is no doubt that many mines will remain to be cleared once the immediate crisis has been addressed, but these will be in lower-priority areas and can be methodically cleared by teams of indigenous deminers.

Which countries receive assistance for mine-clearance programs is another important question. Most of the funding to date has been devoted to the four or five countries commonly identified as the most heavily mined. But what about other countries that face severe mine problems? The status of programs in countries such as Azerbaijan, Chad, Georgia, Lebanon, Sri Lanka, Tajikistan, Vietnam, and Western Sahara will be an important indication of the state of mine action in the coming years. An equally important indication will be the level of support for countries like Laos that have very few mines but an enormous problem with other unexploded ordnance.

A second set of important questions relates to the linkage between humanitarian demining and the Ottawa Convention. Article 5 requires that signatories destroy all anti-personnel mines within their jurisdiction as soon as possible, but not later than 10 years after entry-into-force. Exemptions may be granted in extraordinary circumstances. In an earlier draft of the treaty, a distinction was drawn between military minefields and mined areas. Ultimately abandoned, it was nevertheless an attempt to grapple with the tension in the document between arms control and humanitarianism. From an arms control perspective it is important to clear military minefields along borders and around military installations, but these seldom contribute to the humanitarian crisis. Lives depend on resources not being diverted from urgently needed humanitarian mine action to clear low-priority land simply to comply with the treaty.

Another important issue is whether support for mine action should be conditional on compliance with the Convention. The World Bank has adopted this approach in its loans to Croatia, and other donors may follow suit. The rationale for conditionality is twofold: a desire to ensure that resources devoted to mine clearance are not squandered due to the continued use of mines, and an attempt to encourage states hoping to secure foreign assistance for landmine clearance to comply with the treaty. The judicious use of scarce development funds certainly demands that mine-clearance operations be supported only where it is highly unlikely that the areas will be remined. But linking the provision of assistance to the signing of the treaty violates a basic principle of humanitarianism—that assistance is provided to individuals on the basis of need, irrespective of political considerations.

The effectiveness of future humanitarian mine clearance operations will also depend on better co-ordination among the various actors. The role of the United Nations is particularly important in this context, and its record over the past decade has been inconsistent at best. The UN's Department of Humanitarian Affairs (DHA) was established in 1992 in large part to improve the co-ordination of humanitarian activities. Two years later it was designated the focal point for mine-related activities within the UN system. Although its field operations were frequently plagued with difficulties, it played an important role in developing the broader concept of mine action. As part of the Secretary-General's 1997 reform package, the DHA was disbanded and responsibility for mines transferred to the Department of Peacekeeping Operations. The decision met with widespread opposition due to fears that activities in support of peacekeeping operations would be given priority, and that attention would be given primarily to the technical rather than humanitarian elements of mine clearance. A more pressing concern, however, may be the increasing competition among UN agencies and departments for newly available resources and the resulting diffusion of relevant expertise within the system.

The remarkable role played by non-governmental organizations in securing a treaty banning mines is a central theme running through this volume, and the discussion above illustrates that NGOs have played a critical role in the field of humanitarian demining as well. Not only are NGOs managing large demining operations in a number of mine-affected counties, they have also made important contributions in demining technique and in operationalizing the broader concept of mine action. But unlike the effort to ban mines, no concerted advocacy campaign has been undertaken to promote a common mine action agenda. The practical demands of field operations and the constraints of limited resources partly explain this somewhat surprising omission. But it is also the result of differences of opinion and approach among the prominent mine action NGOs. Success in reaching agreement on basic principles for mine action during the Oslo

Conference in September 1997 and the creation of a working group on humanitarian mine clearance within the steering committee of the ICBL both indicate that the NGO community is becoming more directly engaged in the larger debates surrounding humanitarian demining. Given their effectiveness during the ban campaign, this attention should be welcomed. It is crucial that these organizations, and, indeed, all involved actors, closely monitor the state of mine action in the coming years to ensure that scarce resources are used most effectively to assist those whose lives and livelihoods are affected daily by the scourge of mines.

NOTES

The author would like to thank the Killam Trust, the Social Sciences and Humanities Research Council of Canada, and the Canadian Department of Foreign Affairs and International Trade for their generous support while the research for this chapter was undertaken.

1. Colin King, *Mines and Mine Clearance 1996–97* (London: Jane's Information Group, 1997), 25–6.
2. Patrick Blagden, 'The Use of Mines and the Impact of Technology', in Kevin Cahill, ed., *Clearing the Fields: Solutions to the Global Landmines Crisis* (New York: Basic Books and the Council on Foreign Relations, 1995), 115.
3. Shawn Roberts and Jody Williams, *After the Guns Fall Silent: The Enduring Legacy of Landmines* (Washington: Vietnam Veterans of America Foundation, 1995), 43.
4. Department of Humanitarian Affairs, *Afghanistan: The Development of Indigenous Mine Action Capacities* (New York: United Nations, 1998), 12–13.
5. Ibid., 23.
6. Colin King, 'Landmines in Cambodia', *Jane's Intelligence Review* 7, 6 (June 1995): 273.
7. Jim Sawatzky, 'Canadian Forces Support of Demining Operations in Cambodia', *Strategic Datalink* 58 (Jan. 1997): 1.
8. UNDP, *The Role of the United Nations Development Program in Demining* (New York: UNDP, 1997), 3.
9. Roberts and Williams, *After the Guns Fall Silent*, 261.
10. General Accounting Office (GAO), *Unexploded Ordnance: A Coordinated Approach to Detection and Clearance is Needed* (Washington: GAO, 1995), 7; Roberts and Williams, *After the Guns Fall Silent*, 262.
11. Human Rights Watch Arms Project, *Still Killing: Landmines in Southern Africa* (New York: Human Rights Watch, 1997), 69.

12. For a more detailed account, see ibid., 81–99; and Department of Humanitarian Affairs, *Mozambique: The Development of Indigenous Mine Action Capacities* (New York: UN, 1998), 15–25.
13. Department of Humanitarian Affairs, *Mozambique*, 19.
14. Human Rights Watch Arms Project, *Still Killing*, 88.
15. Colin King, 'Former Yugoslav Landmines', *Jane's Intelligence Review* 7, 1 (Jan. 1995): 15.
16. International Crisis Group, *Ridding Bosnia of Landmines: The Urgent Need for a Sustainable Policy* (Brussels: ICG, 1997), 7–8.
17. Ibid., 17–19.
18. Ibid., 14, 16.
19. UNDP, *The Role of the United Nations Development Program*, 7.
20. International Crisis Group, *Ridding Bosnia of Landmines*, 2.
21. Department of Humanitarian Affairs, *Angola: The Development of Indigenous Mine Action Capacities* (New York: UN, 1998), 5, 37–9.
22. Roberts and Williams, *After the Guns Fall Silent*, 275.
23. Ibid., 252.
24. Department of Humanitarian Affairs, *Study Report: The Development of Indigenous Mine Action Capacities* (New York: UN, 1998), 27.
25. Department of Humanitarian Affairs, *Study Report*, 40–1.
26. Ibid., 49
27. Department of Humanitarian Affairs, *United Nations Demining Database*. [http://www.un.org/Depts/Landmine/index.html]
28. Department of Humanitarian Affairs, *Afghanistan*, 30.
29. For a more detailed discussion of mine action, see Justin Brady, 'A New Paradigm in Mine Action: Mine Action Teams in Moxito Angola', MA thesis, Clark University, 1998.
30. Department of Humanitarian Affairs, *Study Report*, 1.

Cambodia: a prayer for landmine victims. Courtesy of John Rodsted.

For a world free of landmines. Courtesy of John Rodsted.

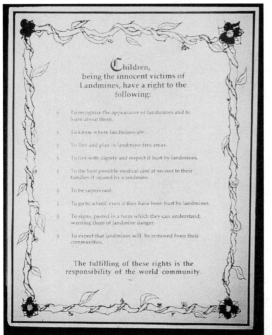

The children's treaty.

Children,
being the innocent victims of
Landmines, have a right to the
following:

- To recognize the appearance of landmines and to learn about them.
- To know where landmines are.
- To live and play in landmine-free areas.
- To live with dignity and respect if hurt by landmines.
- To the best possible medical care at no cost to their families if injured by a landmine.
- To be supervised.
- To go to school, even if they have been hurt by landmines.
- To signs, posted in a form which they can understand, warning them of landmine danger.
- To expect that landmines will be removed from their communities.

The fulfilling of these rights is the
responsibility of the world community.

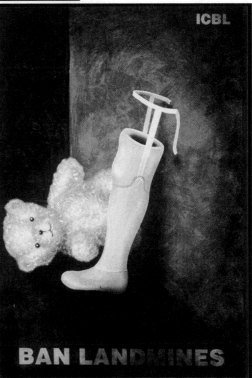

Poster. Courtesy of ICBL.

Ban bus crosses the United States en route to Ottawa. Courtesy of John Rodsted.

Red Cross truck distributes crutches in Cambodia. Courtesy of John Rodsted.

Courtesy of John Rodsted.

PART THREE

LEGACIES OF THE OTTAWA PROCESS

CHAPTER 17

COMPLIANCE WITH INTERNATIONAL NORMS AND THE MINES TABOO

Richard Price

INTRODUCTION

A new international norm has emerged that proscribes the use, stockpiling, production, and transfer of anti-personnel landmines. The previous chapters examined how the international community arrived at this point.[1] This chapter examines what it got. To say that there is a new norm tells us little or nothing about the strength or weakness of that norm. There are many norms in the international system—norms proscribing slavery, apartheid, chemical warfare, torture, the use of ozone-damaging chemicals, the killing of elephants for ivory, and so on. Some of these norms are very robust, while others are relatively weak and routinely violated. Which norms are effective? Is the emergent AP mines norm likely to be one of them? What factors are likely to bolster or undermine the prospects for its effectiveness?

The aim of this chapter is to assess, as far as possible, the robustness of the AP mines taboo by comparing it to other international norms and the factors that have facilitated or undermined compliance. To assess which international norms matter and why, I analyse two major sets of factors: (1) the broader international environment in which a norm is embedded, and (2) features of the norm itself. The former encompasses contextual factors: when and under what conditions do norms matter? I examine the relevance of the structure of the international system, the influence of democratization, the role of technology, and trends in the evolution of warfare in fostering or detracting from compliance with the AP mines taboo. For the second set of considerations I focus more on the properties of the norm and norm-governed activity to examine what features exert a pull towards compliance. In this regard I consider issues of concordance, clarity and simplicity, legitimacy, durability, the role of violations, and enforcement.

INTERNATIONAL ENVIRONMENT

End of the Cold War and Multilateralism

The end of the Cold War was important in opening space for the generation of the AP mines norm in the first place, and the resulting international security environment is conducive for nurturing compliance for a number of reasons. The end of the Cold War has facilitated the strengthening and expansion of other prohibitionary weapons regimes, particularly those controlling the use, testing, and possession of chemical and nuclear weapons. The international arms control environment is characterized by a historically unprecedented degree of transparency and intrusiveness to ensure compliance with these regimes governing weapons of mass destruction,[2] producing a hospitable environment for the AP mines norm.

More generally, the development and entrenchment of norms of multilateralism also encourage the spread and co-ordinated international policing of the mines taboo. As Franck has argued, ad hoc rules may exert a compliance pull, but a 'weaker one than is evinced by primary rules of obligation that are reinforced by a hierarchy of secondary rules which define the rule-system's "right process"'. That is, 'a rule is more likely to obligate if it is made within the framework of an organized normative hierarchy, than if it is merely an ad hoc agreement between parties in a state of nature.'[3] The embeddedness of the mines taboo in a web of multilateralism anchors the norm in ways that could help offset some of the negative effects of the lack of hegemonic leadership.

Hegemonic stability theory posits that compliance with international regimes is only likely with a hegemon willing to enforce compliance and sustain the burden of free riders. While numerous studies have shown the fallibility of the theory, a related argument can emphasize the importance, if not outright necessity, of the participation of hegemonic powers for a regime to be effective. Krasner, for example, has argued that human rights norms are only as successful as far as they are imposed and enforced by dominant states—for Krasner, the campaign against slavery only succeeded because Britain, then the world's pre-eminent naval power, could enforce a ban on the slave trade upon other states in the nineteenth century.[4] The US currently has no rival as a global military power, and although the formal acceptance of the mines taboo by the United States has not been necessary to the formation of a new regime, its further spread and implementation would no doubt be significantly enhanced by the active and vigilant policing of the regime by the world's dominant military and economic power. The routine application of principles of multilateralism ideally involve the non-discriminatory application of agreed principles of conduct, the rule of law instead of the rule of power.[5] However, many enforcement measures potentially available to the international community in response to a violation are not specified in the landmines treaty, but would rather be left to diplomatic will; this means that the mobilization of an energetic multilateral response to violations would only be enhanced with the active participation of a hegemonic power that could stimulate timely multilateral co-ordination, as evidenced with the leading role of the US in its attempts to enforce Iraq's compliance with multilateral sanctions. Moreover, the failure of the US to join the treaty opened a controversy in 1998 over the US contention that it should be permitted to retain its AP mines stockpiles on the soil of NATO allies that have joined the treaty; the lack of participation of the leading NATO member undermines compliance with the multilateral regime.

Democratization
The end of the Cold War also provided a spur to the longer-term historical process of democratization. While the process is very uneven, a relative empowerment of civil society has occurred with the fall of authoritarian regimes from Eastern Europe and the former Soviet Union, as well as in such diverse locales as Latin America, the Philippines, South Africa, and South Korea. While democratization is not a sufficient condition for support of the AP mines taboo (Finland, United States, South Korea), and public opinion in democratic polities can encourage defection from international norms and agreements (e.g., US public opinion on waging chemical warfare against the Japan in World War II or nationalist sentiment in trade disputes), the democratic space created for civil society is an important factor facilitating the maintenance and spread of the taboo in several respects.

First, the vastly decreased security pressures that democratic states enjoy in their relations among themselves facilitate acceptance of the norm; the more reduced the security pressures are on a given state, the more likely it is to join and comply with the AP mines regime. For this reason, any reversals in democratization are likely to degrade prospects for compliance. Second, some scholars have argued that democracies have a higher rate of compliance with international norms and laws than other types of states. This is a controversial question, in part because it is impossible to verify empirically—there is no way of establishing the universe of cases.[6] Burley suggests that liberal democracies are more law-abiding due to the institutionalization of liberal constitutionalism.[7] The focus on domestic legal institutions points us to a key mechanism for compliance with the mines taboo—the convergence of domestic penal legislation among signatory states—that essentially provides a de facto if proto-transnational criminal regime in the absence of a permanent international criminal court. Third, while Florini has argued that democratization does not necessarily facilitate voluntary transparency (states of all kinds have jealously protected their sovereign security secrets),[8] the disclosure of information is facilitated by democratization none the less by the availability of information in more open societies. All other things being equal, would-be violators would have a much harder time keeping the existence and source of violations secret in democratic states than they would in a police state that sought to strictly control information. Democracy creates a structural space for the role of civil society in verifying compliance; the watchdog role of civil society in ensuring that governments live up to their compliance commitments is greatly contracted in non-democratic regimes such as China.

Technology
The surveillance capability of civil society has been greatly facilitated by the development of communications technologies that make it difficult for governments to monopolize information. 'Hypermedia'[9]—the global web of electronic media, including telecommunications, fax machines, and especially the Internet and World Wide Web—have played an unprecedented role in facilitating the growth of a global network of concerned individuals and groups around the landmines issue. Web sites and e-mail traffic have proliferated around the landmines issue, providing a wealth of instantaneously available information that focuses the spotlight on recalcitrants, whether combatants using mines or industries producing them.

Such information politics opens an important crack in the edifice of state autonomy that creates additional pressures towards compliance by considerably removing the manoeuvring room for non-complying practices. Hypermedia facilitate the role of communities of experts who are outside of government and who are able to monitor states' compliance with desired norms of behaviour. Beyond the case of landmines, cases such as nuclear and chemical weapons demonstrate that knowledge is not necessarily a debilitating handicap for non-state actors in issues of national security; some of the foremost experts on these weapons systems are scientists active in the arms control community. 'Networks' is indeed an apt term for the transnational society facilitated by the Internet, the worldwide web of information that states are enmeshed within.

Trends in Warfare
Technology also figures in the forms in which violence is waged. Martin van Creveld, among others, has argued that the social institution of war is undergoing a transformation. For van Creveld, the rules of the game are changing such that elaborate high-technology warfare controlled by states is becoming obsolete in favour of low-intensity conflict. Not incidentally, he argues that such a transformation plays to the strengths of the downtrodden and weak: 'Refusing to play the game according to the rules that "civilized" countries have established for their convenience, they

developed their own form of war and began exporting it.'[10] As epitomized by the US in Vietnam or the Russians in Chechnya, the unwillingness of states to employ all of their technological might—nuclear weapons—against irregular forces suggests there is some truth to such observations. These trends in warfare are, of course, what precipitated the landmines issue in the first place—the proliferation of civil and guerrilla conflicts dominated by the use of readily available, relatively low-technology weaponry—trends that seem to bode poorly for the robustness of the regime. If the deployment of organized violence continues to be predominantly of the 'low-intensity' sort that often involves terrorizing civilian populations, non-signatories (states and non-state actors) seem likely to continue to rely on AP mines as a weapon well suited to that type of warfare.

These are serious potential obstacles to a robust and effective mines taboo. Still, the place of AP mines amid patterns of warfare actually presents an important avenue by which compliance could be encouraged and not just discouraged. The place of AP mines as a favoured means in insurgencies and guerrilla-style tactics may, over time, work against their legitimacy among state powers in the international system. Apart from nuclear weapons, those weapons that have been delegitimized most successfully in the international system are those that have been condemned as 'weapons of the weak'. Poison, chemical weapons, and biological weapons have been castigated as unfair, cheap equalizers because they have been understood to undermine the exclusive advantages of centralized high-technology state violence, both within the state and among the hierarchy of states.[11] That is, states seek to monopolize their internal control over significant means of destruction *vis-à-vis* society, and powerful states seek to maintain their technological advantage over weaker states by denying the legitimacy of low-cost equalizers. Similarly, while some versions of AP mines are touted by proponents as a high-technology advantage, AP mines have been depicted as low-cost equalizers that appeal and play to the strengths of the technologically, financially, or industrially disadvantaged.[12] With the emergence of the prohibitionary norm, AP mine proponents have been put on the defensive to such an extent that, to cite a prominent example, US proponents of the Gator mixed anti-tank/anti-personnel mines system have sought to redefine the latter component not as an AP mine but as a 'submunition'. The significance of such specious semantics for this discussion is their effect of further removing from the category of AP mines the image of a high-technology glamour weapon of the powerful. Because AP mines are an easily available and significant means of destruction, technologically advanced, powerful states are increasingly likely to define their delegitimization as in their interests *vis-à-vis* less powerful states. Similarly, states are likely increasingly to understand the availability of AP mines as undercutting the state monopoly of violence *vis-à-vis* non-state wielders of violence, providing an incentive for all states to circumscribe their availability. In other words, the AP mines taboo establishes a new normative context that shapes how states redefine their interests.

This development would have three further implications. First, the price of a robust international norm proscribing landmines is an increase in the policing power of the state; for this reason, it is too simplistic to regard the successful generation of a new norm prohibiting AP mines as a victory of civil society over the state. Second, the contemporary resistance to the chemical weapons taboo among a small group of nations (and potential non-state actors such as terrorists) demonstrates that one effect of such disciplinary discourses might actually be to increase the allure of the proscribed means for 'the weak', those deemed outside the club of 'civilized' states. Third, while AP mines may be attractive to non-state actors, to the extent that the members of insurgencies and guerrilla conflicts aspire to self-determination (and almost all of them do: their goal is their own state), a pull towards compliance will be exerted by the expectation of the international community that a legitimate member of the community of states abides by the AP mines regime. Thus, while compliance with the mines taboo may be undermined by the fact that many who use mines are not states (and thus, not parties to the treaty), most of those actors are not immune from incentives to comply based on recognition. The international community has withheld diplomatic recognition and all of its benefits from perpetrators of war crimes such as genocide and rape; so, too, could compliance with the landmines taboo be deemed part of the portfolio of necessary practices to be recognized as a legitimate member of the international community and to avoid isolation as a pariah. Even though they are not recognized as states, the Taliban regime in Afghanistan and rebel groups in Sudan and Senegal have pledged not to use AP mines. The inclusion of the use of AP landmines as a war crime in any future International Criminal Court would mark a very important avenue by which to further this pull towards compliance.

A final consideration related to the future course of warfare is an assessment of what might happen should the norm prove efficacious. Many scholars have demonstrated the importance of a shock or crisis in precipitating international change. Ironically, while the carnage caused by AP mines provided a sense of urgency leading to the Ottawa ban, improvements on the ground could conceivably remove the sense of urgency in furthering the ban. That is, if the effects of a ban and demining programs fulfilled the most optimistic projections, the sense of crisis conceivably could be dampened as figures of casualties begin to drop. As issues such as the population crisis, the energy crisis, and the global warming crisis show, the international attention span for a 'crisis' can be difficult to sustain. This provides one reason for underscoring the importance of early ratification and universalization of treaty; if the crisis were to abate significantly, the political will for pressure on recalcitrant states to join and entrench the norm may lessen. This underscores the importance of responding to violations, examined later: the less that violations occur, the more intolerable they must become.

WHAT KIND OF NORMS MATTER?

Concordance

In an effort to develop non-tautological gauges for the robustness of international norms, Legro has posited 'concordance', arguing that the 'more widely endorsed a prescription is, the greater will be its impact.'[13] This criterion is implicit in the criticism that has been voiced that the landmines Convention is a 'feel-good treaty' due to the lack of support among countries that contain well over half of the world's population, including key military powers such as Russia, China, India, and states of the Middle East. The genuine endorsement of the landmines treaty by these countries would, of course, enhance its prospects, but the criticism that the taboo is all but meaningless in their absence is overwrought for a number of reasons. While support for the ban is not universal, the vast majority of AP mine victims have not been in the major hold-out countries. The treaty has widespread acceptance among the most-mined countries (with some exceptions, including Egypt, Iran, and Iraq); this means that, unlike some international norms such as those embodied in human rights instruments, the treaty has support where it needs it most—in countries where the pernicious effects of the now-deviant practice have been most prevalent. In short, the impact of the non-participation of resistant states, while important, is not nearly as great as it would be if those rejecting the new norm included Cambodia, Mozambique, Bosnia, Croatia, Angola, and the Taliban regime in Afghanistan.

Shortfalls in universal concordance should also be put in historical perspective when trying to assess the eventual robustness of the AP mines regime. The pace of the extension of the landmines taboo is quite impressive when compared historically to the spread of other norms of warfare. The poison taboo took hundreds of years to consolidate in Renaissance Europe.[14] The chemical weapons taboo originated in a minor diplomatic declaration at the Hague Conferences of 1899, a document far from the formal institutionalized detail of the landmines treaty. The Geneva Protocol outlawed the use (but not the stockpiling, production, or transfer) of chemical weapons in 1925, and two key military powers—the United States and Japan—did not ratify the agreement until the 1970s. Even though the chemical weapons taboo none the less has been rather successful, it still does not enjoy universal support, with key states in the Middle East the most prominent hold-outs of the Chemical Weapons Convention (CWC) of 1993. It should also be noted that it took over 90 years to extend the chemical weapons taboo from a ban on use to a prohibition on stockpiling, production, and transfer. In short, the signing of a comprehensive landmines taboo by 124 states, as of February 1998, is indicative of an impressive degree of concordance and institutional maturity when put in relief of the century it has taken to consolidate an efficacious chemical weapons taboo.

Third, shortfalls in concordance are offset to a degree by the fact that some key non-signatory states are nevertheless participating in various dimensions of the taboo through policies such as unilateral export bans. Exports are reported to have ceased since 1995, an important achievement since the vast majority of the mines that caused the crisis in the most-infested countries were imported. The United States may present somewhat of a special case, in so far as the US Senate ratification hurdle for international treaties is so high (a two-thirds majority is required to give consent) that security treaties are often difficult to ratify. In lieu of ratification, the executive branch may take unilateral measures that approach the effects of a ban, as occurred with chemical weapons. Even though the US did not ratify the Geneva Protocol until 1975, successive administrations from Roosevelt's in World War II onward none the less refused to sanction the use of lethal chemical warfare. A similar process appears to be under way with respect to landmines—even though the US has not signed the Ottawa Convention, that country has committed itself to eliminating the use of AP mines in Korea by 2006 and everywhere else by 2003. Although one mixed-mine system has been exempted from this search for alternatives, the US has moved significantly towards a de facto AP mine ban despite not being a party to the treaty.

Clarity/Simplicity

Numerous members of the landmines campaign have argued that a major reason for its success is the simplicity of the norm—a blanket taboo is much easier to understand than complex restrictions on how mines can be used. Similarly, a number of scholars maintain that the clarity or simplicity of a norm significantly affects its effectiveness. McElroy contends that 'the clearer the behavioral demands of a moral norm, the greater the compliance with that norm.'[15] Legro has argued that 'specificity' contributes to compliance—the greater the clarity and simplicity of a norm, the more likely it is to be robust.[16] Is this true, and how relevant is this criterion for assessing prospects of compliance with the landmines taboo?

The simplicity of a norm need not by itself facilitate compliance. For one, ambiguous norms could actually be easier to comply with in the sense that it is more difficult to tell what would constitute a true violation; thus, violations on the margin can occur without necessarily being interpreted as invalidating the norm itself. This is illustrated by the case of chemical weapons during the Vietnam War. McElroy claims that it was because the boundaries of the chemical weapons norm were so clear and strong that the use of herbicides and tear gas by the US was condemned by international and domestic criticism.[17] But the reason the US did in fact use such methods in the first place—whereas a strong and clear norm would suggest they would not be used—was because there was some ambiguity about how to interpret the norm proscribing chemical weapons and whether it prohibited means such as tear gas and agent orange. The cause of the violation was the elasticity of the norm, which the US interpreted to mean that it was not violating the norm. The effect, however, was that domestic and international opposition was not content to leave this norm ambiguous to permit flexible interpretations of compliance on the margins, as may happen with international norms, but rather sought to clarify the boundaries of proscribed activity.

Franck, in his analysis of non-coercive pulls towards compliance, has pointed out another reason why simplicity need not facilitate robustness. He has argued that the legitimacy of a norm depends in part on its 'determinacy', which includes the transparency of the standard.[18] He reasons that this exerts a pull towards compliance in so far as 'the more determinate a standard, the more difficult it is to justify non-compliance.'[19] Still, he argues that norm clarity provides no guarantee of compliance, as very clear norms may command an absurdity. For example, a new extradition rule between the US and the UK may be very simple and clear in denying political offences in extradition cases, but President Ronald Reagan felt little pull to comply with such an even-handed standard as it meant abandoning havens for those resisting oppressive regimes. The rule in this case should have been more subtle and complex and taken into account not only what acts had been done, but why and to whom; the simplicity of the norm detracted from its compliance pull.[20] In this way, blanket prohibitions can create more unpredictability than certainty, as almost everyone would choose to make some exceptions.

This is not to say that formulating norms in more subtle or complex terms is not without its costs. The more a rule departs from quantitative measures to qualitative ones, the more it accommodates exculpatory exceptions based on 'good' motives and the more difficult it becomes to determine the rule's content. The more opaque and elastic that content, the less likely it is to control actual behaviour.

What are the implications of these considerations for the AP mines taboo? It is abundantly clear that the previous complex mines norm embodied in the CCW did little to curb the pernicious deployment of AP mines. While the simplicity of the norm banning any use of AP mines means that the taboo is likely to be violated with little ambiguity, the form of the taboo facilitates compliance in several ways seen above. First, would-be incremental violators of the taboo will have little room to finesse questions of violation and compliance by resort to the subterfuge of complex technical rules, as often occurred in the case of chemical weapons.[21] In World War I, belligerent states took advantage of legal technicalities by playing on the wording of the Hague Declaration's ban on 'projectiles the object of which is the diffusion of asphyxiating or deleterious gases', arguing that the use of gas from cylinders did not violate the wording of the agreement and that certain gases were not 'asphyxiating or deleterious'. Subsequently, some states played on the ambiguities of the Geneva Protocol's ban on 'asphyxiating, poisonous or other gases' to initiate forms of chemical warfare from tear gas to napalm and agent orange. The first treaty to regulate AP mines, the CCW, contained language similarly open to abuse by defining an AP mine as a 'mine *primarily* designed to be exploded by the presence, proximity or contact of a person'. The international campaign was insistent on a less ambiguous definition for a comprehensive ban treaty and was successful in excising the qualifier 'primarily' from the Ottawa Convention text.[22] This considerably narrows the scope of interpretive ambiguities that could be taken advantage of and closes one potential avenue of incremental violation, particularly by those not entirely willing to face the full costs of getting caught in outright violation.

Second, it is the absolute form of the taboo (rather than its simplicity *per se*) that is important, in so far as it establishes a higher threshold to be crossed for the use of the weapon. While the deployment of weapons that are to be restricted according to the dictates of proportionality or military necessity ('don't use submarines or aircraft bombing against civilians') may often be left to the discretion of field commanders or individual pilots or soldiers, decisions to use a completely banned weapon may be taken out of such hands if the very availability of the means is restricted. Decisions about use instead become political decisions to be made, often at the highest levels.[23] Thus, the threshold against use may be raised, and the proscribed weapon is more likely to be extracted from standard procedures in doctrine, training, procurement, and deployment than weapons whose use is only restricted and whose deployment is more readily available to the discretion of soldiers under duress in the field.

Legitimacy

Legitimacy, according to Franck, is the belief that a rule is 'just, because it incorporates principles of fairness as these are understood by a moral community'.[24] As he elaborates: 'Legitimacy is a property of a rule or rule-making institution which itself exerts a pull towards compliance on those addressed normatively because those addressed believe that the rule or a rule-making institution has come into being and operates in accordance with generally accepted principles of right process.'[25] Questions of legitimate process were heard prominently after October 1996 as the Ottawa Process overtook other negotiating fora—resistant states and some reluctantly supportive states argued that the Conference on Disarmament was the most appropriate forum for negotiating a ban as it would involve all the major military powers. Other states objected to the Ottawa Process on the grounds that it involved undue influence of civil society in state security policy, as evidenced by the reluctance of many states to include NGOs at international negotiating sessions in Ottawa, Brussels, and Oslo. Despite these objections, the Ottawa Process produced an outcome that secured the widespread legitimacy of an AP mine ban along a different and crucially important axis. The refusal of ban proponents to make a distinction between long-lived and self-deactivating/self-destructing mines was vital for the norm as it forestalled a potentially fatal divide between developed and developing nations. While this process left out some key resistant nations, a majority of the members of the CD eventually came on board, including initially reluctant states such as France, Italy, Australia, Japan, and Brazil. Moreover, the inclusion of most mine-affected states was a more concrete and immediate result than a CD process, which includes few such states and would have had difficulty producing any agreement that went meaningfully beyond the revised Protocol II of the CCW.

Another facet of legitimacy noted by Franck is 'procedural determinacy'—'the extent to which the rule is accessible to legitimate clarifying procedures'.[26] Compliance would be undermined to the extent that there is little confidence that recourse to determinations of compliance and violations will be unbiased. In this regard the reporting, transparency, and compliance procedures of the landmines treaty do not appear to present particular obstacles in ensuring that all parties have the opportunity to participate in the operation of the regime.[27] Indeed, in comparison with treaties in human rights, institutions such as the International Monetary Fund and international negotiations over some issues in the environmental arena such as global warming, the landmines taboo seems likely to be less subject to charges of Western bias that could undermine perceived procedural legitimacy.

The latter consideration points to another facet of legitimacy: a number of scholars have argued that international norms are more likely to be robust the more their proscriptions or prescriptions mesh with domestic norms and discourses. A systemic norm is more likely to attain the status of a salient 'ought' in the domestic arena if it resonates with subsystemic cultures, or at least if there is a normative vacuum or a lack of a cultural clash that provides a hospitable environment for the domestic standing of the international norm.[28] In general, the AP mines taboo fares well on this score—unlike some human rights norms, such as those concerning the status of women or female genital mutilation, the anti-AP mine norm is unlikely to be plagued by cultural backlash of being a 'Western' norm. The mines taboo is, however, likely to meet resistance in entrenched cultures of violence among peoples who have experienced generations of conflict. International organizations, civil society campaigns, support for the norm by political leaders, and the institutionalization of the norm through domestic legislation can play important roles in increasing the domestic salience of the taboo in such circumstances.

Durability

Does the longevity of a norm affect its robustness—is a norm likely to be stronger the longer it has existed? The simple longevity of a norm is, in and of itself, indeterminate as an indicator of robustness—long-held norms can be weakly observed (the centuries-old proscription against the killing of civilians in war) or quickly extinguished (slavery), while relatively new norms can be quite robust (anti-colonialism). However, the case of chemical weapons suggests that longevity can matter for the durability of a weapons taboo in the sense of two phenomena that may accompany durable norms: fear due to unfamiliarity, and the taken-for-grantedness of a tradition of non-use.

In the case of chemical weapons, an important source of the taboo has been their continued status as anachronistically novel instruments of war, especially in terms of their lack of use against civilians. The special apprehension and fear that issue from the confrontation with sheer novelty in human life (what gas proponents historically have called 'ignorance') have held in an almost anachronistic way because massive chemical attacks never became a regular part of war that soldiers and civilians grudgingly had to 'get used to' as another despicable 'inevitability' of warfare. Unfamiliarity has fed into uncertainty, which in turn has enhanced the symbolic status of chemical weapons. This phenomenon obviously is not immediately available as a source for the AP mines norm in the way that it was for the chemical weapons taboo; indeed, unlike chemical weapons, the movement for a taboo came about precisely because of the actual rather than hypothesized devastation of civilians. Boutros-Ghali noted this ambivalence in observing that an

> important avenue to pursue is placing mines in the same legal and ethical category as chemical and biological weapons in order to stigmatize them in the public imagination. The use of mines is so common that for those unfamiliar with their effects they may not invoke the horrific visions of chemical or biological warfare. Were their effects better known, landmines would undoubtedly shock the conscience of mankind into the same public reaction that led to the banning of chemical and biological weapons.[29]

Fear from unfamiliarity is not a source of delegitimization that can bolster compliance with the mines taboo at this point, in so far as this weapon was originally understood as an unremarkable conventional weapon, unlike the unconventional status attributed to chemical or nuclear weapons very soon after or even preceding their appearance.[30] Indeed, delegitimizing AP mines involves their extraction from the already tangled roots of widespread conventional practice rather than an attempt to prevent their maturation from novelty into conventional practice by building on the fear of unfamiliarity. It is often suggested that it is easier to ban weapons on the horizon of invention, before they are developed and deployed, than after they have become part of standard military practice.[31] The historical example of the taboo on poison demonstrates that even weapons that have been widely used can be successfully prohibited, though poison also suggests such a process is apt to take a very long time. The first part of this process, which is already in evidence, is the treatment of AP mine incidents as reportable and even newsworthy events in the daily press. Over time, the degree to which AP mines are genuinely unconventionalized will depend in no small part on the development of a symbolic status of unfamiliarity, which will be persistently in tension with the ready availability of the weapon.

For such an aura of fear and seemingly instinctive revulsion to take root, a tradition of non-use and the accompanying process of forgetting would have to transpire to impart a taken-for-granted quality to the norm. In the case of poison and chemical weapons, generational traditions of the non-use of the weapons have become institutional facts (regardless of the reasons for non-use) that importantly constitute the moral discourses regarding poison and chemical weapons and thus of the international norms proscribing their use. This point can be illustrated with an illuminating episode from the period of the Iran-Iraq war. During US Senate hearings over Iraq's use of chemical weapons in the early 1980s, it was remarked in one exchange that gas weapons surely were reprehensible since even Hitler did not use them against Allied armies or cities. No one present knew why Germany refrained from waging chemical warfare in World War II, but the salient fact remained: 'We do know it did not happen.'[32] Chemical weapons therefore must be odious enough not to use them.

This anecdote has implications for assessing the robustness of the taboo and understanding how norms may exert a pull towards compliance. According to the doctrine of custom in international law, proof of the existence of a legal norm requires not just demonstration of behavioural concordance with a norm, but *opinion juris*—demonstration that conformity was due to belief that the practice was a legal obligation. While the presence of *opinion juris* no doubt bolsters a norm, events and circumstances of a less intentional character can prove of no small importance in the development of a norm. Over time, the process of forgetting the origins and functions of such prohibitions—to the point of never having to question their authority or even feel that *justification is required*—is an indicator of the strength of the norm through its taken-for-granted quality. These dynamics, not longevity *per se*, may contribute to the robustness of a norm; the degree to which they take hold depends in large part on contestation of the norm, particularly the way that agents respond to violations.[33]

Violations

It would seem common sense to maintain that social norms can only be said to be robust to the extent that actors abstain from violating them. On this understanding of norms, the violation of a taboo is indicative of its weakness. However, theoretical and empirical investigations of norms show that there are two ways in which a violation does not necessarily erode or invalidate the norm: (1) if an act is understood and accepted as an extreme and even justifiable departure from a norm, or, if it is not, (2) it is treated as a violation with a disciplinary response. With regard to the former, Kratochwil and Ruggie have stated:

> Precisely because state behavior within regimes is interpreted by other states, the rationales and justifications for behavior which are proffered, together with pleas for understanding or admissions of guilt, as well as the responsiveness to such reasoning on the part of other states, all are absolutely critical component parts of any explanation involving the efficacy of norms. Indeed, such communicative dynamics may tell us far more about how robust a regime is than overt behavior alone.[34]

In other words, not all violations in the sense of 'brute behaviour' are the same. We routinely make a distinction between murder and self-defence; although the brute behaviour—killing—is the same, the occurrence of the former is understood as a threat to undermine the norm proscribing murder while the latter is not. From the perspective of the transgressor, a given violation of a norm need not involve its own rejection of the norm per se but may constitute a justifiable departure from a norm that it otherwise upholds. However, such rationales are unlikely to avoid undermining the broader international social acceptance of a norm unless those justifications gain widespread acceptance among the rest of the international community. One implication of this is that even rhetoric is not altogether insignificant for the robustness of a norm over time. As other studies have shown, the difference between explicit rejection or support of a norm (even if just rhetorical) accompanying a behavioural violation can contribute to the sense of aberration or normalization of the practice, particularly if constituencies develop to hold states to their commitments.[35]

The case of chemical weapons provides an apposite illustration of these processes. Even though there were violations of the norm prohibiting the use of chemical weapons by the Italians in Ethiopia during 1935–6 and the Iraqis in the Iran-Iraq war during the 1980s, the fact that the Italians and Iraqis refused to admit their use is significant when viewed in historical perspective. These states engaged in a process of self-censorship that contributed to the sense of aberration involved in their practice of warfare. When the Iraqis could no longer deny the use of gas in the face of irrefutable evidence, they did not justify it as a humane or even acceptable behaviour in war, as the Germans did in World War I. Indeed, the Iraqis went so far as to argue that they upheld the international norm prohibiting chemical warfare. One need not attribute any credence to such claims to notice that the Iraqis contributed to the anomalous status of chemical weapons; they did not seek to conventionalize the weapon. Indeed, the Iraqis subsequently sought to capitalize on this special status of chemical weapons as terror weapons of last resort during the Gulf War of 1990–1, portraying them as a 'weapon of mass destruction' on par with nuclear weapons. The treatment of chemical weapons represented anything but a normalization process of the weapon as just one more standard component of the world's arsenal. In short, even in the face of violations, such discursive practices have helped sustain the notion that gas warfare is not wholly accepted as an unquestioned and unremarkable standard procedure for the community of nations.

Still, the question arises: given such blatant violations, what can be said about the robustness of the norm? One way to gauge the efficacy of norms is to assess how extreme a situation must be to justify its violation. On this score, the chemical weapons norm can be seen as becoming more robust over time. It amounted to far less than a powerful inhibition on the Germans in World War I or the Italians in Ethiopia; neither was driven to use gas only as a desperate defensive measure for their own survival. For the Iraqis, in contrast, initial resort to chemical weapons was taken only as a desperate measure at a point when it appeared they might lose the war to Iran.

The establishment of such thresholds is a principal way that norms work in social life. Norms that are less than profoundly taken for granted do not render transgressions impossible, but instead make such practices unlikely by raising the threshold of what counts as a legitimate exception to the rule. Few people would feel the need to deliberate over the legitimacy of violating societal norms against murder in the event of a deadly attack on oneself—self-defence is a widely accepted exception to the injunction not to kill. The existence of such exceptions does not mean that the norm is otherwise not robust, however; it simply means that there is a very high threshold in accepting a violation as an exception, and that those exceptions are not undertaken lightly. The chemical weapons taboo can be said to be a 'settled' norm in the sense that violation of it requires extraordinary justification.[36] The campaign to ban AP mines has already had the effect of politicizing the issue to such an extent that in most states it is political decision-makers at the highest levels—and not just soldiers or military decision-makers acting autonomously—who will be involved in making decisions about deployment. Where this has occurred, unusual justifications increasingly will be required for the use of AP mines as a weapon that had been politicized or even removed from standard military procedure, and these conditions are likely to be crossed more rarely than are the thresholds of military necessity or proportionality as left to be decided by soldiers in the field. Thus, while Australia and the United Kingdom were criticized by the ICBL in 1997 for policies that reserved the use of mines in exceptional circumstances, that position reflects how norms of warfare actually tend to work during conflict: military decisions become political ones subject to a higher threshold of justification, providing additional barriers to non-complying behaviour.

A second reason that the violation of a norm need not signal its erosion or death is that, as Foucault observed, violations provide the most opportune moments to define and discipline a particular practice as an aberration.[37] Steven Lee similarly has observed that, 'paradoxically, the *success* of legal deterrence is dependent on its *failure* . . . because its success depends on the belief that the state is willing to carry out its threats, which depends on a history of threat executions.'[38] As with social norms in general, the taboo banning AP mines can withstand future violations without being altogether extinguished, but the way that potential disciplinarians respond to violations assumes importance for the strengthened efficacy of the norm over time. Violations need to be treated precisely as that—violations—and selective responses to violations will tend to undermine the integrity of the norm. This means that in the absence of an acceptable justification, the 'inconsistent application of a rule or general principle undermines its capacity to elicit compliance.'[39] The failure of the international community to sanction Iraq for its use of chemical weapons against Iran in the 1980s is exemplary of this phenomenon. The lack of a plausible legal justification for not sanctioning Iraq—one that could be consistently and impartially applied—undermined the integrity of the chemical weapons taboo and greatly enhanced the allure of chemical weapons for a number of states in the international system.

As it is not a party to the AP mines treaty, the United States will be unable to participate actively in disciplinary measures to enforce violations, such as the organization of widespread international sanctions. Similarly, the absence of two other members of the UN Security Council—Russia and China—effectively removes this powerful institution that has become an increasingly frequent tool to enforce norm compliance in the post-Cold War world. States and international institutions are not the only actors that can respond to violations; transnational civil society has played an important role in enforcing normative conformity in other issue-areas through techniques such as consumer boycotts. Similarly, members of civil society can identify and stigmatize mine producers, but ultimately they must rely on shaming to sway the political will of the consumers—states or insurgent groups. To this point, public reaction to reports of continued use of AP mines, such as in Cambodia, has been non-existent, as was past response to violations of the CCW. While quiet diplomacy may on occasion be preferable to publicizing a determined flouting of the regime, less tepid reactions need to be forthcoming over time if the mines taboo is to avert a disastrous development into the kind of bifurcation that characterizes the chemical weapons taboo—violations in 'less civilized' areas of the world, while still formally taboo, seem less intolerable to the international community than violations within the zone of industrialized democracies.

Enforcement

The above discussion underscores the utmost importance of the political will of states in reinforcing the landmines taboo in the face of violations if this norm is to be taken seriously by potential violators. Even assuming that there was adequate political will among states to enforce the mines taboo, could this new regime be effective? In his analysis of international prohibition regimes, Nadelmann argued that the most difficult activities to suppress are those requiring readily available resources that are easily concealed and not readily substituted for by alternatives.[40] How does the mines taboo fare on these dimensions?

With respect to the availability of alternatives, it is to be noted that one of the main effects of the stigmatization of AP landmines has been the stimulation of the search for alternatives by militaries around the world. While some states have concluded that adequate alternatives do not yet exist for them, many other states have arrived at a different conclusion. As but one example of the latter, in the Philippines 'it has been demonstrated that good intelligence, normal vigilance and tactical flexibility are viable alternatives to the use of AP mines, and can make static defense systems such as the AP mine decreasingly relevant.'[41] The Philippines is virtually and remarkably free of landmines despite decades of conflict. Even though the US has not formally joined the ban treaty, President Clinton directed the Pentagon to find alternatives to mines beginning in 1996, and by January 1997 a Pentagon spokesman stated that doctrinal and tactical changes have been initiated 'such that there will not be a requirement for' AP landmines.[42] In September 1997 Clinton directed that alternatives be found to end the use of all AP mines by 2003 except in Korea, where alternatives are to be ready by 2006. While Pentagon and White House spokespersons have indicated the intention to exempt one mixed self-destructing system (AP mines used to protect anti-tank mines) from this commitment by redefining it as a 'submunition' instead of an AP mine,[43] it is evident that the drive for alternatives is well under way in the US and elsewhere.[44]

While the development of alternatives may be least likely for those for whom AP mines are most attractive—irregular fighting forces—for many states AP mines are amenable to substitution by alternatives.[45] The long-range potential for substitution becomes even more clear when compared to a number of other cases of norm substitutability. The first is other weapons systems that have been the topic of restraint, and for which alternatives have been roundly rejected by state proponents of the weapons (e.g., submarines, nuclear weapons). The second is other practices subject to prohibitionary regimes in the international system such as narcotics or trade in women for prostitution, for which alternatives are not available. The third is the case of chemical weapons. Chemical weapons have always retained some unique utility for certain missions, such as for the US in battling Japanese tunnel and cave defences in World War II. Due in no small part to their delegitimization, however, chemical weapons have been gradually weeded out of the repertoire of strategy and doctrine in most states to the point that it is often claimed they can be banned simply because 'we don't need them any more'. In the case of AP mines a comparable search for alternatives has occurred in a widespread fashion and at a significantly more accelerated pace than occurred with chemical weapons.

None the less, the ease with which AP mines may be produced and concealed creates significant concerns about the effectiveness of a ban. As observed in a study undertaken for the US Department of Defense, 'Few arms control agreements can promise total effectiveness, and landmine controls may be easier to circumvent than most, given how easily such small weapons can be concealed compared with, say, tanks or aircraft.'[46] The authors conclude:

> The monitoring and enforcement provisions of a treaty are unlikely to impose high costs on landmine users. A major cost increase is likely to be required, however, to persuade many developing world armies to forgo mine use on military or economic grounds. While some will respect even an unenforceable treaty rather than use weapons stigmatized by an international ban, no evidence has yet been produced to show that this will be a widespread response.[47]

The analysis of this chapter has been focused mostly on identifying sources for the latter: potential pulls towards compliance with an AP mine taboo arising from issues of legitimacy, moral and legal obligation, and reputation. The efficacy of these factors needs to be weighed against more tangible cost-benefit incentives for defection from the regime. The chief costs of a mines regime on landmine users are 'evasion (or concealment) costs associated with disguising the activity, and punitive sanctions imposed on violators if discovered'.[48] The former includes the costs of disguising production, stockpiling, transfer, and use. The reporting and compliance procedures of the landmine Convention, while short of ensuring 100 per cent verification of compliance, will increase transparency and raise costs of defection. Still, the Institute for Defense Analysis study identifies a number of ways that detection of these activities can be evaded—producers and exporters can relocate to non-party states, and monitoring cannot ensure the end of all production or stockpiling, particularly at undeclared sites but even perhaps at declared sites.[49] Even proving responsibility for mine use is subject to numerous ambiguities.[50] The best that can be hoped for, perhaps, is that by driving production underground the treaty may have an effect of making more difficult the large-scale production and export of AP mines, reducing the vast scale of AP mines flooding the market that would otherwise exist if their production and use were seen as a perfectly legitimate activity.

In other words, while the ease with which even crude AP mines can be made in workshop conditions is seen as making a treaty unverifiable, such production, at least, is unlikely to be of the vast industrial scale that has precipitated the enormity of the landmines problem. The fact that the financial benefits to mine purveyors are comparatively modest in comparison to other contraband activities increases the ratio of costs to benefits relative to other prohibited activities. Overall, however, the relative ease of concealment poses comparable or even greater difficulties of enforcement (due to the low levels of technology involved) when compared to other restricted weapons systems such as chemical or nuclear weapons, and these difficulties are comparable to those that plague international efforts to curb the trade in narcotics.

Domestic penal legislation of states party to the treaty is the key institutional mechanism of enforcement available in this regard. Similar legislation implementing the chemical and biological weapons conventions has led to criminal convictions of individuals, and such dynamics have transpired already in the case of AP mines. A Cape Town entrepreneur was apprehended in 1996 for selling landmines as personal and property protection devices in South Africa. This ran afoul of that country's moratorium on the manufacture and supply of AP mines, as the government argued that the Defense Act applied not only to government but to individuals as well.[51]

CONCLUSION

The growth of global norms of multilateralism and increased transparency in weapons regimes have created an international political environment hospitable for a new international norm proscribing AP landmines. While democratization and the spread of communications technologies are also conducive towards compliance, the effect of other broad historical developments, such as changes in patterns of warfare, are more deleterious or mixed, pending future developments. The absolute form of the taboo, its legitimacy, and its relative institutional maturity carry the potential for norm effectiveness over time, though the elusiveness of AP mines for an enforcement regime significantly detracts from immediate prospects of widespread and robust compliance. However, it would be premature to jump to the conclusion that since the AP mines regime is not fully enforceable and verifiable, it is fated to be a weak norm with low levels of compliance (or further, that the effort to ban mines itself is entirely misconceived).

The criticism that the norm cannot prevent the use of AP landmines (and is therefore not worthwhile) is both true and trivial. Laws prohibiting murder do not prevent murder from occurring, but no one suggests we therefore ought to do away with such laws. Immanuel Kant observed that laws are not for angels or devils, for the former need not be deterred by laws, while the latter will violate them regardless. Laws, for Kant, were aimed primarily at those in between who occasionally are tempted to cross the line, but who are susceptible to the variety of costs of social sanction, from shame to punishment. Similarly, it would be misguided, indeed, to measure the success of the landmines taboo by its immediate ability to prevent any use of AP mines by those most desperate to use them under any circumstances. To place such high demands on norms embodied in treaties is to misunderstand how social norms work in domestic and international society. Initially, it would be appropriate to gauge a successful level of compliance with the norm according to its contribution to ameliorating the problem it was designed to solve—26,000 casualties per year.[52] Without a norm prohibiting the use of AP mines, demining efforts would be but a Sisyphean exercise. A number of indications, analysed above, suggest that over time it is not at all impossible or even improbable that the AP mines taboo has the capacity to function in such a way as to contribute meaningfully to a decrease in the tragedies wrought by landmines.

NOTES

An earlier version of this chapter appeared in *Canadian Foreign Policy* 5, 3 (Spring 1998).

1. See also Richard Price, 'Reversing the Gun Sights: Transnational Civil Society Targets Land Mines', *International Organization* (forthcoming).

2. Ann Florini, 'The Evolution of International Norms', *International Studies Quarterly* 40 (1996): 382–7.

3. Thomas Franck, *The Power of Legitimacy Among Nations* (New York: Oxford University Press, 1990), 184.

4. Stephen Krasner, 'Sovereignty, Regimes, and Human Rights', in Volker Rittberger, ed., *Regime Theory and International Relations* (Oxford: Clarendon Press, 1995), 141.

5. John G. Ruggie, *Multilateralism Matters: The Theory and Praxis of an Institutional Form* (New York: Columbia University Press, 1993).

6. Abraham Chayes and Antonia Handler Chayes, 'On Compliance', *International Organization* 47, 2 (Spring 1993): 177.

7. Anne-Marie Burley, 'Law Among Liberal States: Liberal Internationalism and the Act of State Doctrine', *Columbia Law Review* 92, 8 (Dec. 1992): 1907–96.

8. Florini, 'The Evolution of International Norms', 382.

9. Ronald Diebert, *Parchment, Printing and Hypermedia* (New York: Columbia University Press, 1997).

10. Martin van Creveld, *The Transformation of War* (New York: Free Press, 1991), 178.

11. Richard Price, *The Chemical Weapons Taboo* (Ithaca, NY: Cornell University Press, 1997).

12. US resistance to a ban is largely grounded in the Pentagon's view that the US has technological superiority in AP mines systems. A *New York Times* editorial tried to push the US to support the Ottawa Process by arguing that 'land mines are the poor man's weapon, offering no advantage to the high-tech American military.' See 'Banishing Land Mines', *New York Times*, 12 Aug. 1997. [http://www.nytimes.com/yr/mo/day/editorial/12tue2html]

13. Jeffrey Legro, 'Which Norms Matter? Revisiting the "Failure" of Internationalism', *International Organization* 51, 1 (Winter 1997): 35.

14. Price, *The Chemical Weapons Taboo*.

15. Robert McElroy, *Morality and American Foreign Policy* (Princeton, NJ: Princeton University Press, 1992), 177.

16. Legro, 'Which Norms Matter?', 34–5.

17. McElroy, *Morality and American Foreign Policy*, 177.

18. Franck, *The Power of Legitimacy*, 67.

19. Ibid., 54.

20. Ibid., 68–74.

21. For other examples of ambiguity, such as the Soviet violation of the ABM treaty with the Krasnoyarsk radar, see Chayes and Chayes, 'On Compliance', 188–92.

22. During treaty negotiations at Oslo the ICBL also mobilized support to reject a US proposal to define anti-handling devices placed 'near' an anti-tank mine,

a definition that would have opened a large loophole for continued deployment of AP mines.

23. This is not to argue that restrictions on weapons may not also be subject to political decisions at the highest levels, as evidenced by Jeffrey Legro's analysis of the norms against unrestricted submarine warfare, civilian bombing, and chemical warfare in World War II. See Legro, *Cooperation Under Fire* (Ithaca, NY: Cornell University Press, 1995). I simply argue that the additional potential source of restraint of not having adequate weapons on hand is not available to non-absolute taboos.

24. Franck, *The Power of Legitimacy*, 38.

25. Ibid., 24.

26. Ibid., 67.

27. See Oran Young, 'The Effectiveness of International Governance Systems', in Young, George Demko, and Kilaparti Ramakrishna, eds, *Global Environmental Change and International Governance* (Hanover, NH: University Press of New England, 1996), 238.

28. See, e.g., Jeffrey Checkel, 'International Norms and Domestic Politics: Bridging the Rationalist-Constructivist Divide', *European Journal of International Relations* 3, 4 (Dec. 1997): 473–95; Andrew Cortell and James Davis, 'How Do International Institutions Matter? The Domestic Impact of International Rules and Norms', *International Studies Quarterly* 40 (1996): 451–78; Neta Crawford, 'Decolonization as an International Norm: The Evolution of Practices, Arguments, and Beliefs', in Laura Reed and Carl Kaysen, eds, *Emerging Norms of Justified Intervention* (Cambridge, Mass.: American Academy of Arts and Sciences, 1993), 37–61; Audie Klotz, *Norms in International Relations: The Struggle Against Apartheid* (Ithaca, NY: Cornell University Press, 1995); Legro, 'Which Norms Matter?'.

29. Boutros Boutros-Ghali, 'The Land Mine Crisis: A Humanitarian Disaster', *Foreign Affairs* 73 (1994): 13.

30. Richard Price and Nina Tannenwald, 'Norms and Deterrence: The Nuclear and Chemical Weapons Taboos', in Peter Katzenstein, ed., *The Culture of National Security: Norms and Identity in World Politics* (New York: Columbia University Press, 1996), 114–52.

31. L.C. Green, *Essays on the Modern Law of War* (Dobbs Ferry: Transnational Publishers, 1985), 173.

32. US Congress, Senate, *United States Policy Toward Iraq*, Hearing before the Committee on Foreign Relations, 101st Cong., 2nd sess., 15 June 1990, 51.

33. Thus, in proffering 'duration' as an indicator of the robustness of norms, Legro, 'Which Norms Matter?', 34, is careful to define it not simply in terms of 'how long the rules have been in effect' but also 'how they weather challenges to their prohibitions'.

34. Friedrich Kratochwil and John G. Ruggie, 'International Organization: A State of the Art on the Art of the State', *International Organization* 40 (1986): 768.

35. Thomas Risse-Kappen and Kathryn Sikkink, 'The Socialization of Human Rights Norms into Domestic Practices: Introduction', unpublished manuscript; McElroy, *Morality and American Foreign Policy.*

36. Mervyn Frost, *Ethics in International Relations: A Constitutive Theory* (Cambridge: Cambridge University Press, 1996), 105, regards 'a norm as settled where it is generally recognized that any argument denying the norm (or which appears to override the norm) requires special justification.'

37. Michel Foucault, *Discipline and Punish* (New York: Random House, 1979).

38. Steven Lee, *Morality, Prudence, and Nuclear Weapons* (Cambridge: Cambridge University Press, 1993), 101.

39. Franck, *The Power of Legitimacy*, 138, 163.

40. Ethan Nadelmann, 'Global Prohibition Regimes: The Evolution of Norms in International Society', *International Organization* 44, 4 (Autumn 1990): 525.

41. International Committee of the Red Cross, *Anti-Personnel Landmines: Friend or Foe?* (Geneva: ICRC, 1996), 33.

42. US Office of the Assistant Secretary of Defense (Public Affairs), Background Briefing on Landmine Policy, 23 Jan. 1997. [http://www.dtic.mil/defenselink/news/jan97/x011797_x0117 ldm.html]

43. White House, Press Briefing by Robert Bell, 17 Sept. 1997, 1, 4–5. [http://www.pub.whitehouse.gov/urires/12R?urn:pdi://oma.eop.gov.us/1997/9/18/16.text]

44. See 'Alliant Techsystems Awarded Army Contracts to propose Alternatives to Anti-Personnel Landmines', 15 Jan. 1998, 1. [http://biz/yahoo.com/prnews/980115/mn_alliant_1.html]

45. Stephen Biddle, Julia Klare, Ivan Oelrich, and Johnathan Wallis, *Landmine Arms Control* (Washington: Institute for Defense Analysis, May 1996), 28–30.

46. Ibid., 5.

47. Ibid., 3–4.

48. Ibid., 9.

49. Ibid., 12–21.

50. Ibid., 21–4.

51. *The Star* (Johannesburg), 5 Nov. 1996, 1.

52. On criteria for successful compliance, see Chayes and Chayes, 'On Compliance', 201–5; Young, 'The Effectiveness of International Governance Systems', 8–14.

CHAPTER 18

(RE)PRESENTING LANDMINES FROM PROTECTOR TO ENEMY: THE DISCURSIVE FRAMING OF A NEW MULTILATERALISM

Miguel de Larrinaga and Claire Turenne Sjolander

[T]he 'new multilateralism' will not come from piecemeal reform of old multilateral institutions but rather as part of a recomposition of civil society and political authority from the bottom up. . . . The reconstitution of civil society and political authority . . . would require a different sense of the polity, one that put emphasis on arousing capacities for collective action inspired by common purposes. . . . This would be the indispensable basis for a 'new multilateralism'.[1]

The Ottawa Process[2] leading to the signature of the Convention on the Prohibition of the Use, Stockpiling and Transfer of Anti-Personnel Mines and on Their Destruction has been portrayed as an example of the potential for movement towards a New Multilateralism.[3] At first glance, some of the arguments supporting this claim appear persuasive: middle-power countries, together with an international coalition of non-governmental organizations, were quickly able to generate momentum for an international ban on anti-personnel (AP) mines that bypassed traditional institutional structures and procedures. These claims to a New Multilateralism notwithstanding, the Ottawa conference in December 1997 showcased some of the most telling imagery of the 'old': for two days, a seemingly endless parade of (almost exclusively male) state representatives spoke eloquently about their governments' enthusiasm for the Convention and then walked across the corridor to sign for 'their' government on 'their' dotted line. Down the hall, some distance away, representatives of non-governmental organizations and 'ordinary' citizens, representing only themselves, affixed their signatures to a civil society treaty,[4] pledging to keep those states that had signed the 'real' Convention honest and to pressure those that had not into doing so. The end product of this New Multilateralism was another state treaty, although to be fair, one with many more signatories than originally anticipated and one about which many civil society actors were justifiably proud. Still, one can be forgiven for asking what is so very 'new' about the New Multilateralism?

In order to think about the 'newness' of the multilateralism embodied in the Ottawa Process and the period leading up to it, we need first to reflect on what would constitute a truly 'new' multilateralism. Such reflection is not merely a game of semantics; rather than signalling a change in or transformation of established practices, the way in which New Multilateralism is defined can serve to reinvigorate and restore the practices of existing multilateral structures, and thus reinforce the 'institutionalization and regulation of existing order'.[5] Making multilateralism more efficient, or more responsive, does not inherently make it 'new'. A truly new multilateralism (distinguished here from the New Multilateralism of the Ottawa Process by the use of lower-case text), we argue, is not to be found in the amelioration of existing structures, nor, indeed, in the emergence of their 'new and improved' variants, for such structures are founded on an a priori framing that allows for their existence. Multilateral institutions and structures cannot exist in the absence of a prior consensus on mandates, rules, procedures, and practices. It is rather in the *moment* of contestation over meanings, and the ability to *perceive* the moment as such, that transformation is possible and the new multilateralism can be found. These moments of contestation are revealed when a plurality of voices and practices are constituting themselves in relation to each other, and not in the reinforcement of a consensual order. In this sense, the new multilateralism is not a set of institutions and structures, but rather a moment that reveals antagonisms and thus highlights transformative potential.

In adopting a view of the new multilateralism as an explicitly transformative process rather than a project that seeks to change multilateral practices at the margins,[6] this chapter assesses the extent to which the Ottawa Process represents such a transformation of multilateral practices and structures. The assessment highlights the difficulties inherent in moving beyond existing conceptions of ('old') multilateralism. The theory and practice of multilateralism is inherently political, and in the absence of a serious questioning of how its discourse and practice have been articulated, the context in which multilateralism is anchored limits its transformative potential. In essence, while the global movement to ban landmines suggests avenues and practices that are potentially transformative, the Ottawa Process cannot in itself transcend the practices and discourses of multilateralism that find their roots in modernity. It is not through the simple addition of the moniker 'New' that the New Multilateralism portends transformation.

MULTILATERALISM: FROM REINVIGORATION TO TRANSFORMATION

During the past decade, there has been a resurgence of scholarly interest in multilateral practices and institutions as forms of global governance appropriate to the emerging New World Order.[7] In part, this renewed interest is intimately linked to the end of the Cold War. The conclusion of the super-power stalemate appeared to herald the arrival of an era of unlimited possibilities, at least in terms of those governance practices and structures managing international conflict and co-operation. Coupled with the acceleration of the economic and social processes linked to globalization, the end of the Cold War led to assessments that multilateral practices both *could* work and *would need* to work if the scope of contemporary global transformation was to be managed effectively. From this perspective, multilateralism needed to be reinvigorated because it could now work more efficiently (as a result of the end of superpower rivalry) and more effectively (since globalization effectively creates a need for multilateralism to circumscribe greater numbers of spheres of human activity).

Such understandings of multilateralism are derived explicitly from a perspective defined by the interstate system. On the one hand (in terms of peace and security issues), multilateralism focuses on 'relations among states through diplomatic channels or interstate organizations', while on the other (in terms of the management of the global economy), multilateralism 'refers to relations among the economic actors of civil society within a framework regulated by states and international organizations.'[8] Viewed through this prism, a New Multilateralism must necessarily focus on how international governance practices and structures can be modified to reflect more closely and more appropriately the interests and desires of a potentially greater number of states and key economic agents.[9]

The characterization of the Ottawa Process as a manifestation of the potential for a New Multilateralism is consistent with this attempt to redefine or broaden the practices of international governance. Highlighting 'the potential of a new form of multilateralism predicated on the use of emerging sources of diplomatic influence in the post-cold war era', the process is heralded for its success in 'harnessing . . . new sources of influence'.[10] These sources of influence, residing in '[i]nternational public opinion, transnational NGOs, and revolutions in telecommunications and the mass media' importantly 'serve to expand dramatically the "diplomatic tool-kit" available for use in lobbying decision-makers at state, regional, and global levels.'[11] The New Multilateralism within the context of the Ottawa Process, despite pointing to a greater openness in diplomatic practice, leaves unasked some fundamental questions, however. Who is harnessing the new sources of influence, and whose 'diplomatic tool-kit' is being enhanced? To what extent does this New Multilateralism represent a challenge to the existing practices of international governance, or, alternatively, to what extent does it provide certain states (in this case, middle powers) with new levers of influence to define the international agenda?

From the vantage point of diplomats, state managers, and some scholars, the Ottawa Process invariably represents a new series of multilateral practices. Viewed from the prism of the state, the New Multilateralism requires a different understanding of civil society, of the possibilities for coalition-building, and of the opportunities for public mobilization and rapid response created by new information technologies. There is much that is new in this interpretation of the Ottawa Process,[12] but the extent to which this 'newness' is potentially transformative remains in some doubt. This New Multilateralism does not necessarily or inevitably drive us to a new way of conceptualizing, or a new way of thinking about, the world. It is only in rethinking the world, however, that the possibilities for a new multilateralism can be imagined.

Multilateralism and the State

In positing a vantage point *from* the state, the New Multilateralism assumes an a priori position, that *of* the state, from which multilateralism is understood or given meaning. In this construction, the state becomes essentialized as the inevitable starting point or foundation for multilateralism. On the other hand, the imagination of a new multilateralism starts by positing a non-essentialized state, thereby de-centring multilateralism, putting into question the state as its inevitable starting point or foundation. More importantly, withdrawing the state as a foundational point allows us to see the process by which the state is itself constituted by the practices of Multilateralism. If the state has no inherent a priori position (or no prior ontological status), it must define itself by reference to what it is not, through the discourse and practices in which it participates. In taking the state as non-essentialized, the new multilateralism turns the old on its head; the state is a product, and maintains its privileged position as a result, of discourses and practices such as those of Multilateralism.

From such a perspective, the fact that the question of *whose* 'diplomatic tool-kit' is sidestepped is unsurprising. The state does not define the 'diplomatic tool-kit', but rather, the 'tool-kit' participates in defining what the state 'is'. From the vantage point of the state, transnational public opinion, non-governmental organizations, and new information technologies contribute tools to the diplomatic kit that can be chosen at random to enhance the effectiveness or efficiency of Multilateralism. In the absence of a particular vantage point, the state and the elements of the enhanced 'diplomatic tool-kit' lend meaning and identity to each other, that is, each is in part constituted by what is exterior to, or outside of, itself.

Moving beyond the understanding of the state as the inevitable foundational point within Multilateralism thus raises the more significant question of the construction of meaning and identity. In eschewing an essentialist approach to multilateralism, meaning and identity are always relational—i.e., meaning and identity can never be fixed since there is no 'underlying principle [or *essence*] fixing—and hence—constituting the whole field of differences'.[13] From a non-essentialist perspective, meaning and identity are not intrinsic. Any identity—a subject, a structure, an institution, a concept—is always relational, never self-present or self-engendered, and thus is unstable and in constant need of reiteration. Meaning is constructed as *difference* in that what something *is* is relationally defined by what it *is not*. Meaning is in a perpetual process of being fixed through this exclusion and articulates this exclusion through a series of dichotomies in which the first term is privileged with respect to the second (e.g., man/woman, order/anarchy, state/non-state, white/black).[14] This play of constant identity construction through difference, and the attempt to limit this play or to create a vantage point from which to fix meaning, we will call *discourse*.[15]

What does this insight contribute to our understanding of the new multilateralism as a potentially transformative process? If one ascribes to the concrete empirical practices of the Ottawa Process a system of meaning premised on the unproblematized vantage point of the state, the New Multilateralism can only reinforce existing practices. The transformative potential of the new multilateralism is effectively foreclosed, limiting itself to the expansion of the 'diplomatic tool-kit'. If, on the other hand, one acknowledges that these empirical practices have been constructed *as* the vantage point of the state—i.e., if one adopts a non-essentialist perspective—the entire terrain upon which the Ottawa Process was constructed becomes one where meanings are contested. This contestation over meanings creates an inherently political space, and understanding it reveals the inherently political character of the Ottawa Process. Only by opening up an analysis of the Ottawa Process to the political can we conceive of its transformative potential. This is the project of the new multilateralism.

From the unproblematized vantage point of the state, the success of the Ottawa Process as an exercise in democracy is illustrated by the broad consensus achieved between a large number of civil society actors and compliant states as to the essential nature of landmines and the steps to be taken to confront the problems they present. The inclusion of non-state actors in the Ottawa Process and the achievement of a consensus position on landmines become the definitive markers of the democratic nature of the 'People's Treaty'. In our view, this understanding of democracy significantly eclipses the political and thus veils the transformative dimension of the global movement to ban landmines. The democratic exercise is successful inasmuch as it permits the emergence of a rational consensus around the nature of landmines (landmines defined as a scourge against humanity). The construction of that consensus, we argue, is not the space in which the political takes place. Rather, the political is found in the delimitation of an arena, that is, in a prior distinction between what is 'reasonable' (the legitimate subject of politics) and what is not. This view of a circumscribed arena, where fundamental conflict and antagonism are excluded, permits us to rethink the democracy of the Ottawa Process, for the 'democratic' process takes place within an equally delimited arena. In this sense, democracy is an exchange among the converted, those who already participate in the dominant language games of an international community/consensus. Those who do not share in the consensus, who do not participate in the dominant language games, are deemed 'unreasonable' and are thus excluded from 'democratic' dialogue. From our perspective, however, the democratic and the political components of the global process to ban landmines are to be found in the contestation of meanings over landmines and their construction either as part of a state security discourse or as part of a humanitarian discourse. This antagonism 'opened up' political space and democratic possibilities. From the time the 'official' Ottawa Process was launched, based on a common understanding of landmines as a humanitarian scourge, political space and potentially transformative democratic possibilities were effectively foreclosed. The global movement to ban landmines illustrates some of the transformative potential of the new multilateralism, potential that is eroded as the movement becomes domesticated by the Ottawa Process and is brought into the orbit of existing state diplomatic practices.

DISCURSIVE FRAMING AND THE OTTAWA PROCESS

Landmines and the State Security Discourse

While the history of landmines can be traced back to the US Civil War, mines as they are known today were first developed in World War I to defend against tanks.[16] Paradoxically, as early as the US Civil War, military commanders 'on both sides of that conflict called the weapon an indiscriminate killer', one commander going so far as to characterize its use as 'murder, not war'.[17] Despite the suggestion of mines as indiscriminate instruments of murder at the time of their initial use, AP mines found their place within the arsenals of states as a legitimate weapon of war. This early questioning of their military utility did not prevent their later uncontested use. As with other weapon systems, AP mines became an artifact of the state security discourse framed around an essentialized notion of state sovereignty. Landmines were 'necessary' to the preservation of the state, and the possibility of their removal from state arsenals was conceived as a threat to the state. The extent to which landmines were thus constructed as central to the state security discourse resonated even during the Ottawa Process: 'What the proposed ban will do, of course, is deprive the United States of an important weapon in our arsenal, made even more important by the continued shrinkage afflicting our armed forces. The fact is that the smaller your army, the more important landmines become to stop enemy forces and reinforce your positions.'[18]

How do we understand the articulation of the state security discourse? Framed around an essentialized notion of state sovereignty, mines were a part of the war machine that served to preserve the state from its enemies. Such a discourse is confined to a logic of *raison d'état, realpolitik,* or its more recent mutation into the realist concept of 'high politics'. The very idea of *raison d'état, realpolitik,* or 'high politics' embodies relations of subordination. Certain issues and concerns simply are defined as more important than others, and can be sacrificed if needed. As such, in the discourse framed around securing the existence of the sovereign state, the question of landmines, as, indeed, of other weapon systems, was effectively off limits to civil society. After all, the sovereign state provided the *possibility* of civil society in the first place, instituting a demarcation between civil society within the state and anarchy and contingency without.[19] Significantly, however, the discourse surrounding state sovereignty constrains our ability to conceive of alternative configurations of political space in modernity since 'states have managed to more or less monopolize our understanding of what political life is and where it occurs.'[20] The sovereign state, as the demarcation between civil society and anarchy, equally claims a monopoly on legitimate authority as well as on the instruments and use of force. The implications in terms of security are quite clear, in that '[t]he security of states dominates our understanding of what security can be, and who it can be for',[21] and effectively forecloses the capacity of civil society to contest or to question the weapons of war that secure its existence.

In a similar sense, the discourse surrounding state sovereignty is also profoundly gendered. Mirroring the Western conceptual dichotomies used to describe male/female differences,[22] the state security discourse rests on inherently masculinist and patriarchal assumptions.[23] Sovereign states are constructed as protectors, mandated as such through their legitimate authority over the instruments and use of force. The gendered construction of the state as masculine confers a position of privilege and hierarchy that reinforces the closing off of civil society contestation of the 'protector' role of the state and the instruments of force that make this role possible. In this double foreclosure of state sovereignty and gender, the state security discourse is depoliticized (inasmuch as it is not open to question). At the same time, this depoliticization is profoundly political in that it makes a (prior) distinction between what is a 'reasonable' subject of politics and what is not. The discourse around state sovereignty would present a tremendous challenge to the repoliticization of landmines by civil society.

The Construction of a Counter Discourse

For the question of landmines to be placed on the international agenda of states and civil society, the discourse surrounding state sovereignty/state security of necessity had to be challenged. This challenge was met by the formation of a counter discourse around landmines as a scourge against humanity. On the one hand, the constitution of a counter discourse providing an alternative construction to what landmines 'are' (a scourge against humanity rather than a legitimate instrument in the state's weapons arsenal) opened up political space through the creation of an antagonism between landmines as a scourge against humanity, an 'epidemic',[24] a 'pattern of excruciating human folly',[25] and landmines as a legitimate weapon with military utility supporting the state's role as protector. On the other hand, the articulation of a counter discourse was of necessity equally essentialized and depoliticized in order to confront effectively the essentialized and depoliticized state security discourse.[26] In other words, the only way to shift the terrain defining what landmines are was to reproduce or mimic the structure of the discourse surrounding state sovereignty/state security. In the discursive strategies[27] behind this new essentialization and depoliticization demarcating a new discursive terrain we find the political dimension of the Ottawa Process. This new essentialization and depoliticization redefine the boundaries of what is 'reasonable' and what is not; or of what is a legitimate subject of politics.

The question therefore becomes, what discursive strategies permit the construction of a new essentialized and depoliticized terrain framing the understanding of landmines? The first pillar of this counter discourse is to be found in the Cold War/post-Cold War dichotomy, which in many respects becomes the 'enabling' dichotomy upon which other markers of the discourse are constructed. The end of the Cold War provides an empirical justification, a historical 'grounding', for the redefinition of what landmines 'are'. Where the Cold War and the omnipresent nuclear threat were constructed as a period in which state military security was the primordial axis through which international relations were given meaning, the post-Cold War period appeared to lift the veil cast over the way wars are 'really' fought. In the construction of the counter discourse, important possibilities for new understanding and action are opened up by the end of the Cold War. Jody Williams argues that: '[w]ith the end of the Cold War and the accompanying perception of decreased nuclear threat, there has been growing attention to other weapons which have, in fact, inflicted far more casualties in the wars of the past few decades than nuclear and chemical weapons combined.'[28] During the Cold War, the nuclear fetish prevented the world from 'seeing war the way it is fought on the ground', and its end allowed the world to turn its attention to landmines, the 'legal legacy of the Cold War'.[29] Landmines were revealed as a 'weapon of mass destruction, albeit one moving in slow motion, taking one victim at a time'.[30]

If the end of the Cold War made transparent the reality of war on the ground and revealed the true devastation wrought by landmines,[31] it also created new possibilities in thought and action. 'During the Cold War,' Anita Parlow, a former consultant for Human Rights Watch, wrote in explaining how a global movement to ban landmines became possible, 'policy-makers viewed civilian deaths in wars of national liberation primarily in geopolitical terms. Under the moral mantle of anti-Communism, humanitarian questions were often confused with or subordinated to ideological considerations.'[32] Bob Lawson argues that the success of the Ottawa Process was made possible in part by the potential for new multilateral coalitions arising out of the post-Cold War era, a point similarly argued by Jessica Mathews.[33] Speaking at the opening of the Mine Action Forum, Canadian Minister of Foreign Affairs Lloyd Axworthy went further than this, arguing that the end of the Cold War had fundamentally changed the nature of security, and the question of security for whom:

> with the end of the Cold War, the threat of major conflicts between states has lessened. . . . Threats to human security—human rights abuses, inter-ethnic tension, poverty, environmental degradation and terrorism—have grown, fuelling recurring cycles of violence. Civilians are their primary victims. . . . Security is [now] found in the conditions of daily life . . . rather than primarily in the military strength of the state.[34]

As a historical marker, the contrast between Cold War and post-Cold War worlds becomes a central dichotomy in framing the counter discourse. Where the state security discourse depoliticized the use of landmines and foreclosed their questioning by civil society, the end of the Cold War enabled civil society's problematization of landmines as a legitimate weapon of war.[35] Where the ideological battleground of the Cold War became a prism through which the state security discourse was expressed, the end of the Cold War opened the possibility of perceiving humanitarian questions in non-ideological terms. Where the state security discourse legitimated states as the sole actors within multilateral practices and structures, the end of the Cold War offered up the potential for new international coalitions between state and non-state actors (the New Multilateralism). Finally, where the state security discourse of necessity defined security only in terms of states, the end of the Cold War created the space to define security in terms of humanity—and thus, the space to identify threats to humanity.

Axworthy's interpretation of the effects of the post-Cold War era is particularly illustrative in this regard. He argues, as cited above, that security is now to be found in the conditions of daily life rather than in the military strength of states. Daily life is now to be understood as part of the 'security' umbrella, which, during the Cold War, had only been about the security of states in military terms. In framing the question of security in this manner, Axworthy is signalling that the issue of landmines falls under a broader security rubric, one he characterizes as 'human security'. Parallels can be drawn between Axworthy's reference to human security and those authors who have sought to broaden the traditional application of the concept of security. For example, within the environmental sphere, the use of the security discourse to bring political attention to environmental problems presents the argument that, by broadening the notion of security to include environmental threats, it is possible to engender increased domestic support for environmental issues, as well as international support through increased co-operation between nations. In this sense, the notion of environmental security attempts to distance itself from traditional notions of national security by claiming to be a positive and inclusive concept.[36] Human security (and landmines as an important threat to that security) similarly claims to be a positive and inclusive concept around which it is possible to engender domestic and international support and increase the possibility for international co-operation.

As Simon Dalby has argued within the context of environmental issues, however, '[s]imply tacking on "ecological" or "common" or "sustainable" may not be enough to shift the focus away from . . . the practices of security as imposed force.'[37] What Dalby is pointing to here is the tendency for new issues to become *securitized* through an expansion of the boundaries of the state security discourse. The global movement to ban landmines does not reveal this tendency, however. It is not and, in fact, cannot be constructed around an expansion of the state security discourse, since landmines were already part of that discourse as an instrument of protection. Within the state security discourse, landmines 'protect national borders, military and economic assets, and fighting forces themselves.'[38] While

Axworthy suggests that the issue of landmines has been incorporated into a broadened notion of security (human security) in which the conditions of daily life are security issues, the contrary process to securitization is observable here; landmines are being *humanitarianized*.[39] From a non-essentialist perspective, landmines migrate from being off limits in terms of the state security discourse to being constructed as a legitimate concern for civil society—a humanitarian issue.

The end of the Cold War enables landmines to be humanitarianized, or essentialized as a humanitarian issue, in the framing of the counter discourse. In the construction of this discourse, an 'ideological veil' has been lifted in the post-Cold War world, and landmines can now be seen for what they truly are, or are in their essence—'a scourge against humanity'. The identification of the 'true' nature of landmines is made by humanitarian NGOs working on the ground assisting victims. Landmines are recast as a humanitarian concern, a process that depoliticizes them inasmuch as the humanitarian crisis they pose becomes increasingly unquestioned. The positing of the Cold War/post-Cold War dichotomy opens up the possibility of 'seeing' the 'true' nature of war, and by extension, of landmines, and also enables a contestation over the meaning of landmines around a state security/humanitarian scourge dichotomy. A series of books detailing the human cost of landmines are published, including: *Landmines in Cambodia: The Coward's War* (1991), *Landmines: A Deadly Legacy* (1993), *Land Mines in Angola* (1993), *Violent Deeds Live On: Land Mines in Somalia and Somaliland* (1993), *Land Mines in Mozambique* (1994), and *After the Guns Fall Silent: The Enduring Legacy of Landmines* (1995), among many others over the same time period. Each one confirms the 'true' nature of landmines as a scourge against humanity, detailing the havoc wreaked by these weapons with innumerable statistical tables and analyses.

The process of recasting the 'true' nature of landmines is apparent in these texts. A contestation over meanings is evident in the very barrage of these publications, each of which contributes to shifting the terrain underpinning the understanding of landmines from military utility to humanitarian law. Each participates in the redefinition of landmines as a humanitarian crisis, retroactively (re)writing the story of landmines as a humanitarian scourge. The engagement with the state security discourse is very sophisticated; constantly reiterated are two tests of humanitarian law—proportionality and discrimination—that landmines are said to fail. While military utility is acknowledged, the longer-term human costs are seen as far outweighing any security benefits.[40] The subordination of human costs to the legitimate authority of states as protectors is profoundly questioned. Also acknowledged is the implicit need to move the issue of landmines away from the terrain defined by the state security discourse; in practical political terms, to move the interstate discussion of landmines away from negotiations around their use. As Roberts and Williams argue, 'The military perspective is still accepted as the point of departure for negotiations on landmine use, and conventional military doctrine forms the framework of that discussion.'[41] In the absence of a new point of departure, traditional interstate negotiations could never achieve the objective of a total ban espoused by the NGO community. When a failure to reach agreement at the conference of the Convention on Certain Conventional Weapons (CCW) in October 1995 resulted in its postponement until January 1996, Rae McGrath of the Mines Advisory Group complained: 'It is a tragedy that you can bring together politicians and diplomats from all over the world because there is a humanitarian crisis, and that between these statesmen, they are unable to come to a statesmanlike decision for the sake of humanity.' McGrath went on to argue that 'This conference is a fiasco. It's unjust, it's immoral. You cannot horsetrade with people's lives. The situation here has been more like a market place than serious consideration of a massive humanitarian crisis.'[42] As the Geneva conference of the CCW began to collapse, governments were chided for 'dodging their humanitarian responsibility to create a comprehensive ban on the production, use and export of antipersonnel mines'.[43] In the absence of a new point of departure, negotiations framed in terms of landmine use could not be so fundamentally redefined as to discuss a landmine ban.

Expressions of frustration over the CCW process, however, also participate in defining an alternative point of departure. These expressions of frustration are not framed in terms of an evaluation of the military utility or non-utility of mines, but rather, in terms of the inability of states to deal with the seriousness of the humanitarian crisis caused by landmines. As we have argued earlier, however, the alternative point of departure to the military utility argument needs to be grounded as firmly as the state security discourse for the new meanings ascribed to landmines to become 'natural'. To counter successfully the profoundly embedded notion of landmines as part of the arsenals of states as protectors, landmines must be redefined in their very essence. Landmines as a humanitarian scourge seen through the prism of humanitarian law provides such a grounding, an alternative anchor to fix an alternative meaning. In the fixing of the alternative meaning, other discursive dichotomies are invoked to facilitate defining a new terrain. These dichotomies reinforce the state security (military utility)/humanitarian crisis dichotomy central to the new discursive framing.

As we have seen, the state security discourse is profoundly gendered, and gender again is central to the construction of the new discourse around

landmines as a humanitarian crisis. In moving landmines away from the
state security discourse, explicit symbols of the state's military 'responsibility' are eschewed in favour of those that unambiguously represent the
humanitarian scope of the crisis. Victims of landmines are primarily discussed in text and portrayed in images as civilians, and of those civilians,
most are women and children.[44] Boutros Boutros-Ghali, for example, highlights the civilian nature of the crisis by arguing that 'Each year more than
20,000 human beings are wounded or killed by landmines. Most of them
are not combatants: they are farmers, women and children.'[45] The struggle
to ban landmines is characterized as a fight for the children, where
'[p]rocrastination will mean more civilians dead, more limbs torn from
women and innocent children.'[46] Motivation for the struggle will be found
in the images of the young victims: 'May we be horrified and forever
haunted by the images of children torn apart, fitted with prostheses, or simply handicapped for life.'[47] Stephen Lewis, deputy executive director of
UNICEF, exclaims: 'What are the depths of dementia that we plumb which
permit such atrocities to be visited on our children, the most vulnerable
among us?'[48] The victims of landmines are portrayed as innocents, powerless in the face of a destructive weapon. 'This daily killing and maiming of
powerless peasant women and children around the globe generates casualty
totals that far exceed those of Chernobyl, Hiroshima and Nagasaki combined.'[49] The damage caused by the mines is portrayed graphically and
traumatically through firsthand accounts: 'I am still shaken by my vivid
memories of the women and children I watched taking their first laborious
steps on spindly wooden legs with attached shoes.'[50] Pictorial representations of landmine victims (in the posters, brochures, and films produced by
a variety of national campaigns to ban landmines) predominantly show
women and children. Even the promotional video for the Ottawa Process
produced by the Canadian Department of Foreign Affairs and
International Trade portrays three times as many women and children as
men as landmine victims, and its graphic opening sequence shows children
at play in a mined countryside, with tragic consequences.[51]

The irony, of course, is that the victims of landmines are *not* primarily
women and children. The World Health Organization estimates that 30 to
40 per cent of all landmine victims are women and children.[52] The
International Committee of the Red Cross estimates that non-combatants
(children, women, and elderly men) comprise 31 per cent of all mine victims.[53] Similar evidence is available through specific country studies; 25
per cent of mine victims in Afghanistan are women and children, 12 per
cent in Cambodia, 17 per cent in Mozambique, 32 per cent in Iraqi
Kurdistan, while 4 per cent of victims in Croatia and Bosnia-Herzegovina

are children.[54] This evidence, of course, does not prevent the occasional distortion of the truth where landmine victims are concerned: 'Approximately 90 per cent of the 26,000 landmine victims each year are women and children, many of whom were slain as they walked or worked the killing fields of their home countrysides.'[55] Is it that images of maimed women and children simply tell the story of landmines more poignantly?

The portrayal of victims of landmines as overwhelmingly women and children 'genders' the humanitarian counter discourse as feminine. The discourse around the state as protector is, on the one hand, destabilized by images and words revealing the extent to which it has failed to care for the 'protected'. On the other hand, the gendered nature of the state security discourse as protector is reinforced through the gendering of the counter discourse and the emphasis it places on the feminine. The characteristics of feminine dependency are used to define the victims, and it is precisely their passivity and vulnerability that is exaggerated in portraying them as victims. The state's characteristics of masculine autonomy (freedom, control, and heroics) in part legitimate the use of landmines, but at the same time they produce the (gendered feminine) victims and lead to an essentialized and gendered humanitarian discourse.

This period of the process in the global movement to ban landmines *is* the moment of the political, the moment of the new multilateralism. The political is revealed through the contestation over meaning (the military utility of landmines vs the humanitarian crisis, the masculine protector state vs the feminine victimized protected). The political is also found in the lengthy process and the multiple discursive strategies by which landmines are essentialized as a scourge against humanity. At this point, where a new meaning is in the process of being fixed, where there is an antagonistic contestation over meaning, political space is opened up and a plethora of actors (states, NGOs, international organizations, and individuals) espousing often contrary points of view struggle to delimit the terrain. The inherently political and democratic nature of the process is not found in the creation of a rational consensus, but rather in this struggle to define a new discourse around which such a consensus might later be forged. For the new multilateralism, this moment of the political permits 'an identification of the antagonisms generated within . . . [existing world] order'[56] and this contestation over meaning suggests a plurality of vantage points from which to view a multilateral world order. In terms of Multilateralism, however, the emerging discourse around the humanitarian crisis poses a potential problem. Particularly in its gendered representations, the humanitarian counter discourse posits a potentially anti-statist position, for the protector state is shown to be incapable of defending the lives and well-being of the protected. Further, this discourse suggests that the state and its practices are responsible for the scourge of landmines (through its legitimate authority over the instruments and use of force, and its implicit sanctioning of the production of landmines to fill state arsenals), thereby opening the door to the construction of the state as enemy.

The political antagonisms revealed during the lead-up to the Ottawa Process, pushed to their limits, risk marginalizing the state security discourse and, by extension, the state. Through this recasting, a new demarcation line is drawn between what is 'reasonable' and what is not. While the military utility of landmines, or their place within the state security discourse, continues to be espoused by certain states and civil society actors, this discourse is increasingly marginalized as the humanitarian discourse becomes increasingly essentialized. Positing landmines as legitimate weapons of war with military utility becomes an increasingly 'unreasonable' position.

> The military mind argues for self-destruct mechanisms—they are an obvious answer. But the humanitarian perspective knows that land which has self-exploded will, sensibly, not be used, thus ensuring that malnutrition rates remain unnecessarily high. The land will be used if starvation is close.
>
> The military mind argues legitimate use of marked and mapped minefields. The humanitarian perspective knows that marking and mapping does not keep out civilians if poverty forces them to use the land for survival.
>
> The military mind argues responsible use. The humanitarian who has worked in recent conflicts knows that for 95% of mine use this is the exception rather than the norm.[57]

The absolute certainty attributed to the humanitarian discourse (the humanitarian mind 'knows' where the military mind 'argues') is underpinned by an essentialized notion of what landmines are. It is only in the construction of an uncontested and essentialized image of landmines as a scourge against humanity, as unleashing a global humanitarian crisis, that the humanitarian mind can 'know' so definitively. The state security discourse, for its part, is delegitimated in this counter discourse—it is mere 'argument' (and thus, potentially, mere fiction). This rhetorical strategy illustrates the extent to which a shift in terrain has taken place. The humanitarian discourse begins to delimit the arena where rational consensus-building can occur. Following the contrast between military argument and humanitarian knowledge, Woodmansey goes on to argue: 'Until a meeting takes place which includes on an equal footing all the experts on this issue, militaries will continue to talk amongst themselves about military utility and legitimate use. The breakthrough will come when militaries accept that they are not the only experts on mines, and begin to listen. Then, and only then, a proper debate on the value of mines can begin.'[58] This 'proper debate', however, can only take place on the terrain delimited by the humanitarian discourse, at which point the debate is effectively over since the military utility of mines has been completely discounted as a point of departure.[59]

Eclipsing the Political: The (Re)turn of the State

The Ottawa Process, launched by Canadian Foreign Minister Lloyd Axworthy in early October 1996, finds itself within the new discursive terrain upon which a rational consensus based on the understanding of land-mines as a humanitarian problem can be forged. In explaining his decision to call for a treaty banning landmines by the end of 1997 (Axworthy's 'leap of faith'), Axworthy underscored the importance of the humanitarian and personal dimensions of the issue.

> I remember picking up one of these little landmines, these little butterfly mines that you hold in the palm of your hand. . . . I was looking at my son at the time and said, 'God, how many kids around the world at his age would automatically pick up this brightly-coloured little thing that looked like a toy and have their hand ripped off.' And I said this is just craziness. We're continuing to talk but we know this weapon no longer makes any sense.[60]

What is interesting here is that in announcing his decision to launch the Ottawa Process, Axworthy is acting as a state representative. Yet, as we have seen, the counter discourse surrounding landmines is potentially anti-statist—constructing the protector state as not only incapable of safe-guarding the lives and well-being of the protected, but as ultimately responsible for the production and use of landmines. Given this potentially anti-statist position and the obvious challenge it poses, how can Axworthy as a state representative take his 'leap of faith'? In broader terms, how can we understand this positioning of the state within the potentially anti-statist humanitarian counter discourse?

The description of Axworthy's moment of conversion provides some insight into the discursive strategies underlying the possibility of the state's positioning within the humanitarian discourse. Mines are objectified as the 'toy' lying in wait for a child's curiosity and, as such, are seen as no longer making sense. Landmines themselves become the problem, rather than the states or other actors that produce and use them. Landmines become the 'machine' acting against humanity, a dichotomy that not only reinforces the humanitarian discourse, but also effectively forecloses the question of state responsibility for their production and use. The humanitarian discourse through this 'man vs machine' dichotomy is reinforced by the emphasis given to the indiscriminate nature of landmines and their disproportional impact on women and children. Machines lie in wait for their human victims, incapable of telling the difference 'between the footfall of a soldier and that of an old woman gathering firewood. . . . Landmines recognize no cease-fire and, long after the fighting has stopped, they can maim or kill the children and grandchildren of the soldiers who laid them.'[61] Landmines, thus, are seen to be beyond the control of the soldier or the state—in effect, they simply 'are'. The problem becomes the mine, and the solution is to be found in its eradication. Through this discursive strategy, the state can position itself as part of the solution within the new terrain by treating the mines as 'other' or as the enemy. The indiscriminate 'nature' of landmines and their 'disproportionate' toll on civilian populations frame the terrain of the Ottawa Process, making it possible for states to dissociate themselves from the production and use of mines. They become 'weapons unconscionable even in the armouries of war, weapons whose mechanisms are metaphorically tattooed with the insignia "primarily for civilian targets".'[62]

Through this discursive strategy, the cause of the humanitarian crisis is to be found in the landmine itself. As such, '[a]nti-personnel landmines stand accused of practising blind terrorism.'[63] The machine is the author of the humanitarian crisis, against which humanity (and states) must stand united.[64] The landmine is completely dissociated from the state security discourse; it has become a terrorist agent, an 'irresponsible' entity counterposed to the 'responsible' state. Landmines are a 'blind weapon', a 'buried terror . . . the lethal detritus of 20th-century warfare', an 'infernal device'.[65] Under this new mantle of responsibility, through this ultimate (and profoundly political) act of depoliticization, the state can resume its traditional role in the New Multilateralism through the eclipsing of its responsibility in the production and use of landmines.

The speeches and accolades of state representatives showcased during the Ottawa treaty-signing conference in December 1997 confirmed the extent to which this depoliticization had taken place and landmines themselves had been objectified as the enemy. The Tanzanian Minister for Foreign Affairs commented on the moral obligation incumbent on all states to 'get rid of the scourge of this indiscriminate weapon'.[66] For the Slovak Republic's Foreign Minister, the indiscriminate nature of the weapon inevitably motivated action: 'This scourge threatens the lives and livelihood of innocent and defenceless civilian populations, placing civilians in direct and mortal danger, killing or maiming hundreds of them every day.'[67] The British Secretary of State for International Development, Clare Short, argued that 'Landmines have impeded rehabilitation and development after cruel and destructive wars' and thus the international community must act.[68] José Thomaz Nonô, Brazilian member of Parliament and president of the Committee to Promote Respect for International Humanitarian Law, began his speech simply by pointing to the essential nature of landmines: 'Landmines are a terrible evil.'[69] For the representative from Malta, the Ottawa Convention represented an important breakthrough, 'a crucial step towards bringing this scourge to an end . . . the final blow to this "invisible enemy" that kills innocent civilians everyday and robs people of their means of livelihood.'[70] Even among non-signatories, there is a 'shared interest in a world free of landmines'.[71] Despite the radical potential of the counter discourse to destabilize the state within a new multilateralism, the essentialization of landmines as an inherently indiscriminate weapon, a humanitarian scourge lying in wait for innocent women and children, effectively facilitates the positioning of the state within the New Multilateralism. From the perspective of NGO activists, the signing of the Ottawa Convention as a state convention is coincident with the political imagery of the sovereign state; while the counter discourse might suggest a more radical project, the outlines of such a project are difficult to apprehend in a multilateral world of states.

For Richard Gwyn, writing in the *Toronto Star*, 'The paradox is that global human security can only be achieved when one of the old-style nation-states, such as Canada, exercise political will and their diplomatic contacts for the sake of a cause', despite the energies given over to the global movement to ban landmines by NGOs.[72] From a non-essentialist perspective, Gwyn's paradox is not paradoxical at all; the New Multilateralism as a series of practices is understood through the prism of the state.[73] It *is* about old-style nation-states and their diplomatic practices, however more efficient their diplomacy might be in an era of broadly based coalition formation and new information technologies. As Lloyd Axworthy argued in his address to the opening of the Mine Action Forum, 'I speak for my own government, and others as well, to tell you that . . . we have used all the tools of international diplomacy—bilateral meetings and negotiations, *démarche* by ambassadors, phone calls by the Prime Minister to his counterparts—to produce the text of the convention and to build support for it within the community of nations.'[74] The 'diplomatic tool-kit' may be enhanced, but it remains firmly in the hands of the state.

CONCLUSION

We opened this discussion of the Ottawa Process by asking what was so very 'new' about the New Multilateralism? The answer cannot be categorical. Seen from the vantage point of the state, the 'politics' of the Ottawa Process—that period of interstate diplomacy and NGO lobbying between October 1996 and December 1997—is characterized by a more efficient and effective application of the 'tools' of the 'diplomatic trade'. Middle-power states expand their diplomatic leverage through coalition-building with civil society groups and rapid communication facilitated by new information technologies. Founded on an essentialized notion of landmines, the Ottawa Process as an example of the New Multilateralism holds no transformative lessons that can be applied to other policy issues. If landmines are, in their very being, a scourge against humanity, the process is inherently driven by the issue. An assessment of the applicability of the Ottawa Process to other issue-areas is reduced to evaluating the transferability of the consensus-building strategies of a more efficient and effective New Multilateralism. The politics of the Ottawa Process is possible, feasible, and reasonable due to the essential nature of the landmines themselves. The terrain of the Ottawa Process, however, is not the terrain of the 'political' in the global movement to ban landmines. In an important sense, the launching of the Ottawa Process inserts itself into a pre-delimited terrain, a terrain circumscribing what is 'reasonable' and what is 'unreasonable'. We are not advocating here that such a distinction should not be made. In fact, a distinction between the reasonable and unreasonable is *always* made, since it is inherently constitutive of the political, and thus has far-reaching implications that must be recognized.[75]

From a non-essentialist perspective, the global movement to ban landmines is seen in broader terms. The political is found in the contestation over meaning and in the discursive strategies that attempt to fix meaning. As we have argued earlier, at the point at which meaning is in the process of being fixed through an antagonistic contestation, political space is created through the struggle to delimit a new terrain. It is in the *moment* of contestation over meanings and the ability to *perceive* the moment as such that transformation is possible and the new multilateralism can be found. The new multilateralism is not to be found in the

efficiency and effectiveness of the consensus-building strategies that characterized the Ottawa Process, but rather in the ability to recognize the
prior moments of contestation around, and the attempts to fix, the meaning of landmines. In this sense, the new multilateralism is not a set of
institutions and structures that can become 'new and improved', but
rather a moment that reveals antagonisms and thus highlights transformative potential. The political and democratic nature of the Ottawa
Process is thus to be found in the struggles—and years—leading up to its
'official' launching. This inherently political and democratic moment,
however, is eventually brought back into the orbit of the imagination of
the sovereign state. Our examination of the global movement to ban landmines highlights the difficulties inherent in moving beyond existing practices of Multilateralism, constrained by particular political imaginations
constructed around the discourse of the sovereign state. In late modernity,
the sovereign state continues to fix 'an account of where politics occurs,
and what political life itself can be'.[76]

In revealing the New Multilateralism as discursively constructed practice premised on these political imaginations, however, the New
Multilateralism itself is put at risk. New political imaginations become possible despite the entrenched character of the old. What this analysis does
reveal are glimpses of different senses of the polity, which serve continuously to problematize these political imaginations and, at moments, to
effect change in the face of the late-modern human condition.

> For it must be cried out, at a time when some have the audacity to neo-
> evangelize in the name of the ideal of a liberal democracy that has finally
> realized itself as the ideal of human history: never have violence, inequal-
> ity, exclusion, famine, and thus economic oppression affected as many
> human beings in the history of the earth and of humanity. Instead of
> singing the advent of the ideal of liberal democracy and of the capitalist
> market in the euphoria of the end of history, instead of celebrating the
> 'end of ideologies' and the end of the great emancipatory discourses, let us
> never neglect this obvious macroscopic fact, made up of innumerable sin-
> gular sites of suffering: no degree of progress allows one to ignore that
> never before, in absolute figures, never have so many men, women, and
> children been subjugated, starved, or exterminated on the earth.[77]

This ethos, we argue, should infuse the new multilateralism, just as it was
this ethos that motivated the moment of the political in the global movement to ban landmines.

NOTES

An earlier version of this chapter appeared in *Canadian Foreign Policy* 5, 3 (Spring 1998).

The authors would like to thank Caroline Andrew, David Black, Wayne Cox, Michael Dolan, Marc Doucet, Heather Smith, and two anonymous reviewers for their comments on an earlier draft of this chapter.

1. Robert W. Cox, 'Reconsiderations', in Cox, ed., *The New Realism: Perspectives on Multilateralism and World Order* (New York: United Nations University Press, 1997), 253, 258–9.
2. While there is some debate as to when the Ottawa Process was launched, we will delineate it as the period between Lloyd Axworthy's call for a treaty in October 1996 and the Convention signing in December 1997.
3. Bob Lawson, 'Towards a New Multilateralism: Canada and the Landmine Ban', *Behind the Headlines* 54, 4 (Summer 1997). Where New Multilateralism is capitalized in the text, we refer to the relatively unproblematized notion of a renewed multilateralism, which, as we will see, only reinforces existing practices and norms. As with existing Multilateralism (again capitalized), New Multilateralism, regardless of the number or variety of participants, strengthens the voice of state authority. In contrast, the new multilateralism (in lowercase text) emphasizes a multiplicity of voices and practices both inside and outside of state-centric discourses.
4. Interestingly, the Program and Mine Action Forum Roundtable Agenda provided to delegates attending the Ottawa conference in December 1997 makes no mention of this 'People's Treaty' event, while specifying the exact time of the opening of the state Convention to signature. Reinforcing the distinction between the Ottawa Convention and the People's Treaty, Lloyd Axworthy signed both: Axworthy as 'state representative' and Axworthy as 'ordinary citizen'.
5. Robert W. Cox, 'Multilateralism and world order', *Review of International Studies* 16 (1992): 177.
6. In contradistinction to the view of multilateralism as the insitutionalization and regulation of existing order, a transformative view of multilateralism 'proceeds to an identification of the antagonisms generated within . . . [existing world] order which could develop into turning points for structural transformation.' Ibid.
7. For early statements of this renewed interest, see, e.g., Robert O. Keohane, 'Multilateralism: An Agenda for Research', *International Journal* 45 (Autumn 1990), as well as the Summer 1992 issue of *International Organization* devoted to a symposium on multilateralism.
8. Cox, 'Multilateralism and world order', 162.

9. The theoretical origins of this post-Cold War focus on multilateralism can be found in the *rapprochement* between the neo-realists and the neo-liberal institutionalists during the 1980s. A synthesis of these two schools, based on a 'shared "rationalist" research programme, a conception of science, a shared willingness to operate on the premise of anarchy . . . and to investigate the evolution of co-operation and whether institutions matter' became the 'research programme of the 1980s' and opened the possibility for the two dominant approaches to American international relations scholarship to investigate multilateralism seriously. See Ole Weaver, 'The rise and fall of the inter-paradigm debate', in Steve Smith, Ken Booth, and Marysia Zalewski, eds, *International Theory: Positivism and Beyond* (Cambridge: Cambridge University Press, 1996), 163.

10. Lawson, 'Towards a New Multilateralism', 22–3.

11. Ibid., 22, 23.

12. Peter Herby, arms control adviser in the legal division of the International Committee of the Red Cross (ICRC), has raised the question of the 'newness' of the Ottawa Process, even with respect to other international bans on weapons. Speaking on the development of international humanitarian law during the Ottawa Mine Action Forum on 3 December 1997, Herby argued that the Ottawa Process in fact represented a return to traditional international humanitarian law.

13. Ernesto Laclau and Chantal Mouffe, *Hegemony and Socialist Strategy: Towards a Radical Democratic Politics* (London: Verso, 1985), 111.

14. See Barbara Johnson, 'Introduction', in Jacques Derrida, *Dissemination*, trans. Barbara Johnson (Chicago: University of Chicago Press, 1981), viii. Johnson explains: 'Western thought . . . says Derrida, has always been structured in terms of dichotomies or polarities: good vs. evil, being vs. nothingness, presence vs. absence, truth vs. error, identity vs. difference. . . . The second term in each pair is considered the negative, corrupt, undesirable version of the first, a fall away from it. Hence, absence is the lack of presence, evil is the fall from good.' The construction of dichotomies is characteristic of Western metaphysics and finds its apogee in modernity.

15. By discourse, we understand 'an *articulatory practice* which constitutes and organizes social relations'. In this sense, discourse eschews the dichotomy between the 'ideal' and the 'real'; discourse has an intrinsic materiality in that the 'real' is always contingent on the interpretation given to it. See Laclau and Mouffe, *Hegemony and Socialist Strategy*, 96.

　　In apprehending multilateralism in this way, therefore, we are not denying the existence of a concrete and palpable reality. Multilateralism as a set of practices is indissociable from the meanings we ascribe to them. Discourse is neither completely ephemeral (in the sense that an assigned meaning can easily be replaced at will by another), nor is it rigidly structured (in the sense that meaning is so completely anchored in a fixed relational structure that change is inconceivable).

16. Jody Williams, 'Landmines and measures to eliminate them', *International Review of the Red Cross* 307 (July-Aug. 1995): 376; Jody Williams, 'A Realistic Utopia', *CCW News* 3 (4 Oct. 1995): 2.

17. Williams, 'A Realistic Utopia', 2.

18. 'Moral force and landmines', *Washington Times*, 20 Aug. 1997.

19. As R.B.J. Walker has argued, sovereignty 'suggests a spatial demarcation between those places in which the attainment of universal principles might be possible, and those in which they are not.' It implies a demarcation between 'the progress towards universalizing standards possible within states and the mere contingency characterizing relations between them.' Walker, 'Security, Sovereignty, and the Challenge of World Politics', *Alternatives* 15 (1990): 10–12. See also R.B.J. Walker, *Inside/Outside: International Relations as Political Theory* (Cambridge: Cambridge University Press, 1993).

20. Walker, 'Security, Sovereignty, and the Challenge of World Politics', 6.

21. Ibid.

22. These dichotomies include, for example, 'objectivity vs. subjectivity, reason vs. emotion, culture vs. nature, self vs. other or autonomy vs. relatedness, knowing vs. being and public vs. private'. It is important to underline, as well, that these conceptual dichotomies refer to an understanding of masculinity and femininity as a 'set of socially constructed categories that vary in time and place rather than to biological determinants'. J. Ann Tickner, 'Hans Morgenthau's Principles of Political Realism: A Feminist Reformulation', in James Der Derian, ed., *International Theory: Critical Investigation* (New York: New York University Press, 1995), 54–5.

23. The work of V. Spike Peterson is particularly useful in understanding the gendered construction of the state and of state sovereignty. See Peterson, 'Security and Sovereign States: What Is at Stake in Taking Feminism Seriously?', in V. Spike Peterson, ed., *Gendered States: Feminist (Re)Visions of International Relations Theory* (Boulder, Colo.: Lynne Rienner, 1992). On the way in which sovereignty as a gendered construct manifests itself at the level of both the individual and state, see Rebecca Grant, 'The source of gender bias in international relations theory', in Grant and Kathleen Newland, eds, *Gender and International Relations* (Bloomington: Indiana University Press, 1991). For how the militarized discourse around state security is inherently gendered, see V. Spike Peterson, 'Seeing World Order Beyond the Gendered Order of Global Hierarchies', in Cox, ed., *The New Realism*.

24. Jean Chrétien, 'Notes for an Address by Prime Minister Jean Chrétien on the occasion of the Treaty-Signing Conference for the Global Ban on

Anti-Personnel Landmines', Ottawa, Office of the Prime Minister, 3 Dec. 1997.

25. Stephen Lewis, 'Ottawa Process II—An Agenda for Mine Action', Office of the Executive Director, UNICEF, 2 Dec. 1997.

26. Richard Ashley has argued on this point: 'In modern discourse of politics, importantly, only those contributions that replicate this interpretive attitude and invoke a sovereign voice as an absolute ground can be taken seriously.' Ashley, 'Untying the Sovereign State: A Double Reading of the Anarchy Problematique', *Millennium: Journal of International Studies* 17, 2 (1988): 230.

27. By use of the word 'strategy' we are not suggesting that a particular decision was taken at a particular point in time by a particular individual or group. Rather, the 'strategy' is the cumulative result of a 'myriad of daily decisions and actions' at myriad levels that gain their coherence retroactively. Jef Huysmans, 'Securitising Europe, Europeanising Security, the Construction of Migration in the EU', paper prepared for the conference, 'Defining and Projecting Europe's Identity: Issues and Trade Offs', Graduate Institute of International Studies, Geneva, 21–2 Mar. 1996.

28. Williams, 'Landmines and measures to eliminate them', 375.

29. Jody Williams, public lecture, Carleton University, Ottawa, 3 Nov. 1997.

30. Lawson, 'Towards a New Multilateralism', 18.

31. Over 600,000 civilians are said to have been maimed by landmines during the past 25 years; 26,000 civilian casualties are attributed to landmines every year. See Jean-Baptiste Richardier and Philippe Chabasse, 'For the Banning of Massacres in Times of Peace', in Handicap International, *Antipersonnel Landmines: For the Banning of Massacres of Civilians in Time of Peace* (Paris, 1997), 11; Shawn Roberts and Jody Williams, *After the Guns Fall Silent: The Enduring Legacy of Landmines* (Washington: Vietnam Veterans of America Foundation, 1995), 3.

32. Anita Parlow, 'Toward a global ban on landmines', *International Review of the Red Cross* 307 (July–Aug. 1995): 391.

33. Lawson, 'Towards a New Multilateralism', 22; Jessica Tuchman Mathews, 'The new, private order', *Washington Post*, 21 Jan. 1997, A11.

34. Lloyd Axworthy, 'An Address by the Honourable Lloyd Axworthy, Minister of Foreign Affairs, to the opening of the Mine Action Forum', Ottawa, DFAIT, 2 Dec. 1997, 2.

35. Lawson, 'Towards a New Multilateralism', 18. Lawson points out that it was not until the end of the Cold War that ICRC war surgeons and NGO aid workers 'began to alert the world' to the tragedy of landmines.

36. As Michael Renner argues: 'While military security rests firmly on the competitive strength of individual countries at the direct expense of other nations, environmental security cannot be achieved unilaterally; it both requires and

nurtures more stable and cooperative relations among nations.' Renner, *National Security: The Economic and Environmental Dimensions*, Worldwatch Paper No. 89 (Washington: Worldwatch Institute, May 1989), 63. See also Jessica Tuchman Mathews, 'Redefining Security', *Foreign Affairs* 68, 2 (Spring 1989); Norman Myers, 'Environment and Security', *Foreign Policy* 74 (Spring 1989); Ian Rowlands, 'The Security Challenges of Global Environmental Change', *Washington Quarterly* 14, 1 (Winter 1991).

37. Simon Dalby, 'Security, Modernity, Ecology: The Dilemmas of Post-Cold War Security Discourse', *Alternatives* 17 (1992): 121.

38. Roberts and Williams, *After the Guns Fall Silent*, 4.

39. There is nothing in the post-Cold War world that makes the humanitarian-ization of certain questions inevitable. Arguably one of the most 'intrinsically' humanitarian issues, migration has been constructed as a security problem since the end of the Cold War, requiring closer monitoring and policing by states, i.e., requiring the deployment of state security apparatus. See, e.g., Jeff Huysmans, 'Migrants as a security problem: dangers of "securitizing" social issues', in Robert Miles and Deitrich Thranhardt, eds, *Migration and European Integration: The Dynamics of Inclusion and Exclusion* (London: Pinter, 1995). For a broader treatment of securitization, see Ole Weaver, 'Securitization and Desecuritization', in Ronnie D. Lipschutz, ed., *On Security* (New York: Columbia University Press, 1995).

40. Roberts and Williams write: 'Because the actual consequences of landmine use continue for decades after their initial deployment, their immediate battle-field utility is outweighed by the long-term costs to civilian populations.' *After the Guns Fall Silent*, 4.

41. Ibid.

42. 'CCW Conference: Unjust and Immoral', *CCW News* 6 (13 Oct. 1995): 2.

43. 'A moratorium on landmines', *Boston Sunday Globe*, 28 Jan. 1996, A30.

44. This is not to suggest that soldiers or men are never portrayed as landmine vic-tims. In the Canadian campaign to ban landmines, for example, peacekeepers were often depicted as victims to highlight the direct cost of landmines to Canadians. In so far as peacekeepers are gendered feminine (through their portrayal as supportive helpers, assisting and restoring communities), how-ever, the gendered nature of the counter discourse is strengthened.

45. 'Opening Excerpts . . .', *CCW News* 1 (27 Sept. 1995): 2.

46. 'How Many More Will It Take', *CCW News* 12 (3 May 1996): 1.

47. 'God will sort them out', *CCW News* 11 (30 Apr. 1996): 2.

48. Lewis, 'Ottawa Process II', 1.

49. Jack Dunfey, 'Ridding the World of Landmines', *Boston Globe*, 17 May 1996.

50. Ibid.

51. DFAIT, 'Ban Landmines: The Ottawa Process', video, 29 May 1997.

52. Faiz Kakar, *Direct and Indirect Consequences of Land Mines on Public Health* (Geneva: World Health Organization, July 1995). Victims in the WHO study are those who have suffered either physical or emotional trauma as a result of landmines.

53. ICRC, *The Worldwide Epidemic of Land Mine Injuries: The ICRC Health Oriented Approach* (Geneva: ICRC, Sept. 1995).

54. Roberts and Williams, *After the Guns Fall Silent*, 72, 161, 201, 235, 259. The methodologies and time frames employed in the various country studies are different, making more detailed comparisons impossible. Statistics for Croatia and Bosnia-Herzegovina do not distinguish between adult men and women.

55. Dunfey, 'Ridding the World of Landmines'.

56. Cox, 'Multilateralism and world order', 177.

57. Ian Woodmansey, 'Perspectives: Military, Yes; Humanitarian, No', *CCW News* 3 (4 Oct. 1995): 4. Woodmansey is a spokesperson for Oxfam UK and Ireland.

58. Ibid.

59. Interestingly, this definition of a new terrain for 'rational consensus' is mirrored in the evolution of the position of the ICRC. As John English has argued, the February 1996 ICRC report, *Anti-Personnel Landmines: Friend or Foe?*, which questioned the military utility of landmines, contradicted its January 1994 report. This earlier report of an ICRC meeting of military officers 'bluntly concluded that the military did not regard alternative systems [to AP mines] as being viable.' English goes on to state: 'Some military officials have attacked the conclusions of the 1996 report as unrepresentative of military thinking.' John English, 'The Land Mine Initiative: A Worthwhile Initiative?', paper presented at the conference, 'Worthwhile Initiatives? An Appraisal of Canadian "Mission Diplomacy" ', University of Waterloo, Waterloo, Ont., 6–7 Feb. 1998, 8.

60. Allan Thompson, 'How Canada hatched landmine ban', *Toronto Star*, 16 Sept. 1997, A23.

61. Human Rights Watch Arms Project, *Still Killing: Landmines in Southern Africa* (New York: Human Rights Watch, May 1997), 3.

62. Lewis, 'Ottawa Process II', 2.

63. 'Opening Excerpts . . .', *CCW News* 1 (27 Sept. 1995): 2.

64. The human vs machine dichotomy is not lost on opponents of the ban on landmines. The characterization of mines with deactivation mechanisms as 'smart' or the development of an 'advanced intelligent minefield' confers on these technologies human attributes that blur the dichotomy and recapture the possibility for the responsible use of AP mines within the orbit of the state

as protector. For a discussion of the US politics around a new generation of submunitions, see Tom Masland and John Barry, 'Buried Terror', *Newsweek*, 8 Apr. 1996, 24–7.

65. 'The Cry of Millions . . .', *CCW News* 2 (29 Sept. 1995): 3; Masland and Barry, 'Buried Terror', 24; Eric Margolis, 'We should ban infernal device', *Ottawa Sun*, 1 Aug. 1997.

66. Jakaya M. Kikwete, 'Statement by Honourable Jakaya M. Kikwete, MP, Minister for Foreign Affairs and International Co-operation, to the Landmines Signing Conference', Ottawa, 3 Dec. 1997, 2.

67. Zdenka Kramplová, 'The Address of the head of Delegation of the Slovak Republic to the International Conference on Antipersonnel Landmines', Ottawa, 2–4 Dec. 1997, 2.

68. Clare Short, 'Anti-personnel landmines: Speech by Ms. Short at Ottawa Conference', Ottawa, 3 Dec. 1997, 3.

69. José Thomaz Nonô, 'A Global Ban on Landmines: Parliamentarians and the Agenda for Mine Action', keynote speech by Mr José Thomaz Nonô (Brazil), President of the Committee to Promote Respect for International Humanitarian Law, Inter-Parliamentary Union, Ottawa, 3 Dec. 1997, 1.

70. Mark Anthony Micallef, 'A Global Ban on Landmines: Mine Action Forum', Embassy of Malta (Washington), Ottawa, 2–4 Dec. 1997, 4.

71. Kikwete, 'Statement', 2.

72. Richard Gwyn, 'Axworthy's measured diplomacy deserved Nobel', *Toronto Star*, 12 Oct. 1997, F3.

73. Particularly interesting, for example, was the retroactive (re)writing of the UN role in the global movement to ban landmines, exemplified symbolically by the overwhelming presence of UN representatives in the opening plenary of the December 1997 Mine Action Forum. The New Multilateralism of states naturally emphasizes the role of international institutions that reinforce existing state practices. For a discussion of how international organizations reify the role of states in the international arena, see Timothy Luke, 'Discourses of Disintegration, Texts of Transformation: Re-reading Realism in the New World Order', *Alternatives* 18 (1993).

74. Axworthy, 'Address to the Mine Action Forum', 3.

75. As Mouffe argues: 'If it is perfectly legitimate to make a distinction between the reasonable and the unreasonable, such an opposition has implications that must be acknowledged. Otherwise a specific configuration of practices and arrangements becomes naturalized and is put out of reach of critical inquiry. In a modern democracy, we should be able to question the very frontiers of reason and to put under scrutiny the claims to universality made in the name of rationality.' Chantal Mouffe, *The Return of the Political* (London: Verso, 1993), 143.

76. Walker, 'Security, Sovereignty, and the Challenge of World Politics', 14. Walker goes on to argue that state sovereignty 'denies the possibility of alternative arrangements on the ground that only through the state do we now seem capable of resolving all those contradictions—between universality and diversity, between space and time, between men and citizens, between Them and Us—that were once resolved by the subordinations and dominations of feudal hierarchy, monotheistic religion, and empire.'

77. Jacques Derrida, *Specters of Marx: The State of the Debt, the Work of Mourning, and the New International* (New York: Routledge, 1994), 85.

CHAPTER 19

NEGOTIATING IN THE OTTAWA PROCESS: THE NEW MULTILATERALISM

Michael Dolan and Chris Hunt

'Never before have representatives of civil society collaborated with governments so closely, and so effectively, to produce a treaty to outlaw a weapon.' —Senator Patrick Leahy[1]

'Thus, while the CD's task will take longer to accomplish than the Ottawa Process, the resulting treaty will, unlike the Ottawa Process, extend the reach of an APL ban to the major producers, stockpilers and exporters of AP mines .' —Ralph Earle[2]

'It is also clear that this is not the typical negotiation, where at the eleventh hour a deal is cut behind closed doors. That is not going to happen, nor should it.' —Senator Patrick Leahy[3]

'Of all branches of human endeavour, diplomacy is the most protean.' — Harold Nicolson[4]

In May 1996, a revised Protocol II on landmines was agreed to in Geneva at a Review Conference of the 1980 Convention on Certain Conventional Weapons (CCW).[5] The negotiations at this conference and the two that preceded it, as well as the Protocol itself, embodied much of what is considered to be traditional international relations. The negotiation process was almost exclusively interstate (although NGOs had already become well engaged with the issue). The negotiations were 'top-down' as the negotiations reflected the international power structure, with the US, Russia, and China leading the negotiations. State sovereignty reigned as decision-making was made on the basis of consensus. This allowed states to prevent the emergence of substantive changes to the status quo, which hamstrung those states that pushed for tangible reforms to the anaemic regulation of landmines in the 1980 Convention. That the revised Protocol II did little to satisfy the demands of those forces seeking reform, then, is not surprising given the constellation of forces at work within this setting of conventional interstate diplomacy. Under conventional thinking about traditional international relations, one might have expected that the signing of the revised Protocol II would have placed landmines on a diplomatic back-burner. Instead, there emerged a new negotiation process that split from the CCW negotiations and culminated eventually with the Ottawa Convention in December 1997. Rather than the meagre gruel of the revised Protocol, the Ottawa Convention is an outright ban on the production, stockpiling, transfer, and use of anti-personnel (AP) mines.

The topic of this chapter is understanding the multilateralism underpinning the Ottawa Process and how its negotiations competed with the parallel, existing CCW process and with the AP mine discussions in the Conference on Disarmament (CD) in the months prior to the Oslo Diplomatic Conference of September 1997. The Ottawa Process is inexplicable in the context of conventional international relations. Within certain parameters, the Ottawa Process was everything that the CCW process was not. The Ottawa Process was driven by a nexus of NGO and state. Rather than acting at the fringe of negotiations, the International Committee of Red Cross and the many national campaigns of the International Campaign to Ban Landmines were integral to the negotiation process; this was a 'bottom-up' process compared with the CCW process and that represented by the CD. The states pushing the ban campaign, moreover, were for the most part traditional followers rather than global leaders. Rather than following the lowest-common-denominator approach of diplomatic consensus, the pro-ban group formed a set of core positions that governments could accept or reject, thereby maintaining the integrity of the core itself. Finally, compared to the tortoise pace of the CCW process (and any ban treaty that would be negotiated within the CD), the Ottawa Process was a 'fast-track' phenomenon that began with the Ottawa Conference in October 1996 and ended in the signing of the treaty 14 months later.

As our focus is the negotiation process that led to the Ottawa Convention, the unusual nature of the negotiations presents certain analytical challenges. The grist of negotiations analysis usually includes the interests and position of the relevant actors, the bargaining power of those relevant actors, and the give and take of the bargaining process itself. With the ban on landmines, these factors are analysed in the context of the interrelationships between different international fora that discussed the AP mine issue. To make sense of the negotiations of the Ottawa Process, the chapter begins by providing an understanding of the global context in which they emerged. In the negotiations of the Ottawa Convention, pro-ban countries were able to withstand constant pressure and criticism from many quarters, especially the US government, to deviate from core positions. Under conventional international relations, the Ottawa Process could not have happened. We need to know not only how it could happen but the nature of the negotiation process itself.

The first section of the chapter provides a historical and theoretical contextualization of the Ottawa Process, arguing that the negotiations can be best understood by recognizing the contradictory intersection between 'bottom-up' and 'top-down' multilateral processes evident in the current global conjuncture. The following section illustrates this uneasy intersection of old and new forms of multilateral diplomacy through an analysis of the CCW review sessions and the attempt to co-opt the global AP mine ban into discussions of the CD. An examination of the complexities of the final treaty negotiations in Oslo further underscores this dialectical process.

THE SETTING: THE OLD AND NEW MULTILATERALISM

Current students of international relations (IR) appear to be condemned to live in interesting times. With such developments as the end of the bipolarity associated with the Cold War, the concomitant disintegration of the Soviet Union, the proliferation of ethnic nationalism, and the globalization of production and finance, 'reality, it seems, is not what it used to be in IR.'[6] Humanity is said to be on the threshold of a new reality, the onset of which requires a commensurate remoulding of our theoretical and conceptual ways of comprehending and viewing the social world.[7] Of more immediate relevance to this chapter is, of course, how one is to understand, in both its historical and theoretical context, the multilateral negotiation process that led to the signing of the Convention on the Prohibition of the Use, Stockpiling, Production and Transfer of Anti-Personnel Mines and on their Destruction.

Multilateralism has different meanings for various theoretical perspectives. For realist scholars multilateralism is a cloak for the ulterior motives of states. It thus becomes a tool of states, where co-operation exists to the extent that it suits the major powers. For liberal-institutionalists, the ontological purview of IR is expanded by recognizing that states operate in an international community or society in which other actors become important. These actors cohere to develop institutions, rules, norms, and collective principles that form some degree of global governance, thereby mitigating the deleterious effects of the anarchic international system. In this manner, the scope for multilateralism is enlarged from the instrumentalism associated with the realist perspective. As Knight argues, however, liberal-institutionalism's conception of multilateralism is still very much grounded in a state-centric framework. The actions of elements of civil society serve to legitimate or delegitimate decisions made in state-centric multilateral institutions, rather than in any way transform the terrain of political sovereignty. Thus, for Knight, both liberal-institutionalism and realism conceptualize multilateralism in a top-down fashion, thereby obfuscating certain bottom-up elements.[8]

This 'bottom-up' element embodies the reconstitution of civil society, and is most glaringly manifest in the rise of new social movements, which are 'no longer willing to allow governments to act as exclusive agents on its behalf'. The International Campaign to Ban Landmines is one such social movement operating at both the national and global levels. The ICBL is very much issue-specific, though social movements may have global agendas or operate specific spatial scales. These new social movements challenge the notion that rights, obligations, and identity are most appropriately bound up with the nation-state. This, in turn, is a reflection of technological change and globalization. On the one hand, there is a sense that the world is becoming increasingly interconnected as a consequence of the transformative impact on localities of new forms of global production and the hypermobility of capital, and from developments in information technology and global communications. Decisions and activities in one part of the globe can come to have significant consequences in places quite distant from these actions. The state's ability to make decisions autonomously in relation to the global economy is now seriously in question.

On the other hand, a multitude of challenges to the nation-state emanates from below, from the very localities over which it has traditionally claimed sovereignty. Ethnic nationalism and the proliferation of NGOs and social movements attest to the fact that the state can no longer exclusively resolve all the contradictions inherent in society.[9] The nascent world system is therefore characterized by a 'highly decentralized, almost chaotic multicentric system (comprised of subnational and supranational "sovereignty-free" actors) . . . [that] is being forced to intersect with the relatively coherent and structured world of "sovereignty-bound" actors.'[10] This intersection is also being shaped by changes in the geopolitical terrain associated with the end of the superpower rivalry of the Cold War. Political space seems to have opened for small and middle powers to effect change in the international system, while the importance of regional political and economic institutions has increased.

The above discussion points towards a reconceptualization of multilateralism beyond the top-down, state-centric understandings of both realism and liberal-institutionalism and to the development of a 'new' multilateralism.[11] For Knight, this new multilateralism exists at the uneasy intersection of top-down and bottom-up multilateralism, where:

> in some issue areas some NGOs are effectively positioned at the table with states. They have also been included as major partners in some multilateral

conferences (e.g. the sustainable development conference in Rio de Janeiro, the Nairobi and Beijing conferences on women, the Vienna conference on human rights, and the population conference in Cairo). Also, some governments have begun to include backbench members into their delegations at the UN General Assembly sessions, while others have even included NGO representatives in some of their delegations at major multilateral conferences. And, more recently, NGOs have played a major role in helping the UN and other 'top-down' multilateral bodies deal with humanitarian crises, such as in Somalia and Rwanda.[12]

As Knight points out, however, this new multilateralism does not always embody satisfactory outcomes for civil society precisely because of this contradictory and ambiguous relationship between its top-down and bottom-up elements. In a similar vein, Robert Cox notes that multilateralism is highly 'schizophrenic' in that one part is situated in the present predicaments of the state system while another probes the social and political foundations of a future order.[13] Cox's critical IR perspective also points to the way in which the discursive meanings of multilateralism become important in shaping concrete material practices. This brings in an inherently normative aspect to the new multilateralism, in that it seeks to uncover whose voices are represented (or not) in international politics as well as revealing the nature of particular sites of struggle and contestation.

What are the implications of the foregoing analysis for our understanding of the multilateral negotiation process that successfully led to the Ottawa Convention? At one level, the Ottawa Process is said to be an exemplar of the 'new' multilateralism, 'an extraordinary exploration of new forms of multilateral diplomacy in the post-Cold War era'.[14] For Kofi Annan, Secretary-General of the United Nations, the 'fight against landmines has become a model of international co-operation and action',[15] and this proves that a 'coalition of governments, NGOs, international institutions and civil society can set a global agenda and effect change.'[16] Thus, amid the euphoria of the Ottawa Convention a seductive notion exists that this new multilateralism is particularly apposite for the current post-Cold War period, somehow qualitatively different from the old multilateralism that underpinned US hegemony and the geopolitical rivalries of the Cold War. The seductive allure of conceiving the process as heralding new multilateral forms of diplomacy lies, in part, on the middle power/civil society coalition, a partnership seemingly more inclusive, participatory, and egalitarian. Other features, such as the development of alternative diplomatic fora (outside of the UN's Conference on Disarmament and the CCW), the truncated time frame for negotiations, and the non-consensual agreement process, reinforce the innovative image of this open-ended diplomacy.[17] We concur that this multilateral process is certainly innovative in many respects. However, a more sober assessment of the multilateral negotiation process reveals somewhat more ambiguity than perhaps its supporters acknowledge. This ambiguity reflects this 'schizophrenic' nature of multilateralism in the contemporary era.

THEORIZING THE OTTAWA PROCESS

In light of this understanding of multilateralism, what are the implications for international negotiation, and the landmines negotiations, in particular? Similar developments earlier in the century appeared auspicious. Increasing democratization and the incipient League of Nations contrasted with the horrendous Great War and the secret treaties that engendered it. The postwar period ushered in an era of hope for a new way of doing things. Harold Nicolson, in 1933, took this new hope to task in his analysis of negotiations in the Paris Peace Conference. As an official in the British foreign office, Nicolson observed firsthand the conference, and years later he wrote about the conference's negotiation process. The value of the classic work is not to compare that conference with the Oslo Diplomatic Conference, but to use Nicolson's contrast of two partly implicit models of negotiation—the 'old' diplomacy and a 'new' diplomacy *à la* 1919. For brevity, the contrast between the two models can be illustrated with a series of dichotomized characteristics:[18]

Old Diplomacy	*New Diplomacy*
Professional	Amateur
Secret	Open
Undemocratic	Democratic
the few large states	the many small states
Bilateral	Multilateral
Positional	Principled
Pragmatic	Idealistic
Rational	Emotional
Compromise	No compromise

The old diplomacy for Nicolson was classic diplomacy as practised since the eighteenth century, and was the subject of an earlier book on the experiences of his father as a diplomat. Negotiation under this guise was practised by diplomats—experts in the ways of international affairs. Amateurs were heads of government who insisted on playing the role of diplomats: 'Nothing could be more fatal than the habit (the, at present, persistent and pernicious habit) of personal contact between the Statesmen of the World.'[19] Secrecy and autonomy from the dictates of emotional public opinion were essential for compromises to be reached between disparate positions. Secrecy and compromise were best achieved in bilateral or very small groups rather than in large, multilateral settings, such as international conferences. Negotiations reflected the power differences of the respective states; larger powers dominated bargaining with smaller powers. The positions brought to negotiation were not considered in terms of their intrinsic ethic, but their pragmatic, rational value for the state.

The 'new' diplomacy was the Wilsonian diplomacy of the postwar period. The catch-phrase was 'open covenants, openly arrived at'. Many blamed the war on the encumbering secret treaties negotiated by diplomats and did not wish to trust the making of the peace to this same diplomacy. The new diplomacy reflected the increasing democratization of the political process in previous decades. Rather than a factor to be managed if not ignored, as seen in the old diplomacy, public opinion was seen to be important as an influence on both foreign and local affairs. The new diplomacy reflected a sovereignty that rested in the people, not in the state. With emphasis on principles and democracy, small states would have as much influence as more powerful ones in international gatherings, indeed, this made multilateral conferences more attractive to the new diplomacy. Finally, the emphasis on idealism and ethical principles left negotiators little room for compromise.[20]

Relating these models to the landmines negotiations, some of the characteristics of the old and new diplomacy obviously are irrelevant, but aspects of the old diplomacy better reflect the CCW/CD process, while the Ottawa Process has certain aspects in common with Nicolson's new diplomacy. The CCW/CD process is a classic interstate negotiation process with state sovereignty protected by consensus 'voting'. The process is dominated by the large powers. Negotiating is dominated by pragmatic and rational military concerns. Compromise is seen as necessary if agreement is to be reached, although a clash of vital state interests can mean insubstantial agreements, stalemate, or possibly indefinite negotiating. In contrast, the Ottawa Process is seen as an alternative, more democratic method, one in which civil society is integrally involved in the negotiating. The 'amateurs' are the NGOs, although the importance of non-career diplomats, such as Canadian Foreign Minister Lloyd Axworthy, would seem to be in keeping with the model. Negotiating is based on ethical, specifically humanitarian, concerns. The movement was led by small and middle powers (although see below for the importance of middle powers for the Ottawa Process). Compromise is not a salient aspect of the Ottawa Process; governments either sign onto the ban, or they do not. No reservations, please.

Aligning the two negotiating processes with some of the dichotomous characteristics is problematic at best, and self-serving at worst. For instance, it is not clear that the Ottawa Process featured more principled bargaining than the CCW/CD process; it was perhaps more a clash of military principles versus humanitarian concerns. Professional diplomats were integral in both processes, and frequently they were the same people. Similarly, some delegations to both negotiations included representatives of NGOs. As for secrecy, an anecdote indicates the different negotiating styles of states and NGOs. After a potentially embarrassing corridor exchange between two state delegates was reported by the ICBL in its *CCW News* on 3 May 1996, one of the overheard parties rebuked the NGO, arguing that reporting the conversation broke negotiation etiquette and that no agreement could be reached if all private conversations were made public.

Finally, a word about NGOs, which of course are not part of Nicolson's models, and their relation to public opinion and the ban states, respectively.[21] The bottom-up nature of the Ottawa Process should not be taken to mean that spontaneous public opinion moved the ban treaty. The operative word is spontaneous; public support for banning landmines was assiduously sought after by NGOs. This view is neither surprising nor cynical. NGOs both reflected and formed public opinion. What is different about the Ottawa Process is that NGOs, and their capacity to form opinion, were allowed into the process by the core ban states. Indeed, it is not clear that NGOs were 'allowed into the process', in that NGOs were integrally involved in forming the core group of states in the first place. The relationship between the core states and NGOs, then, was a dialectical one. Each depended on the other in propagating the ban message.

We will use this updated view of the old and new diplomacies as our heuristic model to analyse the landmines negotiations processes. Our emphasis, however, is on understanding the Ottawa Process. We will comment on the CCW/CD process because it is a useful contrast to the Ottawa Process and, more importantly, the two are inextricably related to each other.

FROM THE CCW TO THE OTTAWA PROCESS AND THE CONFERENCE ON DISARMAMENT

The use of AP mines is restricted by international law in two ways: first, in terms of the customary laws of war that hold that weapons and warfare must be confined to military targets, and that their indiscriminate use on civilians is prohibited;[22] second, through the 1980 UN Convention on Conventional Weapons (CCW). Protocol II of the CCW deals specifically with landmines through its definition of a landmine, its prohibition against the use on civilians, the setting of rules of employment of landmines, and restrictions of certain types of mines. In this regard, the 1980 Convention only covered specific aspects of the *use* of landmines, with no provisions regulating the production, sale, or possession of these weapons. Moreover, the CCW did not apply to non-international conflicts and contained no compliance or verification procedures.[23] The apparent lack of respect shown for customary humanitarian norms in the context of warfare, the weak provisions of Protocol II of the CCW, and the fact that by the end of 1992 only 32 nations had consented to be bound by the landmines Protocol meant that the existing international regimes proved ineffective in the face of the growing landmines problem.[24]

This growing landmine crisis[25] was being well documented by those in the field, such as the ICRC, the Vietnam Veterans of America Foundation (VVAF), and Medico International (MI).[26] In November of 1991, the VVAF and MI agreed to launch a formal campaign of advocacy to bring together a global NGO movement to ban landmines. This laid the basis for the first NGO Conference on Landmines, held in London in October 1992, where the International Campaign to Ban Landmines (ICBL) took shape. A plethora of publications also emerged documenting the socio-economic and humanitarian costs associated with AP mines. For example, Physicians for Human Rights published *Landmines in Cambodia: The Coward's War* in 1991 and *Hidden Enemies: Landmines in Somalia* in 1992.

The international context for these civil society interventions in the landmines issue was the shifting global terrain ushered in by the end of the Cold War and the concomitant peacekeeping operations in regions historically caught between superpower rivalry and internal strife. As a legacy of the Cold War, landmines exacted untold damage on civilian populations in affected areas. National anti-landmine campaigns sprung up in both the countries of the West and those immediately affected by landmines. These national campaigns, and the ICBL of which they constituted, began to bring the issue of landmines to the attention of both the public and governments. In 1993, for example, Handicap International pressured the French government over its use of landmines. For Handicap International, Protocol II of the 1980 CCW represented a compromise between humanitarian and military needs that implicitly admitted the use of a weapon that it and the ICBL considered illegal under existing international law.[27] This prompted the French government to request the UN Secretary-General to convene a Review Conference of the CCW. After 15 years of ineffectiveness, 44 countries, together with the ICBL and other NGOs, met in Vienna between 25 September and 13 October 1995 to strengthen the existing international landmine regime.

A short assessment of the Vienna conference was that it was a failure. The Review Conference failed to reach a consensus and agreed to suspend proceedings until January 1996. The major sticking-points concerned primarily technical issues of verification, detectability, and scope, and issues relating to anti-handling devices and self-destructing mines.[28] The major obstructionist states were India, China, and Russia, though they were in part responding to specific proposals by the US and its allies to switch from so-called 'dumb' mines to 'smart' mines that self-destruct after a set period. Given differences in military technology between the developed and developing world, the terrain of the debate was primarily concerned with cost calculations of appropriate security needs, although humanitarian concerns were not wholly absent.

Salient from our theoretical viewpoint is the interpenetration of the aforementioned bottom-up elements of civil society into traditional or top-down multilateral fora. The ICBL and other NGOs representing landmine victims, human rights organizations, and environmental, religious, and medical groups addressed delegates at the Vienna conference, demanding an immediate ban.[29] Various national campaigns held days of action marking the opening of the Vienna conference. The ICBL carefully monitored the developments throughout the conference, publishing the 'good' and 'bad' lists of states with respect to their position on landmines. What is also significant is that a number of states (including Sweden, Norway, Germany, Mexico, Denmark, Austria, and Ireland) articulated the need for a total ban on landmines in their statements at the plenary sessions.[30] These pronouncements also reflected the small but growing number of unilateral declarations of states concerning an outright ban or export moratoria.[31] These declarations were themselves the product of the confluence of bottom-up forces within the state policy-making circles of many of these countries. This was the beginning of a pro-ban coalition that had a 'rolling snowball' effect of picking up additional supporters over the following months.[32]

However, the tone of the conference was one of an 'eventual' rather than an 'immediate' ban on landmines. This theme continued at the two subsequent review sessions held in January and May of 1996.[33] These negotiations were completed on 3 May with the revised Protocol II. The issues continued to be ones of a technical nature, contributing to a much weaker than anticipated amended Protocol, at least in relation to the recommendations of the earlier experts' meetings of 1994.[34] Particular improvements in the Protocol 'were a wider application of the regulations regarding landmines, restrictions on transfers, requirements for landmine detectability, inclusion of consultation and compliance procedures, greater protection for humanitarian workers, including humanitarian de-miners, provisions explaining who should be responsible for mine clearance, and a specific date for the next review conference.'[35] Despite these provisions, the revised Protocol was labelled a 'betrayal' by the ICBL for creating a definitional loophole (where dual-purpose mines are outside the Protocol), for not considering anti-tank mines with anti-handling devices, for legitimizing the use of remotely delivered (scatterable) mines, for encouraging the use, design, and production of 'smart' mines, for having weak compliance and verification measures, and, finally, for leaving individual states themselves to determine whether an 'internal' disturbance has become an internal conflict, and therefore subject to the Protocol.[36]

Despite the low expectations during the two review sessions in Geneva and the weak Protocol that emerged by the end, the ICBL was sufficiently encouraged by the nascent pro-ban movement to call for the initiation of a voluntary international regime aimed only at a humanitarian solution to the landmines crisis. This desire provided the foundation for three NGO/state meetings in the back rooms of Geneva, which met to discuss ways that governments and NGOs could work together to advance an international ban. Representatives of eight governments met with the members of the ICBL in January 1996.[37] The figure increased to 14 at the second meeting, hosted by the Quakers on opening night of the April session. By this time the Canadian government had reversed its landmine policy and had joined the maverick group of pro-ban states. Canadian officials hosted a third meeting to discuss the possible timing, range of participation, and agenda for an international strategy meeting to take place in Ottawa later that year.[38] At these meetings various themes emerged that would subsequently evolve into core tenets of the Ottawa Process: first, the need to highlight the debate around the military utility versus the humanitarian impact of AP mines in order to 'contribute to the development of new global norms with respect to landmines';[39] second, the importance of regional initiatives such as 'mine-free zones' and regional institutions; and third, the importance of educational actions designed to attract wider official and public interest in the AP mine campaign. Negotiation in the 'new diplomacy' was beginning to take shape.

The Canadian announcement of its intention to host a meeting in the autumn marks both the assumption of diplomatic leadership of the core group of pro-ban states by Canada and the formative beginnings of the

Ottawa Process. Other developments buttressed the Canadian initiative. Somewhat ironic, as it turns out, the announcement of a review of US policy on AP mines by the National Security Council and the Pentagon prompted other powers to reflect on their own landmines policies.[40] The results of this review reflected less of a hinted-at bold new policy than a rationalization of its position taken during the CCW Review Conference, which would form the basis of its negotiation position at Oslo. The policy included the elimination of 'dumb' mines except in Korea, and the continued use of 'smart' mines indefinitely until an international agreement was reached. The domestic debate within the US was raised with an open letter to President Clinton published in the *New York Times* (3 April) signed by 15 senior retired military officers, who questioned the military utility of landmines and urged the President to pursue a ban on landmines. Further unilateral declarations by states concerning the use, production, and transfer of AP mines during 1996 reinforced the growing global momentum for a comprehensive ban as states, NGOs, and various international organizations met in Ottawa on 3–5 October.

The first international strategy conference, 'Towards a Global Ban on AP Mines', brought together 50 states pledging their support for a total ban, along with 24 observer states. The most significant outcome of the conference was Canadian Minister of Foreign Affairs Axworthy's 'invitation' and 'challenge' to the participants to sign a treaty 'no later than the end of 1997' banning landmines. With this bold pronouncement, the Ottawa Process and the multilateral treaty negotiations were set in motion. The guide to these processes was also explicated at this Ottawa conference in the form of the Ottawa Declaration and the Chairman's Agenda for Action.

The Ottawa Declaration enshrined the call for 'the earliest possible conclusion of a legally-binding international agreement to ban anti-personnel mines', based on 'a recognition that the extreme humanitarian and socio-economic costs associated with the use of anti-personnel mines requires urgent action'.[41] The Agenda for Mine Action developed concrete steps to be undertaken by the international community, based on three interrelated themes of global action, regional action, and landmine clearance, mine awareness, and victim assistance. In terms of the treaty negotiation process, the first two planks of the agenda are more immediately germane to our discussion.

The global action plan called for the successful passage of a UN General Assembly resolution promoting an international agreement to ban landmines. On 10 December, UN Resolution 51/45S was passed in the General Assembly by a vote of 156–0, with 10 abstentions.[42] Canada[43] and its core-group coalitian partners interpreted the wording of the resolution, which urged states to 'pursue vigorously an effective, legally binding international agreement to ban the use, stockpiling, production and transfer of anti-personnel landmines with a view to completing the negotiation as soon as possible', as a tacit endorsement of the Ottawa Process. As it transpired, the US government interpreted the successful resolution as a signal to move the AP mine issue into an alternative (and more 'traditional') negotiating forum to that of the Ottawa Process—the Conference on Disarmament. In fact, the US had originally proposed the General Assembly resolution. The US government's desire to move the AP mine issue into the CD proved to be one of the major points of contention in the negotiation process during 1997, right up until the Oslo Diplomatic Conference.

Negotiation in the CD definitely reflects the 'old' or conventional interstate diplomacy. The CD is the world's single multilateral negotiating forum dealing with the full range of disarmament issues. In the early CD sessions of 1997 in Geneva, the US, France, Germany, Italy, the UK, and Australia, among others, raised the AP mine issue and the need to negotiate a landmine treaty within this forum.[44] Britain, for example, sought a mandate in the CD to negotiate a ban on transfers of AP mines. The ban on transfers would serve as a first step to the subsequent restrictions on production and eventual elimination of stockpiles. Thus, a treaty negotiated in the CD would be a drawn-out affair (reinforced by the consensus decision-making process), proceeding step by step and incorporating weighty national security and verification measures.[45] This can obviously be juxtaposed with the fast-track negotiation of the Ottawa Process.

The CD became the forum of choice of those states opposed to a total ban on landmines, such as China, India, Iran, Pakistan, Libya, Russia, Syria, Cuba, South Korea, and Sri Lanka. For Australia, France, Britain, Germany, Spain, and the US, for example, the CD represented the 'best' forum for pursuing a landmine ban, though they acknowledged the role played by the Ottawa Process. From the US's point of view, the CD was more inclusive, bringing together the major producers and suppliers of landmines (China, Russia, India, and Pakistan) who remained outside the Ottawa Process, as well as former major producers such as South Africa, France, and Britain and those leading the Ottawa Process. As one US official pointed out:

> The value of negotiating an APL ban in the CD can be confirmed simply by looking around this chamber. As of June 27 more than half of the CD members, including the US, had not associated themselves with the

Brussels Declaration. . . . [T]hese countries make up half or more of the world's population and economic output and half or more of the world's historical activity with regard to antipersonnel landmines. Many of them have security concerns about eliminating their landmines in the near future. We believe negotiations in the CD can take these concerns, including our own, into account. Thus, while the CD's task will take longer to accomplish than the Ottawa Process, the resulting treaty will, unlike the Ottawa Process, extend the reach of an APL ban to the major producers, stockpilers and exporters of APLs. . . . The only way to stop the irresponsible use of antipersonnel landmines is to eliminate the source of those mines. To accomplish that objective, an agreement must include the potential exporters. Many such exporters are far more likely to support an agreement negotiated by them, among others, in this Conference that, *inter alia*, would ban the export of antipersonnel landmines.[46]

Cynics charged the US and others of bringing the landmines issue up within the CD simply to stall, or derail, the Ottawa Process, a process outside of the traditional interstate multilateral fora and one that was more open, transparent, and inclusive. Moreover, few of the heavily mine-infested countries belonged to the CD. Canada, while not opposed to discussion of the landmines issue in the CD, noted that the CD 'should move quickly, with clarity of purpose and determination', and respond to the 'political and humanitarian imperatives of the AP mine crisis.'[47] As discussion of the landmine issue proceeded within the CD throughout 1997, it became clear that a timely and successful negotiation of a ban was simply not possible in this forum.[48]

The landmine issue was not even placed on the official 1997 CD agenda. This reflected as much the internal dynamics of the CD itself as it did the broader relationship between the CD and the Ottawa Process. The rupture over the landmine issue involved a complex arrangement of states—some who feared that the CD would derail the Ottawa Process, some who used the CD to deflect pressure to sign the Ottawa Convention, and yet others who wanted nuclear disarmament to be the top priority for the CD.[49] So in the end, the CD track resulted in deadlock. The closest the CD came to agreement was the appointment of Ambassador John Campbell of Australia as special co-ordinator on landmines, essentially to 'conduct talks about having talks'.[50] This deadlock served to strengthen the parallel negotiating fora represented in the Ottawa Process. Eventually, even the US came on board the Ottawa Process with its 18 August announcement that it was going to Oslo despite not having signed the Brussels Declaration.

The Brussels Declaration, initially signed by 97 states and later by another 10, embodied another key element of global action as stipulated in the 1996 Agenda for Mine Action. Austria was given the task of drafting the treaty to be discussed formally at Oslo and subsequently signed in December in Ottawa. Austria first circulated a version of the draft treaty in November of 1996, requesting comments and suggestions. Following these bilateral discussions, Austria hosted a meeting of experts in Vienna on 12–14 February. Aside from debate over the substance of the text, the 111 states in attendance also debated the Ottawa Process versus the CD as competing venues for the landmine debate. Some present questioned the comprehensiveness of the draft treaty: Cuba, Sri Lanka, South Korea, and Ecuador argued that AP mines were essential for self-defence and hence there should be certain exceptions. Most participating states favoured a longer phase-in period for the destruction of stockpiles than the one-year period stipulated in the draft.[51] However, most of the debate at Vienna focused on the 'intrusive inspection regime' outlined in the draft. Few of those present expressed support for stringent verification measures for ensuring compliance.

A further meeting of experts dealing with issues of compliance and verification was held in Bonn on 24–5 April, attended by NGOs and representatives from 120 states. A second round of bilateral discussions, together with the recommendations emerging from the Bonn meeting, formed the final version of the Austrian draft considered at the AP mine meeting held in Brussels on 24–7 June. In the final version the terms 'verification' and 'on-site challenge inspection', originally in the draft, disappeared. In this regard, compliance became a looser and more co-operative concept in the final Austrian draft presented to the Brussels conference.[52]

The Brussels conference identified those states willing to make a political commitment to launch formal negotiations in Oslo with the objective of concluding negotiations and signing the treaty drafted by Austria. Consistent with other meetings within the Ottawa Process, the Brussels meeting was based on a 'self-selection' principle, whereby an individual state, to be a full participant, had to express its willingness to be bound by the substance of the Brussels Declaration. All told, 154 states attended the meeting either as full participants or as observer parties. The ICBL and the Red Cross continued their active role in the negotiation process at Brussels.

Another facet of the global action plan was to encourage the rapid entry into force and universal adherence to the prohibitions and restrictions on AP mines as contained in the amended Protocol II. The 1980 CCW and the 1996 revised Protocol, as the only existing international legal mechanisms to control the indiscriminate use of landmines, were seen as important interim measures despite insufficiently addressing the scope of the humanitarian crisis.[53] In the many regional and functional meetings prior to the Oslo conference, this base requirement was universally repeated. In this manner, a bridge between those not supporting a total ban and those states in the Ottawa Process could be built.[54]

Another crucial element of the negotiation process was building public awareness and political will for a global AP mine ban. The development of public and governmental awareness towards the landmine issue was tied to regional action, the second key element of the Ottawa Process as articulated in the Chairman's Agenda for Action. Indeed, regional initiatives proved to be fundamental to the success of the multilateral negotiations process, with 107 countries committing themselves to the Brussels Declaration. The geographic diversity of the signatories was testimony not only to the global dimension of the landmine crisis but also to the success of regional initiatives in politicizing many nations to the pro-ban cause.[55]

This process was not without its ambiguities and contradictions. For example, the NATO summit, the Commonwealth Heads of Government meeting, and the G–8 conference all reflected positively on the 'useful' and complementary efforts in a variety of fora, including the CD. The Maputo NGO conference, on the other hand, concluded that the CD would be unable to fulfil any meaningful objectives in relation to an international landmine ban. As a rule, the conferences and meetings held as part of the Ottawa Process did not make positive mention of the CD in their respective declarations.[56] This is not surprising in the case of the meetings in Maputo, Harare, and Kempton Park, since the participants were not likely to endorse a forum in which they were severely underrepresented. It is not surprising, either, that in fora where the major powers were present, the complementary and reinforcing role of the CD was highlighted. This tension reflected the uneasy intersection between bottom-up and top-down multilateral processes that was evident in the course of the treaty negotiation process (and its antecedents). This tension was as much about who were appropriate and legitimate actors in the international system as it was about the legitimate venue for international issues to be discussed.

The multilateral negotiation process up to the Oslo conference was also shaped by various contingent factors, such as the timely change (for the pro-ban movement, at least) of governments in France and Britain, which brought two more G–7 members firmly within the pro-ban camp; the energy and determination of particular individuals within the NGO community such as Jody Williams; and the work of Princess Diana in Bosnia-Herzegovina, which did much to publicize the global campaign.

With Britain and France in the pro-ban camp, the negotiations no longer looked like David versus Goliath. By the time of the Oslo conference, only Japan, of the G–7 countries, supported the US.

THE OSLO CONFERENCE

The story of Oslo revolved around the participation of the US. The presence of the US effectively crossed the CD process with its *alter ego*, the Ottawa Process. The US decision to participate at the eleventh hour of the Ottawa Process, only to be eventually rebuffed by the vast majority of delegations, was a last-ditch attempt to divert the Ottawa Process back into the CD channel. That the ill-fated attempt was made against overwhelming odds revealed, perhaps, either the desperation or the isolation of the White House. Caught between an insistent military and a broad and growing coalition of forces, including a majority of the US Senate, that questioned why the US was not participating in the fast-track approach to banning landmines, the White House reluctantly announced in late August that the US would participate actively in Oslo.

In the environment in which the White House made its decision to go to Oslo were entreaties from other governments requesting US participation in Oslo, including, notably, that of Canada. As a member of the core group and leader of the fast-track approach, one might have expected the Canadian government to eschew the US as the proponent of the tortoise-paced CD process. Rather, it laboured hard at the highest level to ensure US involvement. The Canadian government was portrayed as a 'go-between', taking the concerns of the United States into meetings in which the treaty was drafted.[57] Prime Minister Jean Chrétien and Foreign Affairs Minister Lloyd Axworthy both appealed to the US that 'legitimate security interests must also be taken fully into account, and the negotiators in Oslo are prepared to exercise flexibility and ingenuity to accommodate such concerns.'[58] At the same time, Canadian efforts drew the line early on against 'exceptions' to the proposed treaty: 'There is a clear danger that any open-ended exception will lead to demands for other exceptions and would fundamentally weaken the treaty we are seeking.'[59]

It is not difficult to appreciate Canadian efforts to lure the US into the Ottawa Process. As continental neighbour, military ally, and free trade partner, the assumption of leadership by the Canadian government in the fast-track process opposing the leadership of Washington surprised many, including perhaps itself. Getting the US to participate would obviously end a bilateral rift with the neighbouring superpower. Possible US accession to the landmines treaty, however, would be worth pursuing on its own merits. Governments not going to Oslo included some of the most important users of landmines, such as Russia, China, India, and Pakistan—countries that included much of the global population. Having the US onside might well have a virtuous domino effect, leading to Russian accession (via American efforts), and if the Russians foreswore using landmines on its borders, then the Chinese government could more easily contemplate accession (leading perhaps to Vietnamese assent). Finally, US accession effectively on Ottawa's terms would mean a major diplomatic victory almost without rival in Ottawa. For all of these reasons, the calculation could have been that getting the US onside would be worth a few of the treaty's teeth.

Some of the ban supporters had a very mixed reaction to the last-minute American flip-flop. Quite distinct from Axworthy's comments that the American decision was 'a very positive step that further legitimizes the process and makes this into a very significant event', Steve Goose, who as chair of the US Campaign to Ban Landmines had laboured hard to get the US onside, decided that the serious caveats attached to US participation turned wine into vinegar, branding the approach a 'bad-faith position'. Or, as expressed by Cecilia Tuttle, co-ordinator of Mines Action Canada, 'It would be nice to have the US in, but do you kiss every frog, hoping it'll turn into a prince.'[60] While all would have rejoiced in a true US conversion to the fast track, many feared sabotage. In the end, the White House succumbed to pressures for some movement on landmines. While downplaying the embarrassing flip-flop on the Ottawa Process, the White House recognized the stalemated CD and officially shifted 'some of its efforts' to Oslo. Officially, the policy was to proceed simultaneously on both fronts. In reality, the White House goal was to dovetail the Ottawa Process into the CD; what the US wanted was to fashion the landmines treaty into its own image for use in Geneva. The decision was a last-ditch effort to regain leadership in the landmines issue. Prenegotiation as a prelude to negotiation is a phase in which the parties decide that negotiation is a viable way to resolve a particular problem.[61] It is clear, in retrospect, that the US and the ban states entered the negotiations with very different and mutually exclusive expectations—ones that would inevitably disappoint one side or the other.

Eighty-five countries met in the capital of Norway during September 1997 to negotiate the final treaty to ban the use, stockpiling, production, and transfer of AP mines. The task of the negotiations was to turn the draft Austrian treaty—the 'single negotiating text'—into a legally binding convention. The Austrian draft treaty contained 20 articles within 10 pages of text.[62] The general thrust of the treaty was contained in its first article:

> Each State Party undertakes never under any circumstances: a) To use anti-personnel mines; b) To develop, produce, otherwise acquire, stockpile, retain or transfer to anyone, directly or indirectly, anti-personnel mines; c) To assist, encourage or induce, in any way, anyone to engage in any activity prohibited to a State Party under the Convention. Each State Party undertakes to destroy or ensure the destruction of all anti-personnel mines in accordance with the provisions of this Convention.

Anti-tank mines were excluded from the draft treaty, except those with certain anti-handling devices. While the ICBL argued that these were effectively AP mines, classifying them as such reportedly would have made the treaty unacceptable to many supporting governments.[63]

South African Jacob Selebi was elected conference president.[64] Selebi's selection was auspicious for treaty supporters in several ways. First, the election of an African underscored the core group's message that the ban movement was a North-South campaign and not another example of Western-dominated diplomacy (though, in actuality, the Ottawa Process was Western-dominated), and second, having someone from Africa's pre-eminent country in the chair could only have a salutary effect on the large African contingent of delegations. Finally, Selebi had a reputation as a strong, independent individual who could stand up to the US. The rule of the conference agreed to by the participants (by consensus) on opening day was that decisions were to be made with two-thirds majority (as opposed to the consensus of the CD process). The decision-making rule made it easy for the pro-ban coalition to block any changes to the Austrian treaty, while preventing any one state from preventing agreement. Finally, the ICBL was granted official observer status. Without the US presence at the conference, small differences among the participants doubtless would have carried the discussion within and outside the conference halls of Oslo; as a counterfactual, however, we will never know. With its presence and its controversial proposals, the US became a lightning rod, drawing attention for and (mostly) against. The Oslo negotiation, then, was dominated by the US and its proposals that challenged the essence of the landmines treaty.

To the Austrian draft treaty, the US government proposed major changes in five areas (five so-called 'red lines'), which are discussed in detail by Mary Wareham in Chapter 12.[65] We will address each of these briefly in the context of their discussion at Oslo, but their overall impact clearly, and fairly drastically, would have transformed the Austrian draft. The proposed American modifications restricted the types of anti-personnel mines to be included to allow so-called 'smart' landmines; eliminated from the treaty US and Korean landmines in the Korean peninsula; allowed any state to withdraw from the treaty on short notice, and whenever it became involved in an armed conflict; and allowed any signing state to delay its obligations until about 2010 (nine years after the treaty goes into effect, assumed to be about two years after treaty signing). While these were opening positions, it was not clear how negotiable these positions were. Senator Jesse Helms, a conservative Republican from South Carolina, wrote to President Clinton that these positions were being ridiculed in Oslo and that the US should make it clear that the positions were 'bottom lines', not a 'starting point for debate'.[66]

The US delegation had few allies at the conference. Representatives that supported two or more US proposals came from Japan, Australia, Spain, Ecuador, and Poland. Delegates from the United Kingdom and Brazil supported the US proposal to allow countries to withdraw on short notice and during armed conflict (Chile, supported by Venezuela, had a proposal similar to that of the US, but with a six-month time frame for withdrawal). Delegates that spoke consistently against US proposals came from the core group, led by Belgium and Denmark. Other delegations speaking against US proposals included Canada, France, Italy, the Netherlands, Norway, and South Africa. By region, delegations from the many African governments present were the most numerous in speaking against US proposals. From Latin America, the delegates from Mexico spoke the most frequently against US proposals, while their counterpart in the Philippines had this distinction among Asian countries. The most vociferous opponent of the US, however, was not a state but rather the ICBL. Its conference newsletter, the Ban Treaty News, carried on its masthead the mantra, 'NO EXCEPTIONS—NO RESERVATIONS—NO LOOPHOLES'.[67] The five issues of the newsletter dissected American proposals and stridently reported on those countries speaking for and against mostly American proposals. A typical headline read 'Reject US Demands—Don't Kill or Maim the Treaty'. Elsewhere, the newsletter argued that the US proposals 'would have gutted the treaty and made a mockery of the Ottawa Process.'[68] The ICBL also prepared an informative daily fact sheet, which kept participants aware of the campaign's informed presence. Let us return to the specific American proposals.

Several American proposals were raised in plenary session on the opening days of the conference. The American request to specifically exempt the use of AP mines in Korea was, with the exception of Japan, opposed unanimously. Several governments, however, indicated sympathy for the US position and suggested some undefined 'transition period' or other formula that would accommodate American needs. Thirty-two delegates, including most of the core group, spoke against the proposal, frequently noting that the granting of one exception would open the treaty up to other demands for geographic exceptions.

The next US proposal was to allow governments up to nine years to put the treaty into effect. Some of the delegates from African governments were vociferous in their opposition to this proposal, arguing that it was, in effect, a 'reservation' to the treaty, which was disallowed by the treaty. Speaking in favour of the proposal were Australia, Ecuador, Japan, and Poland. However, noting the general lack of support for this proposal, Ambassador Selebi concluded that the original wording of the article should remain. The third US proposal was to delete the prohibition in the treaty against reservations. As noted in the *Ban Treaty News*, 'The US delegation clearly stated that its government would not be able to sign the treaty with a no reservations clause.'[69] Despite this position, no delegation spoke in favour of the proposal. Thirteen delegations spoke in opposition, led again by the core group.

The final proposal raised in plenary was the most controversial and gained the greatest support of the several US proposals. The proposal to reduce from one year to 90 days the time necessary to notify withdrawal from the treaty, and to allow countries in armed conflict to withdraw from the treaty, was supported by some of the largest and most important countries at the conference, including Britain, Australia, Brazil, Spain, and Ecuador. This proposal reduced the commitment of the signatories to banning landmines only in peacetime, clearly and seriously weakening the treaty and calling into question the commitment of the governments whose delegates spoke in favour of the proposal.[70] The *Ban* newsletter indicated that a Canadian delegate led the attack on the proposal, noting the 'absurdity' of the proposal. Notably, the delegates from France and Italy, along with 11 other delegations, assailed the proposal.[71]

In the working group on 'definitions', the US delegation attempted to exclude 'anti-handling devices' and other 'self-deactivating' mines attached to anti-tank and anti-vehicle mines from the ban treaty by defining them as 'submunitions'. This would have allowed the US military to continue to use its Gator, Volcano, and MOPMS weapons, which heretofore had been classified as AP mines and had been included in its AP inventory, which was eventually to be destroyed under existing US policy.[72] If implemented, the proposal would have given a military advantage to those countries with the technology or money to build or buy self-deactivating mines. Only Japan supported the proposal, while eight countries—Belgium, Canada, Ireland, Norway, the Philippines, South Africa, Sweden, and Switzerland—as well as the Red Cross and the ICBL, spoke against the motion.[73] At the beginning of the second week of the conference, faced with opposition to its plan to reclassify various landmines as submunitions, the US delegation moved to classify them as anti-handling devices. This proposal met the same fate as the original proposal, drawing the support only of Japan.

The first 'round' of negotiations, then, closed with a canyon between the positions of the US and its few supporters, primarily Japan, Australia, and Spain, on one side, and the vast majority, the pro-ban delegations, on the other. In between were Britain and Brazil, who both supported withdrawal on short notice and in the event of armed conflict but joined the pro-ban group on the rest of the issues. Such a split was not unexpected in negotiations as opposing sides open with positions designed to stake out particular positions and principles. While representatives from both sides were calling on each other to make concessions to reach agreement, private discussions among the delegations produced no substantial movement. As leader of the pro-ban coalition, the ICBL and most of the core group delegations toiled to maintain what they perceived as the integrity of the draft treaty intact by keeping supporting delegations in line by rejecting compromise with the US. The Canadian government's actions differed in that it searched for a 'bridging' compromise that would get the US onside without threatening the essence of the treaty.[74] Germany was another country that actively sought compromise between the US and pro-ban positions.[75] The one soft area of the pro-ban delegations involved the transition period for implementing the treaty. Canada's Lloyd Axworthy rejected a compromise on exemptions: 'But in saying that, there can be perhaps other ways in which the issue of transitions can be worked out as, in fact, it has been raised by several other countries as well. . . . any convention needs a certain phasing-in period.'[76]

At the end of the second week of the conference, the draft treaty was released for delegates to send back to their home governments. 'As it stands now we cannot sign it', announced Robert Sherman, a US delegate. The US delegation, clearly miffed at the strong opposition it encountered, informed the conference that it might pull out of the negotiations unless it won important concessions.[77] Over the three-day weekend, the White House contacted various national capitals seeking support for a compromise. Reuters reported that Canada was accused by ICBL's Jody Williams of 'carrying the water' by canvassing other countries to accommodate the US:

Canada initiated this process with a challenge to the world to come to Ottawa in December and sign a treaty which would unambiguously ban this weapon. Yet what do we see. The Canadian prime minister is calling other governments around the world. What signal is that giving when the father of this ban treaty is calling governments [to] help the United States?[78]

The US delegation returned to the conference after the long weekend with a compromise package and a request by Eric Newsom, head of delegation, to extend the conference by one day, which the conference president urged the delegations to accept, despite the grousing of the ICBL. The package proposal dropped earlier demands for a reservations clause and the Korea exception. Similarly, references to self-destructing mines were omitted. Instead, the package focused on three remaining elements of the original proposal: (1) the withdrawal clause (Article 20) would allow a party to withdraw in case it or an ally was 'a victim of armed aggression in violation of UN charter'; (2) allow individual states to defer compliance with certain treaty provisions for nine years from signature, rather than from entry-into-force of the treaty, as originally proposed by the US; and (3) modify the definition of anti-handling device to include not only those attached to the protected mine but also those located 'near' the mine.[79] The package was offered on a 'reject one, reject all' basis.

Comparing the proposal with the original indicates only minor changes by the US. The effect of the proposal would give the US nine years to retain its minefields in Korea and continue to seek a replacement weapon for AP mines. After nine years, if no satisfactory replacement were found, the US could either withdraw from the treaty or wait until it or an ally became involved in an armed conflict. However, including the word 'near' in the definition of anti-handling devices, which would allow the US to use many of its 'smart' mines, might make remaining in the treaty more palatable regardless of future weaponry advancements.

The revised proposal did have sweeteners for any fence-sitters at the conference. Removing the specific exemption for Korea and broadening the withdrawal criteria to allow any country to withdraw from the treaty if it or an ally were attacked could have made the revised proposal more attractive to those delegations not firmly in the pro-ban camp. Similarly, expanding anti-handling devices to include AP mines 'near' anti-tank mines broadened the original US proposal, which sanctioned self-deactivating mines, to include any AP mines. This would have had a devastating effect on the ban, because treaty countries could retain AP mines indefinitely—for placement ostensibly 'near' other mines.

Despite the changes, the package proposal attracted little, if any, additional support. The day extension passed and the US compromise proposal failed. On 18 September, the US chairs were empty as the treaty was formally adopted in plenary session. To save face in the aftermath of the conference, President Clinton announced that the United States would unilaterally stop using landmines in 2006. The weeks following the conference the Ottawa Process attracted greater support for the treaty. After discussions with Canada's Prime Minister Chrétien, Russian President Boris Yeltsin agreed publicly to make permanent his country's ban on the export of landmines and pledged to sign on when economic conditions permitted. This announcement was well received in the White House. A day later, the Japanese government reversed its position and announced that it would sign the treaty in Ottawa. This announcement was not received as magnanimously in Washington: 'Senior U.S. officials bluntly reminded Japan of its defence obligations yesterday and make little effort to conceal their annoyance.'[80] Subsequently, holdouts Greece and Australia came on board as well. By the end of the Ottawa conference in December, 122 countries signed the treaty.

CONCLUSION

Earlier in this chapter, we identified a historical parallel between the present international conjuncture and the period at the end of World War I in which to frame our understanding of the multilateral treaty negotiations. Identified more for heuristic purposes, this parallel underlines what we see as the interface between traditional modes of conducting international relations and emerging forces and processes structuring global society. In this manner we juxtaposed the old and new diplomacy in 1919 with the Ottawa Process. Ironically, Nicolson's model of the new diplomacy seems to fit better the negotiations of the Ottawa Process than it did the Paris Peace Conference in 1919. Disheartened after surveying what he considered to be the disastrous peace negotiations, Nicolson concluded that the conference was guilty of disguising an imperialistic peace under the guise of open diplomacy.[81] The Oslo conference was no such sham, where the Ottawa Process remained true to form.

Nevertheless, keeping in mind Nicolson's comments about the variable nature of negotiations, the visible conduct of the negotiations was not radically different in certain respects from what one might have expected in multilateral negotiations. There was a beginning, middle, and end of the negotiations that saw hard opening positions negotiated into compromise proposals, which in the end could not close the gap sufficiently to get everyone on board. Moreover, the assumption of leadership by Canada, and support by the UK, France, and Germany—four G–7 countries—no longer pitted the weak against the strong as it would have been had Belgium and

Austria been the most powerful ban supporters. Nicolson is instructive on this point; he concluded that in reality there was little difference between the old and new ways of negotiating. For him, the difference was one of method, and different negotiating methods stemmed from different representations. In the old model, negotiators represented the state, while under the new, negotiators represented the people. In 1919, negotiators were cognizant of an amorphous public opinion, and that affected the style and the substance of the peace treaty. In 1997, public opinion was concretized in the form of NGOs, some of which were not only clamouring outside the negotiating rooms but were representatives inside the same rooms.

Still, it would be a mistake to conclude that the Oslo negotiations were a case of old wine in new bottles; the agreement contrasts with many other multilateral negotiations. A recent survey of multilateral negotiations concluded that epistemic groups, such as the ICBL, have a 'declining influence' and that 'multilateral negotiations continue to remain hostage to the interests and behaviors of the great powers. Negotiations can proceed in spite of great powers, but agreement is not possible without them. The United States continues to have an important veto power over negotiated outcomes in most settings.'[82] Clearly, the landmines agreement contradicts this finding (although it may capture the mind-set of the US negotiators, who completely underestimated the momentum of the Ottawa Process). The Oslo experience reflects more closely the observation that 'New alliances that cross traditional North-South lines have been forged as small states have banded together in an effort to define agendas, develop negotiating parameters, and shape outcomes. Various transnational social and scientific groups have also made their presence felt'. The survey also concludes that 'the danger with any coalition is that group solidarity and coalition maintenance can become ends in themselves, leading to rigid and inflexible bargaining positions.'[83] However, it is not clear how a more flexible pro-ban coalition could have obtained a comprehensive agreement in the face of rigid and inflexible US positions—the pro-ban coalition opted for a comprehensive agreement over US participation in a partial agreement. In the end, then, the landmines negotiations do reflect a new multilateralism, one in which civil society, via NGO activity, sometimes has a seat at the table.

The Ottawa Process may be the most optimistic representation of an increasingly potent civil society. Herein lie some of the contradictions of the Ottawa Convention negotiation process, since these bottom-up forces of civil society have directly confronted the traditional top-down processes of interstate multilateralism, the results of which have not been an unambiguous discursive shift to a 'new' multilateralism.[84] The treaty itself is an interstate treaty and does not apply to subnational actors (such as guerrilla groups). This proves problematic in the instance of internal conflict, high-lighted in particular by the situation in Somalia where there is no interna-tionally recognized government.[85] Moreover, a divide has opened up between the NGO community and states (including members of the core group) over the generalizability of the Ottawa Process as an exemplar of a profoundly innovative negotiation process. In a discussion at the Ottawa Process forum concluding the treaty signing, state officials tended to emphasize the uniqueness of the process and the inherent dangers in apply-ing the model in a wider context.[86] NGOs seem to be less circumspect in this regard, highlighting the potential for wider applicability to issues such as child labour.[87]

So much for process. What about the substance of the Ottawa Convention? Assuming its widespread ratification and then implementa-tion, the Ottawa Convention will save many lives. For that, it is indeed a triumph. However, we must not lose sight of the fact that major mine users remain outside of the treaty, and its strict terms make it unlikely that these users will sign on in the short or medium term. The venue for discussion for these countries remains the CD process. Quite divergent opinions were in evidence at the various mine action fora held parallel to the treaty-sign-ing conference in Ottawa. Steffen Kongstad, minister counsellor in the permanent mission of Norway to the UN in Geneva, suggested in comments to the Ottawa Process forum in December that the CD is irrelevant to the Ottawa Process and beyond. Kongstad's specific concerns were with the undemocratic nature of this forum, with its underrepresentation of Africa, and its lowest-common-denominator agreement procedures. Interestingly, Joelle Bourgois, France's permanent representative at the CD, viewed the consensus rule as itself a stepping-stone to the universalization of the treaty. While we do not know the effect the Ottawa Convention will have on the CD, the major commitments taken by throngs of countries can only make it easier for the major powers to reach agreement to limit and regu-late landmines.

Notes

An earlier version of this chapter appeared in *Canadian Foreign Policy* 5, 3 (Spring 1998).

The authors wish to acknowledge the research assistance and financial sup-port of the Non-Proliferation Arms Control and Disarmament Division in the Canadian Department of Foreign Affairs and International Trade. We also wish to thank Steve Goose, Jody Williams, and various government officials for providing interviews. Thanks as well to Fen Hampson and two anonymous critics for their comments on an earlier draft. Of course, the authors are responsible for any errors.

1. ICBL, *Ban Treaty News* No. 3 (9 Sept. 1997): 2.
2. Ralph Earle, quoted in J. Wurst, 'Closing in on a Landmine Ban: The Ottawa Process and U.S. Interests', *Arms Control Today* (June-July 1997). [http://www.armscontrol.org/ACT]
3. ICBL, *Ban Treaty News* No. 3 (9 Sept. 1997): 2.
4. H. Nicolson, *Peacemaking 1919: Being Reminiscences of the Paris Peace Conference* (London: Constable Press, 1933, 1945).
5. The formal title is the Convention on Prohibitions on the Use of Certain Conventional Weapons which may be Deemed to be Excessively Injurious or to have Indiscriminate Effects. The Convention entered into force in 1983.
6. J. George, *Discourses of Global Politics: A Critical (Re)Introduction to International Relations* (Boulder, Colo.: Westview Press, 1994), 1.
7. Of course, it can be argued that every generation experiences social, economic, and political change, and therefore the present era is in no way exceptional in this respect. It does seem, however, that we are living through a major transformation in the capitalist economy and the geopolitical terrain of the interstate system. Arguably, these changes are more complex than terms such as 'New World Order' and 'New World Disorder' suggest.
8. A.W. Knight, '"Top-down" and "Bottom-up" Multilateralism: Two Approaches in the Quest for Global Governance', in M. Fortmann, S. MacFarlane, and S. Roussel, eds, *Multilateralism and Regional Security* (Halifax: Canadian Peacekeeping Press, 1997), 15.
9. Given the uneven distribution of economic and political power in the international system, this challenge to state sovereignty is differentiated across the system. For Robert Cox, the US is possibly the 'last Westphalian', retaining the ability to act forcefully and independently—though even American power is circumscribed in important respects. See Cox, ed., *The New Realism: Perspectives on Multilateralism and World Order* (Tokyo: UN University Press, 1997), xv–xxx.
10. Knight, '"Top-down" and "Bottom-up" Multilateralism', 35.
11. For contrasting theoretical conceptions of what a 'new' multilateralism might look like, compare Cox, ed., *The New Realism*, and Fortmann, MacFarlane, and Roussel, eds, *Multilateralism and Regional Security*. The former contains a diverse 'critical' approach to multilateralism, including post-colonial perspectives, whereas the latter is primarily concerned with reconstructing mainstream IR theories (Knight's article is the notable exception), or 'how is cooperation or rule-regulated behaviour possible between self-centred political entities competing for power and influence in an environment devoid of

supranational authority?' (p. 4). The formulation of the question in this man-ner clearly limits the scope of understanding for multilateralism.

12. Knight, ' "Top-down" and "Bottom-up" Multilateralism', 35.

13. Robert Cox, 'Globalization, multilateralism and democracy', in Cox and Tim Sinclair, *Approaches to World Order* (Cambridge: Cambridge University Press, 1996), 534.

14. B. Lawson, 'Towards a New Multilateralism: Canada and the Landmine Ban', *Behind the Headlines* 54, 4 (1997): 18.

15. Kofi Annan, 'A Weapon of the Past and a Symbol of Shame', excerpts from an address to the Oslo Diplomatic Conference, 3 Sept., in DFAIT, *AP Mine Ban: Progress Report* No. 5 (Sept. 1997): 8.

16. L. Axworthy, 'Notes for an address by the Honourable Lloyd Axworthy of Foreign Affairs at the Closing Session of the International Strategy Conference Towards a Global Ban on Anti-Personnel Mines', DFAIT, 5 Oct. 1996.

17. Comments of Steve Goose, member of ICBL, at the Ottawa Process Forum, 5 Dec. 1997.

18. The list could be extended, but additions become more repetitive and idio-syncratic to the Paris Peace Conference.

19. Nicolson, *Peacemaking 1919*, 208.

20. It is interesting that characterizations of 'old' and 'new' diplomacy following World War I have their counterparts today. The hallmark of the current 'new' multilateralism is the 'growing involvement of citizens groups, experts, and epistemic communities in international negotiation and regime formation processes', a development that is quite similar to the greater popular involve-ment of Nicolson's new diplomacy. See F. Hampson and M. Hart, *Multilateral Negotiations: Lessons from Arms Control, Trade, and the Environment* (Baltimore: Johns Hopkins University Press, 1995), 346–7.

21. To put landmine NGOs in the vernacular of contemporary theorizing, they and related groups constitute an epistemic community—groups with shared knowledge about the subject matter. On the efficacy of epistemic communi-ties, see Peter Haas, 'Do Regimes Matter? Epistemic Communities and Mediterranean Pollution Control', *International Organization* 43, 3 (1989).

22. ICRC, *Banning Anti-Personnel Mines: The Ottawa Treaty Explained* (Geneva, 1997), 4.

23. A. Peters, 'Landmines in the 21st Century', *International Relations* 13, 2 (1996): 44.

24. Ibid., 43. Of the estimated 400 million mines laid since World War II, 65 mil-lion were laid after 1980.

25. A crisis may have an ameliorative effect on negotiations, especially if the threat is perceived by all parties. See Janice Gross Stein, ed., *Getting to the*

Table (Baltimore: Johns Hopkins University Press, 1990). The crisis in land-mines was their increasingly widespread use and their continuing danger to civilians following armed conflicts. This threat was felt most keenly by residents of mine-infested countries and by peacekeeping troops assigned to those countries. From a military perspective landmines were not a crisis, but from a humanitarian perspective they were—a difference that was exploited by the ICBL and the Red Cross.

26. It is not possible in the context of this chapter to map the breadth and complexity of these bottom-up multilateral processes and their relationship to state policy formulation *vis-à-vis* the landmines issue. Such an exercise would necessitate unravelling complex internal and external forces that cohered to shape individual state policy. Other chapters in this volume fill these gaps.

27. Handicap International, *Antipersonnel Landmines: For the banning of massacres of civilians in time of peace: Facts and chronologies*, 2nd edn (Paris, 1997), 9.

28. ICBL, *CCW News* No. 5 (11 Oct. 1995): 1–3.

29. At the first preparatory meeting of the CCW Review Conference in February 1994, China was the only country to block participation of any kind by NGOs.

30. At the third preparatory conference for the Vienna Review Conference in August 1994, Sweden officially proposed an amendment to Article 6 of Protocol II to prohibit the use, development, production, stockpiling, or transfer of AP mines and stating that states must destroy such weapons. This proposal received no discussion at Vienna.

31. In March 1995 Belgium became the first country to pass domestic legislation to ban the use, production, procurement, sale, and transfer of AP mines.

32. Thanks to Fen Hampson for this characterization of the pro-ban movement.

33. The 'President's Text' emerging from January's technical session had no mention of a ban, not even as an ultimate objective, reflecting perhaps the diminished expectations of Ambassador Molander, the president of the CCW Review Conference. ICBL, *CCW News* No. 9 (9 Apr. 1996): 3.

34. Ibid., 4.

35. Peters, 'Landmines in the 21st Century', 44.

36. ICBL, *CCW News* No. 12 (3 May 1996): 2.

37. They were Austria, Belgium, Canada, Denmark, Ireland, Mexico, Norway, and Switzerland—countries that provide many peacekeeping troops that are exposed to leftover landmines.

38. On 17 January 1996 Canada announced a comprehensive moratorium on the production, use, stockpiling, and transfer of AP mines.

39. ICBL, 'Meeting of States and Select NGO Representatives Supportive of a Comprehensive Ban on Anti-Personnel Landmines 29 April', *Report of the Second Session of the Review Conference, Geneva*, 1996, 97–8.

40. ICBL, *CCW News* No. 9 update (22 Apr. 1996): 2.

41. Canada, *Towards a Global Ban on Anti-Personnel Mines: Declaration of the Ottawa Conference* (Ottawa, 1996).

42. The 10 abstainees were China, Cuba, Israel, Belarus, Pakistan, the two Koreas, Syria, Russia, and Turkey.

43. As a convenience, country names refer to the central governments and government officials and representatives.

44. S. Walkling, '111 States Consider Draft Treaty Banning Anti-Personnel Landmines', *Arms Control Today* (Mar. 1997). [http://www.armscontrol.org/ACT]

45. Past weapons conventions negotiated in the CD had specified detailed verification rules. This contrasted with the loose verification rules finally outlined in the draft treaty of the Ottawa Process. Part of the explanation for this difference lay with the underlying rationales behind the CD and the parallel Ottawa Process *vis-à-vis* landmines. Within the CD, landmines are a *disarmament* issue, while the Ottawa Process held as its fundamental premise that the issue was a *humanitarian* one.

46. Ralph Earle, quoted in Wurst, 'Closing in on a Landmine Ban'.

47. Mark Moher, 'Statement Before the Plenary of the Conference on Disarmament', Permanent Mission of Canada to the United Nations at Geneva, 21 Jan. 1997.

48. In a speech at the Japanese Conference on Demining and Victim Assistance held in Tokyo, 7 March 1997, Canadian official Ralph Lysyshyn noted that the focus of 'transfers' of AP mines within the CD basically dodged the issue since these transfers were becoming less of an issue with the growing number of export moratoria declarations by individual states. Moreover, the issue of AP mines would be placed on the CD's agenda only if there was consensus among the 61 members. As this consensus was not forthcoming, the CD simply could not adequately respond to the humanitarian dimension of the landmine crisis.

49. On 12 June Mexico blocked the CD from launching negotiations towards a global ban, much to the dismay of the US. Critics argued that Mexico wanted to keep using landmines against the rebellion in Chiapas state and that its decision also reflected its desire to be a 'champion of nuclear disarmament'. Another interpretation, one articulated by Mexico itself (a core group member of the Ottawa Process), was that the CD was not the appropriate forum for the discussion of this humanitarian issue. See 'Mexico Blocks Conclave on World Land-Mine Ban', *Washington Post*, 13 June 1997, A33.

50. Wurst, 'Closing in on a Landmine Ban'.

51. Walkling, '111 States Consider Draft Treaty'.

52. Wurst, 'Closing in on a Landmine Ban'.

53. The revised Protocol II is not expected to come into force until mid-1998. As of late 1997, only six states had ratified the amended Convention. Ibid.

54. This bridge has become even more important since the December 1997 treaty was signed, now that attention has turned to the universalization of the ban treaty.

55. Lawson, 'Towards a New Multilateralism', 21. The regional initiatives are discussed in Chapter 10. The version of this chapter published in *Canadian Foreign Policy* includes a discussion of these initiatives.

56. All made mention of the basic requirement to either join or ratify the 1980 CCW and the 1996 revised Protocol II.

57. Paul Koring, 'Behind the scenes of Canada's quiet land-mine diplomacy', *Globe and Mail*, 19 Sept. 1997.

58. Letter from the Prime Minister to the US President, 8 Sept. 1997. The vocabulary of 'flexibility' and 'ingenuity' was used as well by Axworthy in his entreaty to Madeleine Albright.

59. Ibid.

60. Juliette O'Neill, 'U.S. Joins Canada in drive to ban landmines', *Ottawa Citizen*, 19 Aug. 1997, A7.

61. See William Zartman, 'Prenegotiation: Phases and Functions', and Brian Tomlin, 'The Stages of Prenegotiation: The Decision to Negotiate North American Free Trade', both in Stein, ed., *Getting to the Table*.

62. Comparable treaties are much longer—the Chemical Weapons Convention at 172 pages and the Comprehensive Test Ban Treaty at about 100 pages.

63. Wurst, 'Closing in on a Landmine Ban'.

64. Ambassador Selebi was permanent representative of South Africa in Geneva. Selebi was known to have a strong staff, including Peter Goosen.

65. The US government also proposed changes to Article 4, Destruction of stockpiled anti-personnel mines; Article 5, Destruction of anti-personnel mines laid within minefields; Article 6, Destruction of anti-personnel mines laid in areas outside minefields; Article 8, Transparency; and Article 10, National implementation measures. These were perceived to be of lesser importance by the participants.

66. Senator Jesse Helms, letter to the White House, 8 Sept. 1997.

67. This newsletter is a primary print source for the discussion of the negotiations that follows. See: [http://www.interpost.no/folkehjelp/ngoforum.update/issue]

68. ICBL, *Ban Treaty News* No. 2 (1997): 1.

69. Ibid., 3.

70. The British ban campaign seriously took the UK delegation to task for its actions on this proposal. See ICBL, 'UK remains silent as US tries to destroy Ottawa landmines treaty', press release, 12 Sept. 1997.

71. ICBL, *Ban Treaty News* No. 3 (1997): 3–4.

72. The reclassification would also have allowed the US again to produce and export the weapons in question.

73. ICBL, *Ban Treaty News* No. 3 (1997): 6.

74. Hampson and Hart, *Multilateral Negotiations*, 40.

75. Interviews with governmental and NGO participants at Oslo.

76. Canadian Press, 10 Sept. 1997.

77. Tim Burt, 'US threatens to quit anti-landmine talks', *Financial Times*, 11 Sept. 1997.

78. Reuters news service, Tanya Pang, 16 Sept. 1997.

79. US proposal, US delegation, 13 Sept. 1997.

80. Paul Koring, 'Japan joins club to ban land mines', *Globe and Mail*, 22 Oct. 1997, A1.

81. Nicolson, *Peacemaking 1919*, 187.

82. Hampson and Hart, *Multilateral Negotiations*, 352, 360.

83. Ibid., 360.

84. Cf. Lawson, 'Towards a New Multilateralism'. Interestingly, for Lawson the role of civil society is one of expanding dramatically 'the "diplomatic tool-kit" available for use in lobbying decision-makers at state, regional, and global levels' (p. 23). Thus, this new multilateralism does not imply an ontological problematization of *who* constitutes legitimate decision-makers in international relations. Therefore, the new multilateralism is still very much bounded by the old interstate modes of global governance.

85. Comment by a Somali delegate during question period of the Ottawa Process Forum, 5 Dec. 1997.

86. One participant in a government focus group was quite explicit in suggesting that the Ottawa Process should become the norm for conducting international negotiations. This participant from Latin America questioned the relationship between NGOs and international democracy, explaining that what was needed was a more democratic *international state system*, rather than NGO/government partnerships *per se*.

87. See the 'Highlights of Results: Interactive Survey Groups', p. 5. Canada's DFAIT contracted a polling firm (Ekos) to develop a series of survey instruments, which were used during the Ottawa conference to explore the opinions of delegates who participated in the process.

CHAPTER 20

DEMOCRATIZATION OF FOREIGN POLICY: THE OTTAWA PROCESS AS A MODEL

Maxwell A. Cameron

Does the Ottawa Process leading to the signing of an international treaty to ban anti-personnel (AP) landmines represent an example of the democratization of Canadian foreign policy through the construction of a partnership between government and civil society?[1] There are two contending views of the democratization of foreign policy. The first is that the existing institutions of representative democracy provide an adequate framework for foreign policy-making. The second is that foreign policy would be enhanced by more active public participation. I argue in favour of the second view, and show that public diplomacy modelled on the Ottawa Process has the potential to contribute to the quality and vitality of liberal democratic institutions. Moreover, I find little evidence to support two widely held objections: (1) that a consultative foreign policy leads to the co-optation of non-governmental organizations (NGOs); or (2) that public diplomacy makes policy-makers virtual 'hostages' of the NGOs.

The chapter is divided into three parts. The first part examines the theoretical debate on the sources and objectives of foreign policy and proposes a solution to difficulties that have arisen around the concept of democratization. The second builds on in-depth interviews with participants, as well as a chronology developed by the Centre for Negotiation and Dispute Resolution[2] at Carleton University, to reconstruct the process by which partnerships were built between governments and global civil society. The final part of the chapter returns to the larger issues of democratization of foreign policy and concludes that the Ottawa Process provides an instructive example of how to open policy-making to greater public awareness, which I argue is the central task of democratizing foreign policy.

DEMOCRATIZATION OF FOREIGN POLICY

The idea of democratizing foreign policy, so prominent in the Canadian Liberal Party's *Creating Opportunities* (the Red Book of 1993), as well as its May 1993 *Foreign Policy Platform*, was given little concrete substance in the first term of Prime Minister Jean Chrétien's mandate. Indeed, a volume commissioned to assess the Liberal record on this front in 1995 found little tangible evidence to suggest that the Liberal government was conducting foreign policy any more democratically than its predecessor, and considerable confusion—in both government and academic circles—about what it would actually mean to democratize foreign policy. The implication was that democratization was a failed promise of the Liberal government. One objective here is to revise that assessment in the light of the Ottawa Process.

Any assessment of the Ottawa Process as an example of democratization of foreign policy will need to confront a question that has been left unresolved in academic and policy debates: What does it mean to democratize foreign policy? Since there is no real agreement on what we mean by democratization in this context, it is almost impossible to assess or draw recommendations from policy experiences. Perhaps the best place to begin is by refining our understanding of democracy by distinguishing between the classical ideal of democracy—as a self-governing community of free and equal consociates under the law—and the modern notion of liberal or representative democracy. Liberal democracy traces its ancestry to the classical ideal, but is distinct in a number of ways. First, modern societies are larger and more complex than ancient city-states or medieval republics, and this gives rise to the need for mechanisms of representation. Liberal democracy is not the direct democracy of argumentative citizens congregated in piazzas and streets, but of individual voters in separate urns choosing among parties to constitute assemblies of representatives to speak on their behalf.

Another characteristic of democracy in classical antiquity and Renaissance Italy was its instability. Indeed, for years after these early experiences, democracy was synonymous with chaos and the tyranny of majorities and demagogues. It was the historical achievement of liberalism to place democracy on the foundation of the rule of law and constitutionalism so that the majoritarian impulses that often gave rise to violent fights over alternative conceptions of the good would be replaced by a minimal consensus on procedural norms that afforded protection to minorities and individuals.

Thus, a third characteristic of liberal democracy is what Giovanni Sartori calls 'limited majority rule'.[3] Democracies are governed by majority rule, but the majority is constrained to respect the views of the minority; otherwise, it degenerates into tyranny. No majority is permanent, and opportunities are provided for the opposition to criticize the government openly, without fear of reprisals. In short, liberal democracy rests on the foundations of representation, the rule of law, and limited majority rule.

It is not surprising, then, that when we talk of democratization in Canada many liberal democrats scratch their heads. Does Canada not have a national Parliament to set the direction of foreign policy? Does the Canadian foreign policy establishment not act within the framework of the rule of law established by Parliament and protected by the judiciary? Is there a conflict between Canadian foreign policy and the will of the majority? It is not clear in what ways the framework of laws and parliamentarianism, which is the heart of liberal democracy, would need to be altered to become more democratic.

Kim Richard Nossal recently called attention to this puzzle. He noted that 'the Canadian political system is already marked by the institutions of representative government that exist by the consent, albeit hypothetical, of the broad mass of Canadian adult citizens, exercised periodically in elections that by general concurrence are both fair and free from coercion. . . . In short, if we were to ask whether Canadians themselves have achieved the "democratic ideals" that they are wont to press on others in the international system, the answer would most probably be in the affirmative.' Nevertheless, Nossal notes, if we were to pose the question ' "Is Canadian foreign policy democratic?" the answer from many quarters tends to be a loud and firm "No." '[4] How can Canadian foreign policy be undemocratic if it is implemented within the framework of a legitimately constituted democratic political system?

Advocates of democratization of foreign policy argue that parliamentary procedures—and much of the institutional apparatus of liberal democracy, including mechanisms of foreign policy review—are much less democratic than they appear or, at any rate, could be substantially improved by being more open and consultative. Tim Draimin and Betty Plewes recently articulated the need to change the policy process 'to make it more transparent (through the development of policy options, decision-making, implementation, and monitoring and evaluation) and more accessible (by such means as publishing documents, holding hearings, roundtables and townhalls).' The effect, they argued, would be 'to expand opportunities for people's participation'.[5]

The idea is not merely to hold more meetings with stakeholders. 'The process must have as a goal the expansion of the public's understanding of increasingly complex issues by engaging its attention in ways which develop its capacity to analyse and understand the trade-offs involved in policy choices.'[6] The vision of democracy behind this idea of democratization is that of a deliberative polity, based on thoughtful and active citizenship. For liberal democrats, however, there is something troubling about the idea that foreign policy is made more democratic by being more consultative. Might not consultations derail the public will as easily as reinforce it? What gives stakeholders or individual members of the public authority to speak on behalf of broader communities? In what sense are NGOs or other groups in civil society 'representative'? Draimin and Plewes note that 'NGOs are becoming much more self-critical about their role, their representativeness, and their accountability.'[7] Liberal democrats use the term 'representation' to mean the authorization of a group or individual to speak or act on one's behalf in some sort of public assembly. If making foreign policy more democratic means strengthening representation, there is no obvious reason to believe that NGOs, or civil society generally, have a major role to play—improving the representativeness of political parties and assemblies might be more to the point.

By posing these questions, liberal democrats highlight problematic assumptions behind demands for greater participation. The argument is not necessarily the élitist one that public participation will lead to worse decisions than those taken by the foreign policy experts, although that is a view one also hears expressed with some frequency in government circles. The liberal argument is more subtle. It suggests that a free society is one in which individuals can go about their business with minimal interferences within a framework of legal rules to which they themselves have consented by virtue of participation in legitimate channels and procedures of decision-making. In this view, consultations with non-elected bodies outside the framework of established procedures and rules for political representation and deliberation may be a good or bad thing from a public policy perspective, but they hardly count as democratization of the policy process.

The argument can be pushed further: the preservation of freedom demands respect for the minimal procedural consensus that stabilizes democratic life.[8] Few things are as threatening to this procedural consensus as irreconcilable moral differences. The political system should not be used to promote a particular conception of a morally good life, whether the issue is abortion, suicide, or religious denomination. The same is true of foreign policy. Moral crusades often have negative domestic ramifications because they require a stronger consensus than that which can be advanced through liberal democratic institutions; they challenge the minimal procedural consensus underpinning liberal democracy and impose a moral vision of the good on the collectivity. Moral issues will always divide us because there are no reasonable means of resolving them, and thus they are best left to individual choice and discretion rather than to public debate and disagreement.

The liberal view is profoundly important and should not be dismissed, but at the same time we should note that the process leading to a ban on AP mines highlighted a well-appreciated limitation of the liberal view of democracy: namely, that the proper functioning of liberal institutions requires more active citizenship than the theorists of liberalism typically admit. The puzzle is that a norm so fundamentally consistent with the best traditions of liberal internationalism[9] did not arise from the progressive development of liberal democratic institutions and practices. Why did it require the in-your-face diplomacy of people like Jody Williams and Steve Goose and an international campaign of grassroots organizations to compel liberal democratic states to live up to the norms implicit in existing international law? The answer may have something to do with the limits of the liberal concept of the 'political'. One of the prices of liberalism, as noted by many political theorists, is a passive view of citizenship. In contrast to the classical or republican idea that politics is an ennobling activity, fit for citizens seeking to express the best within themselves and their communities, liberalism instead offers a vision of politics reduced to the narrow pursuit of particular interests. Citizenship in some liberal theories amounts to little more than periodic voting for alternative élites and compromising among interests in pre-established institutions.

A more active, participatory view of citizenship might provide a better optic through which to understand the international movement to ban mines, yet many participatory democrats are loath to accept the notion that democratization is fostered by closer linkages between government and civil society. And they have good reasons. Mark Neufeld, for example, argues that the idea of democratization of foreign policy is a 'sobering example of how "passive revolution" poses a major threat to efforts to articulate a framework of ideas which can serve the creation of an effective counter-hegemonic bloc.'[10]

Conservative critics fear closer links between government and NGOs for diametrically opposed reasons. David A. Lenarcic, for example, warns of the 'unprecedented involvement of non-governmental organizations in the international policy-making process' and suggests that 'Canadians might want to ask themselves if this "new, private order" makes for a government that is more attuned to their national concerns or one that has become beholden to unaccountable special interest groups which are far less concerned with consensus-building than Canadian governments have typically been both at home and abroad.'[11] His answer to this question is that the Canadian government should not become a 'hostage' to special interests.

The notions that the Canadian government might be captured by NGOs or that NGOs would be co-opted by government were very real concerns on the part of both government and NGOs during the movement to ban landmines. Yet they cannot both be right. That such opposite conclusions could be reached suggests the need for clear criteria for determining when a government has been taken 'hostage' by NGOs or when a social movement has been 'co-opted' by the state. For Lenarcic, the possibility that NGOs were too involved in the policy process is confirmed by the fact that Canadian foreign policy took an 'all or nothing and the faster the better' approach. He suggests that 'if Canada really has desired some *modus vivendi* with the United States its failure to craft one can undoubtedly be attributed to an incapacity to persuade NGOs to accept such a settlement and to an indisposition to rub them the wrong way.'[12] For Neufeld, evidence of co-optation lies in the fact that public consultations are not '"neutral" as regards the parameters set for discussion. . . . Most significantly, potential critics from within the NGO community are transformed into "stakeholders."'[13] If fears of co-optation are well founded one should expect to find evidence of a transformation within the NGO coalition from advocates of radical change to stakeholders. Similarly, fears of NGOs capturing government should be reflected, as Lenarcic suggests, in diplomatic inflexibility around issues where the NGOs were strong.

In contrast to the co-optation and capture theses, a third view is possible: namely, that there was a convergence between policy-makers and NGOs as a result of a grassroots campaign that led the public, largely based on the merits of the issue, to support a ban. As public opinion came around to the ban movement and government officials became convinced of the case against mines, government and NGO perspectives began to converge. Public diplomacy, which included the active involvement of NGOs in the policy and diplomatic processes, was a crucial source of accountability to ensure public officials matched their deeds with their words. In this view, the struggle over landmines was not a two-cornered fight between governments and NGOs but a three-ringed fight between governments, NGOs, and global public opinion.

The view I am articulating is rooted in a vision of democracy that emphasizes the role of public deliberation and collective judgement in the formation of public policy.[14] In this view, the solution to the conundrums of liberal democracy—such as its limited view of citizenship—is not to abandon liberal institutions but to revitalize them. Liberal institutions will function at their best when they operate within the context of a vital and dynamic public sphere, which is defined by Jurgen Habermas, a leading exponent of deliberative democracy, as the informal networks for communicating information and points of view through which public opinions are formed and articulated.[15]

Deliberative democrats do not place excessive hopes for democratization in parliamentary institutions. Legislatures are crucial for converting public opinion into legislative action, but their vitality—as the mine ban movement shows—rests on the liveliness of civil society. Ban initiatives in both Canada and the United States have come initially from the legislative branch, and parliaments played a similarly prominent role in Europe. However, the success of such legislation requires public pressure.

One of the central tenets of deliberative democracy is the importance of publicity. In this view, a policy is legitimate if it can be defended in public against criticism in a free and unconstrained debate. With this in mind we may revisit the co-optation/capture debate. The relationship between government and civil society need not involve the surrender of one to the other, as long as policy-making is open and transparent. Distortions in the policy process tend to occur behind closed doors. The Ottawa Process provides a model for a more public form of diplomacy, one that percolated up from below instead of being concocted from above. It suggests lessons for democratic theorists seeking to revitalize liberal institutions by showing how a more open policy process can compel policy-makers and others— experts, firms, lobbies, and states—to expose their arguments to public scrutiny and criticism, thereby improving the quality and performance of democratic institutions. Does such an approach to foreign policy development represent a threat to liberal democracy or, to the contrary, enhance the vitality of liberal democratic institutions by using them to encourage greater public deliberation and participation in decision-making? I argue the case for the latter.

THE OTTAWA PROCESS: A RECONSTRUCTION

The AP mine ban movement can be divided into three stages.[16] In the first instance, NGOs, governments, and the public learned about the merits of the issue. The period from the end of the Cold War until the 1995–6 review of the UN Convention on Certain Conventional Weapons (CCW) was a period of what might be called, for want of a better term, 'consciousness-raising', in which the NGO community took the lead. This stage was followed by a period of working through the issues, during which time governments, NGOs, and the public began to see failure of traditional mechanisms of diplomacy and, linked to that, the need for a closer relation between government and NGOs. With the failure of the CCW, a third stage began, that of the Ottawa Process, which involved the development of a partnership between the Canadian government and NGOs. The Ottawa Process began in earnest in October 1996 when Foreign Minister Axworthy set a deadline of 14 months to sign a ban treaty and ended with the negotiations in Oslo in September 1997 and the signing of the ban treaty in Ottawa in December 1997.

Awareness of the Issue: 1992–1995

According to Jody Williams, the end of the Cold War 'helped bring the lethality of land mines into new focus.' The United Nations brokered peace agreements in a number of countries in the developing world. When peacekeeping missions entered, 'what they found were millions of land mines.'[17] Awareness of the issue came out of the activities of the United Nations, governments involved in peacekeeping missions, and humanitarian relief organizations. In October 1992, a group of NGOs met in New York and agreed to host a first NGO conference in London in May 1993 (see Chapter 2, by Williams and Goose). At that conference, some 70 representatives from 40 NGOs formed a coalition called the International Campaign to Ban Landmines (ICBL). The ICBL was able to bring together a diverse group of refugee and medical relief workers, human rights and development organizations, and arms control and peace advocates into a loosely structured coalition with a single purpose: to ban AP mines.

At the time that the ICBL was established, the public had no clear beliefs or opinions on the mines issue. This made it easier for ban advocates to pose the problem in terms of the trade-off between the limited military utility of mines versus their overwhelming humanitarian costs. This message was hammered home through a series of activities—including a second international NGO conference on landmines in Geneva in May 1994, a series of seminars in Africa during 1995, and a third international conference in Phnom Penh in June 1995.

Through periodic conferences the ICBL was able to develop a consistent set of messages. Pressures would come on policy-makers from local NGOs using the messages developed by the international campaign; at the same time, they would hear identical arguments from foreign governments supportive of a ban. The ICBL acted as a transmission belt for information, via newsletters, the Internet, and faxes, so that shifts in government policy in one country would immediately be brought to the attention of governments and campaigns around the world. As a result, a sense of momentum was built and pressure on states was continuously ratcheted upward. 'These groups knew how to mold public opinion', said one newspaper policy analyst. 'They brought mine blast survivors, with maimed bodies and missing limbs, to Europe and North America to tell their stories. They produced shocking pamphlets showing damage done by land mines. They enlisted prominent figures such as retired General Norman Schwarzkopf, actor Peter Ustinov, and singer Bruce Cockburn to speak out against the scourge.'[18]

The ICBL paved the way for governments to move towards a ban, but the strength of the coalition was in no small measure due to the fact that there were significant supporters of a ban in governments around the world.[19] The first official step was taken by Senator Patrick J. Leahy of Vermont and Congressman Lane Evans of Illinois, who introduced legislation in the US Congress for a one-year moratorium on exports of AP mines in October 1992. This moratorium, which was extended for three years in 1993, had a dramatic impact on other countries. France announced its own moratorium and then initiated the process that would lead to a review of the mines issue in the CCW. In September 1994 the UN Secretary-General endorsed the idea of a ban, and by 1995 comprehensive export moratoria were in effect in 25 countries. Belgium, however, was the first country to implement a total ban on AP mine use, production, procurement, sale, or transfer, and the Minister of Defence promised to destroy Belgium's existing stockpile.

In Canada, Celina Tuttle, a member of Physicians for Global Survival, nearly single-handedly began a small campaign of letter-writing on the landmines issue. In May 1994 she attended the ICBL's Second International NGO Conference to Ban Landmines in Geneva, Switzerland, which was attended by more than 110 representatives of over 75 NGOs from around the world. The ICBL conference was held just as expert groups had begun to prepare for the Review Conference on the 1980 Convention, also to be held in Geneva. At the time, Canada had still not ratified the CCW. The first informal meetings among Canadian NGOs were held in the fall of 1994, and Mines Action Canada (MAC) became a formal organization with over 20 members in early 1995. The groups to join the coalition included Physicians for Global Survival, CARE, CUSO, Oxfam, Project Ploughshares, World Vision, the United Nations Association of Canada, a number of churches, and the Canadian NGO umbrella organization, the Canadian Council for International Co-operation (CCIC). From the outset, the coalition included development, disarmament, humanitarian, and peace groups. MAC's initial objectives included legislation in Canada to ban the use, production, stockpiling, sale, transfer, or export of AP mines and the destruction of existing stockpiles; support for humanitarian mine clearance efforts; assistance to victims of landmines; and the exchange of information at the international level with the ICBL to promote a global ban.[20]

In March 1995, Celina Tuttle became co-ordinator of MAC, responsible for day-to-day activities of the campaign, and Valerie Warmington, of the CCIC, became chairperson responsible for relations with international organizations. A steering committee was formed of six people representing different groups, with decision-making on a consensual basis. From its inception, indeed, before it was formalized, MAC undertook letter-writing campaigns to lobby government officials. In September 1995, MAC began a letter-writing campaign to pressure the government around the CCW meetings. These campaigns were extremely successful, a fact attributed by NGO leaders to the nature of the issue: 'It was black and white and something could be done about it.'[21] Foreign Minister André Ouellet said he received more letters on mines than on any other issue except national unity. By the fall of 1995, one official asked MAC to cease the letter-writing campaign because it was taking up too much of his time to respond to all the letters— the government, he said, had gotten the message. At the same time, in the fall of 1995 and early 1996, MAC also organized a petition and quickly gathered over 50,000 signatures, which were sent in batches of 10,000 to the House of Commons. Under Canadian legislation, the Minister of Foreign Affairs must respond to such petitions in the House. Working with sympathetic members, such as Reform MP Keith Martin, MAC was able repeatedly to shove the mine ban onto the parliamentary agenda. Parliament played an important role, but as one Canadian parliamentarian put it: 'The public leads the debate; Parliament is less courageous. If you play by the parliamentary rules of the game, you don't get anywhere. Adversarial rules do not lend themselves to constructive solutions. In Parliament, your objective is not to solve problems, but to destroy the other side.' Parliament, he concluded, can play a constructive role only when 'public pressure is persistent, consistent, in-your-face, and in the media.'[22]

MAC also sought consultations with government, demanding to meet regularly with officials within the context of the negotiation process. They used the results of the 1994 Foreign Policy Review to assert their prerogative to have consultations with the government. The government statement that came out of the review process had committed Canada to a 'more consultative foreign policy process', especially with the NGO and human rights community.[23] Meetings with government officials were sporadic at first, but these became more regular after November 1995. Some of the early meetings were acrimonious. MAC representatives sought to explain the humanitarian side of the crisis and argued for the need for someone with a humanitarian background on the delegation to the CCW. The initial reaction of government officials was to argue that mines were legitimate and essential to defence; moreover, the government could not take an excessively strong pro-ban position without jeopardizing the credibility of Canada in the eyes of allies. However, some officials at DFAIT were privately beginning to have second thoughts. One official described how he lost conviction in his own arguments for AP mines as he began to sense that the military was 'trotting out reflex arguments' and that the case against mines being made by the NGOs was a good one.[24] His views changed as a result of an 'epiphany' brought about by arguments made by advocates of a ban outside the government as well as from other members of the staff at DFAIT. NGO leaders countered the arguments of Canadian officials, saying that nothing was likely to happen in the CCW and Canada had little to lose by taking the moral high ground.

A breakthrough in Canadian policy came following unscripted comments in which Foreign Minister Ouellet expressed his personal 'epiphany' in favour of a ban in a media scrum in November 1995.[25] Officials in DFAIT's disarmament division were 'secretly delighted' by Ouellet's statement. Jill Sinclair, head of the division, said, 'Okay, we've got some direction from our minister on this one so let's go for it.' Bob Lawson, who had recently joined the division, faxed MAC the text of Ouellet's remarks, which Tuttle e-mailed to every member of the campaign and encouraged them all to respond with letters congratulating the minister. In one such letter, Debbie Grisdale of Physicians for Global Survival congratulated Ouellet for his 'wise and compassionate decision to call for a total ban on land mines', and offered support and assistance to 'turn your call into law.'[26] The effect of this effort was to ensure that the minister's words received the fullest publicity.

The lobbying stimulated by Ouellet's remarks also drove a wedge between the Department of Foreign Affairs and the Department of National Defence (DND). It became clear to members of MAC—and at least one DFAIT official encouraged this perception in an effort to turn up the public pressure on DND—that a public split was developing between the foreign policy and defence establishments. MAC planted this in the media, not by asserting it directly, but by suggesting that journalists investigate whether such a split existed. The media picked up on this theme, thereby placing DND in an even weaker and more defensive posture.

Working Through the Issue: 1995–1996
As public officials, NGOs, and the public began to grapple with the AP mines issue, linkages that were initially tentative, even surreptitious, between NGOs and government developed into a more genuine partnership. Ouellet's comments had helped to make mines a matter of public policy debate. MAC asked the government whether AP mines violated the proportionality rule of the Geneva Convention, and government lawyers determined that landmines would probably fail. Shortly thereafter, in January 1996, Canada became the first G–7 country to announce a comprehensive moratorium on the production, use, stockpile, and transfer of AP mines (a position previously taken only by Belgium, Norway, and Austria).

In March 1996, Canada invited a member of Mines Action Canada, Valerie Warmington, to join the Canadian delegation to Geneva—not to the first session in January-February, which was devoted to technical issues, but to the second, which took place in April-May. There was a precedent for such a decision: in July 1995 Warmington had served on a delegation to a meeting at the United Nations concerning a trust fund for mine clearance. It was common for Canada to send NGO delegates to such meetings, especially since the Canadian government was eager to show it was working with NGOs, but the government had never invited an NGO member to be part of the Canadian delegation in the CCW. Indeed, only months earlier, the Canadian government had dragged its heels on sending a delegate with a background in humanitarian issues.

'This was a huge issue', said one MAC member. 'We did not support the CCW because they were negotiating something we felt had been outlawed in the Geneva Convention. How could we support the CCW when it was negotiating something that would be less than what was already in place? We did not want to legitimize the CCW.' There was still a lack of trust between the government and the NGOs, and some reservations existed about being seen as 'allies' of the government. The unilateral moratorium, after all, was just a press release, not a legal document. On the other hand, MAC's leadership knew the importance of personal relations and of being able to bring information to the attention of policy-makers at key moments of decision-making. Now they were being asked to sit in the bargaining seat as representative of the Canadian government. 'We were concerned about being co-opted', said another MAC leader. However, she noted that if MAC felt it was being misrepresented, its delegate could always quit. 'You have to explore what is possible. You know what your objectives are from the very beginning. Partnership with government means you share objectives. My view was: "I'll support the government as long as I can, but if it goes off track I will be the first to criticize." '

Participation in the government delegation also risked MAC's standing in the ICBL. Only a handful of countries, such as Sweden and Australia, had NGOs on their delegations, and there were concerns that MAC's image would be diminished among other NGOs. Some NGOs, including people in the ICBL, were suspicious of MAC, which they regarded as a newcomer and an organization that was working closely with government. In the end, MAC could not turn away from the opportunity to push the issue forward. The internal debate in MAC was difficult, but the final conclusion was to treat the opportunity as a pilot process.

The inclusion of MAC obeyed a dual objective on the part of the government: to take the heat off policy-makers and to strengthen the Canadian position. As one official put it, 'let's throw open the books. If Valerie [Warmington] can agree there is nothing to be done, then we're at an impasse.' In other words, it would be clear that the government had done everything possible even if the CCW failed. Moreover, by opening the books and giving MAC access to the thinking behind Canadian policy, the 'shutters would be opened' to scrutiny. NGO involvement meant that 'governments are forced to defend their answers publicly.'[27] At the same time, the issue was moving from the back pages to the front page of newspapers across the country and around the world. The net effect of these pressures would be to make it hard to hide behind secrecy or limit discussion to arms control experts.

Ambassador to the CCW in Geneva Mark Moher, the head of the Canadian delegation, made every effort to ensure Warmington was part of the process; she was at all the meetings, and her opinion was solicited in all decisions. Everything that happened in the negotiations was brought back home and discussed among the NGOs, making the issues far more publicly accessible. By this point, MAC represented 30 NGOs and had over 400 other contacts with whom it consulted regularly. A large number of constituent interests were represented in MAC, and it worked in consultation with these groups during the negotiations. There were full-day working sessions on the treaty, typically with 15 to 25 representatives outside the steering committee, who would give instructions on what Warmington should be seeking in the negotiations.

Did NGO involvement in the CCW negotiations co-opt them, turn them into stakeholders, or deflect them from their initial objectives? A founding member of MAC argued that behind-the-scenes involvement did not deflect MAC from its publicly stated objectives. 'Warmington's involvement meant access to a new level of information, but off-the-record discussions mean nothing in the big picture. They don't mean anything unless politicians make their views public so you can hold them to it. We kept hammering away for public declarations and statements, because they had been saying one thing and doing another. By the time they agreed to allow MAC on the delegation, already they had been forced to change and they knew what they had to do. MAC was there because the government did not have a whole lot to lose.'

Although the experiment of including an NGO in the Canadian government delegation was widely regarded as a success in both official and NGO circles, the results of the CCW were, predictably, a disappointment. Advocates of a ban came away 'virtually empty-handed', said Holly Burkhalter of Physicians for Human Rights. 'Slowed by the CCW's consensus rules and swamped in technical detail, the final product was one that even the most enthusiastic users and exporters of landmines (like India, China, and Russia) could endorse.'[28] At this point, Canadian government officials no longer felt they could say 'leave it to us; we have to work through traditional mechanisms',[29] so they began to explore alternative approaches.

Bob Lawson met privately with NGO representatives and pro-ban states in Geneva during the CCW Review Conference to explore the possibility of 'opening a new track of diplomatic action'.[30] Here again, the active participation of NGOs was decisive. There was agreement around the table when Canada proposed to host a meeting that was initially billed as an 'international strategy session' to bring together like-minded states, government agencies, and NGOs to give impetus to multilateral progress on a global ban.[31] As the CCW Review Conference was wrapping up, Canada, with the support of the International Committee of the Red Cross and the United Nations, formally called for an international meeting in Ottawa for later that year. The idea was to make governments that had gone beyond a moratorium to come together in a bloc. If each pro-ban government propped one another up, Jody Williams and others in the ICBL thought, 'each would get some spine.'[32] The momentum would die unless another step was taken forward. Thus, out of the failure of the CCW came the Ottawa Process.

Coming to Resolution: 1996–1997
One of the unique features of the October 1996 Ottawa conference was that its 'ministers and officials shared plenary and workshop platforms with mine-victims, parliamentarians, and NGO representatives . . . the conference successfully linked NGO activism to a call for action by states.'[33] The Canadian initiative became the only game in town and was attended by 74 states instead of the 15 that were expected. Canada worked with the ICBL and MAC in an effort to promote interest in the conference. Initially, the idea was that governments and NGOs would be equal participants in the conference, and both government and NGO delegates would be involved in all discussions. Many states had serious reservations about such a radical notion. Canadian officials were accused of 'selling out to the NGOs' and of being 'overtaken by their agenda'. In the end, a compromise was reached in which the meeting would be held on two tracks: some meetings would be for official delegates and closed to NGOs unless they were on official delegations (like the meetings of the CCW), and other sessions would be open to NGOs (who were called 'observers') as well as official delegates. There were over 20 NGO delegates in total, including a substantial delegation from MAC as well as from the ICBL, and roughly 15 countries brought NGOs on their official delegations, as they had been encouraged to do by the conference organizers.

In the closing session of the conference, Foreign Minister Axworthy made an announcement that was a surprise to all but a handful of officials at DFAIT and the leading representatives of the NGO community (including Williams, Goose, and Warmington). He said to the assembled audience, 'I have one final point to add to your action plan. That point comes in the form of both an invitation and a challenge. The challenge is to see a treaty signed no later than the end of 1997.'[34] The NGO delegates had been told to orchestrate a standing ovation, which they did; meanwhile, government officials gasped for air.[35] The US delegation was particularly furious. The extent to which Axworthy was out on a limb should not be underestimated: in effect, his core coalition at that time consisted of NGOs and a handful of states.

Perhaps Axworthy's challenge could be construed as evidence of a government 'hostage' to NGOs. However, to make this case one would have to argue that the government was somehow constrained by the NGO community from pursuing a course of action that it would otherwise prefer. There is little evidence that Axworthy's initiative was due to pressure from NGOs—most of whom were as stunned by the announcement as were government officials. In fact, this was one of the few moments during the movement to ban landmines when a government official was out in front of the NGOs. Axworthy was offering to go beyond what the ICBL had demanded, which was a ban by the year 2000.

The debate over the Korean exception ostensibly provides a better example of the government-as-hostage thesis. In March 1997 Chrétien, during meetings in Washington, expressed concern to the Americans that they were refusing to engage in any substantive discussions under the Ottawa Process and urged them to get to the table. The next month a senior delegation travelled to Ottawa to discuss US reservations. The US team questioned whether the treaty could be effective without China and Russia, and argued that they could not defend Seoul without landmines. An article in Maclean's magazine picked up on this and reported that Axworthy told the Americans, 'we can look at how you can put some codicils' in the Convention to permit an 'exception for Korea'.[36] MAC was alarmed by this development and issued an action alert to all the other campaigns in the ICBL, calling on them to oppose this sort of erosion of the treaty. No one from the US campaign responded to the action alert and, as a result, some members of MAC began to wonder whether their US counterparts were willing to accept a Korean exemption in return for US approval of the Convention. These suspicions resurfaced in Oslo.

Canadian NGO fears seemed to be warranted in the final weekend in Oslo, when the US requested and obtained a 24-hour delay in the negotiations. The purpose was to enable the US delegation to come up with a proposal to put on the table. The unity of the ICBL, and the NGO-government partnership, could have been jeopardized at that time by any initiative on the part of the US to insist on a Korean exemption. If the US had dropped all of its demands except for special treatment for Korea (in the seemingly innocuous form of, say, permission to use self-destructing mines in UN-sanctioned demilitarized zones for a certain period of time), the partnership between government and NGOs might have been threatened. MAC sought assurances from Canadian officials that they would not accept any exemptions, and its members would surely have walked away from the negotiations had an exemption been given. The leadership of the ICBL, however, particularly members of the US campaign, might well have accepted such an exemption. With the ICBL divided, the core group of states seeking a ban could have collapsed.

The entire enterprise hung in the balance in Oslo. But the negotiations never reached a breaking point because of the refusal of the US delegates to break open their package of conditions and seriously negotiate. Thus, while it was true that some Canadian officials did not want to go too far toward meeting US objections to the Convention because it would have undermined the partnership with NGOs and would have divided the ICBL, they were never ultimately faced with such difficult choices because of the unwillingness of the Americans to negotiate any form of compromise. A representative of the ICRC expressed the unease felt by many NGOs in Oslo:

> We were on the verge, in spite of collaboration, of having a treaty that would have been very difficult for the ICRC to bless. In the end, we could have had high-level deals struck among government leaders not so involved in this process. We were under great pressure to indicate what level of compromise—delays—we would accept. We were getting to the limit of the role independent organizations can play.

In spite of the fears, the final deal was consistent, in both substance and form, with the objectives that MAC, the ICRC, and the ICBL had set out to achieve. Although they were frustrated by having to sit in the hallways during certain expert meetings, especially since they felt they knew more about the issues than many government delegates, the NGOs could claim to have drafted the treaty, to have 'talked about each and every word' in it.[37] Were they turned into co-opted stakeholders? If this is so, it is puzzling to note that the initial objectives of groups like MAC were accomplished, point by point, in the Ottawa Process.

The idea that the NGOs were 'domesticated' (as suggested by Larrinaga and Turrene Sjolander in Chapter 18) is meaningless unless goals are attributed to the NGOs that they never espoused. The connotations of 'domestication' are also belied by the intense disagreements that emerged between the NGO community and government officials—especially Canadians—when it appeared as though Canada was supporting the US request for a 24-hour delay in the Oslo end-game. Impromptu demonstrations by the NGOs at Oslo in which Canada was accused (prematurely, as it turned out) of 'selling out' (see Chapter 3, by Warmington and Tuttle) were hardly the sort of behaviour one would expect from groups with a stakeholder mentality. Commenting on the view that NGOs were co-opted by the Ottawa Process, Jody Williams remarked ironically, 'I feel domesticated!'

The argument that the Canadian government became a hostage of NGOs turns out to have an equally limited factual basis. Rather than being captured by special interests, the story of the ban movement suggests that it was precisely because the government was attuned to the views of the vast majority of the public that it decided to work in partnership with NGOs and like-minded states in pursuit of a ban. The assertion that there was insufficient debate, or that 'the fervent NGO mantra on APLs' became 'a substitute for thought and analysis at the policy-making level',[38] is at odds with the unprecedented expression of public opinion in favour of a foreign policy option. In seeking a ban, the government was responding much more to public opinion than to the presumed 'unified rigidity' of the NGOs. Indeed, had the Canadian government wanted to divide the NGOs, my reconstruction of the Ottawa Process suggests it would have been extremely easy to do so.

The Ottawa Process concluded with a signing ceremony in Ottawa on 2–4 December 1997. In what was probably the largest diplomatic conference ever hosted by Canada, delegates from 157 countries participated in three days of workshops and discussions, and 122 signed the Convention. The results of a survey and focus groups conducted during the signing conference (see Chapter 1) confirm observations central to my argument. First, NGOs felt that the merit of the issue contributed to the success of their movement. The campaign succeeded by framing the issue as a humanitarian, not an arms control, problem and by making the choice 'morally unambiguous'.[39] Second, government officials tended to attribute special importance to international NGOs (essentially, the ICBL) because 'they were there at the negotiating table as the treaty was negotiated.' The mere presence of NGOs at important meetings was 'a major influence because if someone would say something they didn't like, public opinion would know it.'

At the national level, the role of public opinion varied. Government officials from Norway and Australia emphasized that public opinion favouring a ban was ahead of public policy between 1993 and 1995. Delegates from Zimbabwe and Tanzania, on the other hand, suggested public opinion played a less important role in their countries. Likewise, the role of civil society in Japan was limited; the Japanese government shifted in response to international, not domestic, pressures. Third, NGO representatives emphasized the importance of partnership. The movement to ban AP mines was successful largely because 'NGOs and government were working together, they were not opposing each other.' Not all NGO delegates took this view. For example, relations between governments and NGOs were much more difficult in France and the United Kingdom. As a French delegate put it, 'France, until a year ago, would not have NGOs in official delegations. Now they do that, but there is still no partnership.' A Canadian official indicated that partnership requires an acknowledgement of differences: 'NGOs don't want to be public servants. There will always be some mistrust and competition for ideas and leadership; yet I have seen a real change in many issues, leading to co-operation between government and NGOs.' Similarly, a Norwegian official said that 'NGOs provided pressure and support. To the surprise of governments, they turned out to be reasonable people who understood international diplomacy. Without this partnership, there would have been no Ottawa Process.'

Ekos Research Associates Inc.[40] detected little evidence that the NGOs involved in the Ottawa Process perceived themselves to have been co-opted, or that government officials felt they had been held hostage by the NGOs. By contrast, both strongly emphasized the importance of publicity and the power of public opinion in driving the ban movement forward. The NGOs would have had little impact had they not had the sort of issue that could be used to arouse strong views in the public, and governments would not have responded with such determination without the pressures of public opinion orchestrated globally.

CONCLUSION

I began by asking whether the Ottawa Process represents an example of the democratization of foreign policy through the construction of a partnership between government and civil society. The Ottawa Process democratized foreign policy within the framework of existing representative institutions by using a partnership with civil society to expose policy to the test of publicity. Does this argument meet Nossal's objection that 'the democratizers have it all wrong: what they are proposing are not reforms that will "democratize" Canadian foreign policy; rather, these are merely techniques of political management that are being paraded as examples of democracy in action'?[41] I believe it does.

Democracy can be defined as a set of institutions or the ideals they embody. When defined as institutions, an obvious question suggests itself: why one set of institutions and not another? The answer to this question will depend on what we think democracy *should* be. Nossal takes existing representative institutions, examines proposals for reform in light of how these institutions ought to function, and finds the proposals wanting. He then provides his own proposals, which are more consistent with the institutional features of the Canadian system. Specifically, he suggests that 'in a representative democracy such as Canada, the most appropriate forum for the discussion of issues that affect the community as a whole continues to be the national legislature.'[42] The logic of the argument is impeccable, but it rests on the premise that we should start with existing institutions as our normative standard.

I propose a more basic normative standard, which is consistent with a wide range of democratic institutions, including representative ones. Democracy is a system in which those in power must provide public reasons for their actions and defend them against criticism. The use of public reason helps to underpin and justify representative institutions, as well as other variants of democracy such as classical and republican forms.[43] Consider John Stuart Mill's justification of parliamentary institutions. Mill argued that 'the proper office of a representative assembly is to watch and control the government; to throw the light of publicity on its acts; to compel a full exposition and justification of all of them which any one considers questionable; to censure them if found condemnable'.[44] The idea of public reason is an old and venerable argument in favour of legislative assemblies.

The difference between Mill and deliberative democrats concerns whether the light of publicity shines more brightly in Parliament when there is a vigorous civil society. Deliberative democrats see a strong civil society as vital to the health of the public sphere, and that is why participation is important. Nossal's argument that 'would-be democratizers have confused greater *participation* in the policy process with greater *democratization* of that process'[45] may be true. It is tendentious to claim that consultations with élites will lead to a more egalitarian, participatory democracy; it is also evident that the ability of Parliament to shine publicity on the policy-making process depends on the engagement of citizens and the vitality of civil society. Advocates of democratization should rest their defence of civil society-government partnership on publicity, not on participation.

Public diplomacy—meaning the use of public reason in diplomacy—can help achieve the goals Nossal espouses (namely, defining and pursuing the interests of the community as a whole) but cannot achieve them merely by allowing ordinary parliamentarians a larger role in foreign policy debates.[46] Nossal's perspective exemplifies a problem in contemporary liberal democratic theory and practice to which I have already alluded: only more active citizenship than that typically expected by liberal democrats can enhance the meaningfulness and performance of liberal democracy. Participation is important not for the reasons so trenchantly criticized by Nossal, but because, as classical liberal democrats understood, public engagement is the way to overcome particular interests and achieve a larger vision of the interests of the whole community. Mill believed that the citizen participating in public affairs would feel 'called upon, while so engaged, to weigh interests not his own; to be guided, in case of conflicting claims, by another rule than his private partialities; to apply, at every turn, principles and maxims which have for their reason of existence the common good. . . . He is made to feel himself one of the public, and whatever is for their benefit to be for his benefit.'[47]

The public diplomacy practised in the Ottawa Process compelled policy-makers to provide public reasons for their actions and exposed them to criticism from civil society by bringing an NGO coalition into the policy process, both as domestic partners and international allies. Triangulation between policy-makers, NGOs, and the mass public contributed to the success of Canada's foreign policy initiative to ban landmines because it tapped into a deep current of idealism and Pearsonian internationalism that had long been neglected by the pragmatism espoused by the foreign policy establishment.

The global movement to ban landmines raised awareness of the AP mine problem and, by framing the issue in terms of a trade-off between military utility and humanitarian consequences, provided public opinion with tools to work through the complexities of the issue. The consequence was a remarkably strong consensus. This result is consistent with the central finding of deliberative polling: that the views expressed in public opinion polls, which often appear to be contradictory or incoherent, do not reflect ignorance or stupidity so much as the failure to think the issues through to their consequences; and that once the public has been given the opportunity and encouragement to do so, it can arrive at enduring, reasoned judgements on complex issues.[48]

The idea that the government was taken hostage by particular interests makes little sense in the light of public opinion. It is hard to accuse a government of being hostage to particular interests when it is supported by 95 per cent of the public.[49] Nor is there a basis for asserting that NGOs were co-opted. Neufeld's cautionary words are well taken. There are good reasons to be sceptical of promises of democratization of foreign policy when they come from the Minister of Foreign Affairs or are articulated in a government statement or political party program. There are fewer reasons to be sceptical, however, when democratization occurs as the result of the engagement of the *demos* in a policy process that percolates up from below. In the Ottawa Process, government policy was brought around to the parameters of the debate established by NGOs, not the other way around. Democratization of foreign policy was the consequence, not of ministerial directives, but of a grassroots campaign that originated in global civil society.

To his credit, Foreign Minister Axworthy recognized that 'one can no longer relegate NGOs to simple advisory or advocacy roles in this process. They are now part of the way decisions have to be made. They have been the voice saying that governments belong to the people, and must respond to the people's hopes, demands and ideals.'[50] Likewise, advocates of a ban found a unique staff in the Arms Control and Disarmament Division of DFAIT willing to work with NGOs. Once DFAIT officials had decided to pursue a ban, the involvement of NGOs in the policy process helped them to overcome resistance to policy change among arms control experts and bureaucrats who had long been shielded from public scrutiny. Canada's initiative would not have been possible without a civil society movement of global reach, and it is only in retrospect that we can see how the unique partnership forged between states and global civil society contributed to fulfilling the goal of democratizing foreign policy.

Democracy, regardless of the institutional form it takes, is a political system in which those in power must provide public reasons for their actions and defend them against criticism. In the Ottawa Process, policy-makers provided public reasons for their actions and exposed them to criticism from civil society by bringing an NGO coalition into the policy process, both as domestic partners and international allies. The result was one of the most significant Canadian foreign policy achievements in decades.

NOTES

An earlier version of this chapter appeared in *Canadian Foreign Policy* 5, 3 (Spring 1998).

I am grateful to the following people for their comments: Kerry Buck, Steve Goose, Debbie Grisdale, Fen Hampson, Dean Oliver, Dick Price, Brian Tomlin, and two anonymous reviewers. Bob Lawson was a consistently helpful guide for probing the complexities of government-civil society linkages. Faiza Warsame provided invaluable research assistance. Research funding was generously provided by the Non-Proliferation, Arms Control and Disarmament Division in the Canadian Department of Foreign Affairs and International Trade. The author alone is responsible for the interpretations and evidence presented, including all errors.

1. The Ottawa Process had three elements: (1) a partnership between states and global civil society in the conduct of international diplomacy; (2) the practice of bringing small and medium-sized states into a coalition of the like-minded; and (3) a willingness to operate outside of the normal channels and fora on a diplomatic 'fast track' to ban AP mines. Notes from comments by Steve Goose in the Ottawa Process Forum, 5 Dec. 1997.

2. Centre for Negotiation and Dispute Resolution, *A Working Chronology of the International Movement to Ban Anti-Personnel (AP) Mines* (Ottawa: Carleton University, 1997).

3. Giovanni Sartori, *The Theory of Democracy Revisited*, vol. 1, *The Contemporary Debate* (Chatham, NJ: Chatham House, 1987), 31–4.

4. Kim Richard Nossal, 'The Democratization of Canadian Foreign Policy: The Elusive Ideal', in Maxwell A. Cameron and Maureen A. Molot, eds, *Democracy and Foreign Policy: Canada Among Nations 1995* (Ottawa: Carleton University Press, 1995), 31; Nossal, 'The Democratization of Canadian Foreign Policy?', *Canadian Foreign Policy* 1, 3 (1993): 95–105.

5. Tim Draimin and Betty Plewes, 'Civil Society and the Democratization of Foreign Policy', in Cameron and Molot, eds, *Democracy and Foreign Policy*, 64.

6. Ibid.

7. Ibid., 66.

8. John Rawls, *Political Liberalism* (New York: Columbia University Press, 1996), 133–72.

9. Kant argued strongly for international norms governing the conduct of inter-state relations on the grounds that the existence of warfare as a fact or a possibility in international relations was inevitably one of the most important obstacles to the development of democratic institutions.

10. Mark Neufeld, 'Democratization in/of Foreign Policy: Critical Reflections on the Canadian Case', paper prepared for the Joint ISA-AMEI Conference in Manzanillo, Mexico, 1997, 22. By 'passive revolution', Neufeld (p. 10) means 'the co-optation of the potential leaders of subaltern social groups through the strategy of "assimilating and domesticating potentially dangerous ideas by adjusting them to the policies of the dominant coalition"'. See also Chapter 14 in this volume.

11. David A. Lenarcic, *Knight-Errant? Canada and the Crusade to Ban Anti-Personnel Land Mines* (Toronto: Irwin, 1998), 70.

12. Ibid., 71.

13. Neufeld, 'Democratization in/of Foreign Policy', 12.

14. Jurgen Habermas, *Between Facts and Norms: Contributions to a Discourse Theory of Democracy* (Cambridge, Mass.: MIT Press, 1996); Seyla Benhabib, 'Toward a Deliberative Model of Democratic Legitimacy', in Benhabib, ed., *Democracy and Difference: Contesting the Boundaries of the Political* (Princeton, NJ: Princeton University Press, 1996); John S. Dryzek, *Discursive Democracy: Politics, Policy, and Political Science* (Cambridge: Cambridge University Press, 1990).

15. Habermas, *Between Facts and Norms*, 359–66.

16. See Daniel Yankelovich, *Coming to Public Judgement: Making Democracy Work in a Complex World* (Syracuse, NY: Syracuse University Press, 1991).

17. Jody Williams, 'Land Mines: Dealing with the Environmental Impact', *Environment and Security* 1, 2 (1997): 107–8.

18. Carol Goar, 'Dedication, persistence forged plan to ban mines', *Toronto Star*, 6 Sept. 1997.

19. When asked to explain the US refusal to embrace a ban, members of the ICBL pointed to the 'lack of champions' of a ban within the Clinton administration. Seminar at Carleton University, 3 Nov. 1997.

20. See MAC, 'Objectives of Mines Action Canada', mimeo. These objectives were slightly revised on 1 November 1996, but never modified substantially.

21. Unless otherwise indicated, quotations are from interviews in Ottawa, 15–16 Feb. 1998, with leaders of MAC.

22. Interview, Ottawa, 25 Feb. 1998.

23. Canada, DFAIT, *Canada in the World: Government Statement* (Ottawa: Canada Communications Group, 1995), 48–9.

24. DFAIT official, talk given on a not-for-attribution basis at Carleton University, Ottawa, 28 Oct. 1997.

25. Allan Thompson, 'How Canada hatched land mine ban. The minister looked at his son and said, "This weapon no longer makes sense"', *Toronto Star*, 16 Sept. 1997, A23.

26. Correspondence dated 10 Nov. 1995. MAC archives.

27. DFAIT official, talk at Carleton University, 28 Oct. 1997.

28. Holly Burkhalter, 'Phantom Pain: Banning Landmines', *World Policy Journal* (Summer 1997): 31.

29. DFAIT official, talk at Carleton University, 28 Oct. 1997.

30. Bob Lawson, 'Towards a New Multilateralism: Canada and the Landmine Ban', *Behind the Headlines* 54, 4 (1997): 20.

31. As late as September 1996, Foreign Minister Axworthy was describing the purpose of the conference in Ottawa as an effort to 'build consensus on a strong, forward-looking resolution to the 51st session of the General Assembly.' See 'Notes for an Address by the Honourable Lloyd Axworthy, Minister of Foreign Affairs, to the 51st General Assembly of the United Nations', DFAIT Statement, 24 Sept. 1996.

32. Jody Williams, 'The Ban on Landmines', public lecture, Carleton University, 3 Nov. 1997.

33. Lawson, 'Towards a New Multilateralism', 21.

34. 'Notes for an Address by the Honourable Lloyd Axworthy, Minister of Foreign Affairs, at the Closing Session of the International Strategy Conference Towards a Global Ban on Anti-Personnel Mines', Ottawa, 5 Oct. 1996.

35. DFAIT official, Carleton University, 7 Oct. 1997.

36. Bruce Wallace, 'The battle to ban land mines', *Maclean's*, 1 July 1997, 34.

37. Comment by member of the ICBL, Carleton University, 3 Nov. 1997.

38. Lenarcic, *Knight-Errant?*, 71.

39. Quotations in the remainder of this section are taken from the following 1997 surveys by Ekos Research Associates of Ottawa: 'Ban Convention—Interactive Survey Groups—NGOs'; 'Ban Convention—Interactive Survey Groups—Government'; 'Ban Convention—Focus Group—NGOs'; 'Ban Convention—Focus Group—Government'.

40. Ibid.; Ekos Research Associates, *A Global Ban on Landmines. Survey of Participants: Technical Report* (Ottawa, 1997).

41. Nossal, 'The Democratization of Canadian Foreign Policy?', 101.

42. Ibid., 103.

43. Rawls, *Political Liberalism*, 212–13.

44. John Stuart Mill, *Representative Government* (London: Dent, 1968), 240.

45. Nossal, 'The Democratization of Canadian Foreign Policy?', 102.

46. Ibid., 104.

47. Mill, *Representative Government*, 217.

48. See Yankelovich, *Coming to Public Judgement*; James S. Fishkin, *Democracy and Deliberation: New Directions for Democratic Reform* (New Haven: Yale University Press, 1991); Fishkin, *The Voice of the People: Public Opinion and Democracy* (New Haven: Yale University Press, 1995).

49. Bruce Wallace, 'Second wind', *Maclean's*, 1 Dec. 1997, 19.

50. 'Notes for an Address by the Honourable Lloyd Axworthy, Minister of Foreign Affairs, to the Oslo NGO Forum on Banning Anti-Personnel Landmines', DFAIT Statement, Oslo, 10 Sept. 1997.

CHAPTER 21

TOWARDS A NEW MULTILATERALISM
Lloyd Axworthy

The campaign to ban anti-personnel (AP) mines was a defining moment for post-Cold War international relations at a number of levels. It showed that international public opinion will not tolerate the indiscriminate violence of landmines. Increasingly, the public places humanitarian values above military interests in calculations of international security. It showed that, when existing international bodies are not up to a task, new issue-based alliances can make unprecedented progress. Finally, it showed that states can achieve far more when they work in full partnership with civil society.

I believe that the campaign to ban landmines not only produced a significant victory in international disarmament, but also epitomized broader changes that have shaken the foundations of international relations. Driven by global change, new forms of multilateralism are emerging, with new concepts, new tools, new actors, and even new institutions. As both product and exemplar of these changes, the landmine ban campaign deserves to be studied in its broader context. This context is defined by issues and actors new to international relations: issues such as threats to human security and new forms of conflict based on ethnic or religious identity, and actors such as non-governmental organizations (NGOs), the private sector, and new alliances of states.

The campaign and its context clearly have deep implications for the conduct of Canadian foreign policy. In the second part of this chapter I look at how Canada is responding to the challenge and making its mark on the new multilateralism. Canadian foreign policy is focusing on threats to human security ranging from landmines to excessive military expenditures to human rights abuses. It is developing creative new ways to address these threats, from peacebuilding to public diplomacy.

THE LANDMINE CAMPAIGN IN CONTEXT

The success of negotiations for a landmine convention would have been impossible 10, or even 5 years ago. Until recently, there was very little scope for the voices of individuals to be heard in matters of foreign policy. NGOs were barred from most international meetings, and elected democracies were in the minority. States too often operated under an impenetrable cloak of state sovereignty. As a result, the human cost of landmines and other threats to individual security were largely invisible to the international community.

In the past few years, however, international organizations have opened up to a range of non-state actors. Sovereignty has become more diffuse, with a state's treatment of its own citizens now clearly recognized as a legitimate concern of the international community. Democracies are in the ascendancy, and information, ideas, and people are moving across borders at unprecedented rates. The views of individuals are increasingly heard at the international level, and their message is clear: there is no public tolerance for inhumane warfare. Weapons that, by their very nature, cause massive civilian casualties are unacceptable.

The Changing Nature of War

The changing nature of war has led to a fundamental shift in our understanding of international security and of war itself. War will not disappear but, with the end of the Cold War, the threat of major conflict among states has lessened. Military spending in some states has dropped radically, as have global military sales. While the nuclear tests by India and Pakistan in May 1998 show that we cannot lower our guard against nuclear proliferation, the nature of the threat has changed.

Fears of a showdown between major powers have been largely replaced by an epidemic of 'dirty little wars'. The end of the Cold War has had a dramatic effect on the internal stability of states. Human rights abuses, interethnic tension, poverty, environmental degradation, and terrorism create the conditions for recurring cycles of internal violence. Civilians, not soldiers, have become the primary victims of war. The result is a marked increase in the past decade in the number of intra-state wars, accelerating a trend visible since the end of World War II. Bloody confrontations in the Balkans, the Great Lakes region of Africa, Chechnya, and elsewhere have dashed the hopes of those who predicted the 'end of history', and with it the end of war.

What has changed? There has been a proliferation of sources of conflict, with conflicts based on ethnic or religious identity fuelled by the proliferation of small arms and the collapse of state authority. There has been a similar proliferation in the subjects of conflict, that is, of who is fighting, and of sources of authority that might stem or channel conflict. State-sanctioned soldiers share the battlefield with sub-state actors, ranging from organized military groups with political hold over defined territories to loose gangs of thugs.

The main distinguishing factor between these new conflicts and conventional interstate war, however, is the motivation that lies behind the fighting. In this environment, there is an increased risk of identity-based conflicts, which often arise because human dignity is not being upheld and human needs are not being met.

Traditional interest-based conflicts may be amenable to negotiation, but identity-based conflicts tend to acquire a non-negotiable, zero-sum quality. It is not possible to use identity as a bargaining chip in negotiations. That is the lesson of recent history that we have learned so painfully.

In 'traditional' wars among states, injury or death of civilians was seen as 'collateral damage': a by-product of war that was acceptable as long as it was minimized. Now civilians have become the primary, often the intentional, victims of warfare. In identity-based conflicts, the battlefield extends into homes and playgrounds, with individuals targeted because of their affiliation with a specific group. Some analysts have estimated that the civilian casualty rate in today's internal conflicts is around 90 per cent, compared with 50 per cent in World War I and 10 per cent in the nineteenth century.

The Challenge to Humanitarian Law

The changing nature of conflict poses severe challenges for the international system. Foreign policy tools designed to manage the wars of the past are quite simply ill-suited to the wars of today. The stalwarts of humanitarian law, the Geneva Conventions and their Additional Protocols governing the conduct of warfare by military forces and their treatment of civilians, hold little meaning for the bush fighter or the 12-year-old boy armed with a Kalashnikov. Traditional peacekeeping aimed at monitoring peace accords is of little use when there is no peace to keep or when dealing with complex humanitarian emergencies. International arms regimes designed to address nuclear or chemical weapons do little to stop massacres with small arms, home-made landmines, or machetes.

Similarly, diplomatic measures designed to broker peace among warring nation-states are ill-suited to mediating conflict where the range of combatants is more diffuse. Development assistance programs that presume social and political stability may be insufficient to address the needs of these societies in conflict, and may unintentionally exacerbate inter-group tensions and perceptions of inequity.

The international community needs a new approach. The bitter lessons learned from the failure of international action in Rwanda and the former Yugoslavia made this clear. A new international tool-kit is necessary—from intelligence-based early warning systems to UN rapid reaction capability—but it is not sufficient. The starting point for a successful attempt to address new forms of conflict must be a new way of looking at the very notion of security and its preservation. From this flows a sense of how humanitarian law and other diplomatic tools can be most effectively deployed in a new and complex era.

Human Security

As the nature of conflict has changed, it has become clear that individual security is not necessarily a product of national security. Human security is found in the conditions of daily life—food, shelter, arable land, health, employment, and public safety—not primarily in the state's military strength. At the same time, the winds of globalization have levelled many of the barriers between international and domestic issues and exposed individual citizens to their blast. Addressing threats to human security means grappling with issues formerly considered to be internal problems: human rights abuses, internal conflict, crime, and environmental degradation. Labour standards and children's rights, impunity and peacebuilding, military expenditures, and the export of small arms or landmines—all have a human security dimension.

The landmines campaign differed at a fundamental conceptual level from other international efforts to limit or ban landmines because it looked at the issue from a human security viewpoint rather than a disarmament viewpoint. It took as its starting point the effect of AP mines on the ground—a massive humanitarian crisis—rather than the disarmament aspects of the problem. In disarmament terms, a negotiated agreement for a partial ban would have been a success. In humanitarian terms, however, only a complete ban would achieve the desired results.

This new understanding of security has required a shift in focus, from ensuring peace across state borders to building peace within states. As a result, foreign policy choices are increasingly driven by values rather than by military security interests. Geopolitics is gradually being overtaken by geo-governance. The old top-down view of sovereignty has been turned on its head, as a human security perspective looks at international issues from the bottom up. It brings the individual, until now largely invisible at the international level, back into view. It reminds us that states exist to further the human condition, and not vice versa.

Seen through the lens of human security, the focus of international relations is no longer exclusively a dialogue among states. The state may still be the principal channel through which international activities flow, but the subject of international concern is the individual, not the state. As sovereignty becomes a much more nuanced concept, the space for public diplomacy—involving a wider range of actors and concerns—is growing.

New International Actors

The trend towards new actors in international relations runs in two directions through the traditional hierarchy: outward to less powerful states and downward to civil society. During the Cold War era, states were bound into rigid power-based hierarchies and formal alliances. As the severe realities that underpinned these structures have relaxed, the scope for individual action by states and for new issue-based alliances has increased.

Power has not only become more diffuse, but its very nature is changing. In a wired world, knowledge and information confer international influence, and that influence is power. This 'soft power' works by attraction, not coercion. The strategic use of information and the ability to influence others by presenting attractive models and ideas have become central components of a nation's ability to exert political, economic, or cultural influence. Economic and military power are still highly significant, but they are no longer the only basis of a country's international clout. Thus, states that are not at the summit of the 'hard power' hierarchy now have greater ability than before to influence the course of events.

Power has diffused down as well as out. Globalization has radically transformed the role and power of the non-governmental sector to effect change internationally, for good or for bad. Private capital flows dwarf official development assistance. Rebel groups spread their message and seek international support on the Internet. In some instances NGOs provide the only international presence on the ground in countries in crisis.

This 'democratization' poses real challenges to international governance in a system designed by and for states. How does the international community negotiate a peace accord without knowing who really represents the different factions in an internal conflict? How does it temper the social and political effects of nervous investors suddenly pulling billions out of developing markets? How does it enforce international norms of behaviour among those who were not at the table when the agreements imposing these norms were signed?

At the same time, the rise of non-state actors provides real opportunities to tackle international problems in new and more effective ways. The global nature of threats to human security requires a global response. States acting alone or even the combined efforts of a few large powers are insufficient. New alliances are needed, bringing together states, large and small, from all regions of the world, working together in partnership with NGOs, the private sector, and citizens.

New Tools for a New Multilateralism

The need for new partnerships to address global problems and the increased power wielded by a wide range of state and non-state actors intersected in the landmines campaign. One of the primary reasons for the success of the campaign was the way in which it brought together a mixed group of players in a coalition without precedent.

The landmines campaign worked because it brought together not only donors and mine-affected states, but also humanitarian organizations, non-governmental organizations active in the field, and individual victims. It worked because new synergies were created. Each of these players brought particular assets to the table: only states could sign a binding convention; the International Campaign to Ban Landmines had the tools to mobilize public opinion; the International Committee of the Red Cross had the detailed knowledge and practical experience gained from undertaking mine action in the most affected countries.

By working in a genuine partnership, they were able to move the process forward at speeds unheard of in traditional disarmament negotiations. When it became clear that progress on a landmines ban was not possible in the UN Conference on Disarmament, there was sufficient international will, involving states from all regions, to allow progress outside of existing institutions. The success of the landmines campaign was not a unique event, never to be replicated in the world of diplomacy. The Ottawa Process clearly had its own special features. But it also demonstrated that global problems require global solutions. They cannot be addressed effectively by states, even the most powerful of states, acting in isolation. The landmines campaign was the harbinger of the new multilateralism: new alliances among states, new partnerships with non-state actors, and new approaches to international governance. It is within this framework that Canada has been forging a new international identity for itself.

CANADIAN FOREIGN POLICY RESPONSES: NEW DIRECTIONS

Canada has significant capacity to add value internationally in this new international setting. As a G–8 nation, we have considerable status in traditional power hierarchies. At the same time, Canada has important 'soft power' assets: attractive culture and values, a reputation as an honest broker with no colonial past, a tradition of bilingualism and multiculturalism, and much more. Other nations are also well placed to respond to the challenges of the new multilateralism, but I will focus on the area I know best: the new directions that Canada is taking.

Building on our strong tradition of innovation in foreign policy, we are working to identify where and how Canada can bring value to the new multilateralism. The overarching theme of our response is a greater focus on threats to human security. This has meant bringing some new or relatively ignored issues, such as landmines, to the top of the foreign policy agenda, without losing sight of other traditional areas of concern such as nuclear disarmament. A human security approach means viewing the full sweep of foreign policy through a new lens. Any reordering of priorities is a consequence of this overall vision, rather than change for its own sake.

Seen through a human security lens, several specific issues emerge as areas for further action by Canada: excessive military expenditures, child soldiers, human rights abuses and impunity, and small arms. Excessive military expenditures by governments not only destabilize societies and regions, but also retard development both directly and indirectly. They produce the explosive mix of arms and poverty from which conflict is so often sparked. The development assistance community has for some time recognized the link between development and demilitarization.

Canada may not be in a position to affect directly the spending decisions of other governments, but it can work to persuade and influence. We have sponsored research and international discussion under the aegis of the OECD. We support the UN's efforts to provide greater transparency through compilation of standardized statistics on military expenditures and its conventional arms register. On the demand side, we are working to reduce the sense of insecurity that often drives military spending. For example, Canada is helping to develop African capacity in peacekeeping and peacebuilding, including conflict prevention. On the supply side, Canada has one of the strictest regimes to control arms exports in the world. We continue to review and improve this regime to ensure it is effective and transparent.

Work in the area of military expenditures is largely preventive. Where conflict has already broken out, human needs become acute, yet they often fall between the cracks separating traditional development, disarmament, and peacekeeping measures. Holistic approaches are required to end the use of child soldiers and other human rights abuses in times of conflict, and to stem flows of small arms and light weapons.

The recruitment or outright abduction of children to serve as soldiers, labourers, or sexual slaves creates a problem that, like AP mines, has devastating effects long after the war is over. As with landmines, a major first step is simply to recognize the problem and define its nature and scope. We need to ask who these children are and what their situation is. Sometimes they are being used strategically, sometimes to do civilian work, and sometimes to fight. Children who have been taught to kill or brainwashed to support a cause are certainly victims—but they are dangerous victims. Their future has been taken away, with disastrous consequences for them and also for society.

The international community has some way to go in finding solutions to the problems posed by child soldiers, and these solutions are likely to be found in a complex package of measures, not a single convention or ban. The package must address demobilization and reintegration, providing champions for children and establishing new international norms.

Canada is working with civil society, international bodies, and other governments on all these fronts. We are supporting discussions to exchange experiences and advance thinking on the problem. Children affected by conflict need champions who can help them heal and, equally, stand up for them in national and international fora. Canada is developing a joint project with Norway that would help local psychologists in Algeria to heal children traumatized by the violence in that country. Canada is also pressing in negotiations for the proposed International Criminal Court (ICC) for an awareness of children's rights to be built into its foundations, and for the use of child soldiers to be recognized as a war crime. We must explicitly and universally stigmatize the practice of using children in times of war in the same way that we have stigmatized the use of landmines.

This work meshes with our broader efforts on human rights. Respect for international human rights is a long-standing area of concern for Canada and for multilateral institutions generally. Yet, even as the Universal Declaration of Human Rights marks its fiftieth year of existence, much remains to be done. The changes that have swept the international landscape have profound implications for the international human rights regime, not least the breaches made in the previously solid walls of state sovereignty. These provide opportunities for the establishment of new international norms and the implementation of existing ones.

Canada is pressing hard for the establishment of the ICC, for example, because we believe it provides the international community with an important new means to ensure respect of human rights. These rights may be internationally recognized, yet again and again we see them abused with impunity. An independent, effective ICC would be able to pursue the severest offences, including war crimes and crimes against humanity, when state governments are unwilling or unable to do so. It would ensure that we would not see another Pol Pot die unpunished for the crime of genocide.

A structure that gave some teeth to international human rights agreements would promote respect, rather than lip-service, for the international rule of law. It would also go some way to break recurring cycles of internal conflict. Only with justice can there be true reconciliation, and only with reconciliation, true peace.

Like child soldiers, the complex issue of small arms and light weapons received only limited foreign policy attention in the past. There is growing recognition, however, that the day-to-day human impact of these weapons is far greater than that of big-ticket weapons systems. As with landmines, small arms have slipped through the net of previous efforts, in part because they defy traditional categorization. The trade in light weapons and the use of such weapons in international crime and conflict undermine development, regional and local security, crime prevention, and respect for human rights.

The answer may lie in adapting public health models that attack both the supply and demand sides of the equation with a wide range of measures. This means use of measures ranging from more effective controls on illicit trafficking, to buy-back programs within peace operations, to greater accountability of producers. For a public health model to work, there must be 'buy-in' from civil society and concerted action by all the players: governments, regional and multilateral institutions, NGOs, and public opinion. Canada is working with the range of players brought together in the landmine coalition to see how lessons learned from that campaign might be applied in this case.

As we have focused our foreign policy on these human security issues, similarities and differences have become clearer. There are no 'cookie-cutter' solutions to these threats, but certain elements do recur: a firm and constant focus on overall human impact, new alliances that include governments and civil society, co-ordinated action ranging from research to action on the ground, and new tools and structures to address specific needs.

New Tools and Approaches
Developing the tools and institutions of a new multilateralism is a massive task for the international community. Given this, and the multiplicity of international actors, a division of labour makes sense. Within Canada, we are working first to identify areas where we can bring special value, and then to develop new tools and approaches in these areas. In tandem with this we are seeking to improve co-ordination of international efforts.

The landmine campaign is a case in point. Having achieved a Convention, we are now turning our efforts to implementation and mine action. Canada is funding specific projects through the $100 million fund announced by the Prime Minister at the time of signature of the Convention. These include a $10 million Mine Action Program in Bosnia, which will integrate mine action, reconstruction, and local capacity-building among the full range of players, including Canadian peacekeepers. We are also working with partners to launch mine action projects in the Middle East, Central America, Central Asia, and Africa. Canada also hosted a meeting in March 1998 that brought the landmines coalition together again to launch the second phase of the campaign: co-ordinated international mine action.

In other areas, too, Canada has been developing new ways of addressing human security issues. These efforts cover a range of 'soft power' measures falling under the headings of public diplomacy, democratic development, peacebuilding, support to civil society, and building indigenous capacity. But the tool-kit of the new multilateralism also includes 'hard diplomacy': coercive measures such as marshalling international condemnation, imposing sanctions, or sending peacekeepers. The key lies in developing tools of both kinds to fill gaps in the existing diplomatic repertoire and in knowing when and how to apply these tools effectively.

Canada has been working hard, for example, to develop public diplomacy as a tool of the new multilateralism, both at home and internationally. We hold annual consultations with interested NGOs on human rights and on peacebuilding, and sponsor a National Forum on Canadian Foreign Policy open to all interested citizens. In the landmines campaign and elsewhere, we have pressed for increased participation of NGOs in international decision-making. This is not simply a question of consulting NGOs, but involves a full, sustained partnership.

Canada is also developing new government-to-government partnerships by forming new alliances, often around a specific issue, and forging relations with non-traditional partners. We have established bilateral human rights dialogues with China and Cuba to engage them in practical ways on areas of concern. We have become an active member of the Organization of American States, working on areas of mutual concern such as the drugs trade, Aboriginal issues, and trade liberalization. Within the Commonwealth, Canada is one of the members of the Ministerial Action Group, which provides a multilateral forum to address human rights in Nigeria. Most recently, we have formed a partnership with Norway based on our shared interest in tackling the human security agenda.

The new multilateralism requires international institutions that work and that have the means to address current challenges and concerns. Canada has been at the forefront of reform efforts. These efforts involve not only UN reform writ large, but also the capacity of multilateral forums to address the specific substantive issues outlined above. This means developing the capacity of the UN and other multilateral institutions not just to keep the peace internationally, but to build it. It means giving the UN the money and the support it needs to implement the landmines Convention and international human rights agreements. It means creating new institutions such as the international tribunals for Rwanda and the former Yugoslavia, and soon, I hope, the International Criminal Court.

The Minister for International Co-operation, the Honourable Diane Marleau, and I launched the Canadian Peacebuilding Initiative in 1996 to fill out the multilateral tool-kit available to address human security needs. It provides a focal point for Canadian thinking, co-ordination, and capacity-building as well as funding for projects that had been falling through the gaps of existing institutions. It also allows Canada to bring money, expertise, and ideas to the table multilaterally, as a significant contribution to reform efforts.

Work on developing effective foreign policy tools at the level of non-state actors is still in the early stages. Here, too, Canada is on the cutting edge of diplomacy. We are supporting efforts to develop codes of conduct overseas for Canadian businesses and to engage non-state actors in peace-building measures in cases of internal conflict. The landmine Convention makes provision for the non-state sector to be involved in monitoring compliance. Implementation of the Convention will be an important test of this new approach to ensuring respect for international norms.

A further element of working with non-state actors is to ensure that marginalized sectors of society, which are most affected by threats to human security, have a prominent place on the international agenda. The needs of those who are marginalized for whatever reason—gender, age, ethnicity, religion, or other—must have a central place in the discourse of international law. It is not enough to add them as an afterthought to a 'one-size-fits-all' approach. This is why Canada is pressing to include considerations of gender and children's rights in the founding principles of the International Criminal Court.

Marginalized groups are not simply victims of conflict; they are also key players in building capacity for change, and for peace, from within. The Canadian Peacebuilding Initiative includes a focus on gender and on children's issues for that reason. Just as access to micro-credit for the economically marginalized has produced dramatic advances in overall development, access to the tools with which to build peace for the politically marginalized may have similar effects on overall security.

CONCLUSION

The nature of war has changed. Sovereignty, state-citizen relations, and international relations are being fundamentally transformed at the end of the twentieth century. Peacemaking, peacebuilding, and foreign policy itself must evolve, too. Canada is developing new concepts, new tools, and new partnerships to address these challenges and opportunities in foreign policy, and for global human security based on humanitarian values. In taking the lead on landmines, Canada showed we can rise to these challenges and opportunities. Working in partnership with like-minded states, NGOs, and publics at home and across the globe, we were able to 'punch above our weight' to secure a landmines ban.

Was this a one-time exception to the old rules and established practices of the international system? No. Rising public engagement in the previously closed and élite world of foreign affairs, new connections based on the shared power of information, new partnerships within and between societies and states, and the influence of soft power all point the way to differing but continuing successes for human security and humanitarian values. Canada will continue to play a leadership role in setting new goals and forging new partnerships. With that in mind, it is timely to analyse the success of the landmine campaign, reflect on the lessons learned, and look ahead to new international opportunities in the new century.

NOTE

I am grateful for the assistance of Kerry Buck, Sarah Taylor, and John English in the writing of this chapter.

APPENDIX A

List of Signatories to and Ratifications (Deposited with the United Nations) of the Convention on the Prohibition of the Use, Stockpiling, Production and Transfer of Anti-Personnel Mines and on Their Destruction (as of 31 July 1998)

State	Treaty Signatories	Treaty Ratifications
Algeria	3 Dec. 97	
Andorra	3 Dec. 97	29 June 98
Angola	4 Dec. 97	
Antigua and Barbuda	3 Dec. 97	
Argentina	4 Dec. 97	
Australia	3 Dec. 97	
Austria	3 Dec. 97	29 June 98
Bahamas	3 Dec. 97	
Bangladesh	7 May 98	
Barbados	3 Dec. 97	
Belgium	3 Dec. 97	
Belize	27 Feb. 98	23 Apr. 98
Benin	3 Dec. 97	
Bolivia	3 Dec. 97	9 June 98
Bosnia-Herzegovina	3 Dec. 97	
Botswana	3 Dec. 97	
Brazil	3 Dec. 97	
Brunei Darussalam	4 Dec. 97	
Bulgaria	3 Dec. 97	
Burkina Faso	3 Dec. 97	
Burundi	3 Dec. 97	
Cambodia	3 Dec. 97	
Cameroon	3 Dec. 97	
Canada	3 Dec. 97	3 Dec. 98
Cape Verde	4 Dec. 97	
Chile	3 Dec. 97	
Colombia	3 Dec. 97	
Cook Islands	3 Dec. 97	
Costa Rica	3 Dec. 97	
Côte d'Ivoire	3 Dec. 97	
Croatia	4 Dec. 97	20 May 98
Cyprus	4 Dec. 97	
Czech Republic	3 Dec. 97	
Denmark	4 Dec. 97	8 June 98
Djibouti	3 Dec. 97	18 May 98

State	Treaty Signatories	Treaty Ratifications
Dominica	3 Dec. 97	
Dominican Republic	3 Dec. 97	
Ecuador	4 Dec. 97	
El Salvador	4 Dec. 97	
Ethiopia	3 Dec. 97	
Fiji	3 Dec. 97	10 June 98
France	3 Dec. 97	23 July 98
Gabon	3 Dec. 97	
Gambia	4 Dec. 97	
Germany	3 Dec. 97	23 July 98
Ghana	4 Dec. 97	
Greece	3 Dec. 97	
Grenada	3 Dec. 97	
Guatemala	3 Dec. 97	
Guinea	4 Dec. 97	
Guinea-Bissau	3 Dec. 97	
Guyana	4 Dec. 97	
Haiti	3 Dec. 97	
Holy See	4 Dec. 97	17 Feb. 98
Honduras	3 Dec. 97	
Hungary	3 Dec. 97	6 Apr. 98
Iceland	4 Dec. 97	
Indonesia	4 Dec. 97	
Ireland	3 Dec. 97	3 Dec. 97
Italy	3 Dec. 97	
Jamaica	3 Dec. 97	17 July 98
Japan	3 Dec. 97	
Kenya	5 Dec. 97	
Lesotho	4 Dec. 97	
Liechtenstein	3 Dec. 97	
Luxembourg	4 Dec. 97	
Madagascar	4 Dec. 97	
Malawi	4 Dec. 97	
Malaysia	3 Dec. 97	
Mali	3 Dec. 97	2 June 98
Malta	4 Dec. 97	
Marshall Islands	4 Dec. 97	
Mauritania	3 Dec. 97	
Mauritius	3 Dec. 97	3 Dec. 97
Mexico	3 Dec. 97	9 June 98

State	Treaty Signatories	Treaty Ratifications
Moldova	4 Dec. 97	
Monaco	4 Dec. 97	
Mozambique	3 Dec. 97	
Namibia	3 Dec. 97	
Netherlands	3 Dec. 97	
New Zealand	3 Dec. 97	
Nicaragua	4 Dec. 97	
Niger	4 Dec. 97	
Niue	3 Dec. 97	15 Apr. 98
Norway	3 Dec. 97	9 July 98
Panama	4 Dec. 97	
Paraguay	3 Dec. 97	
Peru	3 Dec. 97	17 June 98
Philippines	3 Dec. 97	
Poland	4 Dec. 97	
Portugal	3 Dec. 97	
Qatar	4 Dec. 97	
Romania	3 Dec. 97	
Rwanda	3 Dec. 97	
Samoa	3 Dec. 97	23 July 98
San Marino	3 Dec. 97	18 Mar. 98
São Tomé and Principe	30 Apr. 98	
Senegal	3 Dec. 97	
Seychelles	4 Dec. 97	
Slovak Republic	3 Dec. 97	
Slovenia	3 Dec. 97	
Solomon Islands	4 Dec. 97	
South Africa	3 Dec. 97	29 June 98
Spain	3 Dec. 97	
St Kitts and Nevis	3 Dec. 97	
St Lucia	3 Dec. 97	
St Vincent	3 Dec. 97	
Sudan	4 Dec. 97	
Suriname	4 Dec. 97	
Swaziland	4 Dec. 97	
Sweden	4 Dec. 97	
Switzerland	4 Dec. 97	24 Mar. 98
Tanzania	3 Dec. 97	
Thailand	3 Dec. 97	
Togo	4 Dec. 97	

State	Treaty Signatories	Treaty Ratifications
Trinidad and Tobago	4 Dec. 97	27 Apr. 98
Tunisia	4 Dec. 97	
Turkmenistan	3 Dec. 97	19 Jan. 98
Uganda	3 Dec. 97	
United Kingdom	3 Dec. 97	31 July 98
Uruguay	3 Dec. 97	
Vanuatu	4 Dec. 97	
Venezuela	3 Dec. 97	
Yemen	4 Dec. 97	22 July 98
Zambia	12 Dec. 97	
Zimbabwe	3 Dec. 97	22 June 98

APPENDIX B

THE OTTAWA CONVENTION
18 September 1997

CONVENTION ON THE PROHIBITION OF THE USE, STOCKPIL-
ING, PRODUCTION AND TRANSFER OF ANTI-PERSONNEL
MINES AND ON THEIR DESTRUCTION

Preamble

The States Parties,

Determined to put an end to the suffering and casualties caused by anti-personnel mines, that kill or maim hundreds of people every week, mostly innocent and defenceless civilians and especially children, obstruct economic development and reconstruction, inhibit the repatriation of refugees and internally displaced persons, and have other severe conse-quences for years after emplacement,

Believing it necessary to do their utmost to contribute in an efficient and coordinated manner to face the challenge of removing anti-personnel mines placed throughout the world, and to assure their destruction,

Wishing to do their utmost in providing assistance for the care and rehabilitation, including the social and economic reintegration of mine victims,

Recognizing that a total ban of anti-personnel mines would also be an important confidence-building measure,

Welcoming the adoption of the Protocol on Prohibitions or Restrictions on the Use of Mines, Booby-Traps and Other Devices, as amended on 3 May 1996, annexed to the Convention on Prohibitions or Restrictions on the Use of Certain Conventional Weapons Which May Be Deemed to Be Excessively Injurious or to Have Indiscriminate Effects, and calling for the early ratification of this Protocol by all States which have not yet done so,

Welcoming also United Nations General Assembly Resolution 51/45S of 10 December 1996 urging all States to pursue vigorously an effective, legally-binding international agreement to ban the use, stockpiling, pro-duction and transfer of anti-personnel landmines,

Welcoming furthermore the measures taken over the past years, both unilaterally and multilaterally, aiming at prohibiting, restricting or sus-pending the use, stockpiling, production and transfer of anti-personnel mines,

Stressing the role of public conscience in furthering the principles of humanity as evidenced by the call for a total ban of anti-personnel mines and recognizing the efforts to that end undertaken by the International Red Cross and Red Crescent Movement, the International Campaign to Ban Landmines and numerous other non-governmental organizations around the world,

Recalling the Ottawa Declaration of 5 October 1996 and the Brussels Declaration of 27 June 1997 urging the international community to negotiate an international and legally binding agreement prohibiting the use, stockpiling, production and transfer of anti-personnel mines,

Emphasizing the desirability of attracting the adherence of all States to this Convention, and determined to work strenuously towards the promotion of its universalization in all relevant fora including, *inter alia*, the United Nations, the Conference on Disarmament, regional organizations, and groupings, and review conferences of the Convention on Prohibitions or Restrictions on the Use of Certain Conventional Weapons Which May Be Deemed to Be Excessively Injurious or to Have Indiscriminate Effects,

Basing themselves on the principle of international humanitarian law that the right of the parties to an armed conflict to choose methods or means of warfare is not unlimited, on the principle that prohibits the employment in armed conflicts of weapons, projectiles and materials and methods of warfare of a nature to cause superfluous injury or unnecessary suffering and on the principle that a distinction must be made between civilians and combatants,

Have agreed as follows:

Article 1
General obligations

1.   Each State Party undertakes never under any circumstances:

a)   To use anti-personnel mines;

b)   To develop, produce, otherwise acquire, stockpile, retain or transfer to anyone, directly or indirectly, anti-personnel mines;

c)   To assist, encourage or induce, in any way, anyone to engage in any activity prohibited to a State Party under this Convention.

2.   Each State Party undertakes to destroy or ensure the destruction of all anti-personnel mines in accordance with the provisions of this Convention.

Article 2
Definitions

1.   'Anti-personnel mine' means a mine designed to be exploded by the presence, proximity or contact of a person and that will incapacitate, injure

or kill one or more persons. Mines designed to be detonated by the presence, proximity or contact of a vehicle as opposed to a person, that are equipped with anti-handling devices, are not considered anti-personnel mines as a result of being so equipped.

2. 'Mine' means a munition designed to be placed under, on or near the ground or other surface area and to be exploded by the presence, proximity or contact of a person or a vehicle.

3. 'Anti-handling device' means a device intended to protect a mine and which is part of, linked to, attached to or placed under the mine and which activates when an attempt is made to tamper with or otherwise intentionally disturb the mine.

4. 'Transfer' involves, in addition to the physical movement of anti-personnel mines into or from national territory, the transfer of title to and control over the mines, but does not involve the transfer of territory containing emplaced anti-personnel mines.

5. 'Mined area' means an area which is dangerous due to the presence or suspected presence of mines.

Article 3
Exceptions

1. Notwithstanding the general obligations under Article 1, the retention or transfer of a number of anti-personnel mines for the development of and training in mine detection, mine clearance, or mine destruction techniques is permitted. The amount of such mines shall not exceed the minimum number absolutely necessary for the above-mentioned purposes.

2. The transfer of anti-personnel mines for the purpose of destruction is permitted.

Article 4
Destruction of stockpiled anti-personnel mines

Except as provided for in Article 3, each State Party undertakes to destroy or ensure the destruction of all stockpiled anti-personnel mines it owns or possesses, or that are under its jurisdiction or control, as soon as possible but not later than four years after the entry into force of this Convention for that State Party.

Article 5
Destruction of anti-personnel mines in mined areas

1. Each State Party undertakes to destroy or ensure the destruction of all anti-personnel mines in mined areas under its jurisdiction or control, as soon as possible but not later than ten years after the entry into force of this

Convention for that State Party.

2. Each State Party shall make every effort to identify all areas under its jurisdiction or control in which anti-personnel mines are known or suspected to be emplaced and shall ensure as soon as possible that all anti-personnel mines in mined areas under its jurisdiction or control are perimeter-marked, monitored and protected by fencing or other means, to ensure the effective exclusion of civilians, until all anti-personnel mines contained therein have been destroyed. The marking shall at least be to the standards set out in the Protocol on Prohibitions or Restrictions on the Use of Mines, Booby-Traps and Other Devices, as amended on 3 May 1996, annexed to the Convention on Prohibitions or Restrictions on the Use of Certain Conventional Weapons Which May Be Deemed to Be Excessively Injurious or to Have Indiscriminate Effects.

3. If a State Party believes that it will be unable to destroy or ensure the destruction of all anti-personnel mines referred to in paragraph 1 within that time period, it may submit a request to a Meeting of the States Parties or a Review Conference for an extension of the deadline for completing the destruction of such anti-personnel mines, for a period of up to ten years.

4. Each request shall contain:

a) The duration of the proposed extension;

b) A detailed explanation of the reasons for the proposed extension, including:

   (i) The preparation and status of work conducted under national demining programs;

   (ii) The financial and technical means available to the State Party for the destruction of all the anti-personnel mines; and

   (iii)Circumstances which impede the ability of the State Party to destroy all the anti-personnel mines in mined areas;

c) The humanitarian, social, economic, and environmental implications of the extension; and

d) Any other information relevant to the request for the proposed extension.

5. The Meeting of the States Parties or the Review Conference shall, taking into consideration the factors contained in paragraph 4, assess the request and decide by a majority of votes of States Parties present and voting whether to grant the request for an extension period.

6. Such an extension may be renewed upon the submission of a new request in accordance with paragraphs 3, 4 and 5 of this Article. In requesting a further extension period a State Party shall submit relevant additional information on what has been undertaken in the previous extension period pursuant to this Article.

Article 6
International cooperation and assistance

1. In fulfilling its obligations under this Convention each State Party has the right to seek and receive assistance, where feasible, from other States Parties to the extent possible.

2. Each State Party undertakes to facilitate and shall have the right to participate in the fullest possible exchange of equipment, material and scientific and technological information concerning the implementation of this Convention. The States Parties shall not impose undue restrictions on the provision of mine clearance equipment and related technological information for humanitarian purposes.

3. Each State Party in a position to do so shall provide assistance for the care and rehabilitation, and social and economic reintegration, of mine victims and for mine awareness programs. Such assistance may be provided, inter alia, through the United Nations system, international, regional or national organizations or institutions, the International Committee of the Red Cross, national Red Cross and Red Crescent societies and their International Federation, non-governmental organizations, or on a bilateral basis.

4. Each State Party in a position to do so shall provide assistance for mine clearance and related activities. Such assistance may be provided, inter alia, through the United Nations system, international or regional organizations or institutions, non-governmental organizations or institutions, or on a bilateral basis, or by contributing to the United Nations Voluntary Trust Fund for Assistance in Mine Clearance, or other regional funds that deal with demining.

5. Each State Party in a position to do so shall provide assistance for the destruction of stockpiled anti-personnel mines.

6. Each State Party undertakes to provide information to the database on mine clearance established within the United Nations system, especially information concerning various means and technologies of mine clearance, and lists of experts, expert agencies or national points of contact on mine clearance.

7. States Parties may request the United Nations, regional organizations, other States Parties or other competent intergovernmental or non-governmental fora to assist its authorities in the elaboration of a national demining program to determine, inter alia:

a) The extent and scope of the anti-personnel mine problem;

b) The financial, technological and human resources that are required for the implementation of the program;

c)   The estimated number of years necessary to destroy all anti-personnel mines in mined areas under the jurisdiction or control of the concerned State Party;

d)   Mine awareness activities to reduce the incidence of mine-related injuries or deaths;

e)   Assistance to mine victims;

f)   The relationship between the Government of the concerned State Party and the relevant governmental, intergovernmental or non-governmental entities that will work in the implementation of the program.

8.   Each State Party giving and receiving assistance under the provisions of this Article shall cooperate with a view to ensuring the full and prompt implementation of agreed assistance programs.

Article 7
Transparency measures

1.   Each State Party shall report to the Secretary-General of the United Nations as soon as practicable, and in any event not later than 180 days after the entry into force of this Convention for that State Party on:

a)   The national implementation measures referred to in Article 9;

b)   The total of all stockpiled anti-personnel mines owned or possessed by it, or under its jurisdiction or control, to include a breakdown of the type, quantity and, if possible, lot numbers of each type of anti-personnel mine stockpiled;

c)   To the extent possible, the location of all mined areas that contain, or are suspected to contain, anti-personnel mines under its jurisdiction or control, to include as much detail as possible regarding the type and quantity of each type of anti-personnel mine in each mined area and when they were emplaced;

d)   The types, quantities and, if possible, lot numbers of all anti-personnel mines retained or transferred for the development of and training in mine detection, mine clearance or mine destruction techniques, or transferred for the purpose of destruction, as well as the institutions authorized by a State Party to retain or transfer anti-personnel mines, in accordance with Article 3;

e)   The status of programs for the conversion or de-commissioning of anti-personnel mine production facilities;

f)   The status of programs for the destruction of anti-personnel mines in accordance with Articles 4 and 5, including details of the methods which will be used in destruction, the location of all destruction sites and the applicable safety and environmental standards to be observed;

g) The types and quantities of all anti-personnel mines destroyed after the entry into force of this Convention for that State Party, to include a breakdown of the quantity of each type of anti-personnel mine destroyed, in accordance with Articles 4 and 5, respectively, along with, if possible, the lot numbers of each type of anti-personnel mine in the case of destruction in accordance with Article 4;

h) The technical characteristics of each type of anti-personnel mine produced, to the extent known, and those currently owned or possessed by a State Party, giving, where reasonably possible, such categories of information as may facilitate identification and clearance of anti-personnel mines; at a minimum, this information shall include the dimensions, fusing, explosive content, metallic content, colour photographs and other information which may facilitate mine clearance; and

i) The measures taken to provide an immediate and effective warning to the population in relation to all areas identified under paragraph 2 of Article 5.

2. The information provided in accordance with this Article shall be updated by the States Parties annually, covering the last calendar year, and reported to the Secretary-General of the United Nations not later than 30 April of each year.

3. The Secretary-General of the United Nations shall transmit all such reports received to the States Parties.

Article 8
Facilitation and clarification of compliance

1. The States Parties agree to consult and cooperate with each other regarding the implementation of the provisions of this Convention, and to work together in a spirit of cooperation to facilitate compliance by States Parties with their obligations under this Convention.

2. If one or more States Parties wish to clarify and seek to resolve questions relating to compliance with the provisions of this Convention by another State Party, it may submit, through the Secretary-General of the United Nations, a Request for Clarification of that matter to that State Party. Such a request shall be accompanied by all appropriate information. Each State Party shall refrain from unfounded Requests for Clarification, care being taken to avoid abuse. A State Party that receives a Request for Clarification shall provide, through the Secretary-General of the United Nations, within 28 days to the requesting State Party all information which would assist in clarifying this matter.

3. If the requesting State Party does not receive a response through the Secretary-General of the United Nations within that time period, or deems the response to the Request for Clarification to be unsatisfactory, it may

submit the matter through the Secretary-General of the United Nations to the next Meeting of the States Parties. The Secretary-General of the United Nations shall transmit the submission, accompanied by all appropriate information pertaining to the Request for Clarification, to all States Parties. All such information shall be presented to the requested State Party which shall have the right to respond.

4.   Pending the convening of any meeting of the States Parties, any of the States Parties concerned may request the Secretary-General of the United Nations to exercise his or her good offices to facilitate the clarification requested.

5.   The requesting State Party may propose through the Secretary-General of the United Nations the convening of a Special Meeting of the States Parties to consider the matter. The Secretary-General of the United Nations shall thereupon communicate this proposal and all information submitted by the States Parties concerned, to all States Parties with a request that they indicate whether they favour a Special Meeting of the States Parties, for the purpose of considering the matter. In the event that within 14 days from the date of such communication, at least one-third of the States Parties favours such a Special Meeting, the Secretary-General of the United Nations shall convene this Special Meeting of the States Parties within a further 14 days. A quorum for this Meeting shall consist of a majority of States Parties.

6.   The Meeting of the States Parties or the Special Meeting of the States Parties, as the case may be, shall first determine whether to consider the matter further, taking into account all information submitted by the States Parties concerned. The Meeting of the States Parties or the Special Meeting of the States Parties shall make every effort to reach a decision by consensus. If despite all efforts to that end no agreement has been reached, it shall take this decision by a majority of States Parties present and voting.

7.   All States Parties shall cooperate fully with the Meeting of the States Parties or the Special Meeting of the States Parties in the fulfilment of its review of the matter, including any fact-finding missions that are authorized in accordance with paragraph 8.

8.   If further clarification is required, the Meeting of the States Parties or the Special Meeting of the States Parties shall authorize a fact-finding mission and decide on its mandate by a majority of States Parties present and voting. At any time the requested State Party may invite a fact-finding mission to its territory. Such a mission shall take place without a decision by a Meeting of the States Parties or a Special Meeting of the States Parties to authorize such a mission. The mission, consisting of up to 9 experts, designated and approved in accordance with paragraphs 9 and 10, may collect additional information on the spot or in other places directly related to the

alleged compliance issue under the jurisdiction or control of the requested State Party.

9. The Secretary-General of the United Nations shall prepare and update a list of the names, nationalities and other relevant data of qualified experts provided by States Parties and communicate it to all States Parties. Any expert included on this list shall be regarded as designated for all fact-finding missions unless a State Party declares its non-acceptance in writing. In the event of non-acceptance, the expert shall not participate in fact-finding missions on the territory or any other place under the jurisdiction or control of the objecting State Party, if the non-acceptance was declared prior to the appointment of the expert to such missions.

10. Upon receiving a request from the Meeting of the States Parties or a Special Meeting of the States Parties, the Secretary-General of the United Nations shall, after consultations with the requested State Party, appoint the members of the mission, including its leader. Nationals of States Parties requesting the fact-finding mission or directly affected by it shall not be appointed to the mission. The members of the fact-finding mission shall enjoy privileges and immunities under Article VI of the Convention on the Privileges and Immunities of the United Nations, adopted on 13 February 1946.

11. Upon at least 72 hours notice, the members of the fact-finding mission shall arrive in the territory of the requested State Party at the earliest opportunity. The requested State Party shall take the necessary administrative measures to receive, transport and accommodate the mission, and shall be responsible for ensuring the security of the mission to the maximum extent possible while they are on territory under its control.

12. Without prejudice to the sovereignty of the requested State Party, the fact-finding mission may bring into the territory of the requested State Party the necessary equipment which shall be used exclusively for gathering information on the alleged compliance issue. Prior to its arrival, the mission will advise the requested State Party of the equipment that it intends to utilize in the course of its fact-finding mission.

13. The requested State Party shall make all efforts to ensure that the fact-finding mission is given the opportunity to speak with all relevant persons who may be able to provide information related to the alleged compliance issue.

14. The requested State Party shall grant access for the fact-finding mission to all areas and installations under its control where facts relevant to the compliance issue could be expected to be collected. This shall be subject to any arrangements that the requested State Party considers necessary for:

a)   The protection of sensitive equipment, information and areas;

b)   The protection of any constitutional obligations the requested State Party may have with regard to proprietary rights, searches and seizures, or other constitutional rights; or

c)   The physical protection and safety of the members of the fact-finding mission.

In the event that the requested State Party makes such arrangements, it shall make every reasonable effort to demonstrate through alternative means its compliance with this Convention.

15. The fact-finding mission may remain in the territory of the State Party concerned for no more than 14 days, and at any particular site no more than 7 days, unless otherwise agreed.

16. All information provided in confidence and not related to the subject matter of the fact-finding mission shall be treated on a confidential basis.

17. The fact-finding mission shall report, through the Secretary-General of the United Nations, to the Meeting of the States Parties or the Special Meeting of the States Parties the results of its findings.

18. The Meeting of the States Parties or the Special Meeting of the States Parties shall consider all relevant information, including the report submitted by the fact-finding mission, and may request the requested State Party to take measures to address the compliance issue within a specified period of time. The requested State Party shall report on all measures taken in response to this request.

19. The Meeting of the States Parties or the Special Meeting of the States Parties may suggest to the States Parties concerned ways and means to further clarify or resolve the matter under consideration, including the initiation of appropriate procedures in conformity with international law. In circumstances where the issue at hand is determined to be due to circumstances beyond the control of the requested State Party, the Meeting of the States Parties or the Special Meeting of the States Parties may recommend appropriate measures, including the use of cooperative measures referred to in Article 6.

20. The Meeting of the States Parties or the Special Meeting of the States Parties shall make every effort to reach its decisions referred to in paragraphs 18 and 19 by consensus, otherwise by a two-thirds majority of States Parties present and voting.

Article 9
National implementation measures

Each State Party shall take all appropriate legal, administrative and other measures, including the imposition of penal sanctions, to prevent and suppress any activity prohibited to a State Party under this Convention undertaken by persons or on territory under its jurisdiction or control.

Article 10
Settlement of disputes

1.   The States Parties shall consult and cooperate with each other to settle any dispute that may arise with regard to the application or the interpretation of this Convention. Each State Party may bring any such dispute before the Meeting of the States Parties.

2.   The Meeting of the States Parties may contribute to the settlement of the dispute by whatever means it deems appropriate, including offering its good offices, calling upon the States Parties to a dispute to start the settlement procedure of their choice and recommending a time-limit for any agreed procedure.

3.   This Article is without prejudice to the provisions of this Convention on facilitation and clarification of compliance.

Article 11
Meetings of the States Parties

1.   The States Parties shall meet regularly in order to consider any matter with regard to the application or implementation of this Convention, including:

a)   The operation and status of this Convention;

b)   Matters arising from the reports submitted under the provisions of this Convention;

c)   International cooperation and assistance in accordance with Article 6;

d)   The development of technologies to clear anti-personnel mines;

e)   Submissions of States Parties under Article 8; and

f)   Decisions relating to submissions of States Parties as provided for in Article 5.

2.   The First Meeting of the States Parties shall be convened by the Secretary-General of the United Nations within one year after the entry into force of this Convention. The subsequent meetings shall be convened by the Secretary-General of the United Nations annually until the first Review Conference.

3.   Under the conditions set out in Article 8, the Secretary-General of the United Nations shall convene a Special Meeting of the States Parties.

4.   States not parties to this Convention, as well as the United Nations, other relevant international organizations or institutions, regional organizations, the International Committee of the Red Cross and relevant

non-governmental organizations may be invited to attend these meetings as observers in accordance with the agreed Rules of Procedure.

Article 12
Review Conferences

1.   A Review Conference shall be convened by the Secretary-General of the United Nations five years after the entry into force of this Convention. Further Review Conferences shall be convened by the Secretary-General of the United Nations if so requested by one or more States Parties, provided that the interval between Review Conferences shall in no case be less than five years. All States Parties to this Convention shall be invited to each Review Conference.

2.   The purpose of the Review Conference shall be:

a)   To review the operation and status of this Convention;

b)   To consider the need for and the interval between further Meetings of the States Parties referred to in paragraph 2 of Article 11;

c)   To take decisions on submissions of States Parties as provided for in Article 5; and

d)   To adopt, if necessary, in its final report conclusions related to the implementation of this Convention.

3.   States not parties to this Convention, as well as the United Nations, other relevant international organizations or institutions, regional organizations, the International Committee of the Red Cross and relevant non-governmental organizations may be invited to attend each Review Conference as observers in accordance with the agreed Rules of Procedure.

Article 13
Amendments

1.   At any time after the entry into force of this Convention any State Party may propose amendments to this Convention. Any proposal for an amendment shall be communicated to the Depositary, who shall circulate it to all States Parties and shall seek their views on whether an Amendment Conference should be convened to consider the proposal. If a majority of the States Parties notify the Depositary no later than 30 days after its circulation that they support further consideration of the proposal, the Depositary shall convene an Amendment Conference to which all States Parties shall be invited.

2.   States not parties to this Convention, as well as the United Nations, other relevant international organizations or institutions, regional organizations, the International Committee of the Red Cross and relevant

non-governmental organizations may be invited to attend each Amendment Conference as observers in accordance with the agreed Rules of Procedure.

3. The Amendment Conference shall be held immediately following a Meeting of the States Parties or a Review Conference unless a majority of the States Parties request that it be held earlier.

4. Any amendment to this Convention shall be adopted by a majority of two-thirds of the States Parties present and voting at the Amendment Conference. The Depositary shall communicate any amendment so adopted to the States Parties.

5. An amendment to this Convention shall enter into force for all States Parties to this Convention which have accepted it, upon the deposit with the Depositary of instruments of acceptance by a majority of States Parties. Thereafter it shall enter into force for any remaining State Party on the date of deposit of its instrument of acceptance.

Article 14
Costs

1. The costs of the Meetings of the States Parties, the Special Meetings of the States Parties, the Review Conferences and the Amendment Conferences shall be borne by the States Parties and States not parties to this Convention participating therein, in accordance with the United Nations scale of assessment adjusted appropriately.

2. The costs incurred by the Secretary-General of the United Nations under Articles 7 and 8 and the costs of any fact-finding mission shall be borne by the States Parties in accordance with the United Nations scale of assessment adjusted appropriately.

Article 15
Signature

This Convention, done at Oslo, Norway, on 18 September 1997, shall be open for signature at Ottawa, Canada, by all States from 3 December 1997 until 4 December 1997, and at the United Nations Headquarters in New York from 5 December 1997 until its entry into force.

Article 16
Ratification, acceptance, approval or accession

1. This Convention is subject to ratification, acceptance or approval of the Signatories.

2. It shall be open for accession by any State which has not signed the Convention.

3.   The instruments of ratification, acceptance, approval or accession shall be deposited with the Depositary.

Article 17
Entry into force

1.   This Convention shall enter into force on the first day of the sixth month after the month in which the 40th instrument of ratification, acceptance, approval or accession has been deposited.

2.   For any State which deposits its instrument of ratification, acceptance, approval or accession after the date of the deposit of the 40th instrument of ratification, acceptance, approval or accession, this Convention shall enter into force on the first day of the sixth month after the date on which that State has deposited its instrument of ratification, acceptance, approval or accession.

Article 18
Provisional application

Any State may at the time of its ratification, acceptance, approval or accession, declare that it will apply provisionally paragraph 1 of Article 1 of this Convention pending its entry into force.

Article 19
Reservations

The Articles of this Convention shall not be subject to reservations.

Article 20
Duration and withdrawal

1.   This Convention shall be of unlimited duration.

2.   Each State Party shall, in exercising its national sovereignty, have the right to withdraw from this Convention. It shall give notice of such withdrawal to all other States Parties, to the Depositary and to the United Nations Security Council. Such instrument of withdrawal shall include a full explanation of the reasons motivating this withdrawal.

3.   Such withdrawal shall only take effect six months after the receipt of the instrument of withdrawal by the Depositary. If, however, on the expiry of that six-month period, the withdrawing State Party is engaged in an armed conflict, the withdrawal shall not take effect before the end of the armed conflict.

4.   The withdrawal of a State Party from this Convention shall not in any way affect the duty of States to continue fulfilling the obligations assumed under any relevant rules of international law.

Article 21
Depositary

The Secretary-General of the United Nations is hereby designated as the Depositary of this Convention.

Article 22
Authentic texts

The original of this Convention, of which the Arabic, Chinese, English, French, Russian and Spanish texts are equally authentic, shall be deposited with the Secretary-General of the United Nations.

INDEX

Note: Page numbers in **bold** indicate an illustration.